THE GOSPEL OF MARK
CHAPTER AND VERSE

David G. Palmer

Cover photograph: the author's own Summary Chart of Mark's Gospel, 2013, prepared in acrylics on wood (double A0) for a two-year National Tour, 2015-2017.

First published as *The Markan Matrix: A Literary-Structural Analysis of the Gospel of Mark*, Ceridwen Press, 1999. Re-titled and Revised, 2020.

Codex Sinaiticus, the first folio of The Gospel according to Mark, © The British Library, Add. 43725. Used by permission. See page 340.

The Greek New Testament, Fourth Revised Edition, edited by Barbara Aland, Kurt Aland, Johannes Karavidopoulos, Carlo M. Martini and Bruce M. Metzger in cooperation with the Institute for New Testament Textual Research, Münster/Westphalia, © 1993 Deutsche Bibelgesellschaft, Stuttgart. Used by permission.

The Greek font, Koine TT, 'Koi_.ttf', typeface name **Koine** (also **Koine Italics**), is the one used in this book. Zondervan required no copyright application for its inclusion.

British Library Cataloguing in Publication Data.

A catalogue record for this publication is available from the British Library.

BIC No. HRCG3

ISBN   978-0-9513661-1-0

Prepared for printing and published by **Ceridwen Press**
The (Old) Cottage Inn, 46 Regent Street, Church Gresley, Swadlincote, DE11 9PL, UK

Printed in Great Britain by **Flexpress**
6 Coal Cart Road, Birstall, Leicester, LE4 3BY, UK

Notes on the Author:

David Palmer is from Hull. He trained at University College London as an Architect, registering in 1975, and then at All Nations Christian College, Wesley House and Fitzwilliam College, Cambridge University, prior to his ordination as a Methodist Minister in 1983.

His first three years of ministry were spent in London, in Camden and Islington, as he explored his calling. As a Circuit Minister, he then served seven years in Cardiff, where in 1988 he also self-published his first book, *Sliced Bread: the Four Gospels, Acts and Revelation: their Literary Structures*. Later, in Paisley, he took on the duties of Superintendent Minister for six years, before becoming a founder Director of the Firehouse Ecumenical Centre for Youth, and Proprietor of Moredun House, a Home for the Elderly. During these years, in the 1990s, he worked part-time on his doctoral studies in the Department of Theology and Religious Studies at Glasgow University. In 1998, he received his doctorate and in 1999 he self-published his thesis, *The Markan Matrix: a Literary-Structural Analysis of the Gospel of Mark*.

After Wales and Scotland, it was Sri Lanka for five years as he and his wife Sue served as Mission Partners, first in Colombo, and then in Jaffna where curfews required that they stay indoors from six in the evening till six in the morning. This was because of the continuing distress that followed the civil war. It gave him opportunity, however, to extend his New Testament Studies from the Books to the Letters, which led to the publishing of his third book, *New Testament: New Testimony to the Skills of the Writers and First Readers*. He launched it at the Tamil, Jaffna Central Library, re-built after a sectarian arson attack in 1981. The book launch took place six months after the Asian Boxing Day tsunami.

Returning to England in 2005, he served as Superintendent Minister of the Leicester Trinity Circuit and, towards the end of his time there, ran a trial Exhibition Tour on his New Testament work, prior to becoming a Supernumerary Minister in 2012 and conducting a two-year tour of Great Britain, 2015-2017. The tour itself inspired his Illustrated Exhibition Edition of *New Testament: New Testimony* (the fifth edition) in 2016. The lock-down due to the coronavirus pandemic has now given him his opportunity to up-date *The Markan Matrix*, re-title it, revise and extend its usefulness with a literal English translation.

Such are the essential details of a lifetime's journey in Faith and Learning which he continues to share with his wife, Sue.

To my twin brother Mike, and Diana
as Sue and I share with them
a Fiftieth Wedding Anniversary Year!

THE GOSPEL OF MARK
CHAPTER AND VERSE

David G. Palmer

Preface:

Since my doctoral thesis, *The Markan Matrix*, was first published in 1999, I have been applying to all the books of the New Testament the methodologies of 'parsing' and rhetorical analysis that my research studies raised in the 1990s. I now have a summary chart which I call, 'The Rhetorical Table of the New Testament'. It gives information without which all judgements about the texts and the writers' abilities can be said to be subjective only and nothing more than supposition or the product of wishful thinking. Contrary to mainstream understanding, the literature of the New Testament is disciplined and systematic in all its presentations. Its writers were literary artists and capable writing technicians. We have now, therefore, the opportunity for being objective in what we say about the books and their authors. The clearest indication of this is that we can now jettison all the chapters and verses of all the books! The texts are all self-referencing and, indeed, the structural references the writers embedded in their texts are far superior to Langton's impositions. Every writer made it their business, indeed it was their business, to help their readers through their writings, to discern their leading ideas and set their material to memory, or to read their works out loud with understanding. To achieve this, they wrote to the writing discipline of their day which was appropriate to an oral/aural culture in which the majority only *heard* a writing. That the church imposed its own reading method of chapters and verses on these texts and that both church and academia continue to depend on them is convincing evidence of a long-term collective failure. No one has been reading these texts as the writers meant! But today we have a choice: we can continue reading to chapters and verses, to lectionary systems and any other 'new way' that anyone might deem helpful, or we can choose to read the texts of Christian Faith as the writers always intended.

So, to Mark's Gospel. Since 1999, I have come to understand the Greek text in greater detail and I have learned also to see how hugely important this book is to our understanding of the New Testament and its literature as a whole. It holds central place in the Christian Faith, historically and developmentally. Given the tragic and bewildering times in which the world today experiences the suffering and death caused by a pandemic, we may with greater sympathy, therefore, consider the influence of the events of AD 70 on the early church. Its literary requirements suddenly changed with the events. And, indeed, a million died then, out of a much smaller world population than ours today! Mercifully, thus far, the world is a long way off the same total of deaths, but during these past six weeks of lock-down, I have been happily preparing for my own possible demise by gathering up all my revisions on the Gospel of Mark and preparing up-dates to my notes, to offer 'Chapter and Verse' as I see it now.

I present a clearer presentation of the Greek text than before and I now accompany it with a literal English translation. I do so, that everyone will be able to read the text in the way that serves Mark's requirements and purposes. Few people today have any facility in ancient Greek and those who do, have no ability anyway in reading texts in ancient Greek as first-century readers. If they had, this book would not have been needed. The texts are given in the two languages, so that the whole of Mark's Gospel can be read and enjoyed apart from my notes. One review of *The Markan Matrix* stated that my book would have particular appeal to crossword aficionados! My fathoming of Mark's Gospel *is* a tightly argued read, yes! But the purpose of my notes is to disclose what the text is doing, at each and every turn. My book may have been unreadable then and it may be that it is no better today, but once we have all mastered the reading Mark requires of us, we will be able to throw my notes away anyway! This then is the point of my book. It is not a commentary to replace all commentaries, though all commentaries will need to be replaced. It is intended as a help to us all to read Mark's

Gospel in the way that was always meant. My book is, first and foremost, a reading aid. Given that we will be able to read his work in the way that Mark meant, we will be able to appreciate and understand what it is that he has produced. We will be able to set not-knowing aside. And, as a result, we will be able to tell others what the Gospel is about, without misleading them.

The changes to the text, since 1999, can be summarised here. Days Two and Three of Series B' were deemed to be 9.2-29 and 9.30-50 respectively; they are now viewed as 9.2-32 and 9.33-50. In the same Series, Days Six and Seven were judged to be 10.32-45 and 10.46-52; they are now deemed to be 10.32-46a and 46b-52. No other changes have been required to the overall scheme, other than that the Title has been separated from the Prologue; the Prologue is now 1.2-20. Previously, the 'shaping' of the 'Days' had been judged to have been variously ABB', AA' and compounds of the two. My reading sensitivity having improved, I now declare that all Days are told in the basic shape of ABB'. This follows, of course, from the Title and the Prologue: from the very beginning of his work, the writer tells his reader, that he is writing in this way throughout, from the very beginning to the very end.

The Greek text has continued to go on revealing characteristics otherwise unseen before, either in time for the 1999 publication, or over all time. I have found that charting the contents has helped; dualities and correspondences that otherwise would have gone unnoticed have been revealed. It happened as I was charting Matthew's Gospel, that I suddenly saw that the bits and the pieces that were being prepared for the finished work, numbering 210 in all, were being laid out on a table like pieces of a jigsaw-puzzle being lined up for insertion. I also learned that Matthew's opening and closing pieces held relevant information for his reader for a checking of his reading. In *The Markan Matrix*, I noted that the First Day and the Last Day of the Narrative corresponded in more ways than had been seen before. The first requires to be seen for the sun setting on the old Sabbath and the last for the sun rising on the new Sabbath. Everything in-between tells how this came about, how the Old Covenant came to be replaced with a New Covenant. And this, we note, is a leading idea of Mark. The Jewish War was ending in disaster for Jerusalem and Judea, but beyond it a new age of God's kingdom, his rule, on earth was judged as assured. Its foundations had already been laid. This is the accompanying leading idea of the Gospel. The context of the happenings of the 70s inspired these ideas in Mark. The 30s saw the launch of Christianity in the world. The 70s saw the re-launch, with Mark's Gospel playing a major role.

Beyond the Gospel's Narrative, each side of it, we have to consider what we find in the Prologue and the Epilogue. In the last scene of the Prologue and the first scene of the Epilogue, we need to register what is there. In the last scene of the Prologue, the ABB' parts disclose, in the introduction, A, the setting for the opening of Jesus' ministry, in part B, Jesus' calling two brothers and in part B', his calling of two more brothers. In the first scene of the Epilogue, the number 'seven' has its place in the text; the writer did not need to give this detail here, but he did. Given what I have found in Luke and John as well as in Matthew, all our gospel writers were providing helps in their texts for their readers, so that they might not only read them, but also check that they had been reading them correctly. In Mark's case, there is a Gospel Narrative of Four Series of Seven Days, where two outer (brother) series of seven days enfold two inner (brother) series of seven days. I did not expect this. I did not look for anything like this in any of the four gospels, but when I stood back from the exhibition artworks that I had painted, I saw these things and I grasped their point.

During the past twenty years, a few books have been published which share the same platform as *The Markan Matrix*. I have the opportunity of addressing points of contact and difference later, after my revised presentation of my own work. Particularly pertinent are the publications of Richard A. Burridge, Dennis R. MacDonald and Richard Bauckham. Rather, here, I want to raise the discussion of the importance of Mark's work in the church's development of its understanding of itself, of its message and of how the message could be shared through literature. What I presented 'new' in 1999 provoked a long review in 2001 which ended, 'Much as one respects the scholarship and conviction that has gone into this book, *sadly it runs counter to too many currents and consensuses in Markan Scholarship.*' Over all my forty years of research, I have not found it easy trying to persuade New Testament scholars of anything that was extraordinarily new to them. It may be this that persuaded me in the first place to write such an unreadable book as *The Markan Matrix* and it may even be what is driving me on now to produce it again, but with changes and developments. It has bothered me also for some time now that scholars and publishers of New Testament studies display an aversion to tables, artworks and illustrations of any kind. As an Architect in my former life, they were the stuff of every-day communication. And all of this is a reminder to me that Mark faced similar difficulties. Fascinatingly, we can see today how in the New Testament there are negative reactions to his work as well as (differing) responses of a more positive kind.

Mark's Gospel just doesn't hold the key to our understanding of the writings of the New Testament, it *is* the key. This has become very clear to me over the past twenty years. Prior to Mark's Gospel, the church possessed only the writings of Paul, of the 50s and early 60s. And it was Paul who had set out the terms of Christian Faith in his letters. In his letter to the Galatians, he even declares his source: he received his gospel 'by revelation from Jesus Christ' (Gal. 1.12). In the 70s, after the Fall of Jerusalem, the Destruction of its Temple and the deaths of *over a million people*, the Christian Faith had to be re-presented. Mark was commissioned with the task of sharing 'good news' ('bravo' news) with a 'world' that was reeling at the carnage in Jerusalem and Judea. That 'world', of course, was the Roman Empire. One part of it had just come to a cruel and horrific end. For his Gospel, it appears Mark simply took from Paul's letters all historical references and designations to Christ, his life, his mission, his death and resurrection, and then applied his own days and dates to the presentation he shaped. He was tasked with telling eternal truth in story-form, with presenting Christian Creed in memorable images. What was required was a form of Greek Tragedy for public performance in a popular form of Greek, by recital, or for reading aloud. Those who could have given him eye-witness accounts were dead: they had died in the pogrom, or before then by execution, or in other ways. So, to produce his Epic, he chose to follow the best available good practice. Who would not have turned to Homer?! The structure to Homer's *Iliad* became Mark's model for all four of his Series of Seven Days.

For a time afterwards, the church encouraged similar gospels to be written, adding teachings to Mark, shaping a gospel for Jews and another for Gentiles, and developing the church's spiritual understanding of its Saviour, Jesus. Those who had had only Paul's Letters were initially troubled by these stories, their conflicting genealogies and their contrary claims. But they had their writers and they put them to use (see for example, 1 and 2 Timothy and Titus). Later, partly in response to *these* writings, one wrote saying that what the gospels were saying really happened (see, 2 Peter). Unity among the writers is seen today, however, in that they all shared the view that 'the end' was imminent. But isn't this the strangest thing? The church today contradicts them all and continues to talk about 'the end' that is still to come! The gospel writers, after Mark (after Paul, in the first place), all specifically taught that it was going to happen in their generation. And according to Mark it did, because he wrote after the event, explaining what had happened in the future tense: provision had been made for those who had not sought to save their own lives, but had died in the pogrom. They had been gathered up into heaven by the returning King himself and his angels. To this day, the church and academe struggle with not knowing what the church's literature is and what it is for, struggling between interpretations of myth and 'history', juggling with different views on just about everything and most of all without understanding of what it is to teach about the Parousia, when in fact Mark's Gospel has been making its appeal all along to the church to seize the new Day of God's Kingdom on earth when everything becomes possible through the replacement, or fulfilling (?) of the Old Covenant with the New.

The believability of Christian Faith is at stake. For too long, critical New Testament scholarship has been building on sand. The truth we would gain from the texts, when we know what they are, how they work and what they were written to do, is the rock most people would rather build on in today's scientifically understood world. It is this that inspired me to pursue a literary analysis twenty-one years ago and it is this that inspires me now to complete this up-date.

In my original preface, I gave some history of my project. I share some of it again here. Literary-structural analysis first became an interest of mine while I was preparing in Cambridge for ordination as a Minister of the Methodist Church, 1981-83. As an architect before then, design method had been my stock-in-trade. It surprised me in the 1980s, therefore, to discover that there was still much to be discussed about the 'designs' of the new Testament Books. The 'architect' in me recognised the challenge. Surely, if we were to understand these works and their writers' intentions we needed to know how their contents were arranged. That was my view then and it has not changed since.

I was first attracted in 1982 to examining the 'Central Section' of Luke's Gospel (Lk. 9.43b-19.48). It was the subject of my undergraduate dissertation. This led me, in turn, to an analysis of the whole of Luke's work, the works of the other gospel writers and an analysis too of the Revelation. Because of my excitement in making many discoveries during the early eighties, and my disappointment in the late eighties at not attracting any publisher, I self-published in 1988, *Sliced Bread: The Four Gospels, Acts and Revelation: their Literary Structures*, for the sake of recording and making available my results. In 1999, for similar reasons, I self-published my thesis: *The Markan Matrix: A Literary-Structural Analysis of the Gospel of Mark.* Twenty-one years later, after a string of publications on the New Testament, I now gather up the results of my continuing work and thinking on Mark's Gospel.

In the original preface, I thanked and named many. I am all too aware that of those who have helped me in the past, the majority have died, but happily, not of coronavirus, but at a good age and after a lifelong service to the truths of the New Testament and Christian Faith. Since I last wrote on Mark, I have held the position for three years of Honorary Research Fellow of The Queen's Foundation, Birmingham. I am particularly grateful for this experience of what a college affiliation might have given me throughout an itinerant, pastoral and community ministry. And, as I did in August 1999 at Moredun House in Paisley, I really do acknowledge now once more the faithful and unceasing support of my wife, Sue. I thank also our grown-up children, their spouses and their children, our grandchildren, who have had to live with me and Mark all their lives.

The (Old) Cottage Inn, Church Gresley, 26th May 2020   David G. Palmer

Abbreviations:

AV	Authorized version
Bib	Biblica
BR	Biblical Research
BT	Bible Translator
BThB	Biblical Theology Bulletin
BZNW	Beihefte zur Zeitschrift für die neutestamentliche Wissenschaft
CBQ	Catholic Biblical Quarterly
EKK	Evangelisch-katholischer Kommentar
EphThL	Ephemerides Theological Lovanienses
ER	Epworth Review
EvTh	Evangelische Theologie
ExpT	Expository Times
GNB	Good News Bible
HThR	Harvard Theological Review
IntDB	The Interpreter's Dictionary of the Bible
JBL	Journal of Biblical Literature
JBR	Journal of Bible and Religion
JerB	Jerusalem Bible
JR	Journal of Religion
JSNT	Journal for the Study of the New Testament
JTS	Journal of Theological Studies
LB	Linguistica Biblica
NEB	New English Bible
NIDNTT	The New International Dictionary of New Testament Theology
NIV	New International Version
NovT	Novum Testamentum
NTS	New Testament Studies
OTK	Ökumenischer Taschenkommentar
R&E	Review & Expositor
RS	Religious Studies
RSV	Revised Standard Version
SBLDS	Society of Biblical Literature Dissertation Series
SBLMS	SBL Monograph Series
SBLSPSBL	Seminar Papers
StPB	Studia Post Biblica
TU	Texte und Untersuchungen
UBS	United Bible Society
ZThK	Zeitschrift für Theologie und Kirche

Chapter One
Introduction:

Methodological Issues in the Study of the Gospel of Mark:

Since literary comparison of the Synoptics in the second half of the nineteenth century led to the conclusion that it was the earliest example of the literary genre "gospel", Mark's Gospel has come out from under the shadows of the longer gospels and become a focal point of New Testament study and, therefore, of an ever-increasing volume of monographs and articles. Indeed, it can be stated that the supply of secondary literature on this Gospel is growing so rapidly today that even those who are professionally engaged in Markan studies find it difficult if not impossible to master.

A number of summaries of much effort devoted to understanding and interpreting Mark's work are available[1]. We need not, therefore, see it as a requirement here to rehearse the whole history of the development of approaches to it, for its own sake: rather, I would endeavour to identify, from the methodological approaches that have been and are being made, the key questions that have continued to be raised, and those in particular which patently still require answers, or, at the very least, new attempts at answers.

Over the past one-and-a-half centuries, an appreciation of the three stages in the growth of the Gospels, which focuses on (1) the actual words and deeds of the historical Jesus, (2) a period of oral transmission, and (3) the writings of the evangelists, has led to the development of a multitude of investigative methods. In the nineteenth century, source criticism was developed as New Testament critics were primarily interested in Mark's Gospel as a historical source for the life of Jesus and his life-setting. At the beginning of the present century, scholars became more interested in the life and life-setting of the early church and began to develop and employ form criticism. Halfway through this century, a new generation turned its attention to the evangelist and his theology and the life-setting of his Christian community and began developing the methodology of redaction criticism.

During the last half of this century, a rash of new methodologies has been developing. Some scholars have begun applying the tools of social science to the text, to understand the social structure and values behind the gospel. Others are reading the text with the assistance of categories learned from anthropology. Structuralists have been entertaining both a philosophy and a critical methodology and they have been developing highly abstract categories based on two presuppositions: that "appearances are not reality"; and that deep structures, below the surface, "express themselves as codes". Also literary-critical study has undergone development[2] and rhetorical criticism has been established. It is these latter two methodologies which many would argue are potentially the most fruitful.

The approach of literary and rhetorical critics begins with seeing the text as a unity. Earlier literary criticism focused on the analysis of texts to establish their structure and com-

---

[1]W.G. Kümmel, *Introduction to the New Testament*, SCM Press Ltd, 1979, ch. 6; H. Räisänen, *The "Messianic Secret" in Mark*, T & T Clark, Edinburgh 1990, ch.1; F.J. Matera, *What are They Saying about Mark?*, Paulist Press, New York/Mahwah, 1987; E. Best, *Mark: the Gospel as Story*, T & T Clark, Edinburgh, 1986, ch. XVI; and M.A. Tolbert, *Sowing the Gospel: Mark's World in Literary-Historical Perspective*, Fortress Press, Minneapolis, 1989, p.106.
[2]See the Introduction in particular to *A Complete Literary Guide to the Bible*, eds. Leland Ryken & Tremper Longman III, Zondervan Publishing House, Grand Rapids, Michigan, 1993.

position, their possible use of sources, their integrity and their style. Now much more attention is given to the rhetorical techniques employed by the author to narrate his/her story. We distinguish between two approaches in recent years: some scholars have been attempting to identify the rhetorical genre of the Gospel by comparing it with similar literature of the Greco-Roman world of the first century[3]; others have been employing the tools of contemporary literary criticism, arguing that since Mark's Gospel is a narrative, it is capable of being analysed like any other story, in terms of plot, character, development, narrative technique, and so on[4]. Redaction critics, since the beginning of the third quarter of this century, did indeed view Mark as both author and theologian, but they often read the Gospel in a piecemeal fashion by concentrating primarily on the evangelist's supposed additions and alterations to the traditions he received.

The study of Mark's Gospel has never before been so diversified and the questions being put have never before been so wide-ranging. The methodological tool-box is full to overflowing and specialisms of craftsmanship have grown beyond any early expectation, but the fact remains that fundamental questions, spanning the last century-and-a-half, still remain unanswered to the satisfaction of scholarship in general.

Fundamental Questions in the Study of Mark's Gospel:

Fundamental questions in the study of Mark's Gospel focus upon his leading idea and upon his theological, literary and compositional abilities.

In 1901, Wrede's rigorous historical analysis led him to define Mark's "leading idea" "or purpose" as the constructing of his Gospel on the basis of a dogmatic theory of a messiahship that was to be kept secret until after Jesus' resurrection[5]. He was dissatisfied with his own work, however, because he recognised the limits of his own methodological approach. He identified a need for a literary-critical analysis which would make clear the particular character of the book and the factors which had contributed to its production. In taking this position, he much anticipated the founding of redaction critical study in the fifties and the more recent literary-critical approaches. The situation today, however, is that we still await sure results from these quarters.

In 1919, K.L. Schmidt raised issues in regard to Mark's "framework" to his history of Jesus. Mark's Gospel, he concluded, stemmed from the linking together of material handed on to him as single units of tradition[6]. He further deduced that Mark's framework was "artifi-

---

[3]E.g. and so henceforth: G.G. Bilezikian, *The Liberated Gospel: A Comparison of the Gospel of Mark and Greek Tragedy*, Grand Rapids: Baker, 1977; B. Standaert, *L'Evangile selon Marc: Commentaire*, Lire la Bible 61, Les Editions du Cerf, Paris, 1983; V.K. Robbins, *Jesus the Teacher (A Socio-Rhetorical Interpretation of Mark)*, Fortress Press, Philadelphia, 1984; J. Dewey, *Markan Public Debate: Literary Technique, Concentric Structure, and Theology in Mark 2.1-3.6*, SBLDS 48, Scholars Press, Chico CA, 1980; Tolbert, *Sowing the Gospel...*; John Painter, *Mark's Gospel: Worlds in Conflict*, Routledge, London and New York, 1997; and for an introduction and guide to scholarship in rhetorical criticism, Burton L. Mack, *Rhetoric and the New Testament*, Fortress Press, Minneapolis, 1990.

[4]E.g. and so henceforth: N.R. Petersen, *Literary Criticism for New Testament Critics*, Fortress Press, Philadelphia, 1978; R.M. Fowler, *Loaves and Fishes. The Function of the Feeding Stories in the Gospel of Mark*, SBLDS 54, Scholars Press, Chico CA, 1981; J.D. Kingsbury, *The Christology of Mark's Gospel*, Fortress Press, Philadelphia, 1983; C.H. Tannehill, "The Disciples in Mark: The Function of a Narrative Role", *JR* 57 (1977); D. Juel, *Messiah and Temple: The Trial of Jesus in the Gospel of Mark*, SBLDS 31, Scholars Press, Missoula, Montana, 1977; and D. Rhoads and D. Michie, *Mark as Story. An Introduction to the Narrative of a Gospel*, Fortress Press, Philadelphia, 1982.

[5]W. Wrede, *The Messianic Secret*, Eng. Tr., James Clarke, Cambridge/London, 1971.

[6]K.L. Schmidt, *Der Rahmen der Geschichte Jesu, Literarkritische Untersuchungen zur ältesten Jesusüberlieferung*, Trowitzsch & Sohn, Berlin, 1919. For a recent and most comprehensive challenge to Schmidt's methods of argument, see David R. Hall, *The Gospel Framework: Fiction or Fact? (A critical evaluation of Der Rahmen...)*, Paternoster Press, Carlisle, 1998.

cial", but it was still, even then, only loosely and variously describable. Literary-critical analysis has attempted clearer definition, but it has not yet resolved the issue. A framework exists: it is one framework; there are not two or more options. Just as any building has a structure which can be described objectively and in all its detail, so too Mark's Gospel has a single structure which demands definition. When it is revealed, it will be one with which scholarship will be able to work, with a unanimity of a kind which we have not yet seen.

Since Wrede, we have witnessed an ever-growing number of propositions, but "on the basis of which leading idea has the evangelist conceived his blending of material?" asks Kümmel.[7] Best poses a similar question: "What is the glue or cement which holds the material together?"[8] "The question is extremely difficult to answer," says Kümmel, "since it must be answered exclusively on the ground of an analysis of Mark's Gospel itself."

A study of Bultmann's starting point displays one aspect of the problem. He begins with a recognition of Schmidt's "careful analysis", but in freely addressing the issue of the parts, the units of earlier tradition, he fails to address, in as open and critical a manner, the issue of the whole, which to Schmidt is just as important. Bultmann starts with the preconception that "the most ancient tradition consisted of individual sections and that the connecting together is secondary"[9]. He falls prey to his second preconception that, "when one tries to determine the leading ideas of Mark's arrangement of his material, one has to take into account the collections of material that he had in front of him."[10] This may sound like good, common sense, but before one can determine Mark's reasons for, and method of organising his material, one has to be able to describe the result, that is, the arrangement itself, of his compositional work. Knowing the shape of the Gospel's presentation is not dependent, in the first instance, on understanding Mark's sources. Bultmann was set on a course, from the beginning, which would lead him inexorably to the conclusion that "Mark is not sufficiently master of his material to be able to venture on a systematic construction himself"[11], apart from a turning point at 8.27ff.[12] A tension is well exhibited here. Mark can be credited with creating a new literary genre, but he lacked both the freedom and ability to create and control it. Bultmann's understanding was that Mark's material controlled him.

Where Bultmann gave up on attempting to define Mark's "leading ideas" others ventured. Dodd sought to show that the order of narratives in Mark's Gospel is basically and essentially the traditional sequence of events of the history of Jesus, as discernible in Acts 10.37-41[13]. Farrer proposed a theological scheme, repetitive of typological fulfilment of Old Testament texts[14]. Carrington proposed that the sequence was the result of a liturgical intention for the Gospel[15] (an idea that Goulder later developed further[16]). Beach identified what he thought were six stages in the revelation of Jesus' messiahship[17]. Bowman claimed to have discovered parallels to the Jewish Passover Haggada[18]. And Kümmel despaired, "Close ex-

---

[7]Kümmel, *Introduction...*, p.85.

[8]Best, *Mark: the Gospel...*, p.100.

[9]R. Bultmann, *Die Geschichte der Synoptischen Tradition*, Gottingen, 1931; *The History of the Synoptic Tradition*, tr. John Marsh, Basil Blackwell, Oxford, 1972, p.338.

[10]Bultmann, *The History...*, p.349.

[11]Bultmann, *The History...*, p.350.

[12]My analysis below shows that he is at least right about the one "turning point" he recognises.

[13]C.H. Dodd, "The Framework of the Gospel Narrative", *ExpT* 43 (1932), pp.396ff.

[14]A.M. Farrer, *A Study in St Mark*, Dacre Press, Westminster, 1951: compare J. Marcus, who confines his study of Old Testament texts to Christological considerations only, *The Way of the Lord: Christological Exegesis of the Old Testament in the Gospel of Mark*, T & T Clark, Edinburgh, 1993.

[15]P. Carrington, *The Primitive Christian Calendar: A Study in the Making of the Markan Gospel*, Cambridge University Press, Cambridge, 1952.

[16]M.D. Goulder, *The Evangelists' Calendar (A Lectionary Explanation of the Development of Scripture)*, SPCK, London, 1978.

[17]C. Beach, *The Gospel of Mark: Its Making and Meaning*, Harper & Bros., New York, 1959.

[18]J. Bowman, "The Gospel of Mark: The New Christian Passover Haggada", *StPB* 8 (1965).

amination of all these schemes leads to no proof based on the text itself"[19]. Again we are presented with the same, basic requirement. The text and the text alone requires analysis. Or, to quote Kümmel once more, the question of Mark's leading idea "must be answered exclusively on the ground of an analysis of Mark's Gospel itself."

On Mark's theological, literary and compositional abilities, not surprisingly we meet with a wide range of opinion too. To Bultmann, Mark was simply a collector or hander on of traditions, not a theologian. On the other hand, Marxsen's pioneering redaction critical studies[20] led him, and Schweizer[21] in turn, to the view that Mark was a profound interpreter, whose theology may also be used on the contemporary scene[22]. Schreiber sees the Gospel as a kind of kerygmatic allegory and that "every line of Mark's Gospel must be explored for its allegorical meaning" (the historical form of the Gospel is but an external wrapping)[23]. Pesch argued that Mark handled the tradition in a very conservative way, that his work was "scarcely governed by any sweeping compositional viewpoint", but is rather "a kind of "unliterary writing", and that he did not attempt to "unify the traditional material"[24]. Pesch's hypothesis that the Gospel is an extended passion narrative has not attracted wide support. Best argues that Mark had "a positive respect for the material which he used" and that he altered the individual units as little as possible. He says, therefore, that "we should not look for a coherent and consistent theology in the Gospel, but be prepared to find unevenness"[25]. Meagher takes the view that Mark's Gospel is "clumsy construction", that it has "an air of great ordinariness" and that it "is not egregiously bad... nor memorably good" as a literary work[26]. Schmithals distinguishes between the work of the final redactor (Mark) and the *Grundschrift*, the bulk of the Gospel: Mark is a very ordinary churchman without literary skill; the author of the believed *Grundschift* is an "excellent theologian[27]. Williams contends that Mark is "hardly a collector or editor", but "a maker, a poet in the strict sense."[28]

Räisänen notes that Williams' work is informed by the new literary approach and that in recent years the focus has turned to Mark's Gospel as a narrative. "Historical or tradition historical questions need not be wholly excluded," he says, "but have to be postponed until a purely literary analysis has been carried out. In such an analysis, the plot and the rhetoric as well as the settings and the characters of the gospel are scrutinised."[29] He refers to the pioneering work of Petersen[30] and to the narrative work of Kingsbury on the "messianic secret"[31]. He quotes from Rhoads' and Michie's work: "The study of narrative emphasises the unity of the final text... A literary study... suggests that the author succeeded in creating a uni-

---

[19]Kümmel, *Introduction...*, p.86.

[20]W. Marxsen, *Mark the Evangelist*, Ger. orig. 1956, Eng.tr. J. Boyce, Abingdon, Nashville, 1969.

[21]E. Schweizer, *The Good News according to Mark*, tr. D.H. Madvig, John Knox Press, Atlanta, 1970.

[22]E. Schweizer, "Die Frage nach dem historischen Jesus", *EvTh* (1964), pp.403-419, 411f.: the mystery of Jesus Christ "can always be preached and never really described"; compare also Marxsen, *Mark...*, p.216.

[23]J. Schreiber, "Die Christologie des Markusevangeliums. Beobachtungen zur Theologie und Komposition des zweiten Evangeliums", *ZThK* 58 (1961), pp.154-183.

[24]R. Pesch, *Das Markusevangelium 1. Teil: Einleitung und Kommentar zu Kap. 1.1-8.26*, Herders Theologischer Kommentar zum Neuen Testament II, Herder, Freiburg, 1976.

[25]E. Best, *Disciples and Discipleship: Studies in the Gospel according to Mark*, T & T Clark, Edinburgh, 1986, pp.46f.

[26]J.C. Meagher, *Clumsy Construction in Mark's Gospel: A Critique of Form and Redaktionsgeschichte*, Toronto Studies in Theology 3, New York, 1979.

[27]W. Schmithals, "Das Evangelium nach Markus", 1-2, *OTK* 2/1-2, Guttersloh (1979).

[28]J.G. Williams, *Gospel against Parable. Mark's language of Mystery*, Sheffield University Press, Sheffield, 1985.

[29]Räisänen, *The Messianic Secret...*, p.14; see also Matera, *What are the saying about...?* p.92 for a similar view and for his reflection on the nineteenth century search for the historical Jesus that investigations would have been more profitable if they had begun with a literary critical study.

[30]N.R. Petersen, *Literary Criticism...*; also, "The Composition of Mark 4.1-8.26", *HThR* 73 (1980), pp.185-217.

[31]Kingsbury, *The Christology....*

fied narrative."[32] Räisänen confidently states himself that, "Mark does have a plot. He has a point of view of his own. He has composed his work according to a plan. Let there be no doubt about that. The *question remains*, however, just how much skill and sophistication does Mark's work display? Just how well did he succeed in creating a unified narrative?"[33]

Again, the requirement of a "purely literary analysis" is called for. If Mark has a plot, what is it? If he has a plan, let it be defined. Only when these things are known will it be possible to proceed with anything like an objective evaluation of Mark's theological, literary and compositional abilities. It follows, that a greater degree of unanimity between scholars would be possible also. It is my essential purpose, therefore, to demonstrate that an analysis of the text and the text alone, with the employment of methodologies appropriate to the task, is able to establish what is the Markan framework and Mark's methods of organisation and presentation.

It may be asked, "If Mark employed both a plan and a method of presentation, why have they not been identified before now?" The answer must lie somewhere between the fact that in the biblical- critical era there has been a loss of contact with first century literary-compositional method[34], and the fact that we have not been employing the right analytical methodologies.

Those who have approached the Gospel text as a unified whole and who have attempted a careful and thoughtful outlining of the overall organisation of Mark's Gospel have had their influence on my thesis. In addition to the work of Williams, Petersen, Kingsbury, Rhoads and Mitchie, as referenced above, I include that of Robbins, Trocmé, Faw, Lang, Scott, Stock, Culpepper, Tolbert and Noble.[35] The rhetorical structure I present, however, runs contrary to all their conclusions. And whilst it adds to the list of potential solutions to the still open, fundamental questions regarding Mark's Gospel, it is offered, nevertheless, as an alternative which meets the challenges of criticism levelled at previous attempts.

The Cultural and Historical Context of the Gospel:

The underlying issues which we recognise at the outset concern the functionings of this new literary genre of "gospel". We necessarily consider the life-setting of the early Christian community and of the Gospel itself.

Readily, we acknowledge that the first audiences of Mark's Gospel shared with him the mind-set of the first century populace in religio-cultural ways. In matters literary-cultural, immediately we note that few first century Christians would possess any literature of their own, sacred or secular, and that the populace, on the whole, would be "un-bookish" and

---

[32]Rhoads & Michie, *Mark as Story*...

[33]Räisänen, *The Messianic Secret*..., p.15 (my italics). Further, Robbins, *Jesus the Teacher*..., p.19, identifies with C. H. Holman, when he says, "Virtually every literary document has a formal structure that is a planned framework, and the framework is likely to be a clue to the interrelation of forms in the document."

[34]In his Introduction to *Rhetoric and the New Testament*..., pp.9-11, Mack demonstrates how "the knowledge of rhetoric actually was lost to us in the twists and turns of twentieth-century scholarship. We now know", he writes, "that interest in rhetoric waned around the turn of the century, ushering in approximately four generations of scholarship without formal training in rhetoric and with very little knowledge of the tradition of rhetorical criticism." (p.11).

[35]V. Robbins, *Jesus the Teacher*..., pp.19-51; É. Trocmé, *The Formation of the Gospel According to Mark*, tr. P. Gaughan, London, SPCK, 1975, pp.215-259; C.E. Faw, "The Outline of Mark", *JBR* 25 (1957), pp.19-23; F.G. Lang, "Kompositionsanalyse des Markusevangeliums", *ZThK* 74 (1977), pp.1-24; M.P. Scott, "Chiastic Structure: A Key to the Interpretation of Mark's Gospel", *BThB* 15 (1985), pp. 17-26; A. Stock, "Hinge Transitions in Mark's Gospel", *BThB* 15 (1985), pp.27-31; R.A. Culpepper, "An Outline of the Gospel According to Mark", *R&E* 75 (1978), pp.619-622; M.A. Tolbert, *Sowing the Gospel*...; and D.F. Noble, *An Examination of the Structure of Mark's Gospel*, PhD Thesis, University of Edinburgh, 1972.

mostly illiterate.[36] Only the wealthy will have possessed their own copies of Biblical books. For one indication of this, according to Luke, an Ethiopian eunuch was in possession of a copy of the book of Isaiah, and he was an important official in charge of all the treasury of the Candace of Ethiopia (Acts 8.27,28). Christians from conscientious Jewish family backgrounds will have memorised the Torah in full, or many of its principal parts, and other scriptures too.[37] Some, indeed, will have been well educated in the sacred scriptures. Apollos (Acts 18.24) was one who was named. We know that the scriptures were being read aloud in the assemblies (1Tim.4.13)[38]. Such was the practice of the synagogue, in reading from the Law and the Prophets every Sabbath (Lk. 4.16,17; Acts 13.15, 15.21). And Luke tells us, indirectly, that Jesus himself was literate (Lk. 4.17 again). The first followers of Jesus we are told, however, were not (Acts 4.13, they were "illiterate and uneducated"), but they need not have been without a good oral education.

Even for the majority of people, who remained illiterate, rhetorical conventions permeated their universe and their culture, the way they heard and the way they spoke[39], for the rhetorical theory of the schools found its immediate application in almost every form of oral and written communication[40], of Jews, Greeks and early Christians alike, with none excepted[41]. In the public place and the place of education, everywhere in the first century, there was a considerable degree of dependence on rhetorical conventions for transmitting and for memorising information[42]. A widespread, customary use of rhetorical figures and patterns of

---

[36]William Harris has sought to discover the extent of literacy in the ancient world: using a broad definition of literacy as the ability to read and write at any level, he draws on wide and varied evidence - explicit, circumstantial and comparative - and takes some account of the types and the uses of literacy. Granting regional and temporal variations, throughout the entire period of classical Greek, Hellenistic and Roman imperial civilisation, the extent of literacy was about 10 per cent and never exceeded 15 to 20 per cent of the population as a whole (*Ancient Literacy*, Harvard University Press, Cambridge, Mass., 1989).

[37]According to Josephus (*Contra Apion*. 2.204, *Ant.*. 4.211; cf. T. Levi 13.2; Philo, *Ad Gaium*, pp.115, 210): in first century Judaism it was a duty, even a religious commandment, that children be taught to read. Instruction may have been given in the home by parents, but rabbinical sources suggest that schools were common in towns and were heavily enrolled. Before its destruction in 70AD, Jerusalem is said to have had 480 synagogues, each with a "house of reading" (*bet sefer*) and a "house of learning" (*bet midrash*) attached. The former provided young children with instruction to read scripture: the latter offered older children instruction in the oral Torah. The capacity to read and understand scripture, especially the Torah, stood at the centre of instruction. For the development of Jewish schools, see M. Hengel, *Judaism and Hellenism*, Fortress Press, Philadelphia, 1974.

[38]For extra-biblical evidence, we might turn to Justin Martyr (*Apology*, 1.67) who describes the procedure of Christian assemblies in the middle of the second century (this dating itself, of course, limits this as "evidence"): "And on the day which is called the day of the sun there is an assembly of all those who live in the towns or in the country, and the memoirs of the apostles or the writings of the prophets are read as long as time permits. Then the reader ceases, and the president speaks, admonishing and exhorting us to imitate these excellent examples..."

[39]Tolbert, *Sowing the Gospel...*, p.41.

[40]G.A. Kennedy, *New Testament Interpretation through Rhetorical Criticism*, University of North Carolina Press, Chapel Hill, N.C., 1984, p.10.

[41]Burton L. Mack, *Rhetoric...*, pp.12-17.

[42]Ian H. Thomson, *Chiasmus in the Pauline Corpus*, JSNT, Sheffield Academic Press, Sheffield, 1995, p.17: he writes, "Throughout classical education, learning by heart was given a prominent role. As the pupils progressed through stages of schooling, ever-increasing attention had to be devoted to the *scriptio continua*." And he quotes from A. Stock: "Chiastic Awareness and Education in Antiquity", *BThB* 14 (1984), pp.23-27, p.24. "Thus, in the Greek system, for those 14-21 years, the grammarian based his instruction on poetry, with Homer in the first place. At the beginning of the Christian era, the treatment of an author had four stages: textual criticism; expressive reading (for this the *scriptio continua* had to be broken down: words separated, punctuation determined, phrases and sentences found, questions distinguished, lines made to scan); literal and literary explanation of both form and content; and ultimately moral judgement of the text. Effectively, to sustain this level of attention to the text, it was learned by heart."

"The ancient educational system, both Greek and Roman, made even its youngest pupils much more aware of the movement and structure of a passage than moderns are. Thus in both systems, a child was not deemed to have learned the alphabet until it could be recited both from alpha to omega (A to X in Latin - Y and Z were

argumentation had established itself cross-culturally. Perelman and Olbrechts-Tyteca[43] in their research on ancient rhetoric re-established its classical definition as "the art of persuasion", described a logic of communication that could be applied to widely ranging modes of human discourse, and immersed the study of speech events in social situations. They well demonstrated the importance of the situation or speech context when calculating the persuasive force of an argumentation. And they well rescued the understanding of rhetoric from that of mere ornamentation, or embellished literary style, or extravagance in public oratory, and placed it at the centre of a social theory of language. Like grammar in culture and language, rhetoric in an ancient society and in its discourse had its rules which developed over centuries and which by trial and error and usage became acceptable. It was, therefore, identified, studied and re-applied in succeeding generations.

A full treatise on what features of literacy and methods of learning characterised the early Christian community may not be possible today[44], but we now know that certain common patterns of interaction, communication and education existed throughout the cultural milieu in which Christianity was born, despite the variations within Mediterranean culture. Robbins informs us that "rhetorical forms and the figure and concept of the sage intersected with established traditions to provide a common cultural base for Greek, Roman, Jewish and Christian communities. Within this setting small forms like the proverb, the apophthegma, and the chreia provided a bridge between oral and written culture."[45] Of the larger literary forms, of oration, diatribe, essay, symposium, epistle, biography and novel, Robbins suggests that they "represented the meeting ground for rhetorical forms and patterns of influence from the wise personages in the culture."[46]

Identifying conventional repetitive and progressive forms in Mark's Gospel, Robbins[47] viewed Mark's accomplishment as that of adopting and modifying such forms as were present in prophetic biblical literature and in non-biblical literature associated with Greco-Roman religio-ethical teachers who gathered disciple- companions.

In terms of 'biblical form' sources, he particularly discovered in 1 and 2 Kings (concerning Elijah and Elisha) and Jeremiah a socio-rhetorical pattern containing three essential elements:

1. the word of the Lord comes to the prophet;
2. the prophet does and says the word of the Lord;
3. events occur according to the word of the Lord as pronounced by the prophet.

In terms of extra biblical material, Robbins sees Xenophon's *Memorabilia* (dating: 390-355 BC) as the most informative document. Other similar documents from the second and third centuries AD are known which similarly tell of people possessing wisdom who gathered dis-

---

looked on as "foreign"), and also from omega to alpha, and then both ways at once, alpha-omega, beta-psi... munu." Thomson suggests that "this approach to the alphabet could not but help contribute to chiastic awareness."
[43]Chaim Perelman, and L. Olbrechts-Tyteca, *The New Rhetoric: A Treatise on Argumentation*, University of Notre Dame Press, Notre Dame, Ind., 1969.
[44]In his book, *Books and Readers in the Early Church: A History of Early Christian Texts*, Yale University Press, New Haven and London, 1995, Harry Y. Gamble gathers some evidence on the subject of education and social class, and recognises also the influence of the multicultural and multilingual settings of the church: for instance, a Christian in Palestine would be well versed in Aramaic, less so in Hebrew, in Greek only a little, and in Latin probably not at all; a Christian in Rome would likely know no Aramaic or Hebrew, but would be well-versed in Greek and best of all in Latin.
[45]Robbins, *Jesus the Teacher...*, p.2.
[46]Robbins, *Jesus the Teacher...*, p.2; H.A. Fischel, "Story and History: Observations on Greco-Roman Rhetoric and Pharisaism", *AOS* (1969), pp.59-88, see pp.61-63; and Tolbert, *Sowing the Gospel...*, pp.81-83.
[47]Robbins, *Jesus the Teacher...*, chapters 3 to 6.

ciple-companions. The socio-rhetorical pattern he discerns contains, again, three essential elements:

1. the teacher himself does what he teaches others to do;
2. the teacher interacts with others through speech to teach the system of thought and action he embodies;
3. through his teaching and action the teacher transmits a religio-ethical system of thought and action to later generations through his disciple-companions.

Additionally, Robbins usefully notes how early Christian writers during the second century referred to the gospels as Ἀπομνημονεύματα (Latin: *Memorabilia*)[48].

In Mark's Gospel he discerns a shift in terminology from the Old Testament 'word' to 'gospel' and a development by Mark of what in the biblical material is often only simple repetition, but after the Greco-Roman method is progressive repetition (by which minor changes are introduced). He discerns a three-step pattern that dominates the narrative, as follows:

1. Jesus comes into a place accompanied by his disciples;
2. people interact both positively and negatively with the action and speech of Jesus;
3. Jesus summons his disciple-companions to transmit features of his action and thought that he has enacted before them.

And based on this, he argues that the formal structure of Mark's Gospel as a whole is established on such three-step progressions as he identifies.

For Tolbert, the two major formative influences on Mark's stylistic development were Greco-Roman rhetoric and popular culture. To the evidence of elite, first century Greco-Roman literature[49] which has been much studied already for its Gospel links in terms of aretalogy, biography and memorabilia, Tolbert usefully draws in a consideration of early examples of the ancient popular novel[50]. Whilst she acknowledges that Mark's Gospel does not share with them the same story line, she demonstrates that the similarities, nevertheless, between their rhetorical, stylistic and linguistic features are conspicuous. She writes, "Both are synthetic, conventional narratives that combine historiographic form with epic and dramatic substance. Episodic plots, central turning points, final recognition sequences, dialogic scenes with narrative frames, sparing but crucial use of monologue, repetition, narrative summaries, foreshadowing, and monolithic illustrative characters are some of the elements the Gospel and ancient novels have in common - and all of these are presented in a simple, crude, conventional style suitable to popular dissemination across a broad spectrum of society."[51]

For Hooker, Mark's Gospel functions *like* a drama, after the manner of a contemporary Greek drama as described by Aristotle (in *Poetics* 10-12,18 and *Rhetoric* III.14). Following the basic pattern of a tragedy, after the 'prologue' (which in practice provides the audience with whatever they need to understand the play), the Gospel presents firstly the 'complica-

---

[48]Robbins, *Jesus the Teacher...*, p.65.

[49]E.g. *The Histories* of Herodotus; also Virgil's *Eclogues, Georgics* and *Aeneid*; Homer's *Iliad* and *Odyssey*; Xenophon's *Memorabilia*; the works of Plutarch, Catullus and Thucydides.

[50]Gamble (*Books and Readers...*, p.39) raises the question, "In what sense may we speak of there having been a popular literature in the Roman empire?" He argues that the capacity to read, the interest and leisure to do so and the financial means to procure texts, belonged to a few, and this circumstance must limit the idea of popular literature. But, he reminds us that much ancient reading was aloud and occurred in public, quasi-public and domestic settings where those listening might include the semiliterate and illiterate as well as the literate.

[51]Tolbert, *Sowing the Gospel...*, p.78.

tion', secondly the 'turning point' or 'reversal', and thirdly the 'denouement' (lit. 'untying'). Hooker identifies 8.27 to be the likely candidate for such a 'turning point'. Without conviction, she writes that an Aristotelian Greek tragedy "*may* be rounded off with an epilogue"[52]. In her commentary[53] she identifies 16.1-8 as 'the last section of the Gospel', but titles it 'the Epilogue' as many other commentators do. My reading, however, is that 16.9-20, although generally considered an addition to Mark's writing, appears more separated from the preceding text[54], and exhibits more the qualities, therefore, of an 'epilogue' after the manner of a Greek tragedy.

Mack's interesting observations, about the historical probability of New Testament writers and even bearers of Palestinian traditions being influenced by Greco-Roman rhetorical theory and practice, fuel the argument that Mark deliberately and understandably employed literary conventions available to him from the cultural milieu of his age. In referring to the classical handbooks[55] he summarises the five aspects of the practice of rhetoric that were, in general, addressed[56]:

a) Invention (*heuresis, inventio*): the conceptual process of deciding on the subject to be elaborated, the position one would take on an issue of debate, or the thesis one wished to propose. It also referred to the search for materials one might use which was more a matter of finding or discovering the right material for making a point, and less a matter of creating a brand-new idea (for a 'clever' example, he turns to Mk.2.23-28, because it is taken from the objectors' own literary tradition and used against them[57]).

b) Arrangement (*taxis, disposito*): the work of ordering material into an outline, paying attention to such things as the best sequence to use, or whether one should expand on this or that point, or how best to develop a sub-theme. Skeletal outlines were standard and in crafting a speech in particular, rhetors were expected to "hide the standard outline" (an example of this is possibly the 4-8-4-8-4 scheme of Luke's Sermon on the Plain[58]). Arrangement was as important and creative a process as invention.

c) Style (*lexis, elocutio*): the way in which material was handled in the process of composition. Grammar, syntax, rhythm and the selection and repetition of words were matters of importance. Style was a matter of aesthetic effect and an important factor in persuasion; it also had a mnemonic function.

d) Memory (*mneme, memoria*): the process of memorising the speech so that delivery would be natural. Techniques in writing were devised: the most interesting is the imaginative creating of a scene in which vivid and striking images of persons, objects and events would be set by association with the points, words and figures of speech one wished remembered (*Ad Herennium* III.xvi.28 to xxiv.40).

e) Delivery (*hypocrisis, pronunciato*): it referred to voice, pauses, and gestures appropriate to a speech occasion.

With Robbins, in the literary-structural analysis I present, I will agree on the importance of three-step progressions in the Markan text, but not with his thematic description of the three steps. Rather, I will show that the three-step progressions are of a purely literary-structural kind. Based on syntax, grammar and word repetition, the three steps read as 'introductory', the 'first development', and the 'second and completing development'. I will agree

---

[52]Morna D. Hooker, *Beginnings: Keys that open the Gospels*, SCM Press Ltd., London, 1997, p.4.
[53]Morna D. Hooker, *The Gospel according to St Mark*, Black's New Testament Commentaries, A & C Black, London, 1991, p.382.
[54]See most commentaries for arguments of dislocation between 16.8 and v.9.
[55]Principally: Aristotle's *Ars Rhetorica*, Cicero's *De inventione*, the *Rhetorica ad Herennium* and the Progymnasmata of Theon and Hermogenes.
[56]Mack, *Rhetoric...*, pp.32-34.
[57]Mack, *Rhetoric...*, p.52.
[58]David G. Palmer, *Sliced Bread: The Four Gospels, Acts and Revelation: Their Literary Structures*, Ceridwen Press, Cardiff, 1988, p.70.

with Robbins that three-step progressions indicate the nature of the structure and plan of the Gospel as a whole, but I will not be found to be agreeing with him on his outline of Mark's Gospel. Fundamentally it is because many more three-step progressions exist by this definition than by his. The interest he shows in 1 and 2 Kings and Jeremiah appears justified. A few of the three-step progressions I define do correspond to his. It may well be the case that Mark was influenced by the forms of prophetic biblical literature. Additionally, however, there is the possibility that Mark was also influenced by the methodology and content of the first Priestly document of the Pentateuch (Genesis 1.1-2.4a, dated 538-450BC) and the compositional method of the editors of the Pentateuch (of only a slightly later period).

On the structural parallelism of the first eleven chapters of Genesis, 1.1-7.24 and 8.1-11.26, for parallels between 'creation' (chs.1,2) and 're-creation' (8.1-9.17), and further meaningful parallels, see Barry L. Bandstra[59]. We will see that Mark displays similar sectional, simple parallelism, denoted A:A'. And specifically on the structure of Gen. 1.1-2.4a, Bandstra discerns two three-day sub-series[60]. My literary-structural analysis will demonstrate that Mark repeatedly employs a 'seven day' scheme, and we will see that each of Mark's seven-day schemes (four in all) exhibit similar three-day sub-series, though, in Mark's case, each side of a central day's telling. (Day seven of the Priestly 'creation story' is included in the Epilogue.)

Attention is attracted also to the fact that Mark opens his Gospel Prologue with the words "The *beginning* of the Gospel..." (see Gen. 1.1) and the longer ending includes a reference to "creation" too (Mk. 16.15). Further to this, I observe, as does Painter, that Mark quotes from Gen. 1.27 in Mk. 10.6. In my presentation of my structural analysis, we will see that it significantly falls in the central Day's telling of Mark's third series of seven days, the turning point of the series. Painter's contribution is important and worth mention here: to him, Mark's Gospel "is... an attempt to proclaim the good news of God in a world dominated by evil... While Mark lacks a full account of creation of the world by God, 10.6, 'From the beginning of the creation male and female he made them', is enough to show full dependence on the Genesis account... In earlier Jewish historical writings all being and action were understood as expressions of the will of God, and if Israel suffered it was understood to be a consequence of disobedience to God."[61] We may observe also that in the accounts of the flood, by which God is said to have first dealt with all the evil in the world, there are other references to seven-day passages of time (Gen. 8.10,12), and references also to forty-day periods (Gen. 7.12,17; 8.6; *cf.* Mk. 1.13) and a twenty-seventh day (Gen. 8.14, the day that "the earth was completely dry"; *cf.* Day 27 in Mark's account, the day of Jesus' death and burial). Another possible point of contact is Mark's identification of the Spirit as coming down on Jesus as a "dove" (Mk. 1.10; *cf.* Gen. 8.8-12).

My reading of Gen. 1.1-2.4a, in brief, is as follows:

		Prologue:	1.1,2	God created the heavens and the earth
A	A	Day One:	1.3-5	light; day and night
	B	Day Two:	1.6-8	water/water; sky
	B'	Day Three:	1.9-13	water/land, vegetation
A'	A	Day Four:	1.14-19	lights; day and night
	B	Day Five:	1.20-23	water/sea - creatures; sky - birds; "be fruitful..."
	B'	Day Six:	1.24-31	land; creatures; man; "be fruitful..."; vegetation
		Epilogue:	2.1-4a	(inc. Day 7) the heavens and the earth... created

---

[59] Barry L. Bandstra, *Reading the Old Testament: An Introduction to the Hebrew Bible,* Wadsworth Publishing Co., International Thomson Publishing Inc., 1995, p.72.
[60] Bandstra, *Reading the Old Testament...*, p.62.
[61] Painter, *Mark's Gospel...*, pp.19,20.

ABB' is a denotation which I deem reflects the relationship of the contents of the days within each of the two three-day sub-series, where A is 'introductory', B is the 'first development', and B' is the 'second and completing development'. We will discover similar three-day arrangements in Mark's Gospel, A(ABB'):A'(ABB'), but with an inserted middle day, B, hence A(ABB'):B:A'(ABB'). Further, a literary-structural analysis of Gen. 1.1-2.4a, as a whole, demonstrates AA' formations (in the structures of the contents of the parts) and ABB' formations (in the structures of the sub-parts). We will see how Mark employs these forms.

From the Prologue: A   a In the beginning
                          b God created the heavens
                          b' and <u>the earth.</u>
                A'   a <u>The earth</u> was without form
                          b and darkness was upon the <u>face of the deep</u>
                          b' and the Spirit of God was moving over the <u>face of</u>
                               <u>the waters.</u>[62]
From the First Day: A   a And God said, "Let there be <u>light</u>."
                          b And there was <u>light</u>.
                          b' And God saw that the <u>light</u> was good.
                A'   a And God separated the <u>light</u> from the <u>darkness</u>.
                          b God called the <u>light</u> "day"
                          b' and the <u>darkness</u> he called "night".
                And there was evening/ and there was morning/ one day.
                (*a repeating, concluding formula*)

Tolbert, we note, omits to give consideration to this or any other possible, third formative influence on Mark's style, that is of Old Testament composition. And such composition, as I demonstrate above, itself exhibits a possible 'Greco-Roman' influence. It need not be considered 'out of the question': clearly Homer was being read from the eighth century BC, and his *Iliad* pre-dated the completion of the Pentateuch by several centuries.

Fascinatingly, we will see that the 'arrangement', the skeletal outline of Homer's *Iliad* finds a parallel of a kind, like that of the creation account in Genesis, with that of Mark's Gospel. The whole tale, of the beginnings of Greek civilisation (compare the beginnings of Christian civilisation in Mark's Gospel), is told in fifty-two "days". We will compare Mark's twenty-eight "Days", in his telling, of Gospel Narrative, and other days in its framing, that is in both Prologue and Epilogue. Book one of the *Iliad* covers the following in order: one day, an interval of nine days, one day and an interval of twelve days; the last book (twenty-four) covers the following: an interval of twelve days, one day, an interval of nine days and one day. It is the first book's scheme in reverse. In other words the epic both begins and ends with episodes covering twenty-three days each. The six remaining days of Homer's scheme, that is the main days of his telling, are arranged around a central episode (book nine), the envoy's visit to Achilles, which is the turning point in the whole epic. The first 'three days' are told in books 2-8 (seven in all) and the second 'three days' in books 10-23 (fourteen in all). The scheme, according to my own summary, is:

---

[62]It is interesting to note that Luke, writing anywhere between two and twenty years after Mark, opens his Gospel with a threefold protasis and a threefold apodosis which can be described similarly, in broad terms, by A:A', and in its more detailed form as abb':abb'. Lk. 1.1-4, however, is significantly longer than Gen. 1.1,2.

3 days	Book 1	Days 1, 9, 1, 12	
3 days	Books 2-8	Books 2,3	Day 1 beginning with night
		Books 4-7	Day 2 beginning with Zeus & Hera
		Book 8	Day 3 beginning with dawn
X	Book 9	the turning point	
3 days	Books 10-23	Books 10-14	Day 1 beginning with night
		Books 15-18	Day 2 beginning with Zeus & Hera
		Books 19-23	Day 3 beginning with dawn
23 days	Book 24	Days 12, 1, 9, 1	

We will observe Mark's employment of a similar 'skeletal outline'/'arrangement' for each of his four Gospel Series which is very similar to the above: that is 'three: one: three', where at the centre of each of Mark's seven-day schemes, he has a day's telling (in distinction to Homer's separated 'heavenly' scene of a turning point) which acts as a fulcrum, hinge or turning point to the two sub-series of three days around it.

On the issue of 'style', we will discern only a vague similarity between 'sixes' and 'threes'. In the epic poem it is a hexameter with rich and subtle cadences, and in the 'epic gospel' it is fundamentally a three-piece, ABB' presentation, which we will identify as simultaneously employed at a number of literary levels. Lastly, in this much abbreviated comparison, in terms of 'delivery', the meter of Homer's poetry is based on pronunciation time and not, as in our language, on stress[63], whereas Mark's prose for its clausal constructions will be shown to reflect a breathing rhythm.

The histories of criticism of both 'epics' demonstrate similarity, in consideration of the parts played by oral and written tradition, and of the freedom of the author to control his production and create something new. The uncovering of Homer's structure leads his critics and myself on Mark to similar convictions too: consider Sinclair's two summaries: "the use of words in subtle and recurrent patterns as well as the complex formation of the whole point irresistably to the genius of one man"[64], and "without understanding the complexity of the *Iliad* there can be no understanding of Homer himself"[65]. I am happy to say the same of Mark's work. But I am not saying that Mark modelled his work expressly on Homer's. My understanding is simply this, that the Homeric presentational methods[66] were known in Mark's day and to Mark himself, as likely in the day of the Pentateuch's completion. His rhetorical conventions were learned, imitated and built upon over the centuries, over which time they gained and maintained an acceptance cross-culturally. It may be that we will not be able to identify with certainty the link specifically between Mark's Gospel and any one work, or the collected works of an ancient rhetor, either as reviewed here, or above. It is a matter more of understanding the background literary culture in which Mark's Gospel was fashioned. In

---

[63]Bernard Knox, "Introduction" to Robert Fagles' translation, *The Iliad: Homer*, Viking Penguin, 1990, p.12.
[64]Andrew Sinclair, "Appreciation", *Homer's Iliad*, tr. W.H.D. Rouse, Thomas Nelson & Sons Ltd., London/Heron Books, undated, p.503.
[65]Sinclair, "Appreciation", *Homer's Iliad*, p.496.
[66]See again Introduction, note 42. Further, the chronological scheme for Homer's *Iliad* is interpreted by some, by 'day-reports' (i.e. two in both Prologue and Epilogue), as an eleven-section chiasm (so also *Odyssey*). In my book, *Sliced Bread...*, I present eleven-sectioned chiasms for Matthew's Gospel and for Luke's two books. The case may be put, therefore, that these writers too followed Homeric methods of ancient rhetoric.

Genesis, 1 and 2 Kings, in Tolbert's identification with the ancient popular novel, in Hooker's reference to form in Aristotelian Greek tragedy, and in Mack's specific reference (as with others) to Xenophon's *Memorabilia*, I do find parallels in Mark's Gospel which will be identified in the following chapters.

It is accepted that structure and organisation, of that which was written to be read aloud, had an immediate, two-fold practical purpose of aesthetic[67] and mnemonic[68]. The memorising of texts, by listening to what is read aloud, is in any culture or civilisation assisted and enhanced by rhetorical conventions. It was especially so in the first centuries BC and AD. Examples of these include the organisation of information in listings, acrostics and symmetries of presentation by both simple parallelism and chiasm, also the exercise of rhythm and the repetitions of words, phrases, sentence- constructions, paragraph-forms, and so on. The fact that we are discovering applications of all of these methods and such characteristics within the Biblical corpus (both Old and New Testaments) should not be a surprise to us. Literature which is structured at every level, and which has its repetitions and its rhythms of themes and details, assists not only the process of oral education and clear communication but also the memorising of it, for private recall, at one end of the scale, and for a perfect, public re-presentation, at the other end of the scale.

No literature of the first century will have been without an 'arrangement', a plan and framework[69], nor, we add, its detailed presentational system which is the rhetorical method/'style' the writer employed to construct his sentences and paragraphs[70]. It simply would not have functioned without it. It is difficult to argue otherwise therefore, than that the first requirement of a gospel was that it needed a simple, memorable, rhythmic structure for the whole, and a system, or method of presentation used throughout, for its parts. My analysis of Mark's Gospel will show that its author well met these requirements, and that he did so by employing rhetorical conventions in use in his day. If the new literary genre of gospel was to function well, it had to be compiled and composed to fit its life-setting of the first century.

We turn now to a brief consideration of the likely historical context to Mark's writing of his Gospel. The first issue focuses on the tradition which is judged to link the writing of Mark's Gospel with the time of the death of Peter (in AD 64). According to the tradition of John the elder and passed on (in about AD 130) by Papias, Bishop of Hierapolis, and recorded by Eusebius in his *Ecclesiastical History*[71], we can read the following, that:

"...Mark became the interpreter of Peter and he wrote down accurately, but not in order, as much as he remembered of the sayings and doings of Christ. For he was not a hearer or a follower of the Lord, but afterwards, as I said, of Peter, who adapted his teachings to the needs of the moment and did not make an ordered exposition of the sayings of the Lord. And so Mark made no mistake when he thus wrote down some things as he remembered them; for he made it his especial care to omit nothing of what he heard, and to make no false statement therein."

---

[67]We observe that the aesthetic component, in interior design, artefact, architecture and town-planning today, is often considered separately from function: in first century literature, created for reading aloud, function and aesthetic could not be so separated. Literature functioned through its aesthetic.

[68]See: C.H. Talbert, *Literary Patterns, Theological Themes, and the Genre of Luke-Acts*, SBLMS 20, Scholars Press, Missoula, Montana, 1974, p.81, (in regard to Homer); Birger Gerhardsson, *Memory and Manuscript* (tr. Eric J. Sharpe), C.W.K. Gleerup, Uppsala, 1961, p.147 (in regard to Jewish haggadah).

[69]See note 33 above.

[70]Barthes says: "...there does, of course, exist an 'art' of the storyteller which is the ability to generate narratives (messages) from the structure (the code)." Roland Barthes, "Introduction to the Structural Analysis of Narrative", *Image - Music -Text*, ed. & tr. Stephen Heath, Hill and Wang, New York, 1977, p.80.

[71]Eusebius, *HE*, iii.39.15, also reproduced in Henry Bettenson, *Documents of the Christian Church*, Oxford University Press, 2nd Ed., 1963, p.27, from which the translation quoted is taken.

Those who wish to affirm the historical reliability of Mark's Gospel frequently appeal to this testimony, though there is much that can be discussed about its reliability:

1) it is likely that after the first sentence everything else is what Papias has added;

2) Papias may have identified Mark with Peter's companion on the basis of 1 Peter 5.13 (compare other references to a John Mark in Acts 12.12,25; 15.37-39; and presumably the same person in Col. 4.10, Philemon 24 and 2 Tim. 4.11);

3) though dependency may have been upon Papias, we may still consider the support for the linking of Mark with Peter: of Justin Martyr who refers to the 'memoirs of Peter' (c. 150); of the Anti-Marcionite Prologue (c. 160-180) which tells us that Mark was the interpreter of Peter and that he wrote his Gospel after Peter's death in Italy; of Irenaeus (c. 180-200) who describes Mark as the disciple and interpreter of Peter, who wrote after the deaths of both Peter and Paul; of the several records of Clement of Alexandria (c. 180) which tell of Mark's writing down the words of Peter, but in contrast to the former support, during the latter's lifetime; and of Origen (c. 200) likewise, who tells how Peter instructed Mark.

We cannot here develop the discussion; space does not allow. But it is clear that the tradition that Mark was a "disciple of Peter" could have been either the cause or the result of the early church's view that all the canonical gospels required apostolic authentication. We cannot be certain either way. And the debate about whether or not Mark's Gospel really connects with Peter is an open question too. Nevertheless, we can deduce simply that it is most likely that the 'Gospel' was required because the eye-witnesses of the life of Jesus were dying out. Thus, the church will have had a justifiable need for written material, or written record of the 'beginnings' of the faith. The deduction is that this need did indeed lead Mark to write, and did lead, in turn, to the contributions of the other three evangelists.

Equally, other questions arise and they are still open too. Where was the Gospel written? And what was the date of its writing? (Or given the above: How long after the death of Peter was it written?) They are recognised as important, but they are not best addressed separately at this juncture[72]. Rather, we ask, "Was Mark motivated to write his Gospel because of a significant historical event which marked an upheaval that was both political and religious?" We consider what may have been the possible reaction of Mark and the early church to the fall of Jerusalem and the destruction of its temple in the year 70, because of which the Jewish revolt which began in 66 was coming to its end in 73. If Mark had been in Rome around that time[73], he would have seen for himself the victorious Titus return with the spoils from the temple; if he had been other than in Rome, he would certainly have heard about it.

Clearly, the defeat of the Jews, the destruction of the temple, and the re-occupation of Jerusalem by the Roman legions will have spelt, somewhat emphatically to early Christians and to both insiders and outsiders of the Jewish faith, the end of Judaism, the end of the era of the 'Old Covenant and Temple sacrifices'. We will see from literary-structural analysis that

[72]All commentaries raise these issues and present the evidence for different options. We note that Gamble (*Books and Readers...*, p.102) says of Mark's Gospel that "wherever it was composed, it must have circulated widely within ten to twenty years of its origin. How else might it have come independently into the hands of... Matthew and... Luke...?" Étienne Trocmé, *The Formation of the Gospel according to Mark*, SPCK, London, 1975 (first publ. in Fr. 1963), p.242, asks, "How could a work as distinguished as Mark have circulated widely and enjoyed a measure of authority... despite the competition of Matthew, Luke and John and of its distant claim to descent from an apostolic source? The only plausible explanation is that it was covered by the prestige of a very important church which gave special credit to it, no doubt because the book was written by one of its members and for its own use. All things considered, this important church could only have been the Church of Rome, as ancient tradition suggests."

[73]According to Clement of Alexandria, Mark wrote his Gospel in Rome; the Anti-Marcionite Prologue says he was in "the regions of Italy"; and Irenaeus implies that the Gospel was written in Rome. See note 72 also for Trocme's view. But the belief that he wrote there could have been attributed to the link between Mark and Peter. Further, Chrysostum (in the fourth century) said he wrote in Egypt, and others have suggested Antioch, and still others (ref. Marxsen) Galilee.

there is in Mark's 'arrangement' of his Gospel an important emphasis on 'good news'. 'Good news' is, of course, a counter to 'bad news'. We properly ask, therefore, "Might the 'bad news' that was countered with 'good news' have been, more than anything else, the considered demise of the Old Covenant?" If so, the 'good news' was fundamentally God's establishing of a New Covenant, to replace the Old. We will see from literary-structural analysis that Mark's 'arrangement' does indeed place a strong emphasis on the role of Jesus in establishing a New Covenant, and replacing the Old. Indeed, given what we shall see of the ordering of the contents of his Gospel, we will be able to picture Mark writing at a time when the nationalistic religion of Old Israel was already in ruins, literally in terms of its temple, but also morally- and spiritually-speaking. And his 'good news' about the new, universal faith of a New Israel, in which both Jew and Gentile would share, simply had its focus on the one who, by his call, mission, death, resurrection and ascension, had been demonstrating God's new way of dealing with evil in the world (an evil which was bringing down/had already brought down the Old Covenant); one who was establishing a new kingdom, the Kingdom of God, which would have no boundaries either in creation, or, for that matter, even between heaven and earth.

To summarise at this point, we may simply state that the immediate requirement of the new literary genre of gospel was to fill a vacuum created by the decease of the first witnesses, and to provide for the church a mission statement for a new age that was born of the greatest upheaval the world had ever seen[74]. We will return to such matters when we have a surer understanding of the primary document itself.

There remain many other, open questions. Those which impinge on the actual process of producing the first Gospel, and on the functions for which the Gospel was intended, as well as its status in the church, are numerous indeed. There is every reason to rehearse some of them here. Was the Gospel simply completed in one operation, or was it first written and then re-written by the same person after input or reflective comments from others? Did it attempt to satisfy requirements laid down by any other, or others, than the writer? When it was first read was it publicly or privately? Did it need approval? Or did it attract approval? And when it was first circulated was it as one manuscript, only? When were copies first made? And how many copies...? For what purpose might they have been made? To whom was the task given to read it aloud publicly? Or was it first circulated by being committed to memory for recital in Christian or other gatherings? How many people would have been appointed initially to "present" it? Would they have had training in its presentation, both in how it was composed and how it was to be read? Was it to be read, or presented in one sitting? Or, was it to be serially presented or read over a number of meetings? And when it was read or presented whole, or in parts at a time, what was then expected to follow? Were questions invited and discussion encouraged? Did its reading in public lead to people making commitments, or re-commitments to Jesus? Did it have a mission effect?

Accessibility to the answers to all these and similar questions is not ours today, but they are posed here simply because they need to be asked. In some way or another, the church chose to "own" the Gospel of Mark, to show it respect, to use it for its own purposes, and to preserve it. That it was later re-written by Matthew and Luke in turn and added to for other purposes by them is another, though much associated matter.

---

[74]"The war of the Jews against the Romans was the greatest of our time; greater too, perhaps, than any recorded struggle whether between cities or nations... This upheaval, as I said, was the greatest of *all* time...", so wrote Josephus in his Preface, 1,7, *The Jewish War*, tr. G.A. Williamson, Rev. Ed., Penguin Books, Harmondsworth, 1980.

An Interest in "Days":

A number of readers of Mark's Gospel have identified, almost in a cursory manner, the presence of days. Bultmann[75], whose focus is the first century Hebrew/Palestinian Day which begins and ends with sunset, says, "Jesus' last ministry in Jerusalem is somewhat awkwardly compressed along with the Passion itself into a sequence of seven days, and the components of the last act are divided among the hours of the day: the first watch of the night starts at 14.17...". For Drury, "at both the beginning and the end of the book, days are marked out, together with times of day, with a precision lacking elsewhere. And in both the familiar pattern is discernible." (He sees the correspondence between Jesus' rising up a great while before day, 1.35, "prophesying" his early morning resurrection, 16.2ff. The pattern in both is "action followed by withdrawal leading to further action".) He writes, "The early passage 1.21-38 covers some twenty-four hours from morning to morning...."[76]. As such, Drury shows an interest in what is termed the "civil day" (see my note 82) which can be qualified either as beginning at sunset, or as beginning at sunrise, but which is identified by Drury here as beginning with sunrise. "The last chapters cover a series of days and of times within them, beginning at 14.1," he says.

Drury's list includes 1.21-38 and, it might be deduced (because he does not state), 14.1-11, 14.12-72, 15.1-47 and 16.1-8. These limits satisfy the criterion of the "civil day" as beginning at sunrise. We can add others, on the same principle: 11.1-11; 11.12-19 and 11.20-13.37. (This makes initially eight days in all, by simple reading.) In a number of commentaries[77] these last three days are discerned, and Hooker notes that they are "three successive days". Schweizer, however, fails to discern any of these day-divisions in chapter 11. It would appear from his notes on 11.12-26 that he is distracted fully by the so-called Markan preference (he cites only 5.21-43 as another example at this point) for sandwich construction. Indeed, many scholars see the two-part story of Jesus' withering of the fig tree as a whole (11.12-14 and vv.20-26), enveloping a central part, telling of Jesus' action in the temple (11.15-19)[78]. The arrangement and the possible significance of the arrangement of Markan "Days" is lost on them: their interest is in other matters.

Elsewhere in the Gospel "Days" *seem* not to be important beyond mention of other Sabbaths in 2.23 (possibly 3.1) and 6.2, and references to the passing of days in 2.1, 8.1,2 and 9.2. To the eight "Days" discerned already above we add two Sabbaths (I judge 2.23-3.6 to be one Sabbath day) making now ten "Days" in all. To these ten we now add the three "Days" which, as my analysis will show, begin at 2.1, 8.1 and 9.2. These "Days" begin with summary tellings of other days that are otherwise left unreported. (In this way Mark makes it perfectly clear that he is not reporting every day in the mission of Jesus.) The tally of defined "Days" in Mark's telling is now thirteen. Additionally in the Gospel we discover references to times or periods of days: 1.32, 35; 4.35; 6.35, 47, 48; 11.11, 19, 20; 14.17, 72; 15.1, 25, 33, 34, 42; 16.2 (also 16.9, 14). Given the references to 'evenings' in 4.35 and 6.47 we can discern two more days to add to the list. The first of these can be deduced to begin at 3.7 and the second of these to begin at 6.30. Fifteen "Days" are definable simply from the text.

It is the case that other "Days" are less clearly delineated by Mark. Good story-telling requires no continuing repetition of detail to establish a rhythm, a pattern or a sequence. It is, therefore, most significant that the first "Day" of Mark's narrative (1.21-38) covers a twenty-four hour period from sunrise to before sunrise the following day. He clearly presents it as

---

[75]Bultmann, *The History...*, p.341.

[76]J. Drury, "Mark", *The Literary Guide to the Bible*, eds. R. Alter & F. Kermode, Collins, London, 1987, p.410.

[77]E.g. D.E. Nineham, *Saint Mark*, The Pelican Gospel Commentaries, Penguin Books Ltd., Harmondsworth, 1963, pp.303 and 305; also M.D. Hooker, *The Gospel...*, p.255.

[78]Compare: Eduard Schweizer, *The Good News according to Mark*, tr. Donald H. Madvig, John Knox Press, Atlanta, 1970, pp.229-236; Nineham, *Saint Mark*, pp.297ff.; and Hooker, *The Gospel...*, pp.260ff.

one which begins with the beginning of daylight, proceeds through the daylight hours and the sunset into the evening, and ends in the night before the new dawn. It acts as a model, a type, a pattern. Mark presents it as an indication of what he has in mind for his narrative presentation and the form it will take - a presentation of "Days" - and he establishes it right at the beginning. All other "Days", that is reportings of events and teachings, will fall into the same temporal mould. They will not, indeed they cannot extend beyond the twenty-four hour period defined by Day One. What is reported as an event or succession of events or teachings will be told within the parameters of a twenty-four hour day which begins with sunrise.

It follows, therefore, that other "Days" are inferred, and that they can be deduced from the text. Simple deduction is possible by giving consideration to "Days" which stand in juxtaposition, for instance where a Sabbath day precedes a "Day" in sequence and where the activities of the "Day" following are non-sabbatical. An example of this is the "Day" of 3.7-4.41 which follows that of 2.23-3.6. The "Day" of 3.7-4.41 is the fourteenth "Day" added to the list (see above). The activities described in the introductory passage, 3.7-12, are clearly not introductory activities to a Day's telling which has its beginning in the evening of a Hebrew/Palestinian Day, which begins with sunset. They are the introductory activities with which Mark begins a new Day's telling at a time after sunrise, hence within the temporal parameters of the Civil Day defined as beginning at sunrise. This particular Day's telling takes us to the evening and night-time event (4.35: "And he says to them on that day, evening having come..."). The story which follows, of 5.1-20, is one that is set in the day-time: it allocates to another "Day", the sixteenth for the list.

Other deductions are based on phrases which speak of Jesus' "rising" (see 7.24 and 10.1) meaning "getting up from sleep"[79]; on new journey beginnings (as in 9.30, "And thence, going forth...") or on new arrivals (as at 5.1, "And they came to the other side of the sea..."; or as at 10.46, which is a most interesting juxtaposition of statements, literally, "And they come to Jericho. And as he was going out from Jericho..."). For Bultmann, "the spatial link is also a *temporal* one. This expresses the temporal sequence..."[80] In the presentation of my analysis, in which the Markan "Days" and Series of "Days" are established, these matters are fully presented and discussed. We will see many times over, in his opening pieces to new "Days", and simply nowhere else in his "Day" presentations, that Mark references other days which pass between his formal tellings of "Days", either specifically (by number or dating), or by inference (with brief journey details which suggest numbers of days which are taken up with travel, which are otherwise not reported).

In his discussion of the Markan outline, Taylor makes comment: "It is soon manifest that he (Mark) has no day to day account of the progress of the mission, but he shows a good historical judgement in using an impressive record of a typical day in the life of Jesus (1.21-39)... There is little ordered sequence but *it is notable how particular days stand out*"[81]. He sees 4.1-5.43 as one day, "remembered not only for its teaching but also for its crossing and re-crossing of the lake and a series of events perhaps telescoped, but given in chronological order." A number of issues are raised here. What are the other days that "stand out" for Taylor? Is the 'day' really 1.21-39? And is it really part of the tradition? Or was it compiled, or even created by Mark? Further, could the passage 4.1-5.43 possibly be only one day? We read at 4.35 that evening had come. Is it possible that the stories of 4.35-5.43 were set in the night watches, with so many people about, and without Mark telling us which watch? Or, rather are there not three days of activities told in these verses, so deduced because there is one night-crossing of the lake and one return crossing at the end of another day's episodes?

---

[79]In 1.35, Jesus' rising is 'from sleep'; it is judged that there is no good reason for changing the meaning for 7.24 and 10.1. Further, we observe that the rising of Jairus' daughter in 5.42 is also from 'sleep', see 5.39.
[80]Bultmann, *The History...*, p.340.
[81]V. Taylor, *The Gospel according to St Mark*, MacMillan, London, 1952, p.146: my italics.

Clearly, an examination of the whole text of Mark's Gospel, for "Days", is an exercise waiting to be done. The possibility did indeed exist, contrary to what Taylor understood, as recorded above, that the Gospel Mark consisted of reports of "Days". Another distinct possibility also existed, that the Gospel outline combined both Days and Series of Days in a framework or matrix, artificial or otherwise. In my analyses of Chapters 3 to 6, I present the arguments which support my view that the main Gospel Narrative, from 1.21 to 16.8, consists of twenty-eight Days, in Mark's telling, and that these Days are arranged in four Series each of seven Days. The definition of "Day" which Mark employs consistently, for the purpose of his presentation, as defined by Day One, 1.21-38, is the period from the dawn of one day to the beginning of dawn the next day, that is from sunrise to just before sunrise[82]. I will argue that clear correspondences between Days and Series of Days are evident, with the result that the Markan matrix can be defined in some detail. In Chapters 2 and 7 I give careful consideration also to the "Days preceding" and "following" the main Gospel Narrative, which I define in turn as the Prologue, for which read 1.1-20, and a near representative form of the original Epilogue, for which read 16.9-16, 19-20a.

A Methodology for identifying "Days", their intra- and inter-relationships, and their literary-structures:

It may be that some days do "stand out" more than others but, as we have seen above, any definition of a "Day" needs testing. Fundamental to establishing that the text is actually structured in "Days" is the defining of the beginnings and the endings of the "Days" themselves. Temporal, geographical and place-defining terms all have value and all such references have to be weighed carefully. Arguments based on vocabulary, syntax and style have their value for not only are there Markan introductory formulae to be defined, but also there is a Markan method (of writing) to be understood. Further, a structural relationship exists between Series of Days, Days, their sections, their parts, their sub-parts and their sub-sub-parts, and it requires description. Points in the text where Mark introduced new themes require identifying. And his development of his themes, as also his repetitions of keywords and phrases, needs to be understood for the ways in which they locate within any particular "Day" or within associated "Days" (either in juxtaposition, or in balance through a vertical reading or a horizontal reading of the Gospel's Series).

During the early stages of analysis, because nothing was known with any certainty about Mark's framework and plan, and nothing at all about either Mark's framework of "Days" and his "Series of Days", and further, because so very little was known with any certainty about his rhetorical method (beyond the possibilities of limited chiastic arrangements, his threesomes of details, and some threesomes of construction), it was simply a case of trial and error, of attempt and renewed attempt, of developing one hypothesis after another and

---

[82]From *IntDB*, Vol. 1, (1962) Abingdon, Nashville, 1981, p.783, S.J. De Vries: The civil day can be a space of twenty-four hours, extending from sunrise to sunrise or from sunset to sunset. Early Hebrews reckoned the civil day from one dawn to the next. Gradually, they began to count from sunset to sunset in accordance with the rising importance of their lunar festivals.
We observe that, while we define a 'day' in the world today as being from just after midnight to the next midnight, we now have a 'TV Day' of twenty-four hours which begins with dawn, or thereabouts (see any programme chart). We also often talk of "tomorrow" (even after midnight) as meaning when we wake from sleep. Mark was as aware as we are today of different reference points to the start of the day, for he shows that, while he plans his Days to a dawn beginning, as when Jesus "rises" from sleep, he also understands the other, alternative civil day definition, which is the Hebrew/Palestinian Day, whereby when evening comes prior to a sabbath, see 15.42, the new day's own particular obligations begin.

putting each to the test. It was a "messy" but most important stage in the process of analysis.[83] But once a focus began to be secured upon the signifiers of Mark's primary-structure of "Days" and "Series of Days", and upon meaningful and significant correspondences between these elements, the process of literary-structural analysis became more methodical. To meet the need of a purely literary-structural analysis of the Markan text in the beginning no single methodology on its own was sufficient to the task. Not until 1.1-16.8 disclosed its Prologue (1.1-20) and its Gospel narrative of Four Series of Seven Days (1.21-16.8) did it appear pertinent to examine Mark's work for any systematic presentational-method he may have used to form the elements of his work. In other words, the basic 'structure' of the book had to be discovered first; it was only then that the question could be asked if Mark had a 'construction method' too. For the purpose of presenting the analysis, it was deemed sensible to present the disclosures of these characteristics of his composition simultaneously. The discovery of Mark's repeated use of the same, complete rhetorical constructions qualifies not only the nature of the structural organisation of 1.1-16.8, but also facilitates a new reading of 16.9-20.

That this analysis has been carried out at a time when more methodologies exist than could ever have been dreamed of in ancient times means that it can be well-tested against the propositions which have resulted from many other lines of enquiry. Clearly, commentaries and studies are available for comparisons to be made between my findings and those of others who, through source, form, redaction and, principally, rhetorical criticism, have been exploring for possible answers to age-old questions. The commentaries which we employ include principally four: that of Taylor, which is typical of the British scholars of his period, approaching the Gospel from the stand-point of source critics (the commentary was first published in 1952 and has been judged "a classic" by other commentators); that of Nineham, published in 1963, reflective of the position form critics were then taking; that of Schweizer, published in 1967, which is the first recognised commentary based on the redaction critical method[84]; and that of Hooker, published in 1991, which takes account of many late twentieth-century Markan studies and represents a work of scholarship which is the result of many years of teaching, much valued by her students. In the discussions, we also draw on traditional and contemporary studies for the valuable insights of those who have practised an openness to possibilities, holding at the same time to sound exercise of reason and scholarship.

My Presentation of the Analysed Text:

In Chapters Two to Seven, during the course of our examination of the Gospel's component parts, I re-present the UBS4 (5) Nestle-Aland text which, with annotations and underlinings, demonstrates what I discern to be the literary-structure of each. For each Day's presentation, Mark employs, in simple form or composite forms, an A,B,B' structure, whereby A is introductory, B is the first development, and B' is the second, responding/paralleling and conclud-

---

[83]The similarities between the first stage in the process of examining the 'design' of a text, for its structure and its construction-method, and the first stage of designing a building are worth paralleling. In both it is the most demanding stage. The scheme-design stage (of a building) is literally the most mind-bending and yet the most exciting. Further, it is the stage which is most influential upon the end-outcome. It is typically one in which no single methodology is sufficient to the task, for it is a time for discerning all the influential factors and for considering all the possibilities.

[84]John K. Riches, *A Century of New Testament Study*, The Lutterworth Press, Cambridge, 1993, pp.153f.: Schweizer's commentary on Mark "remains one of the most balanced examples of redaction critical work, even if there is never any real doubt about his commitment to a broadly Barthian conception of the freedom and radical grace of God."

ing development. This phenomenon can be observed throughout the Gospel at several different levels of literary order.

As an example, I present my analysis of the first two verses of Day One, 1.21,22:

A a   *Καὶ εἰσπορεύονται εἰς Καφαρναούμ.*
   b   *καὶ εὐθὺς τοῖς σάββασιν εἰσελθὼν εἰς τὴν συναγωγὴν ἐδίδασκεν*[22]
   b'   *καὶ ἐξεπλήσσοντο ἐπὶ <u>τῇ διδαχῇ</u> αὐτοῦ, <u>ἦν γὰρ διδάσκων</u> αὐτοὺς*
        <u>ὡς ἐξουσίαν ἔχων</u> καὶ <u>οὐχ ὡς</u> οἱ γραμματεῖς.[23]

In Chapter Three, we will sift the evidence for concluding that Day One (1.21-38) comprises three main Parts: **A, B** and **B'**. Here A denotes 1.21,22 as an introductory first part of three. parts which make up the first half's telling. B is the first development, which is vv.23-25. And B' is the second and completing/concluding development, which is vv.26-28. In this way, Part A of the Day's telling is completed. In part a, Mark establishes the geographical place. In part b, his first development, he details the day and the time of day (*καὶ εὐθὺς τοῖς σάββασιν*), movement into the locality of the event, and the activity (teaching) of the subject who is Jesus, un-named here, as in many other similar occurences. In part b', his second and completing development of this construction, Mark reports the response of the people to Jesus' activity (teaching) as well as the reason for their response, in two balancing parts ("for he was teaching them as having authority", "and not as the scribes."). The key words which suggest balance between parts b and b' are underlined.

Further detailed breakdown, at the next level of literary order, can be exhibited:

A a   *Καὶ εἰσπορεύονται*   (a)
            εἰς Καφαρναούμ.   (a')
   b   *καὶ εὐθὺς τοῖς σάββασιν*   (a)
            εἰσελθὼν εἰς τὴν συναγωγὴν   (b)
            ἐδίδασκεν[22]   (b')
   b'   *καὶ ἐξεπλήσσοντο ἐπὶ <u>τῇ διδαχῇ</u> αὐτοῦ,*   (a)
            <u>ἦν γὰρ διδάσκων</u> αὐτοὺς <u>ὡς ἐξουσίαν ἔχων</u>   (b)
            καὶ <u>οὐχ ὡς</u> οἱ γραμματεῖς.[23]   (b')

Part a breaks down into sub-parts (a) and (a'). Part b breaks down into sub-parts (a), (b) and (b'): in this case the (b) (b') relationship holds as (b') completes (b). And part b' breaks down into sub-parts (a), (b) and (b'), where (b) and (b') correspond in a comparison and complete the whole.

It may be judged, quite properly, from these analyses that Mark's rhetorical method at this level of literary-structural order, abb', does not require that these parts are equal either in their number of words, or in their more detailed structural compositions.

Also, further detailed breakdown is possible in b(b) for example:

           <u>εἰσελθὼν</u>   .a
           <u>εἰς</u> τὴν συναγωγὴν   .a'
and elsewhere, severally.

In this way, all the clauses of these verses, 1.21,22, are identified and defined for their settings and their relationships in the complete presentation. We observe here four levels of literary-structural order in all, as annotated by A, a, (a) and .a (as also for B and B'). The annotation, my method of it, may be deemed cumbersome, but it is my best approach. In the following chapters, after a few introductory annotations like this, I will present the text as below, or very similarly, coupling both vertical and horizontal separations to express the structuring of the text without too much annotation:

Καὶ εἰσπορεύονται   A   A
    εἰς Καφαρναούμ.
    καὶ εὐθὺς τοῖς σάββασιν
    εἰσελθὼν
      εἰς τὴν συναγωγὴν
    ἐδίδασκεν[22]
  καὶ ἐξεπλήσσοντο
      ἐπὶ τῇ διδαχῇ αὐτοῦ,
    ἦν γὰρ διδάσκων αὐτοὺς
      ὡς ἐξουσίαν ἔχων
  καὶ οὐχ
    ὡς οἱ γραμματεῖς.[23]

In my analysis of the gospel, I will underline words that will have significance in one way or another in the whole scheme of Mark's telling of "Days". Clearly, explication of every detail would, if provided, become tedious to follow. I judge that few people would want all the evidence at all literary levels. Clearly, once someone has been introduced to the reading method the text requires, he or she will be able to interpret it for themselves. Yet, the evidence at the higher levels of literary ordering will be discussed because it cannot be missed! In this matter, what was useful to me, after my first analysis of the whole of the text, was that I was introduced to a similar analytical work, but with a different purpose from mine. I was introduced to Neirynck's most detailed analysis on *Duality in Mark*[85]. A reading of his work gave me confirmation that I was on the right track and his work was useful to me for that. But what was particularly useful was seeing how he laid out his analysed texts. To present his analysis, Neirynck presented a synthesis of his data in lines and spaces: vertically to portray sections, and horizontally to portray sub-sections and parts. I have followed this now (as above) for the whole of the presentation of my analysed Greek text and my literal English translation. Whilst I cannot agree with Neirynck's synthesis, for the reason that he does not discern what to me is the fundamental 'arrangement' by Mark of material in Days and Series of Days in the higher orders of Mark's literary structure, I do find myself agreeing significantly, nevertheless, with his detailed reading of correspondences in the text, in much of the middle and lower levels of literary order. I did complete a comparison of my reading with that of Neirynck's for the verses of Mark's Prologue and in my publication of 1999, I included it in my Chapter Two. But I have since removed it as it really did not show much more than how the majority of Mark's dualities fall into the b/b' and B/B' parts of my readings of Mark's abb' and ABB' structures, again in the middle and lower orders only.[86]

---

[85]Frans Neirynck, *Duality in Mark: Contributions to the Study of the Markan Redaction*, Rev. Ed., Leuven University Press, Leuven, 1988.
In Part II, he collates dualities and other relationships. His chief categories are listed here:Compound verb followed by the same preposition; Multiplication of cognate verbs; Double participle; Double imperative; Double negative; Double statement: negative-positive; Double statement: temporal or local; Double statement: general and special; Synonymous expression; Translation; Double Group of persons; Series of three; Correspondence in narrative; Command and Fulfilment; Request and Realization; Double question; Correspondence in discourse; Sandwich arrangement; Parallelism in sayings; and Doublets. But for all this analysis, he fails to present any helpful and meaningful synthesis.
[86] Anyone who wants to persue this survey can get a copy of my 1999 edition of *The Markan Matrix*, or getin touch with me..

Is this Gospel a Work of Ancient Rhetoric?

Given that literary structure and style are of paramount importance to any work of ancient rhetoric, we ask, in the end, if there is sufficient evidence to state categorically that this gospel is, indeed, a work of ancient rhetoric. In answering, we will need to re-visit and re-assess the fundamental questions which have remained unanswered in regard to Mark's Gospel and see if they are now answered with the evidence we have always needed. In the last Chapter Eight, we will gather up the result of this literary-structural analysis and take a look at what has resulted from this line of approach. In 1999, I stated it would be the Markan Matrix that we would be seeing. I was attempting a modernising of approach and a justification of a snappy title.

I said then that in turning to any commentary, we usually look to the contents' page or to some presentation in the introduction to see what understanding the writer might have concerning the composition of the book under examination. I observed also that the very positioning of this listing or table and the designation which is given to it seem to say as much about the commentator and his/her attitude to the work as about the biblical text itself. Their terms include: contents, structure, analysis, plan, arrangement, outline, plot and framework.

My choice of "matrix" for the title of my 1999 publication was not chosen because of any structuralist use of the term. Rather, it seemed to me then to hold in one, single term the two aspects of whole design on the one hand and its detailed construction on the other. A "matrix", according to the Concise Oxford Dictionary[87], has six definitions:

1) a mould in which a thing is cast or shaped, e.g. gramophone record;
2a) an environment or substance in which a thing is developed;
2b) a womb;
3) a mass of fine-grained rock in which gems, fossils, etc. are embedded;
4) *(Math.)* a rectangular array of elements in rows and columns that is treated as a single element;
5) *(Biol.)* the substance between cells or in which structures are embedded;
6) *(Computing)* a gridlike array of interconnected circuit elements.

All may be considered to have illustrative and metaphorical value, but it is definition four I had in mind. I was aware, in 1999, that Structuralists[88] establish charts and "sets", for example, for parables, or sayings, and then determine their meaning by both a "serial reading" (horizontal: across, say, listings of meaningful units of each parable) and a "formal reading" (vertical: down the list of parables and their meaningful units), thus proceeding to a definition of the "generative matrix" (out of which, in this illustration, all parables come by means of certain laws of transformation). But while I present something like this, I promise something altogether much simpler. My work is not to be confused with structuralism.

Throughout my examination of the text, we will keep reminding ourselves that Mark was writing to facilitate his reader's reading and memorising of his text. The work called for simplicity, symmetry, repetitions and structural dualities which revealed to the reader all that

---

[87]R.E. Allen (ed.), *Concise Oxford Dictionary of Current English*, Clarendon, Oxford, 8th ed. 1990.
[88]E.g. and so henceforth: R. Funk, *Language, Hermeneutic, and the Word of God*, Harper & Row, New York 1966; E. Guttgemanns, *Offene Fragen zur Formgeschichte des Evangeliums*, Christian Kaiser Verlag, Munchen, 1970; E. Leach, *Genesis as Myth and Other Essays*, Cape, London, 1969; E. Leach & D.A. Aycock, *Structuralist Interpretations of Biblical Myth*, Cambridge University Press, 1983 (reviewed by R.Carroll, *Religious Studies*, 21/1 (1985), pp.116-118); D.O. Via, *The Parables: Their Literary and Existential Dimension*, Fortress Press, Philadelphia, 1974; and *Kerygma & Comedy in the New Testament: A Structuralist Approach to Hermeneutic*, Fortress Press, Philadelphia, 1975.

he (she?) needed to know to present the work as the writer intended. As we discuss the "Days", their Series and their Sub-Series, it will be seen that Mark's Gospel is a work of literature which, in modern terms, employs a "matrix" which reveals at once that the book is systematically arranged and unified in its themes and details through correspondences that are, in fact, horizontal, vertical *and* diagonal.

We could say that we identify the "generative matrix" of Mark's Gospel. Rather, we will speak, I think, in older terms, of a framework which is basically revealed to be read horizontally, across a charting of each Series of seven Days, and vertically, down through the charting of the four Series of Gospel Narrative. For examples of horizontal readings in the second Series, the feeding of the five-thousand lies diametrically opposite the feeding of the four-thousand and in the third Series, in the same positions as the above, in his transfiguration-glory Jesus is accompanied by 'two', and this lies opposite the request of 'two' to be each side of him in his future glory. For examples of vertical readings, the last Days of the middle two Series end with the only descriptions in the Gospel of healings of blind people, and the last Days of the outer two Series end with the Gospel's only "raisings from the dead". Diagonal correspondences are to be found too: they form a *chi*, an X, at the middle of the presentation. The two (large) 'teaching' Days on the kingdom of God lie diagonally opposite each other. The two Days that tell of Jesus' departure at his meals with sinners lie diagonally opposite each other too, thus forming the X. And finally, in its opening and closing pieces, in the Prologue and the (near original) Epilogue, the Narrative is well cradled, though these two elements read separately from it and in correspondence with each other.

We reserve final judgement to the final chapter.

Chapter Two
The Days Beginning the Gospel (1.1/2-20):

The Title and Prologue:

Throughout the years of biblical criticism, the Prologue has been described as consisting of the first eight verses, the first thirteen, or the first fifteen, or even, by one, as the first twenty verses? In recent times, a great many scholars and commentators have thought it thirteen verses[89]; a few, fifteen verses[90]; and possibly only two, the whole twenty verses, and one of these, likely by default, arguing for vv.1-15 and attaching vv.16-20 without comment.[91] Which is the writer's intended introduction? That is our key question here. And the attendant one is, "Is it the writer's intention that the Title be seen as separated from the Prologue?" Clearly, if the Gospel narrative is arranged in "Series" of "Days" from 1.21 as I propose in my Introduction, then there is a literary-structural argument for a focus here on the first twenty verses. In Chapter Three, Day One (1.21-38) will be examined. But here, we will rehearse the now traditional arguments on the first twenty verses and sift new, literary-structural evidence.

Content Considerations:

A glance at the New English Bible will show that the translators who were responsible for it viewed the first thirteen verses of Mark's Gospel as his Introduction. The belief that a division should be made after v.13, goes back to R.H. Lightfoot[92]. He argued that the printed Greek texts of his day were wrong to leave a gap after v.8; rather, it belongs after v.13. Lightfoot's influence has been of great importance; few commentators have ignored his insight that these thirteen verses form a closely connected section. For him, this re-created gap (between v.13 and v.14) defined the limits of an opening, Christological section which provides the key to understanding the rest of the Gospel. The introduction was not just two or three incidents leading up to the ministry of Jesus.

Possibly following Lightfoot's argument, Nineham understood the "Prologue" to be vv.1-13, and that it is "what the reader learns about the secret about Jesus before the story of the ministry begins." He argued that the incidents of these verses, from the evangelist's view, formed a fully coherent unity; that the passage stands apart from the rest of the gospel as a sort of curtain-raiser; and that "the curtain goes up" at v.14.[93] Nineham argued that the Gospel is written from the viewpoint of Jewish eschatological hope and that for Mark this hope found fulfilment in Jesus; that in his life we see the beginnings of God's final intervention in history, the first, but decisive, stage in the overthrow of the powers of evil and the establish-

---

[89]Lightfoot, Wilson, Cranfield, Schweizer, Hooker, Nineham, English, Standaert, Robbins, Kummel, Farrer, Matera, Hengel, Tolbert and Painter.
[90]Keck, Pesch, Drury, Best and Dewey.
[91]Goulder, *The Evangelists' Calendar...* (by default); F. Belo, *A Materialist Reading of the Gospel of Mark*, Maryknoll, New York, 1981: he supports 1-21a.
[92]R.H. Lightfoot, *The Gospel Message of St Mark*, Clarendon Press, Oxford, 1950.
[93]Nineham, *Saint Mark*, p.55.

ment of God's sovereign rule. He further observed that the introduction establishes the identity and authority of Jesus beyond any doubt.

To Hooker also, the "first thirteen verses stand apart from the rest of the gospel and provide the key for what follows".[94] Following Nineham, she sees the similarity between Mark's introduction and that of John (John 1.1-18). Though different in character they both, nevertheless, set out to give information about Jesus which will provide the key to understanding the rest of the gospel. Both prologues explain who Jesus is by comparing him with the Baptist and by stressing Jesus' superiority. For Hooker, the first thirteen verses describe events "different in character from those that take place in most of the remaining pages of the gospel", though she has to recognise some parallels: with chapter 9, for visions and voices (9.2-7), and chapter 3, for mention of the activities of the Holy Spirit and Satan (3.23-29). We are "allowed to view the drama from a heavenly vantage-point before Mark brings us down to earth."

Where the supporters of a thirteen-verse Prologue discuss their case, we observe the similarity of their appeal to evidence. A common argument is that vv.14 and 15 are separate from the Prologue because these verses introduce the first major section of the Gospel, which is Jesus' Galilean Ministry (e.g. see Nineham and Tolbert)[95]. Hooker recognises that other scholars argue that vv.14-15 should be included. "But," she says, "vv.14-15 lead us into the story of the ministry of Jesus with a summary of his proclamation of the Kingdom, whereas vv.1-13 provide us with the key to understanding that story, and the basis for his declaration that the Kingdom is at hand." Later, however, she argues that according to Mark's summary in 1.15, the Kingdom of God was the central theme of Jesus' teaching, borne out by the rest of the gospel. It is exactly this kind of consideration which suggests to me its inclusion in Mark's introduction. For both Drury and Best, vv.14-15 "conclude" the prologue. For Drury, it is an "active" ending, the announcement of "the Gospel" of the first verse of the book, and "the story is set on its way"[96]. For Best, the prologue concludes with an amalgam and summary of terms Jesus himself used ("the Kingdom of God is at hand") and terms the church used ("repent and believe the gospel")[97].

On 1.16-20, Hooker argues that "the theme of discipleship is prominent in Mark's gospel". It may be considered also, therefore, as appropriate for inclusion in the introduction. An introduction, even in much biblical and other ancient literature, opens up a consideration of themes that the book is to address. John 1.1-18 for example does. Hooker argues that the impression given by Mark is that the personality and authority of Jesus were such that four men responded to his call at their first meeting. Mark impresses his readers with Jesus' authority. And for both Nineham and Hooker this authority of Jesus is one of the insights we are given in the introduction, vv.1-13. Vv.16-20 arguably, therefore, extend the introduction. It is this that Belo sees, in judging that the narrative of Mark actually begins at 1.21b. And for him, the story proper begins in Capernaum, with the sabbath[98]. Goulder's support for 1.1-20 being a whole is based on his interest in possible lectionary parallelism: but, he covers only vv.1-15 in his argument[99].

Continuing our discussion centred on matters of content, we might consider the repentance that John looked for (1.4) and the extension of this theme, the repentance which Jesus looked for (1.15). Further, John preaches a "baptism of repentance for the forgiveness of sins", also that the one who is coming is "stronger.....": we observe that Jesus preaches, in addition to repentance (and the Kingdom...) "belief - in the Gospel". Additionally, there is the theme of "attraction", in 1.5, of John, and of "greater attraction", in 1.18 and v.20, of Jesus,

---

[94]Hooker, *The Gospel...*, p.31.
[95]E.g. Nineham, *Saint Mark*, p.67; also Tolbert, *Sowing the Gospel...*, pp.113ff.
[96]Drury, *The Literary Guide...*, p.409.
[97]Best, *Mark: the Gospel...*, p.129.
[98]Belo, *A Materialist Reading...*
[99]Goulder, *The Evangelists' Calendar....*, p.246.

for there is not only a going to Jesus, as to John, but a following and a giving up of life as it had been, which is a fuller expression of the repentance which John the Baptist was preaching. If as both Hooker and Nineham say, the introduction compares and contrasts John and Jesus, then the introduction cannot be concluded at 1.13, leaving such an issue incomplete. 1.14 makes the link so strongly anyway: John's ministry is over, Jesus' is beginning. There is an argument, on content consideration alone, for understanding Mark's Prologue to be the first twenty verses.

We may consider another line of argument, based on contents: the Gospel of Mark, as a single whole, not only presents the story of Jesus, but also includes a call to its reader/its listeners. No-one can just sit there: there are things to be done! Repenting, believing and following are stated early on (1.15,17,20). These are in addition to being "baptised in/with the Holy Spirit" (1.8) and becoming "fishers of men" like the first disciples (1.17). To the introductory content of verses 1.1-13, therefore, we may properly consider adding the contents of vv.14-20[100]. It may well have been in Mark's mind that his Prologue had a two-fold purpose: to present information about Jesus that those who were there around him did not know at first, and to lay down at the outset issues of discipleship and matters which will need to be addressed in future generations.

Content-wise, the first thirteen verses link (according to Schweizer's summary, for example) a résumé of the story of John the Baptist with both the Baptism of Jesus and the Temptation of Jesus. Schweizer sets these under the title of "The Beginning"[101]. The verses which follow are placed under a new, sectional title, "The Authority of Jesus and the Blindness of the Pharisees" (1.14-3.6) and a sub-title, "The Authority over Demons and Illness" (1.14-45) and then the descriptive titles of "Jesus proclaims the Kingdom of God" (1.14-15) and "The Call to Discipleship" (1.16-20). That is a lot of titling, and it is not all helpful. The passages of 1.14-15 and 1.16-20 sit comfortably under the specific headings but uncomfortably under the larger headings. The "blindness of the Pharisees", it may be noted, is not specifically an issue, until 3.5[102]; Jesus' "authority over demons and illness" appears first in 1.23ff.; and the issue of Jesus' "authority" is not verbalised until 1.22. For Schweizer, "The Demonstration of the Authority of Jesus" does come with 1.21-28. Almost as if she were paraphrasing Schweizer, Hooker titles 1.14-3.6, "Authority at work: success and opposition in Galilee." Again, "authority", considering simply her own references, comes into her titling of the piece beginning only at 1.21.[103] The case is similar with Nineham, who identified the section "The Galilean Ministry" as beginning at 1.14 but continuing to 8.26. For Tolbert, Jesus' Galilean Ministry extends from its specific introduction in vv.14,15, from 1.14 to 10.52.[104] It is true that Mark's grasp of Palestinian geography is suspect, but would he have thought that the country of the Gerasenes (5.1) and Tyre and Sidon (7.24 and v.31) were all in Galilee? Clearly, Nineham, ending this section at 8.26, was convinced that Mark did not think that Caesarea Philippi (8.27) was in Galilee. These things, and the fact that Mark himself introduces at 10.1 the Judaean element of Jesus' journeying, bring into question Tolbert's bisectionalising of the Gospel into a Galilean Ministry and a Jerusalem Ministry only. These and other attempts to separate vv.14,15 and vv.16-20 from the earlier verses of 1.1-13 are wholly problematic.

---

[100]To the arguments above, of Hooker, Nineham and Tolbert, that vv.14-20 represent a second, separate Introduction to the Galilean Mission, we can also add those of Painter, from his most recent commentary, *Mark's Gospel*, 1997..., pp.33-37.
[101]Schweizer, *The Good News...*, pp.28ff.
[102]In 2.6, what is raised is the "blindness" of the scribes; in 2.16, the scribes of the Pharisees question only, and in 2.18 the same (it may be judged) question Jesus about fasting only; and in 2.24, the Pharisees question only.
[103]Hooker, *The Gospel...*, pp.52ff.,61.
[104]For Tolbert, following the arguments of R.H. Lightfoot, *Locality and Doctrine in the Gospels*, Hodder & Stoughton, London, 1938, and E.S. Malbon, "Galilee and Jerusalem: History and Literature in Marcan Presentation", *CBQ* 44 (1982) pp.242-248, the Galilean Section of the Gospel extends to 10.52.

Literary-structural Considerations:

We consider now the contributions of literary-structural evidence to the debates over the opening verses of the Gospel, and we begin with Robbins, who identifies three-step progressions in relation to the formal structure of Mark. His "Introduction" is 1.1-13. He says, "The first three-step progression in the narrative... is 1.14-15, 16-18 and 19-20"[105] (he explains: Jesus came...; and passing along...; and going on a little further...). His structural understanding of these verses is one to which I hold, but it is not the earliest three-step progression. An earlier structural threesome can be observed in 1.9, 10-11 and 12-13 (And it came to pass, Jesus....; and immediately... the Spirit...; and immediately... the Spirit....). The earliest, structural threesome of the Gospel, of such scale, however, is that of 1.1-3, 4-5 and 6-8 (The beginning of the gospel of Jesus...; it came to pass, John....; and there was John....). In each of these cases, a structure is identified which might be described by a,b,b &, that is where a is the introductory piece, b is the first development and b & is the second and completing development, where b and b & balance and parallel each other. Simple, literary-structural analysis does indeed suggest that the Prologue *is* the first twenty verses of the Gospel. It suggests that the Prologue itself is a three-step progression, of vv.1-8, 9-13 and 14-20. We will return to a consideration of this after we have reviewed the literary-structural propositions of others.

It is presently the case that published structural-analyses of pieces of Mark's writing concentrate much upon his possible chiastic organisation of material. We consider three such serious analyses of the Prologue: Dewey's (1.1-8 of 1.1-15)[106], Drury's (1.1-15)[107] and Tolbert's (1.1-13)[108]. It may be argued straightway, because they all differ appreciably, that they cannot all be what Mark had in mind. Chiasm, it is noted, is the simplest thing to argue wrongly[109]. In the attempt to establish any pattern by one set of criteria, another set of criteria either is rejected, or simply unidentified. A later and simple illustration of this, chosen particularly because it arose in my search for Mark's 'design criteria', is found in 11.12-25. For many scholars it is a typical example of Markan envelope-structuring (11.12-14, the first part of the fig-tree incident; vv.15-19, Jesus' clearing of the Temple; vv.20-25 the second part of the fig tree episode). The "Day"-division at 11.19,20, however, which to me is Mark's clearest signal of his structural method, slashes right through such a scheme.[110]

In presenting her scheme, Dewey[111] first describes the larger rhetorical unit of the prologue as 1.1-15 and as delimited by the *inclusio* of the word "gospel". For her the prologue divides into two parts, vv.1-8 which is concerned with John, and vv.9-15 which is concerned with Jesus. The second part, vv.9-15, is marked off by its own *inclusio*, "came Jesus", vv.9, 14. Further, the conclusion of the first part, "John's preaching concerning the coming of Jesus" (vv.7,8), parallels the conclusion of the second part, "Jesus' preaching concerning the coming of the kingdom of God" (vv.14,15). She sees the two parts as closely interrelated by extensive and varied use of word repetitions (e.g., wilderness, baptism, spirit, preaching, repentance and messenger). She restricts her analysis after this to vv.1-8 and presents a five-part chiasm for the first eight verses:

[105]Robbins, *Jesus the Teacher...*, pp.27ff: for Robbins, three-step progressions begin all the sections of the Gospel's formal structure.
[106]Dewey, *Markan Public Debate...*, pp.144ff.
[107]Drury, *The Literary Guide...*, p.408; and in "Mark 1.1-15: An Interpretation", *Alternative Approaches to New Testament Study*, ed. A.E. Harvey, SPCK, London, 1985.
[108]Tolbert, *Sowing the Gospel...*, pp.108-113.
[109]See Thomson, *Chiasmus...*, pp.290-292.
[110]Refer to Chapter Six, The Fourth Seven-Day Series, and the discussions on Days Twenty-three and Twenty-four.
[111]Dewey, *Markan Public Debate...*, pp.144ff.

A	1,2a	Jesus
B	2b,3	description of John
C	4,5	a pair of presentations on John's ministry
B	6	description of John
A	7,8	Jesus.

The symmetrical rhythm is indicated by the content. She sees it as significant that in the opening verses of the Gospel, "Mark's audience is alerted from the very beginning to Mark's use of symmetrical and chiastic patterns"[112].

At first sight, it appears a most promising analysis of not only vv.1-8, but also of vv.1-15. Yet it begs several questions: can we really say that A parallels A (when v.2 might connect better with v.3, and Jesus' name is missing in vv.7,8), that B parallels B (when the issues regarding John are so different, and when v.4 and v.6 mention John only, and in their opening phrases), and that C is a pair of central statements (when there are really more than two statements, and the ministry of John well covers vv.4-8, in all)? Further, given that her basic contents' reason, for her identification of two parts to the Prologue, is that the first is concerned with John and the second with Jesus, she does seem to be simplifying the argument too much as Jesus and John are mentioned in both. We move on, but we will continue to consider her case.

When Drury's analysis was first published[113], he claimed that the first fifteen verses of the gospel were set in a four-part chiasm, ABBA: where in the outer pieces, Jesus is announced in the first and arrives in the last; and where in the inner pieces, John is announced in the first and arrives in the second. It is left to his readers to unravel. It may be read as: A: v.1, B: vv.2,3, B: vv.4-8 or vv.4-13 and A: vv.9-15 or vv.14,15. Drury's second attempt[114] describes a six-part chiasm of ABCCBA:

A	1	(Gospel)
B	2,3	Wilderness
C	4-8	Jordan
C	9-11	Jordan
B	12,13	Wilderness
A	14,15	(Gospel).

Immediately, comparison with Dewey's chiasm demonstrates that Drury and she are identifying different content criteria (to which problem for defining chiasm, refer above). Drury's focus for his middle four pieces is on 'place'; Dewey's is on 'persons'; though they both refer to the locating of the word 'gospel' in similar ways. We consider Tolbert's analysis.

Tolbert's contribution to the debate is that of a four-part chiasm for the first thirteen verses. For her, the first thirteen verses comprise the prologue, and the prologue she argues is "carefully organised rhetorically into four sections by patterns of word repetition". Her sections are:

A	1-3	Ἀρχή	Jesus, Son of God, messenger, voice, in the wilderness
B	4-8	ἐγένετο	John, baptising, Jordan
B'	9,10	καὶ ἐγένετο	Jesus, baptised, John, Jordan
A'	11-13	καὶ φωνὴ ἐγένετο	Jesus, beloved Son, voice, in the wilderness, angels.

---

[112]*ibid.*
[113]Drury, *The Literary Guide...*, p.408.
[114]Drury, "Mark 1.1-15...".

She identifies that, after the opening three verses, an anaphoric[115] use of the impersonal *ἐγέ-νετο* begins each section. (Immediately, we see that her criteria for delimiting the parts are different again from Dewey and Drury.) Additionally, she identifies that the four sections are related to each other by an anastrophe, whereby a keyword or hook word[116] near the end of each section is repeated near the beginning of the next: that is, between sections A and B: *ἐν τῇ ἐρήμῳ*, between B and B': *ἐβάπτισα, βαπτίσει* and *ἐβαπτίσθη*, and between B' and A': *οὐρανοὺς, τὸ πνεῦμα* and *ἐκ τῶν οὐρανῶν, τὸ πνεῦμα*.

She says, "The tendency to supply linking words or phrases, often but not always indicative of major themes, close to the end of one division and near the beginning of the next, is a very common practice. It serves to alert the reader to the shift in material while at the same time smoothing the transition." She further recognises that this type of stylistic feature is what Lucian, writing in about 165AD, had in mind on a grander scale in recommending that the historian adopt a smooth, even style of narration. He wrote: "Only when the first point has been completed should it lead on to the next, which should be, as it were, the next link of the chain. There must be no sharp break, no multiplicity of juxtaposed narratives. One thing should not only lie adjacent to the next, but be related to it and overlap it at the edges."[117] Tolbert views her four sections of the prologue as distinct but that "they overlap one another at the edges".

She rightly sees further thematic and verbal correspondences between the sections, which I have included in the above summary presentation of her work. We can observe some problems, however. Whilst her fourth section, 1.11-13, is about "Jesus" it does not mention his name. Further, her section B is twice as long as her other sections; it mentions John twice. In regard to anastrophes, the matter of "baptism" is rehearsed more times than she acknowledges. And much more material is found here which does not connect with any in section B'. Further, her appeal to anastrophes is unconvincing. Besides the problem of the link between sections B and B' on "baptism", there is mention of the "spirit" at the end of B, but not at the beginning of B'. If it is that a keyword is identified in one section, the same *key*-word cannot, surely, be identified as a 'non-keyword' (such as "spirit", in B, v.8) in another section within the same construction.

Reviewing these three proposals for chiasm, we expose the difficulties which are always faced when attempts are made to define structure from such a mix and repetition of themes, details and words. To these proposals, and to Dewey's additional proposal for 2.1-3.6[118], I will present counter arguments that lead me to the view that the first detailed chiasm in the gospel appears only at 5.3-5.[119] Literary-structural analysis of the first twenty verses of the Gospel persuades me that chiasm was not in Mark's mind as he composed his Prologue. To this method of analysis we now return.

While reviewing Robbins' analysis I stated that the evidence suggested the Prologue comprises the first twenty verses of the Gospel, on the grounds that it is basically a three-step progression itself of vv.1-8, 9-13 and 14-20. Below we annotate these A, B and B' in turn, because step A may be considered introductory, step B may be considered to be the first development, and step B' may be considered to be the second and concluding/completing development. We identified above that each of these steps were themselves three-step progres-

---

[115]Anaphora (or epanaphora) is the repetition of the same word or phrase at the beginning of successive clauses, sentences or sections. See, eg., Demetrius, *On Style*, pp.59-62; and *Rhetorica ad Herrenium* 4.13.19.

[116]She agrees with Dewey (*Markan Public Debate*. p.32) that "hook word" is probably a better term for this type of repetition, because it is more neutral. See also H. Parunak, "Oral Typesetting: Some uses of Biblical Structure", *Bib* 62 (1981): pp.153-168.

[117]Lucian, *De conscribenda historia* p.55 (tr. D.A. Russell in *Ancient Literary Criticism: The Principal Texts in New Translations*, eds. D.A. Russell and M. Winterbottom, Clarendon Press, Oxford, 1972, p.545.

[118]Dewey, *Markan Public Debate...*, pp.109ff., which we discuss under The First Seven Days.

[119]We discuss this under The First Series of Seven Days, and at Day Six.

sions: vv.1-3,4-5,6-8; vv.9,10-11,12-13; and vv.14-15,16-18,19-20. I present below the results of my literary-structural analysis of the first twenty verses of the Gospel. Contrary to all previous proposals, The Title is revealed as 1.1 with an abb' presentation and The Prologue as 1.2-20 with an ABB' construction:

1.1:   Ἀρχὴ / τοῦ εὐαγγελίου / Ἰησοῦ Χριστοῦ

Beginning / of the Gospel / of Jesus Christ.

Careful inspection of 1.1-8 requires that we identify v.2 as beginning an A part, v.4 a B part and v.6 a B' part, given the parallels between 'There came to pass, John…' and 'And there was John…'. Both parts, in turn, complete the construction which begins with 'As it has been written…' The likely original title is favoured as the variant reading which adds 'Son of God' to 'Jesus Christ' does now look, even more than before, like a later addition.[120]

Καθὼς γέγραπται   **A**
            ἐν τῷ Ἡσαΐᾳ
            τῷ προφήτῃ,
      Ἰδοὺ
            ἀποστέλλω τὸν ἄγγελόν μου
                  πρὸ προσώπου σου,
            ὃς κατασκευάσει τὴν ὁδόν σου·
      φωνὴ βοῶντος ἐν τῇ ἐρήμῳ,
            Ἑτοιμάσατε τὴν ὁδὸν κυρίου,
            εὐθείας ποιεῖτε τὰς τρίβους αὐτοῦ,
Ἐγένετο Ἰωάννης
            ὁ βαπτίζων ἐν τῇ ἐρήμῳ
            καὶ κηρύσσων βάπτισμα μετανοίας
                  εἰς ἄφεσιν ἁμαρτιῶν. [5]
      καὶ ἐξεπορεύετο πρὸς αὐτὸν
            πᾶσα ἡ Ἰουδαία χώρα
            καὶ οἱ Ἱεροσολυμῖται πάντες,
      καὶ ἐβαπτίζοντο ὑπ' αὐτοῦ
            ἐν τῷ Ἰορδάνῃ ποταμῷ
            ἐξομολογούμενοι τὰς ἁμαρτίας αὐτῶν. [6]
Καὶ ἦν ὁ Ἰωάννης
            ἐνδεδυμένος τρίχας καμήλου
                  καὶ ζώνην δερματίνην
                  περὶ τὴν ὀσφὺν αὐτοῦ,
                  καὶ ἐσθίων / ἀκρίδας / καὶ μέλι ἄγριον. [7]
            καὶ ἐκήρυσσεν
            λέγων,
      Ἔρχεται
            ὁ ἰσχυρότερός μου
            ὀπίσω μου,
      οὗ οὐκ εἰμὶ ἱκανὸς
                  κύψας
                  λῦσαι τὸν ἱμάντα τῶν ὑποδημάτων αὐτοῦ· [8]
            ἐγὼ ἐβάπτισα ὑμᾶς ὕδατι,
            αὐτὸς δὲ βαπτίσει ὑμᾶς ἐν πνεύματι ἁγίῳ.

---

[120] Codex Sinaiticus, for example, clearly shows 'Son of God' as squeezed into the text on a later occasion. See also my first book, *Sliced Bread: the Four Gospels, Acts and Revelation: their Literary Structures*, Ceridwen Press, Cardiff, 1988, p.22, where I first argued for a separated title after the suggestions of many others.

B

Καὶ ἐγένετο
  ἐν ἐκείναις ταῖς ἡμέραις
ἦλθεν Ἰησοῦς
  ἀπὸ Ναζαρὲτ
  τῆς Γαλιλαίας
καὶ ἐβαπτίσθη
  εἰς τὸν Ἰορδάνην
  ὑπὸ Ἰωάννου. [10]
Καὶ εὐθὺς
  ἀναβαίνων
  ἐκ τοῦ ὕδατος
εἶδεν σχιζομένους τοὺς οὐρανοὺς
  καὶ τὸ πνεῦμα
  ὡς περιστερὰν καταβαῖνον εἰς αὐτόν· [11]
καὶ φωνὴ ἐγένετο ἐκ τῶν οὐρανῶν,
  Σὺ εἶ ὁ υἱός μου ὁ ἀγαπητός,
  ἐν σοὶ εὐδόκησα.
Καὶ εὐθὺς
  τὸ πνεῦμα αὐτὸν ἐκβάλλει
  εἰς τὴν ἔρημον. [13]
καὶ ἦν ἐν τῇ ἐρήμῳ
  τεσσεράκοντα ἡμέρας
  πειραζόμενος ὑπὸ τοῦ Σατανᾶ.
καὶ ἦν μετὰ τῶν θηρίων,
  καὶ οἱ ἄγγελοι διηκόνουν αὐτῷ.

Μετὰ δὲ τὸ παραδοθῆναι τὸν Ἰωάννην   Β'
   ἦλθεν ὁ Ἰησοῦς
       εἰς τὴν Γαλιλαίαν
    κηρύσσων τὸ εὐαγγέλιον τοῦ θεοῦ[15]
    καὶ λέγων
   ὅτι Πεπλήρωται ὁ καιρὸς
      καὶ ἤγγικεν ἡ βασιλεία τοῦ θεοῦ·
    μετανοεῖτε
    καὶ πιστεύετε
      ἐν τῷ εὐαγγελίῳ.
Καὶ παράγων
      παρὰ τὴν θάλασσαν
      τῆς Γαλιλαίας
    εἶδεν Σίμωνα
     καὶ Ἀνδρέαν
     τὸν ἀδελφὸν Σίμωνος
   ἀμφιβάλλοντας ἐν τῇ θαλάσσῃ·
    ἦσαν γὰρ ἁλιεῖς. [17]
  καὶ εἶπεν αὐτοῖς ὁ Ἰησοῦς,
   Δεῦτε ὀπίσω μου,
   καὶ ποιήσω ὑμᾶς γενέσθαι ἁλιεῖς ἀνθρώπων. [18]
  καὶ εὐθὺς
   ἀφέντες τὰ δίκτυα
   ἠκολούθησαν αὐτῷ.
Καὶ προβὰς ὀλίγον
   εἶδεν Ἰάκωβον
        τὸν τοῦ Ζεβεδαίου
     καὶ Ἰωάννην
        τὸν ἀδελφὸν αὐτοῦ,
    καὶ αὐτοὺς
    ἐν τῷ πλοίῳ
    καταρτίζοντας τὰ δίκτυα, [20]
  καὶ εὐθὺς
   ἐκάλεσεν αὐτούς.
  καὶ ἀφέντες
     τὸν πατέρα αὐτῶν
     Ζεβεδαῖον
   ἐν τῷ πλοίῳ
    μετὰ τῶν μισθωτῶν
  ἀπῆλθον
    ὀπίσω αὐτοῦ.

And below: my literal English translation which is laid out in a similar way
to the Greek to communicate parts ABB', abb', (a)(b)(b'), .a,.b,.b', etc.

As it has been written   **A**
      in Isaiah
      the prophet,
  'Behold! (*Idou*)
      I send the) messenger of me (-*ou*)
            before your (-*ou*) face (-*ou*),
      who will prepare your way (-*ou*).
  A voice of one crying in the desert,
       "Prepare the way of the Lord (-*ou*),
        make straight the paths of him (-*ou*)."'
There came to pass John,
        the one baptizing in the desert,
        and preaching a baptism of repentance
           for the forgiveness of sins.
  And went out to him
      all the Judaean country
      and all the Jerusalemites.
  And they were baptized by him
      in the Jordan river,
      confessing their sins.
And there was John,
          clothed in camel hairs,
            and a leather belt
            around his waist,
         and eating
          locusts
         and wild honey.
    and he preached,
    saying,
  'There comes
    one stronger than me,
    after me,
Of whom I am not fit,
      kneeling,
      to loosen the thong of his sandals:
    I baptized you in water;
    but he will baptize you in Holy Spirit.'

And it came to pass in those days,

B

        came Jesus

            from Nazareth

            in Galilee,

       and he was baptized

            in the Jordan

            by John.

And immediately,

            coming up

            out of the water,

       he saw the heavens being opened,

            and the Spirit

            as a dove coming down into him,

       and there was a voice out of the heavens,

            'You are my beloved Son,

            in you I have been well pleased.'

And immediately,

            the Spirit threw him out

            into the desert.

       And he was in the desert

            forty days,

            tempted by Satan.

       And he was with the wild animals,

            and the angels ministered to him.

And after the imprisonment of John   B'
    <u>came Jesus into Galilee</u>,
        <u>preaching</u> the Gospel of God
        <u>and saying</u>,
    'The time has been fulfilled
        and the kingdom of God has drawn near,
      repent
      and believe in the Gospel.'
  <u>And passing along</u> beside the Sea of Galilee,
      he saw Simon
        and Andrew,
        the brother of Simon,
      casting into the sea,
        for they were fishermen.
    And he said to them, Jesus,
      'Come after me,
      and I will make you to become fishers of men.'
    And immediately,
      leaving the nets,
      they followed him.
  <u>And going forward a little</u>,
      he saw James,
          the son of Zebedee,
        and John,
          his brother,
      and they
        in the boat
        mending the nets.
    And immediately,
      he called them.
    And leaving their father
        Zebedee
    in the boat,
        with the hired servants,
      they went away,
        after him.

In this literary-structural presentation, I have underlined not only the significantly re-peated name of "Jesus" but also what is likely an equally important signifier of the structure and, therefore, of the literary-structural completeness of Mark's introduction. His use of ἔρχομαι, apparently so strategically[121], warrants close attention. In part A of the Prologue, we read about the one who "is coming" (Ἔρχεται). In B, he has come: Jesus came (ἦλθεν) to John. And in B' also: Jesus came (ἦλθεν) into Galilee to begin his ministry, according to Mark, after John was imprisoned. The overall structure of the Prologue is expressed, there-fore, by ABB'.

The analysis breaks down the text of the Prologue into five different levels of literary order expressed in turn by: ABB', abb', (a) (b) (b'), (.a) (.b) (.b') and (.a) (.a'), (..a) (..b) (..b') and (..a) (..a'). We may discern Mark's use of his literary-structural three-part presentational principle at all these levels, and note at the lower and, therefore, more detailed levels only, his use of an alternative 'two-part' construction-method. The basic principle of his writing method is that he establishes an introductory part, follows it with a first development, and then completes the whole piece with a second development, whereby the first and second de-velopments balance each other. By employing this method throughout his Gospel presenta-tion (at every level of literary order) he signals his definition of sections, parts, sub-parts, etc. This uncovering of his rhetorical method and use of writing style is of fundamental assistance in the establishing of his framework and plan for the Gospel as a whole, as well as in the de-fining of its constituent parts. In the larger constructions (of ABB', abb' and (a) (b) (b')) his presentations balance for content and detail, and in the smaller constructions (of (.a) (.b) (.b'), (.a) (.a') and (..a) (..b) (..b'), (..a) (..a')) the parts and sub-parts balance by reason of their de-tail and their function in the text (for qualifying and completing purposes).

At the start of my analysis of the Gospel text, I could not have known where the analysis would take me. Simply, it is the case that as the analysis was once begun it devel-oped its own momentum and could not be stopped. As a result, it demonstrates how much the three-part presentational method of Mark's choice governed his writing effort. The breaking down of the text into clauses and words had its purpose!

The literary-structural/rhetorical analysis of the Gospel's Prologue provides, then, an excellent example of how Mark's rhetorical method signals the delimiting of his Gospel sec-tions, pieces and parts. It is a method, as we will see, which he applies consistently from be-ginning to end of his Gospel. Not only is his method, on discovery, a cause of some amaze-ment, but also is his ability to work it at so many levels of literary order simultaneously.

In the Introduction, page 21, I promised a case study which would determine whether or not there was a meeting point between Neirynck's analysis[122] and mine. The apparent dif-ference between our findings is due to the fact that he seeks and discerns dualities whereas I discern three-part presentations which include dualities as part of the construction, at any lit-erary level at any one time. In all he discerns forty-four dualities in the verses which make up Mark's Prologue. He places them under nineteen of his thirty Group headings. We could ex-amine them group by group, but rather I choose to present my summary. Of Neirynck's forty-four 'dualities', in my reading of the Prologue:

25 link first and second 'developments', hence they have ABB' relationship;
 9 link introduction and first development, hence ABB';
 9 link introduction and second development, hence ABB'; and only
 1 displays no relationship at all.

---

[121]See under Day Two for further examples of the importance to Mark of ἔρχομαι.
[122]Neirynck, *Duality...*, Part II, pp.73-135.

It is, of course, particularly telling that over one half of Neirynck's identified dualities correspond in simple BB' relationship. The remainder which link introduction and first development, and introduction and second/completing development are positively significant also. Indeed all three identifications of relationship serve to demonstrate that Mark is creating three-part wholes. This identification of Mark's 'style' of presentation in his Prologue is important. It is the writing method which he adopts for the whole of his Gospel.

We can now review my presentation of the literary-structure of the first twenty verses, in the rhetorical terms in which Tolbert presents her own.

In the Title and at the beginning of the second and third parts of the Prologue, we identify the anaphora of "Jesus'" name: consider 1.1, 1.9 and 1.14. We observe that the anaphora is strengthened at 1.9 and 1.14 by the common application of $\tilde{\eta}\lambda\theta\epsilon\nu$. The name of Jesus is given the definite article in the third and final case, and its use suggests emphasis. The placings of the name of "Jesus", as described above in my literary-structural analysis, would appear to be more convincing than the $\dot{\epsilon}\gamma\dot{\epsilon}\nu\epsilon\tau o$ of Tolbert's three of four sections. "Jesus" is the central figure of Mark's work, beyond any question.

The relationships between the three sections of the Prologue can be described. The first part A introduces the scriptures which are fulfilled with the presence of John the Baptist and his announcements concerning the one who is coming. The second part B continues the story with Jesus coming to John from Galilee: his baptism at the hands of John leads on to the heavenly disclosures and his John-/Moses-/Elijah-like time in the desert. And the third part B' completes the threefold Prologue: John's imprisonment marks the time of Jesus' return to Galilee and the beginning of his preaching the 'Gospel' (linking back to the opening of A) and his calling followers. A is introductory; it is developed by B, and in turn B' develops B and completes the whole.

Anaphoras are in evidence also at the next level of literary order, in sections b and b': in A, at 1.4 and 1.6, the name, $'I\omega\acute{a}\nu\nu\eta\varsigma$; in B, at 1.10 and 12, in the term, $K\alpha\grave{\iota}\,\epsilon\grave{\upsilon}\theta\grave{\upsilon}\varsigma$; and in B', at 1.16 and 19, in repetitions: of place; of $\epsilon\grave{\iota}\delta\epsilon\nu$; and of pairs of brothers who immediately respond to Jesus' call. Close investigation of the lower literary orders shows also, at their levels, many verbal correspondences, hence further anaphoras. At all levels, what is discerned, is the paralleling of b and b', the second two parts, over and against the introductory role of a, the first part of the construction. These are not heavily dependent on verbal paralleling: rather, at the more detailed scales of presentation, (.a) (.b) (.b') and (..a) (..b) (..b'), they are more dependent on meaning, syntax and balance.

Additionally, we identify a fine example of parechesis in the Title of the Gospel and in the opening lines of the Prologue, a repetition of the same sound in immediately following words. A welter of them can be identified in fact in the opening piece and all conclude b and b' clauses:

$$'A\rho\chi\acute{\eta}\,\tau o\hat{\upsilon}\,\epsilon\grave{\upsilon}\alpha\gamma\gamma\epsilon\lambda\acute{\iota}o\upsilon\,'I\eta\sigma o\hat{\upsilon}\,X\rho\iota\sigma\tau o\hat{\upsilon}$$

$$K\alpha\theta\grave{\omega}\varsigma\,\gamma\acute{\epsilon}\gamma\rho\alpha\pi\tau\alpha\iota$$
$$\dot{\epsilon}\nu\,\tau\hat{\omega}\,'H\sigma\alpha\acute{\iota}\alpha$$
$$\tau\hat{\omega}\,\pi\rho o\phi\acute{\eta}\tau\eta,$$
$$'I\delta o\grave{\upsilon}$$
$$\dot{\alpha}\pi o\sigma\tau\acute{\epsilon}\lambda\lambda\omega\,\tau\grave{o}\nu\,\acute{\alpha}\gamma\gamma\epsilon\lambda\acute{o}\nu\,\mu o\upsilon\,\pi\rho\grave{o}\,\pi\rho o\sigma\acute{\omega}\pi o\upsilon\,\sigma o\upsilon,$$
$$\grave{o}\varsigma\,\kappa\alpha\tau\alpha\sigma\kappa\epsilon\upsilon\acute{\alpha}\sigma\epsilon\iota\,\tau\grave{\eta}\nu\,\acute{o}\delta\acute{o}\nu\,\sigma o\upsilon\cdot$$
$$\phi\omega\nu\grave{\eta}\,\beta o\hat{\omega}\nu\tau o\varsigma\,\dot{\epsilon}\nu\,\tau\hat{\eta}\,\dot{\epsilon}\rho\acute{\eta}\mu\omega,$$
$$'E\tau o\iota\mu\acute{\alpha}\sigma\alpha\tau\epsilon\,\tau\grave{\eta}\nu\,\acute{o}\delta\grave{o}\nu\,\kappa\upsilon\rho\acute{\iota}o\upsilon,$$
$$\epsilon\grave{\upsilon}\theta\epsilon\acute{\iota}\alpha\varsigma\,\pi o\iota\epsilon\hat{\iota}\tau\epsilon\,\tau\grave{\alpha}\varsigma\,\tau\rho\acute{\iota}\beta o\upsilon\varsigma\,\alpha\grave{\upsilon}\tau o\hat{\upsilon},$$

It would appear that Mark has given thought not only to what he was going to write, but also to how it was going to sound. Reworking the LXX and MT versions of scriptures, which he chose to knit together and ascribe to Isaiah, he has also applied a rhetorical device which would enhance, for his audience, his opening presentation. We will find more of them later in the Gospel: one to introduce each of the two middle Series and a final one to end the Epilogue, rather like a rhyming couplet (a survivor from Greco-Roman literature?) at the end of an Act in a Shakespearean play.

Readers of the Greek and literal English translation above will now be able to summarise for themselves the writer's intentions for his Title and Prologue, given this exposure of the technical details of his rhetorical constructions that fulfil both the rules of ancient rhetoric and the writing practices of that era. More will be revealed towards the end of this book about the writer's harmonising of his Prologue with his intended Epilogue. That the writer inserted other 'helps' too for his readers is something I can introduce here: there are aids in the text that are given the reader so that they can check they are reading the structural presentation correctly. Mark does not fail to surprise! His text works at two levels: overtly, for the writer's audience, it communicates linked and succeeding stories of happenings which are salvific, theological and even creedal, but under the surface, for the reader alone, are messages that can be called 'checks', so the reader can know that he of she is reading the work in the required way. Look at Codex Sinaiticus, for example, at the rows of letters in columns without gaps between words and little more than edentations (see page 340) for punctuating the text. It is the writer's writing style that provides the punctuation and works at the micro- and macro-levels throughout the text. The Prologue concludes with Jesus calling two brother fishermen by the lakeside and then, a little further along the shore, his calling two more brother fishermen. The last part of the Prologue bears a message for the reader alone, just as the first part of the Epilogue does. By the time the reader has reached the end of the script, he/she will see this. The number introduced in the opening part of the Epilogue is 'seven'. Cradling the Narrative of the Gospel, therefore, are signifiers of structure: the Gospel narrative comprises 'two' inner 'brother' Series, around which are 'two' outer 'brother' Series. Both Series consist of seven Days. The Gospel's scheme is 'four' times 'seven'. We will see later, in the Series themselves, just how much numbers do matter to this writer. But for now, we will note that he will have written in 'helps' about which no reader will have known anything in the last seventeen hundred years!

In summary, the contents of the Prologue's three sections hold together on the theme of beginnings. Further, John and Jesus are compared and contrasted. The beginning of Jesus' mission proceeds after the imprisonment of John. He is preaching the Gospel of God (1.14) and is calling followers. Repentance and belief, immediacy of following, these are the true responses. The first twenty verses, we may conclude, describe fully and adequately for Mark (and presumably, therefore, his Church) the background and beginning to the Days of Jesus' messianic mission: "the time is fulfilled", the waiting is over.

I refer to a classic essay on stylistics, in which Ian Watt demonstrated that all of the major themes in Henry James's "The Ambassadors" could be found in its first paragraph alone. As many commentators have pointed out, finding the themes depended upon having read all of "The Ambassadors" and not just the first paragraph.[123] It is also the case with Mark's Prologue and its inclusion of Jesus' calling of disciples. I have never really understood why so many scholars and commentators on Mark have taken the view that the Prologue stopped short of the calling of disciples. The fact is, of course, that they came with their own view to the text of the Prologue (and the views of those before them) that it was meant only to communicate mysteries we would otherwise have known nothing about. The Prologue introduces the main themes. And now we can say also, without contradiction, that the Prologue demonstrates also Mark's presentational style which he applies to his gospel in its

---

[123] I. Watt, "The First Paragraph of *The Ambassadors*: An Explication", in *Contemporary Essays on Style: Rhetoric, Linguistics, and Criticism*, eds. G. Love and M. Payne, Scott, Foresman and Co., Glenview, Ill., 1969, pp.266-283.

every part! Whether it is in its ABB', simple form, or in compounds of the same, ABB'/ABB'/ABB', Mark uses the same basic method of writing to complete all his individual "Days", always completing any succession of three-part wholes before he starts upon another, for the 'telling' of another "Day".

And finally, as we complete the structural argument provoked by the Prologue, we may observe that one of the earliest manuscripts lends also some support to the view that 1.1-20 describes fully Mark's opening presentations. Codex Vaticanus (B) clearly exhibits its first edentation[124], a sure sign of a recognised break in the text, at 1.21. This edentation is a single protruding letter in the left hand margin which has its parallel in our traditional, paragraph signifying indentation, of the type that I am using here. In the Codex, in the line above, it was preceded by a varying amount of space, of an incomplete line of characters, just as I am employing for my work. Furthermore, other spaces (much smaller) appear prior to 1.4, 9, 14, 16 and 19, that is, at each of the major sub-divisions of the text as we identify (1.1, 9 and 14) and at three of the six minor sub-divisions (1.4, 16 and 19). It might be argued, therefore, that Codex Vaticanus has preserved a number of Mark's signifiers of structure, but demonstrates, at the same time, how the loss of his signifiers of paragraphs resulted as copies, and copies of copies, were made.

The Prologue's three-sections with its nineteen verses of introduction may be judged, only very broadly, to have covered fifty days or more. To the forty days of Jesus' sojourn in the desert we add the days (unstated by Mark) which John spent in the desert before Jesus, and the days (also unstated) between the end of Jesus' forty days in the desert and John's imprisonment. What follows thereafter, from 1.21, is a narrative which has as its framework a presentation of twenty-eight "Days", through the telling of which Mark captures the full extent and implication of Jesus' mission, for those who read his gospel and those who have it read or recited to them. It is not as such a day-to-day account (in consecutive terms) as we shall see; Jesus is no 'twenty-eight day wonder'. In Mark's reporting of "Days" he makes reference to many more days than he actually tells, by report and by suggestion. In his introductory pieces to three of his "Days" (at 2.1ff, 8.1ff. and 9.2ff), he makes it plain that there are other days to Jesus' mission which he does not report. Simply, Mark adopts, from 1.21, a particular method of presentation, which he employs to the end of his narrative, 16.8. We will discuss these matters much more in the chapters ahead.

---

[124]Codex Vaticanus displays only nine edentations in all: compare: Sinaiticus which has 319 and Alexandrinus which has 316.

Chapter Three
The First Series of Seven Days (1.21-5.43):

Day One: 1.21-38:

Arguably, the Day is 1.21-34, 1.21-38 or 1.21-39.

Drury[125] sees the day, 1.21-38, as "some twenty-four hours from morning to morning". Nineham[126] writes of 1.21-34 as "a specimen day" and of vv.35-39 that "we are meant to take this incident closely with what precedes - as a sort of appendage to the "specimen day"[127]. Wilson titles the day, 1.21-39, "A Day in the Life of Jesus"[128]. Hooker speaks of 1.21-39 as a "closely knit series of events"[129] (but see below). Schweizer treats 1.21-28, 29-31 and 32-39 as separate stories[130], though he suggests that it is likely "that vv.23-26, 29-32, 34a, 35-38 had been told in a connected form before Mark"[131]. Pesch discerns a pre-Markan tradition also, and terms it "a day in Jesus' ministry at Capernaum"; though he estimates that it is 1.21a, 29-39[132]. Kuhn, quite differently, sees 1.16-39 as pre-Markan[133].

The Day begins: *Καὶ εἰσπορεύονται εἰς Καφαρναούμ, καὶ εὐθὺς τοῖς σάββασιν εἰσελθὼν εἰς τὴν συναγωγὴν ἐδίδασκεν.* The day's telling begins with an introductory, 'dramatic' historical present[134]. For Nineham[135], "the day opens after an unspecified interval." For Schweizer[136], Mark here begins a new unit (i.e. vv.21-28); "not only is nothing said of any disciples accompanying Jesus, but most important is the fact that the events in vv.16-20 could not have happened on the Sabbath, when fishing and the repairing of nets were strictly forbidden." Schweizer's method of argument may be correct in terms of distinguishing the break between vv.20 and 21, but as all four disciples (who are called in 1.16-20) make their re-appearance in 1.29-31, the first part of his argument appears too strong. Also we may note that he undermines his own argument somewhat and shows perhaps a little too much confidence in considering v.32. He says of the verse that it "has little significance unless the setting sun marks the end of the Sabbath, so that from that time on it was permissible, once more, to carry the sick." He says, "It does not have this meaning for Mark, since whenever he refers to Jewish customs he explains them to his readers (7.3f.)." We note, nev-

---

[125]Drury, *The Literary Guide...*, p.410.
[126]Nineham, *Saint Mark*, pp.73,82.
[127]Nineham, *Saint Mark*, p.83.
[128]R McL. Wilson, "Mark", *Peake's Commentary on the Bible*, Eds. Black & Rowley, Nelson, Sunbury-on Thames,1977, p.801; see also Taylor, *The Gospel...*, p.146.
[129]Hooker, *The Gospel...*, p.77.
[130]Schweizer, *The Good News...*, pp.49-56.
[131]Schweizer, *The Good News...*, p.50.
[132]Pesch, *Das Markusevangelium...*, p.67.
[133]H-W. Kuhn, *Ältere Sammlungen im Markusevangelium*, Studien zur Umwelt des Neuen Testaments No. 8, Vandenhoeck & Ruprecht, Gottingen, 1971.
[134]H. St. John Thackeray, *The Septuagint and Jewish Worship: A Study in Origins*, 2nd Edn., The Schweich Lectures, Oxford University Press, London, 1923, pp.20-22: speaking of the dramatic type of historical present, he says (p.21), "The tense as a rule is ... "dramatic" in the sense that it serves to introduce new scenes in the drama. It heralds the arrival of a new character or a change of locality or marks a turning-point in the march of events... The main function is... to introduce a date, a new scene..., in other words a fresh paragraph in the narrative." For a discussion of the historical present, see under Day Two.
[135]Nineham, *Saint Mark*, p.73.
[136]Schweizer, *The Good News...*, p.50.

ertheless, that at 1.32 Mark has at least defined "evening" for his audience by the phrase, "when the sun set". One might deduce from this that Mark assumed his audience would understand the significance of this moment of the day for the Jew.

Contrary to what Schweizer suggests, Mark does have an understanding of the Hebrew/Palestinian Day which begins with *sunset* and which in the case of the *beginning* of a Sabbath involves new obligations for the Jews (see 15.42). He would seem to have a comprehensive grasp of its structure. He is informed about the four watches of the night and the twelve hours of daylight, for on the third day on which Jesus is in the Temple, Mark records all four watches as late, midnight, cock-crowing and early (13.35), and on the day of Jesus' crucifixion, he refers to the third, the sixth and the ninth hours of daylight (15.25, 33 and 34). Bultmann[137] may think that Mark begins a new day at 14.17 with the first watch of the night, that 14.27-65 takes up the second, 14.66-72 the third, and the fourth (πρωΐ) begins at 15.1, but, given Mark's own evidence, while he understands the Hebrew/Palestinian Day to begin with *sunset*, he chooses to present his gospel scheme of "Days" in terms of the civil day which is qualified as from *sunrise* to (just before) *sunrise*[138].

The key question is then, what does Mark mean by καὶ εὐθὺς τοῖς σάββασιν in 1.21? Does he mean 'from the evening of the day' (thus following the Jewish Day, as beginning with sunset), or does he mean 'beginning with daylight' (i.e. from sunrise, so following the "civil day" as qualified by beginning with sunrise)? It is clearly the second of these; the contents of 1.21-38 demand this understanding because the action is continuous through the daylight hours to the evening and the hours of darkness (1.32, Ὀψίας δὲ γενομένης) and well into the night (1.35, Καὶ πρωΐ ἔννυχα λίαν). As was stated in the Introduction, Mark chose to present *all* his Days' reports for his Gospel according to the "civil day" which is qualified as beginning with sunrise and ending just before the following sunrise. We will keep on returning to this matter because it is a most important feature in the literary-structural analysis of Mark's Gospel.

Linking the first two sentences of this Day's report, Hooker[139] expunges any possible reference to 'the disciples' by her translation "And he entered Capernaum", so substituting "he" for "they" for which there is no textual support. (She sees vv.21-28 as a separate unit, also vv.29-31, 32-34, 35-39, 40-45, and so on: twelve units in all from 1.14 to 3.6.) The literal translation "And they entered into Capernaum" in itself points to the coupling of 1.21-28 to what follows from 1.29. This coupling can be suggested because the four who were called by Jesus to follow him (in 1.16-20), who together with Jesus justify the "they" of 1.21, are all named in vv.29-31. In 1.32-34 no disciples are mentioned, but in 1.35-38 Simon is. It is not until 3.16, on Day Five, when Jesus is choosing the twelve, that Simon is mentioned again.

Mark may well have "revised extensively the style of the tradition he received"[140], for the overall outcome of his presentation has its unity as a Day primarily in the temporal references at 1.21 ("And immediately on the Sabbath"), at 1.32 ("And when evening came") and at 1.35 ("And rising very early in the night"). Consider also Mark's references to 'place': in 1.21 ("And immediately on the Sabbath entering into the synagogue"), in 1.23 ("And immediately there was in their synagogue") and in 1.29 ("And immediately leaving the synagogue"). References to both time and place bind the separate units into a whole. Consider also the day-time exorcism and the day-time healing and the night-time multiplications of both, and the common emphatic editorial record of Jesus' commands to the demons to silence (1.24 and v.34) because "they knew" him. The presentation following, of the literary-structure of Day One, shows how well Mark created a balanced structure of three parts. At the beginning of

---

[137]Bultmann, *The History...*, p.341.
[138]See note 82, in the Introduction.
[139]Hooker, *The Gospel...*, p.61.
[140]Schweizer, *The Good News...*, p.54.

the first part, Jesus arrives in Capernaum and enters the synagogue; at the beginning of the second, Jesus leaves the synagogue and goes to Simon's house; and at the beginning of the third, Jesus leaves Simon's house for 'a desert place'. Key to the defining of the three parts of this Day's telling are Jesus' changes of location. We will discuss this feature further, but after we have rehearsed the arguments regarding the day's conclusion.

1.35a requires discussion: *Καὶ πρωῒ ἔννυχα λίαν ἀναστὰς ἐξῆλθεν...* Schweizer uses the Good News translation "Very early the next morning, long before daylight, Jesus got up and left the house..." Hooker translates similarly, "And early in the morning, while it was still dark, he got up, left the house..."[141]. Clearly, both Schweizer and Hooker (and others), on this basis, appear to argue that a new day starts at this juncture. In our normal, Western parlance it is surely the case, because for us a new day starts at midnight, but in Mark's terms a new Day of his reporting does not start until dawn. We ask then, how should we translate and interpret *πρωῒ ἔννυχα λίαν*, which Cranfield characterises as "odd but vivid"[142] and which Drury, as above mentioned, sees as prefiguring 16.2?[143]

Problems of translation and, therefore, of interpretation, in these matters, are not solved simply by recourse to Greek, which here is ambiguous in its use of *πρωῒ*. The word can mean "early", but it can also be understood to be the technical term for the fourth watch of the night. The problem occurs most acutely for Hooker at 16.2. Here, she translates *καὶ λίαν πρωῒ τῇ μιᾷ τῶν σαββάτων ἔρχονται ἐπὶ τὸ μνημεῖον ἀνατείλαντος τοῦ ἡλίου,* "And very early in the morning on the first day of the week they came to the tomb just after sunrise"[144]. She points out an inconsistency between the first and last temporal parts of the sentence. For her, the first means "in the early hours before dawn". She is determined to see the expression in its technical usage, but it cannot be squared with "just after sunrise". She notes that attempts were made "at an early stage to tidy up this anomaly by altering one phrase or the other" but explains weakly, "probably Mark was not being as precise as his critics". Rather, the explanation would seem to be that nowhere outside of 6.48 and 13.35 does Mark appear to have written about the fourth watch, and nowhere outside of 13.35, in a listing of the night watches, does he use *πρωῒ* in the technical sense. We note that at 6.48 he might have written *πρωῒ*, but he in fact writes, "at about the fourth watch of the night...". His use of *πρωῒ* elsewhere (in 11.20; 15.1; and 16.2) describes the time soon after dawn and, therefore, defines the beginning of new days.

1.35a may translate literally and perfectly acceptably therefore, in Mark's terms, as "And very early in the night...". Mark makes no reference to any watch; it may have been the fourth watch or it may have been the third. (It is unlikely that any implication is intended of either the second or the first: 1.32-34 records Jesus beginning his healing-work at sunset, and he healed many; and when he rises (1.35) it is surely from sleep.) Rather, Mark qualifies *πρωῒ* by *ἔννυχα λίαν.* Compare then 16.2 *καὶ λίαν πρωῒ,* but note the contrast: there is no reference to "night" in this verse. In the telling of the Gospel's last Day, the "night" lies between 16.1 and 16.2; Mark's report of the Day is 16.2-8. 16.1 is purely introductory to that report, in that it gives the names of the women, and the reason for their going to the tomb.

We continue with our consideration of the text, and note that Schweizer[145] sees vv.32-39 as a whole: it is surely the case as Mark presents, that knowing who Jesus was (v.34) and what he was present to do (v.38) are issues which are indissolubly joined. (See also, as above, Schweizer's suggestion that vv.23-26, 29-32, 34a, 35-38 were connected before Mark edited

---

[141]Hooker, *The Gospel...*, p.75.
[142]C.E.B. Cranfield, *The Gospel according to St Mark*, gen. ed. C.F.D. Moule, The Cambridge Greek Testament Commentary, Cambridge University Press, Cambridge, 1959, rev. 1977, p.88.
[143]Drury, *The Literary Guide...*, p.410; see also Hooker, *The Gospel...*, p.76.
[144]Hooker, *The Gospel...*, pp.382-384.
[145]Schweizer, *The Good News,* p.54.

them.) Concerning verses 1.35-39, Taylor[146] says the passage "derives its significance from (the) three preceding stories... *The story ends* with the words of Jesus, 'Let us go elsewhere into the neighbouring towns, that I may preach there also, for to this end came I forth' (1.38)." The case can be put, therefore, in terms of temporal connections (1.21, 32 and 35) and in matters of place and related content, for understanding Mark's First Day as continuous from 1.21 to 38/39. And Taylor himself thinks there is a good case for ending the passage at 1.38.

Where does 1.39 belong: at the end of the first Day, or at the beginning of the following Day? We refer to Taylor again who appears to be contradicting himself: "The statement in v.39 is a summary passage which rounds off the section and prepares the way for what follows." We have three choices before us: it may have been in Mark's mind that v.39 performed as a conclusion to his First Day; it may have been in his mind that it was introductory to the second; or it may have been his deliberate link between the two. Both Hooker[147] and the Good News Bible which Schweizer uses read, "So he travelled... ". Nineham uses the RSV, "And he went throughout ...". Hooker and Schweizer have strengthened the link between 1.38 and 39 by their acceptance of a looser translation of $\kappa\alpha\iota$. And there is another consideration: the verb is either $\mathring{\eta}\lambda\theta\epsilon\nu$ or $\mathring{\eta}\nu$. The latter has the support of ACDW and the great majority of MSS. Cranfield[148] suggests that $\mathring{\eta}\nu$ is probably to be preferred. It is "supported by the Lukan parallel; the periphrastic imperfect is characteristic of Mark; and $\mathring{\eta}\lambda\theta\epsilon\nu$ looks like a grammatical improvement due to $\epsilon\iota\varsigma$ (which if $\mathring{\eta}\nu$ is read, is equivalent to $\acute{\epsilon}\nu$)." The choice is an awkward one. On balance, as the earlier and more reliable witnesses read $\kappa\alpha\iota\ \mathring{\eta}\lambda\theta\epsilon\nu$ and other new days begin similarly (5.1 and 9.33, $\kappa\alpha\iota\ \mathring{\eta}\lambda\theta\epsilon\nu$, 6.1 and 8.27, $\kappa\alpha\iota\ \acute{\epsilon}\xi\mathring{\eta}\lambda\theta\epsilon\nu$, 8.22 and 10.46, $\kappa\alpha\iota\ \acute{\epsilon}\rho\chi o\nu\tau\alpha\iota$), v.39 more likely begins the next Day in Mark's telling, and v.38 does more likely end the telling of this first Day, with Jesus speaking (as in the days ending at 2.22, 8.20, 26, 9.1, 50, 10.31, 45 and 13.37) and with emphasis (as in the days ending at 3.6, 4.41, 5.20, 43, 6.52, 7.30, 37, 9.29, 10.52, 14.11, 72 and 16.8). Additionally, 1.35-38 (the ending of Day One) compares for content with 1.45 (the ending of Day Two): this will be presented under the examination of Day Two, 1.39-45.

We come to the point now where the literary-structure of Day One as a whole can be presented. We first summarise the literary-structure of Day One as we will do for each Day. It is properly described as having an ABB' form (of ABB'/ABB'/ABB' in its composite state). Mark well created this structure: in part A, Jesus enters the synagogue; in part B he enters Simon's house and in part B' he leaves Simon's house. It is well represented by ABB' where B and B' parallel for place. In the first of these, part A (1.21,22) introduces the new town, but also day and time of day ($\kappa\alpha\iota\ \epsilon\mathring{v}\theta\grave{v}\varsigma\ \tau o\hat{\iota}\varsigma\ \sigma\acute{\alpha}\beta\beta\alpha\sigma\iota\nu$), entry into a place, the activity of the main character, Jesus, and the response of the people and their reason for their response. Part B (1.23-25), in the same setting (and connected by $\kappa\alpha\iota\ \epsilon\mathring{v}\theta\grave{v}\varsigma$), first introduces a new character into the scene who because of what he says evokes a response from Jesus. Part B' (1.26-28) completes B by first reporting the effect of Jesus' response and then two outcomes. In the second, part A (1.29), linking with what has gone before (by reference to 'synagogue' and by $\kappa\alpha\iota\ \epsilon\mathring{v}\theta\grave{v}\varsigma$), establishes the new setting and introduces Jesus' four companions. Part B (1.30,31) relates a healing and what follows it. And Part B' (1.32-34), in the same setting ('at the door'), and establishing the new time of the day (the end of the Sabbath), tells of many healings and castings out of demons. In the third, Part A (1.35) states a new time and tells how the main character, Jesus, left for a desert place, to pray. Part B (1.36,37) tells of the arrival of Simon and the others. Part B' (1.38) gives Jesus' response, making clear his purpose. The Day's focus is on how Jesus becomes known in Capernaum, in all Galilee (1.28) and how his purpose was in other local towns too.

---

[146]Taylor, *The Gospel...*, p.182, my italics.
[147]Hooker, *The Gospel...*, p.75.
[148]Cranfield, *The Gospel...*, p.90.

The literary structure of Day One is viewed, in the Greek, as:

Καὶ <u>εἰσπορεύονται</u> εἰς Καφαρναούμ.		a	A	**A**
καὶ εὐθὺς τοῖς σάββασιν	(a)	b		
<u>εἰσελθὼν εἰς τὴν συναγωγὴν</u>	(b)			
ἐδίδασκεν[22]	(b')			
καὶ ἐξεπλήσσοντο ἐπὶ τῇ διδαχῇ αὐτοῦ,	(a)	b'		
ἦν γὰρ διδάσκων αὐτοὺς .a	(b)			
ὡς ἐξουσίαν ἔχων .a'				
καὶ οὐχ ὡς οἱ γραμματεῖς. [23]	(b')			

<u>Καὶ εὐθὺς</u>   B

        ἦν ἐν τῇ συναγωγῇ αὐτῶν
        ἄνθρωπος ἐν πνεύματι ἀκαθάρτῳ,
     καὶ ἀνέκραξεν[24]
           λέγων,
       Τί ἡμῖν
          καὶ σοί,
            Ἰησοῦ Ναζαρηνέ;
       ἦλθες ἀπολέσαι ἡμᾶς;
         οἶδά σε τίς εἶ,
         ὁ ἅγιος τοῦ θεοῦ.
     καὶ ἐπετίμησεν αὐτῷ ὁ Ἰησοῦς
           λέγων,
       Φιμώθητι
         καὶ ἔξελθε ἐξ αὐτοῦ. [26]

Καὶ σπαράξαν αὐτὸν τὸ πνεῦμα τὸ ἀκάθαρτον   B'
        καὶ φωνῆσαν φωνῇ μεγάλῃ
        ἐξῆλθεν ἐξ αὐτοῦ.
     καὶ ἐθαμβήθησαν ἅπαντες,
           ὥστε συζητεῖν πρὸς ἑαυτοὺς
           λέγοντας,
       Τί ἐστιν τοῦτο;
       διδαχὴ καινὴ κατ᾽ ἐξουσίαν·
         καὶ τοῖς πνεύμασι τοῖς ἀκαθάρτοις ἐπιτάσσει,
         καὶ ὑπακούουσιν αὐτῷ. [28]
     καὶ ἐξῆλθεν ἡ ἀκοὴ αὐτοῦ
        εὐθὺς πανταχοῦ
        εἰς ὅλην τὴν περίχωρον τῆς Γαλιλαίας.

Καὶ εὐθὺς ἐκ τῆς συναγωγῆς ἐξελθόντες   A   **B**
    ἦλθον εἰς τὴν οἰκίαν Σίμωνος καὶ Ἀνδρέου
    μετὰ Ἰακώβου καὶ Ἰωάννου. [30]
ἡ δὲ πενθερὰ Σίμωνος κατέκειτο   B
    πυρέσσουσα,
    καὶ εὐθὺς λέγουσιν αὐτῷ περὶ αὐτῆς. [31]
    καὶ προσελθὼν
    ἤγειρεν αὐτὴν
    κρατήσας τῆς χειρός·
    καὶ ἀφῆκεν αὐτὴν ὁ πυρετός,
    καὶ διηκόνει αὐτοῖς.
Ὀψίας δὲ γενομένης,   B'
    ὅτε ἔδυ ὁ ἥλιος,
    ἔφερον πρὸς αὐτὸν
    πάντας τοὺς κακῶς ἔχοντας
    καὶ τοὺς δαιμονιζομένους· [33]
    καὶ ἦν ὅλη ἡ πόλις
    ἐπισυνηγμένη
    πρὸς τὴν θύραν. [34]
    καὶ ἐθεράπευσεν πολλοὺς
    κακῶς ἔχοντας
    ποικίλαις νόσοις,
    καὶ δαιμόνια πολλὰ ἐξέβαλεν,
    καὶ οὐκ ἤφιεν λαλεῖν τὰ δαιμόνια,
    ὅτι ᾔδεισαν αὐτόν.

Καὶ πρωῒ ἔννυχα λίαν   A   **B'**
    ἀναστὰς
    ἐξῆλθεν
    καὶ ἀπῆλθεν εἰς ἔρημον τόπον
    κἀκεῖ προσηύχετο. [36]
καὶ κατεδίωξεν αὐτὸν Σίμων   B
    καὶ οἱ μετ' αὐτοῦ, [37]
    καὶ εὗρον αὐτὸν
    καὶ λέγουσιν αὐτῷ
    ὅτι Πάντες ζητοῦσίν σε.
καὶ λέγει αὐτοῖς,   B'
    Ἄγωμεν ἀλλαχοῦ
    εἰς τὰς ἐχομένας κωμοπόλεις,
    ἵνα καὶ ἐκεῖ κηρύξω·
    εἰς τοῦτο γὰρ ἐξῆλθον. [39]

And in literal English:

And they go into Capernaum.
     And immediately on the Sabbath,
          entering into the synagogue,
          he began to teach.
     And they were amazed at his teaching,
          for he was teaching them as having authority,
          and not as the scribes.
And immediately,
          there was in their synagogue
          a man with an unclean spirit.
     And he cried out
          saying,
     'What to us
          and to you,
          Jesus of Nazareth?
     Have you come to destroy us?
          I know who you are:
          the holy one of God.'
     And Jesus scolded him,
          saying,
     'Be quiet.
     and come out of him.'
And the unclean spirit throwing him,
          and shouting loudly,
          came out of him.
     And all were astonished,
          so that they debated among themselves,
          saying,
     'What is this?
          A new teaching with authority,
             and he commands the unclean spirits,
             and they obey him.'
     And news went out about him,
          immediately everywhere,
          into all the environs of Galilee.

A

And immediately   **B**
                          out of the synagogue
                          going forth,
                they came to the house of Simon and Andrew,
                with James and John.
        Now Simon's mother-in-law was laid low,
                        fever-stricken
                and immediately they tell him about her.
            And approaching,
                    he raised her up,
                            taking her hand,
                    and the fever left her.
            And she began to serve them.
        And as evening came,
                        when the sun set,
                    they bring to him
                        all the sick
                        and the demon-possessed,
                    and there was all the city
                            gathered
                            at the door.
            And he healed many
                    who were ill
                    with various diseases.
            And he expelled many demons,
                    and he did not allow the demons to speak,
                    because they knew him.

And very early in the night,   **B'**
                        getting up,
                        he left there,
                and he went away to a desert place,
                and there he prayed.
            And hunted him down,
                    Simon
                    and the ones with him.
                And they found him.
                And they say to him,
                        'Everyone is looking for you.'
            And he says to them,
                    'Let us go elsewhere,
                            into neighbouring towns,
                            in order that I may preach there also.
                    For this purpose I came.'

In the above, the initial notations, ABB', abb' and (a)(b)(b'), give way to vertical spacings and indents to express this literary style which operates at every level, where the first part A is introductory, the second B is the first development and the third part B' is the second and concluding development, whereby the third part qualifies and completes the second part, and so completes the whole. At the lowest levels of literary order, as was stated in the Introduction, abb' can give way to aa', reducing from three to two parts. The most significant words, for the purpose of structural analysis, are underlined.

Further, in the Introduction is a preview of the more detailed structural breakdown and method of annotation, with 1.21-22 provided for an example.[149] All the parts which make up the whole of this Day's report perform in very similar ways. It is the writer's writing-style that punctuates his text and defines all the units of his text at all literary levels. This is the writer's biggest help to his reader, who, if he received a text in the character of Codex Sinaiticus, in colums of rows of letters with no gaps between words, would be able to establish from the Greek text all of its major and minor divisions and sub-divisions. To present detailed argument for them all is unnecessary. The New Testament scholar today will be able to develop his/her own reading skill quite quickly and so become the equivalent of a first century reader. Further explications of the text, however, will continue to be shared as we proceed and seek evidence of Mark's consistency and to thoroughly understand his rhetorical method.

Mark's rhetorical style is simple, tightly-controlled and rhythmic. It will be demonstrated that he repeats it consistently for all his presentations of the "Days". Here, it can be stated that this discovery of his "compositional-structure", because it confirms "Day" presentation completion in the completed composite form of ABB'/ABB'/ABB', is as important a signifier in the setting of the parameters of the "Days" as the temporal, geographical, locational, verbal and material evidence which Mark also supplies.

Day Two: 1.39-45:

We begin with the consideration that the Day's telling which follows that of Day Two clearly begins at 2.1, *Καὶ εἰσελθὼν πάλιν εἰς Καφαρναοὺμ δι' ἡμερῶν.* It follows, therefore, that 1.45 ends Mark's telling of Day Two. In this closing verse to his second Day we see features as found in 1.35-38, the closing verses to the first Day. In both, Jesus chooses "desert places", and just as he was known by "everyone" in Capernaum (at the end of the first Day) so he is now known in "all" Galilee (at the end of the second Day). Day One tells both where and how Jesus first became known and where and how popular knowledge of him increased; Day Two continues the telling, presenting a further stage in the same process. The incident of the healing of the leper and the leper's disobedience in telling all, added to the summary account of Jesus' continuing work in Galilee (1.39), leads to the result described in v.45.

We continue with consideration of 1.39. In this opening verse to the second Day, we see that what Mark says took place in Capernaum is what all of Galilee experienced in turn: previously they had only heard (see 1.28). Hooker writes, "It matters little, therefore, whether the closely knit series of events from v.21 to v.39 are understood as they have often been understood, as the recollection of the first Sabbath that the (four) disciples spent with Jesus, or whether we interpret the links as artificial, and see the narrative as an account of a typical Sabbath; whether or not this particular series of events took place in Capernaum during one particular period of 24 hours, Mark uses them to present to us the impact Jesus made, not only there, but in the whole of Galilee."[150]. This comment, of course, bridges both Days One and

---

[149]See pages 20-21.
[150]Hooker, *The Gospel...*, p.77.

Two: it is in the report of Day Two that we learn how it is that people came to Jesus from all over Galilee. 1.39 summarises Jesus' mission in Galilee and v.45 details the outcomes of the Day's specific incident. But, how is 1.39 to be viewed as introductory to vv.40-45?

Clearly 1.39 describes activities over many days, even maybe several weeks: κηρύσσων / εἰς τὰς συναγωγὰς αὐτῶν / εἰς ὅλην τὴν Γαλιλαίαν suggests the possibility of a number of Sabbaths. The verse is a summary with which Mark defines the context for this new Day's report. At the beginnings of other days Mark also defines or infers a passage of time between his last Day's report and his next Day's report in his introductory, scene-setting, context-establishing opening pieces. We note the temporal links which he defines clearly: 2.1 "after some days"; 2.23 "And it came to pass on the Sabbath" (we note, it is likely not consecutive with the Day before); 8.1,2 "In those days.... three days"; 9.2 "And after six days" (we list further examples: 11.12; 11.20; 14.1; 14.12; 15.1 and 16.1,2).

Further, Bultmann noticed how Mark employs geographical links which behave temporally.[151] All these that are of my listing below begin new Days of Mark's telling:
1.21 "And they entered Capernaum" (we have noted above its disjunction with preceding verses, for reasons of Sabbath prohibitions);
6.30 "And the apostles assemble to Jesus" (they have been places and carried out their mission - the whole verse behaves like that of 1.39; the parenthetical placing of the story about John's death, from 6.14-29, strengthens the impression that days have passed[152]);
7.24 "And from there rising up he went away" (see 10.1, which is very similar: notably, these begin the middle Days of the two middle Series of seven Days, 7.24-30 and 10.1-16); one was written with the other to hand/in mind);
7.31 "And again, going out of the city of Tyre he came through Sidon to the sea of Galilee";
8.22 "And they came to Bethsaida";
8.27 "And Jesus went forth and his disciples to the villages of Caesarea Philippi";
9.30 "And from there going forth they passed through Galilee";
9.33 "And they came to Capernaum";
10.1 "And from there rising up he went into the territory of Judaea and beyond the Jordan";
10.17 "And as he went forth into the way"; and
10.46 "And they came to Jericho. And as he was leaving Jericho".

And at the beginning of other Days, we note that Mark employs a combination of geographical and temporal links:
1.21 "And they entered Capernaum. And immediately on the Sabbath";
3.7 "And Jesus with his disciples departed to the sea and a large crowd from Galilee followed" (a temporal change is inferred, for with 3.6 the sabbath day's activities conclude. Compare Schweizer's argument on the temporal change between 1.20 and 21 above);
5.1 "And they came to the other side of the sea into the country of the Gerasenes" (after a "night crossing");
5.21 and 6.53 are similar to 5.1; and
6.1f. "And he went from there and came into his own country... and when the Sabbath came".

The content of 1.39, reflective of many of Mark's opening verses of accounts of Days, gives both a temporal and a geographical context to the content which begins at 1.40. The verse also provides a material context for the record of a new day, for Jesus is journeying and missioning as he goes. Hooker is surely mistaken in saying that this episode is "introduced abruptly into the narrative"[153], though she is correct in saying that "it is not part of the close complex of stories which is just ended". Clearly, she does not see the significance of 1.39 as introductory to 1.40-45.

---

[151]Bultmann, *The History...*, p.340.
[152]Inserting a unit of tradition "within another" is said to be a particularly Markan feature, found elsewhere: see 3.22-30; 5.25-34; 11.15-19; 14.3-9, but see our discussions on these matters, under the appropriate "Days".
[153]Hooker, *The Gospel...*, p.78.

We consider also the further matter of Mark's predilection for a compositional grammatical feature much repeated in the openings to his presentations of Days[154]. 1.39,40 reads:

$$\textit{Καὶ ἦλθεν}$$
$$κηρύσσων$$
$$εἰς τὰς συναγωγὰς αὐτῶν$$
$$εἰς ὅλην τὴν Γαλιλαίαν$$
$$καὶ τὰ δαιμόνια ἐκβάλλων.$$
$$\textit{καὶ ἔρχεται πρὸς αὐτὸν λεπρὸς}$$
$$παρακαλῶν αὐτὸν$$
$$καὶ γονυπετῶν$$
$$καὶ λέγων αὐτῷ$$
$$ὅτι Ἐὰν θέλῃς$$
$$δύνασαί$$
$$με καθαρίσαι...$$

We observe: 1.39 "<u>And he went</u>..."/1.40 "<u>And there comes to him a leper</u>...", which in 1.40 is one kind of literal translation of a historical present that comes before the subject's introduction. In the whole of the Gospel, we encounter 151 historical presents in all.[155] Because they are "highly characteristic of Mark's style"[156], we devote a little space to considering them.

In note 10 above, in our discussion of Day One, we referred to Thackeray's observation that the "tense as a rule is... 'dramatic' in the sense that it serves to introduce new scenes in the drama. It heralds the arrival of a new character or a change of locality or marks a turning-point in the march of events... The main function is... to introduce a date, a new scene..., in other words a fresh paragraph in the narrative." Writing specifically on Mark, he says, ($\textit{λέγει}$ excluded) they are used in a precisely similar way to introduce new scenes and characters... *They are a feature which to the observant reader serves to divide the gospel* into rough paragraphs."[157] Standard grammars and recent writers describe this as part of the "discourse function" of the historical present.[158] For Fanning, historical presents are used in the New Testament on the whole "to bring a past occurrence into immediate view, portraying the event as though it occurs before the readers' eyes." He adds, "Although the historical present appears in different specific patterns of usage through ancient Greek literature, it does appear that *vivid or dramatic narration* of past events is the common characteristic of its use."[159]

Osburn (see Taylor, note 32) instances examples of historical presents signalling a "shift from background matters to principal action" (e.g. 1.30, with $\textit{λέγουσιν}$; also 4.13, with $\textit{λέγει}$).[160] It is most surely the case that $\underline{\textit{καὶ ἔρχεται}}$ at 1.40 behaves this way, by introducing principal action against the background Mark gives in his introductory verse of v.39.

The historical present, as we find at 1.40 for Day Two, and at 1.21 for Day One, features strongly in many of the verses of Mark's opening passages to his Days and at the begin-

---

[154]Best, *Disciples...*, p.50, and note 10.

[155]J.C. Hawkins, *Horae Synopticae,* Clarendon Press, Oxford, 2nd edn. 1909, pp.143-149.

[156]See Taylor, on vocabulary, syntax and style, item 5, pp.46f.

[157]Thackeray, *The Septuagint...*, p.22; my italics.

[158]Cf. Ernest DeWitt Burton, *Syntax of the Moods and Tenses in New Testament Greek*, 3rd ed., T. & T. Clark Edinburgh, p.271; F. Blass & A. Debrunner, *A Greek Grammar of the New Testament and other Early Christian Literature,* tr. & rev. R.W. Funk, University of Chicago Press, Chicago, 1957, para.321; Randy Buth, "Mark's use of the Historical Present", *Notes on Translation*, 65 (1977), pp.7-13; Carroll D. Osburn, "The Historical Present in Mark as a Text-Critical Criterion", *Bib* 64 (1983), pp.486-500.

[159]B. M. Fanning, *Verbal Aspects in New Testament Greek*, Clarendon Press, Oxford, 1990, p.226.

[160]It is Hawkins (*Horae Synopticae*) who discerns, from his study of the Westcott-Hort text, not only the number of historical presents in Mark's Gospel but also that 72 are levgei/levgousin.

nings of new sections in his reporting of those Days: in Days 1, 2, 3, 4, 5, 7, 8, 9, 10, 12, 14, 16, 20, 21, 22, 23, 24, 26, 27 and 28 (that is, twenty out of the total number of twenty-eight days). They are, with the first reference being the beginning of the Day: 1.21/21; 1.39/40*; 2.1/3*/15/18b*/...18c; 2.23/25/3.3.&4; 3.7/13/20*/31*; 5.21/22*/38*; 6.1/1b*; 6.30/30; 6.53/7.1; 7.31/32 (cf. 2.3); 8.22/22a*/22b (see 7.32); 9.2/2; 10.32/35; 10.46/46a*/46b; 11.1/1a/1b/7a/7b; 11.12/15*; 11.20/27*/12.13/18*; 4.12/12/13/17*/32*/37*/37/41*/41/43; 15.1/20b/21/22/... 24/27; 16.1/2*.

In this list, we include some present participles (e.g. 10.46b) and some λέγει references (e.g. 2.25 and 3.3,4), which are found to introduce new paragraphs. The eighteen examples which are marked* are the present middle historical present, καὶ ἔρχεται or καὶ ἔρχονται. They are worth singling out because Mark shows a particular preference for these.

Twice only in Mark's Gospel do they begin new Days: at 8.22a and at 10.46a, where their use may be described as 'dramatic' ("as they serve to introduce new scenes", ref. Thackeray). In both instances καὶ ἔρχονται εἰς is found; it is followed in the first of these by "Bethsaida", and in the second by "Jericho". 8.22b and 10.46b can also be compared: in their different ways they both introduce blind men into the reportings of the Days. In 8.22b we read "and they bring to him a blind man". Significantly it is another historical present which follows the one in 8.22a; it behaves like καὶ ἔρχεται at 1.40 by introducing principal action against the background just previously stated (following Osburn's argument), and it behaves also like καὶ ἔρχεται at 1.40 by introducing the principal character of the report of the Day (in a 'dramatic' way, after Thackeray's understanding). In 10.46b Mark employs a present middle participle to introduce the principal action (against the background of v.46a) and then proceeds to introduce blind Bartimaeus who is the principal character of the report of this Day. (Notably, these Days of Mark's telling are the last Days of his two middle Series of seven Days, 8.22-26 and 10.46-52; again,[161] one was written with the other to hand.) Mark's employment of the historical present in the general sense, his use of καὶ ἔρχεται also in the general sense, and his exceptional use of ἔρχονται in two introductory settings, in one followed by a further historical present and in the other by a present middle participle, all support the conclusion that 1.40-45 continues a Day's telling which is introduced in 1.39.

The literary structure of Day Two is as follows:

---

[161] See above, for reference to the two middle Days of the two middle Series of seven Days, 7.24-30 and 10.1-16, where also one was written with the other in mind.

Καὶ ἦλθεν   A   **A**

    κηρύσσων

       εἰς τὰς συναγωγὰς αὐτῶν

       εἰς ὅλην τὴν Γαλιλαίαν

    καὶ τὰ δαιμόνια ἐκβάλλων.

καὶ ἔρχεται πρὸς αὐτὸν λεπρὸς   B

    παρακαλῶν αὐτὸν

      καὶ γονυπετῶν

      καὶ λέγων αὐτῷ

    ὅτι Ἐὰν θέλῃς

      δύνασαί

      με καθαρίσαι.

καὶ σπλαγχνισθεὶς   B'

      ἐκτείνας τὴν χεῖρα

      αὐτοῦ ἥψατο

    καὶ λέγει αὐτῷ,

      Θέλω,

      καθαρίσθητι· [42]

Καὶ εὐθὺς

      ἀπῆλθεν ἀπ᾽ αὐτοῦ ἡ λέπρα,

      καὶ ἐκαθαρίσθη.

καὶ ἐμβριμησάμενος αὐτῷ   A   **B**

    εὐθὺς

      ἐξέβαλεν αὐτόν, [44]

    καὶ λέγει αὐτῷ,

  Ὅρα μηδενὶ μηδὲν εἴπῃς,   B

ἀλλὰ ὕπαγε   B'

      σεαυτὸν δεῖξον τῷ ἱερεῖ

    καὶ προσένεγκε

      περὶ τοῦ καθαρισμοῦ σου

      ἃ προσέταξεν Μωϋσῆς,

    εἰς μαρτύριον αὐτοῖς. [45]

Ὁ δὲ ἐξελθὼν   A   **B'**

    ἤρξατο κηρύσσειν πολλὰ

    καὶ διαφημίζειν τὸν λόγον,

ὥστε μηκέτι αὐτὸν δύνασθαι   B

    φανερῶς

    εἰς πόλιν εἰσελθεῖν,

ἀλλ᾽ ἔξω   B'

    ἐπ᾽ ἐρήμοις τόποις ἦν·

    καὶ ἤρχοντο πρὸς αὐτὸν πάντοθεν.

And in literal English:

And he went,   **A**
       preaching
          in their synagogues
          in all of Galilee,
     and casting out demons.
And there comes to him a leper,
     beseeching him,
          and falling on his knees,
          and saying to him,
     'If you are willing,
       you are able
       to cleanse me.'
And being full of compassion,
          stretching out his hand,
       he touched him,
   and he says to him,
       'I am willing,
       be cleansed.'
And immediately,
       the leprosy left him,
       and he was cleansed.

And strictly warning him,   **B**
       immediately he cast him away
       and he says to him,
  'See, you tell no one anything.
  But go,
       yourself show
       to the priest,
    and offer
       for your cleansing
       what Moses commanded,
    for a testimony to them.'

But as he went,   **B'**
       he began to proclaim many things,
       and to spread about the word,
   so that he was no longer able
     openly
     to enter a city,
  but outside,
       in desert places he was,
       and they came to him from every direction.

Again, the reasons for the annotations and underlinings are as for the Prologue and for Day One.

The literary-structure of Day Two may be described, therefore, as a simple **ABB'** form: **A** introduces the Day's principal event (in A, with a contextualising report of Jesus' activity in Galilee; in B, with an introduction of the new character, the leper, with his request to Jesus; and in B', with the active response of Jesus: the leper is cleansed); **B** is the first development of the Day's story (in A, Jesus takes further action and casts the leper out with an order; in B, with the first part, 'Say nothing'; and in B' the second part, 'Go, show...'); and in **B'** the Day's report concludes (in A, with the leper's ignoring of Jesus' command; in B, with the first result of the leper's response; and in B', with a qualification of that result). As we have observed above (in the opening paragraphs) Day Two is in sequence with Day One. They both present on the theme of the spreading of the news of Jesus and his developing need of 'desert places'. We will see also below how Day Three is in sequence with Day Two, how the first three Days are a three-step progression in Mark's scheme of presenting "Days".

Day Three: 2.1-22:

In considering Day Two, we identified Day Three as clearly beginning at 2.1. The opening phrase is *Καὶ εἰσελθὼν πάλιν εἰς Καφαρναοὺμ δι' ἡμερῶν*. A passage of "some days" between Days Two and Three of Mark's telling is clearly established by Mark, if a little unusually.[162] As stated in the Introduction, Mark tells us that he is not reporting all the Days of Jesus' mission: here he gives clear indication of that.[163] Within the gospel context, this introduction of 2.1 informs us that Jesus re-enters Capernaum for a second time, for a return visit[164]. It recalls the material of Day One (1.21-38). The opening participle is singular but at 2.13 and v.18 the disciples have their place within the linked stories of this Day, as they did in Day One.

Necessarily we refer to the identification of the importance and the purposes for Mark of historical presents (presented as part of Day Two's analysis) and here in this instance to 2.3, to the words *Καὶ ἔρχονται* (a historical present) and *φέροντες* (a present participle) with which Mark begins the telling of this Day's first specific event by introducing its principal character. The purpose of 2.1,2 is to establish the setting for the event of the telling of the Day's first part. The content of 2.3-7 is the first development of the event itself, and that of 2.8-12 is the second and completing development. But before we discuss this further, we note a particular constructional feature. Just as there is the geographical link with the beginning of Day One (Capernaum) we find also a verbal link with the ending of Day Two: see 1.45 for *τὸν λόγον, ὥστε μηκέτι* and *εἰσελθεῖν*. In 2.1,2 they are found in reverse order. Properly, they may be identified as anastrophes. Dewey sees these as "hook words, reverse repeated, which link the two stories"[165] (according to our designation of 1.39-45 and 2.1-12). Rather, the point may be made, because of the geographical links between 1.21 and 2.1, and the verbal links between 1.45 and 2.1,2, that the first three Days (of Mark's telling), 1.21-38, 1.39-45 and 2.1-22 are held together as a threesome of days in the telling. A case may be built on these connections, but not only these details.

---

[162]The preposition with the genitive has the idea of "through" but is used here temporally as "after", F. Blass & A. Debrunner, *A Greek Grammar of the New Testament and other Early Christian Literature*, tr. & rev. R.W. Funk, University of Chicago Press, Chicago, 1957.

[163]For a discussion of 2.1, 8.1,2 and 9.2, the introductory passages to Days which speak clearly of other days untold by Mark, see under "An Interest in Days" in the Introduction.

[164]It is not until 9.33 that we have a report of Jesus being in Capernaum again.

[165]Dewey, *Markan Public Debate...*, pp.117f.

Days One and Two lend credence to the expressive second verse of this third Day's setting: καὶ συνήχθησαν πολλοὶ ὥστε μηκέτι χωρεῖν μηδὲ τὰ πρὸς τὴν θύραν. We have already compared the endings of Days One and Two above for indication of Jesus' rapidly growing popularity. Now the people of Capernaum are gathered where they have been before, at the door of Simon's house (1.33, Day One), only now there is no longer space for everyone! Further to this, people have come to Jesus before "carrying" their sick (see 1.32). In Day Three we are presented with a specific healing episode, rather like Days One and Two (Simon's mother-in-law and the leper), and just as it can be said that the earlier healings lead to other matters, here specifically it is to the issue of Jesus' authority to forgive sins (sinners), a presentation which concludes at 2.12, with "all" being astonished and glorifying God. This ends the first part, **A**, in this Day's telling. 2.13 begins the second part, **B**, and "all the crowd" gather around Jesus.

But we first complete our reading of 2.1-12 and its three parts. Vv.1,2 are clearly introductory and establish the setting, the audience, and the principal character's role in regard to the audience; vv.3-5 begin the telling of the first specific event of the day, with the Markan historical present which introduces new characters and so establishes a new "paragraph" (see my note 10); and vv.6-12 complete the story. The ABB' construction shows itself as the earlier ones, with abb' and (a)(b)(b') detailing. We observe how the two B and B' parts end with a focus on what Jesus says to the paralytic; the two uses of λέγει τῷ παραλυτικῷ are found in exactly the same literary-structural locations, Bb(b') and B'b(b').

Now we will see how 2.13-22 connects with 2.1-12. We discuss firstly the temporal reference at 2.13 which is worthy of close attention. We read, _Καὶ ἐξῆλθεν πάλιν παρὰ τὴν θάλασσαν._ At this point, many commentators see a clear correspondence with 1.16-20, Jesus' calling of two pairs of named brothers by the sea[166] (see page 59 for an earlier discussion on the common words and details of these passages). As a result, the Greek word πάλιν (found 28 times in the Gospel) is simply translated "again". Hence, πάλιν enjoys its _rursus_ (_Latin:_ back, return) usage. Without taking anything away from this, the case can be put, however, for πάλιν here at 2.13 to mean also "thereupon" or "immediately after", or "without hesitation".

We turn firstly to Taylor: he records that the word originally meant "back", but that in later Greek it came to be used in the sense of "again"[167]. He recognises also that it is used as an inferential conjunction with the meaning, "further", "thereupon". Bultmann previously noted, "Sometimes πάλιν is added... simply as a succession formula", as translated from the Aramaic[168]. But, Taylor notes Howard's belief that in many of the Markan instances, the meaning of πάλιν is really iterative, and that where it is inferential it is unnecessary to go back to the Aramaic. Bultmann discerns the following possible candidates: 2.1,13; 3.1; 4.1 and 11.27. He omits consideration of 15.13: here we might read, "And they again cried out, 'Crucify him!'" But, this, according to Mark, is the first time the crowd so shouted. "And they immediately cried out...", might be considered the more literal rendering. (The N.I.V. records simply, "'Crucify him!' they shouted.") It may be argued, against Bultmann, that 2.1 and 11.27 best reflect _rursus_ usage. In the case of 2.1, the temporal reference suggests no _immediacy_ of return (consider "after some days") and at 11.27 we are reading about Jesus' visiting Jerusalem for the third day in a row (see Days 22, 23 and 24 which are all consecutive in Mark's telling: 11.1-11; vv.12-19; and vv.20-13.37).

The possibility that πάλιν is used as a succession formula at 2.13, 3.1 and 4.1, is particularly interesting because in these positions it appears three "Days" in succession (in Mark's telling) and at similar points in each Day's reporting. (Especially, do we note in Day

[166]Nineham, _Saint Mark_, p.95; Schweizer, _The Good News..._, p.63; Hooker, _The Gospel..._, p.94.
[167]Taylor, _The Gospel..._, p.192.
[168]Bultmann, _The History..._, p.339.

Three, that the B part begins: "And he went out without hesitation by the sea and all the crowd came to him and he taught them." In Day Five, a B part begins: And without hesitation he began to teach by the sea, and a huge crowd gathered to him." We will see below how Days Three, Four and Five are the three central days of this first Series of seven Days and for each of them I favour the rendering of $\pi \acute{a} \lambda \iota \nu$ as akin to "thereupon" or "immediately after".[169] It powerfully connects the parts of these Days and no more especially than in Day Four, the very central day of the Series. In the case of this Day Three, compare especially the beginnings of 2.1 and 2.13: *Καὶ εἰσελθὼν πάλιν εἰς Καφαρναούμ* and *Καὶ ἐξῆλθεν πάλιν.* They do have the appearance of a deliberate match. Part **A** is set in Simon's house and part **B** begins by the sea but settles in Levi's house. What contrasts is the meaning of $\pi \acute{a} \lambda \iota \nu$. at 2.1 it cannot be inferential, given the summary of 1.45, but at 2.13 it is more likely to be inferential than iterative, given that "all the crowd" of 2.1-12 comes to Jesus.

We continue with our examination of 2.13-22 which contains parts **B** and **B'**. Below, we discover further "paragraph"-defining, structurally-significant use by Mark of the historical present, the kind we have observed already in Days One and Two: they are at 2.14, 15,16,18b and 18c. This list includes *καὶ ἔρχονται* at v.18b, and present participles at vv.14 and 16. We note that Nineham, Schweizer and Hooker[170] all see 2.13-17 as a Markan whole because of the linkage between vv.13,14 and vv.15-17 of "outcasts". For me 2.13-17 describes the limits of Part **B**. 2.13 establishes the new setting and begins a new contribution to our understanding of Jesus' ministry. In v.14, Jesus calls Levi who follows. In vv.15-17, Jesus eats with tax collectors and sinners which provokes a challenge to Jesus and his response. In this way, we identify the three parts, A, B and B'. We may observe that in B', Mark introduces "scribes" for their response to Jesus' activity just as he did in vv.6,7 (significantly, both occupy the same structural position of B').

In vv.18-22, Part **B'**, Jesus has to answer challenges as his disciples are eating when others are fasting. Again, we discover ABB' and abb'presentations. In vv.20-22, for example, in the (b) and (b') positions, we have a pair of presentations beginning in turn with *οὐδεὶς* and *καὶ οὐδεὶς* which illustrate Jesus' introductory statement, of part (a), v.20 (structural discoveries of this kind do aid exegesis). And again, a three-part presentation is defined which can be characterised as an introduction followed by two connecting stories. Much later in the Gospel we are going to read of a similar scene of a meal Jesus shares with his disciples. The stories of this Day correspond to the stories of that day, when Jesus is taken from them. What the writer is setting up is a diagonal correspondence across his Gospel from his First Series of Days and his Day Three to his Fourth (and last) Series of Days and his Day Five. It is the first diagonal of a diagonal cross, a chi in Greek, the first part of a central chiasm that holds the Gospel presentation together. The one we are happy to call Mark for convenience is showing his rhetorical and literary skills and is showing incontrovertibly that he is very much in control of what he is doing. Day Three itself holds together well. The parts are closely related and what is key to the whole is what is revealed of Jesus' ministry which is "demonstrating again his authority to forgive sinners"[171] (see v.17b). Mark is showing his liking for linking like units of tradition, here, of 'eating and fasting' (though they may have been linked already in earlier oral or written tradition)[172]. The ending of Day Three is at 2.22 because at 2.23 Mark turns the focus onto a Sabbath day.

I present the literary structure of Day Three (with annotations as before) which, in the composite form of ABB'/ABB'/ABB' as for the structure of Day One:

---

[169]See Alexander Souter, *A Pocket Lexicon to the Greek New Testament*, Clarendon Press, Oxford, 1976.
[170]Nineham, *Saint Mark*, pp.94f.; Schweizer, *The Good News...*, pp.62f.; and Hooker, *The Gospel...*, pp.93f.
[171]Hooker, *The Gospel...*, pp.93,94.
[172]See for another example 2.23-28 and 3.1-6, for what is 'not lawful on the sabbath'.

Καὶ εἰσελθὼν πάλιν εἰς Καφαρναοὺμ   A   **A**
    δι᾽ ἡμερῶν
    ἠκούσθη
       ὅτι ἐν οἴκῳ ἐστίν. [2]
   καὶ συνήχθησαν πολλοὶ
   ὥστε μηκέτι χωρεῖν
   μηδὲ τὰ πρὸς τὴν θύραν,
  καὶ ἐλάλει αὐτοῖς τὸν λόγον. [3]
καὶ ἔρχονται   B
     φέροντες πρὸς αὐτὸν παραλυτικὸν
     αἱρόμενον ὑπὸ τεσσάρων. [4]
   καὶ μὴ δυνάμενοι προσενέγκαι αὐτῷ
     διὰ τὸν ὄχλον
    ἀπεστέγασαν τὴν στέγην ὅπου ἦν,
    καὶ ἐξορύξαντες
      χαλῶσι τὸν κράβαττον
      ὅπου ὁ παραλυτικὸς κατέκειτο. [5]
   καὶ ἰδὼν ὁ Ἰησοῦς τὴν πίστιν αὐτῶν
    λέγει τῷ παραλυτικῷ,
    Τέκνον, ἀφίενταί σου αἱ ἁμαρτίαι.
ἦσαν δέ τινες τῶν γραμματέων ἐκεῖ   B᾽
    καθήμενοι
    καὶ διαλογιζόμενοι ἐν ταῖς καρδίαις αὐτῶν, [7]
  Τί οὗτος οὕτως λαλεῖ;
  βλασφημεῖ·
    τίς δύναται ἀφιέναι ἁμαρτίας
    εἰ μὴ εἷς ὁ θεός;
  καὶ εὐθὺς ἐπιγνοὺς ὁ Ἰησοῦς τῷ πνεύματι αὐτοῦ
    ὅτι οὕτως διαλογίζονται ἐν ἑαυτοῖς
    λέγει αὐτοῖς,
   Τί ταῦτα διαλογίζεσθε ἐν ταῖς καρδίαις ὑμῶν; [9]
  τί ἐστιν εὐκοπώτερον,
    εἰπεῖν τῷ παραλυτικῷ,
      Ἀφίενταί σου αἱ ἁμαρτίαι,
    ἢ εἰπεῖν,
      Ἔγειρε
        καὶ ἆρον τὸν κράβαττόν σου
        καὶ περιπάτει; [10]
 ἵνα δὲ εἰδῆτε
    ὅτι ἐξουσίαν ἔχει ὁ υἱὸς τοῦ ἀνθρώπου
     ἀφιέναι ἁμαρτίας
     ἐπὶ τῆς γῆς
    λέγει τῷ παραλυτικῷ, [11]
  Σοὶ λέγω,
     ἔγειρε
    ἆρον τὸν κράβαττόν σου
    καὶ ὕπαγε
      εἰς τὸν οἶκόν σου. [12]
   καὶ ἠγέρθη

καὶ εὐθὺς ἄρας τὸν κράβαττον
ἐξῆλθεν
ἔμπροσθεν πάντων,
ὥστε ἐξίστασθαι πάντας
καὶ δοξάζειν τὸν θεὸν λέγοντας
ὅτι Οὕτως οὐδέποτε εἴδομεν.

Καὶ ἐξῆλθεν   A   **B**
        πάλιν
        παρὰ τὴν θάλασσαν·
καὶ πᾶς ὁ ὄχλος ἤρχετο πρὸς αὐτόν,
καὶ ἐδίδασκεν αὐτούς. [14]
Καὶ παράγων   B
                εἶδεν Λευὶν
                        τὸν τοῦ Ἀλφαίου
                        καθήμενον ἐπὶ τὸ τελώνιον,
                καὶ λέγει αὐτῷ,
                        Ἀκολούθει μοι.
                καὶ ἀναστὰς
                        ἠκολούθησεν αὐτῷ.
καὶ γίνεται κατακεῖσθαι αὐτὸν ἐν τῇ οἰκίᾳ αὐτοῦ,   B'
                καὶ πολλοὶ τελῶναι καὶ ἁμαρτωλοὶ συνανέκειντο
                        τῷ Ἰησοῦ
                        καὶ τοῖς μαθηταῖς αὐτοῦ·
                ἦσαν γὰρ πολλοὶ
                        καὶ ἠκολούθουν αὐτῷ. [16]
        καὶ οἱ γραμματεῖς τῶν Φαρισαίων
                ἰδόντες
                        ὅτι ἐσθίει μετὰ τῶν ἁμαρτωλῶν καὶ τελωνῶν
                ἔλεγον τοῖς μαθηταῖς αὐτοῦ,
                        Ὅτι μετὰ τῶν τελωνῶν καὶ ἁμαρτωλῶν ἐσθίει;
        καὶ ἀκούσας
                ὁ Ἰησοῦς λέγει αὐτοῖς
                ὅτι Οὐ χρείαν ἔχουσιν οἱ ἰσχύοντες ἰατροῦ
                        ἀλλ᾽ οἱ κακῶς ἔχοντες·
                οὐκ ἦλθον καλέσαι δικαίους
                        ἀλλὰ ἁμαρτωλούς.

Καὶ ἦσαν οἱ μαθηταὶ Ἰωάννου καὶ οἱ Φαρισαῖοι νηστεύοντες.　　A　　**B'**
　　　　　καὶ ἔρχονται
　　　　　καὶ λέγουσιν αὐτῷ,
　　Διὰ τί οἱ μαθηταὶ Ἰωάννου
　　　　　καὶ οἱ μαθηταὶ τῶν Φαρισαίων
　　　　　νηστεύουσιν,
　　οἱ δὲ σοὶ μαθηταὶ οὐ νηστεύουσιν;
καὶ εἶπεν αὐτοῖς ὁ Ἰησοῦς,　　　　　　　　　　　　　　　B
　　　　Μὴ δύνανται οἱ υἱοὶ τοῦ νυμφῶνος
　　　　　ἐν ᾧ ὁ νυμφίος μετ᾽ αὐτῶν ἐστιν
　　　　　νηστεύειν;
　　　　ὅσον χρόνον ἔχουσιν τὸν νυμφίον μετ᾽ αὐτῶν
　　　　　οὐ δύνανται νηστεύειν· [20]
ἐλεύσονται δὲ ἡμέραι　　　　　　　　　　　　　　　　　B'
　　　　ὅταν ἀπαρθῇ ἀπ᾽ αὐτῶν ὁ νυμφίος,
　　　　καὶ τότε νηστεύσουσιν ἐν ἐκείνῃ τῇ ἡμέρᾳ.
　　 <u>οὐδεὶς ἐπίβλημα ῥάκους ἀγνάφου</u>
　　　　　　ἐπιράπτει
　　　　　　ἐπὶ ἱμάτιον παλαιόν·
　　　　<u>εἰ δὲ μή αἴρει τὸ πλήρωμα ἀπ᾽ αὐτοῦ</u>
　　　　　τὸ καινὸν
　　　　　τοῦ παλαιοῦ,
　　καὶ χεῖρον σχίσμα γίνεται. [22]
　<u>καὶ οὐδεὶς βάλλει οἶνον νέον εἰς ἀσκοὺς παλαιούς·</u>
　　　　εἰ δὲ μή ῥήξει ὁ οἶνος τοὺς ἀσκούς
　　　　καὶ ὁ οἶνος ἀπόλλυται καὶ οἱ ἀσκοί·
　　　　(ἀλλὰ οἶνον νέον εἰς ἀσκοὺς καινούς.)t

And now in literal English:

And coming again to Capernaum,   A   **A**
    after some days,
    it was heard that he was in the house.
And many gathered,
    so that there was no longer room
    even at the door.
And he spoke/ to them/ the word.
And they come,   B
    bringing a paralytic to him,
    carried by four men.
And being unable to get to him,
      because of the crowd,
    they unroofed the roof over where he was,
    and having made an opening,
      they lower the stretcher
      on which the paralytic was lying.
And Jesus seeing their faith,
    he says to the paralytic,
    'Child, your sins are forgiven.'
Now there were some of the scribes there,   B'
      sitting
      and reasoning in their hearts,
    'Why does this man speak like this?
    He blasphemes:
      who can forgive sins,
      but God alone?'
And immediately, Jesus, knowing in his spirit
      that thus they reasoned in themselves,
      he says to them,
    'Why do you reason these things in your hearts?
    Which is easier:
      to say to the paralytic,
        "Your sins are forgiven",
      or to say,
        "Get up, and pick up your stretcher, and walk"?
But that you may know
      that the son of man has authority
        to forgive sins
        on earth.'
      he says to the paralytic,
    'To you I say, "Get up,
      pick up your stretcher
      and go
        to your home".'
And he got up,
      and immediately picking up the stretcher
        he went out
        in front of everybody,
      so that everyone was astonished
        and glorified God saying,
        'We've never seen anything like this before!'

And he went out, *without hesitation*, by the sea,   A   **B**
    and all the crowd came to him,
    and he taught them.
And passing along,   B
      he saw Levi,
        son of Alphaeus,
        sitting on the custom seat.
    And he says to him,
      'Follow me.'
    And getting up,
      he followed him.
And it comes to pass that he sat at table in his house,   B'
      and many tax-collectors and sinners sat at table
        with Jesus
        and with his disciples,
      for there were many,
        and they followed him.
    And the scribes of the Pharisees,
      seeing that he eats with sinners and tax-collectors,
      say to his disciples,
        'Does he eat with tax-collectors and sinners?'
    And hearing, Jesus says to them,
      'The strong do not have need of a doctor,
        but those who are ill;
      I did not come to call righteous people,
        but sinners.'

And there were the disciples of John and the Pharisees fasting,   A   **B'**
      and they come
      and they say to him,
      'Why do the disciples of John and the disciples of the Pharisees fast,
      but your disciples do not fast?'
    And Jesus said to them,   B
      'Can the sons of the bride-chamber fast
        while the bridegroom is with them?
      While they have the bridegroom with them
        they cannot fast.
    But days will come   a   B'
      when the bridegroom is taken away from them,
      and then they will fast in that day.
    <u>No one</u> / a patch / of unshrunk cloth   b
        sews
        on an old garment,
      <u>otherwise</u> it takes the fullness from itself
        the new
        from the old,
      and a worse tear will result.
    <u>And no one</u> puts new wine into old wineskins,   (a)   b'
      <u>otherwise</u> the wine will burst the wineskins   (b)
      and both wine and wineskins will perish.'   (b')
      (*but new wine requires new wineskins.**)

A word on the final line*: to me it is an unnecessary, later addition by some fastidious and over zealous scribe. The phrase, *but new wine requires new wineskins,* actually lies outside of the abb' constructions of the b' which is written to harmonise with the earlier b part.

Clearly, the first three Days tell where and how Jesus first became known and where and how his fame spread. The first Day (1.21-38) tells of Jesus in Capernaum, the second Day (1.39-45) of Jesus in Galilee after a number of days (or weeks?), and the third Day (2.1-22) of Jesus' return to Capernaum also after some days, and his attracting his biggest crowd so far. This is the first threesome of Days in Mark's Gospel narrative presentation. Mark has made it very clear that many other days could have been reported, but he has chosen to tell this first phase of Jesus' mission in only three reported Days. On the grounds of geographical place consideration alone, Capernaum/Galilee/Capernaum, it would be tempting to view this sub-Series of Days as being an ABA' scheme. But when we take into acccount the verbal links (for example, as identified between the ending of Day Two and the beginning of Day Three) an ABB' scheme is suggested. I judge that the thrust of Mark's three-Day story-line is the most important signifier of what he intended. On the grounds of Jesus' rising popularity, I view this sub-Series to be an ABB' rhetorical scheme because this best expresses the progression of these three Days' tellings (given the definition above of his rhetorical style, ABB', whereby A is introductory, B is the first development, and B' is the second and concluding development which completes, therefore, the whole). I hold the view that this is what Mark had in mind, and that he chose to write systematically to these levels of literary order, composing consistently to his early-adopted rhetorical method and 'style'. It would seem that he really did have Homer's plan for the *Iliad* as his template. It would seem be true also to say that he never lost sight of the needs of the future readers of his gospel. He was always aware of the help they would need from him and his own responsibilities to them.

Day Four: 2.23-3.6:

The Day begins: *Καὶ ἐγένετο αὐτὸν ἐν τοῖς σάββασιν παραπορεύεσθαι διὰ τῶν σπορίμων.* The Sabbath day is the setting: the plural is used with a singular meaning as in 1.21, in Day One[173]. A number of translations begin reading, "One sabbath..." and weaken Mark's presentation of linked days. Mark's effort is in treating the reader/the listener to a created, connected narrative, be it still an artificial framework.[174] The Greek requires something a little more sympathetic, such as "On the Sabbath...". Both Mark's framework of Days and his connections between his reportings of Days are expressive of continuity.

We may refer here to Mark's use of *καὶ*, to parataxis, which is one of the most noticeable characteristics of Mark's style, whereby he sustains a connectedness of the parts and achieves a unified whole. Hawkins points out that of the 88 sections in the Wescott-Hort text 80 begin with *καὶ* and only 6 have *δέ* as the second word.[175] For comparison, Matthew has 159 sections and the numbers are 38 and 54 respectively, and Luke has 145 sections and 53 and 83 respectively. In fact *δέ* is found in all in Mark's Gospel only about 156 times which is less than half the number we should expect to find if it was used as freely as in Matthew or Luke. The possibilities that LXX-use or Aramaic-use had an influence on Mark have been entertained[176] but Moulton thinks that "in itself the phenomenon proves nothing more than

---

[173]Cranfield, *The Gospel...*, pp.71,72,114.
[174]K.L. Schmidt, *Der Rahmen...* In his penetrating investigation in 1919, he may have claimed correctly that as a whole the outline of Mark's Gospel was a purely artificial construction, but too sweeping, surely, is his conclusion that it *reduced* to "only single stories, *pericopae*, which are put into a framework."
[175]Hawkins, *Horae Synopticae*, p.151.
[176]J.H. Moulton & G. Milligan, *The Vocabulary of the Greek Testament (*London, 1914-29), Eerdmans, Grand Rapids, 1972, pp.57-58,314.

would a string of "ands" in an English rustic's story." To Taylor too, it is "elementary culture".[177] To Tolbert, however, parataxis, also asyndeta (the absence of the connecting links
supplied by particles and conjunctions), as well as ordinary diction and brevity of narration,
which are all striking features of Mark's style, all "find a home in Greek rhetorical theory".[178]
"In Demetrius' terms," she writes, "the Gospel's style attempts to blend the clarity and simplicity of ordinary speech with the emotion of dramatic delivery."[179]

Literary-structural analysis does demonstrate that καί dominates the opening of the
lines of literary order at many levels. Its *absence* from such positions, interestingly, is illuminating also. In a valuable study, Paul Ellingworth[180] shows how the *absence* of καί functions
in Mark's work, particularly: how it features frequently in direct speech; how it marks new
pericopae or paragraphs ("thus a new narrative or a new stage in the narrative"); where sentences begin with a pronoun followed by δέ (in several passages, "where chains of such sentences have the apparent effect of heightening the cut and thrust of dialogue"); also, in three
places, how it indicates that Mark takes up the thread of his narrative again after a digression;
and in other cases how it tends to mark some kind of new phase or step within a narrative[181].
In this Day's account καί introduces all the major sectional and part divisions (the first and
second halves, and parts A, B and B'), and of the twelve sub-parts, five of the six b sub-parts
and three of the six b' sub-parts. We examine those instances where καί is *absent* in this
Day's reading:

1) 2.25 b ὅτε χρείαν ἔσχεν   2) 2.26 b' (πῶς) εἰσῆλθεν
3) 2.28 b' ὥστε κύριός ἐστιν   4) 3.4b b' οἱ δὲ ἐσιώπων.

Examples 1), 2) and 3) all occur in direct speech. In 1) and 2) they give the "when" and the
"how" to the opening, "what David did". In 3) it introduces the consequence clause, the third
and concluding part of Jesus' argument of vv.27,28. Example 4) is a clear case of a pronoun
followed by δέ. And though it stands individually here, it still has dramatic "effect".

We have to look beyond this Day's report for other examples of Ellingworth's listing.
They are best raised now, nevertheless, as we here address this matter of the non-καί sentence. We will consider *his own samples* under *his own group headings*, but as they may be
judged to function given my literary-structural analysis:

1) How the non-καί sentence marks new pericopae or paragraphs (and "thus a new
narrative or a new stage in the narrative"): we consider those at: 1.14 - it opens the third section, B', of the Prologue; 5.11 - it opens a new development in the telling of Day 6; 5.35 - it
opens the last section of Day 7; 7.24 - it opens Day 11; 8.1 - it opens Day 13; 9.30 - it opens
Day 17; 10.32 - it opens Day 20; 9.38 - it opens part B in the middle section of Day 17; 13.14,
24, 28, 32 ("distinct phases in the eschatalogical discourse: all in direct speech") - to these, I
add 13.7 which opens a 'B' Section A; 13.14 - it opens the 'B' Section B'; I add 13.18 which
opens a 'B" Section A; 13.24 - it opens 'B" Section B; 13.28 - opens 'B" Section B, part b; and
13.32 - it opens the concluding section 'B" Section B'; 14.1 - it opens Day 25; and 15.6 - it
opens 'A' Section B of Day 27. To the fourteen examples which Ellingworth gives, I have
added two. Five begin Days; nine begin Sections (four of which are in the eschatalogical discourse); and two begin major parts of sections. None are found in my analysis which do not
hold structural significance. There is reason here to record agreement on our findings.

[177]Taylor, *The Gospel...*, p.49.
[178]Tolbert, *Sowing the Gospel...*, pp.42,43.
[179]See: Demetrius, *On Style*, pp.221-222.
[180]Paul Ellingworth, "The Dog in the Night: A Note on Mark's non-use of καί, BT 46 (1995) pp.125-128.
[181] I here consider five of Ellingworth's eight categories only. Space does not allow a complete presentation. For
a full listing of his groups of non- καί sentences, see his article, "The Dog in the Night...".

2) In three places, how the non-*καὶ* sentence indicates that Mark takes up the thread of his narrative again after a 'digression':

6.16: given my analysis the non-*καὶ* beginning most certainly follows a three-part whole (6.14b, 15a, 15b) and so opens another three-part whole (another *new section*). Ellingworth says of v.16, "When Herod heard it", that it recalls v.14a, "Now King Herod heard about all this". He describes, therefore, vv.14b,15 (these verses "record various opinions about Jesus") as a "digression"[182]. But my reading is that there is no "digression" as such. 6.14a records Herod's *hearing* about Jesus' *disciples' mission*; it ends the telling of Part **B** of Day 8's account. 6.16 represents the *particular view of Herod*, against 16.14b,15 which begins the second half with the introductory *views of the people*.

7.20: the non-*καὶ* sentence here does follow what may be termed a 'digression' ("In saying this, Jesus declared that all foods are fit to be eaten", GNB). But in my analysis 7.20 opens another *new section*, the last section of Day 10.

8.25: if the man's comment that he sees "people... like trees walking about" is a 'digression' from the action, then here again the non-*καὶ* sentence following a digression opens another *new section* in my analysis.

On the evidence of these three samples, the issue of "digressions" would appear to be less important than the fact that all three non-*καὶ* sentences open new sections and so *mark new pericopae or paragraphs*: it appears that they might be best placed under a sub-category of category 1).

3) How the non-*καὶ* sentence tends to mark some kind of new phase or step within a narrative:

1.32: Ellingworth argues that it represents "a transition from a particular healing to a general statement". In this fashion, in Day 1 of my analysis, this non-*καὶ* sentence opens another *new section*. Whether it belongs in this category, or in category 1) is debatable. There is certainly little to separate 1's "new stage" from 3's "new phase or step". If scale *is* the point of difference, then 1.32 does belong under category 1.

9.24a: in my analysis of Day 16, I find that six of the nine parts in Part **B** open with non-*καὶ* beginnings (that is A<u>abb'</u>, <u>b'</u> here being 9.24a, B<u>abb'</u> and B'<u>abb'</u>, as underlined). They are each classifiable under Ellingworth's (eight) groupings. We may note that although 9.24a is not classifiable elsewhere, under any of his other headings, it does not *alone* of these mark a "new step" as such in the narrative: see 9.22b,25 and v.27. Again as above, if it is scale that separates categories 1) and 3), then 9.24a and those like it that are not classifiable elsewhere can be identified as "marking some kind of *new step* within a narrative".

Further to the issues, for literary-structural analysis, of *καὶ* and non-*καὶ* sentences, we observe that Mark frequently adds *εὐθύς* to *καὶ*. We may observe that it intensifies Mark's simple linking of parts in succession, and that it is frequently to be found at the beginning of new lines, and we note, at the more significant levels of literary order. Again Paul Ellingworth supplies a useful study[183]. We review his major points. To him, the use of "Immediately" at the beginning of a section shows that Mark is moving "from one story to a closely related one" (he cites 1.12 as an example). In my analysis of the Prologue, 1.12 does link *closely* sub-sections b and b', 1.10,11 and 1.12,13 (see page 49). The use of "and immediately" can show also that Mark is moving "from one stage in a longer story to the next" (for which he cites 6.45; 14.43 and 15.1). In my analysis of Day 9, 6.45 marks the beginning of the Day's third and final main section. In my analysis of Day 26, 14.43 begins 'B' Section B'. In my analysis of Day 27, 15.1 begins the Day's telling, "And immediately early" ("early" is qualified by "immediately"; Mark provides an immediate and dramatic quickening of the pace of events, for this Day's telling). In the analysis of the Prologue, we further saw how "and

---

[182]Ellingworth, "The Dog...", p.126.
[183]Paul Ellingworth, "How Soon is 'Immediately' in Mark?", *BT* 29 (1978) pp.414-419.

immediately" can be used twice to introduce a pair of stories: we observed these links between sub-sections a, b and b', 1.9 with 1.10,11 and 1.12,13.

We have discussed already πάλιν and seen it function as a strong succession formula[184]. We remind ourselves that it is discovered at the level of literary order whereby it connects major parts of a Day's report, in the middle days, Days Three, Four and Five, of this first Series of seven Days. It would seem that we are beginning to identify a Markan hierarchy of succession formulae, and that his use of Καὶ (and non-καὶ), Καὶ εὐθύς and Καὶ πάλιν are to be taken seriously.

We return to our examination of Day Four. The introduction to the Day recalls Day One (see 1.21), though the Day's focus is different from anywhere else in the Gospel: only here is the subject of conflict over the Sabbath addressed. Likely, the stories of the Day, 2.23-28, "doing what is unlawful: plucking ears of corn", 3.1-5, "doing what is unlawful: the healing", and 3.6, that which results from Jesus' silencing of the Pharisees, were at one time separate units of tradition. Or alternatively, of course, Mark may have created either one or all three of these pieces to construct this Day's report. What is certain is that the conjunction of Καὶ... πάλιν at 3.1a is Mark's. My view is that Mark compiled this succession of stories.

At this point, regarding 3.1a we should note that a number of translations struggle. For example, the N.I.V. reads, "Another time he went in to the synagogue...", and the N.E.B. reads, "On another occasion when he went to the synagogue..." Both bring disjunction into the Markan text. In the Jer.B. and the R.S.V., however, πάλιν is translated simply, "again" and the connection is still made between the two episodes. In the G.N.B., the link, we notice, is strengthened with, "Then Jesus went back to the synagogue..." It is judged that this is nearer to Mark's intention because of its use of "then" as a succession formula and because it says also that he "went back" (Jesus has been in synagogues before, in 1.21 and 39); πάλιν here may reasonably be judged to retain its common *rursus* usage also[185]. For a simple, literal translation, for reasons already stated above, the following may be suggested too: "And *immediately after this* he entered into a synagogue..." My preference now is to render it, "And without hesitation…" as this would show Mark's Jesus to be in combative mood, taking it to the Pharisees! This, I judge, is Mark's intention.

We continue with our consideration of the linking of the three parts of this Day's telling. It may be judged that the subject of the verb παρετήρουν in 3.2 is 'the Pharisees' of 2.24, for the reasons that the two stories in juxtaposition share the same focus on what is 'lawful on the Sabbath' and that the Pharisees were responsible for introducing the question in the first place, in 2.24. Mark does intend the two incidents to be read together as one Day's activities.

The Day clearly ends with 3.6: the content of 3.7-12 and all that follows on Day Five is non-Sabbatical.[186] Interestingly, arguments vary as to the purpose and the effect of 3.6. Nineham sees it as a clear conclusion "not only to this (second) story (of the day), but also to the whole series of conflicts[187]. Hooker rightly points out, however, that the conflict theme is taken up again at 3.20ff.[188] It is this very fact that undermines somewhat the abiding deduc-

---

[184]See under my examination of Day Three

[185]It is the case also that as 2.13 reflects Jesus' first time "by the sea" in 1.16 the common usage of πάλιν may be retained in addition to its being a succession formula there: so too 4.1 for the same reasons.

[186]See my notes also, under Day One, for the separation of 1.16-20 from 1.21ff. for reasons of the sabbath's obligations. The question, of course, arises in the same way as before: does the new Day at 3.7 begin with a new sunrise or at the sunset at which the Jewish Sabbath ends? Clearly 3.7-12 describes a new Day's activities as after a sunrise: 1) Mark would have told us if it was evening: see 1.32, 4.35, 6.47, 14.7 and 15.42; or that it was "late": see 6.35, 11.11 and 11.19; and 2) he in fact describes in 3.7-12 the beginning of a succession of events which will lead to an evening (4.35)/night-time event (consider the "boat" of 3.9 which re-appears in 4.1 and 4.36).

[187]Nineham, *Saint Mark*, p.110.

[188]Hooker, *The Gospel...*, p.109.

tion, which she also makes, that 2.1-3.6 represents a pre-Markan group of conflict stories.[189] It is true that it can be argued that Mark may have added another conflict story to a pre-existent collection, but what more weakens the prevailing view are the literary-structural analyses of each Day (so far presented) and the uncovering of a Markan Series of seven Days which has in the first part of its scheme a threesome of the first three days, followed by a fourth and middle Series pivotal day, prior to a further and final, balancing threesome of days. We will be looking at this after the analysis of Days Five, Six and Seven. Mark appears less a conservative editor with each disclosure of the elements of his framework and the features of his rhetorical style: he appears, rather, more a chronicler or compiler[190], and one who exhibits a good control of his material and of his own presentation methodology.

On 3.6 again, both Taylor and Nineham[191] judge that the allusion to the death plot of the Pharisees and the Herodians appears "too early in the Gospel". ut there is a case for supposing that Mark knew exactly what he was doing: this fourth and middle Day of his first Series of seven has its parallel in the fourth and middle Day of the final series (14.1-11). Both speak of the plottings against Jesus' life. We may note now that conflict stories are present in Days Three, Four and Five of the first series of Days; we may note also that these are the middle three days. We will see later that conflict stories, with similar emphases, are present in Days Two, Three, Four, Five and Six, the middle five days, in the final series (11.12-19; 11.20-13.37; 14.1-11; 14.12-72 and 15.1-47).[192] Another possibly significant parallel is seen: just as Judas Iscariot is first introduced in Day Five (last in the listing of the twelve) of the first Series, as being "the one who betrayed" Jesus, so he is presented in Day Five of the final Series, in the very act of betrayal (14.43-46). We will come to such considerations later.

We may notice that in Day Four there is a total absence of any mention of either crowds, or of Jesus' (growing) popularity (compare the first three Days), but the fact that Day Four climaxes with something of a complete contrast to what we have witnessed up to now, the announcing of a death plot against Jesus, does not mean that it is totally detached from what has preceded it, in terms of its subject matter and content. Jesus' growing popularity in Days Two and Three was accompanied by a growing opposition in Days Three and Four. Further, the crowds may not be very far from Mark's mind. The very mention of Herodians at this point[193], in 3.6, may be intended by Mark to suggest that Jesus was being seen, even early on in his mission, not only as a threat to Old Israel's religious leadership, but also as a threat to political order in Palestine. One who was attracting such a popular following was a potential cause of political unrest.

Before I present my literary-structural analysis for this day, Day Four, we consider the construction of 2.1-3.6, concerning which Dewey[194] and others[195] have recognised symmetri-

[189]Since the seventies, a number of scholars have begun to argue against a pre-Markan Galilean controversy collection: G. Minette de Tillesse, *Le secret messianique dans l'Évangile de Marc*, LD 47, Éditions du Cerf, Paris, 1968 (for the reason that the stories reflect Mark's overall theology); A.B. Kolenkow, "Beyond Miracles, Suffering and Eschatology", *1973 Seminar Papers*, ed. G. MacRae, SBLSP 109 (1973), pp.155-202 (on form critical and redactional grounds as well as on theological grounds); D.-A. Koch, *Die Bedeutung der Wundererzahlungen für die Christologie des Markusevangeliums*, BZNW 42, Walter de Gruyter, Berlin, 1975 (neither 3.6 nor 2.28 need to be explained as pre-Markan redactional conclusions to a collection; the use of "Son of Man" in 2.10,28 are in conformity with the authority-theme begun at 1.21; to place together related traditions would occur to an evangelist as well as to any other compiler of tradition).
[190]See Farrer, *A Study in St Mark...*, p.4.
[191]Taylor, *The Gospel...*, p.146, and Nineham, *The Gospel...*, p.110.
[192]We note: other days of conflict stories exist too, in the middle two series of seven days.
[193]Though it is not certain who they really were, the usual view is that they were friends and supporters of Herod Antipas, not a religious sect.
[194]Dewey, *Markan Public Debate...*
[195]Giuseppe G. Gamba, "Considerazioni in margine alla poetica di Mc.2.1-12", *Salesianum* 28 (1966), pp.324-349; P. Mourlon Beernaert, "Jésus controversé: Structure et théologie de Marc 2.1-3.6", *NRT* 95 (1973), pp.129-149; David J. Clark, "Criteria for Identifying Chiasm", *LB* 35 (1975), pp.63-72.

cal patterning of its *pericopae*, though they differ in their views. Dewey's own proposition, which has attracted much support, is as follows:

A	2.1-12	The healing of the paralytic
B	2.13-17	The call of Levi/eating with sinners
C	2.18-22	The sayings on fasting and on the old and the new
B'	2.23-28	Plucking grain on the sabbath
A'	3.1-6	The healing on the sabbath.

And she adds a qualification, "Further, B is rhetorically related to A, and B' to A', while both B and B' are related to C".[196] This "concentric literary pattern is definitely to be found in the text itself," she says. I cannot agree, for a number of reasons.

Firstly, I *will* agree that chiasm[197] is to be found extensively in the New Testament. I will agree also that it is to be found in Mark's Gospel, but it will be demonstrated that chiasm is to be found only sparingly in the detail of Mark's narrative, and regularly, only in his larger structurings of his Series of seven Days, and in his overall Gospel plan. 2.1-3.6 may have the appearance of chiasm when it is separated from its Gospel context, but when it is set where it should be, between 1.45 and 3.7, it does not work as a chiasm anything like so well: details of 2.1-3.6 have their relationships with the text each side of it and beyond, elsewhere in the Gospel, and some details feature more importantly because it is only in 2.1-3.6 that they appear at all in the whole Gospel.

Dewey's analysis may appear to be complete, but it is not. She shows those passages which seem to parallel, and in many instances do parallel in their details, but she fails, with her overall structure, to take account of those that do not parallel. She lacks a detailed summary which takes account of all the parts that make up her supposed whole. Above all, she has had to select one set of structuralising criteria over and against another, as she tries to establish the overall arrangement in her second reading from information from her first reading. She is led to simplify, erroneously, her argument of arrangement, and reject other correspondences which are equally deserving of as much prominence in any scheme.

I give just one example (and there are a number) which provokes this criticism. Dewey's rhetorical critical analysis leads her to the judgement that 3.1-6 "builds on the narra-

---

[196]Dewey, *Markan Public Debate...*, pp.110 and 116.

[197]Chiasm or "chiasmus" is not truly a term of ancient rhetoric: the first clear reference to it as a technical term is found around the 4th century AD in Hermogenes (*On Invention*, 4.3, H. Rabe (ed.) Rhetores Graece Vol. 6, in Bibliotheca Scriptorum Graecorum et Romanorum Teubneriana, Leipzig, 1913) , who uses it in terms of, but limits it to, the crosswise interchange of the clauses in a four-clause sentence. A. Di Marco, "Der Chiasmus in der Bibel 1. Teil", *LB* 36, 1975, pp.21-97, p.23, suggests that a number of other terms were used instead in ancient rhetoric to describe what is now called chiasmus, but this must be treated with caution. Chiasm, or chiasmus, defines a broad range of literary devices, all of which have their similarity only in that a crossing, or an inversion occurs. We use the term in this way here.
In regard to the Gospels and Acts in particular, there is a case to be put for chiasmus in Matthew (J.C. Fenton, "Inclusio and Chiasmus in Matthew", *Studia Evangelica*, International Congress on New Testament Studies, Vol. 73, eds. Kurt Aland, et al.; Akademie-Verlag, Berlin, 1959, pp.174-179; Angelico Di Marco, "Chiasmus: 3. Teil", pp.38-57); in Luke-Acts (C.H. Talbert, *Literary Patterns, Theological Themes and the Genre of Luke-Acts*, SBL, Scholars Press, Missoula, Montana, 1974; Craig Blomberg, "Midrash, Chiasmus, and the Outline of Luke's Central Section" pp.217-259, *Gospel Perspectives (Studies in Midrash and Historiography)* Vol. III, eds. France & Wenham, JSOT Press, Sheffield, 1983; M.D. Goulder, "The Chiastic Structure of the Lucan Journey", *TU* 87 (1963), pp.195-202; K.E. Bailey, *Poet and Peasant: A Literary Cultural Approach to the Parables*, Eerdmans, Grand Rapids, 1976; Angelico Di Marco, "Chiasmus: 3. Teil", pp.62-68); and in John (David Deeks, "The Structure of the Fourth Gospel", *NTS* 15 (1968-69), pp.107-129; Angelico Di Marco, "Chiasmus: 3. Teil", pp. 69-85). In Matthew, Luke-Acts and John, I contribute to the debate on the Gospels and Acts, adding the Revelation to John, in *Sliced Bread...*
For a classical tretament of chiasmus, see A. Vanhoye's, *La Structure Litteraire de l'Epitre aux Hebreux*, Desclee de Brouwer, Paris-Bruges, 1976.

tive of" 2.23-28, yet she *chooses* to parallel 2.1-12 with 3.1-6, because "they show a striking similarity" for their rhetorical pattern: the miracle is begun, then interrupted, then completed, in both. She defines their similar frames: she says, "As the debate section in 2.1-12 is framed by Jesus' two addresses to the paralytic" (compare my presentation of my analysis: in both parts, at 2.5 and v.10, at the exact same points we read, λέγει τῷ παραλυτικῷ,...) "...here (in 3.1-6) Jesus' answer to the opponents is framed by his two commands to the sick man..." (compare here my presentation again: in both parts, B and B' (3.3 and v.5), we read in the opening lines, denoted by a, λέγει τῷ ἀνθρώπῳ). "Both are clearly delineated ring compositions," Dewey says. "*Unlike 2.6-10a, however, the central portion of 3.1-6 should not be considered an interposition. It is not sufficiently set off from the outer ring in which the opponents also feature strongly.*" This point of difference, identified in her first reading, is important. In her second reading, she summarises an impressive number of parallels, but the counter-logic is not there summarised as well. The clearest undermining of Dewey's scheme is that in their Gospel context, 2.23-28 and 3.1-6 are the only passages which focus on what is 'lawful on the sabbath' (see 2.24 and 3.4 in particular): they are parallels of each other above all else, and if they were part of a chiasm this would be indicated by their parallel positioning.

The difference between Dewey's approach and mine here is fundamental. Dewey's parts A, B and C by my analysis are one Day's telling and her parts B' and A' are another Day's telling. The two most important signifiers of Markan structure, his rhetorical style of ABB' employed from beginning to end of his Gospel in his constructing of his Prologue and his Days, and his determinative matrix of Series of seven Days, govern all his work of arrangement. Due to the uncovering of these for the Gospel as a whole, I cannot support the method of her analysis for what is, even on form-critical grounds[198], an arbitrarily-defined Gospel piece. Dewey cannot account for her concentric literary pattern starting and finishing where it does because she cannot present anything meaningful before it and after it.

Another approach to analysing the text of Mark is that of 'rhetorical analysis' as exemplified by Mack[199], on 2.23-28. (Why he presented the classical rules af ancient rhetoric and failed then to test them against Mark's text, I should like to know! Rather he focused on chreia.) The chreia[200] as it stands now, he says, "is elaborated as if the objection were to eating on the Sabbath." The argument unfolds, for Mack, in this way:

Narrative:	Plucking grain on the Sabbath (v.23)
Issue:	It is not lawful (v.24)
Argument (Rebuttal):	
Citation:	Read the scriptures (v.25)
Example:	What David did (vv.25,26)
Analogy:	Eating when hungry (v.25)
Maxim:	Sabbath made for people (v.27)
Conclusion:	The Son of man is Lord even of the Sabbath (v.28).

This format, he says "gives the impression that the argument unfolded inductively when, as a matter of fact, the elaboration had to be crafted with the 'pronouncement' (v.28) in mind all along. One sees from this that the construction of a pronouncement story (like this one) was an exercise in thinking backward, starting with the conclusion and then crafting an inductive

---

[198]'Conflict stories' are present elsewhere in the Gospel, in Days delimited by 3.7-4.41, 6.53-7.23, 8.1-21, 10.1-16, 11.12-19, 11.20-13.37, 14.1-11, 14.12-72 and 15.1-47.

[199]Mack, *Rhetoric...*, pp.52,53.

[200]Chreia is defined in very similar ways in the ancient handbooks. For Theon, it is "a concise statement or action which is attributed with aptness to some specified character or to something analogous to a character." For Hermogenes it is "a reminiscence of some saying or action or a combination of both which has a concise resolution..."

approach to it." These comments are helpful to understanding Mark's work of compositon. But my view is that Mark first established 3.6 for the climax to this Day's telling, the whole of 2.23-3.6, where Part **A**, 2.23-28 is introductory, Part **B**, 3.1-5, is the first development and Part **B'**, 3.6, is the second and concluding development.

I present the literary structure of Day Four:

Καὶ ἐγένετο   **A**

> αὐτὸν ἐν τοῖς σάββασιν παραπορεύεσθαι
> διὰ τῶν σπορίμων,
> καὶ οἱ μαθηταὶ αὐτοῦ ἤρξαντο ὁδὸν ποιεῖν
> τίλλοντες τοὺς στάχυας. [24]
> καὶ οἱ Φαρισαῖοι ἔλεγον αὐτῷ,
> Ἴδε
> τί ποιοῦσιν
> τοῖς σάββασιν
> ὃ οὐκ ἔξεστιν;
> καὶ λέγει αὐτοῖς,
> Οὐδέποτε ἀνέγνωτε
> τί ἐποίησεν Δαυίδ,
> ὅτε χρείαν ἔσχεν καὶ ἐπείνασεν
> αὐτὸς καὶ οἱ μετ᾽ αὐτοῦ; [26]
> εἰσῆλθεν
> εἰς τὸν οἶκον τοῦ θεοῦ
> ἐπὶ Ἀβιαθὰρ ἀρχιερέως
> καὶ τοὺς ἄρτους τῆς προθέσεως ἔφαγεν,
> οὓς οὐκ ἔξεστιν φαγεῖν
> εἰ μὴ τοὺς ἱερεῖς,
> καὶ ἔδωκεν καὶ τοῖς σὺν αὐτῷ οὖσιν;
> καὶ ἔλεγεν αὐτοῖς,
> Τὸ σάββατον
> διὰ τὸν ἄνθρωπον ἐγένετο
> καὶ οὐχ ὁ ἄνθρωπος
> διὰ τὸ σάββατον· [28]
> ὥστε κύριός ἐστιν ὁ υἱὸς τοῦ ἀνθρώπου
> καὶ τοῦ σαββάτου.

Καὶ εἰσῆλθεν   **B**
        πάλιν
        εἰς τὴν συναγωγήν.
    καὶ ἦν ἐκεῖ ἄνθρωπος ἐξηραμμένην ἔχων τὴν χεῖρα· [2]
    καὶ παρετήρουν αὐτὸν
        εἰ τοῖς σάββασιν θεραπεύσει αὐτόν,
        ἵνα κατηγορήσωσιν αὐτοῦ. [3]
  καὶ λέγει τῷ ἀνθρώπῳ
      τῷ τὴν ξηρὰν χεῖρα ἔχοντι,
      Ἔγειρε εἰς τὸ μέσον.
    καὶ λέγει αὐτοῖς,
          Ἔξεστιν τοῖς σάββασιν
     ἀγαθὸν ποιῆσαι
        ἢ κακοποιῆσαι,
     ψυχὴν σῶσαι
        ἢ ἀποκτεῖναι;
   οἱ δὲ ἐσιώπων.
  καὶ περιβλεψάμενος αὐτοὺς μετ᾽ ὀργῆς,
      συλλυπούμενος ἐπὶ τῇ πωρώσει τῆς καρδίας αὐτῶν,
     λέγει τῷ ἀνθρώπῳ,
        Ἔκτεινον τὴν χεῖρα.
    καὶ ἐξέτεινεν,
    καὶ ἀπεκατεστάθη ἡ χεὶρ αὐτοῦ. [6]

καὶ ἐξελθόντες   **B'**
    οἱ Φαρισαῖοι εὐθὺς μετὰ τῶν Ἡρῳδιανῶν
        συμβούλιον ἐδίδουν
        κατ᾽ αὐτοῦ
    ὅπως αὐτὸν ἀπολέσωσιν.

And in literal English:

And it came to pass   A   A
        that he on the Sabbath
        passed through the cornfields,
    and his disciples began to make way,
        plucking the ears of corn
    and the Pharisees began to say to him,
        'Look,
         why do they do
            on the Sabbath
            what is not lawful?'
And he says to them,   B
        'Have you never read -
    What David did,
        when he had need and was hungry,
        he and the ones with him?
    He entered
            into the house of God
            in the days of Abiathar the High Priest
        and ate the shewbread
            which it was not lawful to eat,
            except by the priests,
        and gave also to the ones with him?'
And he said to them,   B'
        'The Sabbath
        on account of man was,
    and not man
        on account of the Sabbath
    so that the Son of man is Lord
        also of the Sabbath.'

And he entered,   A   **B**
    without hesitation,
    into the synagogue.
And there was a man there with a withered hand.
And they watched him carefully,
    if on the Sabbath he might heal him,
    in order that they might accuse him.
And he says to the man with the withered hand,   B
    'Rise,
    into the middle.'
And he says to them,
     'Is it lawful on the Sabbath
    to do good,
     or to do evil,
    to save life,
     or to kill?'
And they were silent.
And looking round at them with anger,   B'
    greatly grieved at their hardness of heart,
    he said to the man,
     'Stretch out your hand.'
And he stretched it out,
And was restored the hand of him.

And going forth,   a   **B'**
    the Pharisees immediately with the Herodians, b
     held counsel
     against him,
    how they might destroy him.   b'

The Day's telling is properly described, like all the previous days as having the form ABB which could be called a composite ABB'/ABB'/ABB' scheme. In the first Part, **A**, A (2.23,24) introduces the new day, the sabbath, and begins reporting also the first event of the Day; B (vv.25,26) beginning with a 'dramatic' historical present records Jesus' first response, which is his reply to the Pharisees' question; and B' (vv27,28) gives Jesus' second response (exegetically, here the two responses beg comparison because, for the first time in the Gospel, the potential for associating Jesus with David is raised). In the second part, **B**, A (3.1,2) tells how Jesus entered without hesitation into the synagogue (in anger) and was presented with a new opportunity to address the Pharisees (but, who is being challenged here: is it Jesus, or is it the Pharisees?); in B (vv.3,4) beginning with a 'dramatic' historical present, Jesus takes charge of the scene and silences the Pharisees; and in B'(v.5) Jesus looks round at the Pharisees in anger (and we find the same words as in B, λέγει τῷ ἀνθρώπῳ) and heals the man. In the third part, **B'**, as if to add to the drama, the Day's presentation finishes abruptly: part a reports the Pharisees' leaving; part b tells how they joined (in heated conversation?) with the Herodians; and part b' tells how they wanted to destroy him.

This middle day's telling of Mark's First Series of seven Days ends on a highly dramatic note. What is more, its parallel day (Day Four) in the Fourth and Final Series of the gospel is similarly constructed with a final short part which is just as dramatic. Between them, the first presents tha first plot against Jesus' life and the second presents the last.

Day Five: 3.7-4.41:

Several propositions are presented: that Day Five has the limits of 3.7 and 4.41, and that it comprises three sections (3.7-19; vv.20-35; 4.1-41) which are each created by Mark according to his ABB' rhetorical method; that with Day Five Mark begins his second sub-Series and threesome of Days (Day Five, 3.7-4.41; Day Six, 5.1-20; and Day Seven, 5.21-43); and that Mark uses this sub-Series (3.7-5.43) to conclude his first Series of seven Days (1.21-5.43) for which Mark's focus is "Jesus' first days of mission (in Galilee and in particular, in the region of its Sea)". We rehearse the pertinent judgements and arguments of others as we examine the text.

Hooker notes that most commentators make a major break and, therefore, a new beginning at 3.7, but she says, "such divisions are largely arbitrary". She points out two links with previous material; stories of conflict (2.1-3.6 and 3.21-35) and the injunction of Jesus to silence unclean spirits (1.25, 34 and 3.12).[201] Yet, she notes too the change to a new theme, which she calls "the commissioning of the twelve" (later, "the appointment of the twelve"[202]). She observes also the important theme which is sustained throughout the next three chapters (we note: Days Five, Six and Seven); it is "the response which men and women make to Jesus: the truth about him is spelt out in a series of parables and miracles, but this truth is hidden from the majority of those in the story, who hear and see but fail to comprehend".[203]

We observe also that Jesus' exercise of great authority binds these three days into a threesome. At the end of the first (Day Five, 3.7-4.41) he displays his power over the wind and waves. In the second (Day Six, 5.1-20), after an extravagantly detailed description of a demoniac's possession by evil spirits and the attempts by others to restrain him, he demonstrates his power over immense evil. And in the third (Day Seven, 5.21-43) he shows his power to heal an incurable (whose ailment and whose attempts to find a cure are again spelt out in much detail), and at the climax of the Day's report shows his power to raise even the

---

[201]Hooker, *The Gospel...*, p.109.
[202]Hooker, *The Gospel...*, p.110.
[203]Hooker, *The Gospel...*, p.109.

dead. Nineham argues similarly, and I agree with him, that these stories make up "one of the groups of three of which Mark is so fond".[204]

On 3.7-12, both Nineham and Hooker view the passage as a major editorial summary statement of Jesus' activity[205]. And they compare it with those of 1.14,15 and 1.32-34. For Nineham the question arises, "Why here?" Schweizer's answer to this is simple; he sees 3.7-12 as introductory to part III of the Gospel 3.7-6.6a, on "Jesus' ministry in parables and signs and the blindness of the world"[206]. Contrary to Schweizer, I would argue that the summary introduced at 3.7 is included in the text by Mark at this point as a beginning to his new three-day presentation with which he concludes his first Series of seven Days, 1.21-5.43. At the end of the first of these days, Day Five, there is a night-crossing of the lake, and at the end of the second day's activities (Day Six)[207] there is a return crossing, with the result that the last of the three days, Day Seven, tells what then takes place at, or near the same setting of the first of these three days. It would appear that Mark has deliberately created a geographical scheme which echoes that of the first threesome of days, 1.21-2.22, where the first and last days of that series also have a common setting (which is Capernaum).

Taylor's estimate that 4.1-5.43 is one day's telling[208] is challenged for the reason, as stated in the Introduction, that all that Mark tells us about, in 4.35-5.43, cannot have happened in one day: fundamentally the argument against his proposition has much to do with the fact that 4.35 tells us that 'evening had come'. The content of 4.35-5.43 could not all have taken place in one day, in night-watches; much occurs in successive daylight periods. Other reasons, not raised in the Introduction, are added below. My first point of difference with Taylor is that this Day's telling begins at 3.7 and not at 4.1. As presented under Day Four, the content of 3.7-12 is non-sabbatical and so separates from 3.6 and what precedes it. In my note 62, the notion that the new Day might begin at 3.7 with the sunset at which the Jewish sabbath ends is untenable fundamentally because the reportings of the Day's activities continue to evening (4.35) and beyond, without any hint of a night disrupting the flow of events. (See note 62 for other reasons.)

We continue with a consideration of 3.7-12. Nineham's interest in the first instance is as with Lightfoot[209] in the relationship between 3.7-12 and vv.13-19. As "a typical Markan insertion" (between 2.1-3.6 and 3.20ff. which are stories of conflict) these verses, he says, "provide a foil to the dark picture of mounting misunderstanding and hostility"[210]. Given the appointing of the "twelve" (in vv.13-19), against the description of 'all Israel' gathered to him (in vv.7,8) and the frenzy of an enthusiastic and excitable crowd (in vv.9-12), with Nineham and Lightfoot we may see here "the foundation of the new Israel"[211]. The Day begins, certainly, with the most extended list yet of peoples present, from every part of the Holy Land inhabited by Jews. All "old Israel" gathers to Jesus.

We may judge, therefore, that 3.7-19 is the opening presentation, Part A. of this Day's telling and that it comprises the three parts Nineham suggests: vv.7,8; vv.9-12; and vv.13-19. Robbins also identifies the same divisions. For him 3.7-19 represents the first three-step progression since 1.14-20:[212] The first unit of the progression, vv.7,8, he calls a "re-statement" of

---

[204]Nineham, *Saint Mark*, p.157.

[205]Nineham, *Saint Mark*, p.112; Hooker, *The Gospel...*, p.109.

[206]Nineham, *Saint Mark*, pp.78ff.

[207]See in the discussion on this day, a more detailed consideration of "night-crossings".

[208]Taylor, *The Gospel...*, p.146; see my Introduction, p.32.

[209]R.H. Lightfoot, *The Gospel Message...*

[210]Nineham, *Saint Mark*, p.112.

[211]Lightfoot, *The Gospel Message...*, p.39.

[212]Vernon K. Robbins, *Jesus the Teacher...*: Essentially, Robbins identifies three-step progressions in ways similar to myself. But in all the Gospel, he identifies only six possibilities: at 1.14-20; 3.7-19; 6.1-13; 8.27-9.1; 10.46-11.11 and 13.1-37. Upon these six three-step progressions alone, he attempts to build a case for his presentation of the formal structure of the Gospel. Because his next three-step progression after 3.7-19 is at 6.1-13, he argues the new section of material introduced by 3.7-19 ends at 5.43, our three days, Days Five, Six and

1.14-20; the second unit, vv.9-12, he says, is a "re-statement" of 1.21-3.6, with the addition of new features; the third and final unit, vv.13-19, he says, parallels units two and three in the first progression, that is 1.16-18 and vv.19f. and "establishes expectations that were not explicit there"[213]. He identifies what will be the three roles of the "twelve" at 3.14,15: they are: "to be with him", "to be sent out to preach" and "to have authority to cast out demons". Robbins develops this: "the expectation to 'be with' Jesus was evident from 1.16-20 where the men were asked to leave everything and follow; the expectation to be 'sent out to preach' was probably implicit in the promise that the disciples would be made 'fishers of men'. The assertion that the disciples would acquire 'authority to cast out demons' is new information". I would only question, why separate the two mission activities in this way? Preaching and casting out demons were Jesus' own two mission activities, as we read in 1.39. As it is, Mark presents them together, consider: (.a) *καὶ ἵνα ἀποστέλλῃ αὐτούς,* (.b) *κηρύσσειν,* (.b') *καὶ ἔχειν ἐξουσίαν ἐκβάλλειν τὰ δαιμόνια.* Again we discern an (.a) (.b) (.b') sequence.

Robbins' references to chapter one have their parallels in the writing of most commentators on 3.7-12. Likewise, his designation of gospel sections, 1.14-3.6 and 3.7-5.43 has the near agreement of a number of commentators (compare 1.14-3.6 and 3.7-6.6a/.13 of Taylor, Schweizer and Hooker). I take a contrary view for the reason stated above, that the evidence points to Mark's creation of two sub-Series of three Days in balance around a middle Day, to form his first Series of seven Days. Other support will be given to this after the completion of the examination of the first seven Days.

As 3.7-19 is the opening section of Day Five, it is not surprising to find within it a particular detail of important literary-structural significance for the construction of the Day as a whole. The 'boat' of 3.9 is an important linkage, because it re-appears in 4.1 and again at 4.36 (though the Greek differs a little: compare: *πλοιάριον, εἰς πλοῖον* and *ἐν τῷ πλοίῳ*). It links all three parts of the Day's construction. The strong link at 4.1, *Καὶ πάλιν ἤρξατο διδάσκειν παρὰ τὴν θάλασσαν,* has been discussed under Day Three, above. In this Day's telling, it links the first and second pieces of Part **B**, 3.20-4.23. It may be translated: "And immediately afterwards, he began to teach by the sea...", but for now I rather prefer, "And without hesitation, he began to teach...", because I think Mark intends to show Jesus as frustrated with the kinds of challenges he *had just had to face* from both his own family and the scribes (as told in 3.20-35). The same opening 'sits' Jesus in 'the boat' as he begins his teaching, to his own agenda, on the Kingdom of God.

Part **B**'s opening piece, 3.20-35, is clearly a 'whole' presentation. To Best, the opening phrase is attributable to Mark since he regularly introduces "the house" as a place where instruction is given[214]. Hooker sees its connection with what precedes by translating 3.20a *Καὶ ἔρχεται εἰς οἶκον* as "Then he went indoors...". With this section, she says, "we move back into the atmosphere of conflict... but move another step forward in the development of this theme, since now Jesus' opponents do not merely watch him and criticize, but offer their own - utterly false - interpretation of the source of his authority and power."[215] With regard to this section's form, she argues that a number of stories have been woven together, probably by Mark, and she sees another example of intercalation of incidents "of which he is so fond", describing the structure as 3.20,21, vv.22-30 and vv.31-35 (i.e. material about the scribes is "sandwiched" between material about his relatives and friends). While I can agree with the limits of this section, I cannot agree with Hooker in the other matters. Understanding Mark's

---

Seven. We may value Robbins' analysis so far as it goes. His identification of three-step progressions and his judgement that they are a clue to the formal structure of Mark's Gospel is close to what is being uncovered here in this analysis. That he argues the limits of gospel-sections on the grounds that no other than these six three-step progressions exist, which is really what he does, is an argument, of course, with which I cannot agree. Neither can I agree with him on all his identified progressions.

[213]Robbins, *Jesus the Teacher...*, see pp.31-33.

[214]Best, *Disciples...*, p.50.

[215]Hooker, *The Gospel...*, p.114.

rhetorical method differently, for its ABB' form, it can be argued that the compositional work of Mark was to bring only two stories together, and that this is expressed by the following divisions: vv.20-22 (the opening part, introducing firstly the setting, and secondly the two sets of people who are raising issues: in the first place Jesus' family, and in the second, scribes from Jerusalem); vv.23-30 (the first development: Jesus anwering the scribes); and vv.31-35 (the second and completing development: Jesus speaking about 'family'). Mark's literary-constructional method of ABB' and abb' is in evidence again in its parts and sub-parts.

The first parts of Mark's Day Five, Part **A** and Part **B**'s opening part, are covered sufficiently. For our examination of the remaining verses, 4.1-41 we will draw in the efforts of Dewey and Fay on 4.1-34 first of all, and then rehearse the challenge of Räisänen, for whom chapter 4 is a suitable test-case for any theory about the nature of Mark's composition. For Dewey these verses are a five section concentric structure[216]; for Fay, they are a seven section scheme[217].

Dewey:			Fay:	
A vv.1,2a	Introduction X		A vv.1,2a	Introduction X
B vv.2b-20	Parable material		B vv.2b-9	Parable material
			C vv.10-13	Parabolic method
			D vv.14-20	Interpretation (the Sower)
C vv.21-25	Sayings material		C' vv.21-25	Parabolic method
B' vv.26-32	Parable material		B' vv.26-32	Parable material
A' vv.33,34	Conclusion		A' vv.33,34	Conclusion

The first difficulty I encounter is with 4.1-2a which they both view as a chiasm. They present:

a   *Καὶ πάλιν ἤρξατο διδάσκειν παρὰ τὴν θάλασσαν.*

b   *καὶ συνάγεται πρὸς αὐτὸν ὄχλος πλεῖστος,*

c   *ὥστε αὐτὸν εἰς πλοῖον ἐμβάντα καθῆσθαι ἐν τῇ θαλάσσῃ,*

b' *καὶ πᾶς ὁ ὄχλος πρὸς τὴν θάλασσαν ἐπὶ τῆς γῆς ἦσαν.* ²

a' *καὶ ἐδίδασκεν αὐτοὺς ἐν παραβολαῖς πολλά,*

The notion that this is a five-part chiasm does not reflect the three-sentence structure of my analysis. In defining would-be chiastic structures, it depends on selecting one set of criteria over and against the selecting of another. The choice of *διδάσκειν* and *ἐδίδασκεν* as key words defining the outer framing sentences is a 'choice'. Choose *θάλασσαν* and the other two uses of the word, in all, in lines a, c and b', and no chiasm is suggested! One would have to say that Mark overlooked what might be read as other hook words if he did intend the chiastic arrangement as Dewey and Fay suggest. I might have been interested in seeing a three-part chiasm: (a) (bcb') (a'), rather I present my analysis below, which to me demonstrates another Markan composite abb' form:

---

[216]Dewey, *Markan Public Debate...*, pp.147-152,167, after Jan Lambrecht, *Marcus Interpretator: Stijl en Boodschap in Mc.3.20-4.34*, Desclee de Brouwer, Brugge-Utrecht, 1969.
[217]Greg Fay, "Introduction to Incomprehension: The Literary Structure of Mark 4.1-34", *CBQ* 51 (1989), pp.65-81.

		(a)	a
Καὶ πάλιν			
ἤρξατο διδάσκειν		(b)	
παρὰ τὴν θάλασσαν.		(b')	
καὶ συνάγεται πρὸς αὐτὸν ὄχλος πλεῖστος,		(a)	b
ὥστε αὐτὸν	.a	(b)	
εἰς πλοῖον ἐμβάντα καθῆσθαι	.b		
ἐν τῇ θαλάσσῃ,	.b'		
καὶ πᾶς ὁ ὄχλος	.a	(b')	
πρὸς τὴν θάλασσαν	.b		
ἐπὶ τῆς γῆς ἦσαν. [2]	.b'		
καὶ ἐδίδασκεν αὐτοὺς		(a)	b'
ἐν παραβολαῖς		(b)	
πολλά.		(b')	

It may be said at the outset that we do at least all identify the same five lines. But my reading is that (my) 'a' (immediately above) is 'introductory' to the B part of the Day's **B** part. I am seeing the Introductory, A Part to the Day's telling as 3.7-19; the **B** part as 3.20-4.23; and the **B'** Part as 4.24-41. *Καὶ πάλιν* (see my earlier arguments for the role of *Καὶ πάλιν* linking parts together strongly in the tellings of Days Three, Four and Five) here pulls together the presentations of the Parable of the Sower and its interpretation in a truly Markan fashion in the B and B' pieces. These pieces even end with similar words: compare

Ὃς ἔχει ὦτα ἀκούειν ἀκουέτω with
Εἴ τις ἔχει ὦτα ἀκούειν ἀκουέτω.

See also, for a similar example of parallelism: the following two presentations of parables on the Kingdom of God now predictably occupy B and B' positions also. Yes, it may be said that Dewey's and Fay's chiasm is simpler and more balanced, but that does not make their analysis right. For Mark, balance is achieved by his basic construction-use of ABB' and his writing style of abb' which he employs throughout his book.

I have to say that I view the larger concentric arrangements of Dewey and Fay with a little scepticism. If they discern chiasm where there is no chiasm in just one-and-a-half verses only, how can we judge they are able to see the chiastic structure of thirty-four verses? Again, anyone can establish a chiasm just about anywhere in the text (any text?) if they are not too bothered about what happens beyond its limits, that is, each side of the 'chiasm'. Further, if Fay can propose an expanding of Dewey's pattern, to bring different passages into new parallelisms, he raises doubts in my mind that any paralleling can be established at all, on the basis of a concentric pattern. I judge that his 'centring' of the interpretation of the 'sower' parable is a bad move, as it clearly belongs alongside the parable.

We turn briefly to the challenge of Räisänen. In his study on the "Messianic Secret" in Mark's Gospel[218] he says, "Any theory about the nature of Mark's composition must prove good in practice. A theory must be capable of making sense of crucial passages in the gospel. For such a test, the parable chapter of Mk. 4 is as suitable a section as any." I think he has a good point. It is the largest concentrate of Jesus' teaching thus far and it is not until 13.5-37 that we find anything of the same order. But, there is a but. Prior to chapter 4, in 3.23-35 is a large teaching block and that is within the same day's telling and that includes parables too!

We continue, and we discuss the three difficulties which have been observed by scholars in regard to 3.23-30, 4.33,34 and 4.10-'?' It has been said of 3.23-30 that it ends a little clumsily at 3.30: "for they said, 'He has an unclean spirit.'" Taylor calls it "an elliptical

---

[218]Heikki Räisänen, *The Messianic Secret...*, p.28.

passage which is an explanatory Markan comment." It is the evangelist's way of saying, "This is the reply of Jesus to the charge, 'He has Beelzebul' (in 3.22)." Taylor sees 4.33,34 in the same category, as the evangelist's explanation. Just as the GNB which Schweizer uses puts 3.30 (see above) in parenthesis, so 4.33,34 may be put in brackets, as Taylor sees it "as similar" to 3.30. The bigger problem, clearly, is with 4.10-'?'. We return to the question asked, at what point, if at all, does Jesus resume his teaching of the crowd, because as 4.36 says, he was still in the boat? As presented above, the case can be put for the insertion being 4.10-23. In short all three difficult passages (3.30, 4.33,34 and 4.10-23) may be regarded as set in parentheses as explanations. 3.30 is Mark's explanation for Jesus' teaching on what "will not be forgiven" (3.28,29); 4.33,34 is Mark's explanation of Jesus' use of parables and how he interpreted them for his disciples; and 4.10-23 is Mark's insertion by which he features Jesus' explaining the reason for his speaking in parables, and explaining the first of the parables in his teaching block (4.1-32). All three 'insertions', however, have their proper place within Mark's systematically presented rhetorical scheme. Mark has built them into this Day's framework: they were not added later.

The literary-structural argument for the ending of the larger parenthetical piece (4.10-23) still requires presenting. The question is: at what point, if at all, in Mark's mind, is Jesus talking again to the crowds[219]? To assist enquiry, we have the evidence of Mark's presentation methodology, though here it *is* tested to the limit. It is certainly extended, though it does retain the ABB' form, overall.[220] Fundamental to the exposing of the rhythm of presentation is Mark's frequent repetition of "And he said...". (See the presentation of the literary-structure of the Day, following these notes.) What helps establish 4.23 as the end of the parenthetical piece beginning at 4.10 is the repetition of 4.9, "...has ears to hear let him hear." In commentaries on 4.21-25, the inclusion of 4.23 is given either very little or no consideration at all. Taylor, however, does consider it and ruminates on its linkage initially with vv.21f. and comments too, "but it has the appearance of a connecting link relating the sayings to the parable of the sower"[221]. He does not say if he means all the four sayings of vv.21-25 or just the two with which he thinks it was first associated.

Clearly, in 4.24-32, after the introductory piece a (vv.24,25), the pair of "Kingdom of God" parables (vv.26-29 and vv.30-32) fall perfectly into parallel positions (b and b') as we should expect them to, after the manner of Mark's rhetorical structuring elsewhere. The literary-structural analysis I present does appear to answer Räisänen's challenge. With this piece, 4.24-32, I judge that Part **B'** of the Day's telling begins. We here examine 4.33-41 which contains the two remaining parts: Part B, vv.33-34. the summary on Jesus' teaching in parables and explaing them to his disciples, and Part B', vv.35-41, the story of Jesus' stilling the storm. 4.33-34 displays an abb' composition; 4.35-41 does so too. The three parts of the latter show an introduction, a first development, about a storm of wind, Jesus asleep and awakened, and a second development, on how the wind dropped, the fearful disciples and their fearing a great fear. The subjects of Faith and Jesus' identity are raised at the last.

It remains only to summarise the overall sectional-structure of Day Five. Several times already, the three Parts have been stated as 3.7-19; 3.20-4.23 and 4.24-41 and they are laid out to Mark's repeating composite form, ABB'/ABB'/ABB'. (As discussed in Day Two above, we again observe key use by Mark again of historical presents.)

As a final point, we ask, should we be concerned that the numbers of the verses of the parts are not 'too equal'? They number in turn: 13, 39 and 18. We have found unenumbers already, particularly in the middle Day, Day Four. Or we could argue that this Day's telling, compared with those we have already examined, is exceptional: 1) it is the longest so far (in

---

[219]Which would also include the disciples, that is the twelve and the others.
[220]See also, 3.16-19, where the description of "the twelve" is another extension.
[221]Taylor, *The Gospel...*, p.262.

terms of the whole Gospel it is the second longest report, with 70 verses, after Day Twenty-four, 11.20-13.37, which has 90 verses); and 2) it is the first so far to contain much teaching (Day Twenty-four is the next we encounter and it contains even more and, very interestingly it lies diagonally opposite, so completing the central *chi*, X, in the Markan 'matrix': *cf.* Day Three with Day Twenty-Six and Day Five with Twenty-Four).

In the Introduction we looked for possible repetitive and progressive forms in biblical and non-biblical literature which might have influenced Mark in his choice of 'arrangement' and 'style'. It is clearly the case that in the Genesis account of creation, 1.1-2.4a, and in Homer's *Iliad* there is evidence of wide variation in the sizes of the presentations of the Days' accounts themselves. (See page 10, for the verses of the days of the Genesis account which vary widely, and page 12, for the marked differences in the numbers of 'Books' which the Days of the *Iliad* comprise.) The analysis of Mark's work shows it, in this regard, to be little different from these comparable compositions. What seems important, therefore, in the writing of such ancient literature, is that the *constructions* were themselves complete, in their ABB' forms. In regard to Day Five's sectional variation, we might then say simply that it follows earlier precedent, and that the variation in sizes of presentations was less important to ancient writers than the completing of their constructions. And we might say of Mark's rhetorical method, from all that we have seen already: it matters not to him how long the elements are, or how much they vary; it matters only that all the main component parts, A, B, B' and a, b, b' are present, and so on, at every literary level.

What I have stated previously though, may be correct. Up until this Day's telling, Mark's structural method had not really been put to the test, with teaching blocks like these to include. His method here has been stretched to the limit, it seems, as it clearly shows extensions to his presentations, in 4.1-32 especially. But this is evidence of the capability of the writing style he uses, to expand its capacity to accommodate a greater amount of material when it is needed to do so. The basic ABB' unit can accommodate abb' pieces for A, for B and for B': nine lines, therefore. In turn, the abb' pieces can accommodate three parts per unit: that takes it to twenty-seven possible lines. The next level takes it to a possible 81 lines and the next to 243! So long as the writer is continuing with his use of ABB', whether it is in three lines or 243, he is helping his reader define the reading units of the text. Mark is such a writer. Below is the literary structure of Day Five:

Καὶ ὁ Ἰησοῦς   A   A
      μετὰ τῶν μαθητῶν αὐτοῦ
      ἀνεχώρησεν πρὸς τὴν θάλασσαν·
   καὶ πολὺ πλῆθος ἀπὸ τῆς Γαλιλαίας ἠκολούθησεν·
      καὶ ἀπὸ τῆς Ἰουδαίας[8]
         καὶ ἀπὸ Ἱεροσολύμων / καὶ ἀπὸ τῆς Ἰδουμαίας
      καὶ οἱ πέραν τοῦ Ἰορδάνου
         καὶ περὶ Τύρον / καὶ Σιδῶνα,
πλῆθος πολύ,
      ἀκούοντες ὅσα ἐποίει
      ἦλθον πρὸς αὐτόν.[9]
καὶ εἶπεν τοῖς μαθηταῖς αὐτοῦ   B
         ἵνα πλοιάριον προσκαρτερῇ αὐτῷ
      διὰ τὸν ὄχλον

ἵνα μὴ θλίβωσιν αὐτόν· [10]
πολλοὺς γὰρ ἐθεράπευσεν,
ὥστε ἐπιπίπτειν αὐτῷ
ἵνα αὐτοῦ ἅψωνται / ὅσοι εἶχον μάστιγας. [11]
καὶ τὰ πνεύματα τὰ ἀκάθαρτα,
ὅταν αὐτὸν ἐθεώρουν,
προσέπιπτον αὐτῷ
καὶ ἔκραζον λέγοντες
ὅτι Σὺ εἶ ὁ υἱὸς τοῦ θεοῦ. [12]
καὶ πολλὰ ἐπετίμα αὐτοῖς
ἵνα μὴ αὐτὸν φανερὸν ποιήσωσιν.
Καὶ ἀναβαίνει εἰς τὸ ὄρος   Β᾽
καὶ προσκαλεῖται οὓς ἤθελεν αὐτός,
καὶ ἀπῆλθον πρὸς αὐτόν. [14]
<u>καὶ ἐποίησεν δώδεκα,</u>
(οὓς καὶ ἀποστόλους ὠνόμασεν,) not original?
ἵνα ὦσιν μετ᾽ αὐτοῦ
καὶ ἵνα ἀποστέλλῃ αὐτοὺς
κηρύσσειν [15]
καὶ ἔχειν ἐξουσίαν ἐκβάλλειν τὰ δαιμόνια· [16]
<u>καὶ ἐποίησεν τοὺς δώδεκα,</u>
<u>καὶ ἐπέθηκεν</u> ὄνομα τῷ Σίμωνι
Πέτρον, [17]
καὶ Ἰάκωβον τὸν τοῦ Ζεβεδαίου
καὶ Ἰωάννην τὸν ἀδελφὸν τοῦ Ἰακώβου,
<u>καὶ ἐπέθηκεν</u> αὐτοῖς ὀνόματα
Βοανηργές / ὅ ἐστιν Υἱοὶ Βροντῆς· [18]
καὶ Ἀνδρέαν καὶ Φίλιππον καὶ Βαρθολομαῖον
καὶ Μαθθαῖον καὶ Θωμᾶν καὶ Ἰάκωβον
τὸν τοῦ Ἀλφαίου
καὶ Θαδδαῖον καὶ Σίμωνα τὸν Καναναῖον [19]
καὶ Ἰούδαν Ἰσκαριώθ,
ὃς καὶ παρέδωκεν αὐτό<u>ν.</u>

<u>Καὶ ἔρχεται εἰς οἶκον·</u>   a   A   **B**
καὶ συνέρχεται πάλιν ὁ ὄχλος,
ὥστε μὴ δύνασθαι αὐτοὺς μηδὲ ἄρτον φαγεῖν. [21]
καὶ ἀκούσαντες
οἱ παρ᾽ αὐτοῦ ἐξῆλθον κρατῆσαι αὐτόν,
<u>ἔλεγον γὰρ</u>
ὅτι ἐξέστη.
καὶ οἱ γραμματεῖς
οἱ ἀπὸ Ἱεροσολύμων καταβάντες
<u>ἔλεγον</u>
ὅτι Βεελζεβοὺλ ἔχει,
καὶ ὅτι ἐν τῷ ἄρχοντι τῶν δαιμονίων
ἐκβάλλει τὰ δαιμόνια.

Καὶ προσκαλεσάμενος αὐτοὺς   b
         ἐν παραβολαῖς
         ἔλεγεν αὐτοῖς,
     Πῶς δύναται Σατανᾶς Σατανᾶν ἐκβάλλειν; [24]
     <u>καὶ ἐὰν βασιλεία ἐφ᾽ ἑαυτὴν μερισθῇ,</u>
         οὐ δύναται σταθῆναι ἡ βασιλεία ἐκείνη· [25]
     <u>καὶ ἐὰν οἰκία ἐφ᾽ ἑαυτὴν μερισθῇ,</u>
         οὐ δυνήσεται ἡ οἰκία ἐκείνη <u>σταθῆναι.</u> [26]
     καὶ εἰ ὁ Σατανᾶς ἀνέστη ἐφ᾽ ἑαυτὸν καὶ ἐμερίσθη,
         οὐ δύναται στῆναι
         ἀλλὰ τέλος ἔχει. [27]
     ἀλλ᾽ οὐ δύναται οὐδεὶς
         εἰς τὴν οἰκίαν τοῦ ἰσχυροῦ εἰσελθὼν
         τὰ σκεύη αὐτοῦ διαρπάσαι
     ἐὰν μὴ πρῶτον τὸν ἰσχυρὸν δήσῃ,
         καὶ τότε τὴν οἰκίαν αὐτοῦ διαρπάσει. [28]
   Ἀμὴν λέγω ὑμῖν
     ὅτι πάντα ἀφεθήσεται τοῖς υἱοῖς τῶν ἀνθρώπων,
     τὰ ἁμαρτήματα καὶ αἱ βλασφημίαι
     ὅσα ἐὰν βλασφημήσωσιν· [29]
     ὃς δ᾽ ἂν βλασφημήσῃ εἰς τὸ πνεῦμα τὸ ἅγιον
     οὐκ ἔχει ἄφεσιν εἰς τὸν αἰῶνα,
     ἀλλὰ ἔνοχός ἐστιν αἰωνίου ἁμαρτήματος.
   ὅτι ἔλεγον,
     Πνεῦμα ἀκάθαρτον
     ἔχει.

<u>Καὶ ἔρχεται</u>   b'
         ἡ μήτηρ αὐτοῦ
         καὶ οἱ ἀδελφοὶ αὐτοῦ
     καὶ ἔξω στήκοντες
         ἀπέστειλαν πρὸς αὐτὸν
         καλοῦντες αὐτόν. [32]
     καὶ ἐκάθητο περὶ αὐτὸν ὄχλος,
         καὶ λέγουσιν αὐτῷ,
         Ἰδοὺ
     ἡ μήτηρ σου καὶ οἱ ἀδελφοί σου
     ἔξω ζητοῦσίν σε.
   καὶ ἀποκριθεὶς αὐτοῖς
     λέγει,
     Τίς ἐστιν ἡ μήτηρ μου καὶ οἱ ἀδελφοί μου;
   καὶ περιβλεψάμενος τοὺς περὶ αὐτὸν
     κύκλῳ καθημένους
     λέγει,
     Ἴδε ἡ μήτηρ μου καὶ οἱ ἀδελφοί μου. [35]
     ὃς γὰρ ἂν ποιήσῃ τὸ θέλημα τοῦ θεοῦ,
         οὗτος ἀδελφός μου
         καὶ ἀδελφὴ
         καὶ μήτηρ ἐστίν.

Καὶ *πάλιν*   a   B

ἤρξατο διδάσκειν
παρὰ τὴν θάλασσαν.
καὶ συνάγεται πρὸς αὐτὸν ὄχλος πλεῖστος,
ὥστε αὐτὸν
εἰς πλοῖον ἐμβάντα καθῆσθαι
ἐν τῇ θαλάσσῃ,
καὶ πᾶς ὁ ὄχλος
πρὸς τὴν θάλασσαν
ἐπὶ τῆς γῆς ἦσαν. [2]
καὶ ἐδίδασκεν αὐτοὺς
ἐν παραβολαῖς
πολλά,

καὶ ἔλεγεν αὐτοῖς   b

ἐν τῇ διδαχῇ αὐτοῦ, [3]
Ἀκούετε.
ἰδοὺ
ἐξῆλθεν ὁ σπείρων
σπεῖραι. [4]
καὶ ἐγένετο ἐν τῷ σπείρειν
ὃ μὲν ἔπεσεν παρὰ τὴν ὁδόν,
καὶ ἦλθεν τὰ πετεινὰ καὶ κατέφαγεν αὐτό. [5]
καὶ ἄλλο ἔπεσεν ἐπὶ τὸ πετρῶδες
ὅπου οὐκ εἶχεν γῆν πολλήν,
καὶ εὐθὺς ἐξανέτειλεν
διὰ τὸ μὴ ἔχειν βάθος γῆς· [6]
καὶ ὅτε ἀνέτειλεν ὁ ἥλιος
ἐκαυματίσθησαν,
καὶ διὰ τὸ μὴ ἔχειν ῥίζαν
ἐξηράνθη. [7]
καὶ ἄλλο ἔπεσεν εἰς τὰς ἀκάνθας,
καὶ ἀνέβησαν αἱ ἄκανθαι καὶ συνέπνιξαν αὐτό,
καὶ καρπὸν οὐκ ἔδωκεν. [8]
καὶ ἄλλα ἔπεσεν εἰς τὴν γῆν τὴν καλήν,
καὶ ἐδίδου καρπὸν ἀναβαίνοντα καὶ αὐξανόμενα,
καὶ ἔφερεν *ἓν τριάκοντα*
καὶ ἓν ἑξήκοντα
καὶ ἓν ἑκατόν.

καὶ ἔλεγεν,   b'

Ὃς ἔχει ὦτα ἀκούειν
ἀκουέτω.

Καὶ ὅτε ἐγένετο κατὰ μόνας,   a   B'

ἠρώτων αὐτὸν
οἱ περὶ αὐτὸν
σὺν τοῖς δώδεκα
τὰς παραβολάς. [11]
καὶ ἔλεγεν αὐτοῖς,
Ὑμῖν τὸ μυστήριον δέδοται τῆς βασιλείας τοῦ θεοῦ·

ἐκείνοις δὲ τοῖς ἔξω ἐν παραβολαῖς τὰ πάντα γίνεται, [12]
ἵνα βλέποντες βλέπωσιν καὶ μὴ ἴδωσιν,
 καὶ ἀκούοντες ἀκούωσιν καὶ μὴ συνιῶσιν,
 μήποτε ἐπιστρέψωσιν καὶ ἀφεθῇ αὐτοῖς.
καὶ λέγει αὐτοῖς,   b
 Οὐκ οἴδατε τὴν παραβολὴν ταύτην,
 καὶ πῶς πάσας τὰς παραβολὰς γνώσεσθε; [14]
ὁ σπείρων τὸν λόγον σπείρει. [15]
      οὗτοι δέ εἰσιν οἱ παρὰ τὴν ὁδὸν
           ὅπου σπείρεται ὁ λόγος,
      καὶ ὅταν ἀκούσωσιν
           εὐθὺς ἔρχεται ὁ Σατανᾶς
           καὶ αἴρει τὸν λόγον τὸν ἐσπαρμένον εἰς αὐτούς. [16]
 καὶ οὗτοί εἰσιν ὁμοίως οἱ ἐπὶ τὰ πετρώδη σπειρόμενοι,
      οἳ ὅταν ἀκούσωσιν τὸν λόγον
           εὐθὺς μετὰ χαρᾶς λαμβάνουσιν αὐτόν, [17]
      καὶ οὐκ ἔχουσιν ῥίζαν ἐν ἑαυτοῖς
           ἀλλὰ πρόσκαιροί εἰσιν·
                εἶτα γενομένης θλίψεως ἢ διωγμοῦ
                διὰ τὸν λόγον
           εὐθὺς σκανδαλίζονται. [18]
 καὶ ἄλλοι εἰσὶν οἱ εἰς τὰς ἀκάνθας σπειρόμενοι·
      οὗτοί εἰσιν οἱ τὸν λόγον ἀκούσαντες, [19]
      καὶ αἱ μέριμναι τοῦ βίου
           καὶ ἡ ἀπάτη τοῦ πλούτου
           καὶ αἱ περὶ τὰ λοιπὰ ἐπιθυμίαι
      εἰσπορευόμεναι
      συμπνίγουσιν τὸν λόγον,
           καὶ ἄκαρπος γίνεται. [20]
 καὶ ἐκεῖνοί εἰσιν οἱ ἐπὶ τὴν γῆν τὴν καλὴν σπαρέντες,
      οἵτινες ἀκούουσιν τὸν λόγον καὶ παραδέχονται
      καὶ καρποφοροῦσιν
           <u>ἓν τριάκοντα</u>
                <u>καὶ ἓν ἑξήκοντα</u>
                <u>καὶ ἓν ἑκατόν.</u>
Καὶ ἔλεγεν αὐτοῖς,   b'
      Μήτι ἔρχεται ὁ λύχνος
           ἵνα ὑπὸ τὸν μόδιον τεθῇ
           ἢ ὑπὸ τὴν κλίνην;
      οὐχ ἵνα ἐπὶ τὴν λυχνίαν τεθῇ; [22]
      οὐ γάρ ἐστιν κρυπτὸν
           ἐὰν μὴ ἵνα φανερωθῇ,
      οὐδὲ ἐγένετο ἀπόκρυφον
           ἀλλ᾽ ἵνα ἔλθῃ εἰς φανερόν. [23]
 εἴ τις ἔχει ὦτα ἀκούειν
      ἀκουέτω.

Καὶ ἔλεγεν αὐτοῖς,   a   A   **B'**

    Βλέπετε τί ἀκούετε.

  ἐν ᾧ μέτρῳ μετρεῖτε

        μετρηθήσεται ὑμῖν

        καὶ προστεθήσεται ὑμῖν. [25]

    ὃς γὰρ ἔχει,

        δοθήσεται αὐτῷ·

  καὶ ὃς οὐκ ἔχει,

        καὶ ὃ ἔχει ἀρθήσεται ἀπ' αὐτοῦ.

Καὶ ἔλεγεν,   b

    Οὕτως ἐστὶν ἡ <u>βασιλεία τοῦ θεοῦ</u>

ὡς ἄνθρωπος βάλῃ τὸν σπόρον ἐπὶ τῆς γῆς [27]

  καὶ καθεύδῃ καὶ ἐγείρηται

    νύκτα καὶ ἡμέραν,

    καὶ ὁ σπόρος βλαστᾷ καὶ μηκύνηται

        ὡς οὐκ οἶδεν αὐτός. [28]

  αὐτομάτη

    ἡ γῆ καρποφορεῖ,

    πρῶτον χόρτον,

        εἶτα στάχυν,

        εἶτα πλήρη σῖτον ἐν τῷ στάχυϊ. [29]

ὅταν δὲ παραδοῖ ὁ καρπός,

  εὐθὺς ἀποστέλλει τὸ δρέπανον,

  ὅτι παρέστηκεν ὁ θερισμός.

Καὶ ἔλεγεν,   b'

    Πῶς ὁμοιώσωμεν <u>τὴν βασιλείαν τοῦ θεοῦ</u>,

  ἢ ἐν τίνι αὐτὴν παραβολῇ θῶμεν; [31]

ὡς κόκκῳ σινάπεως,

  ὃς ὅταν σπαρῇ ἐπὶ τῆς γῆς,

  μικρότερον

    ὂν πάντων τῶν σπερμάτων

    τῶν ἐπὶ τῆς γῆς, [32]

καὶ ὅταν σπαρῇ,

  ἀναβαίνει

    καὶ γίνεται μεῖζον πάντων τῶν λαχάνων

    καὶ ποιεῖ κλάδους μεγάλους,

  ὥστε δύνασθαι

    ὑπὸ τὴν σκιὰν αὐτοῦ

    τὰ πετεινὰ τοῦ οὐρανοῦ κατασκηνοῦν.

Καὶ τοιαύταις παραβολαῖς πολλαῖς   a   B

    ἐλάλει αὐτοῖς τὸν λόγον,

    καθὼς ἠδύναντο ἀκούειν· [34]

χωρὶς δὲ παραβολῆς οὐκ ἐλάλει αὐτοῖς,   b

κατ' ἰδίαν δὲ τοῖς ἰδίοις μαθηταῖς ἐπέλυεν πάντα.   b'

Καὶ λέγει αὐτοῖς   a   B'

        ἐν ἐκείνῃ τῇ ἡμέρᾳ
        ὀψίας γενομένης,
      Διέλθωμεν
        εἰς τὸ πέραν. [36]
    καὶ ἀφέντες τὸν ὄχλον
      παραλαμβάνουσιν αὐτὸν
      ὡς ἦν ἐν τῷ πλοίῳ,
    καὶ ἄλλα πλοῖα ἦν μετ' αὐτοῦ. [37]
καὶ γίνεται λαῖλαψ μεγάλη ἀνέμου,   b
      καὶ τὰ κύματα ἐπέβαλλεν εἰς τὸ πλοῖον,
      ὥστε ἤδη γεμίζεσθαι τὸ πλοῖον. [38]
    καὶ αὐτὸς ἦν ἐν τῇ πρύμνῃ
        ἐπὶ τὸ προσκεφάλαιον
        καθεύδων·
    καὶ ἐγείρουσιν αὐτὸν
        καὶ λέγουσιν αὐτῷ,
      Διδάσκαλε,
        οὐ μέλει σοι
        ὅτι ἀπολλύμεθα;
    καὶ διεγερθεὶς
      ἐπετίμησεν τῷ ἀνέμῳ
      καὶ εἶπεν τῇ θαλάσσῃ,
        Σιώπα,
        πεφίμωσο.
καὶ ἐκόπασεν ὁ ἄνεμος,   b'
    καὶ ἐγένετο γαλήνη μεγάλη.
    καὶ εἶπεν αὐτοῖς,
      Τί δειλοί ἐστε;
      οὔπω ἔχετε πίστιν;
    καὶ ἐφοβήθησαν φόβον μέγαν,
        καὶ ἔλεγον πρὸς ἀλλήλους,
      Τίς ἄρα οὗτός ἐστιν
      ὅτι καὶ ὁ ἄνεμος καὶ ἡ θάλασσα ὑπακούει αὐτῷ;

And now in literal English:

And Jesus,   A   **A**
        with his disciples,
        departed to <u>the sea</u>.
    And a great crowd from Galilee followed
        and from Judea
            and from Jerusalem
            and from Idumaea
        and beyond the Jordan
            and around Tyre
            and Sidon.
    A very great crowd,
        hearing what he was doing,
        came to him.
And he told his disciples to have <u>a little boat</u> ready for him   B
        because of the crowd,
        lest they should press upon him,
    For he healed many people
        so that they fell on him
        in order that they might touch him,/ as many as suffered sickness.
    And the unclean spirits,/ whenever they saw him,/ fell before him
        And they cried out, saying, 'You are the Son of God.'
        And much he warned them/ that they should not make him known.
And he went up into a mountain,   B'
        and he called to him whom he wished,
        and they went to him.
    <u>And he appointed twelve</u>
        that they might be with him
        and that he might send them out
            to preach
            and to have authority to cast out demons.
    <u>And he appointed twelve</u>
        and he added a name to Simon,
        'Peter',
      and James son of Zebedee
        and John the brother of James,
        and he added names to them,
            Boanerges,
            which is 'Sons of Thunder',
      and Andrew, and Philip, and Bartholomew,
        and Matthew, and Thomas, and James
            son of Alphaeus,
        and Thaddeus, and Simon, the Canaan,
            and Judas Iscariot
            who indeed betrayed him.

And he comes into a house,   a   A   **B**
       and the crowd comes together again,
       so that they were not able even to eat bread.
    And hearing,
       his relatives set out to seize him,
       for they were saying, 'He is out of his mind!'
   And scribes,/ coming down from Jerusalem,/ were saying,
       'He is possessed by Beelzebul,
        and by the ruler of demons he expels demons.'
And calling them to him,   b
         in parables
         he began to speak to them,
      'How is Satan able to cast out Satan?
         And if a kingdom is divided against itself, that kingdom cannot stand.
         And if a house is divided against itself, that house cannot stand.
      And if Satan stood up against himself and was divided,
          he is unable to stand,
           but has an end.
       But no one is able,
          entering the house of a strong man,
          to plunder his goods,
       Unless he first binds the strong man
          and then he plunders his house.
    Truly, I tell you:
      all will be forgiven the sons of men,
         the sins and the blasphemies,
         whatever things they blaspheme;
      but whoever blasphemes against the Holy Spirit
         he has no forgiveness in this age,
         but is in danger of eternal sin.'
    Because they said,
      'An unclean spirit
      he has.'
And they come, his mother and his brothers.   b'
      And standing outside,
         they sent for him,
         calling him.
      And a crowd sat around him,
          and they say to him,
          'Behold,
        your mother and your brothers
        outside they are looking for you.'
    And answering them,
      he says,
      'Who is my mother and my brothers?
    And looking round at the ones round him, / sitting in a circle, / he says,
      'Behold,/ my mother/ and my brothers.
       For whoever does the will of God,
         this is my brother/ and sister/ and mother.'

And *without hesitation*,   a   B
        he began to teach
        <u>by the sea</u>.
     And a huge crowd is gathered to him,
       so that he/ got into <u>a boat</u> to sit/ in the sea,
       and all the crowd were towards the sea on the land.
     And he taught them/ in parables/ many things.
   And he began to say to them,   b
         in his teaching,
     'Hear!
     Behold,
        a sower went out
        to sow.
     And it came to pass in the sowing
        some fell by the way
        and came the birds and devoured it.
      and other fell on rocky ground,
         where it had not much earth,
       and immediately it sprouted up,
         because it had no depth of earth,
       and when the sun rose
          it was scorched,
        and because it had no root
         it withered,
      and other fell among thorns,
        and the thorns came up and choked it,
        and it gave <u>no fruit</u>.
     And others fell into good earth,
       and gave <u>fruit</u>,/ coming up/ and growing,
       and bore thirty,/sixty/ and an hundredfold.'
   And he said,   b'
     'He who <u>has ears to hear</u>,
     <u>let him hear</u>!'

And when he was alone,   a   B'
            asked him,/ the ones around him,/ with the twelve,
            about the parables.
And he said to them,
         'To you the mystery has been given of the kingdom of God,
         but to those,/ the ones outside,/ all things are in parables.
That seeing,/ they may see/ and not perceive,
        and hearing,/ they may hear/ and not understand
        lest they should turn/ and it should be forgiven them.'
And he says to them,   b
        'Do you not know this parable?
        How then will you know all the parables?
The one sowing, sows the word
           and these are the ones by the way,
               where the word is sown
           and when they hear
               immediately Satan comes
               and he takes the word sown in them.
And these are the ones sown in rocky ground,
           who when they hear the word
               immediately they receive it with joy,
           and they do not have root in themselves
               but are short-lived,
                   when affliction or persecution comes
                   on account of the word,
               immediately they are offended.
And others are the ones sown among thorns,
           these are the ones hearing the word,
           and the cares of the age
               and the deceitfulness of riches
               and the desires about other things,
             coming in,
             choke the word
               and it becomes <u>fruitless</u>.
And those are the ones sown in good earth,
           who hear the word and welcome it
           and <u>bear fruit</u> in thirty,/ and in sixty/ and in a hundredfold.'
And he said to them,   b'
        'Comes the lamp
           that it may be placed under the tub,
           or under a couch?
Not that it may be placed on the lampstand?
        For there is nothing hidden,
           except that it may be known.
        Nor became covered,
           but that it may come into the open.
If anyone <u>has ears to hear,</u>
           <u>let him hear</u>!'

<u>And he said</u> to them,   a   **A**   **B'**
      'Take heed what you hear.
      With what measure you measure,
           it will be measured for you,
           and it will be added to you.
      For he who has,
           it will be given to him
      but to he who has not,
           even what he has will be taken from him.'
   <u>And he said</u>,   b
      'Thus is <u>the kingdom of God</u>:
as a man might throw seed on the earth
      and might sleep and rise,
           night and day,
           and the seed sprouts and lengthens as he knows not,
      of its own accord,
           the earth bears fruit,
           first the grass, then an ear, then full corn in the ear;
but when the fruit forms,
      immediately he sends for the sickle
      because the harvest has come.'
   <u>And he said</u>,   b'
      'How may we liken <u>the kingdom of God</u>?
      Or by what parable may we place it?
As a grain of mustard seed,
      which,
           when it is sown
           in the earth
      is smaller
           than all the seeds
           of the earth.
And when it is sown,
      it comes up
           and becomes greater than all the herbs,
           and makes great branches,
      so that are able
           in the shade of it
           the birds of heaven to dwell.

And with many such parables   a   B
      he spoke to them the word,
      as they were able to hear,
     and without a parable he did not speak to them,   b
     but privately to his own disciples he explained all things.   b'

And he says to them,   a   B'
              on that day,
           evening having come,
           'Let us cross to the other side.'
       And leaving the crowd,
          they take him
          as he was <u>in the boat</u>,
       And other <u>boats</u> were with him.
And a great storm of <u>wind</u> occurs,   b
          and the waves struck into the boat,
          so that now the boat filled.
       And he was in the stern,
            on a cushion,
            sleeping.
         And they waken him,
           and they say to him,
        'Teacher,
           doesn't it matter to you
           that we are perishing?'
      And being awakened,
         he rebuked the wind,
         and he said to the sea,
           'Be still,
           be muzzled.'
And the <u>wind</u> dropped,   b'
         and there was a great calm.
      And he said to them,
         'Why are you fearful?
         How have you no faith?'
      And they feared a great fear,
           and they began to say to each other,
         'Who then is this?
         That even the winds and the waves obey him?'

Day Six: 5.1-20:

The Day begins: *Καὶ ἦλθον εἰς τὸ πέραν τῆς θαλάσσης εἰς τὴν χώραν τῶν Γερασηνῶν...* The point has been made above that Day Five (3.7-4.41) ends with the story of a crossing of the sea; it is a crossing which begins in the evening (4.35,36). Four crossings of the sea, in all, are reported by Mark, and there is reason to see them all as night-crossings which separate the telling of the Day on which the crossing begins from the Day on which the crossing ends, with an arrival in a new place. Bultmann's acknowledgement that "the spatial link (in many of his examples beginning with *εἰς*) is a temporal one"[222] is supportive of the argument. We examine this feature of the night-time sea-crossing because it is an important indicator Mark uses to help his reader/listeners understand that new Days in his telling begin with new locations and new activities after sunrise.

The first sea-crossing of the Gospel begins on Day Five, at 4.35,36 ("When evening had come"). A storm arises and to the amazement of the disciples travelling with him Jesus stills the storm. The sea-journey is concluded with the words "And they came to the other side of the sea into the country of the Gerasenes", at 5.1 which is the beginning of Day Six of Mark's telling and, therefore, the beginning of a new report. And Day Five's report is concluded with the completing of the story of the stilling of the storm. A 'space' exists, we note, between the ending of Day Five and the beginning of Day Six. But it is not incumbent on Mark to fill the void with a Pepysian "and so to bed"[223] kind of comment. Night-time equates with sleep-time, and that may be perfectly understood without any reference to sleep, though in Day Five's closing account of the stormy crossing we are told, of course, that Jesus *was* "sleeping on a pillow".

The second sea-crossing begins on Day Six, at 5.18 ("And as he embarked into the boat..."). It ends at 5.21 ("And when Jesus had crossed over in the boat again to the other side a great crowd..."). Two primary questions need to be put as there is no reference (as there is in the first example of a sea-crossing) to the time of embarkation. Was it a night-time crossing? And was the crossing's completion, therefore, coincident with the beginning of a new Day's telling? Estimates of the timings and the times taken by the events of the proposed Day Six (5.1-20) and/or estimates or information of the timings of the events of the proposed Day Seven (5.21-43) are required.

The events of the proposed Day Six begin with a meeting of Jesus and the man who Mark says called himself "Legion" (there is no mention of it being night-time and the story's events are continuous and suggest that they all occur in daylight). Due to the time-taking episodes, whereby the pig-herders witness the drowning of the two thousand or so pigs, and flee to report "*in the city and in the fields*", and the ones to whom they report come out to Jesus and then beg him to go, it may be judged that Jesus' return crossing began late that day. The events of the proposed Day Seven begin with Jesus and an assembled crowd by the sea. Jesus is there long enough for Jairus to learn where he is and to come to him to beg Jesus to go with him to his home to heal his dying daughter. A land-journey ensues, during which Jesus is delayed (by a woman who takes her healing from him), by which time messengers come with news of Jairus' daughter's death, after which Jesus resumes his land-journey, arrives at the house and gives her back her life. The events of 5.21-43, it may be judged, are themselves sufficient for one Day's telling in Mark's scheme. (It also begins to look like another ABB' presentation.)

Additionally, in estimating the possible time lapse between the proposed Days Six and Seven, and given their designations in terms of their chapter and verse, there is the evidence of a sequence of disclosures of 4.35-41 (at least), 5.1-20 and 5.21-43 which is "one of those

[222]Bultmann, *The History...*, p.340.
[223]Samuel Pepys, *Diary*, 6 May, 1660, *et passim*.

groups of three of which Mark is so fond" (according to Nineham: see Day Five's examination). We note too that the two other night crossings, of Days Nine and Thirteen, the case for which will be put below, both end the second Day's tellings (underlined) of threesomes of Days in Mark's scheme (the sub-Series are Days Eight, Nine and Ten, and Days Twelve, Thirteen and Fourteen). The proposed night-crossing, beginning (late in the Day) at 5.18 and ending (near the sunrise of the new Day) at 5.21, would play the same role in the telling of Days Five, Six and Seven.

The weight of evidence would seem to suggest that Mark did intend this return crossing as a foil between Days Six and Seven as defined by 5.1-20 and 5.21-43.

The third sea-crossing (of the disciples alone) begins on Day Nine (6.30-52), at 6.45, before sunset: Jesus tells his disciples to embark into the boat and to go ahead of him to the other side, to Bethsaida. "And when evening came the boat was in the middle of the sea and he (Jesus) was alone on land" (6.47). The disciples were having trouble with their rowing because the wind was against them. "About the fourth watch of the night" Jesus goes to them "walking on the sea..." (6.48). As he reached them and got into the boat, the wind ceased (6.51). The sea-journey ends on Day Ten (6.53-7.23), at 6.53, "And crossing over onto land they came to Gennesaret and anchored. And as they came out of the boat immediately..." (because it was daylight, we can deduce) people brought to him their sick. This third example of a sea-crossing makes it perfectly clear that a crossing (a maximum eight miles across and sixteen miles from top to bottom) could take all night[224].

The fourth sea-crossing begins on Day Thirteen (8.1-21), at 8.13, "...embarking, he went away to the other side". The sea-journey concludes on Day Fourteen (8.22-26), at 8.22, "And they 'come' to Bethsaida. And they 'bring'...". In this story of a sea-crossing, no time of embarkation is stated in the telling. How are we to estimate it? We may compare Days Nine and Thirteen for some help in the matter, and also examine a detail of the Day itself.

We consider firstly the parallel contents (pertinent to this issue) of the Days (as proposed) in which these stories of the third and fourth sea-crossings occur. Day Nine (6.30-52) reports the feeding of the five thousand: it records a short sea-journey (not a crossing, in 6.32) to a "solitary place" (which we can assume is just down the coast-line) and records a night-time crossing which was supposed to be to Bethsaida. Day 13 (8.1-21) reports the feeding of the four thousand: it records a short sea-journey (not a crossing, 8.10) down the coast to Dalmanutha and records a crossing to Bethsaida. Mark is setting these two tellings of Days in parallel: it is logical to conclude that he intended the crossing of Day Thirteen to behave as for Day Nine, as a Day-separating indicator. We may now see if there is any support for this in the examination of a particular detail of Day Thirteen.

In 8.2, it is reported that the crowd had been with Jesus three "days" and had had nothing to eat. According to rhetorical analysis, the introduction to the telling of the Day's events is 8.1-3: it is the A part of Mark's ABB' construction with which he forms the first half of his whole presentation. It begins reading literally: "In those days there being again a great crowd, and not having anything they might eat, calling to him the disciples he says to them, 'I have compassion on the crowd, because now *three days* they remain with me, and they have nothing they might eat...'" The question arises as to the timing of Jesus' calling his disciples to him. The most likely explanation is that the crowd has been with Jesus all of the day (here reported) and that prior to it they have been with him two days. He, therefore, calls his disciples to him *late on* in the Day being reported. Again we might compare this Day's telling with that of Day Nine. The feeding of the five thousand takes place "late" (6.35) in the Day (when people regularly ate their main meal of the day). The feeding of the four thousand (of Day Thir-

---

[224]Whether rowing or sailing, reasonably short stretches of water, because of wind and storm in the first case and because of a lack of wind in the second, can be perceived to be very long indeed. (I have had the worrying experience of both.)

teen) can be similarly timed, as late in the day, and the timing of Jesus' meeting with the Pharisees would, therefore, have been later, and the crossing later still.

We assess that four times in his gospel narrative, Mark uses the night-crossing of the sea as an important indicator to his audience that new Days in his telling begin with new locations and new activities after (meaning: 'immediately after', 'sometime after', or 'anytime after') sunrise. This exercise establishes the limits of a number of Days in Mark's telling and establishes also the principle that Mark uses new geographical locations to signal his beginning of new Days. We can continue now with our analysis of Day Six (5.1-20).

The Day's story is without exception viewed by commentators as a unity, but over the years attitudes have varied as to how much Mark's hand is evident in the presentation we have here. Bultmann[225] points out that the narrative has the form characteristic of the miracle-story which he suggests is in its original form, save transitional phrases in v.1 and the redactional verse 8. Because of the "unevenness of the narrative", its vivid and emphatic details, and because v.8 "appears to reflect the Evangelist's embarrassment in coping with an excess of material", Taylor explains that the passage was not yet reduced to the rounded form of miracle-stories and was, therefore, a clear piece of oral tradition which is Petrine in origin[226]. Nineham particularly sees its connection with the previous day's story of "the stilling of the storm": the question is posed, he says, "Who then is this that such immense power is at his disposal?" but of its present form, he says, "It has clearly passed through a number of stages" of development[227]. In relation to this, he devotes space to the problem of the setting, "the country of Gerasene", which is thirty miles from the lake shore. Commentators over the years have remarked on Mark's poor geographical knowledge. It is proper to point out, however, in this context, that Mark makes nothing of the fact that this is predominently Gentile country, neither that the man who is healed is a Gentile, nor that those who were attending the pigs were Gentiles, nor those also who then came out to Jesus. No argument from silence is satisfactory, but in contrast, in Day Eleven (7.24-30), a turning point Day in his second Series of seven Days, Mark spells it out loudly and clearly that Jesus is ministering in Tyre, to "a Greek, a Syrophoenician by race" (7.25) and through her to her daughter. It would seem that in presenting Day Six in the way that he does, Mark intends his readers and listeners to see the possibility at least of God's intention for the New Covenant, which appears to have had its launching, on Day Five, with the appointment of 'the twelve' (from an impressive 'seven' geographical areas), to be open to Gentiles in the future, even though they appear to be rejecting Jesus here on this day.

Hooker describes this day's story as one which contains "an embarrassing amount of detail"[228] and as a "narrative that does not run smoothly". She says that vv.3-5 are "somewhat obtrusive", that v.6 "seems strange" after v.2b, that v.8 is "clumsy", and that we have two proofs of the demoniac's cure, in vv.11-13 and v.15[229]. These are evidences to her of the stages of development the story has gone through, for to her it is possible that two accounts are combined by Mark (5.1-2, 7-8 and 15; and vv.2-6 and 9ff.). According to others[230] it is a combination of a miracle-story and a popular tale about an unknown exorcist who tricked some demons into self-destruction. For the duplicating of v.2 by v.6 she describes one possibility, that Mark "has forgotten what he wrote there"!

The structure of 5.1-20 to Taylor is expressed as an arrangement of scenes, four in all: vv.1-10 the man; vv.11-13 the swine; vv.14-17 the townspeople and vv.18-20 back to the man by the lakeside. To Taylor, it is a four-act drama "and yet we do not receive the impres-

---

[225]R. Bultmann, *The History*..., p.224.
[226]Taylor, *The Gospel*..., pp.22f.: few commentators today would feel able to write like this.
[227]Nineham, *Saint Mark*, p.152.
[228]Perhaps suggested to her by Taylor's comments recorded above.
[229]Hooker, *The Gospel*..., p.141.
[230]Hooker, *The Gospel*..., p.142.

sion of imaginative artistic creation"[231]. But the story's analysis presented below demonstrates well the Markan style, a,b,b': it is a story again told in three parts: Part **A**, 5.1-8, is introductory; Part **B**, vv.9-13 is the first development; and Part **B'**, 5.14-20, is the second and completing development. All but two of the openings to the main pieces begin with *καὶ*. Those that do not are 5.8 and v.11: 5.8 is an editorial clarification, "For he was saying to him..."; and v.11 begins, *Ἦν δὲ ἐκεῖ*, "Now there were there, on the mountains, a herd of pigs..." At 5.15, we discover another of Mark's favourite historical presents. Mark again demonstrates that he is in control of his writing and presentational method. There is no need to look for two stories behind his presentation. It is one drama and clarity is the result.

What for some time I thought was a six-part chiasm at 5.3-5, turns out to be just another example of Mark's abb' presentational approach which works at various literary levels simultaneously. It disappoints me a little to say this! I had been thinking about the "embarrassing amount of detail" that Hooker speaks about and believed that I had spied the first chiasm of the Gospel; I surmised that legion's problems were given the chiastic treatment for maximum effect. The man's problems were severe indeed: the form of their presentation was to strengthens further the 'impossibility' of Jesus being able to do anything for him. Chiasm is a Greco-Roman rhetorical device[232] and both Fay and Dewey have thought they have seen it in Mark's Gospel. But see below. My proposal was as follows, for 5.3-5:

a   *ὃς τὴν κατοίκησιν εἶχεν ἐν τοῖς μνήμασιν·*

b   *καὶ οὐδὲ ἁλύσει οὐκέτι οὐδεὶς ἐδύνατο αὐτὸν δῆσαι,*

c   *διὰ τὸ αὐτὸν πολλάκις πέδαις καὶ ἁλύσεσιν δεδέσθαι*

c'   *καὶ διεσπάσθαι ὑπ' αὐτοῦ τὰς ἁλύσεις καὶ τὰς πέδας συντετρῖφθαι,*

b'   *καὶ οὐδεὶς ἴσχυεν αὐτὸν δαμάσαι·*

a'   *καὶ διὰ παντὸς νυκτὸς καὶ ἡμέρας ἐν τοῖς μνήμασιν*
        καὶ ἐν τοῖς ὄρεσιν ἦν κράζων καὶ κατακόπτων ἑαυτὸν λίθοις.

But now compare the larger piece in literal English:

And as he came out of the boat,		(a)	a	B
immediately,	.a	(b)		
met him out of the tombs,	.b			
a man with an unclean spirit,	.b			
who the dwelling had		(b')		
among the tombs.				
And no one anymore was able to bind him with a chain,			b	
because he had often been bound with fetters and chains				
and the chains were burst by him				
and the fetters were broken.				
and no one was able to subdue him.				
And always by night and by day			b'	
among the tombs				
and in the mountains				
he was crying out				
and he was cutting himself with stones.				

It is as I say above. The 'parsing' of this piece into its parts shows that it is not a chiasm of any kind, yet 'extravagant' the piece is – in its detail of the man's disorder. Both reader and

---

[231]Taylor, *The Gospel...*, p.277.
[232]Consider, for Markan composition: Joanna Dewey, and Benoit Standaert, *L'Évangile...*; and for pre-Markan: Rudolf Pesch *op.cit.* and Paul J. Achtemeier, *Toward the Isolation...*, pp.265-291 and *The Origin...* pp.198-221; see above, under Day Four, for a fuller discussion.

audience in the first century would likely recognise the change of rhythm.[233] The first chiasm just might be spied in the story with which the Final Series begins, in 11.1-11. We'll have to see. But here we note that the description of the 'incurable' woman with the "issue of blood" (5.25) in the next Day's telling, that of Day Seven, is similarly deliberately full in detail, and non-chiastic. In Day Six, Jesus works such amazing power against the forces of evil, that Nineham is right that it raises again the question posed by Jesus' stilling of the storm in Day Five, "Who then is this that such immense power is at his disposal?" In Day Seven, Mark tells us that Jesus can heal the incurably sick, but more than that, Jesus has the power even to raise the dead!

The literary structure of Day Six may be characterised as an ABB' construction in its shorter form, and an ABB'/ABB'/ABB' construction in its longer form. The literary structure of Day Six is viewed as follows:

```
Καὶ ἦλθον                                                        A      A
      εἰς τὸ πέραν τῆς θαλάσσης
      εἰς τὴν χώραν τῶν Γερασηνῶν. 2
Καὶ ἐξελθόντος αὐτοῦ ἐκ τοῦ πλοίου                               B
            εὐθὺς
                        ὑπήντησεν αὐτῷ
                        ἐκ τῶν μνημείων
                  ἄνθρωπος
                        ἐν πνεύματι ἀκαθάρτῳ, 3
            ὃς τὴν κατοίκησιν εἶχεν
                  ἐν τοῖς μνήμασιν·
      καὶ οὐδὲ ἀλύσει οὐκέτι οὐδεὶς ἐδύνατο αὐτὸν δῆσαι, 4
            διὰ τὸ αὐτὸν πολλάκις πέδαις καὶ ἀλύσεσιν δεδέσθαι
            καὶ διεσπάσθαι ὑπ᾽ αὐτοῦ τὰς ἀλύσεις
            καὶ τὰς πέδας συντετρῖφθαι,
      καὶ οὐδεὶς ἴσχυεν αὐτὸν δαμάσαι·5
      καὶ διὰ παντὸς νυκτὸς καὶ ἡμέρας
                  ἐν τοῖς μνήμασιν
                  καὶ ἐν τοῖς ὄρεσιν
            ἦν κράζων
            καὶ κατακόπτων ἑαυτὸν λίθοις.
Καὶ ἰδὼν τὸν Ἰησοῦν ἀπὸ μακρόθεν                                B'
      ἔδραμεν
      καὶ προσεκύνησεν αὐτῷ, 7
      καὶ κράξας φωνῇ μεγάλῃ
            λέγει,
            Τί ἐμοὶ καὶ σοί, Ἰησοῦ
                  υἱὲ τοῦ θεοῦ τοῦ ὑψίστου;
            ὁρκίζω σε τὸν θεόν,
                  μή με βασανίσῃς. 8
      ἔλεγεν γὰρ αὐτῷ,
            Ἔξελθε τὸ πνεῦμα τὸ ἀκάθαρτον
            ἐκ τοῦ ἀνθρώπου.
```

---

[233]For a discussion of such matters, refer to the Introduction, to the section "The Cultural and Historical Context of the Gospel", and specifically footnote 42 of Chapter One.

Καὶ ἐπηρώτα αὐτόν,   A   **B**
        Τί ὄνομά σοι;
    καὶ λέγει αὐτῷ,
        Λεγιὼν ὄνομά μοι,
        ὅτι πολλοί ἐσμεν. [10]
    καὶ παρεκάλει αὐτὸν πολλὰ
        ἵνα μὴ αὐτὰ ἀποστείλῃ
        ἔξω τῆς χώρας.

  Ἦν δὲ ἐκεῖ   B
        πρὸς τῷ ὄρει
        ἀγέλη χοίρων μεγάλη βοσκομένη· [12]
    καὶ παρεκάλεσαν αὐτὸν
        λέγοντες,
        Πέμψον ἡμᾶς εἰς τοὺς χοίρους,
        ἵνα εἰς αὐτοὺς εἰσέλθωμεν. [13]
    καὶ ἐπέτρεψεν αὐτοῖς.
Καὶ ἐξελθόντα   B'
        τὰ πνεύματα τὰ ἀκάθαρτα
        εἰσῆλθον εἰς τοὺς χοίρους,
    καὶ ὥρμησεν ἡ ἀγέλη κατὰ τοῦ κρημνοῦ
        εἰς τὴν θάλασσαν,
        ὡς δισχίλιοι,
    καὶ ἐπνίγοντο ἐν τῇ θαλάσσῃ.

Καὶ οἱ βόσκοντες αὐτοὺς ἔφυγον   A   B'
    καὶ ἀπήγγειλαν
      εἰς τὴν πόλιν
       καὶ εἰς τοὺς ἀγρούς·
    καὶ ἦλθον
      ἰδεῖν
       τί ἐστιν τὸ γεγονός. [15]
Καὶ ἔρχονται πρὸς τὸν Ἰησοῦν,   B
    καὶ θεωροῦσιν τὸν δαιμονιζόμενον
      καθήμενον ἱματισμένον καὶ σωφρονοῦντα,
      τὸν ἐσχηκότα τὸν λεγιῶνα,
    καὶ ἐφοβήθησαν. [16]
   καὶ διηγήσαντο αὐτοῖς οἱ ἰδόντες·
    πῶς ἐγένετο τῷ δαιμονιζομένῳ
    καὶ περὶ τῶν χοίρων. [17]
   καὶ ἤρξαντο παρακαλεῖν αὐτὸν
    ἀπελθεῖν
    ἀπὸ τῶν ὁρίων αὐτῶν.
Καὶ ἐμβαίνοντος αὐτοῦ εἰς τὸ πλοῖον   B'
    παρεκάλει αὐτὸν ὁ δαιμονισθεὶς
    ἵνα μετ' αὐτοῦ ᾖ. [19]
   καὶ οὐκ ἀφῆκεν αὐτόν,
    ἀλλὰ λέγει αὐτῷ,
   Ὕπαγε εἰς τὸν οἶκόν σου πρὸς τοὺς σούς,
   καὶ ἀπάγγειλον αὐτοῖς
    ὅσα ὁ κύριός σοι πεποίηκεν
    καὶ ἠλέησέν σε. [20]
  καὶ ἀπῆλθεν
   καὶ ἤρξατο κηρύσσειν
    ἐν τῇ Δεκαπόλει
    ὅσα ἐποίησεν αὐτῷ ὁ Ἰησοῦς,
  καὶ πάντες ἐθαύμαζον.

And in literal English:

And they came   A   A
       to the other side of the sea,
       to the region of the Gerasenes.
   And as he came out of the boat,   B
        immediately
           met him out of the tombs,
           a man with an unclean spirit,
        who the dwelling had
           among the tombs.
  And no one anymore was able to bind him with a chain,
        because he had often been bound with fetters and chains
           and the chains were burst by him
           and the fetters were broken.
        and no one was able to subdue him.
  And always by night and by day
         among the tombs
         and in the mountains
       he was crying out
       and he was cutting himself with stones.
  And seeing Jesus from afar   B'
       he ran
       and he worshipped him.
  And crying out in a loud voice,
        he says,
         'What to me, and to you, Jesus,
           Son of the most high God?
        I plead with you by God,
           that you may not torment me!'
  For he was saying to him,
        'Come out unclean spirit,
       from the man!'

And he questioned him,
       'What is your name?'
  And he says to him,
      'Legion is my name,
       because we are many.'
  And he begged him much
      that he would not send them
      outside the country.
Now there was there
      on the mountains
      a great herd of pigs feeding.
  And they begged him,
       saying,
     'Send us into the pigs,
      that we may enter them.'
  And he allowed them.
And coming out
      the unclean spirits entered
      into the pigs.
  And rushed the herd over the precipice
      into the sea,
      about two thousand.
  And they drowned in the sea.

A   **B**

B

B'

And the ones feeding them fled.   A   **B'**
        And they reported
            in the town
            and in the fields.
        And they came
            to see
            what had happened.
   And they come to Jesus.   B
        And they see the demoniac,
            sitting,/ clothed,/ and in his right mind,
            the man who had had the legion.
        And they were afraid.
     And the ones seeing related to them
        what had happened to the demoniac
        and about the pigs.
     And they began to beg him
        to go away
        from their region.
And as he embarked into the boat,   **B'**
        the demoniac begged him
        to let him be with him.
     And he did not permit him,/ but he said to him,
        'Go/ to your home,/ to your people.
          And report to them
             what the Lord has done for you,
            and that he pitied you.'
     And he went away.
        And he began to spread the news
            in the Decapolis,
            what Jesus had done for him.
        And all marvelled.

Day Seven: 5.21-43:

This third Day of this threesome of Days, Days Five, Six and Seven, begins after Jesus has completed his return night-crossing of the sea[234]; it has a similar setting to that of the first of the three days, Day Five. In all three of these Days, the stories begin by the sea, though in the second of these it is on the opposite side of the sea.

Day Eight begins at 6.1f.: *Καὶ ἐξῆλθεν ἐκεῖθεν, καὶ ἔρχεται εἰς τὴν πατρίδα αὐτοῦ, καὶ ἀκολουθοῦσιν αὐτῷ οἱ μαθηταὶ αὐτοῦ. καὶ γενομένου σαββάτου ἤρξατο διδάσκειν ἐν τῇ συναγωγῇ·* All the underlined words have significance in one way or another, in Mark's constructional method, for establishing a new Day's telling[235]. Further, the action of 5.21-43 is uninterrupted by a night. The telling of Day Seven, therefore, ends at 5.43.

5.21-43 is viewed as a unity by all our four commentators, but as we noted in Day Six, they vary in their understanding as to how much of the story's parts and details were connected before Mark came to handle them. Taylor agrees with Bultmann on the classification of this narrative as a miracle-story[236] but totally rejects any suggestion that it is a community-product. Taylor treats this story in the same way as he treated the preceding story of the demoniac, "It is not rounded by repetition but a record based on personal testimony." In this way only, he says, "can we account for its distinctive characteristics: the vivid portraiture of Jairus and his agonized cry for aid, the incident of the woman on the way to his house, the sceptical attitude towards Jesus of the messengers, his refusal to be dissuaded, the picture of the mourners, the saying, 'The child is not dead but sleeps', the mockery thereby provoked, the command in Aramaic addressed to the girl, the compassionate regard for her welfare shown by Jesus."[237] To Taylor, compared with the parallel stories in the Gospels of Matthew and Luke, Mark's account impresses "with its greater originality".

Clearly, however, we have two stories here, the raising of Jairus' daughter and the healing of the woman with the issue of blood. Taylor sees their connection as historical and not merely literary. Schmidt holds also to the view that "the interweaving is due to historical recollection"[238]. With Taylor, we might acknowledge that a story may be told to fill an interval, such as with 6.14-29, but his point that an intercalation of narratives is not a feature of Mark's method is suspect. Hooker would seem to differ from him; see under Day Five for her view on 3.20-35 and, though my sub-dividing differs from hers, I would identify there also Mark's grafting of two stories together. In the case of 5.21-43, Nineham sees 5.25-34 as "more probably a Markan insertion", an insertion with a style "distinctly different in the Greek from that of the rest of the passage."[239] But he does not say in what way it is "distinctly different". To me, I see ni difference in style. We may conjecture: what is "distinctly different" is the specific wording of the woman's medical problem, and not the construction which again clearly follows Mark's ABB' form.

Hooker too takes Nineham's position that 5.25-34 is a Markan insertion, but for reasons that the life Jesus restored to the 'twelve-year-old' girl is paralleled in his restoration of the woman who had suffered 'twelve' years.[240] She further notes that the stories are linked by issues of "faith" and that much of the vocabulary would be appropriate to the resurrection

---

[234]See under the examination of Day Six for the evidence that this is a night-crossing.

[235]Mark's use of historical presents has been discussed under Day Two; his use of *καὶ γενομένου σαββάτου* is a clear instance of his defining a new Day; his use of *εἰς* in his introductory passages is highlighted under Day Six as an accessory to the spatial link which expresses a temporal development; and his use of *Καὶ ἐξῆλθεν* and *ἐκεῖθεν* will be discussed under Days Eight and Fifteen.

[236]Bultmann, *The History...*, pp.228-230; Taylor, *The Gospel...*, pp.285f.

[237]Taylor, *The Gospel...*, p.285.

[238]Schmidt, *Der Rahmen...*, p.148.

[239]Nineham, *Saint Mark*, p.157.

[240]Hooker, *The Gospel...*, p.147.

hope of the Christian community: consider v.23 "save" and "live"; v.39 (the contrast between death and sleep); v.41 "get up" (cf. 2.9 and 3.3) and v.42 (the mockery of the bystanders). Richardson[241] comments on v.40, "they laughed at him", as the way in which the world often laughs at Christian hopes of resurrection. That there are correspondences between the last Day of the first Series and the last Day (16.1-8) of the fourth and final Series of Mark's Gospel, the only resurrection accounts in the gospel, is a discussion to which we will come as we take these studies of Mark's Days and interpret Mark's Gospel matrix.

Lohmeyer[242] viewed the story of the raising of Jairus' daughter as consisting of four stages: vv.21-24, by the lakeside; vv.35-37 on the road; vv.38-40 in the court of the house and vv.41-43 in the maiden's chamber. I would agree with his major sub-divisions of the story, on literary-structural grounds, but the arrangement by Mark of the whole of Day Seven is fundamentally another composite of his ABB' tightly-organised rhetorical style. The first, introductory (and observably shorter) Part **A**, 5.21-24 is followed by the first development, Part **B**, vv.25-34 and the second and completing development, Part **B'**, vv.35-43. The Parts, 5.21-24 and 5.35-43, can hardly be described as an "envelope structure" to 5.25-34, or 5.25-34 as an 'insertion'.[243] The signifier of the ABB' form is found in the introductory section and at 5.24: it reads, "And he went away with him / and a great *crowd* followed him / and they *pressed upon* him." Both the second and the third Parts are well introduced by the first, and there are the verbal links too, as italicised, between 5.24 and 5.31. In regard to the way the text divides up, we may note again the use of $\kappa\alpha i$ linked with the historical present and, in particular, Mark's favourites[244] at v.22 ($\kappa\alpha i$ $\check{\epsilon}\rho\chi\epsilon\tau\alpha\iota$) and v.38 ($\kappa\alpha i$ $\check{\epsilon}\rho\chi o\nu\tau\alpha\iota$): both are in the same Ba position, in the first and last Parts. In the same Ba position in the second section is another of Mark's favourite signifiers of a new 'paragraph', $\kappa\alpha i$ $\epsilon\dot{\upsilon}\theta\dot{\upsilon}\varsigma$.[245] And as we observed on page 64, there is also the signifier of a non-$\kappa\alpha i$ sentence beginning Part **B'** at 5.35.

Parts two and three report amazing changes of state for both the woman and Jairus' young daughter. We observe the detail that the woman has been suffering twelve years, $\delta\dot{\omega}\delta\epsilon\kappa\alpha$ $\check{\epsilon}\tau\eta$ (5.25), and the girl's age, $\mathring{\eta}\nu$ $\gamma\grave{\alpha}\rho$ $\dot{\epsilon}\tau\tilde{\omega}\nu$ $\delta\dot{\omega}\delta\epsilon\kappa\alpha$ (5.42). The two parts are, therefore, further bonded together as B and B' parts in any ABB' scheme. And we note for the first time in the Gospel a potential interest of Mark in the significance of numbers[246]. 'Twelve' is a number traditionally associated with the elective purposes of God and, therefore, with Israel[247] (for the obvious link, consider the twelve tribes in O.T. use). We recall Mark's report of Jesus' appointment of 'twelve' disciples (3.14, 16) in Day Five, the first of this sub-Series of Days. We dare to interpret Mark's references in these contexts to 'twelve': a new Israel is being established and echoes of Old Israel redound to it. A New Covenant is in preparation.

The literary structure of Day Seven is presented in full:

---

[241]A. Richardson, *The Miracle Stories of the Gospels*, SCM, London 1941.

[242]E. Lohmeyer, *Das Evangelium des Markus*, Meyer K., 11th ed., Vandenhoeck & Ruprecht, Gottingen, 1951, Orig. 1937, p.104.

[243]See Nineham, *Saint Mark*, p.157; and Hooker, *The Gospel...*, p.147.

[244]See under Day Two above.

[245]See under Day Four above.

[246]In the reports of Days Nine and Thirteen, on the feedings of the five-thousand and the four-thousand respectively, especially because of 8.19-21, listeners are as challenged as the disciples to understand the significances of "5", "5,000" and "12", and also "7", "4,000" and "7". This will be discussed as we examine Days Nine and Thirteen, and as we review the form of Series Two at the end of chapter Four. We will return to the subject of Mark's possible numerological interest and the possible meanings of "deep" structures in chapter Eight as we resume the discussion of Mark's literary intentions which were introduced in chapter One.

[247]From "Numbers" in *NIDNTT* and *IntDB*.

Καὶ διαπεράσαντος τοῦ Ἰησοῦ   A   **A**
          ἐν τῷ πλοίῳ
              πάλιν εἰς τὸ πέραν
      συνήχθη ὄχλος πολὺς ἐπ᾽ αὐτόν,
      καὶ ἦν παρὰ τὴν θάλασσαν. [22]
Καὶ ἔρχεται   B
          εἷς τῶν ἀρχισυναγώγων,
          ὀνόματι Ἰάϊρος,
      καὶ ἰδὼν αὐτὸν
          πίπτει πρὸς τοὺς πόδας αὐτοῦ [23]
          καὶ παρακαλεῖ αὐτὸν πολλὰ
             λέγων
      ὅτι Τὸ θυγάτριόν μου ἐσχάτως ἔχει,
      ἵνα ἐλθὼν
              ἐπιθῇς τὰς χεῖρας αὐτῇ
      ἵνα σωθῇ
          καὶ ζήσῃ. [24]
Καὶ ἀπῆλθεν μετ᾽ αὐτοῦ.   B᾽
      καὶ ἠκολούθει αὐτῷ ὄχλος πολύς,
      καὶ συνέθλιβον αὐτόν. [25]

Καὶ γυνὴ   A   **B**
          οὖσα ἐν ῥύσει αἵματος
          δώδεκα ἔτη[26]
   καὶ πολλὰ παθοῦσα
          ὑπὸ πολλῶν ἰατρῶν
   καὶ δαπανήσασα τὰ παρ᾽ αὐτῆς πάντα
          καὶ μηδὲν ὠφεληθεῖσα
          ἀλλὰ μᾶλλον εἰς τὸ χεῖρον ἐλθοῦσα,[27]
  ἀκούσασα περὶ τοῦ Ἰησοῦ,
     ἐλθοῦσα ἐν τῷ ὄχλῳ ὄπισθεν
     ἥψατο τοῦ ἱματίου αὐτοῦ·[28]
  ἔλεγεν γὰρ
     ὅτι Ἐὰν ἅψωμαι κἂν τῶν ἱματίων αὐτοῦ
     σωθήσομαι.
Καὶ εὐθὺς ἐξηράνθη ἡ πηγὴ τοῦ αἵματος αὐτῆς,   B
     καὶ ἔγνω τῷ σώματι
     ὅτι ἴαται ἀπὸ τῆς μάστιγος.
  καὶ εὐθὺς
     ὁ Ἰησοῦς
          ἐπιγνοὺς ἐν ἑαυτῷ
          τὴν ἐξ αὐτοῦ δύναμιν ἐξελθοῦσαν
     ἐπιστραφεὶς ἐν τῷ ὄχλῳ
          ἔλεγεν,
          Τίς μου ἥψατο τῶν ἱματίων;
  καὶ ἔλεγον αὐτῷ οἱ μαθηταὶ αὐτοῦ,
     Βλέπεις τὸν ὄχλον συνθλίβοντά σε,
     καὶ λέγεις,
          Τίς μου ἥψατο.
Καὶ περιεβλέπετο   B᾽
     ἰδεῖν τὴν τοῦτο ποιήσασαν.[33]
  ἡ δὲ γυνὴ
          φοβηθεῖσα καὶ τρέμουσα,
          εἰδυῖα ὃ γέγονεν αὐτῇ,
     ἦλθεν καὶ προσέπεσεν αὐτῷ
     καὶ εἶπεν αὐτῷ πᾶσαν τὴν ἀλήθειαν.[34]
  ὁ δὲ εἶπεν αὐτῇ,
     Θυγάτηρ,
          ἡ πίστις σου σέσωκέν σε·
     ὕπαγε εἰς εἰρήνην,
          καὶ ἴσθι ὑγιὴς ἀπὸ τῆς μάστιγός σου.

Ἔτι αὐτοῦ λαλοῦντος   A   **B'**
        ἔρχονται ἀπὸ τοῦ ἀρχισυναγώγου
        λέγοντες
    ὅτί Η θυγάτηρ σου ἀπέθανεν·
  τί ἔτι σκύλλεις τὸν διδάσκαλον;
ὁ δὲ Ἰησοῦς
       παρακούσας τὸν λόγον λαλούμενον
       λέγει τῷ ἀρχισυναγώγῳ,
   Μὴ φοβοῦ,
   μόνον πίστευε.
 και οὐκ ἀφῆκεν
    οὐδένα μετ᾽ αὐτοῦ
    συνακολουθῆσαι
  εἰ μὴ τὸν Πέτρον καὶ Ἰάκωβον
  καὶ Ἰωάννην
  τὸν ἀδελφὸν Ἰακώβου. [38]
καὶ ἔρχονται εἰς τὸν οἶκον τοῦ ἀρχισυναγώγου,   B
  και θεωρεῖ θόρυβον
  και κλαίοντας καὶ ἀλαλάζοντας πολλά, [39]
 και εἰσελθὼν
   λέγει αὐτοῖς,
  Τί θορυβεῖσθε καὶ κλαίετε;
 το παιδίον οὐκ ἀπέθανεν
  ἀλλὰ καθεύδει. [40]
 και κατεγέλων αὐτοῦ.
αὐτὸς δὲ   B'
       ἐκβαλὼν πάντας
       παραλαμβάνει τὸν πατέρα τοῦ παιδίου
         καὶ τὴν μητέρα
         καὶ τοὺς μετ᾽ αὐτοῦ,
    και εἰσπορεύεται
      ὅπου ἦν τὸ παιδίον· [41]
    και κρατήσας τῆς χειρὸς τοῦ παιδίου
      λέγει αὐτῇ,
    Ταλιθα κουμ,
      ὅ ἐστιν μεθερμηνευόμενον
    Τὸ κοράσιον, σοί λέγω, ἔγειρε. [42]
 και εὐθὺς ἀνέστη τὸ κοράσιον
  και περιεπάτει,
  ἦν γὰρ ἐτῶν δώδεκα.
 και ἐξέστησαν εὐθὺς
    ἐκστάσει μεγάλῃ. [43]
  και διεστείλατο αὐτοῖς πολλὰ
    ἵνα μηδεὶς γνοῖ τοῦτο,
  και εἶπεν
    δοθῆναι αὐτῇ
    φαγεῖν.

And in literal English:

And when Jesus had crossed over,   A   A
             in the boat,
             again to the other side,
        a great crowd was assembled to him,
        and he was by the sea.
And there comes   B
           one of the synagogue chiefs,
           by name, Jairus.
And seeing him,
           he falls at his feet,
           and begs him much,
              saying,
'My daughter is at the point of death,
           coming,
               lay your hands on her
           that she may be healed
             and live.'
And he went away with him.   B'
        And a great crowd followed him.
        And they pressed upon him.

Now a woman   A   **B**

          having a flow of blood
          twelve years
     and suffering many things
          by many doctors
     and having spent all she had
          and profiting nothing,
          but rather becoming worse,
  hearing about Jesus,
     coming up in the crowd from behind,
     she touched his garment,
  for she said,
     'If I may touch even his garments,
     I will be healed.'
And immediately her fountain of blood was dried up,   B
     and she knew in her body
     that she was cured of the condition.
  And immediately,
    Jesus,
         knowing in himself
         the power going out from him,
     turning on the crowd,
      he began to say,
       'Who touched my garments?'
  And his disciples said to him,
     'You see the crowd pressing upon you
     and you say,
       "Who touched me"?'
And he looked round   B'
     to see the one
     who had done this.
  And the woman,
        fearing and trembling,
        knowing what had happened to her,
     came and fell before him,
     and she told him all the truth.
  And he said to her,
     'Daughter,
        your faith has healed you,
     go in peace,
        and be whole from your condition.'

And while he was still speaking,   **A**   **B'**
> they come from the house of the synagogue chief,
> saying,
>> 'Your daughter has died.
>> Why trouble the teacher anymore?'

But Jesus,
> overhearing the word being spoken,
> says to the synagogue chief,
>> 'Do not fear.
>> Only believe!'

And he did not allow
> anyone with him
>> to accompany him,
> except Peter and James
>> and John,
>>> the brother of James.

And they come into the house of the synagogue chief,   **B**
> and he witnesses an uproar,
> and much weeping and crying aloud.

And entering,
> he says to them,
>> 'Why do you make an uproar and weep?
> The child did not die,
> but sleeps.'

And they ridiculed him.

But he,   **B'**
> putting them all out,
> takes the father of the child,
>> and the mother,
>> and the ones with him.

And he goes into where the child was.
And taking hold of the hand of the child,
> he says to her,
>> 'Talitha coum',
>>> which is,
>>> being interpreted,
>> 'Girl, to you I say, "Get up!"'

And immediately the girl got up,
> and she walked,
> for she was twelve years old.

And they were astonished/ (immediately) / with a great astonishment.
> And he ordered them much / that no-one should know this.
> And he said,
>> 'Give her
>> to eat.'

A Summary of the First Seven Days:

The literary-structural features of this first Series of the Gospel of Mark are summarised in tabular form, following a synopsis here of what Mark has been telling us.

The first threesome of "days" (Days One, Two and Three, 1.21-2.22) which Mark presents tells where and how Jesus first became known and where and how his fame spread. Capernaum and neighbouring towns in Galilee were the places Jesus missioned. It was his teaching (in the synagogues, Simon's house and by the lakeshore) and expelling of demons and healing of all manner of sick folk which led to people talking about him and an ever-increasing number of people gathering to him. No-one was unreachable by his ministry: the "unclean", sinners and tax collectors feature prominently in the actual stories of his missioning. And Mark demonstrates so early in his Gospel that such a ministry leads to a clash (a charge of 'blasphemy' and other challenges) between Jesus, whose ministry is "new", and others, whose "old" positions are being challenged (so expressed at its climax, in 'parables', and attached to a an enigmatic saying about "the time when the bridegroom will be taken..", which will be a "day" of fasting).

The second threesome of "days" (Days Five, Six and Seven, 3.7-5.43) tells firstly how all "old Israel" gathers to Jesus and how Jesus lays down the foundations for a "new Israel" (by appointing the twelve). In the course of these days, he exhibits immense power and authority, stilling a raging storm, subduing evil in the form of a 'legion' of spirits, healing a woman with a 'twelve- year' bleeding-problem, and (at its climax) raising a dead 'twelve year old' girl. With parables, 3.20-35 and 4.1-32, Jesus teaches what his actions demonstrate, the coming complete defeat of the kingdom of Satan and the establishment of the kingdom of God on earth. In his mission, Jesus is reaching out to all, but in no way will all have their place in God's kingdom.

The two three-day series have their rich common seams and their many points of contact. They are arranged around the central, singular and individualistic Day Four which is different from all the other days of this Series, and which in its conclusion and at its climax alludes to the opposition to Jesus (of Pharisees and Herodians) which will ultimately result in his death. In the first messianic-type reference of its kind in the gospel narrative, Jesus himself likens his presence and practice to that of King David. In literary-structural terms, this Day Four has a central, pivotal, or fulcrum role between the sub-Series/threesomes of Days.

The short title I suggest for this, Mark's first Series of seven Days is, "Jesus' First Days of Mission, Confined to Galilee and the Region of its Sea."

For the sake of clarity, we rehearse the points made in this chapter concerning the number of days Mark judged his first stage of Jesus' mission to have covered. In his presentations of only seven Days he has made it plain that there were many more days than these for the telling. His first three Days' reports (in sub-Series, and the first, a Sabbath) summarise activity which extended over possibly many weeks (see pages 50 and 63). Further, the Sabbath of Day Four is presented as though it is in succession with the previous Day's telling, but it could have been up to six days later. Mark's telling of the beginning of Day Five's report links it to Day Four as consecutive. The second sub-Series, his balancing three Days' reports, are presented as three days runnning consecutively. (Mark's method in his Day-presentations is to give notice, only in his introductory pieces, of other days which he otherwise does not report.) The first Series of seven Days, in the way that Mark tells it, may be judged, therefore, to cover many weeks.

In addition, we consider the role of the "Sabbath" in Mark's scheme. Beyond direct mention of the two Sabbaths in this Series, there is a hint only that Jesus did preach on other Sabbaths. That two Sabbaths are reported, one being the first day and the second being at the turning point of the Series, suggests that the "Sabbath" was important to Mark. We may judge their significance in this Series: the first with demonstrating that Jesus' mission was firstly to the Jews; and the second which was a most suitable backdrop to a demonstration of conflict over the law. The second Series, on its first day, begins also with a Sabbath (see pages 151,194). Though these mentions of the Sabbath have their importance in Mark's thematic presentation, they have no importance structurally-speaking beyond these Series' opening days and the middle day of the first Series. Though Mark presents 'seven Day' Series it is not the case that we should interpret them as 'weeks', with each containing a single Sabbath. Rather, his use of 'seven' for a format may be interpreted to express "completion"[248], the completion of a 'stage' in the mission of Jesus. In each Series, as we have seen above for the first Series, Mark demonstrates that he covers more than seven days. He chooses simply to report a stage in Jesus' mission by telling the activities of seven days only, as if he were taking them from a diary. The construct is clearly artificial.

The structure of Mark's first Series of seven Days, may now be summarised. Overall, I interpet it to be an ABA' form, where A represents the first threesome of Days and A' represents the second threesome of Days, around a middle, pivotal Day, designated B. It is a three-part chiasm, but which, in terms of the seven Days it comprises, can be expressed by:

$$A(ABB') - B - A'(ABB').$$

A qualification is called for, however. In analysing the middle three Days of the Series, it was observed that their presentations each included $K\alpha i \ \pi \acute{\alpha} \lambda \iota \nu$ in similar literary-structural positions, 'pulling' parts together in a significant way. The issue of 'conflict' also appeared to see these three days as working together. Additionally, we might consider that these three days similarly report activities of Jesus' disciples (compare 2.16,18-20; 2.23; 3.9,14-19, 4.10-23, 33-41). Further, we can observe some balance of material between Days Three and Five for parables, untitled as such in Three, but present nevertheless (towards its end, 2.19-22). It may be seen also that in the tellings of Days Two and Six, Jesus ministers to male individuals in each (one is 'unclean', the other has 'an unclean spirit'). And in Days One and Seven, Jesus ministers to individual women; he also raises two from their beds. Given these kinds of observations, the seven day Series could look more like a *seven*-part chiasm.

Several points need to be made. Whilst there may be some evidence of an *inclusio* between Days One and Seven, this may be interpreted only in this way, that the seven Day presentations make a Series. That is, the series could still be chiastic in terms of three parts (three days, one day, three days), or seven parts (the seven Days: 1, 2, 3, C, 3', 2', 1'). In the very same way, the similarities between the second and sixth Days do not help determine the choice, because they still lie symmetrically opposite each other as the middle days of the three-day sub-Series A(A<u>BB</u>') - **B** - A'(A<u>BB</u>'). To these arguments, we need to introduce other observations: that individuals with 'unclean spirits' appear not only in Days Two and Six, but also in Days One and Five; and that Day One includes much more than Jesus ministering to a woman (Simon's mother-in-law). Most importantly, Days One and Five have been shown to relate firmly to each other. Further, at the beginning of Day Five there is an emphatically clear new stage in the presentation. And for content and theme development, we have seen how Days One to Three connect, and how Days Five to Seven connect as linear, three-day sub-series, each with their own *inclusio* of geographical location, in the first, Capernaum, and in the second, a similar shore of the Sea of Galilee (due to a crossing and a return crossing).

The structural scheme of this Series of seven Days *is* indeed best described by ABA'. And given the above considerations, it is properly stated that the ending of A (Day Three) and

---

[248]'Seven' is a sacred number in many of the world's religions, and as it stands for 'fulfilment' or 'completion' in Hebrew usage (*IntDB*, Vol.3, 1961, Twelfth reprinting, p.564), we, who have not been encouraged in the modern Western world to think in these terms, do have to consider seriously this likely reason for Mark's choice of it for his rhetorical plan.

the beginning of A' (Day Five) both connect with the turning point B (Day Four) in their structural forms and some of their content. It is a characteristic of ancient rhetoric that one part "should not only lie adjacent to the next, but be related to it and overlap it at the edges" (Lucian[249]). Further, the Series' three-part chiasm well reflects in the first part 'the complication', the second the 'turning point', and the third the 'dénouement' of Greek tragedy (Aristotle[250]). In the first three-day sub-series is the material which sets out the events that will lead inevitably to tragedy (Jesus' mission against evil and sickness leads not only to his rising popularity, but also to a charge of 'blasphemy' and challenges over other issues); at the centre is the turning point when something of the significance of what is taking place is grasped (at its climax, Pharisees and Herodians plot to kill Jesus); and in the last three-day sub-series is a working out of the tragedy (which in this opening series is a prefiguring of the Gospel's final series; it shows that Jesus is effective in dealing with contrary powers, all evil, sickness and even death).

A Tabular Summary of the literary-structure of the First Seven Days:

	1	2	3	4	5	6	7
DAYS: number identified							
chapters and verses	1.21-38	1.39-45	2.1-22	2.23-3.6	3.7-4.41	5.1-20	5.21-43
SERIES' STRUCTURE	A		B		A'		
DAYS: in literary-terms, in series□	A	B	B'		A	B	B'
DAYS' sections	A B B'	A	A B B'	A	A B B'	A B B'	A B B'
DAYS' sectional sub-divisions	A B B' A B B' A B B'	A B B'	A B B' A B B' A B B'	A B B'	A B B' A B B' A B B'	A B B' A B B' A B B'	A B B' A B B' A B B'
DAYS' number of verses	18	7	22	12	70	20	23
SUB-SERIES' number of verses	47				113		
SERIES' number of verses	172						

---

[249]Lucian, *De conscribenda...*; see my page 47 for a brief discussion of this and particularly, the anastrophe.
[250]Aristotle, *Poetics...*; see my page 19.

In summary then, we have identified a Series of seven Days which comprises a three-day series, a middle day and turning point, and another three-day series. We are given reports of seven Days, but they tell (in their opening pieces) that this stage in Jesus' mission covered many weeks. We have titled this stage, "Jesus' First Days of Mission, Confined to Galilee and the Region of its Sea". Superficially, the text gives us the impression that Mark has provided for us a distillation of the main features of the first phase in Jesus' mission, as if he has chosen particular days to report, as from a diary. Rather, what we discover is the first stage of a tale which is both tragic and wondrous. Its meaning focuses clearly upon Jesus, on who he is and the New Covenant which he will establish.

Addendum to the analysis of 'The First Seven Days':

During the course of this first chapter (of four) on the literary-structural analysis of Mark's Gospel narrative, a number of studies and observations have been made of the signifiers of Mark's structure, and of his rhetorical method in organising his contents. Some of these studies were initiated in the Introduction, others were introduced in Chapter Two. They are foundational to the analysis of the three remaining Series, and they are listed here in summary:

Under Day One:	1)	Mark's understanding of the Hebrew/Palestinian day (see also Introduction: An Interest in "Days");
	2)	Mark's definition of "Day" which he uses for the purpose of his presentation: the civil day beginning with sunrise (see also Introduction: An Interest in "Days" and note 60);
	3)	$\pi\rho\omega\dot{\iota}$ and other times of day;
Under Day Two:	4)	Temporal links;
	5)	Geographical links which behave temporally;
	6)	Historical Presents;
Under Day Three:	7)	$Ka\dot{\iota}\ \pi\acute{a}\lambda\iota\nu$,
Under Day Four:	8)	$Ka\dot{\iota}$ and parataxis;
	9)	non-$\kappa a\dot{\iota}$ sentences;
	10)	$Ka\dot{\iota}\ \epsilon\dot{\upsilon}\theta\dot{\upsilon}\varsigma$,
	11)	Chiasm: an alternative to it, part I (see also Introduction: The Cultural and Historical Context... and Chapter Two: The Days beginning the Gospel);
Under Day Five:	12)	Three-step progressions and formal structure;
	13)	Sandwich construction: an alternative to it, part I (see also Introduction: an Interest in "Days");
	14)	Chiasm: an alternative to it, part II;
	15)	Numbers of verses and the versatility of ABB' to accommodate varying numbers of lines (3 to 243?);
Under Day Six:	16)	"Night-crossings of the sea of Galilee": new Days begin with new locations and new activities after sunrise;
Under Day Seven:	17)	Sandwich construction: an alternative to it, part I;
	18)	Mark's numerological interest.

What is clear from the analyses of Mark's Prologue and First Series, and what is worth stating here, is that the sizes of Mark's rhetorical units, whether sub-Series of Days, Days, Day-sections, parts, sub-parts, and so on, vary according to the amount of content he wishes to include for each. Consider the Days themselves, from the tabular summary: they vary by a factor of ten (the longest is seventy verses; the shortest is seven verses). It is the general case that Mark's process of composition at every level is not governed by a need to balance his presentations by numbers of verses, lines of text, or numbers of words. What does matter to him (and in ancient rhetoric) is that these constructions, whether ABA', or ABB', or abb' or (a)(b)(b'), etc. are in themselves completed.

Chapter Four
The Second Series of Seven Days (6.1-8.26):

Day Eight: 6.1-29:

The Day begins with a three-part opening:

> A   a   *Καὶ ἐξῆλθεν ἐκεῖθεν,*
>   b   *καὶ ἔρχεται εἰς τὴν πατρίδα αὐτοῦ,*
>   b'   *καὶ ἀκολουθοῦσιν αὐτῷ οἱ μαθηταὶ αὐτοῦ.*

The first line of Mark's opening construction is introductory; the second line is the first development; and the third is the second and completing development. The plan exhibits his usual method of presentation.

For the first time in the Gospel, however, we encounter Mark's use of *ἐκεῖθεν.* in all, he uses the word six times; significantly three are found in this Day's telling at 6.1,10 and 11; and of the other three, two are to be found, as at 6.1, introducing new Days, at 7.24 and 10.1. The other use is at 9.30 and will be discussed under Day Sixteen. *Καὶ ἐξῆλθεν* (and variants, in the aorist), *ἔρχεται* (and variants, all in the historical present) and *εἰς*[251] are found principally at important turning points in the Markan text, but never before in such close combination as we find here[252]. To these Mark now adds *ἐκεῖθεν* to signify strongly a new beginning.[253] But that is not all there is to the matter.

To the commonly-used historical present at the beginning of a b line, Mark has added another at the beginning of line b', *ἀκολουθοῦσιν.* These two 'developing' lines of Mark's introductory piece represent classically Markan story-telling. Further, when these two lines, b and b', are read with the first line of the following Part B, that is, *καὶ γενομένου σαββάτου*, we observe what can only be a deliberate repeat on Mark's part of parechesis, the ou sound which we identified richly in the Title and at the beginning of the Prologue. The word *ἀκολουθοῦσιν* twice also repeats the sound, and this word is first used in 1.18 of the Prologue (though it is also found in the intervening material at 2.14 *bis*, 2.15, 3.7, and 5.24). We observe also the poetic nature of the first line, *Καὶ ἐξῆλθεν ἐκεῖθεν.* These observations serve to show two things: that Mark was writing his Gospel for the purpose of it being read aloud; and that he was using rhetorical conventions available to him to indicate his rhetorical

---

[251]Bultmann, *The History...*, p.339, identifies all four words (and others) as significant in Mark's 'editing of traditional material': but because of the pervasive evidence of Mark's rhetorical style in all the units themselves, they may rather be viewed as significant within his work of composition as a whole.

[252]*ἐξῆλθεν* 2.13, 6.34,54, 7.31, 8.27, 9.30, 16.8; and *ἔρχεται* 1.40, 2.3, 3.20,31, 5.15,22,38, 8.22, 10.1,46, 11.15,27, 12.18, 14.32,37: see under Day Two, for further discussion on *ἔρχομαι*, and under Days Six and Eleven for *εἰς.* See also note 112 in chapter three.

[253]Nineham, *Saint Mark*, p.165: on v.1, he says, "The connecting formula is vague and no doubt purely conventional." We reflect on his terminology. In one sense, we are identifying a "disconnecting" formula in v.1: that is, that which is presented from 6.1 has its separation from 5.43 and what precedes it. As a "connecting" formula, it is not "vague" for it well forms a link between what has preceded it and what now takes place in a new setting and circumstance. If it is that the connecting formula is "purely" conventional then we note the fact in no derisory way, as Nineham does, but with some satisfaction at discerning Mark's method.

plan to his audience[254]. This additional identification of the use by Mark of parechesis and the poetic here establish beyond any doubt that at 6.1 a new Series begins.

Again this is not all there is to the matter. Significant correspondences exist between this first Day of Mark's second Series and the Prologue. In 6.1, *καὶ ἔρχεται εἰς τὴν πα-τρίδα αὐτοῦ*, has its earlier counterpart in the Prologue, in 1.9 and 14. The content on the telling of how John the Baptist died, in 6.14-29, clearly has its connection too with the Prologue, in 1.14. And the 'calling to repentance', not mentioned anywhere else in the Gospel, except of John in 1.4, and of Jesus in 1.15 is what the disciples now do too, in 6.12. Further, significant verbal correspondences exist between this first Day of Mark's second Series and the first Day of his first Series: in 6.2, 1.21 *σαββάτου, διδάσκειν, συναγωγῇ*, in 6.2, 1.22 *ἐξεπλήσσοντο*, in 6.7, 1.22 *ἐξουσίαν*, in 6.7, 1.23,27 *τῶν πνευμάτων τῶν ἀκαθάρτων*, in 6.13, 1.34 *καὶ δαιμόνια πολλὰ ἐξέβαλλον*, and in 6.13, 1.34 *καὶ ἐθεράπευον*. And they all follow in exactly the same order.

Given these features, it can be argued that Mark established this new beginning in his Gospel narrative in parallel to his beginning of the Gospel itself, in the Prologue, and to the beginning of the narrative, in his Day One. It might be argued also that he fashioned this his eighth Day out of material which he had been considering using in his Prologue and his first Day's telling. The Prologue might have included the report that "John the Baptist was beheaded by Herod", and the first Day's telling might have reported that Jesus was "not easily recognised for who he really was in his home town". But we may surmise that he could do neither of these things. He could not have started his Gospel with two negative accounts; rather, he saved these matters for the first Day's telling of his second Series.

Clearly, two fundamental propositions are being raised: 1) that this Day's telling begins a new Series; and 2) that as it begins with a brilliantly fashioned Markan opening its telling will be sectionalised in ways that we have discerned already. We, therefore, consider the contributions of our earlier selected commentators, Taylor for his 'old' literary-critical approach, Nineham for his form-critical sensitive approach, Schweizer for his redaction-critical approach, and Hooker for her more recent overview of all approaches:

	Gospel Section:	6.1-29 sub-divisions:			Gospel section:	
		I		II	III	
Taylor:	3.7-6.13	6.1-6a		6b-13 }{	14-29	6.14-8.26
Nineham:	1.14-8.26	6.1-6a		6b-13	14-29	1.14-8.26
Schweizer:	3.7-6.6a	6.1-6a	}{	6b-13	14-29	6.6b-8.26
Hooker:	3.7-6.6a	6.1-6a	}{	6b-13	14-29	6.6b-8.26
and compare:	(1.21-5.43) }{	6.1-6a		6b-14a	14b-29	6.1-8.26

They are tabulated along with my own which is based on rhetorical/literary-structural analysis.

For Nineham no sectional break appears, but for Taylor there is one and it is between 6.13 and 14. For Schweizer and Hooker a sectional break is discernable between 6.6a and 6b. Our different methodologies lead us to the same view, nevertheless, that 8.26 ends the section[255]. In terms of the verses which the units comprise, the four commentators all agree with

---

[254]For the general use of ancient rhetorical conventions, see Tolbert, *Sowing the Gospel...*, p.41, and Kennedy, *New Testament Interpretation...*, p.10.

[255]Though Hooker rightly points out (*The Gospel...*, p.197) that "some commentators" (we find: Trocmé, *The Formation...*, pp.80, 84, and Best, *Disciples...*, p.2), seeing the similarity between 8.22-26 and 10.46-52 for stories (we note: the only such stories in the Gospel) of the healing of blind people, divide the Gospel at 8.22, judging the healings to form an 'inclusio' to the material about the way of the cross and the meaning of discipleship. We will see below that these two stories, the tellings of Days 14 and 21, conclude the two middle Series of the Gospel.

each other. A number of popular editions of the Bible reflect the same[256]. The JerB stands out, however, with an additional and titled division between v.13 and v.17[257], that is vv.14-16, "Herod and Jesus", and a further untitled division at 6.21, "First miracle of the loaves".[258] It is at vv.14-16 where rhetorical analysis helps. And it will explain my division between vv.14a and 14b.

Taylor reasons that 6.14 begins a new section which he titles "The Ministry beyond Galilee"[259], and that specifically 6.1-6a represents the ending of the period of Jesus' "synagogue preaching".[260] We compare Nineham's titling: for him, the section from 1.14-8.26 is "The Galilean Ministry".[261] The issue of defining geographical place in terms of an overall region is clearly compounded by what appears to be Mark's own lack of geographical understanding[262]. In non-Markan terms, that is, in strictly factual terms, events do take place both in Galilee and outside of Galilee.

All four commentators argue that the division between v.6a and v.6b is justified because v.6a well completes the story of Jesus' rejection in his home town (it is likely that Mark does mean Nazareth). Taylor also rehearses the other argument that v.6b better links Jesus' movement from village to village with the mission on which he sends his disciples (vv.7ff.), than connects Jesus' movement with his rejection at Nazareth (6.1-6a). But what Taylor rejects, Wellhausen[263] and Schmidt[264] support. The position I take is that Mark presents the two passages, 6.2-6a and 6.6b-14a, in the closest possible way, as B and B' Sections, thus demonstrating that the reports of *the beginnings* of *two new activities*, in B' (vv.6b-14a), have their cause in B (vv.2-6a). We will expound this later.

On 6.1-6, Hooker writes, "It can fairly be seen as the climax to the previous section of the gospel, and as a parallel to 3.1-6. Just as 1.14-3.6 ended with the rejection of Jesus by the Pharisees, so 3.7-6.6 ends with the rejection of Jesus by his neighbours...." Schweizer's presentation is similar and may have influenced Hooker.[265] Clearly, they are both reasonably certain, by their methods of analysis, that Mark has organised his material to a plan, and that they have discerned that plan. But Hooker continues, "This new section of the gospel begins (at 6.6b), like the two previous ones, with a summary of Jesus' activity (this time very brief - 6.6b only!), followed by a section dealing with the disciples..." In her case, following the path she has set herself, she finds herself at a place where she feels uncomfortable, for 6.6b is too brief! So she writes, "Once again, however, we must remember that the divisions we are making are artificial and are not necessarily part of Mark's own understanding. *It is possible to arrange the material differently...*"[266]

Up to this point in the presentation, I have sought to show that the Title is 1.1 and the Prologue 1.2-20; that the first full section of the narrative is a Series of Seven Days, 1.21-5.43; and that the Series includes two threesomes of days, 1.21-2.22 and 3.7-5.43, around a central Day, 2.23-3.6. Here I am seeking to demonstrate that 6.1 begins a new Day, with limits of 6.1-29; that here begins a new threesome of Days with limits of 6.1-7.23; and also a

---

[256]AV, NEB, GNB, NIV; the RSV shows 6.1, 6b, 7 and 14.

[257]To achieve this, is a very loose translation of αὐτὸς γὰρ ὁ Ἡρῴδης ἀποστείλας ἐκράτησεν τὸν Ἰωάννην."Now it was this same Herod who had sent to have John arrested...". Vv.17 and 18 both contain γὰρ as the second word; vv.17 and 18 parallel each other; and they complete v.16 and form a three-verse whole.

[258]V.21, in my judgement, completes a larger three-part whole, vv.16-21: vv.16-18 is introductory and vv.19,20 and in turn v.21 complete the 6 verse whole.

[259]Taylor, *The Gospel...,* p.307.

[260]Taylor, *The Gospel...,* p.298.

[261]Nineham, *Saint Mark,* pp.65-220.

[262]See the same problem above, in Day Six (5.1-20).

[263]Wellhausen, J., *Das Evangelium Marci,* Reimer, Berlin, 2nd Ed., 1909, p.42.

[264]Schmidt, *Der Rahmen...,* pp.158-162.

[265]See Schweizer, *The Good News...,* pp.122,123; Hooker, *The Gospel...,* p.154.

[266]Hooker, *The Gospel...,* p.154, my italics.

new Series of Seven Days, 6.1-8.26 (with which 'section', three of our four commentators so nearly agree[267]), which is the first of two middle Series. The discovery of Mark's rhetorical style, ABB', at many levels of literary order, and his determining his plan to "Days" and "Series of Days" has served us well so far. We will continue, given this understanding, to plot divisions and sub-divisions which are not impositions of mine, but are of Mark's own creation. Mark's arrangement, not mine of Mark, is what I am attempting to present. I proceed gingerly to a presentation of what, in my judgement, is the literary-structure of Day Eight, for I know it is provocative.

Literary-structural analysis demonstrates that all the Days' telling are constructed as either simple ABB' or composite ABB'/ABB'/ABB' structures. In simple terms, Part **A**, I propose, is 6.1-6a, Part **B**, vv.6b-14a and Part **B'**, vv.14b-29[268]. Part **A** is introductory: 6.1 tells how Jesus returns to his own country with his disciples (Mark establishes the new geographical setting for the day this way, as usual); 6.2-4, in the first line explains that it is a Sabbath and the location (for this Series, the only time) is in the synagogue where Jesus is rejected, the issue is to do with his identity; and 6.5-6a states the consequence which leads to the next part of the day's story. Part **B** is the first development of the Day's construction: 6.6b-7 tells of a mission initiative on the part of Jesus; in 6.8-11 Jesus begins to give authority to his disciples and their mission instructions; and in 6.12-14a we read what follows from their going out. Part **B'** is the second and completing development od the Day's presentation: 6.14b-15 raises immediately again Part A's opening issue of Jesus' identity (see 6.2-6a); in 6.16-21 we get the first half of the story of John's beneading; and in 6.22-29, after a dramatic pause, we get the second half and the completion of the story (and with it the completion of the Day's contribution to our understanding).

The reason I stand out from the commentators with the division between vv.14a and 14b is due primarily to my discernment of Mark's three-part structures of both vv.12-14a and vv.14b,15. In vv.14b,15, we identify an indisputable abb' construction; the parts begin:

a   *Καὶ ἔλεγον ὅτι*...
b   *ἄλλοι δὲ ἔλεγον ὅτι*...
b'   *ἄλλοι δὲ ἔλεγον ὅτι*...

In vv.12-14a, it is less obvious immediately, but the same construction as found everywhere else is discernible, hence the addition of v.14a to vv.12 and 13:

a   *καὶ ἐξελθόντες*
          ἐκήρυξαν
          ἵνα μετανοῶσιν, [13]
b   *καὶ δαιμόνια πολλὰ ἐξέβαλλον,*
          καὶ ἤλειφον ἐλαίῳ πολλοὺς ἀρρώστους
          καὶ ἐθεράπευον.
b'   *καὶ ἤκουσεν ὁ βασιλεὺς Ἡρῴδης,*
          φανερὸν γὰρ
          ἐγένετο τὸ ὄνομα αὐτοῦ.

In both constructions, the first part, a, is introductory; the second, b, is the first development; and the third, b' is the completing development. The argument of juxtaposition

---

[267]Taylor, Schweizer and Hooker: see the tabular summary above.
[268]See the discussions with which I end the analyses of Day Five, and the First Series: it matters not how the elements of Mark's ABB' scheme weigh with each other in terms of their numbers of verses, but that they weigh with each other in terms of their function, as introductory, of first development and of second.

arises also, because v.14a plays no part structurally in 14b-15. Properly, they may be said to relate contents-wise, but Mark did not mean them to be read without a break between them. And I make an observation: no translation of v.14a, or v.14b, or v.15a I have come across reflects either Mark's structure, or his Greek.

The rhetorical function of v.14a is more than that of completing Part **B**: it is an anastrophe which makes connection with Part **B'**. And equally the connection itself is not established by 14a alone. The introductory passage of **B'**, vv.14b-15, reports the questioning which results from the success of Jesus' continuing personal mission, and the mission of the disciples, by which Jesus' name is promoted. We note that Jesus was already known in his own native place for his powerful deeds (v.2) performed elsewhere and before his arrival. He was being talked about everywhere: the first Series of Days makes that plain. But contrast Jesus' lack of success in his own country, in 6.1-6a, with the success that is now attributed to him in the much wider area, because of his disciples' mission, 6.6b-14a.

Because the disciples' mission is the cause of Herod's hearing in Jerusalem, Mark links v.14a with vv.12,13 in one of his rhetorical units to show that it is very definitely the case. The GNB translation of v.14a is: "Now Herod heard about all this, because Jesus' reputation had spread everywhere". I would only replace "Now" with "And", and omit "had" in order to maintain Mark's continuity. And Herod, we note, in terms of the drift of the story presented, could only have heard (v.14a) if these mission activities of the disciples, begun on a Sabbath, had continued over a number of days, and over a wide area, and been talked about first by the general populace. Vv.14b-15 report that "people were saying" who they thought Jesus was; further, a verbal link is provided by προφήτης of v.4 and v.15.

The structural significance of vv.14b,15 is very important for two reasons: 1) It well begins vv.14b-29; and 2) it further anchors this Day the first of a new Series of seven Days.

We take 1) first. On page 65, when we were discussing Mark's 'new section use' of non-καί sentences, we observed that 6.16 so began, after vv.14b,15 (a three part whole). The argument is that, in v.16, the *particular view of Herod* about Jesus' identity is set against, in vv.14b,15, the introductory *views of the people*. With v.16 begins the first of two B parts, B and B'.

In regard to 2), vv.14b,15 has an important doublet in 8.28[269], which in 8.27-9.1 helps establish Day Fifteen as the first of the next Series of seven Days.[270] It is an important, introductory parallel betweeen the two seven-Day Series, 6.1-8.26 and 8.27-10.52, which are the middle two Series of the Gospel. We expose what is common between 6.14b,15 and 8.28:

6.14b,15:
Καὶ ἔλεγον

ὅτι Ἰωάννης ὁ βαπτίζων ἐγήγερται ἐκ νεκρῶν,
καὶ διὰ τοῦτο ἐνεργοῦσιν αἱ δυνάμεις ἐν αὐτῷ.
ἄλλοι δὲ ἔλεγον
ὅτι Ἡλίας ἐστίν·
ἄλλοι δὲ ἔλεγον
ὅτι προφήτης ὡς εἷς τῶν προφητῶν.

---

[269]Our four commentators all observe this doublet, but fail to see any literary-structural significance in it.

[270]On v.15, Schweizer (*The Good News...*, p.132) expresses his opinion, unsupported, that it "originally must have been connected with 8.27f." On vv.14-29, he says, "It is the only story in Mark which is not directly a story about Jesus (most commentators indeed say this) and it is written in a cultured style which shows that it must have been established in written form before Mark." Schweizer displays here no understanding at all of Mark's ability to compose, construct and create both his Gospel to a plan and the pieces he needed to complete it. The text here continues to exhibit Mark's masterful control, and most clearly his abb' rhetorical style. In his handling of tradition, either oral or previously written, he is most certainly re-presenting it himself.

8.28:
οἱ δὲ εἶπαν αὐτῷ
        λέγοντες
        ὅτι Ἰωάννην τὸν βαπτιστήν,
καὶ ἄλλοι,
        Ἠλίαν,
ἄλλοι δὲ
        ὅτι εἷς τῶν προφητῶν.

The corresponding words and annotations (given that 8.28 is set in a different rhetorical context) all follow the same order. We observe what we may call the 'minor difference' of the Greek that qualifies John as "the baptising one" in 6.14 and "the Baptist" in 8.28, for we note that they are both used in Day Eight's telling (see v.24 and v.25).

Mark's creation of 6.1-29 as the presentation of a whole "Day" is not yet addressed. Likewise, the discussion of the division at 6.14b is not yet completed. To do both, we have to return to 6.1-14a and focus on the *key literary feature* here of *verbs in the imperfect tense*.

What none of the selected commentators sees is the important presence of a whole rash of imperfects in 6.1-29, which number sixteen in all. (The next rash, of five, appears in the introductory passage, 6.53-56, of the third Day of this Series.) The three imperfects of vv.14b,15 are clearly continuous[271]. Mostly, the others are inceptive: it is these which are important for establishing 6.1-29 as a single "Day" in Mark's scheme.

Strictly speaking, *only* vv.2-11 tell the happenings of this particular, single, Sabbath day, but I argue below that vv.12-14a, being basically inceptive, have their place too. V.1 is purely introductory, and in typical Markan fashion it simply, in the opening piece, gives details of a journey which has been made, and the characters who have made it. Vv. 2-14a tell about *two* new activities that were *begun* on that day which would continue for a number of days: 1) Jesus' going round "the villages in circuit teaching" in 6.6b; and 2) the disciples' mission in 6.7-14a where: vv.6b-7b introduce both activities; vv.7c-11 record Jesus' mission instructions; and vv.12-14a complete the three-part presentation.

The imperfects require to be understood as continuous action or inceptive (they are nowhere here conative). We will not discuss them all. The first, of real significance in my judgement is in 6.6b: I read, "He began to go round..."[272] It is an activity which begins on that day, and continues beyond it. As in v.7b, καὶ ἤρξατο, "and he began..." ("to send them out..."), so also we read in v.7c, "And he began to give them authority..."[273] In v.13, we might read also, "They began to cast out many demons; and they began to anoint many sick with

---

[271]Max Zerwick & Mary Grosvenor, *A Grammatical Analysis of the Greek New Testament*, Biblical Institute Press, Rome, 1981, p.121 · ἔλεγον. 3rd pl. impers. meaning "people were saying".

[272]Hooker says (*The Gospel...*, p.162) "Mark does not describe what Jesus did while his disciples were absent: the gap until their return has been filled by the story of the Baptist's death." My argument is that Mark did tell us what Jesus was doing, and that the Baptist's death was not simply a lacuna-filler. For reasons stated above, it would seem that Mark chose not to report the Baptist's death in the Prologue, likely because of its negative tones, but created his moment of opportunity here to include it.

[273]Nineham, *Saint Mark*, pp.167, 168: Nineham admits disappointment, "We should have expected this (the sending out of the twelve) to be a decisive stage in the development of the Gospel, but as Wellhausen points out, it is not... We may say, in fact, that this incident... plays no vital part in the structure and development of the Gospel. And in line with that is the extremely sketchy way in which the story is told. Why did Jesus send the twelve at precisely this point, and what did he do while they were away?" He adds puzzlement to disappointment. But, the truth is that Mark does tell us what Jesus was doing while the disciples were away, and Mark does tell us why Jesus sent them out at this point. Attention to Mark's rhetorical style, his literary-structure, and his verbal tenses repays all effort.

oil; and they began to heal."[274] That is, in terms of the Day's report, these activities and even that of v.12, "they preached" (though here an aorist), began on that day and were to continue beyond it. V.14a alone of vv.12-14a, with two verbs in the aorist, might be said to speak of the mission of the disciples as then concluded, but that is not the case as Mark presents its completion only in 6.30 when the disciples return to Jesus. V.14a is Mark's reporting of the ultimate effect of the disciples' mission.

By designing his construction in the way that he has, Mark gives himself the opportunity, in 6.14b-29: 1) to use material which he could not use, either in his Prologue, or in the First Day's telling of the First Series; 2) to use material which would help him establish a succession of closely-related points in his first three-day sub-series (Days Eight to Ten; see the discussion at the close of Day Ten); and 3) to use material which he could duplicate, in part, and parallel, in part, in the opening Day's telling of his next Series (see Day Fifteen's presentation).

Lastly, before the Day's presentation is given in the Greek and literal English, we need to note that many commentators and scholars say that the story about John the Baptist's death is the only story in the Gospel which is not directly a story about Jesus.[275] It is, however, a story which is well attached to the issue of who Jesus is. Consider 6.2-6a and vv.14b-15. And as a story in a succession of stories (as we will see at the conclusion of Day Ten's presentation), Mark does see it, at this point in the Gospel, as prophetic of Jesus' future destiny (see also Day Sixteen, as it follows Day Fifteen which is the parallel day in the following Series). But this Day's telling in total is as much prophetic of the disciples' future mission (16.15,16, 20a; ref. 6.14a, kings will hear about Jesus in the future), and their mission will begin ultimately, after Jesus' death, from his own 'native country'[276] (14.28 and 16.7).

The literary structure of Day Eight is as follows:

---

[274]Neither Fritz Rienecker (*A Linguistic Key to the Greek New Testament: Matthew-Acts*, tr & rev. Cleon L. Rogers, Jr., S. Bagster & Sons, London, 1977) nor Max Zerwick and Mary Grosvenor (*A Grammatical Analysis...*) interpret the imperfects (as either inceptive or continuous action). The presence of the aorist in v.12 may support the interpretation of continuous action, but the presence of $\mathring{\eta}\rho\xi\alpha\tau o$ $\alpha\mathring{v}\tau o\mathring{v}\varsigma$ $\mathring{\alpha}\pi o\sigma\tau\acute{e}\lambda\lambda\epsilon\iota\nu$ and the inceptive of v.7 support the inceptive.

[275]Nineham, *Saint Mark*, pp.167, 168.

[276]Two points: 1) I risk here a reference to verses from the supposed non-Markan 'longer ending', which will be discussed in Chapter 7; and 2) ref. 6.1: $\pi\alpha\tau\rho\acute{\iota}\varsigma$ may be translated 'native town' (Nazareth) or 'native place' (Galilee) (Souter, *A Pocket Lexicon...*).

Καὶ ἐξῆλθεν ἐκεῖθεν,   A   **A**
     καὶ ἔρχεται
        εἰς τὴν πατρίδα αὐτοῦ,
     καὶ ἀκολουθοῦσιν αὐτῷ
        οἱ μαθηταὶ αὐτοῦ. [2]
καὶ γενομένου σαββάτου   B
        ἤρξατο διδάσκειν ἐν τῇ συναγωγῇ·
     καὶ πολλοὶ ἀκούοντες ἐξεπλήσσοντο
        λέγοντες,
       Πόθεν τούτῳ ταῦτα,
        καὶ τίς ἡ σοφία ἡ δοθεῖσα τούτῳ
        καὶ αἱ δυνάμεις τοιαῦται
          διὰ τῶν χειρῶν αὐτοῦ
          γίνωνται; [3]
      οὐχ οὗτός ἐστιν ὁ τέκτων,
        ὁ υἱὸς τῆς Μαρίας
        καὶ ἀδελφὸς Ἰακώβου
          καὶ Ἰωσῆτος καὶ Ἰούδα καὶ Σίμωνος;
       καὶ οὐκ εἰσὶν αἱ ἀδελφαὶ αὐτοῦ
        ὧδε
        πρὸς ἡμᾶς;
     καὶ ἐσκανδαλίζοντο ἐν αὐτῷ.
        καὶ ἔλεγεν αὐτοῖς
        ὁ Ἰησοῦς
       ὅτι Οὐκ ἔστιν προφήτης
        ἄτιμος
       εἰ μὴ ἐν τῇ πατρίδι αὐτοῦ
        καὶ ἐν τοῖς συγγενεῦσιν αὐτοῦ
        καὶ ἐν τῇ οἰκίᾳ αὐτοῦ. [5]
καὶ οὐκ ἐδύνατο ἐκεῖ ποιῆσαι οὐδεμίαν δύναμιν,   B'
     εἰ μὴ ὀλίγοις ἀρρώστοις
        ἐπιθεὶς τὰς χεῖρας
        ἐθεράπευσεν· [6]
     καὶ ἐθαύμαζεν
        διὰ τὴν ἀπιστίαν αὐτῶν.

Καὶ περιῆγεν τὰς κώμας   A **B**
   κύκλῳ
   διδάσκων, [7]
  καὶ προσκαλεῖται τοὺς δώδεκα,
  καὶ ἤρξατο
    αὐτοὺς ἀποστέλλειν
    δύο δύο.
 καὶ ἐδίδου αὐτοῖς ἐξουσίαν τῶν πνευμάτων τῶν ἀκαθάρτων· B
  καὶ παρήγγειλεν αὐτοῖς
   ἵνα μηδὲν αἴρωσιν
    εἰς ὁδὸν
    εἰ μὴ ῥάβδον μόνον,
   μὴ ἄρτον, μὴ πήραν, μὴ εἰς τὴν ζώνην χαλκόν, [9]
    ἀλλὰ ὑποδεδεμένους σανδάλια
    καὶ μὴ ἐνδύσησθε δύο χιτῶνας. [10]
  καὶ ἔλεγεν αὐτοῖς,
   Ὅπου ἐὰν εἰσέλθητε εἰς οἰκίαν,
    ἐκεῖ μένετε
    ἕως ἂν ἐξέλθητε ἐκεῖθεν. [11]
   καὶ ὃς ἂν τόπος μὴ δέξηται ὑμᾶς
    μηδὲ ἀκούσωσιν ὑμῶν,
    ἐκπορευόμενοι ἐκεῖθεν
      ἐκτινάξατε
      τὸν χοῦν
      τὸν ὑποκάτω τῶν ποδῶν ὑμῶν
    εἰς μαρτύριον αὐτοῖς.
 καὶ ἐξελθόντες   B'
   ἐκήρυξαν
   ἵνα μετανοῶσιν, [13]
  καὶ δαιμόνια πολλὰ ἐξέβαλλον,
   καὶ ἤλειφον ἐλαίῳ πολλοὺς ἀρρώστους
   καὶ ἐθεράπευον.
  καὶ ἤκουσεν ὁ βασιλεὺς Ἡρῴδης,
   φανερὸν γὰρ
   ἐγένετο τὸ ὄνομα αὐτοῦ.

Καὶ ἔλεγον   A   **B'**
       ὅτι Ἰωάννης ὁ βαπτίζων ἐγήγερται ἐκ νεκρῶν,
       καὶ διὰ τοῦτο ἐνεργοῦσιν αἱ δυνάμεις ἐν αὐτῷ.
    ἄλλοι δὲ ἔλεγον
       ὅτι Ἡλίας ἐστίν·
    ἄλλοι δὲ ἔλεγον
       ὅτι προφήτης
       ὡς εἷς τῶν προφητῶν.

Ἀκούσας δὲ   B
           ὁ Ἡρῴδης ἔλεγεν,
           Ὃν ἐγὼ ἀπεκεφάλισα
             Ἰωάννην,
                οὗτος ἐκ νεκρῶν ἠγέρθη.
       αὐτὸς γὰρ ὁ Ἡρῴδης ἀποστείλας
                ἐκράτησεν τὸν Ἰωάννην
                καὶ ἔδησεν αὐτὸν ἐν φυλακῇ
            διὰ Ἡρῳδιάδα
               τὴν γυναῖκα Φιλίππου
               τοῦ ἀδελφοῦ αὐτοῦ,
            ὅτι αὐτὴν ἐγάμησεν· [18]
       ἔλεγεν γὰρ ὁ Ἰωάννης τῷ Ἡρῴδῃ
            ὅτι Οὐκ ἔξεστίν σοι
            ἔχειν τὴν γυναῖκα τοῦ ἀδελφοῦ σου. [19]
    ἡ δὲ Ἡρῳδιὰς ἐνεῖχεν αὐτῷ
           καὶ ἤθελεν αὐτὸν ἀποκτεῖναι,
           καὶ οὐκ ἠδύνατο· [20]
       ὁ γὰρ Ἡρῴδης ἐφοβεῖτο τὸν Ἰωάννην,
           εἰδὼς αὐτὸν ἄνδρα δίκαιον καὶ ἅγιον,
           καὶ συνετήρει αὐτόν,
       καὶ ἀκούσας αὐτοῦ
           πολλὰ ἠπόρει,
           καὶ ἡδέως αὐτοῦ ἤκουεν.
   καὶ γενομένης ἡμέρας
          εὐκαίρου
     ὅτε Ἡρῴδης
          τοῖς γενεσίοις αὐτοῦ
          δεῖπνον ἐποίησεν
     τοῖς μεγιστᾶσιν αὐτοῦ
          καὶ τοῖς χιλιάρχοις
          καὶ τοῖς πρώτοις τῆς Γαλιλαίας, [22]

Καὶ εἰσελθούσης   Βʼ

       τῆς θυγατρὸς αὐτοῦ Ἡρῳδιάδος
       καὶ ὀρχησαμένης,
    ἤρεσεν τῷ Ἡρῴδῃ
    καὶ τοῖς συνανακειμένοις.
εἶπεν ὁ βασιλεὺς τῷ κορασίῳ,
    Αἴτησόν με ὃ ἐὰν θέλῃς,
    καὶ δώσω σοι·²³
καὶ ὤμοσεν αὐτῇ,
    Ὅ τι ἐάν με αἰτήσῃς
    δώσω σοι
        ἕως ἡμίσους τῆς βασιλείας μου.
καὶ ἐξελθοῦσα
    εἶπεν τῇ μητρὶ αὐτῆς,
        Τί αἰτήσωμαι;
    ἡ δὲ εἶπεν,
        <u>Τὴν κεφαλὴν Ἰωάννου τοῦ βαπτίζοντος.</u>
καὶ εἰσελθοῦσα εὐθὺς
    μετὰ σπουδῆς
       πρὸς τὸν βασιλέα
    ᾐτήσατο
       λέγουσα,
    Θέλω
       ἵνα ἐξαυτῆς δῷς μοι
          ἐπὶ πίνακι
       <u>τὴν κεφαλὴν Ἰωάννου τοῦ βαπτιστοῦ.</u>
καὶ περίλυπος γενόμενος ὁ βασιλεὺς
    διὰ τοὺς ὅρκους
       καὶ τοὺς ἀνακειμένους
    οὐκ ἠθέλησεν ἀθετῆσαι αὐτήν·²⁷
καὶ εὐθὺς
       ἀποστείλας ὁ βασιλεὺς
       σπεκουλάτορα
    ἐπέταξεν ἐνέγκαι τὴν κεφαλὴν αὐτοῦ.
    καὶ ἀπελθὼν
       ἀπεκεφάλισεν αὐτὸν
       ἐν τῇ φυλακῇ²⁸
καὶ ἤνεγκεν τὴν κεφαλὴν αὐτοῦ ἐπὶ πίνακι
    καὶ ἔδωκεν αὐτὴν τῷ κορασίῳ,
    καὶ τὸ κοράσιον ἔδωκεν αὐτὴν τῇ μητρὶ αὐτῆς. ²⁹
καὶ ἀκούσαντες
       οἱ μαθηταὶ αὐτοῦ ἦλθον
    καὶ ἦραν τὸ πτῶμα αὐτοῦ
    καὶ ἔθηκαν αὐτὸ ἐν μνημείῳ.

And now in literal English:

And he went away from there   **A**   **A**
       and he comes into his own country (*ou*)
       and his disciples follow with him. (*ou*)
    And as the Sabbath came (*ou, ou*)   **B**
           he began to teach in the synagogue
    And many hearing were astounded,
               saying:
        'Where did this man get these things,
           and what is this wisdom given to this man,
           and such powerful works happening through his hands?
       Is not this the carpenter,
             the son of Mary,
          and brother of James
             and Joses and Judas and Simon
         and are not his sisters here with us?'
    And they were offended by him
         and he said to them,
          Jesus,
       'Is not a prophet without honour
      in his own country
         and among his relatives
         and in his house?'
   And he could not do there any powerful work   **B'**
      except on a few sick people,
         laying on his hands,
         he healed them
     and he marvelled
         because of their unbelief.

  And he began to go round the villages   **A**   **B**
         in circuit
         teaching.
    And he calls the twelve to him.
    And he began to send them out two by two.
  And he began to give them authority over unclean spirits   **B**
    And he charged them
       that they should take nothing on the way
          except a staff only
      no bread, no wallet, no copper in their belt,
         but tied-on sandals,
         and not to put on two coats.
    And he began to say to them,
       'Wherever you enter into a house,
         there remain
         until you leave there,
       and whatever place does not receive you,
         nor do they hear you,
         leaving there
            shake off the dust under your feet
            for a testimony against them.'

And going out,

        they preached

        that they should repent.

And they cast out many demons,

        and they anointed with oil many sick,

        and they healed.

And King Herod heard,

        for widely known

        became the name of him.

              B' (top right)

And they were saying,

        'John the Baptist has been raised from the dead,

        and therefore the powerful works operate in him.'

But others were saying,

        'He is Elijah.'

And others were saying,

        'A prophet,

        like one of the prophets.

            A   **B'**

But hearing,

                 Herod said,

              'The one whom I beheaded,

              John,

              this one is raised.'

            B (right)

For Herod himself sending,

          seized John

          and bound him in prison,

        on account of Herodias,

          the wife of Philip,

          his brother,

        because he married her.

For John said to Herod,

        'It is not lawful for you

        to have your brother's wife.'

Herodias, therefore, had a grudge against him

        and wished to kill him,

        but she was not able.

For Herod feared John,

        knowing him a just and holy man,

        and he kept him safe.

And hearing him,

        he was much puzzled,

        but gladly he heard him.

A suitable day came,

        however,

      when Herod,

        for his birthday,

        held a banquet

      for his courtiers

        and the chiliarchs

        and the chief men of Galilee.

Now when entered   B'
      the daughter of Herodias herself
      and danced,
    she pleased Herod
    and those reclining with him.
And the king said to the girl,
    'Ask me whatever you want
    and I will give to you.'
And he swore to her,
    'Whatever you ask
    I will give to you
      up to half
      of my kingdom.'
And going out,
    she said to her mother,
      'What may I ask?'
    And she said,
      'The head of John the Baptist.'
And entering immediately,
    with haste
    to the king,
    she asked,
      saying,
    'I wish
    that at once you give me
      on a dish
    the head of John the Baptist.'
And becoming deeply grieved,
    because of the oaths,
      and those reclining with him,
    he did not wish to reject her.
And immediately,
    sending the king,
    an executioner,
    he gave orders to bring his head
    and going
    he beheaded him
    in the prison.
And he brought his head on a dish.
    And he gave it to the girl.
    And the girl gave it to her mother.
And hearing,
    his disciples came
    and they took his body
    and they placed it in a tomb.

Day Nine: 6.30-52:

The day begins:

> *Καὶ συνάγονται οἱ ἀπόστολοι πρὸς τὸν Ἰησοῦν,*
> *καὶ ἀπήγγειλαν αὐτῷ*
> *πάντα*
> *   ὅσα ἐποίησαν*
> *   καὶ ὅσα ἐδίδαξαν.*

Commentators have noticed what must have been a passing of a number of days between Jesus' sending out his disciples and their return[277]. Consequently, as for 5.25-34 (in Day Seven), they have viewed 6.14-29 as expressive of an interval of time. Day Eight's analysis makes clear, however, that it is not the only reason it is positioned there. In literary-structural and rhetorical terms, given that 6.14-29 is more fully integrated into the presentation than previously discerned, its primary function is re-established: it reflects the issue of Jesus' identity raised in the synagogue scene, 6.2-6a, firstly in vv.14b,15, and then in vv.16ff; and it springs from the mission, in 6.6b-14a, of Jesus' disciples, which enjoys success from the moment it begins. A new Day's telling well begins at 6.30.

   In the introduction to this Day, 6.30-33, in the first part (A, v.30) we read of the return and the reporting of the disciples to Jesus; in the second part (B, v.31) we have Jesus' suggestion that they rest somewhere privately; and in the third part (B', vv.32,33) we read of their going there, by boat, but that they were not going to be alone.

   The main story of the Day, the Feeding of the Five-thousand, is found in vv.34-44. It is a story which has its parallel in the symmetrically-opposite Day Thirteen (8.1-21), the Feeding of the Four-thousand. Again, we can discern the Markan hand of careful planning.[278] The story of the Feeding is presented in three parts: after the short introduction (A, v.34) in which Jesus, coming out of the boat, is met by a large crowd, it is said that he has compassion for the crowd. What follows is a miracle event which expresses his compassion. In the two balancing parts (B, vv.35-38 and B', vv.39-44), v.35 first establishes the lateness of the hour, and in v.36 the disciples establish the need of the crowd to eat (they too will have had need, we interpret, see v.31 of the introduction to the Day).

   The closing, third part of the Day relates an evening/night-time crossing of the lake and the second miracle of the Day, Jesus' walking on the sea. For a discussion on the ending of this day, Day Nine, at 6.52, see Day Six, for with Days Five and Six we have identified already the importance of the "night-crossing" of the Sea of Galilee in Mark's scheme; that is, how it concludes one day, prior to the beginning of a new one. As in the earlier examples, so here too the night-crossing of 6.45-52 brings Days Nine and Ten into juxtaposition. Given that Days Five, Six and Seven are a threesome of days, this fact alone suggests that Days

---

[277]It may, of course, have been weeks if Jesus' "teaching in circuit around the villages" (6.6b) included teaching in synagogues on the sabbaths. On this point, consider I. Sonne, *IntDB*, Vol. 4, "Synagogue", pp.481, 487: "Bigger villages must have had some kind of synagogue"; the synagogue had "the character of an educational institution... reading from the Scriptures and exposition of the Law constituted the focal point in the sabbatical gatherings".

[278]The fact that there are two 'feeding stories' has long intrigued interpreters of the Gospel of Mark. They have been viewed as a 'doublet', two variants of a single story. And for some considerable time now, virtually every interpreter has observed material clusterered around the feeding stories that is also similar in content and form. In chs.6-8, they have been viewed as two parallel cycles of stories. Pre-Markan cycles or catenae have been sought out in chs.6-8, 4-6, and even 4-8. To the approaches, in particular, of Fowler, *Loaves and Fishes...*, and Achtemeier, "Towards the Isolation.." and "The Origin and Function...", (in this literary-structural analysis of Mark's second Series) we bring the additional evidence of the importance of "days" in Mark's scheme, and his ABB' presentational method.

Eight, Nine and Ten may form another threesome. We will be able to discuss this later, after the presentation of the literary-structure and contents of Day Ten.

The limits of Day Nine are relatively easily defined, so too is the overall structure of the Day which may be described, from the above, as a composite ABB' form. Mark's rhetorical style is clearly identified again. His abb' literary-structural principle is demonstrated consistently at the higher levels of literary order, here at ABB' and abb', and again with variations at the lower orders of (a) (b) (b') and (a) (a'), (.a) (.b) (.b') and (.a) (.a'), (..a) (..b) (..b') and (..a) (..a').

We observe two comparatively long parts B and B' in the middle section, that is vv.35-38 and vv.39-44, but they are entirely compatible with what we find in other Day's tellings, with the major parts of the Days' contents[279]. We make another observation: compared with 6.1-29, 6.30-52 has not attracted anything like the interest of commentators and scholars, in its divisions and sub-divisions. This may be explained by the fact that there is little that is controversial here about Mark's presentation, unlike the Day prior to it. It is also the case that there is little attention paid by commentators to the divisions in the text following, and covering a number of the Days which we will be delimiting. One of the reasons for this is that some of these Days are much smaller units than those previousy defined; another reason is that no major divisions, generally speaking, are proposed by commentators up to 8.21.

Below, I present the literary structure of Day Nine. Verbal correspondences, significant historical presents, and Markan sectional introductory formulae are all underlined.

Καὶ συνάγονται οἱ ἀπόστολοι πρὸς τὸν Ἰησοῦν,　　　　　　A　　A
　　　καὶ ἀπήγγειλαν αὐτῷ
　　πάντα
　　　　　　ὅσα ἐποίησαν
　　　　　καὶ ὅσα ἐδίδαξαν. [31]

καὶ λέγει αὐτοῖς,　　　　　　　　　　　　　　　　　　B
　　　Δεῦτε ὑμεῖς αὐτοὶ
　　　　　κατʼ ἰδίαν
　　　　　　εἰς ἔρημον τόπον
　　　καὶ ἀναπαύσασθε ὀλίγον.
　ἦσαν γὰρ οἱ ἐρχόμενοι καὶ οἱ ὑπάγοντες πολλοί,
　καὶ οὐδὲ φαγεῖν εὐκαίρουν.

καὶ ἀπῆλθον ἐν τῷ πλοίῳ　　　　　　　　　　　　B'
　　　　　　εἰς ἔρημον
　　　τόπον
　　　κατʼ ἰδίαν. [33]
　καὶ εἶδον αὐτοὺς ὑπάγοντας
　　　καὶ ἐπέγνωσαν πολλοί,
　καὶ πεζῇ
　　　　　　ἀπὸ πασῶν τῶν πόλεων
　　　　συνέδραμον
　　　　　　ἐκεῖ
　　　καὶ προῆλθον αὐτούς. [34]

---

[279]See note 268 on the lengths of parts in Mark's constructions. See Day Five, in section 4.1-32, the parabolic teachings of Jesus, for an example of longer parts.

Καὶ ἐξελθὼν   A   **B**

        εἶδεν πολὺν ὄχλον,

    καὶ ἐσπλαγχνίσθη ἐπ᾽ αὐτοὺς

      ὅτι ἦσαν ὡς πρόβατα

      μὴ ἔχοντα ποιμένα,

  καὶ ἤρξατο διδάσκειν αὐτοὺς πολλά.

καὶ ἤδη ὥρας πολλῆς γενομένης   B

        προσελθόντες αὐτῷ

        οἱ μαθηταὶ αὐτοῦ ἔλεγον

    ὅτι Ἔρημός ἐστιν ὁ τόπος,

      καὶ ἤδη ὥρα πολλή·[36]

      ἀπόλυσον αὐτούς,

    ἵνα ἀπελθόντες εἰς τοὺς κύκλῳ ἀγροὺς καὶ κώμας

      ἀγοράσωσιν ἑαυτοῖς

      τί φάγωσιν.

  ὁ δὲ ἀποκριθεὶς

      εἶπεν αὐτοῖς,

      Δότε αὐτοῖς ὑμεῖς φαγεῖν.

    καὶ λέγουσιν αὐτῷ,

      Ἀπελθόντες

    ἀγοράσωμεν δηναρίων διακοσίων ἄρτους

      καὶ δώσομεν αὐτοῖς φαγεῖν;

  ὁ δὲ λέγει αὐτοῖς,

      Πόσους ἄρτους ἔχετε;

      ὑπάγετε ἴδετε.

    καὶ γνόντες

      λέγουσιν, Πέντε,

    καὶ δύο ἰχθύας.

καὶ ἐπέταξεν αὐτοῖς ἀνακλῖναι πάντας   B'

      συμπόσια συμπόσια

      ἐπὶ τῷ χλωρῷ χόρτῳ.[40]

    καὶ ἀνέπεσαν

      πρασιαὶ πρασιαὶ

    κατὰ ἑκατὸν

      καὶ κατὰ πεντήκοντα.[41]

καὶ λαβὼν τοὺς πέντε ἄρτους καὶ τοὺς δύο ἰχθύας

      ἀναβλέψας εἰς τὸν οὐρανὸν

    εὐλόγησεν καὶ κατέκλασεν τοὺς ἄρτους

      καὶ ἐδίδου τοῖς μαθηταῖς αὐτοῦ

      ἵνα παρατιθῶσιν αὐτοῖς,

    καὶ τοὺς δύο ἰχθύας | ἐμέρισεν | πᾶσιν.[42]

καὶ ἔφαγον πάντες καὶ ἐχορτάσθησαν·[43]

    καὶ ἦραν κλάσματα

      δώδεκα κοφίνων πληρώματα

      καὶ ἀπὸ τῶν ἰχθύων.[44]

    καὶ ἦσαν

      οἱ φαγόντες

      πεντακισχίλιοι ἄνδρες.

Καὶ εὐθὺς   A   **B'**

        ἠνάγκασεν τοὺς μαθητὰς αὐτοῦ
        ἐμβῆναι εἰς τὸ πλοῖον
    καὶ προάγειν πρὸς Βηθσαϊδάν,
    ἕως αὐτὸς ἀπολύει τὸν ὄχλον. [46]
καὶ ἀποταξάμενος αὐτοῖς
    ἀπῆλθεν εἰς τὸ ὄρος
    προσεύξασθαι.
καὶ ὀψίας γενομένης
    ἦν τὸ πλοῖον ἐν μέσῳ τῆς θαλάσσης,
    καὶ αὐτὸς μόνος ἐπὶ τῆς γῆς. [48]
καὶ ἰδὼν αὐτοὺς   B
    βασανιζομένους ἐν τῷ ἐλαύνειν,
    ἦν γὰρ ὁ ἄνεμος ἐναντίος αὐτοῖς,
περὶ τετάρτην φυλακὴν τῆς νυκτὸς
    ἔρχεται πρὸς αὐτοὺς
        περιπατῶν ἐπὶ τῆς θαλάσσης·
    καὶ ἤθελεν παρελθεῖν αὐτούς. [49]
οἱ δὲ
    ἰδόντες αὐτὸν
    ἐπὶ τῆς θαλάσσης περιπατοῦντα
  ἔδοξαν ὅτι φάντασμά ἐστιν,
  καὶ ἀνέκραξαν· [50]
    πάντες γὰρ αὐτὸν εἶδον
    καὶ ἐταράχθησαν.
ὁ δὲ εὐθὺς ἐλάλησεν μετ᾽ αὐτῶν,   B'
    καὶ λέγει αὐτοῖς,
  Θαρσεῖτε,
    ἐγώ εἰμι·
  μὴ φοβεῖσθε. [51]
καὶ ἀνέβη πρὸς αὐτοὺς
    εἰς τὸ πλοῖον,
    καὶ ἐκόπασεν ὁ ἄνεμος.
καὶ λίαν ἐκ περισσοῦ ἐν ἑαυτοῖς ἐξίσταντο, [52]
    οὐ γὰρ συνῆκαν ἐπὶ τοῖς ἄρτοις,
    ἀλλ᾽ ἦν αὐτῶν ἡ καρδία πεπωρωμένη.

And in literal English:

And assemble the apostles to Jesus   A   **A**
    and they reported to him
    everything
      that they had been doing
      and that they had been teaching.
  And he says to them,   B
      'Come you yourselves
        privately,
        to a desert place
      and rest a little.'
  For there were many coming and going
  and they did not have opportunity to eat.
  And they went away   B'
      in the boat
    to a desert place
    privately.
  And they saw them going
    and many knew.
  And on foot
      from all the cities,
    they ran together
      there,
    and arrived before them.

And going forth   A   **B**
        he saw a great crowd.
And he had compassion on them,
        because they were like sheep,
        not having a shepherd.
And he began to teach them many things.
And now as it was becoming late,   B
            approaching him,
            his disciples began to say,
      'This is a desert place,
          and now the hour is late,
          dismiss them,
      that going away into the fields and villages near by,
          they may buy for themselves
          something to eat.'
But he, answering, said to them,
          'You give them something to eat.'
    And they say to him,
          'Going away,
      may we buy two-hundred denarii of loaves,
          and shall we give them to eat?'
And he says to them,
          'How many loaves have you?
    Go.
         See?'
    And knowing,
        they say, 'Five,
        and two fish.'
And he instructed them to sit everyone down,   B'
          group by group,
          on the green grass.
    And they sat down,
          group by group,
      in hundreds
        and fifties.
And taking the five loaves and the two fishes,
        looking up to heaven,
      he blessed and broke the loaves
         and gave them to the disciples
          that they might set them before them,
      and the two fishes/ he divided/ to all.
And they all ate and were satisfied.
      And they collected the scraps
        twelve full baskets
        and of the fish.
      And were/ the ones eating/ five thousand males.

And immediately   A   **B'**
                 he made his disciples
                 embark in the boat,
           and go ahead/ to Bethsaida,
            while he dismissed the crowd.
      And when he had sent them away,
           he went away into a mountain
           to pray.
      And when it became evening,
           the boat was in the middle of the sea,
           and he was alone on the land.
   And seeing them   B
           distressed with rowing,
           for the wind was against them,
     about the fourth watch of the night,
           he comes towards them,
                walking on the sea,
           and he wished to go by them.
     But they,
               seeing him
               on the sea walking,
           thought that it was a ghost
           and cried out,
               for all saw him
               and were troubled.
  But he immediately spoke with them,   B'
            and he says to them,
          'Take courage,
           it is I.
       Don't be afraid.'
     And he went up to them
           into the boat
           and the wind ceased.
    And very much exceedingly in themselves they were amazed,
          for they did not understand about the loaves,
          but their hearts were hardened.

Day Ten: 6.53-7.23:

The opening three-part piece is 6.53-56. V.53 reports the landing at Gennesaret, not Bethsaida as was the proposed destination of 6.45. Mark gives no direct explanation for this fact, though it may be argued reasonably that he leaves us to judge from his report of the storm the night before that a change was necessitated. Alternatively, because the destination is eventually reached, in 8.22, there are those who want to suggest that Mark has split up an earlier collection of narratives and has inserted 6.53-8.21, and forgotten to amend his geographical reference.[280] Literary-structural analysis, however, challenges this opinion. Everywhere in the text, Mark is demonstrating much control of his material and care in presenting his detailed points. The probability is that there is some kind of deliberate compositional intention expressed here.

This Day Ten, we note, is the third day of this Series' first threesome of days. Day Fourteen, which begins with 8.22, is the third day of this Series' parallel threesome of days. Mark's reference to 'Bethsaida' in both sub-Series is just one detail which connects and, therefore, reinforces the balance between his presentations of Days Eight to Ten and Days Twelve to Fourteen. The thrust of these two sub-Series, 6.1-7.23 and 7.31-8.26, is in similar direction. They both include feeding stories, stories of Sea journeyings, and stories of controversy with Pharisees, in the same order[281]. They also both include accounts of healings, but in different literary settings, and in different forms. And the one noticeable point of real contact between the feeding stories is in 8.19-21, which is where Mark shares a conundrum with his audience. We will return to these issues in the summary of this Series.

The proposal that 6.53-56 is the introductory piece to this Day, a single Day's telling, requires examination. It clearly speaks of activities over several days. As under Day Eight (6.1-29) we considered a glut of imperfects (sixteen), so here also we have the next rash of them (five, in vv.53-56) to consider. The imperfect of part B, vv.54,55, may be interpreted as inceptive and, therefore, as descriptive of activity that "began" (only) to take place. As in Day Eight, so also here $\mathring{\eta}\rho\xi\alpha\nu\tau o$ significantly features and suggests this inceptive interpretation of $\mathring{\eta}\kappa o\upsilon o\nu.$ The four imperfects of part B', v.56, may be interpreted as continuous or repeated action descriptive of the activity that surrounded Jesus, in the general case, "wherever" he went. It is judged, therefore, that 6.53-56 functions as Mark's introduction to his telling of a single day, this Day Ten.

Overall, Day Ten is structured as Day Nine, in an ABB' form (see all the Days so far). As with the lower levels of literary order, so here too the three parts perform similarly: Part A, 6.53-56, introduces the whole by setting the context; the second part, Part B, 7.1-13, is the first development, and the third part, Part B', 7.14-23, is the second and completing development.

---

[280]E.g. Hooker, *The Gospel...*, p.171.

[281]Ref. Luke H. Jenkins, "A Marcan Doublet", in *Studies in History and Religion: Presented to Dr. H. Wheeler Robinson*, ed. Ernest A. Payne, Lutterworth, London, 1942, pp.87-111: Jenkins describes what he thought was a "sustained doublet": 6.31-7.37 and 8.1-26; Taylor, *The Gospel...*, revised and reduced it to 6.35-56 and 8.1-10, to his own satisfaction. Since then many attempts have been made at defining the Markan, or the Pre-Markan double cycle, but with no certain results.Much more recently, Fowler, *Loaves and Fishes...*, has focused principally on the feeding stories, and he has concluded that the feeding of the four thousand is the tradition and that of the five thousand is Mark's own creation. For an examination of the function of this duality, he turns to 8.4 (which is the "crucial verse for the interpretation of the two stories as a *doublet*", p.93) and the irony of it is that the disciples "have no concept of the self-condemnation implied by their words", p.99. He does not focus on the irony of 8.14,16. And most lacking of all is any consideration of 8.19-21, which are surely the key, as we will see, to understanding the way these stories really do connect and function in their Gospel settings.

Part **A**, 6.53-56, is introductory in that it opens the Day's telling; it defines the place Gennesaret, which neither Taylor nor Nineham appear to appreciate[282]; and it establishes the activity that surrounded Jesus there and 'wherever' he went. The historical present at 7.1 is the link which Taylor and Nineham miss.

In true Markan fashion (see Thackeray's understanding of the historical present, under Day Two) this historical present of 7.1 introduces the new section, Part **B**, 7.1-13, by introducing new characters into the frame who in turn raise the issue for the Day, which is, first of all, to do with the fact that Jesus' disciples "eat bread with unclean/unwashed hands" (v.2)/"unclean hands" (v.5). It is in the repetition of the question, at v.5, that another question is attached, in regard to the "tradition of the elders". Lambrecht properly points out that vv.1-5, my part A, raises the questions; vv.6-13, my parts B and B', deal with the tradition; and vv.14-23, my Day's Part **B'** deals with the matter of unclean hands.[283] Part A, vv.1-5, contains a Markan 'aside'[284], vv.3,4. Parts B and B' commence at vv.6 and 9: compare the beginnings of:

v.6   ὁ δὲ εἶπεν αὐτοῖς, Καλῶς...

and v.9   Καὶ ἔλεγεν αὐτοῖς, Καλῶς...

In the first of these two parts, Mark quotes from Isaiah 29.13 (closer to the LXX than to the Hebrew text), which he fits into his rhetorical style:

a   ὁ δὲ εἶπεν αὐτοῖς,

         Καλῶς ἐπροφήτευσεν Ἡσαΐας περὶ ὑμῶν τῶν ὑποκριτῶν,

b   (a)   ὡς γέγραπται

    (b)   ὅτι Οὗτος ὁ λαὸς τοῖς χείλεσίν με τιμᾷ,

         ἡ δὲ καρδία αὐτῶν πόρρω ἀπέχει ἀπ' ἐμοῦ·

    (b')   μάτην δὲ σέβονταί με,

         διδάσκοντες διδασκαλίας ἐντάλματα ἀνθρώπων.

b'   ἀφέντες τὴν ἐντολὴν τοῦ θεοῦ

         κρατεῖτε τὴν παράδοσιν τῶν ἀνθρώπων.

The quotation has its introduction in b(a), its first part presentation in (b), and its second part in (b'). Overall, the introduction to part b is in a, the quote is in b, and Jesus' application of the quote is in b'. (In the symmetrically opposite Day, Day Twelve (7.31-37), there appears to be an inclusion of a deliberate parallel to Isaiah 29.13, on Mark's part, which is an allusion to Isaiah 35.5,6.)

The Day's Part **B'**, 7.14-23, is again made up of three parts: the opening part A, vv.14,15, describes Jesus' calling the crowd to him and addressing them on the first issue raised (raised, structurally-speaking in the parallel Part **B**, 7.1-13). Parts B and **B'** have a new setting, in a house, away from the crowd (see vv.17-19 and vv.20-23); here "his disciples begin to question Jesus about the *parable*". We can see, in vv.21,22, how Mark lists *twelve* examples of 'evil thoughts' in two lists: the first six are in the plural form and the second six are in the singular. At the fifth (?) level of order, in (b) and (b'), he presents the two listings, in .a and .a' (the sixth order (?)) the words themselves.

At vv.14,15 the abb' presentation of the parts clearly suggests the rejection of v.16, "If anyone has ears to hear, let him hear", which is not supported by our principle witnesses, Codices Siniaticus and Vaticanus. The idea expressed by the enthusiastic copyist, that this

---

[282]Taylor, *The Gospel...*, p.334, writes, "Unlike the three preceding stories, there is no link between this narrative and the rest, no temporal or local statement which tells us when and where the incident took place." Nineham, *Saint Mark*, p.188, writes, "The evangelist makes no attempt to locate this section either in space or in time."
[283]J. Lambrecht, "Jesus and the Law: an Investigation of Mark 7.1-23", *EphThL* 53 (1977), pp.24-79.
[284]See also 7.2b ("this is unwashed"), v.19 ("purging all foods"), in this same Day's telling.

verse might be included, is an interesting one, however: it comes from Day Five (3.7-4.41) and specifically from the parables-section, from 4.9 and v.23. The explanation of 4.33,34 is well rehearsed in this Day's Part **B'**: in part A, Jesus addresses the crowd with the *parable*; in part B, *in private*, the disciples question Jesus about it, so he begins his explanation; and in part B', he completes his explanation.

The literary structure of Day Ten is viewed as:

Καὶ διαπεράσαντες ἐπὶ τὴν γῆν		A A
ἦλθον εἰς Γεννησαρὲτ		
καὶ προσωρμίσθησαν. [54]		
καὶ ἐξελθόντων αὐτῶν ἐκ τοῦ πλοίου		B
εὐθὺς		
ἐπιγνόντες αὐτὸν [55]		
περιέδραμον ὅλην τὴν χώραν ἐκείνην		
καὶ ἤρξαντο		
ἐπὶ τοῖς κραβάττοις τοὺς κακῶς ἔχοντας περιφέρειν		
ὅπου ἤκουον ὅτι ἐστίν. [56]		
καὶ ὅπου ἂν εἰσεπορεύετο		B'
εἰς κώμας		
ἢ εἰς πόλεις		
ἢ εἰς ἀγροὺς		
ἐν ταῖς ἀγοραῖς		
ἐτίθεσαν		
τοὺς ἀσθενοῦντας,		
καὶ παρεκάλουν αὐτὸν		
ἵνα κἂν τοῦ κρασπέδου τοῦ ἱματίου αὐτοῦ		
ἅψωνται·		
καὶ ὅσοι ἂν ἤψαντο αὐτοῦ		
ἐσῴζοντο.		

Καὶ συνάγονται πρὸς αὐτὸν	a	A	**B**
οἱ Φαρισαῖοι			
καί τινες τῶν γραμματέων			
ἐλθόντες ἀπὸ Ἱεροσολύμων [2]			
καὶ ἰδόντες τινὰς τῶν μαθητῶν αὐτοῦ			
ὅτι κοιναῖς χερσίν,			
τοῦτ' ἔστιν ἀνίπτοις,			
ἐσθίουσιν τοὺς ἄρτους [3]		continued below	

οἱ γὰρ Φαρισαῖοι καὶ πάντες οἱ Ἰουδαῖοι   b
  ἐὰν μὴ πυγμῇ νίψωνται τὰς χεῖρας
   οὐκ ἐσθίουσιν,
    κρατοῦντες τὴν παράδοσιν τῶν πρεσβυτέρων, [4]
  καὶ ἀπ᾽ ἀγορᾶς ὅταν ἔλθωσιν
   ἐὰν μὴ βαπτίσωνται
   οὐκ ἐσθίουσιν,
  καὶ ἄλλα πολλά ἐστιν
   ἃ παρέλαβον κρατεῖν,
   βαπτισμοὺς ποτηρίων
    καὶ ξεστῶν
    καὶ χαλκίων
καὶ ἐπερωτῶσιν αὐτὸν   b'
  οἱ Φαρισαῖοι
  καὶ οἱ γραμματεῖς,
  Διὰ τί οὐ περιπατοῦσιν οἱ μαθηταί σου
   κατὰ τὴν παράδοσιν τῶν πρεσβυτέρων,
  ἀλλὰ κοιναῖς χερσὶν
   ἐσθίουσιν τὸν ἄρτον;
ὁ δὲ εἶπεν αὐτοῖς,   B
  Καλῶς ἐπροφήτευσεν Ἡσαΐας περὶ ὑμῶν τῶν ὑποκριτῶν,
ὡς γέγραπται
  ὅτι Οὗτος ὁ λαὸς τοῖς χείλεσίν με τιμᾷ,
   ἡ δὲ καρδία αὐτῶν πόρρω ἀπέχει ἀπ᾽ ἐμοῦ·
  μάτην δὲ σέβονταί με,
   διδάσκοντες διδασκαλίας ἐντάλματα ἀνθρώπων.
ἀφέντες τὴν ἐντολὴν τοῦ θεοῦ
  κρατεῖτε τὴν παράδοσιν τῶν ἀνθρώπων.
Καὶ ἔλεγεν αὐτοῖς,   B'
  Καλῶς ἀθετεῖτε τὴν ἐντολὴν τοῦ θεοῦ,
  ἵνα τὴν παράδοσιν ὑμῶν τηρήσητε. [10]
Μωϋσῆς γὰρ εἶπεν,
  Τίμα τὸν πατέρα σου καὶ τὴν μητέρα σου,
  καί, Ὁ κακολογῶν πατέρα ἢ μητέρα θανάτῳ τελευτάτω· [11]
ὑμεῖς δὲ λέγετε,
  Ἐὰν εἴπῃ ἄνθρωπος τῷ πατρὶ ἢ τῇ μητρί,
  Κορβᾶν,
   ὅ ἐστιν, Δῶρον,
   ὃ ἐὰν ἐξ ἐμοῦ ὠφεληθῇς, [12]
  οὐκέτι ἀφίετε αὐτὸν
   οὐδὲν ποιῆσαι τῷ πατρὶ
   ἢ τῇ μητρί, [13]
  ἀκυροῦντες τὸν λόγον τοῦ θεοῦ
   τῇ παραδόσει ὑμῶν
    ᾗ παρεδώκατε·
   καὶ παρόμοια τοιαῦτα
    πολλὰ ποιεῖτε.

Καὶ προσκαλεσάμενος πάλιν τὸν ὄχλον   A   B'
     ἔλεγεν αὐτοῖς,
     Ἀκούσατέ μου πάντες καὶ σύνετε. [15]
οὐδέν ἐστιν ἔξωθεν τοῦ ἀνθρώπου
     εἰσπορευόμενον εἰς αὐτὸν
     ὃ δύναται κοινῶσαι αὐτόν·
ἀλλὰ τὰ ἐκ τοῦ ἀνθρώπου
     ἐκπορευόμενά ἐστιν τὰ κοινοῦντα τὸν ἄνθρωπον.
Καὶ ὅτε εἰσῆλθεν   B
     εἰς τὸν οἶκον
     ἀπὸ τοῦ ὄχλου,
ἐπηρώτων αὐτὸν
     οἱ μαθηταὶ αὐτοῦ
     τὴν παραβολήν. [18]
καὶ λέγει αὐτοῖς,
     Οὕτως καὶ ὑμεῖς ἀσύνετοί ἐστε;
     οὐ νοεῖτε
          ὅτι πᾶν τὸ ἔξωθεν
               εἰσπορευόμενον εἰς τὸν ἄνθρωπον
               οὐ δύναται αὐτὸν κοινῶσαι, [19]
          ὅτι οὐκ εἰσπορεύεται
               αὐτοῦ εἰς τὴν καρδίαν
               ἀλλ' εἰς τὴν κοιλίαν,
          καὶ εἰς τὸν ἀφεδρῶνα
               ἐκπορεύεται;
               καθαρίζων πάντα τὰ βρώματα.
ἔλεγεν δὲ   B'
          ὅτι Τὸ ἐκ τοῦ ἀνθρώπου ἐκπορευόμενον
          ἐκεῖνο κοινοῖ τὸν ἄνθρωπον· [21]
     ἔσωθεν γὰρ
          ἐκ τῆς καρδίας τῶν ἀνθρώπων
          οἱ διαλογισμοὶ οἱ κακοὶ ἐκπορεύονται,
     πορνεῖαι, κλοπαί, φόνοι, [22]
          μοιχεῖαι, πλεονεξίαι, πονηρίαι,
     δόλος, ἀσέλγεια, ὀφθαλμὸς πονηρός,
          βλασφημία, ὑπερηφανία, ἀφροσύνη· [23]
     πάντα ταῦτα τὰ πονηρὰ
          ἔσωθεν ἐκπορεύεται
          καὶ κοινοῖ τὸν ἄνθρωπον.

And in literal English:

And crossing over onto land,   **A**   **A**
        they came to Gennesaret,
        and they anchored.
And as they came out of the boat,   **B**
        immediately
                knowing him,
                they ran through all that region,
        and they began
                to carry around on stretchers those who were ill,
                where they heard that he was.
And wherever he entered,   **B'**
                into villages,
                        or into cities,
                        or into the countryside,
                in the market places,
                    they placed
                    their sick.
And they begged him
                that if even the fringe of his cloak
                they might touch.
And as many as touched him
                were healed.

And assemble to him   A   **B**
    the Pharisees,
    and some of the Scribes,
  coming from Jerusalem
  and seeing some of his disciples
    that with unclean hands
      (this is unwashed)
    they eat bread.
(For the Pharisees and all the Jews
    unless they wash hands carefully
      they do not eat,
    holding the tradition of the elders
  and when they come from market places,
    unless they wash,
    they do not eat.
  And there are many other things
    which they received to hold:
    washings of cups
      and of utensils
      and of bronze vessels)
And questioned him/ the Pharisees/ and the Scribes,
  'Why walk not your disciples
    according to the tradition of the elders,
  but with unclean hands
    eat bread?'
And he said to them,   B
  'Well has Isaiah prophesised concerning you hypocrites.
As it is written:
  "This people honours me with the lips
    but their heart is far away from me
  And in vain they worship me
    Teaching teachings which are commands of men."
Leaving the commandment of God,
  you hold the tradition of men.'
And he said to them,   B'
  'Well you reject the commandment of God
  that you may keep your tradition,
For Moses said,
  "Honour your father and your mother."
  And "The one speaking evil of father or mother let him die."
But you say,
    "If a man says to his father or to his mother,
    "Corban
      which is a gift
      whatever you might have profited from me.""
No longer do you allow him
  to do anything for the father
  or the mother,
annulling the word of God
  by your tradition / which you pass on,
  and such similar things / many you do!'

And calling the crowd to him again,   A   B'
      he began to say to them,
       'Hear me, everyone, and understand:
   There is nothing from outside a man,
      entering into him,
      which can make him unclean.
   But the things coming out of a man
      they are the ones defiling a man.'
And when he entered   B
      into a house
      away from the crowd,
   questioned him
      his disciples,
      about the parable
  and he says to them,
      'Thus also you are without understanding?
      Do you not understand
          that everything from outside
            entering into a man
            cannot defile him,
        because it enters not
          into his heart,
          but into the belly
        and into the drain
          it goes out.'
        (purging all foods).
And he began to say,   B'
      'The thing out of a man coming forth,
      that defiles a man,
   For from within,
      out of the heart of men,
      evil thoughts come forth:
   sexual immoralities, thefts, murders,   *(6 plural terms)*
      adulteries, greeds, iniquities;
   deceit, lewdness, envy,   *(6 singular ones)*
      blasphemy, arrogance, foolishness.
  All these evil things
      from within come forth
      and defile a man.'

Before we continue with an examination of Day Eleven, we can determine the relationship of Days Eight, Nine and Ten. In a geographical and temporal sense, Nine and Ten are more closely related, by the night crossing, and because there is a passing of days between Eight and Nine. This might suggest an ABB' relationship of the Days, but the first threesome of Days in the Gospel (of Days 1,2 and 3), if it had been judged on these grounds alone, would have been judged an ABA' relationship. The overriding consideration in that case, as indeed in the second case also (Days 5, 6 and 7), was the linear movement of the three-day story.

Day Eight, we might say, begins low key, with a rejection of "*the prophet*" Jesus by *those who*, we might have thought, *would have been his keenest supporters*. Jesus' sending out of his disciples clearly raises both key and tempo. After instructions, amongst which "take *no bread and no money*" (*God will provide?*), they begin the mission, and many hear and talk about what is happening. Indeed, as a result, "*King*"[285] Herod himself hears about it, and about Jesus. And Herod, like the people, wonders who he is. Then we are given a story about Herod's "*banquet*" and that which leads to the beheading of John[286]. In all, Jesus, the rejected prophet, is *likened to three prophets: John raised from the dead, Elijah and another*.

On Day Nine, the disciples, tired from their mission, *rejoin Jesus*. Their futile attempt to find a quiet place, because of the growing crowd, leads to them all taking a boat elsewhere. But a large crowd gathered nevertheless. To Jesus, they were like "sheep without a shepherd". (There was *no prophet around* who was worthy to be their "*shepherd*".) And then there is the 'banquet in the desert' for which, in a fashion like that of *Elijah/Elisha*, but much more miraculously (for *Jesus is greater*, he feeds more with less), *bread* and fish are multiplied for the five thousand (as *God provides*/as *Jesus provides* it; *money was not needed*, the disciples *had* five *loaves*...). Jesus has already *confounded his disciples* with this miracle, but he goes on to "*terrify*" them. After they have struggled at oar in the face of a contrary heavy wind through three watches of the night, Jesus appears to them walking on the sea. *He re-joins them*. And all is calm. But they are not. They still have <u>*not understood*</u> about the "*loaves*": "<u>*their hearts were hardened*</u>".

Day Ten tells, when Jesus stepped out of the boat, how he was immediately recognised, and how *people ran* through the countryside *to him* bringing their sick wherever they heard he was. In village, town and farm they laid down their sick in open spaces: just a touch of his cloak was all they needed. (It is action-packed, dramatic presentation. *The people needed him.*) And just as his disciples *had gathered round him*, in Day Nine (6.30), so now, in Day Ten, also Pharisees and some scribes who had heard *in Jerusalem*, came and *gathered round him* (7.1). At the last, *those who might have recognised who Jesus really was* demonstrate to Jesus, who quotes from *Isaiah (the prophet)* that "<u>*their hearts were hardened*</u>", that they had "let go of the commands of God", holding to man's traditions on what is "*clean*" and "*unclean*". (They are *not true shepherds* of the people; they have no compassion...). *They will not acknowledge Jesus to be greater than John the Baptist, King Herod, Elijah or any <u>prophet</u>.*

This threesome of Days has its many vivid connections. Key words, themes and interpretations are in italics. The first day is clearly introductory; its themes and sub-themes are picked up and developed, in turn, in the two days which follow it. It is indeed arranged to an ABB' scheme. It has its movement of story-line best expressed in this way.

---

[285]Herod was no "king", but Mark probably chose to use the title for the purpose of showing Jesus in a still greater light.
[286]Compare: Herod/Pilate, 6.26/15.15; contrast: John/Jesus, 6.29/15.46 (no disciples buried Jesus).

Day Eleven: 7.24-30:

This Day is the middle Day of the first of two middle Series of Seven Days. The Day begins like Day Eight, with use of the significant word Ἐκεῖθεν, with which Mark begins the telling of four Days in all.[287] The opening line reads:

Ἐκεῖθεν δὲ ἀναστὰς ἀπῆλθεν εἰς τὰ ὅρια Τύρου.

We may translate literally: "And from there, rising up" (after the night, from sleep) "he went away to the region of Tyre." In 1.35, ἀναστὰς is used for the first time, but there within the context of a pre-dawn activity. Here, at the beginning of Day Eleven, Mark appears to use it in a post-dawn, pre-journey sense.[288] He does exactly the same in the opening line of the corresponding middle day, Day Eighteen (10.1-16), of the second middle Series of Seven Days, where (at 10.1) he repeats his use of no less than five words in all:

Καὶ ἐκεῖθεν ἀναστὰς ἔρχεται εἰς τὰ ὅρια τῆς Ἰουδαίας...

The corresponding words are all underlined. We note too that ἀπῆλθεν is a variant of ἔρχεται. It may be judged, therefore, that Mark deliberately composed the beginning of one of these two days, both of them significant for their positions, with the other in mind.

We observe that the introductory piece to this Day's telling (and that of Day Eighteen, 10.1, therefore) is similar in structure and content to that of Day Eight (6.1), in that Mark tells us that Jesus left the place of the earlier Day's telling (in the first part) and arrives in another, the place of Mark's new Day's telling (in the second part). It is an introductory formula which he repeats also at 7.31 (the beginning of Day Twelve), at 8.27 (beginning Day Fifteen), and at 9.30/33 (beginning Day Seventeen?). Further, the formula is detected at 6.53 (beginning Day Ten): it is only slightly different in that the 'place' left behind is the sea (from the closing section of the previous Day's telling). Interestingly, the last similar example at 10.46a/46b is a reversal of the norm: at the ending of Day Twenty, the arrival is told, and at the beginning of Day Twenty-one the departure is told (before the telling of what takes place on Jesus' departure from Jericho). This introductory formula (and its variant) is a development of the one defined (under Day Six) by the analysis of night-crossings of the Sea of Galilee, which is that new Days begin with new locations and new activities after sunrise. What makes this formula (uncovered here) a development therefore, is the additional information of the leaving of the place of the previous Day's telling. Eight Days in Mark's scheme (we include that of the reversal, Day Twenty-one) begin, therefore, in like manner. The common words are as follows:

Ἐκεῖθεν	four times	(6.1, 7.24, 9.30, 10.1);
Καὶ ἐξῆλθεν	four times	(6.1, 7.31, 8.27, 9.30);
ἦλθον, -εν	three times	(6.53, 7.31, 9.33);
ἔρχεται, -ονται	three times	(6.1, 10.1,46);
εἰς	in all eight cases	(6.1,53, 7.24,31, 8.27, 9.33, 10.1,46a/46b).

Additional information is provided in each introductory piece regarding place names, or descriptions of place, and in a number of cases the journey between the place left and the place

---

[287]Refer to page 117.

[288] Just for now, I want to draw attention to the fact that neither the GNB or the NIV translate this word ἀναστὰς. It is, in fact an important word, for the way it is distributed in Mark's Gospel: at the beginning, at the introductions of the two middle days and at the end.

arrived at is suggestive of a day or more between the tellings of Mark's reported Days. For example, for this Day's telling the place of departure is Gennesaret and the destination is the District of Tyre. The only difficulty we might have is that our estimate of the days of the journey might differ from Mark's; his geographical knowledge, as we have now stated twice above, does not seem too accurate.

As the discovery of this introductory formula is helpful to us now for the purpose of discerning the turning points between Mark's sub-Series of Days, it may be judged that it will have been helpful to Mark's first audience of readers, reader-reciters and listeners. I present the literary structure to Day Eleven:

Ἐκεῖθεν δὲ   A
    ἀναστὰς
    ἀπῆλθεν εἰς τὰ ὅρια Τύρου.
  καὶ εἰσελθὼν εἰς οἰκίαν
    οὐδένα ἤθελεν γνῶναι,
    καὶ οὐκ ἠδυνήθη λαθεῖν·[25]
  ἀλλ' εὐθὺς ἀκούσασα γυνὴ περὶ αὐτοῦ,
    ἧς εἶχεν τὸ θυγάτριον αὐτῆς πνεῦμα ἀκάθαρτον,
    ἐλθοῦσα προσέπεσεν πρὸς τοὺς πόδας αὐτοῦ·[26]
ἡ δὲ γυνὴ ἦν Ἑλληνίς,   B
    Συροφοινίκισσα
    τῷ γένει·
  καὶ ἠρώτα αὐτὸν
    ἵνα τὸ δαιμόνιον ἐκβάλῃ
    ἐκ τῆς θυγατρὸς αὐτῆς.
  καὶ ἔλεγεν αὐτῇ,
    Ἄφες πρῶτον
      χορτασθῆναι τὰ τέκνα,
    οὐ γάρ ἐστιν καλὸν
      λαβεῖν τὸν ἄρτον τῶν τέκνων
      καὶ τοῖς κυναρίοις βαλεῖν.
ἡ δὲ ἀπεκρίθη   B'
    καὶ λέγει αὐτῷ,
    Ναί, κύριε·
  καὶ γὰρ
    τὰ κυνάρια ὑποκάτω τῆς τραπέζης ἐσθίουσιν
    ἀπὸ τῶν ψιχίων τῶν παιδίων.
  καὶ εἶπεν αὐτῇ,
    Διὰ τοῦτον τὸν λόγον
    ὕπαγε,
    ἐξελήλυθεν ἐκ τῆς θυγατρός σου τὸ δαιμόνιον.
  καὶ ἀπελθοῦσα εἰς τὸν οἶκον αὐτῆς
    εὗρεν τὸ παιδίον βεβλημένον ἐπὶ τὴν κλίνην
    καὶ τὸ δαιμόνιον ἐξεληλυθός.

And in literal English:

And from there,   (see Day 18, for parallels)   A
       rising up,
       he went away into the region of Tyre.
    And entering into a house,
       he wished no-one to know,
       and he could not be hidden,
    But immediately a woman hearing about him,
       whose daughter had an unclean spirit,
       coming/ she fell/ at his feet.
Now the woman was a Greek,   B
       a Syrophoenician
       by race.
    And she asked him
       that he expel the demon
       from her daughter.
    And he said to her,
       'Permit first
          the children to be satisfied,
       For it is not good
          to take the bread of the children
          and throw it to the dogs.'
But she answered,   B'
          and says to him,
       'Lord,
       and yet
          the dogs under the table
          eat of the crumbs of the children.'
    And he said to her,
       'Because of this word,
          go,
       the demon has gone out of your daughter.'
    And going away to her house,
       she found the child laid upon the bed
       and the demon gone.

The presentation structure of this Day is a simple ABB' form. Part A, vv.24,25, in three parts, is introductory, in that it establishes the change of geographical place and sets Jesus in a house, seeking privacy; inevitably he is known to be there, and a woman who had a daughter with an unclean spirit comes to him. Part B, vv.26,27, develops the story and Part B', vv.28-30, concludes it. The first of the three parts of B fills out the details of the woman and the reason for her approaching Jesus; she is a Greek, a Syrophoenician and she asks Jesus to cast out the demon from her daughter. The first part of Jesus' reply, part b is balanced by the second, part b': the connection, as frequently elsewhere, is made by γάρ. In B', the first part is the woman's reply, which in part b gains Jesus' approval (parts b in both B and B' begin similarly), and as he says, so in part b', it is done.

The basic reasons for the judgement that 7.30 ends Day Eleven's telling are that 7.31 clearly begins the next new Day's telling in Mark's scheme, see above, and that Mark's three-part rhetorical presentation is complete. Day Eleven, therefore, is equal to the shortest Day in Mark's telling so far encountered (compare Day Two, for the number of verses).

In content terms, as for the middle day of the first Series, 2.23-3.6, whilst the crowds are not very far away, they are only alluded to. The story moves along with Jesus in centre stage, on his own, without even mention of his disciples (who do of course have an introductory part to play in the earlier middle day). In 7.31ff. the crowd features again (in v.33). The story of 7.24-31 paints a 'quieter' scene than the ones before or after it. Furthermore, for the first time in the Gospel, Mark makes plain that Jesus' ministry is to a Gentile (we might deduce that the demoniac of 5.1-20 is a Gentile, but Mark there makes absolutely no reference at all to the matter). This Day's story, with limits of 7.24 and 30, well performs as a hinge or fulcrum to the presentation of this Series of seven Days. Symmetrically balanced around it, in Days Nine and Thirteen are the feedings of the Five-thousand and the Four-thousand, each with their numerical details which are summarised in the presenting of a numerological puzzle, after the telling of the second of the two stories. Clearly, in the conversation between the woman and Jesus is the issue of bread for the Jews and bread for the Gentiles. The Feeding of the Five-thousand, since Augustine's time at least, has been associated with the Jews and the Feeding of the Four-thousand with the Gentiles (for a recent study on this, see Drury[289] and my development, under Day Thirteen). The mention of "bread" or "loaves", in Greek the same, $\check{\alpha}\rho\tau o\varsigma$, is found in five of the seven days of this Series: Day Eight, 6.8; Day Nine, 6.36, 37, 38, 41 *bis*, 44, 52; Day Ten, 7.2, 5; Day Eleven, 7.27; Day Twelve, none; Day Thirteen, 8.4, 5, 6, 14 *bis*, 16, 17, 19; and Day Fourteen, none. The only other references to bread in the Gospel are at 2.26 (the shewbread) 3.20 and 14.22: that is, nineteen of the twenty-two references are found in this Series. In Day Thirteen's telling, Jesus wants his disciples to 'understand' the significance of the numbers of the loaves and the baskets: Mark wants his readers/listeners to understand too, because he has set the Days of this Series, and their contents, therefore, to disclose that this first of two middle Series of the Gospel marks the extension of Jesus' ministry, which was not to Jews alone, but to Gentiles also.

Given the arrangement of the Days of this Series and these and numerous additional features (such as the inclusion of disciples in the mission work, the wider geographical area he covers, and the first, *amazing* healing of a blind man), I am titling the Series, "Days of Increase in the Mission of Jesus".

Day Twelve: 7.31-37:

The day begins:

> *Καὶ πάλιν / ἐξελθὼν / ἐκ τῶν ὁρίων Τύρου*
> *ἦλθεν διὰ Σιδῶνος*
> *εἰς τὴν θάλασσαν τῆς Γαλιλαίας*
> *ἀνὰ μέσον τῶν ὁρίων Δεκαπόλεως.*
> *καὶ φέρουσιν αὐτῷ κωφὸν καὶ μογιλάλον,*

It is part A, the introductory piece, vv.31,32a, and it sets the scene for vv.32b-37. It displays a link with the previous Day's telling by *Καὶ πάλιν ἐξελθὼν ἐκ τῶν ὁρίων Τύρου*. It is

---

[289]Drury, *The Literary Guide...*, pp.414-416.

demonstrated under Day Eleven that this content and construction follows the scheme of an introductory formula which Mark uses eight times in all to define the ending of one of his Day's reports and the beginning of a new one. The first line tells of Jesus' going from one place; the second line tells of his arrival in another; and the third line introduces those also in the scene. The beginning of Day Eight, the first Day of this Series, is the first such example in the Gospel (see 6.1 and the rhetorical analysis as presented); others in this second Series of seven Days include the openings of Days Ten (6.53-56) and Eleven (7.24,25). In all, they are the first and the three middle Days.

We observe further, significant correspondence between 6.1 and 7.31,32a. As Day Eight's telling begins, here too we discover a historical present, with *Kaì*, in the balancing part b' with which the introductory section to the Day is completed. Again, we may judge that Mark began composing one of these two Days with the other as his reference. (Days Eight and Twelve have their significance in Mark's seven Day scheme here as the introductory Days of sub-Series/threesomes of Days.)

For a discussion on *ἐξῆλθεν* and variants, see under Day Eight. In regard to *Kaì πάλιν* (see under Day Three), here it might be judged to qualify *ἐξελθὼν* / *ἐκ τῶν ὁρίων Τύρου* (observe also here: *ἐξ* and *ἐκ*) in like manner as in 2.13, 3.1 and 4.1, meaning "immediately after", "thereupon" or "without hesitation". It would express an immediacy in Jesus' setting out to return to Galilee. In other words his journeying back would be interpreted as starting, not at or just after dawn as at other times (7.24 and 10.1), but before evening (in the previous Day's telling, 7.24-30). To argue this does not impugn the principle of Mark's presenting his tellings of Days as beginning with sunrise and ending just before the following sunrise, though in this case it is, uniquely in the Gospel, Mark's next reported Day's introduction which tells how the previously reported Day concluded. A passage of days is inferred for the journeying between the earlier Day's report and this (of 7.31-37). The place of departure is Tyre and the place of arrival is mid Decapolis, sixty miles away[290]. We might estimate that the journey would have taken a minimum of three days or so. Mark's method as with other Days' tellings is to give temporal and geographical information which sets his next, new Day's context in the opening lines. Here this information is in the first two lines, in v.31; a new Day's telling is begun with v.31.

The alternative reading of *Kaì πάλιν*, as meaning "again", does not fit the verbal context. Jesus' arrival in Tyre (7.24) was his first, according to Mark, so he could not have been leaving there "again". Further, *Kaì πάλιν* cannot qualify *ἐξελθὼν* only: *ἐξελθὼν* and *ἐκ τῶν ὁρίων Τύρου* occupy parallel positions in the b and b' parts. And the final point must be stated clearly: *Kaì πάλιν* here is not used to link 7.24-30 and 7.31-37 as one Day's telling as at 2.13, 3.1 and 4.1, simply because the introductory link here at 7.31 demonstrates that a journey of days separates the two tellings.

The Day's presentation is a simple ABB'. The introductory part, A, vv.31,32a, well establishes the new geographical setting and the new principal character. Again, we see clearly Mark's hand at work composing. And as we see elsewhere, in a simple ABB' formation for a Day's telling, Part B begins the development of the story and Part B' completes it. Part B, vv.32b-34, relates the new and ardent request to Jesus and Jesus' actions in response. Part B', vv.35-37, in three parts, tells of the resulting double healing and what follows. In the first of the two parallel sub-parts Jesus orders the crowd's silence, but it is a futile request. In the second, the reason is given: their excitement is such that they cannot be quiet. (As in Day Eight, at 6.2 (and also Day One, at 1.22), Mark, at 7.37, uses the word *ἐξεπλήσσοντο*.) The Day is completed with what seems an allusion to Isaiah 35.5,6; the matter of the 'blind seeing' is the subject for Day Fourteen, with which Day Twelve holds many correspondences; and the

---

[290] All my distances of Jesus' journeys are measured from the maps of Aharoni and Avi-Yonah, *The Macmillan Bible Atlas*, Rev. Ed., Macmillan Publishing/New York & Collier Macmillan Publishers/London, 1977.

composition here of one has much influenced the other. These are the first and last Days of a new threesome of Days.

The literary structure of Day Twelve is viewed as:

Καὶ πάλιν   A
        ἐξελθὼν
        ἐκ τῶν ὁρίων Τύρου
   ἦλθεν διὰ Σιδῶνος
        εἰς τὴν θάλασσαν τῆς Γαλιλαίας
        ἀνὰ μέσον τῶν ὁρίων Δεκαπόλεως. [32]
   καὶ φέρουσιν αὐτῷ
        κωφὸν
        καὶ μογιλάλον,
καὶ παρακαλοῦσιν αὐτὸν   B
        ἵνα ἐπιθῇ αὐτῷ
        τὴν χεῖρα.
   καὶ ἀπολαβόμενος αὐτὸν
           ἀπὸ τοῦ ὄχλου
           κατ᾽ ἰδίαν
        ἔβαλεν τοὺς δακτύλους αὐτοῦ εἰς τὰ ὦτα αὐτοῦ
        καὶ πτύσας ἥψατο τῆς γλώσσης αὐτοῦ, [34]
   καὶ ἀναβλέψας εἰς τὸν οὐρανὸν ἐστέναξεν,
        καὶ λέγει αὐτῷ,
        Εφφαθα,
        ὅ ἐστιν, Διανοίχθητι. [35]
καὶ εὐθέως ἠνοίγησαν αὐτοῦ αἱ ἀκοαί,   B'
        καὶ ἐλύθη ὁ δεσμὸς τῆς γλώσσης αὐτοῦ,
        καὶ ἐλάλει ὀρθῶς.
   καὶ διεστείλατο αὐτοῖς ἵνα μηδενὶ λέγωσιν·
        ὅσον δὲ αὐτοῖς διεστέλλετο,
        αὐτοὶ μᾶλλον περισσότερον ἐκήρυσσον. [37]
   καὶ ὑπερπερισσῶς
        ἐξεπλήσσοντο
        λέγοντες,
        Καλῶς πάντα πεποίηκεν·
           καὶ τοὺς κωφοὺς ποιεῖ ἀκούειν
           καὶ τοὺς ἀλάλους λαλεῖν.

And in literal English:

And again   A

        going forth
        out of the region of Tyre,
    he came through Sidon
        to the Sea of Galilee
        in the midst of the region of Decapolis,
   and they bring to him a man,
        deaf
        and speaking with difficulty.
And they beg him   B
        to place on him
        his hand.
   And taking him away
           from the crowd
           privately,
        he put his fingers into his ears
        and with spittle touched his tongue.
   And looking up to heaven he groaned,
           and he says to him,
        'Ephphatha',
        which is, 'Be opened!'
And immediately his ears were opened,   B'
        and his tongue was loosened,
        and he began to speak clearly.
   And he ordered them that they should tell no-one,
        but as much as he ordered them,
        they more exceedingly proclaimed.
   And most exceedingly they were astounded,
        saying,
        'He has done everything well,
           and both the deaf he makes to hear
           and the dumb to speak.'

Day Thirteen: 8.1-21:

The day begins Ἐν ἐκείναις ταῖς ἡμέραις..: compare the beginnings of Days Three (2.1-22), Four (2.23-3.6), and Sixteen (9.2-29), for Mark's explicit mention of other days passing between his reports. That days do pass between the tellings of Days Twelve and Thirteen is made clear in v.2, Σπλαγχνίζομαι ἐπὶ τὸν ὄχλον ὅτι ἤδη ἡμέραι τρεῖς προσμένουσίν μοι καὶ οὐκ ἔχουσιν τί φάγωσιν. Days Twelve and Thirteen are not consecutive, unlike Days Thirteen and Fourteen which are linked by another late-day/night-crossing of the Sea of Galilee, which sees Jesus and his disciples, in this case, arriving at Bethsaida (for our earlier discussions on night-crossings, see Days Six and Nine; and for our earlier discussions on the goal of Bethsaida, see Day Ten).

Day Thirteen, as we have noted above, begs comparison with Day Nine, for Feedings and for many details in the telling (such as Σπλαγχνίζομαι which we have already seen above, in 8.2: compare 6.34), but also for the summaries of the Feedings in 8.16-21, and for night-crossings of the Sea of Galilee. We have observed already that the two days lie symmetrically opposite each other in Mark's scheme for this, his first middle Series of Seven Days. Clearly, one of these two days has been composed by Mark with the other much in mind.

Fowler[291] concludes from his studies that the story of the feeding of the four-thousand is the tradition, and that the story of the feeding of the five-thousand is Mark's own creation. Comparison of the structural forms of the two stories, given my analysis, appears to offer some support to his conclusion. The form of the story of the feeding of the five-thousand is much more balanced, or weighted, and in a fashion which is more regularly found in the Gospel, than that of the feeding of the four-thousand. It appears he constructed the former with greater freedom. This whole issue of the freedom with which Mark wrote is an interesting one. We might wonder how much he was constrained in handling tradition, and whether or not he was more constrained by his own method. Similarly, in his handling of already written tradition and oral tradition, was he constrained by one more than the other? We will return to such matters in chapter Eight.

We have noted that the chreia of 2.23-28 is likely composed backwards, that is from the conclusion and point to be established. This Day's telling ends with 8.16-21. And it is clear that this concluding piece is important to the functioning of the two feeding stories in Mark's scheme. We might judge, therefore, that Mark here too composed back from his conclusion and from the point that he was wishing to make. We go now to the beginning of the Day.

We observe that in the opening part of this Day, Part **A**, 8.1-9, Mark records no geographical setting, only a temporal reference, and a qualification of it, in v.2, which helps us determine easily that this is a new Day in his telling (for our discussion on this being a single Day's reporting, see Day Six and the presentations on night-crossings). As we have done before, so we do again, and seek from the preceding passage what is immediately missing. We have to go back to 7.31 to establish the geographical setting (it is not at all unreasonable to do this when it is understood that 7.31 begins a new threesome of Days). And it is an important setting for making sense of Mark's emphasis for the Day, and not only the Day, but also the sub-Series and the Series in full. Jesus and his disciples are in the Decapolis (lit. 'ten cities') which was a confederation of ten Greek cities, on the east of the Jordan, mainly, under the protection of the Roman Governor of Syria, but enjoying a certain degree of independence. In other words, the setting for Days Twelve and Thirteen places Jesus and his disciples among a people who were predominantly Gentile. The man, of Day Twelve, who was deaf and had a speaking disorder whom Jesus healed, is likely, therefore, to have been a Gentile.

---

[291]Fowler, *Loaves and Fishes...*, see note 281.

Who, then, were the four-thousand that Jesus fed this Day? In a very round-about way, in 8.16-21, Mark is telling us that they were Gentiles. We will discuss this after the presentation of the literary-structure for the telling of this Day.

The Day's telling is a composite ABB'/ABB'/ABB', 8.1-9/10-12/13-21. The literary structure of Day Thirteen is viewed as:

Ἐν ἐκείναις ταῖς ἡμέραις   A   A
         πάλιν πολλοῦ ὄχλου ὄντος
         καὶ μὴ ἐχόντων τί φάγωσιν,
προσκαλεσάμενος τοὺς μαθητὰς
         λέγει αὐτοῖς, [2]
         Σπλαγχνίζομαι ἐπὶ τὸν ὄχλον
         ὅτι ἤδη ἡμέραι τρεῖς προσμένουσίν μοι
         καὶ οὐκ ἔχουσιν τί φάγωσιν· [3]
         καὶ ἐὰν ἀπολύσω αὐτοὺς νήστεις εἰς οἶκον αὐτῶν,
         ἐκλυθήσονται ἐν τῇ ὁδῷ·
         καί τινες αὐτῶν ἀπὸ μακρόθεν ἥκασιν.
καὶ ἀπεκρίθησαν αὐτῷ
         οἱ μαθηταὶ αὐτοῦ
         ὅτι Πόθεν τούτους δυνήσεταί τις ὧδε
         χορτάσαι
         ἄρτων ἐπ' ἐρημίας;
         καὶ ἠρώτα αὐτούς,
         Πόσους ἔχετε ἄρτους;
οἱ δὲ εἶπαν,
         Ἑπτά.
καὶ παραγγέλλει τῷ ὄχλῳ   B
         ἀναπεσεῖν
         ἐπὶ τῆς γῆς·
         καὶ λαβὼν τοὺς ἑπτὰ ἄρτους
         εὐχαριστήσας
         ἔκλασεν
         καὶ ἐδίδου τοῖς μαθηταῖς αὐτοῦ
         ἵνα παρατιθῶσιν
         καὶ παρέθηκαν τῷ ὄχλῳ. [7]
         καὶ εἶχον ἰχθύδια ὀλίγα·
         καὶ εὐλογήσας αὐτὰ
         εἶπεν καὶ ταῦτα παρατιθέναι. [8]
καὶ ἔφαγον   B'
         καὶ ἐχορτάσθησαν,
         καὶ ἦραν περισσεύματα κλασμάτων
         ἑπτὰ σπυρίδας. [9]
      ἦσαν δὲ ὡς τετρακισχίλιοι.
      καὶ ἀπέλυσεν αὐτούς. [10]

Καὶ εὐθὺς   A   **B**
    ἐμβὰς εἰς τὸ πλοῖον
      μετὰ τῶν μαθητῶν αὐτοῦ
      ἦλθεν εἰς τὰ μέρη Δαλμανουθά.
  Καὶ ἐξῆλθον οἱ Φαρισαῖοι   B
      καὶ ἤρξαντο
    συζητεῖν αὐτῷ,
    ζητοῦντες παρ' αὐτοῦ σημεῖον   *ἀπὸ τοῦ οὐρανοῦ,*
    πειράζοντες αὐτόν. [12]
 καὶ ἀναστενάξας τῷ πνεύματι αὐτοῦ   B'
      λέγει,
    Τί ἡ γενεὰ αὕτη ζητεῖ σημεῖον;
    ἀμὴν λέγω ὑμῖν,
      εἰ δοθήσεται τῇ γενεᾷ ταύτῃ σημεῖον. [13]

Καὶ ἀφεὶς αὐτοὺς   A   **B'**
    ἐμβὰς πάλιν εἰς τὸ πλοῖον
    ἀπῆλθεν εἰς τὸ πέραν.
  Καὶ ἐπελάθοντο λαβεῖν ἄρτους,
    καὶ εἰ μὴ ἕνα ἄρτον
    οὐκ εἶχον μεθ' ἑαυτῶν ἐν τῷ πλοίῳ. [15]
  καὶ διεστέλλετο αὐτοῖς
      λέγων,
    Ὁρᾶτε,
    βλέπετε
      ἀπὸ τῆς ζύμης τῶν Φαρισαίων
      καὶ τῆς ζύμης Ἡρῴδου.
καὶ διελογίζοντο πρὸς ἀλλήλους   B
      λέγοντες
    ὅτι Ἄρτους
    οὐκ ἔχομεν.
καὶ γνοὺς   B'
      ὁ Ἰησοῦς λέγει αὐτοῖς,
    Τί διαλογίζεσθε
        ὅτι ἄρτους οὐκ ἔχετε;
    οὔπω νοεῖτε
    οὐδὲ συνίετε;
    πεπωρωμένην ἔχετε τὴν καρδίαν ὑμῶν; [18]
     ὀφθαλμοὺς ἔχοντες οὐ βλέπετε
     καὶ ὦτα ἔχοντες οὐκ ἀκούετε;
  καὶ οὐ μνημονεύετε, [19]
    ὅτε τοὺς πέντε ἄρτους ἔκλασα εἰς τοὺς πεντακισχιλίους,
     πόσους κοφίνους κλασμάτων πλήρεις ἤρατε;
     λέγουσιν αὐτῷ, Δώδεκα.
    ὅτε καὶ τοὺς ἑπτὰ εἰς τοὺς τετρακισχιλίους,
     πόσων σπυρίδων πληρώματα κλασμάτων ἤρατε;
     καὶ λέγουσιν αὐτῷ, Ἑπτά.
  καὶ ἔλεγεν αὐτοῖς,
    Οὔπω συνίετε;

And in literal English:

In those days,   A   A
      again there being a great crowd,
      and not having anything that they might eat,
   calling the disciples to him,
       he says to them,
     'I have compassion on the crowd,
        because they have been with me three days now,
       and they have nothing that they may eat.
    And if I dismiss them without food to their houses,
       they will faint on the way,
       and some of them are from afar.'
  And answered him
        his disciples,
      'How will anyone here be able
        to satisfy these people
        with bread in a desert?'
    And he asked them,
      'How many loaves have you?'
    And they said,
      'Seven.'
And he commands the crowd   B
    to sit down
    on the ground,
  And taking the seven loaves,
      giving thanks,
      he broke them
    and gave them to his disciples
      that they might serve them
    and they served the crowd.
  And they had a few fish,
    and blessing them,
    he told them to serve these also.
And they ate   B'
    and they were satisfied
    and they collected the excesses of scraps,
      seven baskets.
  Now they were about four-thousand.
  And he dismissed them.

And immediately   A   **B**
    embarking in the boat
      with his disciples,
    he came into the area of Dalmanutha.
And Pharisees came out   B
    and they began
    to debate with him,
    seeking from him a sign from heaven,
    testing him.
And groaning in his spirit,   B'
    he says,
  'Why does this generation seek a sign?
  Truly I say to you.
    No sign will be given to this generation.'

And leaving them,   A   **B'**
    again embarking,
    he went away to the other side.
And they forgot to take loaves,
    and, but for one loaf,
    they had none with them in the boat.
And he charged them,/ saying, /'See,
    beware of the leaven of the Pharisees,
    and of the leaven of Herod.'
And they reasoned with each other   B
  saying,
  'Loaves we have not.'
And knowing,   B'
    Jesus says to them,
  'Why do you reason,
    that you have no loaves?
  Do you not yet understand,
  or realise?
Have your hearts been hardened?
  Having eyes, do you see not?
  And having ears, do you hear not?
And do you not remember?
  When I broke the five loaves for the five-thousand,
    how many basketfuls of scraps did you collect?'
  They say to him, 'Twelve.'
  'When the seven to the four-thousand,
    how many basketfuls of scraps did you collect?'
  And they say, 'Seven.'
And he said to them,
  'Do you still not realise?'

We examine the structure of the Day's presentation. Clearly, the opening part is Part A, 8.1-9, the feeding of the four-thousand. Again, it is made up of the usual three parts. Part A, vv.1-5, communicates Jesus' concern for the crowd to have food before they depart, but the there is little bread and fish available. Part B, vv. 6-7, tells how these provisions multiplied in Jesus' hands. Part B', vv.8-9, tells how they were all filled, all four-thousand of them. Part **B**, 8.10-12, tells of a sea-trip to Dalmanutha, (v.10), of Pharisees who seek a sign from heaven (v.11) and Jesus' response (v.12). It is another three-piece presentation which fits the description, ABB'. Part **B'**, 8.13-21, presents the beginning of another sea crossing, but it begins badly as they had forgotten to bring loaves; Jesus uses the opportunity to warn the disciples of the 'leaven' of the Pharisees and of Herod. Mark thus completes his opening part A, vv.13-15. Part B, v16, tells how the disciples were discussing the matter of their lack of loaves. In this way, Mark sets up the climax to this Day's teaching. In Part B, vv.17-21, Jesus questions them about what they are discussing. It raises the puzzle of the Day and, indeed, of the Series. It is one of the most baffling even[292], of the Gospel. How does Mark intend us to interpret the numerological conundrum which Jesus poses in regard to the feedings of the five-thousand and the four-thousand? Clearly, Mark wants us, his readers, to solve this?

Tradition requires us to interpret that Jesus first fed the Jews and then fed the Gentiles. This is supported principally by both the structure of this Series and the geography of the Days of the Series. We consider, first of all, the three references to bread or loaves which are *not included* in this Series. The ones in 3.20 and 14.22 lie significantly opposite each other in Mark's scheme, in the fifth Days of the First and Fourth Series, that is in Day Five (3.7-4.41) and in Day Twenty-Six (14.12-72). In the first of these, Jesus is with his disciples in a house, but a crowd is present and "they were not able to eat bread" (as in v.20 which follows directly on from Jesus' choosing the twelve, 3.13-19). In the second of these, the setting is the Last Supper when Jesus is alone with his disciples. It is a (vertical) correspondence which is one of many which suggest the deliberate creation, on Mark's part, of a paralleling of Series One and Four. The remaining reference to bread, 2.26, to which Drury appears rightly to turn for assistance, is found in the "hinge" day, Day Four, of the First Series. In this present Series, the "hinge" day, Day Eleven, is most significant also in Mark's scheme, as we have already shown in the analysis of that Day's report (for *bread* for Jews and Gentiles). In the summary of this Series it will be further developed and expressed. In Day Four, 2.26, Jesus' reference to what David did with the shewbread (*twelve loaves*) 'gets him off the hook' with the Pharisees, but only for a while on that day, for later they watch him carefully in the synagogue to see if they might find an accusation that 'could stick'.

Drury refers to Leviticus 24 in which are set out the regulations, regarding the *twelve* loaves.[293] David takes *five* of these loaves: *seven* are left. David's story is somewhat fulfilled by the miraculous feeding of *five* loaves to Jews, but Jesus goes further than David: he completes the distribution, by his miraculous feeding of the remaining 'seven' to the Gentiles. Thus far, we can go with Drury, but, clearly, the conundrum is only part answered. What of the numbers five-thousand and four-thousand, and of the baskets twelve and seven? Drury recognises 'seven' to be the sacred number of fulfilment (or completion), but he does not discuss the other numbers in terms of their rhetorical, cultic or symbolic uses, which were common in the civilisations and religions of the Ancient near East, and still evident in the then modern world of the first century.[294]

'Twelve', 'five', 'four' and 'a thousand' have their own early numerological significance, but what we cannot be sure of, is their precise meaning to Mark. 'Twelve' has been a

---

[292]Drury, *The Literary Guide...*, p.414.
[293]Drury, *The Literary Guide...*, pp.414-416.
[294]It may be today that we do not think of numbers as having any symbolic significance, but clearly, we do have to consider first century rhetorical uses. In the years since, the church may have been guilty of 'gross excess' in interpreting them, but it is still no reason, for example, for Hooker (*The Gospel...*, p.166) to say, "It is unlikely that Mark saw any such significance in numbers." Vv.16-21 sets a puzzle: there is no way of skirting around it.

number traditionally associated with the elective purposes of God and, therefore, with Israel (for the obvious link, consider: the twelve tribes). 'Five', as half the basic number ten, is frequently referenced in the books of the Bible: we have the Decalogue, the five books of the Law of Moses and the five books of the Psalms. 'Four' is a sacred number the world over and derives its significance from the 'four winds', the four points of the compass: all the world is signified. Multiples of 'a thousand' are used frequently for hyperbole.[295] We may, thus, deduce that the feeding of the *five-thousand* with *five* loaves and the left-over *twelve* baskets of fragments are all indicative of Jews and that the feeding of the *four-thousand* with *seven* loaves and the left-overs in *seven* baskets are indicative of the Gentiles (all the other nations of the world?), whose inclusion within the 'new Israel' for its completeness is a fulfilment of the divine purpose.

Day Fourteen: 8.22-26:

The telling of Day Fourteen, we note at the outset, is the most concise of all Mark's twenty-eight Days; it is the shortest for its number of verses. It consists of a simple three-part structure, ABB'. As was stated under Day Twelve, when compared for correspondences with Day Twelve, 7.31-37, we have to see them as a pair, as one day's telling has most clearly influenced the other.

The introductory Part A comprises three parts which all begin with *καί* and a historical present. The first part, v.22a, begins with one of Mark's favourite indications of a new turning point, *Καὶ ἔρχονται*: it establishes the new geographical place (see also 6.45 and discussions on Bethsaida). The balancing second and third parts, v.22b and v.22c, in turn introduce the new character on the scene and, as in Day Twelve, another ardent request which is put to Jesus. The two historical presents and pronouns, *καὶ φέρουσιν αὐτῷ...* and *καὶ παρακαλοῦσιν αὐτόν...* are exactly the same as in Day Twelve, and are positioned also in exactly the same way, at b and b'.

Parts B and B', vv.23,24 and vv.25,26, relate a two-part healing, which is a unique event in itself in the Gospel. Further, that this is the first healing of a blind person in the Gospel attracts to it special status also. The only other healing of a blind person is recorded in the last Day of the following Series, that is Day Twenty-one, 10.46-52. The two middle Series end in the same way (as they also begin in the same way and turn in the same way).

The introductory part of Part B, v.23a, as in Day Twelve's report, sees Jesus taking the man away alone (compare here, *καὶ ἐπιλαβόμενος* and *καὶ ἀπολαβόμενος*). In the second part, v.23b, Jesus spits in his eyes (in the parallel story, "spitting he touched his tongue"), places his hands on him (*cf.* "he put his fingers in his ears"), and begins to ask the man if he can see. In the third part, v.24, the man responds: he sees partially. In Part B' and the first part, v.25a, which begins with a non-*καί* sentence, Jesus again places his hands on the man, here expressed as, "on his eyes". In the closing, balancing, two parts, v.25b and v.26, in the first, the man begins to see clearly (the imperfect tense, as in Day Twelve at this point, is again inceptive), and in the second, Jesus sends him to his home, forbidding him to enter the village (*cf.* the ending of Day Twelve).

The literary structure of Day Fourteen follows, firstly in the Greek and then in literal English:

---

[295]I am condensing much information here on 'numbers', from *NIDNTT* and *IntDB*.

Καὶ ἔρχονται εἰς Βηθσαϊδάν.   A
    καὶ φέρουσιν αὐτῷ τυφλὸν
    καὶ παρακαλοῦσιν αὐτὸν
        ἵνα αὐτοῦ ἅψηται. [23]
καὶ ἐπιλαβόμενος τῆς χειρὸς τοῦ τυφλοῦ   B
    ἐξήνεγκεν αὐτὸν
    ἔξω τῆς κώμης,
  καὶ πτύσας εἰς τὰ ὄμματα αὐτοῦ,
    ἐπιθεὶς τὰς χεῖρας αὐτῷ,
    ἐπηρώτα αὐτόν,
        Εἴ τι βλέπεις;
  καὶ ἀναβλέψας
       ἔλεγεν,
    Βλέπω τοὺς ἀνθρώπους,
    ὅτι ὡς δένδρα ὁρῶ περιπατοῦντας.
εἶτα πάλιν   B'
    ἐπέθηκεν τὰς χεῖρας
    ἐπὶ τοὺς ὀφθαλμοὺς αὐτοῦ,
  καὶ διέβλεψεν,
    καὶ ἀπεκατέστη,
    καὶ ἐνέβλεπεν τηλαυγῶς ἅπαντα. [26]
καὶ ἀπέστειλεν αὐτὸν εἰς οἶκον αὐτοῦ
    λέγων,
    Μηδὲ εἰς τὴν κώμην εἰσέλθῃς.

And they come to Bethsaida.   A
    And they bring to him a blind man.
    And they beg him
        that he would touch him.
  And taking the hand of the blind man,   B
    he led him out,
    outside the village.
  And with spittle in his eyes,
    putting his hands on him,
    he questioned him,
        'Can you see anything?'
  And looking up,
        he began to say,
    'I see men
    that look like trees walking.'
Then again   B'
    he put his hands
    on his eyes,
  And he looked steadily
    and he was restored,
    and he saw everything clearly.
  And he sent him to his house,
    saying,
    'Do not enter into the village.'

Clearly, because of the story's parallel in Day Twelve, I judge that 8.22-26 attaches to that which precedes it as the seventh Day of the Gospel's second Series of seven Days, the first of two middle Series. Most commentators indeed do take 8.27 (which follows) to begin a new section in Mark's Gospel, but a number entertain the possibility that 8.22 begins it.[296] In his discussion of what he calls "the great central section of the Gospel, 8.22-10.52", Best[297] sees the healings of blind men, 8.22-26 and 10.46-52, as the beginning and the ending of the section. He sees the accounts as "transition sections", but fails to support his view when he argues: 1) "To understand them we need to accept the widespread conception that the restoration of sight is a metaphor for the gift of spiritual understanding"; and 2) that the two-stage healing, of 8.22-26, "represents two stages of enlightenment" and that this is reflected in the next account of 8.27ff, which tells of two stages in Peter's enlightenment (I have other alternative interpretations to this which will be explained below as we discuss this threesome of Days, 7.31-8.26, and as we summarise this Series). Best's understanding and his interpretation of the two passages have their supporters, but neither of his arguments supports his positioning of them as an *inclusio* within 8.22-10.52. I judge other issues determine the two passages' true positionings in Mark's scheme: 1) that 8.22-26 clearly reflects 7.31-37 and, therefore, belongs in sub-Series with it; 2) that 8.27-9.1 reflects 6.1-29 (we discuss this under Day Fifteen) with the result that the first Days of the two middle Series correspond; and 3) that 8.22-26 and 10.46-52, the only two stories in the Gospel on the healings of blind people, in turn, complete the two "central sections" (not *one*, as Best says), so that the last Days of the two middle Series correspond. The symmetries of 2) and 3) are compelling evidence of Mark's plan.

We consider again the last three Days of this Series, not separately now, but together. Days Twelve, Thirteen and Fourteen appear to form a threesome of Days in the style ABA'. The similarity between Days Twelve and Fourteen would seem to require it. But, temporal details suggest otherwise; that it is an ABB' formation. There is a disjunction between Days Twelve and Thirteen: there is a passing of other days between. Between Days Thirteen and Fourteen there is the link of a late/night-crossing; no days between are suggested or inferred. In geographical terms, however, we might judge that Days Twelve and Thirteen are specially linked by the location in the Decapolis, and judge the scheme is AA'B. We ask again, as we did before, in considering the first threesome of Days in this Series, "Is there a 'movement' or a seam running through the telling of these Days, Days Twelve, Thirteen and Fourteen, that suggests a clear intention on Mark's part?"

Day Twelve tells simply of a healing, in the Decapolis, of a deaf man with a speaking difficulty. Jesus is the prophet who fulfils prophecy. But, he has only partially fulfilled it. From the Isaianic allusion, at its conclusion, the healing of the *lame* and the *blind* are missing. In Day Fourteen we *do*, however, find a report of Jesus' healing of a *blind* man, who sees men as trees "*walking*" in the first stage of his cure. Is this at all significant? If it is, then it suggests an ABA' arrangement of this sub-Series.

Day Thirteen, in between, however, raises a number of issues about 'blindness' in terms of a 'lack' or 'a want' of 'understanding'. It tells of the second miracle-feeding of the Gospel, and immediately after it, Pharisees ask for a "sign from heaven". They want, like Mark's audience to see something from Jesus that will prove to them who he is. To the reader/listeners, of course, the Pharisees' request is incredible. Were the Pharisees *blind* to what was going on, and *deaf* to reports? Hooker helpfully observes that miracles and parables function similarly in Mark's Gospel[298]. "To those who have eyes to see and ears to hear, both miracles and parables demonstrate the power of the Kingdom of God," she says. (For which,

---

[296]See note 255 above.
[297]Best, *Disciples...*, pp.2-4.
[298]Hooker, *The Gospel...*, p.191.

compare 8.18.) And in the first sub-Series (in the summary on page 146) we notice the link between 'not understanding' and 'hardened hearts'. Both Jesus' disciples and the Pharisees provide the examples of this. The same is found in this sub-Series also, at the very point where Mark begs understanding of the feeding miracles, in 8.17. Only now it is the disciples alone who provide the example, and *they are here being challenged by Jesus about it*. It is clearly the case that the disciples provide Mark with the vehicle for this teaching. In Day Thirteen we read that the disciples are amazingly 'blind'. Just before the feeding of the four-thousand, they would appear to have no recollection at all of how Jesus fed the five-thousand. Furthermore, in 8.15, we see a demonstration of Jesus' concern for his disciples (and, there-fore, for all who would follow him) that they are not 'taken in' by the Pharisees, or by Herod (8.15 recalls 6.14bff. in the first sub-Series). To Jesus, the disciples demonstrate a worrying 'blindness' to the meaning of the 'feedings' (in 8.16-21). And Best, as we have seen already above, identifies the link in Mark's Gospel between 'restoration of sight' and 'understanding'.

Day Thirteen raises a number of problems and issues. Day Fourteen ends the sub-Series with a resolution to them all for everyone. Day Fourteen tells how Jesus is able to heal even the blind, and so fulfill all the prophecy alluded to earlier. Only now, the healing is not simply a healing. It is a healing of a blind man, uniquely in the Gospel *in two stages*. It is a metaphor, an acted parable, especially so, given the previous Day's issues raisings. The heal-ing in two stages has to be interpreted. Yes, he can heal the blind, but he can give enlighten-ment too, so that *all* can "see clearly all things".

In this sub-Series, Mark certainly touches a raw nerve in the minds and hearts of his audience. Pharisees and all like them want an easy step to faith. Jesus' denies the Pharisees and those like them such a sign. Signs are not to be relied upon. Our 'hearts' should tell us that Jesus is the one. (In our discussion of the longer ending, we will return to the matter of 'signs'.)

In summary, the introductory Day to the sub-Series, 7.31-37, reports a simple healing miracle, but it does not, in itself, fulfil the whole of the prophecy alluded to. The middle Day, 8.1-21, reports a miracle feeding and raises a number of issues about 'understanding' and the 'feeding of faith'. The concluding Day, 8.22-26, tells of a healing miracle which completes the earlier prophecy, but it fundamentally points beyond itself, in its unique way, to the very means to 'understanding'. The sub-Series exhibits an *inclusio* between the first and the last days, but it is best expressed as an ABB' scheme like those we have already encountered, 1.21-2.22, 3.7-5.43 and 6.1-7.23.

A Summary of the Second Series of Seven Days:

Again, as for the First Series of Seven Days, the findings of my analysis are summarised and presented in tabular form.

The first threesome of "days" of this second Series, 6.1-7.23, is discussed under Day Ten. It can be summarised in terms very similar to the first threesome of "days" of the first Series. It tells initially where and how Jesus' fame spread further (through the mission of his disciples and "Jesus' going round in circuit"). Nazareth and neighbouring villages in Galilee were the places of mission, after Jesus' teaching in the synagogue. The disciples' preaching, casting out of demons and healing work led to people talking about Jesus, wondering who he was, and gathering to him in huge numbers. This time, even Herod hears and wonders, as well as reflects on what he had done to John the Baptist. The feeding of the five-thousand is presented, overall in the Markan scheme, as a symbolic and Messianic meal for Jews. Again, as in the first threesome of "days" of the first Series of the Gospel, Mark demonstrates how Jesus' continuing ministry, wherever he went, in villages, towns or countryside, leads to a clash between Jesus, whose ministry is "powerfully new", and Pharisees and scribes, whose "old" positions are being challenged. This sub-Series raises issues of 'understanding' who Jesus is and what he is doing.

The second threesome of "days", 7.31-8.26, likewise compares with the second threesome of "days" in the first Series of seven Days, as well as with the first threesome of "days" of this Series. Given Jesus is in predominantly Gentile territory (compare also 5.1-20, in the first Series and its second threesome), the continuing work of establishing 'new Israel', which will include Gentiles, begins with a healing, and proceeds to a feeding of four-thousand, a symbolic meal for Gentiles and another clash with Pharisees, before the first account of its kind in the Gospel, an amazing healing, back in predominantly Jewish territory, of a blind man, in *two stages*. This sub-Series raises issues of 'understanding' who Jesus is and what he is doing, and also the source of this 'understanding'.

The two three-day sub-Series have their rich common seams, their many points of contact. They are arranged around a central, singular and individualistic day, Day Eleven. In literary-structural terms, this Day Eleven has a central, pivotal, or fulcrum role between the sub-Series/threesomes of Days, and as we discussed in Day Eleven's analysis it focuses on the issue of the tension between Jesus' mission to Jews and Gentiles: Jews are first in order, but Gentiles are included, and second. It discloses very clearly that Mark is a creative writer who demands to be read and understood for what he has created. When did anyone last hear a sermon on the feeding of the five-thousand that included the feeding of the four-thousand and, at its heart, the incident of the Syrophoenician woman whose reply is provoked by Jesus' supposed reference, first-of-all, to Gentile 'dogs'! The Series well included 'increase' in its title; Jesus' ministry is not just to Jews, but to Gentiles.

The balance of the Series is clearly evident. The first sub-Series includes Jesus' symbolic meal for Jews (in the telling of the middle day), and after the pivotal Day, the second sub-Series (again, in the telling of the middle day) his symbolic meal for Gentiles. The summary of the structure of Mark's Second Series of Seven Days, therefore, is now presented: it is in an ABA' form, as is the First Series of Seven Days, where A represents the first threesome of Days, B the singular Day Eleven, and A' the second threesome of Days. In examining the first Series, we had to consider the possibility that it was a seven-Day chiasm. Such a possibility has not surfaced in the examination of this Series' structure.

This Series well indicates the steady and inventive control which Mark exercised over the material he had to hand. This material has been variously described as oral or written, as single, independent units of tradition, or as already-linked units. The miracle stories themselves have been viewed by Hooker, as already-formed, independent cycles of tradition, 6.32-7.37 and 8.1-26[299]; by Achtemeier, as a pre-Markan cycle of miracles consisting of two catenae[300], which he incorporated; and by others as an earlier, original cycle, 6.32-52, 8.22-30[301] which Mark has split up, and into which he has inserted 6.53-8.21, to create his own double cycle. Additional to the material he had to hand, we have to consider the material which he created[302]. All options need to be weighed very carefully against the new evidence of his rhetorical method, his Day-compositional planning, and his creation of a Series of seven Days, with limits of 6.1 and 8.26. It never has been an easy task to separate the tradition Mark employs from his editing: it will be no easier now to determine *what material he had to hand* before he began composing, because it would appear that, if he did have written tradition in his possession, he has re-written everything to his abb' presentational method.

As I stated under Day Eleven, given the contents of the seven Days of this Series, in terms of the incidents/events themselves and their interpretations, and the wider geographical

---

[299]Hooker, *The Gospel...*, p.163.
[300]Achtemeier, "Towards the Isolation...".
[301]Hooker, *The Gospel...*, p.171.
[302]Fowler, *Loaves and Fishes...*, p.181.

area Jesus covers, I am choosing to title this Series simply, "Days of Increase in the Mission of Jesus".

As I did at the conclusion of the analysis of the First Series, so I will do here. For the sake of clarity, the point is emphasised that while Mark chose to report a second stage in the mission of Jesus in seven Days, he intimated that there were other days he was not reporting. Between the telling of the last Day of the first Series and the telling of the first Day of the second Series, Day Eight, a journey took place (of a minimum of about 18 miles) which will itself have taken at least one day; and the story of Day Eight takes place on a Sabbath, up to six days later. Between Days Eight and Nine, under Day Nine's analysis, we noted that weeks may have passed. Days Nine and Ten are consecutive. Between Days Ten and Eleven is a 60 mile journey to Tyre which will have taken three days minimum. Between Days Eleven and Twelve a return journey is made taking the same length of time. Between Days Twelve and Thirteen is a passing of three days minimum. Days Thirteen and Fourteen are consecutive. The point is then made, without any attempt to add up the days to establish Mark's under-standing of the actual time this stage of Jesus' mission took. Simply, he summarised what to him was a stage in Jesus' mission of possibly several weeks, in only seven Days of reports.

In completing this presentation on the Second Series, we return to the issue of the fi-nal Day, 8.21-26, and to how Mark meant us to interpret the healing of the blind man, *in two stages*. I have already nailed my colours to the mast, by interpreting it in its sub-Series con-text. But it may be that it has significance also in its Series context, or in the Gospel's context as a whole.

To many, as to Best (see above) it appears to look *forward* to the revelation of Peter that Jesus is the Christ, which is completed by Jesus in turn, in terms of the suffering and death he would have to undergo. Given that it concludes the Second Series, it appears much more certain that, for Mark, it initially looks *back*, and completes his Series' presentation. Given the localities mentioned (which include Jerusalem more than once) and the 'feeding of the Jews' in the first sub-Series (6.1-7.23), Jesus' mission is *firstly to the Jews*, and after the turning point of the middle Day (7.24-30), given the localities and the 'feeding of the Gen-tiles' in the second sub-Series (7.31-8.26), Jesus' mission is *secondly to the Gentiles*. It would appear that Mark wants his audience to interpret the ministry of Jesus in this way, for which purpose 8.21-26 is a more than adequate, though somewhat mysterious conclusion to the Se-ries. (And we note, the ending of his previous Day's telling in (8.17-21) is no less mysteri-ous.)

Additional support for this conclusion comes from reference to the 'Sabbath'. In the first Series of the Gospel, its two reports were deemed to have significance. The first was that Jesus' ministry was firstly to the Jews (see pages 111f.). This Day is the first Day of that Se-ries. On the first Day of this second Series, it is a Sabbath also. Again, the significance is the same, and it is re-inforcing for its repetition. Sabbaths are not encountered in Mark's Day scheme beyond this point, until 16.1, when one is reported in the introductory piece to the fi-nal Day's presentation, which tells of the events of the first day of the week.

Lastly, we ask, "Are Best *et al.* right in seeing the two-stage healing of 8.22-26 as pre-emptive of the two stages of disclosure about Jesus in the following pericope, 8.27ff.?" (For their proposal and for my views about the positioning of the pericope, see page 162.) Clearly, there are arguments for seeing that this unique healing, in two stages, has its interpre-tation firstly within the three-day sub-Series of its report, and secondly within the Series it-self. Whether or not it has its interpretation in the Gospel as a whole, that is, outside of the second Series, is judged best by reference to ancient, rhetorical convention.

Best's interpretation is that 8.22-26 and 8.27ff. are structurally related. My literary-structural analysis sees the relationship in this way: 8.22-26 is the last Day of a Series and 8.27ff. is (part of) the first Day's telling of the next Series. Normally in ancient rhetoric effort is made to "smooth the transition" between the ending of one section and the beginning of the next. Normally this is achieved by a link *word* or *phrase*, an anastrophe (see page 30). There is a clear example of an anastrophe between Series, in the last Day of the third Series and the first Day of the fourth. In 10.46-52, we read "*Son of David*" twice; and in 11.1-11 we read, "Blessed is the coming Kingdom of *our father David*". These are the first mentions of "David" since 2.25; the next follow at 12.35,36 and 37.

Is it then the case that Mark uses a 'link motif' instead of a standard anastrophe to "smooth the transition" between the ending of the second Series and the beginning of the third? If there is clear indication that Mark himself intended a 'two-stage' parallel, the firmest literary-structural evidence (given our findings so far) would be a presentation of the two stages of revelation in the B and B' parts of a three-part whole. An examination of the first Day of the next Series will show that this is in fact the case. Best and others appear, therefore, to be right about the connection, but wrong in their structural argument. We must conclude, therefore, that there is justification for interpreting the 'two-stage' healing of 8.22-26 in three different contexts: in the sub-Series it concludes, in the Series it ends and in its Gospel setting, where it precedes the telling of the first Day of the next Series.

A Tabular Summary of the literary-structure of the Second Seven Days:

DAYS: number identified in series	1	2	3	4	5	6	7
number identified in Gospel	8	9	10	11	12	13	14
chapters and verses	6.1-29	6.30-52	6.53-7.23	7.24-30	7.31-37	8.1-21	8.22-26
SERIES' STRUCTURE	A		B		A'		
DAYS: in literary-terms, in series	A	B	B'	A	B	B'	
DAYS' sections	A B B'	A B B'	A B B'	A	A	A B B'	A
DAYS' sectional sub-divisions	A B B' A B B' A B B'	A B B' A B B' A B B'	A B B' A B B' A B B'	A B B'	A B B'	A B B' A B B' A B B'	A B B'
DAYS' number of verses	29	23	27	7	7	21	5
SUB-SERIES' number of verses		79				33	
SERIES' number of verses				119			

Addendum to the analysis of 'The Second Seven Days':

During the course of this chapter, a further signifier of literary-structural division between Days has been added to the list of those established in the analysis of the First Series. It is an introductory formula which is basic to understanding eight of the Day-divisions, four in this Series and four in the following Series. It is added to the list of the features of Mark's rhetorical method, for which reason it continues the numbering:

Under Day Eleven: 19)   The leaving of the place of the earlier Day's telling and the arriving in another: an introductory formula.

Again as in the first Series, we note in the second Series a wide variation in the sizes of Mark's rhetorical units of Days, parts of Days, and so on. The Days themselves vary between 29 and 5 verses, by a factor of just less than six (which is much less than the factor of ten of the first Series). We observe that each of the Days in the first sub-Series are longer in the telling than each of those in the second. No symmetry of size in the arrangements of the Days of the two sub-Series appears intended by Mark; in the first sub-Series the middle of the three is the shortest; in the second sub-Series the middle Day is the longest in the telling. What matters to Mark, in literary terms, above all else, is that his constructions, whether they are ABA', ABB', ABB'/ABB'/ABB', or abb', are in themselves complete. That way, the reader is given every help to interpret correctly the script he is supplied, of columns of rows of letters and little else, into its parts, its Days and its Series. Similarly, the listeners, as well as the reader-reciter, are given every help to set the text to memory for performing in exactly the way that the writer intended.

Chapter Five
The Third Series of Seven Days (8.27-10.52):

Day Fifteen: **8.27-9.1:**

The Day begins:

> Καὶ ἐξῆλθεν ὁ Ἰησοῦς   a
> καὶ οἱ μαθηταὶ αὐτοῦ   b
> εἰς τὰς κώμας Καισαρείας τῆς Φιλίππου.   b'

We compare it with the beginning of Day Eight:

> Καὶ ἐξῆλθεν ἐκεῖθεν,   a
> καὶ ἔρχεται εἰς τὴν πατρίδα αὐτοῦ,   b
> καὶ ἀκολουθοῦσιν αὐτῷ οἱ μαθηταὶ αὐτοῦ.   b'

Significantly, Day Eight begins the first middle Series (6.1-8.26) and Day Fifteen begins the second middle Series (8.27-10.52). Both these Days begin with the introductory formula of leaving one place and arriving in another (found eight times in all: four times in the Series 6.1-8.26, and also at 9.30/33, 10.1 and 10.46 in this Series); see under Day Eleven for a discussion of this. We can observe, in addition to the same detailed structure in each (but with b and b' in reversal, for contents), seven common words between them, and in each the same repeating use of parechesis (the same sounding endings of *οῦ*, at the endings of the last two lines of each, as discovered in abundance in the opening of the Gospel, in 1.1 and 1.2,3)[303]. It is compelling evidence that as Mark composed one of these two opening parts to these Days' tellings, he did so with an eye on the other. I further deduce that the significant positionings and roles of these two Days, at the beginnings of new Series, 6.1-8.26 and 8.27-10.52[304], caused Mark to compose these introductions with even greater attention to detail than elsewhere, by reflecting the clear characteristic of the Prologue's opening parechesis.

Other significant correspondences with Day Eight can be identified. The structure of this Day's telling, is the same composite ABB'/ABB'/ABB' structure, with a short A Part. The primary correspondence in content terms concerns what people were saying about Jesus, see 6.14b,15 and 8.28, and yet in this Day's telling we get to know who he is, through the declaration of Peter. (See Day Eight's analysis for this.) A common phrase between these two days is ἤρξατο διδάσκειν (compare 6.2 and 8.31), though it is found also in other introductory elements of Mark's rhetorical units, for example, in 4.1 and 6.34.

The disclosures of Day Fifteen are themselves supremely important in Mark's Gospel scheme, and in this seven Day Series too, and we will discuss them below, but first of all we note the views of Taylor, Schweizer and Hooker on the literary structure, with which also

---

[303]Other examples of parechesis in the Gospel only occur at 13.1, the beginning of a new half in the telling of 11.20-13.37, Day Twenty-four, the longest Day's telling in terms of verses, and in 16.19b,20 in the longer ending. Their likely significance will continue to be discussed.
[304]Taylor (*The Gospel...*), Nineham (*Saint Mark*), Schweizer (*The Good News...*), Hooker (*The Gospel...*) and myself, all agree on the limits of this section of the Gospel, though we vary in our designation of it, as the second, the third, the fourth or the fifth section.

Robbins and Best[305] agree. Nineham does not discuss the matter. It is the case, that, for the first time, we do all agree! The Parts I, II and III are 8.27-30, vv.31-33 and vv.34-9.1, though I will show that they can best be described as Parts ABB'. Given my presentation above, I judge v.27abc to be the introductory piece to this Day's telling, for its mention of the principal characters, Jesus and his disciples, and the place to which they were going. Part A, 8.27-30, first develops with the important words, *καὶ ἐν τῇ ὁδῷ*. Jesus and the disciples were nowhere in earshot of anyone else. It is the setting for the first disclosure that Jesus is the Christ. Part B, 8.31-33, opens with the second disclosure of the Day, of what will happen to Jesus. The Part is completed with 'rebukings', Peter of Jesus and, in turn, Jesus of Peter. Part B', 8.34-9.1, begins with Jesus calling a crowd. The third disclosure of this Day is for the people, even for all who are listening to this Gospel: it is a message on self-denial, carrying one's own cross and following. Thus is the opening part, v.34. The following part B is itself made up of three parts which each begin with the word *ὅς*. 9.1 provides the final part B', telling that there will be some among them who will live to see the kingdom of God come.

The Day reads as follows:

Καὶ ἐξῆλθεν ὁ'Ιησοῦς   A   A
     καὶ οἱ μαθηταὶ αὐτοῦ
     εἰς τὰς κώμας Καισαρείας τῆς Φιλίππου.
   καὶ ἐν τῇ ὁδῷ
     ἐπηρώτα τοὺς μαθητὰς αὐτοῦ
     λέγων αὐτοῖς,
   Τίνα με
     λέγουσιν οἱ ἄνθρωποι
     εἶναι;
οἱ δὲ εἶπαν αὐτῷ   B
     λέγοντες
     ὅτι'Ιωάννην τὸν βαπτιστήν,
   καὶ ἄλλοι,
     'Ηλίαν,
   ἄλλοι δὲ
     ὅτι εἷς τῶν προφητῶν.
καὶ αὐτὸς ἐπηρώτα αὐτούς,   B'
     'Υμεῖς δὲ
     τίνα με λέγετε εἶναι;
   ἀποκριθεὶς
     ὁ Πέτρος λέγει αὐτῷ,
     Σὺ εἶ ὁ Χριστός.
   καὶ ἐπετίμησεν αὐτοῖς
     ἵνα μηδενὶ λέγωσιν
     περὶ αὐτοῦ.

---

[305]Robbins, *Jesus the Teacher...*, pp.37-41; Best, *Disciples...*, p.6.

Καὶ ἤρξατο διδάσκειν αὐτοὺς   A   **B**
       ὅτι δεῖ τὸν υἱὸν τοῦ ἀνθρώπου
         πολλὰ
         παθεῖν
       καὶ ἀποδοκιμασθῆναι ὑπὸ τῶν πρεσβυτέρων
          καὶ τῶν ἀρχιερέων
          καὶ τῶν γραμματέων
       καὶ ἀποκτανθῆναι
       καὶ μετὰ τρεῖς ἡμέρας ἀναστῆναι. [32]
    καὶ παρρησίᾳ   B
       τὸν λόγον
       ἐλάλει,
     καὶ προσλαβόμενος
       ὁ Πέτρος
       αὐτὸν
    ἤρξατο
       <u>ἐπιτιμᾶν</u>
       αὐτῷ.
  ὁ δὲ ἐπιστραφεὶς   B'
       καὶ ἰδὼν τοὺς μαθητὰς αὐτοῦ
       <u>ἐπετίμησεν Πέτρῳ</u>
     καὶ λέγει,
       Ὕπαγε ὀπίσω μου,
      Σατανᾶ,
    ὅτι οὐ φρονεῖς
       τὰ τοῦ θεοῦ
       ἀλλὰ τὰ τῶν ἀνθρώπων.

Καὶ προσκαλεσάμενος τὸν ὄχλον   A   **B'**
       σὺν τοῖς μαθηταῖς αὐτοῦ
       εἶπεν αὐτοῖς,
    Εἴ τις θέλει
       ὀπίσω μου
       ἀκολουθεῖν,
   ἀπαρνησάσθω ἑαυτὸν
       καὶ ἀράτω τὸν σταυρὸν αὐτοῦ
       καὶ ἀκολουθείτω μοι. [35]
  ὃς γὰρ ἐὰν θέλῃ   B
       τὴν ψυχὴν αὐτοῦ σῶσαι
       ἀπολέσει αὐτήν·
    ὃς δ' ἂν ἀπολέσει τὴν ψυχὴν αὐτοῦ
         ἕνεκεν ἐμοῦ
         καὶ τοῦ εὐαγγελίου
       σώσει αὐτήν. [36]
     τί γὰρ ὠφελεῖ ἄνθρωπον
       κερδῆσαι τὸν κόσμον ὅλον
       καὶ ζημιωθῆναι τὴν ψυχὴν αὐτοῦ; [37]
     τί γὰρ δοῖ ἄνθρωπος
       ἀντάλλαγμα
       τῆς ψυχῆς αὐτοῦ; [38]
  ὃς γὰρ ἐὰν ἐπαισχυνθῇ με
       καὶ τοὺς ἐμοὺς λόγους,
       ἐν τῇ γενεᾷ ταύτῃ
         τῇ μοιχαλίδι
         καὶ ἁμαρτωλῷ,
   καὶ ὁ υἱὸς τοῦ ἀνθρώπου ἐπαισχυνθήσεται αὐτὸν
   ὅταν ἔλθῃ
       ἐν τῇ δόξῃ τοῦ πατρὸς αὐτοῦ
       μετὰ τῶν ἀγγέλων τῶν ἁγίων.
  καὶ ἔλεγεν αὐτοῖς,   **B'**
      Ἀμὴν λέγω ὑμῖν
    ὅτι εἰσίν τινες
     ὧδε
     τῶν ἑστηκότων
   οἵτινες οὐ μὴ γεύσωνται θανάτου
       ἕως ἂν ἴδωσιν τὴν βασιλείαν τοῦ θεοῦ
       ἐληλυθυῖαν ἐν δυνάμει.

And in literal English:

And Jesus went forth,   A   **A**
      and his disciples, (*ou*)
      to the villages of Caesarea Philippi. (*ou*) (for *ou*, see Day 8)
   And on the way,
      he questioned his disciples (*ou*),
      saying to them,
  'Whom
     do men say
     that I am?'
And they told him,   B
      saying,
      <u>'John the Baptist,</u>   (for parallels, see Day 8)
   <u>and others,</u>
     <u>Elijah,</u>
  <u>but others,</u>
     <u>one of the prophets.'</u>
And he questioned them,   B'
    'But you,
     whom do you say that I am?'
  Answering
    Peter says to him,
    'You are the Christ.'
  And he rebuked them
    that they should tell no one
    about him.

And he began to teach them,   A   **B**
    'It is necessary for the son of man
      many things
      to suffer.
    And to be rejected by the elders
        and the chief priests
        and the scribes
     and to be killed,
     and after three days to rise again.'
And openly / the word / he spoke   B
   and taking aside
     Peter
     him
  he began
     to rebuke
     him.
But he turning round   B'
    and seeing his disciples,
    rebuked Peter
  and he says,
    'Go behind me,
     Satan,
  because you do not have in mind
    the things of God,
    but the things of men.'

And calling the crowd to him,   A   **B'**
        with his disciples,
        he said to them,
    'If anyone wishes
        after me
        to come,
   Let him deny himself
        and let him take up his cross
        and let him follow me.
<u>For whoever</u> wishes   B
        to <u>save</u> <u>his soul</u>
        <u>will lose</u> it.
   And whoever <u>will lose</u> <u>his soul</u>,
            for my sake
            and the gospel,
        he will <u>save</u> it.:
     <u>for what</u> profits a man
        to gain the whole world
        and to forfeit <u>his soul</u>;
     <u>for what</u> might a man give
        in exchange
        for <u>his soul</u>?
<u>For whoever</u> is ashamed of me
        and the words of me,
        in this generation
        adulterous
        and sinful,
     also the son of man will be ashamed of him
     when he comes
        in the glory of his father
        with the holy angels.'
And he said to them,   B'
      'Truly, I tell you,
   there are some
     here
     of the ones standing
  who by no means will taste death
     until they see the kingdom of God
     having come in power.'

The key words and phrases and the repeating detailed parallels and correspondences are significant within this Day's presentation and as we consider this Day and its parallel Day Eight. We necessarily now list and discuss these features. They play an important part in the Markan scheme, in his Gospel as a whole and to this particular Series:

1) *Καὶ ἐν τῇ ὁδῷ*

The mention of 'And on the way…' introduces a phrase much in evidence in the Days of this Series. In the Gospel, the word for "way" is found at 1.2,3; 8.3,27; 9.33,34; 10.17,32,46,52; and 11.8. In the Prologue (see 1.2,3), the term is used in the accusative case, in the manner of "prepare the way".[306] At 10.17, the phrase is *εἰς ὁδόν* "into the way", and at 11.8, similarly, *εἰς τὴν ὁδόν* "in the way". At 10.46, the phrase is *παρὰ τὴν ὁδὸν* "by/at the side of the way". The word by itself is also found at 4.4,15, in the parable of the sower and its interpretation, and in 12.14, when Pharisees and Herodians question Jesus, and acknowledge that he teaches "the way of God". A variant use may be recognised in 13.34, in *ἀπόδημος* "on a far journey". In all the other cases, the phrase is *καὶ ἐν τῇ ὁδῷ* "on the way".

Of the fifteen Gospel uses in total, seven are found in this Third Series, in Days 15, 17 *bis*, 19, 20 and 21 *bis*, that is, in the first and third Days of the first threesome of Days, and in all three Days of the second threesome. We note that they are found twice over in the last Days of both threesomes. The much systematic use of the word itself does much to bind these seven Days themselves together, in Mark's scheme.

This Series contributes much to the notion (derived in the first place from consideration of the Prologue) that Mark's Gospel is "the gospel of the Way", but because its final narrative-use is in the first Day's telling of the fourth and last Series of the Gospel, "the Jerusalem Days", at 11.8, it provokes a narrow interpretation, however, that the destination of this "way", in narrative terms alone, is Jerusalem. See also 10.32. Such an argument justifies the first part of the title suitable for this Third Series: "The Days of Jesus' Journeying to Jerusalem, to the Cross and Glory".

2) *οἱ δὲ εἶπαν αὐτῷ λέγοντες ὅτι Ἰωάννην τὸν βαπτιστήν,*
καὶ ἄλλοι, Ἠλίαν,
ἄλλοι δὲ ὅτι εἷς τῶν προφητῶν.

The comparison between 8.28 and 6.14b,15 provokes a comparison between the functions of the first days of the two middle series of the Gospel. The question of Jesus' identity is firmly raised at the beginning of both. In 6.1-6a it is introduced in the opening scene of Jesus' teaching in the synagogue in his home town, and developed in 6.14bff. in which three possibilities are entertained by the people. Herod thinks he knows which of the choices is to be made. In 8.28-30, in the opening of this Day's, it leads to the answer of Peter: Jesus' identity is not any one of the three entertained by the people; he is "the Christ".

3) *Σὺ εἶ ὁ Χριστός*, 8.29. For the first time since the opening phrase of the Prologue, "The beginning of the gospel of Jesus Christ...", this status is given Jesus. The term next appears, on Jesus' own lips, at 9.41, noticeably in Day Seventeen, the third day of this Series and of the first sub-Series (the use in these Days suggests that Mark intended an *inclusio* be

---

[306]In his discussion on 8.22-10.52, Best refers to the Prologue and Mark's use of O.T. scripture and states, "Mark's Gospel is the.... gospel of The Way. It is a way in which Jesus, the Lord, goes and it is a way to which he calls his followers..." See Best, *Disciples...,* p.5.
Marcus, in fine detail sifts the arguments for this same proposition and concludes, "It would be no exaggeration... to say that the way of Jesus/the way of the Lord is not only the double theme of Mark's Gospel, but also the controlling paradigm for his interpretation of the life of his community." See Marcus, *The Way of the Lord...,* p.47.

read). In the Fourth Series, it is applied at 12.35, 13.21, 14.61 and 15.32. Most significantly, in this first Day's telling of this third Series, it is introduced in the first part, Part **A**, and then elaborated upon in Part **B**, before being further elaborated upon in Part **B'**. In the first of the two '**B**' parts, the disclosure is about Jesus' suffering, death and rising again and in the second it is about Jesus' coming in glory and the coming kingdom of God, in power. It is an opening to a new series which focuses on an exposition on Jesus and what his followers are to do.

At this juncture, it is worth drawing attention to a title for Jesus which suddenly appears in the Gospel for the first time in the last Day of this Series, Day Twenty-One. Twice over (in 10.47,48) we read that "Son of David" is the cry of the blind beggar Bartimaeus. To our four commentators, it is a messianic title synonymous with "Christ". In Mark's presentation, this Series ends as it begins, and another Markan *inclusio* is observed.

4)　　*Καὶ ἤρξατο διδάσκειν αὐτοὺς*
　　　　　ὅτι δεῖ τὸν υἱὸν τοῦ ἀνθρώπου
　　　　　πολλὰ
　　　　　παθεῖν
　　　　καὶ ἀποδοκιμασθῆναι ὑπὸ τῶν πρεσβυτέρων
　　　　　καὶ τῶν ἀρχιερέων
　　　　　καὶ τῶν γραμματέων
　　　　καὶ ἀποκτανθῆναι
　　　　καὶ μετὰ τρεῖς ἡμέρας ἀναστῆναι.

We observed above a parallel of this opening phrase in 6.2, at the opening of the first Day of the earlier middle Series. The view of many commentators is that Mark intended his report on the death of John the Baptist to be indicative of what would happen to Jesus: this view is supported here by literary-structural analysis. It demonstrates that for the composition of these first Days of the middle Series, Mark had the parallel between John the Baptist and Jesus in mind. The next Day's telling, without actual mention of John's name, but of Elijah[307], continues Mark's train of thought, 9.12,13, and expresses another prediction much overlooked[308] of a similar kind to the above: compare 8.31 and 9.12:

8.31:　　*ὅτι δεῖ τὸν υἱὸν τοῦ ἀνθρώπου πολλὰ παθεῖν*
9.12:　　*καὶ πῶς γέγραπται ἐπὶ τὸν υἱὸν τοῦ ἀνθρώπου ἵνα πολλὰ πάθῃ*

The first sub-Series of three Days contains a prediction each Day, therefore, because on the third Day, Day Seventeen (9.30-50), the second of what is commonly termed 'three predictions' is found at 9.31 (with the response of the disciples again, in 9.32). At 10.32-34, the middle day of the second threesome of Days of this Series, in the telling of Day Twenty, is the so-called third prediction of 'three'. This Day too contains at its close, another prediction, from Jesus' own lips, and it is another "Son of man" saying, 10.45,

　　　　　καὶ γὰρ ὁ υἱὸς τοῦ ἀνθρώπου
　　　　　　οὐκ ἦλθεν
　　　　　　διακονηθῆναι
　　　　　ἀλλὰ διακονῆσαι
　　　　καὶ δοῦναι τὴν ψυχὴν αὐτοῦ
　　　　　　λύτρον
　　　　　　ἀντὶ πολλῶν.

---

[307]See page 146 for a reference to the Elijah/Elisha like feeding by Jesus of the five-thousand. The second Days of both middle Series have their points of contact as do the first Days: see Days Nine and Sixteen.

[308]Attention is much more paid by commentators to the so-called "three predictions" (of this Series), 8.31, 9.31 and 10,33,34.

We discern, then, not three only but five such predictions in this Series. After the two very different "Son of man" sayings so far encountered in the Gospel, at 2.10 and v.28, in Series One, the seven which appear in this Series (8.31,38; 9.9,12,31; 10.33,45) are clearly grouped. The next references come at 13.26, 14.21 *bis*, 14.41,62. The "Son of man" predictions continue in 14.21 and v.41: in 13.26 and 14.62, they are, as for 8.38, to do with Jesus' return.

5) Εἴ τις θέλει
 ὀπίσω μου
 ἀκολουθεῖν,
 ἀπαρνησάσθω ἑαυτὸν
 καὶ ἀράτω τὸν σταυρὸν αὐτοῦ
 καὶ ἀκολουθείτω μοι.

Jesus' journey through suffering to glory is not his alone; suffering to glory awaits his disciples also. It is a theme which is introduced here and pursued in this Day in vv.35-9.1 and in this Series in 10.35-39 (and in different terms too, of self-denial, in 9.33-37 and 10.17-31). It is a subject which will appear again in Series Four, in 13.9-13.

6) ἐν τῇ δόξῃ τοῦ πατρὸς αὐτοῦ

"Glory" is another key word and issue which this Day's telling introduces. For the first time in the Gospel it is found at 8.38. Jesus' transfiguration glory is the first subject of the following Day, Day Sixteen. Though the word is not mentioned there itself, it is indicated in the episode. The chiastically parallel Day of the Series, Day Twenty, 10.32-45 (compare the second day with the sixth, around the fourth, the central day), contains the second use of the word, at 10.37. In the first of these, two chief characters of the Old Covenant appear with Jesus: in the second, two leading characters of the New Covenant express their wish to be seated each side of Jesus in his "glory". Just as in the first of the two middle Series, where days two and six, in the succession of days, parallel each other for feedings of the five- and the four-thousand in symbolically messianic feasts, so too in the second of the two middle Series, in the same locations, are episodes which point to Jesus' messianic status and function. The third use in the Gospel of the word "glory" is found at 13.26,27, in the same teaching as we discerned above, which additionally speaks of the sufferings that awaited the disciples. It is a saying which reflects the sayings of 8.38-9.1. It has a clear parallel also in 14.62, but again without use of the word itself.

7) τὴν βασιλείαν τοῦ θεοῦ

Up to this point in the Gospel, this phrase is discovered in the Prologue, and in the parables of the first Series only (in 1.15; 4.11,26,30). On this first Day of this Series, it is well introduced again at 9.1: it appears further at 9.47, 10.14,15,23,24,25 (the only other uses are at 12.34, 14.25 and 15.43). In this Series it appears in the telling of the first and third Days of the first sub-Series, the middle day, and the first Day of the second sub-Series, that is in each of the Series' major rhetorical units[309]. Because our focus is on literary-structural issues, we restrict discussion here of the term to a summary of Mark's use of it in this Series: "the kingdom of God" will come with the glorified Jesus and with power (8.38, 9.1) and will only be entered/received by his disciples/followers if they meet certain conditions (9.47 and following, as above).

---

[309]We noted in the first Series' summary that the middle Days of that Series shared similar structurings and contents. We observed that the last Day of the first sub-Series, the middle Day of the Series, and the first Day of the completing sub-Series, were characteristic of ancient rhetoric. Whilst they represented separate rhetorical units, they related and overlapped at the edges (page 112). These three middle Days of this Series, likewise, contain similar contents (teachings on the kingdom of God), and relate and overlap as they function in the same way structurally.

This third Series of Seven Days will be shown to be structured like the first and the second. Day Fifteen, therefore, as Day Eight, begins a Series and begins a sub-Series of three Days. The force of the argument Mark presents for this Day can be expressed in terms similar to that of Mack[310] but more fully and more specifically: Jesus is not only the founder teacher, but also the crucified and risen Christ, predictive prophet and apocalyptic judge.

Day Sixteen: 9.2-32:

The day begins *Καὶ μετὰ ἡμέρας ἕξ*. Clearly, there can be no argument that a new Day in Mark's telling does not commence here. As at 2.1, and 8.1,2, here for the last time in the Gospel Mark has given explicit information of days passing between the telling of two Days' reports. Indeed, this is the clearest reference in the whole Gospel because it numbers them (even at 8.1,2 the matter of the number is open to interpretation[311]). Because it is so specific, some have tried to interpret the reason for the "six". A number of commentators point to Exodus 24.16 which tells how Moses and Joshua went up Mount Sinai, where the glory of the Lord settled, and a cloud covered it for six days.[312] As Taylor points out, Ex.24.15f. may have coloured the account, but the "temporal statement is used differently" (compare the six days that pass *before* the incident, in Mark's account).

Day Sixteen's literary structure[313] is:

```
Καὶ μετὰ ἡμέρας ἕξ                                          a    A    A
    παραλαμβάνει ὁ Ἰησοῦς τὸν Πέτρον                         b
        καὶ τὸν Ἰάκωβον
        καὶ τὸν Ἰωάννην,
    καὶ ἀναφέρει αὐτοὺς εἰς ὄρος ὑψηλὸν                      b'
        κατ᾽ ἰδίαν
        μόνους.
καὶ μετεμορφώθη ἔμπροσθεν αὐτῶν, 3                           a    B
    καὶ τὰ ἱμάτια αὐτοῦ ἐγένετο στίλβοντα λευκὰ λίαν
    οἷα γναφεὺς ἐπὶ τῆς γῆς οὐ δύναται οὕτως λευκᾶναι. 4
    καὶ ὤφθη αὐτοῖς                                          b
        Ἠλίας σὺν Μωϋσεῖ,
        καὶ ἦσαν συλλαλοῦντες τῷ Ἰησοῦ.
    καὶ ἀποκριθεὶς
        ὁ Πέτρος λέγει τῷ Ἰησοῦ,
        Ῥαββί,
```

---

[310]Mack, *Rhetoric...*, pp.80,81: concluding his examination of 8.34-9.1, he summarises the roles of Jesus, as that of "founder teacher, crucified Christ, predictive prophet, and apocalyptic judge". For this summary he appears to be reading Mark's Gospel as a whole, the plot for which he usefully defines as a combination of "martyrological passion narrative with an apocalyptic resolution". I read these roles of Jesus to be the essential disclosures of this Day's telling.

[311]See under Day Six and the discussion of night-crossings, and under Day Thirteen (8.1-21).

[312]Taylor, *The Gospel...*, p.388; Schweizer, *The Good News...*, p.181.

[313]In his Christological exegesis of the Old Testament in the Gospel of Mark, Marcus opens each of his studies with line by line presentations of the texts and an annotation partitioning the verses. Though it appears he has not analysed for structure beyond this, his definitions of 'lines' in the scanning compare well with mine in my analysis of 9.2-8 and 9.11-13. See Marcus, *The Way of the Lord...*, pp.80 and 94.

καλόν ἐστιν ἡμᾶς ὧδε εἶναι,
καὶ ποιήσωμεν τρεῖς σκηνάς,
σοὶ μίαν
καὶ Μωϋσεῖ μίαν
καὶ Ἠλίᾳ μίαν. [6]
οὐ γὰρ ᾔδει
τί ἀποκριθῇ,
ἔκφοβοι γὰρ
ἐγένοντο.
καὶ ἐγένετο νεφέλη   b'
ἐπισκιάζουσα αὐτοῖς,
καὶ ἐγένετο φωνὴ ἐκ τῆς νεφέλης,
Οὗτός ἐστιν ὁ υἱός μου ὁ ἀγαπητός,
ἀκούετε αὐτοῦ.
καὶ ἐξάπινα
περιβλεψάμενοι
οὐκέτι οὐδένα εἶδον
ἀλλὰ τὸν Ἰησοῦν
μόνον μεθ᾽ ἑαυτῶν.
Καὶ καταβαινόντων αὐτῶν   a   Β'
ἐκ τοῦ ὄρους
διεστείλατο αὐτοῖς
ἵνα μηδενὶ
ἃ εἶδον
διηγήσωνται,
εἰ μὴ ὅταν ὁ υἱὸς τοῦ ἀνθρώπου
ἐκ νεκρῶν
ἀναστῇ. [10]
καὶ τὸν λόγον ἐκράτησαν πρὸς ἑαυτοὺς
συζητοῦντες
τί ἐστιν τὸ ἐκ νεκρῶν ἀναστῆναι.
καὶ ἐπηρώτων αὐτὸν   b
λέγοντες,
Ὅτι λέγουσιν οἱ γραμματεῖς
ὅτι Ἠλίαν δεῖ ἐλθεῖν πρῶτον;
ὁ δὲ ἔφη αὐτοῖς,   b'
Ἠλίας
μὲν ἐλθὼν πρῶτον
ἀποκαθιστάνει πάντα,
καὶ πῶς γέγραπται
ἐπὶ τὸν υἱὸν τοῦ ἀνθρώπου
ἵνα πολλὰ πάθῃ
καὶ ἐξουδενηθῇ· [13]
ἀλλὰ λέγω ὑμῖν
ὅτι καὶ Ἠλίας ἐλήλυθεν,
καὶ ἐποίησαν αὐτῷ
ὅσα ἤθελον,
καθὼς γέγραπται
ἐπ᾽ αὐτόν.

Καὶ ἐλθόντες πρὸς τοὺς μαθητὰς   A   **B**
     εἶδον ὄχλον πολὺν περὶ αὐτοὺς
     καὶ γραμματεῖς συζητοῦντας πρὸς αὐτούς. [15]
   καὶ εὐθὺς πᾶς ὁ ὄχλος
     ἰδόντες αὐτὸν
     ἐξεθαμβήθησαν,
   καὶ προστρέχοντες
     ἠσπάζοντο αὐτόν.
καὶ ἐπηρώτησεν αὐτούς,   B
     Τί συζητεῖτε πρὸς αὐτούς;
   καὶ ἀπεκρίθη αὐτῷ
     εἷς ἐκ τοῦ ὄχλου,
     Διδάσκαλε,
     ἤνεγκα τὸν υἱόν μου πρὸς σέ,
      ἔχοντα πνεῦμα ἄλαλον· [18]
      καὶ ὅπου ἐὰν αὐτὸν καταλάβῃ
       ῥήσσει αὐτόν,
        καὶ ἀφρίζει
        καὶ τρίζει τοὺς ὀδόντας
       καὶ ξηραίνεται·
     καὶ εἶπα τοῖς μαθηταῖς σου
      ἵνα αὐτὸ ἐκβάλωσιν,
      καὶ οὐκ ἴσχυσαν.
   ὁ δὲ ἀποκριθεὶς αὐτοῖς / λέγει,
     Ὦ γενεὰ ἄπιστος,
      ἕως πότε πρὸς ὑμᾶς ἔσομαι;
      ἕως πότε ἀνέξομαι ὑμῶν;
   φέρετε αὐτὸν πρός με.
καὶ ἤνεγκαν αὐτὸν πρὸς αὐτόν.   a   B'
     καὶ ἰδὼν αὐτὸν
      τὸ πνεῦμα εὐθὺς συνεσπάραξεν αὐτόν,
     καὶ πεσὼν ἐπὶ τῆς γῆς
      ἐκυλίετο
      ἀφρίζων.
   καὶ ἐπηρώτησεν τὸν πατέρα αὐτοῦ,   b
     Πόσος χρόνος ἐστὶν
     ὡς τοῦτο γέγονεν αὐτῷ;
   ὁ δὲ εἶπεν
      Ἐκ παιδιόθεν· [22]
     καὶ πολλάκις
      καὶ εἰς πῦρ αὐτὸν ἔβαλεν
      καὶ εἰς ὕδατα
      ἵνα ἀπολέσῃ αὐτόν·
     ἀλλ' εἴ τι δύνῃ,
      βοήθησον ἡμῖν
      σπλαγχνισθεὶς ἐφ' ἡμᾶς.
   ὁ δὲ Ἰησοῦς εἶπεν αὐτῷ,
     Τὸ Εἰ δύνῃ,
     πάντα δυνατὰ τῷ πιστεύοντι.

εὐθὺς κράξας   b᾽
  ὁ πατὴρ τοῦ παιδίου
  ἔλεγεν,
 Πιστεύω·
 βοήθει μου τῇ ἀπιστίᾳ.
ἰδὼν δὲ ὁ Ἰησοῦς
  ὅτι ἐπισυντρέχει ὄχλος
  ἐπετίμησεν τῷ πνεύματι τῷ ἀκαθάρτῳ
   λέγων αὐτῷ,
 Τὸ ἄλαλον καὶ κωφὸν πνεῦμα,
  ἐγὼ ἐπιτάσσω σοι,
 ἔξελθε ἐξ αὐτοῦ
 καὶ μηκέτι εἰσέλθῃς εἰς αὐτόν.
καὶ κράξας
 καὶ πολλὰ σπαράξας
 ἐξῆλθεν·
  καὶ ἐγένετο ὡσεὶ νεκρός,
  ὥστε τοὺς πολλοὺς λέγειν ὅτι ἀπέθανεν. [27]
 ὁ δὲ Ἰησοῦς
  κρατήσας τῆς χειρὸς αὐτοῦ
   ἤγειρεν αὐτόν,
  καὶ ἀνέστη.
καὶ εἰσελθόντος αὐτοῦ εἰς οἶκον
 οἱ μαθηταὶ αὐτοῦ κατ᾽ ἰδίαν ἐπηρώτων αὐτόν,
 Ὅτι ἡμεῖς οὐκ ἠδυνήθημεν ἐκβαλεῖν αὐτό;
καὶ εἶπεν αὐτοῖς,
 Τοῦτο τὸ γένος ἐν οὐδενὶ δύναται ἐξελθεῖν
 εἰ μὴ ἐν προσευχῇ.

Κἀκεῖθεν ἐξελθόντες   A B᾽
 παρεπορεύοντο διὰ τῆς Γαλιλαίας,
 καὶ οὐκ ἤθελεν ἵνα τις γνοῖ· [31]
  ἐδίδασκεν γὰρ τοὺς μαθητὰς αὐτοῦ
  καὶ ἔλεγεν αὐτοῖς
ὅτι Ὁ υἱὸς τοῦ ἀνθρώπου παραδίδοται εἰς χεῖρας ἀνθρώπων, B
 καὶ ἀποκτενοῦσιν αὐτόν,
 καὶ ἀποκτανθεὶς
  μετὰ τρεῖς ἡμέρας
  ἀναστήσεται. [32]
οἱ δὲ ἠγνόουν τὸ ῥῆμα,   B᾽
 καὶ ἐφοβοῦντο
 αὐτὸν ἐπερωτῆσαι.

And now in literal English:

And after six days   A   **A**
      Jesus takes Peter
         and James
         and John
      and he leads them up into a high mountain
         privately
         alone.
And he was transfigured before them,   B
         and his garments became exceedingly gleaming white,
         such as no fuller on earth could whiten.
      And appeared to them,
         Elijah and Moses,
         and they were conversing with Jesus.
        And answering
           Peter says to Jesus,
           'Rabbi,
         It is good that we are here
         and let us make three tents,
           for you one
             and for Moses one
             and for Elijah one.'
      For he did not know
         what he answered,
        for exceedingly afraid
        they became.
    And there came a cloud
        overshadowing them.
      And a voice came out of the cloud,
        'This is my beloved Son,
        listen to him.'
      And suddenly,
         looking round,
        no longer did they see anyone,
        but Jesus alone with them.
And as they came down   B'
        from the mountain
      he ordered them
        that to no-one
          the things they had seen
          they should relate
        until the Son of Man
         from the dead
         should rise.
      And they kept the word to themselves,
        debating
        what is the rising from the dead.
      And they questioned him,
        saying,
        Why do the scribes say
        that it is necessary for Elijah to come first?'
      And he said to them,

'Elijah,
    indeed coming first
    first restores all things.
And how is it written
    concerning the Son of Man?
    That he should suffer many things
    and be counted nothing.
But I say to you
    that Elijah has indeed come,
    and they did to him
      what things they wished,
    as it is written
      concerning him.'

And coming to the disciples   A   **B**
    they saw a great crowd around them
    and scribes debating with them.
And immediately all the crowd,
    seeing him,
    were exceedingly astonished.
And running up to him,
    they greeted him.
And he questioned them,   B
    'What are you debating with them?'
And answered him,
    one of the crowd,
    'Teacher,
I brought my son to you,
    having a dumb spirit,
    and wherever it seizes him,
      it tears him and he foams and grinds his teeth
      and he wastes away.
And I spoke to your disciples
    that they might expel it
    and they were not able.'
And answering them,
    he says,
    'O unbelieving generation.
      How long shall I be with you?
      How long shall I endure you?
    Bring him to me.'
And they brought him to him,   B'
    and seeing him,
      the spirit immediately threw him violently,
    and falling on the earth
      he swallowed,
      foaming.
And he questioned his father,
    'How long ago is it
      when this began happening to him?'
And he said,

'From childhood,
and often,
both into fire it threw him
and into water,
that it might destroy him.
But if you can do anything,
help us,
having compassion on us.'
And Jesus said to him,
'"If you can"?
All things are possible to the one who believes.'
Immediately crying out,
the father of the child
began to say,
'I believe,
help my unbelief.'
And Jesus seeing
that a crowd was running together,
he rebuked the unclean spirit,
saying to it,
'Dumb and deaf spirit, / I command you,
"Come out of him
and no more may you enter him!"'
And crying out,
and much convulsing him,
it came out,
and he was as dead,
so that many said he was dead.
But Jesus,
taking hold of his hand, / raised him,
and he stood up.
And when he entered into a house,
his disciples privately questioned him,
'Why were we not able to expel it?'
And he told them,
'This kind by nothing can come out,
except by prayer.'

And from there going forth   A   B'
they began to pass through Galilee
and he did not wish anyone to know,
for he was teaching his disciples,
and he was saying to them,
'The Son of Man is to be betrayed into the hands of men   B
and they will kill him
and being killed
after three days
he will rise up.'
And they did not understand the word   B'
and they feared
to question him.

The second and third lines, b and b', of the Day's introductory part A (9.2abc) exhibit historical presents in a now observed, classically Markan way: see Days Eight (6.1-29), Twelve (7.31-37) and Fourteen (8.22-26). Overall, the Day's telling is structured in three parts. The structure, again, is a composite ABB'/ABB'/ABB' arrangement.

Part **A**, 9.2-13, tells how Jesus took Peter, James and John (compare also 5.37, 13.3 and 14.33 for their participation in special events) from the other disciples and up onto a high mountain to witness his transfiguration. It tells of the ensuing discussion on their way back down. The first part, part A, 9.2, is introductory; Jesus takes Peter, James and John up a mountain. Part B, vv3-8, is the first development, the scene of Jesus' transfiguration, his meeting with Moses and Elijah and a voice out of the cloud. Part B', vv.9-13, relates the descent, Jesus' order to the disciples and a discussion about Elijah.

We look at a few of the details. 9.2 includes an opening temporal clause. In 9.5, Peter addresses Jesus as "Rabbi"; it is the first mention of this title for Jesus in the Gospel (for others, see 11.21 and 14.45). 9.4 and v.5 display a reversing of order of the names of Moses and Elijah; it is a convention of ancient rhetoric which indicates an author's intention to show that two parts are in correspondence. 9.6 and v.7 display, an anastrophe[314] which connects the two 'b' pieces, b and b'. The scene and the words of the voice, 9.7,8, are reminiscent of the scene just after Jesus' baptism, told in 1.11. The "Christ" of Day Fifteen (8.27-9.1) is, in this Day Sixteen, the "beloved Son of God" (see also 1.1) who is to be "listened to" (we note: the prophet[315] whom God would raise up like Moses had to be listened to: see Deut. 18.14,15,17,18). In Part **A**, we read Jesus' command to the disciples to be quiet about the event until "the Son of man should rise from the dead". The three debate the meaning of "rising from the dead", but ask Jesus, not about that, but about Elijah and the necessity of his coming first. In his reply, Jesus speaks not only about Elijah's coming but also about himself (and his own suffering), and also about Elijah (John the Baptist is inferred) who, already, has come, to whom others "did what things they wished". Both 'b' parts speak of what "is written". The first part of the Day's telling, given its variety of subjects and O.T. allusions, is clearly a conflation on Mark's part of several traditions and expectations.

Part **B**, 9.14-29, tells of their return to the other disciples and of an exorcism. At first sight, there is little to connect these first two Parts of Day Sixteen, but for the return (*cf.* 9.2b). The scene now is of a large crowd around the disciples and some scribes who are debating with them; 'scribes', therefore, also lonk these two parts (see v.11 for this further connection). And there is something more: something about Jesus, when he was seen, astonished the crowd. The likely interpetation Mark's audience is meant to appreciate is Jesus' 'identification' with Moses, who, in Ex. 34.29f., reflects the 'glory of God' to a 'large crowd' on coming down from the mountain. The introductory part A, 9.14,15, is followed by part B, 9.16-19, which tells how the disciples were not able to cast out the dumb spirit (in v.25, it is a 'dumb and deaf spirit'). Part B', 9.20-29, tells how Jesus was able to heal the boy and to teach his disciples that such healing is a matter of faith and prayer. Part **B** is beautifully told. It 'parses' fascinatingly to the abb' rhythms.

Again, we look at a few of the details of 9.14-29. Part A, vv.14-15, sets the scene and places Jesus again firmly in the centre. In part B, vv.16-19, Jesus takes the lead, and, as we have seen before in Days Six (5.1-20) and Seven (5.21-43) he heals when no one could have expected him to do so: the needs of the boy are so great, and the disciples could not help, even though they they had healed others before (see Day Eight). Part B begins with Jesus' question, "What are you debating?" and a man answers from the crowd, "Teacher...". In 9.17, Διδάσκαλε is an address to Jesus which we find five times in this Series: see also 9.38,

---

[314]See note 28 and the accompanying text under my analysis of the Prologue.
[315]Identification maybe being made by Mark with the prophet of 6.15 and 8.28. See Fowler, *Loaves and Fishes...*, pp.126-128, who thinks "there can be little doubt" about it.

10.17,20 and v.35. Part B ends with Jesus' lament for their unbelief and a call to "bring" the boy to him. Part B' begins, "And they brought him to him…", continues with Jesus questioning the father and raising the matter of believing, which evokes from the father the cry, "I believe; help my unbelief!" (It is the cry of a typical disciple.[316]) The crowd grows. Jesus commands the dumb and deaf spirit to leave. It does so, leaving the boy "as dead". The scene closes with Jesus raising the boy and explaining to his disciples ("when he had entered into a house") that prayer alone succeeds in a case like this.

And now to 9.30-32: for a long time, I used to think that 9.29 ended this Day's telling. I was prompted to think that 9.30 was an opening verse. The words, *Κἀκεῖθεν ἐξελθόντες* (see Day Eight), seemed like an opening, suitable to a Day, given what we find at 6.1, 7.24 and 10.1. As it is, of Mark's six uses, it seems that three begin days and three begin sections (parts). What persuaded me, in this case, was: 1) that the opening verses, vv.30-32, continue the theme of Jesus' instructing his disciples; 2) that this travel reference is a resumption only of their journeying and a beginning of a journeying that was to happen over future days; 3) that *ἐξελθόντες* fails to cut it for a dramatic opening to a new Day's action; *Καὶ ἐξῆλθεν ἐκεῖθεν* would have worked (as for Day Eight); and 4) when the details of this Series are laid out, end to end, this prediction of Jesus lies opposite its parallel, in Days Sixteen and Twenty, the B Days of the two ABB' sub-Series, either side of the central Day. Symmetry is important to Mark. So far, in the first of the two middle Series, we have established the duality of Feasts in the Desert, in the B Days. Day Sixteen is the first of the two B Days in this Series. In Day Twenty we will see how two disciples want to be with Jesus in his glory, a mirroring of this day's opening part, when two share with Jesus in his glory. For these reasons, I now judge vv.30-32 to be the three-part closing Part **B'** of Day Sixteen.

As the second Day of this Series, as also for the first Day (Day Fifteen), we find Jesus instructing his disciples: four witness the disclosure of who Jesus is and all learn, or struggle to learn, from Jesus' further disclosures. Given the soteriological components of the Day's telling, Schweizer is surely right to point out that the story of the transfiguration unites "two expectations which were alive in Judaism: the coming of the prophet of the end-time who is like Moses, and the appearing of Elijah at the dawning of the end-time"[317] The most important Christological disclosure, of course, of this Day's telling is that Jesus is the "Son of God"!

Day Seventeen: 9.33-50:

The day begins similarly to Days One, Two, Three, Six, Ten and Fourteen, so far. Day Seventeen begins, *Καὶ ἦλθον εἰς Καφαρναούμ.* In Days One and Three, it is Capernaum they enter, in Ten, it is Gennesaret and in Day Fourteen, it is Bethsaida. In all these days, bar Day One the verb is *ἦλθον* or a variant of it. See under Day Eight for a brief discussion on 6.1, 7.24 and 10.1: in regard to Day Seventeen, 10.1 is clearly introducing another Day. The limits, therefore to this Day are 9.33 and v.50.

Mark's literary-structural presentation for Day Seventeen is his commonly-used, ABB' plan of three sections, and is presented here:

---

[316]Hooker, *The Gospel…*, p.224.
[317]Schweizer, *The Good News…*, p,183. The other commentators of my selection write similarly.

Καὶ ἦλθον εἰς Καφαρναούμ.   A   **A**
    καὶ ἐν τῇ οἰκίᾳ γενόμενος
      ἐπηρώτα αὐτούς,
    Τί ἐν τῇ ὁδῷ διελογίζεσθε; [34]
οἱ δὲ ἐσιώπων,   B
    πρὸς ἀλλήλους γὰρ διελέχθησαν ἐν τῇ ὁδῷ
    τίς μείζων.
  καὶ καθίσας   B'
      ἐφώνησεν τοὺς δώδεκα
      καὶ λέγει αὐτοῖς,
    Εἴ τις θέλει
      πρῶτος
      εἶναι
    ἔσται
      πάντων ἔσχατος
      καὶ πάντων διάκονος.

καὶ λαβὼν παιδίον   A   **B**
      ἔστησεν αὐτὸ
        ἐν μέσῳ αὐτῶν
      καὶ ἐναγκαλισάμενος αὐτὸ
        εἶπεν αὐτοῖς, [37]
    Ὃς ἂν ἓν τῶν τοιούτων παιδίων δέξηται
      ἐπὶ τῷ ὀνόματί μου,
      ἐμὲ δέχεται·
    καὶ ὃς ἂν ἐμὲ δέχηται,
      οὐκ ἐμὲ δέχεται
      ἀλλὰ τὸν ἀποστείλαντά με.
  Ἔφη αὐτῷ ὁ Ἰωάννης,   B
      Διδάσκαλε,
    εἴδομέν τινα
      ἐν τῷ ὀνόματί σου
      ἐκβάλλοντα δαιμόνια,
    καὶ ἐκωλύομεν αὐτόν,
      ὅτι οὐκ ἠκολούθει ἡμῖν.
  ὁ δὲ Ἰησοῦς εἶπεν,   B'
      Μὴ κωλύετε αὐτόν,
      οὐδεὶς γάρ ἐστιν
        ὃς ποιήσει δύναμιν ἐπὶ τῷ ὀνόματί μου
        καὶ δυνήσεται ταχὺ κακολογῆσαί με· [40]
    ὃς γὰρ οὐκ ἔστιν καθ' ἡμῶν,
      ὑπὲρ ἡμῶν ἐστιν. [41]
    ὃς γὰρ ἂν ποτίσῃ ὑμᾶς ποτήριον ὕδατος ἐν ὀνόματι
      ὅτι Χριστοῦ ἐστε,
      ἀμὴν λέγω ὑμῖν
        ὅτι οὐ μὴ
        ἀπολέσῃ τὸν μισθὸν αὐτοῦ.

Καὶ ὃς ἂν σκανδαλίσῃ   A   **B'**
       ἕνα τῶν μικρῶν τούτων
       τῶν πιστευόντων εἰς ἐμέ,
    καλόν ἐστιν αὐτῷ
    μᾶλλον
       εἰ περίκειται μύλος ὀνικὸς περὶ τὸν τράχηλον αὐτοῦ
       καὶ βέβληται εἰς τὴν θάλασσαν. [43]
Καὶ ἐὰν σκανδαλίζῃ σε ἡ χείρ σου,   B
       ἀπόκοψον αὐτήν·
    καλόν ἐστίν σε κυλλὸν
       εἰσελθεῖν
       εἰς τὴν ζωὴν
     ἢ τὰς δύο χεῖρας ἔχοντα
       ἀπελθεῖν
            εἰς τὴν γέενναν,
            εἰς τὸ πῦρ τὸ ἄσβεστον. [45]
    καὶ ἐὰν ὁ πούς σου σκανδαλίζῃ σε,
       ἀπόκοψον αὐτόν·
    καλόν ἐστίν σε
       εἰσελθεῖν
       εἰς τὴν ζωὴν χωλὸν
     ἢ τοὺς δύο πόδας ἔχοντα
       βληθῆναι εἰς τὴν γέενναν.
    καὶ ἐὰν ὁ ὀφθαλμός σου σκανδαλίζῃ σε,
       ἔκβαλε αὐτόν·
    καλόν σέ ἐστιν μονόφθαλμον
       εἰσελθεῖν
       εἰς τὴν βασιλείαν τοῦ θεοῦ
     ἢ δύο ὀφθαλμοὺς ἔχοντα
       βληθῆναι εἰς τὴν γέενναν, [48]
       ὅπου
            ὁ σκώληξ αὐτῶν οὐ τελευτᾷ
            καὶ τὸ πῦρ οὐ σβέννυται·
  πᾶς γὰρ πυρὶ ἁλισθήσεται.   B'
    καλὸν τὸ ἅλας·
       ἐὰν δὲ τὸ ἅλας ἄναλον γένηται,
       ἐν τίνι αὐτὸ ἀρτύσετε;
    ἔχετε ἐν ἑαυτοῖς ἅλας,
       καὶ εἰρηνεύετε
       ἐν ἀλλήλοις.

And in literal English:

And they came to Capernaum.   A   **A**
       And being in the house,
           he began to question them,
      'What, on the way, were you debating?'
    And they were silent,   B
       for with one another they debated on the way
       who was the greatest.
   And sitting,   B'
          he called the twelve,
          and he says to them,
      'If anyone wishes
        first
        to be,
     he shall be
        last of all
        and servant of all.'

And taking a child,   A   **B**
         he set him
           in the midst of them,
         and folding him in his arms,
           he said to them,
      'Whoever receives one such child
        <u>in my name</u>
        receives me.
     And whoever receives me,
        receives not me
        but the one who has sent me.'
    John said to him, 'Teacher,   B
     we saw someone
        <u>in your name</u>
        expelling demons
     and we forbade him
        because he was not following us.'
    But Jesus said,   B'
        'Do not forbid him,
        For there is no-one
          who will do a miracle <u>in my name</u>
          and will be able quickly to speak evil of me.
      <u>For he who</u> is not against us
        is for us.
      <u>For whoever</u> gives you a cup of water
          <u>in my name</u>,
        because you are of Christ,
        truly I tell you
          by no means will he lose his reward.

And whoever causes to sin   A   **B'**
> one of these little ones,
> <u>believing in me,</u>
> it is better for him,
> rather,
>> if a heavy millstone were hung round his neck
>> and he be thrown into the sea.

And if your hand causes you to sin,   B
> cut it off.
> It is better to enter into life maimed
> than with two hands to go away into Gehenna,
>> into the unquenchable fire.

And if your foot causes you to sin,
> cut it off.
> It is better to enter into life lame
> than with two feet to be thrown into Gehenna.

And if your eye causes you to sin,
> pluck it out.
> It is better to enter the kingdom of God one-eyed
> than with two eyes to be thrown into Gehenna,
>> where "their worm dies not,
>> and the fire is not quenched".

For everyone will be salted with fire.   B'
> Salt is good,
> but if the salt becomes saltless,
> by what will you season it?
> Have in yourselves salt,
> and be at peace / among each other.'

Part **A**, 9.33-35, first establishes the geographical location as Capernaum[318] and the setting "in a house"[319]. 9.30-32 tells us that Jesus is travelling with his disciples; in 9.33-35 the same are assumed. Jesus asks what they were discussing *ἐν τῇ ὁδῷ*[320]. They were silent; they had been discussing who was 'the greatest'. Jesus, therefore, sits and calls the twelve and what he says about being 'first' is balanced by 'last' and 'servant of all'. Study the presentations in both Greek and literal English and you will see that Mark has delicately balanced all the pieces of this opening Part **A** to his abb' template.

Parts **B**, vv.36-41, and **B'**, vv.42-50, follow, balancing each other in their introductions: in the first, Jesus takes a child and stands him in the midst of them; in the second, the child (who is a 'believer', so v.42 suggests) is again Jesus' model. Again, we see Mark's constructive hand so clearly at work. In Part **B**, the first part introduces the phrase *ἐπὶ τῷ ὀνόματί μου*, this sets up the teaching for the second two parts, both of which include reference to the same. In Part **B'**, the opening part introduces *ὃς ἂν σκανδαλίσῃ* and *καλόν*. the first of the two completing parts comprises three very similar sayings which in the concluding sub-part climaxes with entry "into the Kingdom of God"[321]; the completing second

---

[318]See Days One and Three for earlier references, 1.21 and 2.2.
[319]See also for "in a house": 2.1,15, 3.19, 7.17,24, 9.28 and 10.10.
[320]For a discussion on the importance of *ἐν τῇ ὁδῷ* in this Series of Days, see 1) under Day Fifteen.
[321]For a discussion on the importance of "the kingdom of God" in this Series of Days, see 7) under Day Fifteen for a brief discussion.

part links fire (from before) with salt, in its first line, and in its concluding two lines presents the illustration of salt.

With this collection of sayings, Mark concludes a sub-Series of three Days of Jesus' teaching addressed to his disciples. Hooker[322] observes that 9.41-50 possesses a unity and an emphasis remarkably close to that of 8.34-38. We draw attention also to the obvious parallel between 8.31 and 9.31. When Mark composed Day Seventeen, he had Day Fifteen (8.27-9.1) in mind. Again, this kind of observation tends to a summarising of Mark's plan for these three Days in terms of an ABA' form. That they are a threesome of Days is well supported, but how did Mark himself view his composition? References to changes in geographical place (that is, as opposed to change of local setting) and to the Days, as to whether or not two of the three are consecutive, have proved futile in all previous cases. We will not be discussing such, therefore. It is the movement of the story-line and the revelations that indicate the form.

The view I take is that Day Fifteen is clearly and emphatically introductory. It introduces new information in the Gospel narrative both about Jesus and about discipleship. Day Sixteen continues these two themes and develops them. And Day Seventeen in completing the sub-Series returns in part to Day Fifteen's Christological disclosures, thus providing an *inclusio*, but again continues to develop the theme of discipleship. In all three Days, the focus is on Jesus and on discipleship.

When we look at the presentations of the Christological disclosures of these three days, we can identify another important link. To the first Day's disclosure that Jesus is the Christ attaches the command to silence, on the part of the disciples, 8.30 (here the Messianic secret, specifically the Messianic secret, is introduced). To the second Day's disclosure of Jesus' transfiguration glory (and his Sonship of God?) attaches a second command to silence till Jesus 'was risen' from the dead (9.9). (They had to be silent about "what they had seen", and "heard" too, we might add to be consistent.) At the end of the second Day's telling (9.30,31), we read that Jesus' teaching of his diciples, about his death and resurrection, was for them only to know, at that time[323]. In contrast to the third Day's telling (i.e. Day Seventeen's telling), the next (Day Eighteen) begins with reference to "the crowds who go with him again", 10.1. Day Eighteen includes no reference to any Messianic secret. Clearly, Days Fifteen to Seventeen are a sub-Series, and they are arranged as before in the earlier Series, in an ABB' form.

Day Eighteen: 10.1-16:

Commonly, commentators view 10.1 as introductory in geographical terms to a collection of narratives, based on topical arrangement:[324]

10.2-12	on Adultery
10.13-16	on Children
10.17-22	The Rich Man and Eternal Life
10.23-27	The Conversation on Riches
10.28-31	The Question of Rewards.

---

[322]Hooker, *The Gospel...*, pp.230f.

[323]The "Messianic secret" is discussed below, in the summary of this Series and in Chapter 8.

[324]Taylor, *The Gospel...*, p.415. Compare J. Jeremias, *Infant Baptism in the First Four Centuries*, tr. by D. Cairns, SCM Press, London, 1971, p.50: Jeremias sees 10.1-31 as a pre-Markan complex. Kuhn argues that it is 10.1-45 which goes back to an original complex of pre-Markan material containing three pericopae relating to divorce, wealth and position, approx. vv.2-12, 17-32 and 35-45 (H.W. Kuhn, *Ältere Sammlungen im Markusevangelium*, Vandenhoeck & Ruprecht, Göttingen, 1971, pp.146-191).

The reason I break after 10.16, and so discern this Day's telling ends at v.16, is that a new Day's journeying is inferred by the opening of 10.17: *Καὶ ἐκπορευομένου αὐτοῦ εἰς ὁδόν.* It compares with 8.27a-d:

> *Καὶ ἐξῆλθεν ὁ Ἰησοῦς*
> *καὶ οἱ μαθηταὶ αὐτοῦ*
> *εἰς τὰς κώμας Καισαρείας τῆς Φιλίππου.*
> *καὶ ἐν τῇ ὁδῷ ...*

and the beginning of Day Twenty,

> *Ἦσαν δὲ ἐν τῇ ὁδῷ ἀναβαίνοντες εἰς Ἱεροσόλυμα.*

To these, we could also add 10.46b, because the character whose story is related, sat *παρὰ τὴν ὁδόν.* Hence, we may discern that the beginnings of five of the seven Days of this Series employ *ἐν τῇ ὁδῷ* or variants, and that Mark used the term in such a position to signal the beginnings, or to reinforce the beginnings of the tellings of these new Days. The pericopae of 10.17-22, 23-26, 27-31 in the table above, so separated from the others by 10.17, approximate to my **A**, **B** and **B'** Parts of Day Nineteen's three-part presentation.

Day Eighteen's telling is organised by Mark (here also) to his ABB' scheme. The longer Part **A**, 10.1-9 (compare that of Day Fifteen, and others), in its opening part establishes the new geographical location in a, the accompaniment of crowds in b, and a common activity of Jesus, which is teaching, in b' (elsewhere in introductory verses: teaching: 1.21, 6.2, (8.2), 9.31; preaching: 1.39; speaking the word: 2.2; telling them: 10.32). The second part commences with the approaching Pharisees and their question to Jesus about the law and divorce, "testing him". The third part states Jesus' response. Part **B**, vv.10-12, commences with the relating of a re-location ("in the house again", v.10), and establishes that it is Jesus and his disciples who are now present only (which reminds us of scenes described in the previous three days). The disciples question Jesus and Jesus responds: the matter is about re-marriage, divorce and adultery. Part **B'**, vv.13-16, tells how children are now brought to Jesus; they become an illustration (compare Day Seventeen, 9.30-50, v.36) to the disciples of how they must receive the kingdom of God; and in conclusion to the Day's telling (the third part of Part **B'**), Jesus is "repeatedly blessing" the children.

I present the literary structure of Day Eighteen. The levels of literary order follow again the abb' presentational approach of Mark at every level: they exhibit again his careful creating of introductory pieces to balancing pairings of contents.

Καὶ ἐκεῖθεν   A   **A**
    ἀναστὰς
    ἔρχεται
        εἰς τὰ ὅρια τῆς Ἰουδαίας
        καὶ πέραν τοῦ Ἰορδάνου,
  καὶ συμπορεύονται
    πάλιν
    ὄχλοι πρὸς αὐτόν,
  καὶ ὡς εἰώθει
    πάλιν
    ἐδίδασκεν αὐτούς.
καὶ προσελθόντες   B
    Φαρισαῖοι
    ἐπηρώτων αὐτὸν
  εἰ ἔξεστιν ἀνδρὶ γυναῖκα ἀπολῦσαι,
  πειράζοντες αὐτόν.
ὁ δὲ ἀποκριθεὶς
  εἶπεν αὐτοῖς,
    Τί ὑμῖν ἐνετείλατο Μωϋσῆς;
οἱ δὲ εἶπαν,
  Ἐπέτρεψεν Μωϋσῆς βιβλίον ἀποστασίου γράψαι
  καὶ ἀπολῦσαι.
ὁ δὲ Ἰησοῦς εἶπεν αὐτοῖς,   B'
  Πρὸς τὴν σκληροκαρδίαν ὑμῶν
  ἔγραψεν ὑμῖν τὴν ἐντολὴν ταύτην. [6]
ἀπὸ δὲ ἀρχῆς κτίσεως
    ἄρσεν καὶ θῆλυ
    ἐποίησεν αὐτούς· [7]
  ἕνεκεν τούτου
    καταλείψει ἄνθρωπος
    τὸν πατέρα αὐτοῦ καὶ τὴν μητέρα
    (omit? *καὶ προσκολληθήσεται πρὸς τὴν γυναῖκα αὐτοῦ,*) [8]
  καὶ ἔσονται οἱ δύο εἰς σάρκα μίαν·
    ὥστε οὐκέτι εἰσὶν δύο
    ἀλλὰ μία σάρξ. [9]
  ὃ οὖν
    ὁ θεὸς συνέζευξεν
    ἄνθρωπος μὴ χωριζέτω.

Καὶ εἰς τὴν οἰκίαν πάλιν   A   **B**
    οἱ μαθηταὶ περὶ τούτου ἐπηρώτων αὐτόν. [11]
    καὶ λέγει αὐτοῖς,
  Ὃς ἂν ἀπολύσῃ τὴν γυναῖκα αὐτοῦ   B
    καὶ γαμήσῃ ἄλλην
    μοιχᾶται ἐπ' αὐτήν, [12]
  καὶ ἐὰν αὐτὴ ἀπολύσασα τὸν ἄνδρα αὐτῆς   B'
    γαμήσῃ ἄλλον
    μοιχᾶται.

Καὶ προσέφερον αὐτῷ παιδία   A   B'
        ἵνα αὐτῶν ἄψηται·
        οἱ δὲ μαθηταὶ ἐπετίμησαν αὐτοῖς. [14]
ἰδὼν δὲ   B
                ὁ Ἰησοῦς ἠγανάκτησεν
                καὶ εἶπεν αὐτοῖς,
        Ἄφετε τὰ παιδία ἔρχεσθαι πρός με,
                μὴ κωλύετε αὐτά,
                τῶν γὰρ τοιούτων ἐστὶν ἡ βασιλεία τοῦ θεοῦ. [15]
        ἀμὴν λέγω ὑμῖν,
                ὃς ἂν μὴ δέξηται τὴν βασιλείαν τοῦ θεοῦ
                        ὡς παιδίον,
                οὐ μὴ εἰσέλθῃ εἰς αὐτήν. [16]
καὶ ἐναγκαλισάμενος αὐτὰ   B'
        κατευλόγει
        τιθεὶς τὰς χεῖρας ἐπ᾽ αὐτά.

And in literal English:

And from there,   (see Day 11, for parallels)   A   A
                rising up,
                he comes
                        into the region of Judea,
                        beyond the Jordan.
                And they go together
                        again,
                        crowds to him.
                And as he was accustomed,
                        again
                        he taught them.
        And approaching,   B
                        Pharisees
                        questioned him,
                        'Is it lawful for a man to dismiss his wife?'
                        testing him.
                And he answering,
                        said to them,
                        'What did Moses command you?'
                And they said,
                        'Moses permitted a man to write a divorce certificate
                        and to dismiss his wife.'

And Jesus said to them,   B'
      'For your hardheartedness,
      he wrote you this commandment.
  But from the beginning of creation,
        male and female
        he made them,
    for the sake of this,
        will leave a man
        his father and mother,
            (and be united to his wife)   *omit?* *
    and the two will become one flesh,
        so that no longer are they two,
        but one flesh.'
  What, therefore,
      God has joined together,
      let no man separate.'

And in the house again,   A   **B**
      the disciples began to question him about this
      and he says to them,
  'Whoever dismisses his wife   B
      and marries another
      commits adultery with her,
  And if she having dismissed her husband   B'
      marries another,
      she commits adultery.'

And they were bringing children to him,   A   **B'**
      that he might touch them,
      but the disciples rebuked them.
  And seeing,   B
        Jesus was angry
        and he said to them,
  'Let the children come to me.
        Do not prevent them,
        for of such is the kingdom of God.
    Truly I say to you,
        whoever does not receive the kingdom of God
            as a child,
        by no means will he enter into it.'
  And folding them in his arms,   B'
      he blesses them,
      putting his hands on them.

* *Not all manuscripts support this.*

Day Eighteen opens, in 10.1, without any reference to $\dot{\epsilon}\nu\ \tau\hat{\eta}\ \dot{o}\delta\hat{\omega}$ (see 1, on page 175). We can observe the complete absence of this Series' familiar feature in the Day's telling, and also, in this Series of seven Days so far, the absence of any new Christological disclosures or predictions about Jesus. The opening itself is very similar to that of Day Eleven, 7.24-30, which itself is the middle day of the first of the two middle Series of the Gospel. (See under Day Eleven, for a discussion on this). The common opening words are $\dot{\epsilon}\kappa\epsilon\hat{\imath}\theta\epsilon\nu$, $\dot{\alpha}\nu\alpha\sigma\tau\dot{\alpha}\varsigma$ and $\epsilon\dot{\imath}\varsigma\ \tau\dot{\alpha}\ \ddot{o}\rho\iota\alpha$. Clearly, Mark composed one of these two days with the other in mind. That in itself suggests that it was also in his mind that he was composing here the middle Day to his second and corresponding middle Series.

The Day indeed stands alone in this Series: Pharisees are present (in vv.2-9, the first major part of the Day's telling, and nowhere else in the Series) to "test" Jesus by questioning him on *marriage and divorce*, not specifically adultery. In the second and final major part (vv.10-16) in a new setting, "in the house", the disciples question Jesus on the subject which becomes that of *adultery*; they then cause Jesus to be "angry" by turning away those who were bringing children to him. 'Marriage' and 'family' do link the two major sections, and the Day's point ends on discipleship matters again (as in all the Days of this Series).

In the first of these two major sections, vv.2-9, in his reply to the Pharisees, Jesus quotes interestingly from Genesis 1.27 *and* 2.24, connecting them together in a way which to Nineham[325] is reminiscent of rabbinical exegesis. Because of my interest in Genesis 1.1-2.4a, that it had possible influence on Mark's choice of literary structure (see page 10, in my Introduction), I find this matter particularly noteworthy. Its inclusion here, in a Series' middle Day and turning point, does suggest that this reference to the Genesis account of creation is indeed significant. It is especially so, because the middle Day and turning point of the first Series, on 'what is lawful on the Sabbath', connects clearly also with the creation story, in Genesis 2.1-4a, its epilogue. This matter will be addressed in Chapter 8.

On the inclusion of vv.13-16, Isaksson is one who prefers to connect it to 10.1-12 and regards the two together, as they are found in Matt. 19.1-15 as a church marriage catechism.[326] My literary-structural analysis establishes this link: 'marriage' (even marriage stability) and 'children' are the subjects (of sections B and B', in turn) which here seem to be linked in Mark's mind. In regard to the exemplary qualities of children in matters of discipleship many suggestions have been made. They include: a child's innocence, simplicity, ingenuousness, and receptiveness. Barclay's traditional stance[327] that 'a child trusts adults', however, still offers the most strightforward interpretation, that a disciple is to trust God. Entry into/receiving the Kingdom, for the disciple, promises 'repeated blessing'; he/she has simply to allow God continuous rule in his/her life. Moral and salvific issues here combine in Mark's presentation.

The question now put is: how does this middle day of this Series of seven Days function as a pivot to the sub-Series each side of it if, that is, it is any more than just a buffer between them? The middle day, Day Eleven, of the first middle Series looks both ways, that is to what precedes and to what follows it. We might expect this Day, therefore, to perform a similar function, especially as we identify Mark's interest in starting it like Day Eleven.

In terms of the major component, we may identify the subject to be 'discipleship: marriage, divorce and adultry' (not 'parenting' as such). The emphasis is on what is ethical. It is "representative of the kind of controversy in which the church frequently was engaged, as, e.g., in its quarrel with Judaism", says Schweizer[328]. Children then feature in the Day's tell-

---

[325]Nineham, *Saint Mark*, p.265: on "For this reason", v.7, he notes that "Jesus makes it refer to something different - the fact (in Gen 1.27) that the human race was created from the beginning in two sexes", and not 2.23, that woman was created from man.

[326]A. Isaksson, *Marriage and Ministry in the New Temple*, Lund, 1965, pp.119, 121.

[327]Wm. Barclay, *Mark*, Daily Study Bible, St Andrew Press, Edinburgh, 1954, p.251.

[328]Schweizer, *The Good News...*, p.201.

ing, but as an illustration of a salvific point, which has to do with the Kingdom of God. In the previous Day's telling, Jesus uses a child as an illustration for discipleship teaching. And we note in the day following that Jesus, for the only time in the Gospel, addresses his disciples, "Children..." (10.24).

We may make the observation that this Series re-introduces the concept of the Kingdom of God to the Gospel, in its first Day's telling, at 9.1 (see 7, on page 177). It is a term not otherwise found in the Series outside of the three middle days. Issues are raised over "entering", or "receiving" the Kingdom of God. In Day Seventeen, there is one reference, at 9.47 (on entry); in the telling of Day Eighteen there are two references, at 10.14,15 ("of such (of children) is..."/receiving, entry); and in Day Nineteen, there are three references, at 10.23,24,25 (on entry, three times). In the handling of the Kingdom of God concept in the central Day's telling we may note, therefore, a different emphasis from that of the Day preceding and the Day following, which mirror each other. The central day expresses uniquely that the kingdom of God is a gift to be received. The Kingdom of God is to be full of childlike disciples, who receive it as a gift, through trusting God. All discipleship hinges on this. Day Eighteen is a hinge day's telling in itself, therefore, a fulcrum to the presentations of 'teachings on discipleship'. There is more to the argument, however.

The opening reference to the Kingdom of God, in 9.1 which is coupled to 8.38 by Mark, in the first Day's telling of this Series is further illuminating. This first Day establishes that Jesus is the Christ, that he is to suffer, be rejected, be killed and after three days rise again (the Series variously, but consistently reminds the reader/listeners of this: five predictions in all are identified[329]). Further to these things, Jesus is to come in the glory of his father, and the kingdom of God is to come in power with him. These 'Christological-disclosures' link firmly with Jesus' 'teachings on discipleship', but fundamentally they make it plain that the Kingdom of God (God's rule) becomes possible through his suffering, death, resurrection and return. Day Eighteen is pivotal in this Series because it establishes that the Kingdom of God, secured for all by Jesus, is a gift to be received. The Day is central because it calls for this understanding of the two major components which make up the Series, and it gives guidance as to what must be the reader's/listeners' response to these matters.

The contents' repetitions, of 'children' and 'the Kingdom of God' in the middle three Days of this Series, may be judged to be evidence again of what we discovered particularly clearly in the first Series (see page 113), of the characteristic in ancient rhetoric whereby smooth transitions between rhetorical units were established by hook words and phrases.

Day Nineteen: 10.17-31:

For the arguments for seeing 10.17 and 10.32 as beginning new Days, refer to the discussions under Day Eighteen.

On the structure of 10.17-31, Taylor, Schweizer, Hooker and Best[330] all agree that these verses form a Markan whole with 10.2-16 and that these divide: vv.17-22, vv.23-27, and vv.28-31. Bultmann's analysis sees 10.17-31 as a whole, where the first unit, vv.17-22, is the base unit to which 'supplements' are attached: vv.23-27, vv.28-30 and v.31.[331] Literary-structural analysis demonstrates to me that this Day's telling is constructed of the following

---

[329]See 4) under Day Fifteen and the features of the Series.
[330]Taylor, *The Gospel...*, p.424; Schweizer, *The Good News...*, p.208f.; Hooker, *The Gospel...*, p.239f.; Best, *Disciples...*, p.17.
[331]Bultmann, *The History...*, p.20. Hooker allows also that the section may originally have been these four separate units, *The Gospel...*, p.240.

three parts, vv.17-22, vv.23-26 and vv.27-31 (thus, differently divided) and that their relationship is best expressed by ABB'. The literary structure of Day Nineteen is as follows:

Καὶ ἐκπορευομένου αὐτοῦ   A   A
        εἰς ὁδὸν
   προσδραμὼν εἷς
       καὶ γονυπετήσας
   αὐτὸν ἐπηρώτα αὐτόν,
  Διδάσκαλε ἀγαθέ,
τί ποιήσω
   ἵνα ζωὴν αἰώνιον
   κληρονομήσω;
ὁ δὲ Ἰησοῦς εἶπεν αὐτῷ,   B
   Τί με λέγεις ἀγαθόν;
   οὐδεὶς ἀγαθὸς
      εἰ μὴ εἷς
      ὁ θεός. [19]
τὰς ἐντολὰς οἶδας·
   Μὴ φονεύσῃς,
     Μὴ μοιχεύσῃς,
     Μὴ κλέψῃς,
   Μὴ ψευδομαρτυρήσῃς,
     Μὴ ἀποστερήσῃς,
     Τίμα τὸν πατέρα σου καὶ τὴν μητέρα.
ὁ δὲ ἔφη αὐτῷ,
   Διδάσκαλε,
 ταῦτα πάντα ἐφυλαξάμην
 ἐκ νεότητός μου.
ὁ δὲ Ἰησοῦς   B'
      ἐμβλέψας αὐτῷ
   ἠγάπησεν αὐτὸν
 καὶ εἶπεν αὐτῷ,
     Ἕν σε ὑστερεῖ·
 ὕπαγε
    ὅσα ἔχεις
      πώλησον
       καὶ δὸς τοῖς πτωχοῖς,
     καὶ ἕξεις θησαυρὸν
       ἐν οὐρανῷ,
   καὶ δεῦρο
    ἀκολούθει μοι.
ὁ δὲ στυγνάσας ἐπὶ τῷ λόγῳ
 ἀπῆλθεν λυπούμενος,
 ἦν γὰρ ἔχων κτήματα πολλά.

Καὶ περιβλεψάμενος   A   **B**
           ὁ Ἰησοῦς λέγει
           τοῖς μαθηταῖς αὐτοῦ,
       Πῶς δυσκόλως οἱ τὰ χρήματα ἔχοντες
           εἰς τὴν βασιλείαν τοῦ θεοῦ
           εἰσελεύσονται.
       οἱ δὲ μαθηταὶ ἐθαμβοῦντο
           ἐπὶ τοῖς λόγοις αὐτοῦ.
     ὁ δὲ Ἰησοῦς πάλιν ἀποκριθεὶς   B
           λέγει αὐτοῖς,
           Τέκνα,
       πῶς δύσκολόν ἐστιν
           εἰς τὴν βασιλείαν τοῦ θεοῦ
           εἰσελθεῖν·
       εὐκοπώτερόν ἐστιν
           κάμηλον διὰ τῆς τρυμαλιᾶς τῆς ῥαφίδος διελθεῖν
           ἢ πλούσιον
               εἰς τὴν βασιλείαν τοῦ θεοῦ
               εἰσελθεῖν.
     οἱ δὲ περισσῶς ἐξεπλήσσοντο   B'
           λέγοντες πρὸς ἑαυτούς,
           Καὶ τίς δύναται σωθῆναι;

ἐμβλέψας αὐτοῖς   A   **B'**
                    ὁ Ἰησοῦς λέγει,
              Παρὰ ἀνθρώποις ἀδύνατον
                 ἀλλ᾽ οὐ παρὰ θεῷ,
                πάντα γὰρ δυνατὰ
                   παρὰ τῷ θεῷ.
        Ἤρξατο λέγειν   B
                    ὁ Πέτρος
                      αὐτῷ,
              Ἰδοὺ ἡμεῖς ἀφήκαμεν πάντα
              καὶ ἠκολουθήκαμέν σοι.
        ἔφη ὁ Ἰησοῦς,   B'
                 Ἀμὴν λέγω ὑμῖν,
              οὐδείς ἐστιν ὃς ἀφῆκεν οἰκίαν
                        ἢ ἀδελφοὺς ἢ ἀδελφὰς ἢ μητέρα
                        ἢ πατέρα ἢ τέκνα ἢ ἀγροὺς
                    ἕνεκεν ἐμοῦ
                    καὶ ἕνεκεν τοῦ εὐαγγελίου, [30]
                 ἐὰν μὴ λάβῃ
                        ἑκατονταπλασίονα
                           νῦν
                        ἐν τῷ καιρῷ τούτῳ
                    οἰκίας καὶ ἀδελφοὺς καὶ ἀδελφὰς
                        καὶ μητέρας καὶ τέκνα καὶ ἀγροὺς
                        μετὰ διωγμῶν,
                    καὶ ἐν τῷ αἰῶνι τῷ ἐρχομένῳ
                        ζωὴν αἰώνιον. [31]
                 πολλοὶ δὲ ἔσονται
                    πρῶτοι ἔσχατοι
                    καὶ οἱ ἔσχατοι πρῶτοι.

And in literal English:

And when he went out   A   **A**
        into the way,
    one running up to him
         and kneeling,
        began to question him,
        'Good Teacher,
    What may I do
        that I may inherit
        eternal life?'
  And Jesus said to him,   B
         'Why do you call me good?
       There's no one good
           except one,
           God.
    Do you know the commandments:
        Do not kill;
           Do not commit adultery;
           Do not steal;
        Do not bear false witness;
           Do not defraud;
           Honour your father and mother?'
  And he said,
         'Teacher.
        I have observed all these things
        from my youth.'
  And Jesus,   B'
        looking at him,
        loved him.
  And he said to him,
         'One thing you lack.
       Go!
           What things you have
             sell
             and give to the poor
          and you will have treasure
             in heaven.
        And come!
         Follow me!'
  But he being sad at the word,
        went away grieving,
        for he had many possessions.

And looking around,   A   **B**
        Jesus says
        to his disciples,
    'How hard for the ones having riches
        that into the kingdom of God
        they might enter.'
  And the disciples were amazed
        at his words.

And Jesus again answering,   B
       says to them,
       'Children,
   How hard it is
       into the kingdom of God.
       to enter.
   It is easier
       for a camel to go through the eye of a needle,
       than for a rich man
          into the kingdom of God
          to enter.'
And they were exceedingly astonished,   B'
   saying to each other,
   'And who can be saved?'

Looking at them,   A   **B'**
       Jesus says,
   'With men it is impossible,
       but not with God,
   for all things are possible
       with God.'
  Began to say,   B
       Peter,
       to him,
   'Behold we have left everything
   and we have followed you.'
  Said Jesus,   B'
       'Truly I tell you,
   There is no-one who has left house,
          or brothers, or sisters, or mother,
          or father, or children, or fields,
       for my sake
       and for the sake of the gospel,
     but he receives
       a hundredfold
          now,
          in this time
       houses and brothers and sisters
          and mothers and children and fields,
          with persecutions
     and in the age coming,
       eternal life.
  And many will be:
     the first last,
     and the last first.'

Part **A**, 10.17-22, part a, tells how 'on the way', a rich man 'runs' up to Jesus to question him about 'inheriting eternal life'. 'Entry into life' is an issue twice raised by Jesus in Day Seventeen (9.30-50, in 9.43,45), day three of the first sub-Series (of this Series). It is, therefore, one of the correspondences between the first and second sub-Series (of this Series), for this Day begins the second sub-Series. (For references also to the 'Kingdom of God', see the discussion at the end of Day Eighteen's examination.) 'Eternal life' is a phrase which is found again, later in this Day's telling, at v.30 (and nowhere else in the Gospel). In part b, the rich man's address to Jesus, "Good Teacher..." is questioned by Jesus, before he questions the man as to his understanding of the law. The Part concludes with the man's affirmative answer, prefaced now by "Teacher" only: the man is challenged to sell what he has, to give it to the poor and to follow Jesus, rather, he walks away sad.

Part **A** introduces the issues of 'riches and eternal life' (10.17,21,22) which is addressed in Part **B** (vv.23-26) and of 'giving up what one has and following Jesus' (v.21) which is addressed in Part **B'** (vv.28-31). Again Mark's three-part rhetorical method is in evidence whereby **A** sets up **B** and **B'**. It distinguishes vv.17-31 as Mark's own composition. It is difficult to define which if any of these units (but v.31) had an earlier separate existence: I can neither agree, therefore, with Bultmann that sections B and B' are 'supplements' only, nor with Hooker or others that the parts pre-existed independently. So what about my re-divisioning of these units? I am persuaded that Mark, in completing Part **A** with ὁ δέ Ἰησοῦς ἐμβλέψας αὐτῷ... saw his opportunity to start Part **B** with Καὶ περιβλεψάμενος ὁ Ἰησοῦς λέγει... and Part **B'** with ἐμβλέψας αὐτοῖς ὁ Ἰησοῦς λέγει... Hence, and also for interpreting the abb' constructions, my differences of sub-division from those named. Further, I like the possibility that as Mark introduces the phrase with 'looking at him, he loved him', he means his reader to interpret that he loved his disciples as he looked upon them.

In Part **B**, the first part, Jesus raises the issue of riches and entry into the kingdom of God (three times in this section: the phrase is synonymous with 'eternal life'). The additional two parts develop Jesus' teaching on the subject. A unique address by Jesus of the disciples appears, Τέκνα (see the discussion on the role of the central Day of this Series, Day Eighteen). In Part **B'**, the first part, Jesus speaks of what is possible. Peter is provoked to raise his question, the issue of leaving "all" and following Jesus; this is part two. Jesus' response is given in part three; the two b parts, the second and third parts, complete the presentation.

On 10.17-31, Mack states, "This material belongs to a section of Mark that is notoriously difficult to parse (Mark 9.38-10.31). The section falls between the second and third prediction units, and appears to serve a function similar to that of the 'confession of Peter' (for the first prediction unit) and the transfiguration (for the second prediction unit) by preparing for the prediction and for a set of discipleship sayings to follow."[332] My observation is that it is expressedly the function of 10.17-31. Simply, Mark *has* begun his second sub-Series of this Series in a way that reflects the beginning of his first. (Knowing Mark's literary structure of both Series and Days makes 9.38-10.31 much easier to parse, than Mack states, as other passages too, I suggest.)

Additionally, we may note Mark's reference to "gospel" in both these sub-Series' opening Days, at 8.35 and 10.29. Its mention further links these Days. Altogether the word appears only four times in his Gospel narrative. Outside of this third Series, it is found only in 13.10, where it combines with "the Gentiles", and in 14.9, the middle Day of the final Series, where it is linked with the "world". In the Title, it is found once, in the Prologue twice and the longer ending once, where it is linked with "the world" and "all creation"[333]. We will see in Chapter 8 that the word "gospel" has its significance in terms of Mark's overall plan for reasons of its incidence.

---

[332]Mack, *Rhetoric...*, p.54.
[333]See my discussion under Day 18 on Genesis and the creation story, and its possible influence in Mark's arranging of his "Gospel".

For further parallels of the teaching content of this Day, see my presentations on 8.34-37 (in Day Fifteen) and 9.35 (in Day Seventeen, the third Day of the sub-Series, begun on Day Fifteen). We may observe too how Days Seventeen and this Day end with concise sayings, 9.50 (on "salt") and 10.31 (on "first" and "last")[334]. For other reasons as well, such as teachings on "the Kingdom of God", and the setting which after a Day's break (in the middle Day of the Series) is 'on the way' again (as first introduced in Day Fifteen), we may observe that this Day's telling does indeed function in Mark's scheme as the first of a new threesome of Days.

Day Twenty: 10.32-46a:

The Day begins, as we observed under Day Eighteen, with another reference to $\dot{\epsilon}\nu\ \tau\hat{\eta}\ \dot{o}\delta\hat{\omega}$ [335], but now 'the way' is qualified, as the way 'to Jerusalem'. This Day is the second Day of this new threesome of Days, and as on Days Fifteen (8.27-9.1) and Seventeen (9.30-50), it includes, early in the telling, the third of the three similar 'Son of man' predictions by Jesus, by which he says what is going to happen to him. Only now the earlier predictions are doubly qualified: what will happen to Jesus will happen to him in Jerusalem (vv.33,34); and what will happen to him (in the co-sequent Day of the following and final Series)[336] will be at the hands of the "Gentiles". Part A relates these matters. In the opening piece, we come across four imperfects expressing continuous action; Jesus leads the way to the astonishment and fear of those behind him[337]. The Day's presentation is another, simple ABB' scheme[338]. The contents set it apart, however. But for the introduction which refers to "the ones following" (v.32), the Day's episodes include only Jesus and "the twelve"[339] in the telling. And here attaches an important point. Just as in the first sub-Series of this Series, in matters of Jesus' disclosures to his disciples of his death and resurrection, (8.30, 9.30,31) and of his Sonship of God (9.9), here also, in the second sub-Series, we see that Jesus' disclosures of his death and resurrection are for a limited audience. Here, expressedly, it is for "the twelve" alone.

This Day's Parts are: **A**, vv.32-34; **B**, vv.35-40 and **B'**, vv.41-46a and they each comprise three pieces, abb'. Taylor, Nineham, Schweizer and Hooker all describe the outer limits of these units as vv.32-34; vv.35-40 and vv.41-45.[340] For me, I have to include v.46a with vv.41-45. Codex Alexandrinus shows a break after v.46a. It is needed in literary-structural terms, but more than that it begs a dramatic pause before the new Day starts. Mark wants his audience to reflect on Jesus' sorrow; he is going to Jerusalem to die there and his disciples are still thinking and behaving in worldly ways.

---

[334]9.34,35; 10.31 and 10.43,44 all beg comparison. 9.34,35 (in Day 17), in response to "greater" has a single saying on "first" and "last", to which "and servant of all" is attached. 10.31 (Day 19) has a double, reverse saying: "first"/"last"; "last"/"first". And 10.43,44 (Day 20), in response to "great" has "servant"; and in response to "first" has "slave of all". They demonstrate a close relationship. They clearly link sub-Series one with sub-Series two, but in the last of these is the final Series' development of the issues.

[335]See 8.27, 9.30/33, 10.17 for similar Day-beginnings.

[336]"... the Gentiles,... will mock him and spit on him, flog him and kill him." *cf.* Day 27: the Gentiles flog Jesus, mock him, spit on him, and kill him.

[337]We observe in v.32 that these emotions precede the third prediction. Could it be that the disciples have understanding now, *before* Jesus tells them in more detail what is to happen?

[338]For other 'simple' ABB' constructions of Days so far uncovered, see Days Two, Eleven, Twelve, Fourteen, Fifteen, Eighteen and Nineteen. Days Seven, Nine, Ten and Seventeen are the larger 'composite' ABB' constructions.

[339]Day Seventeen, 9.30-50, is the next nearest to telling that only Jesus and the 'twelve' were present (vv.30,35). Jesus sets a child in their midst (v.36), so others are about.

[340]Taylor, *The Gospel...*, pp.436-443; Nineham, *Saint Mark*, pp.277-280 (for Nineham 10.32-52 should be read together); Schweizer, *The Good News...*, pp.216-218; and Hooker, *The Gospel...*, pp.244-246.

All the parts of this Day's telling behave in relation to each other as we would (now) expect them to, where A is introductory, B is the first development and B' is the second, corresponding and completing devlopment. Discipleship and the want of seats of "lordship" and "authority" (as James and John wanted, each side of Jesus 'in his glory') are not compatible. Servanthood is expected of (the) disciples, because Jesus himself has come "to serve and to give his life...".

Clearly, this Day's telling, the second of this sub-Series of three, begs comparison with the transfiguration story of Day Sixteen, the second Day of the first sub-Series of three. Day Sixteen tells about two who *meet* with Jesus in his glory. Day Twenty tells about two who would *sit* with Jesus in his glory. The first are Moses and Elijah, representative of the Law and the Prophets, or leaders of the Old Covenant. The second are James and John who, with the other disciples, have been called to leadership under the New Covenant. Specifically, in Day Twenty's telling, the disciples are taught by Jesus about the qualities of leadership which he expects from them. His illustration is not that their leadership must be like that of the leaders of Moses and Elijah. The disciples might not have aspired too easily to such. Rather, it is that their leadership must not be anything like that of the leaders of the "Gentiles" (v.42). In v.33, τοῖς ἔθνεσιν is well translated "to the Gentiles". In v.42, τῶν ἐθνῶν could be translated "of the nations", to include both Israel and Gentile nations, because Jesus nowhere commends Israel's leadership (see 6.34 for an indication of this).

Under the examination of Day Nineteen, on page 203, I drew attention to the importance of Mark's distribution of the word "gospel" in matters of understanding Mark's plan. Outside of the Prologue, it links to "the world" (in 14.9, 16.15), "all creation" (in 16.15, in the possible Epilogue) and "the Gentiles" (in 13.10). I here draw attention similarly to the importance of the word meaning either "Gentiles" or "nations". References include the above, 10.33 and v.42, and in addition only: 11.17, 13.8 and v.10. These are found solely in the second and third Days of the final Series. In chapter 8, we will discuss Mark's spared use of both.

The literary structure of Day Twenty follows:

Ἦσαν δὲ ἐν τῇ ὁδῷ   A   **A**
       ἀναβαίνοντες εἰς Ἱεροσόλυμα,
     καὶ ἦν προάγων αὐτοὺς ὁ Ἰησοῦς,
       καὶ ἐθαμβοῦντο,
     οἱ δὲ ἀκολουθοῦντες
       ἐφοβοῦντο.
  καὶ παραλαβὼν πάλιν τοὺς δώδεκα   B
       ἤρξατο αὐτοῖς λέγειν
     τὰ μέλλοντα αὐτῷ συμβαίνειν, [33]
  ὅτι Ἰδοὺ   B'
         ἀναβαίνομεν
         εἰς Ἱεροσόλυμα,
    καὶ ὁ υἱὸς τοῦ ἀνθρώπου παραδοθήσεται
       τοῖς ἀρχιερεῦσιν
        καὶ τοῖς γραμματεῦσιν,
     καὶ κατακρινοῦσιν αὐτὸν θανάτῳ
  καὶ παραδώσουσιν αὐτὸν τοῖς ἔθνεσιν [34]
       καὶ ἐμπαίξουσιν αὐτῷ
       καὶ ἐμπτύσουσιν αὐτῷ
    καὶ μαστιγώσουσιν αὐτὸν
       καὶ ἀποκτενοῦσιν,
      καὶ μετὰ τρεῖς ἡμέρας
       ἀναστήσεται.

  Καὶ προσπορεύονται αὐτῷ·   A   **B**
       Ἰάκωβος καὶ Ἰωάννης
      οἱ υἱοὶ Ζεβεδαίου
    λέγοντες αὐτῷ,
        Διδάσκαλε,
     θέλομεν
       ἵνα ὃ ἐὰν αἰτήσωμέν σε
      ποιήσῃς ἡμῖν.
   ὁ δὲ εἶπεν αὐτοῖς,
      Τί θέλετέ με
      ποιήσω ὑμῖν;
  οἱ δὲ εἶπαν αὐτῷ,   B
     Δὸς ἡμῖν
       ἵνα εἷς σου ἐκ δεξιῶν
        καὶ εἷς ἐξ ἀριστερῶν
     καθίσωμεν
       ἐν τῇ δόξῃ σου.
   ὁ δὲ Ἰησοῦς εἶπεν αὐτοῖς,
       Οὐκ οἴδατε
       τί αἰτεῖσθε.
     δύνασθε
       πιεῖν τὸ ποτήριον
        ὃ ἐγὼ πίνω,
     ἢ τὸ βάπτισμα
       ὃ ἐγὼ βαπτίζομαι

βαπτισθῆναι;
οἱ δὲ εἶπαν αὐτῷ,
Δυνάμεθα.
ὁ δὲ Ἰησοῦς εἶπεν αὐτοῖς,   Β'
Τὸ ποτήριον ὃ ἐγὼ πίνω
πίεσθε
καὶ τὸ βάπτισμα
ὃ ἐγὼ βαπτίζομαι
βαπτισθήσεσθε, 40
τὸ δὲ καθίσαι
ἐκ δεξιῶν μου
ἢ ἐξ εὐωνύμων
οὐκ ἔστιν ἐμὸν δοῦναι,
ἀλλ᾽ οἷς ἡτοίμασται.

Καὶ ἀκούσαντες   Α   Β'
οἱ δέκα ἤρξαντο ἀγανακτεῖν
περὶ Ἰακώβου καὶ Ἰωάννου. 42
καὶ προσκαλεσάμενος αὐτοὺς   Β
ὁ Ἰησοῦς λέγει αὐτοῖς,
Οἴδατε
ὅτι οἱ
δοκοῦντες ἄρχειν τῶν ἐθνῶν
κατακυριεύουσιν αὐτῶν
καὶ οἱ μεγάλοι αὐτῶν
κατεξουσιάζουσιν
αὐτῶν. 43
οὐχ οὕτως δέ ἐστιν
ἐν ὑμῖν·
ἀλλ᾽ ὃς ἂν θέλῃ
μέγας γενέσθαι ἐν ὑμῖν,
ἔσται ὑμῶν διάκονος, 44
καὶ ὃς ἂν θέλῃ
ἐν ὑμῖν εἶναι πρῶτος,
ἔσται πάντων δοῦλος· 45
καὶ γὰρ ὁ υἱὸς τοῦ ἀνθρώπου
οὐκ ἦλθεν
διακονηθῆναι
ἀλλὰ διακονῆσαι
καὶ δοῦναι τὴν ψυχὴν αὐτοῦ
λύτρον
ἀντὶ πολλῶν.
Καὶ ἔρχονται εἰς Ἰεριχώ.   Β'

And in literal English:

Now they were in the way,   A   A
      going up to Jerusalem,
    and Jesus was going ahead of them,
      and they were astonished,
   and the ones following
     were afraid.
And taking again the twelve,   B
   he began to tell them
   the things about to happen to him,
'Behold,   B'
      we are going up
      to Jerusalem.
    And the Son of Man will be betrayed
     to the chief priests
     and to the scribes.
    And they will condemn him to death.
  And they will deliver him to the Gentiles.
    And they will mock him.
    And they will spit on him.
  And they will scourge him.
    And they will kill him.
    And after three days
      he will rise again.'

And approach him,   A   B
    James and John,
    the sons of Zebedee,
  saying to him,
     'Teacher,
   we wish
    that whatever we ask you,
  you may do for us.'
And he said to them,
    'What do you wish me
    to do for you?'
And they said to him,   B
    'Grant us
     that one on your right
     and one on your left,
   we may sit
    in your glory.'
And Jesus said to them,
     'You don't know
     what you are asking!
   Are you able
    to drink the cup
    which I drink?
   Or to be baptised
    in the baptism
    in which I am baptised?

And they said to him,
    'We are able!'
And Jesus said to them,   **B'**
    'The cup which I drink,
      you will drink.
    And you will be baptised
      in the baptism
      in which I am baptised.
    But to sit
          on my right,
          or on my left,
        is not mine to grant,
        but for whom it has been prepared.'

And hearing,   A   **B'**
    the ten began to be incensed
    about James and John.
  And calling them to him,   B
        Jesus says to them,
        'You know
      that the ones
        thinking to rule over the Gentiles,
        lord it over them,
      and the great of them
        exercise authority
        over them.
    But it is not so
        among you.
    But whoever wishes
        to be great among you,
        he will be your servant.
    And whoever wishes
        to be first among you,
        he will be slave of all.
    For even the Son of Man
        did not come
        to be served,
      but to serve
      and to give his life
        a ransom
        for many.'
And they come to Jericho.   **B'**

Day Twenty-one: 10.46b-52:

This last Day of this second of two middle Series begins in a new way:

Καὶ ἐκπορευομένου αὐτοῦ ἀπὸ Ἰεριχώ...

We are left to judge, therefore, whether we should interpret days, hours or just minutes between Jesus' arrival and departure.

Ending the presentation of the preceding Day, we have *Καὶ ἔρχονται εἰς Ἰεριχώ.* Some may view this as *the proper beginning* for this new Day's presentation, especially as we have found already similar phrasing to begin a number of new Days.[341] For a long time, I was satisfied that in literary-structural terms this Day did indeed begin with the telling of Jesus' arrival. But now I think I have my reading right, for reasons chiefly given under Day Twenty. As for the ending of the Day, it is clearly at v.52. What follows in 11.1-11 belongs to a new sequence of Days. What is clear too is that this Day features the healing of a blind man, just as the final Day of the first of the two middle Series does (for more, see Day Fourteen). Nowhere else in the Gospel are there reports of a blind man being healed. (This has its significance for the arrangements of the middle Series and the way they relate.)

Given that Jericho was a major town on Jesus' route to Jerusalem and that it is reasonable to consider that Jesus might have stayed there, it may be considered more likely that Mark meant our interpretation to be that he did indeed stay there a few days. What implies this is that when Jesus does leave, with his disciples, he does so also with a considerable crowd. He will have needed (in realistic terms) a few days at least, over which to gather a very large crowd. Mark, I think, is not underplaying the drama. The days of Jesus journeying to Jerusalem, to suffering, to death and to glory, are coming to their end and their climax!

Others have had to judge before us where this Day's telling begins; the scribe of Codex Alexandrinus is one of them and he was persuaded that *Καὶ ἔρχονται εἰς Ἰεριχώ* belonged with the contents of the preceding Day's telling. He either introduced a space himself, between Jesus' arrival and departure, or he simply faithfully repeated what he had in the earlier manuscripts that he had to hand.

The full opening piece deserves a little attention:

Καὶ ἐκπορευομένου αὐτοῦ ἀπὸ Ἰεριχώ	a
καὶ τῶν μαθητῶν αὐτοῦ	
καὶ ὄχλου ἱκανοῦ	
ὁ υἱὸς Τιμαίου	b
Βαρτιμαῖος,	
τυφλὸς	
ἐκάθητο	b'
παρὰ τὴν ὁδὸν	
προσαιτῶν.[47]	

The first part, a, is told in a way that the details accrue line after line: firstly 'as he is leaving' then 'and his disciples', then and a considerable crowd! The second part, b, simarly introduces 'the son of Timaeus', 'Bartimaeus', 'a blind man'. And the third part, b', completes the description of the man, he was 'sat', 'by the way', 'begging'. It well sets the scene, for this short presentation. See under Day Fifteen for the importance to this Series of *ἐν τῇ ὁδῷ.* With the same phrase, the Day's telling ends too.

---

[341] See the Days beginning 6.1, 53, 7.24, 31, 8.27 and 10.1 for their similar introductory pieces.

The literary structure of Day Twenty-one is viewed as:

Καὶ ἐκπορευομένου αὐτοῦ ἀπὸ Ἰεριχὼ   A
            καὶ τῶν μαθητῶν αὐτοῦ
            καὶ ὄχλου ἱκανοῦ
      ὁ υἱὸς Τιμαίου
          Βαρτιμαῖος,
          τυφλὸς
      ἐκάθητο
          παρὰ τὴν ὁδὸν
          προσαιτῶν. [47]
    καὶ ἀκούσας
          ὅτι Ἰησοῦς ὁ Ναζαρηνός
          ἐστιν
      ἤρξατο
          κράζειν
          καὶ λέγειν,
      Υἱὲ Δαυὶδ
          Ἰησοῦ,
          ἐλέησόν με.
    καὶ ἐπετίμων αὐτῷ πολλοὶ
          ἵνα σιωπήσῃ·
      ὁ δὲ πολλῷ μᾶλλον ἔκραζεν,
      Υἱὲ Δαυίδ,
          ἐλέησόν με.
  καὶ στὰς   B
      ὁ Ἰησοῦς εἶπεν,
      Φωνήσατε αὐτόν.
    καὶ φωνοῦσιν τὸν τυφλὸν
      λέγοντες αὐτῷ,
      Θάρσει,
          ἔγειρε,
          φωνεῖ σε. [50]
    ὁ δὲ ἀποβαλὼν τὸ ἱμάτιον αὐτοῦ
      ἀναπηδήσας
      ἦλθεν πρὸς τὸν Ἰησοῦν.
  καὶ ἀποκριθεὶς αὐτῷ   B'
      ὁ Ἰησοῦς εἶπεν,
      Τί σοι θέλεις ποιήσω;
    ὁ δὲ τυφλὸς εἶπεν αὐτῷ,
      Ραββουνι,
      ἵνα ἀναβλέψω.
    καὶ ὁ Ἰησοῦς εἶπεν αὐτῷ,
          Ὕπαγε,
          ἡ πίστις σου σέσωκέν σε.
      καὶ εὐθὺς ἀνέβλεψεν,
      καὶ ἠκολούθει αὐτῷ
          ἐν τῇ ὁδῷ.

And in literal English:

And as he was leaving Jericho   A
     and his disciples
     and a considerable crowd,
   the son of Timaeus,
     Bartimaeus,
     a blind man
  sat
     by the way
     begging.
  And hearing
     that it was Jesus
     the Nazarene,
   he began
     to cry out,
     and to say,
   'Son of David,
     Jesus,
     have mercy on me!'
  And many rebuked him,
     that he be quiet,
   But he much more cried out,
   'Son of David,
     have mercy on me!'
 And standing,   B
    Jesus said,
    'Call him!'
  And they call the blind man,
    saying to him,
    'Be of good courage,
     rise up,
     he calls you.'
  And casting off his garment,
    rising up,
    he came to Jesus.
 And answering him,   B'
    Jesus said,
    'What do you wish I do?'
  And the blind man said to him,
    'Rabboni,
    that I may see.'
  And Jesus said to him,
     'Go,/ your faith has healed you.'
    And immediately he could see.
    And he began to follow him on the way.

Again, the structure is a simple ABB' form, where A is introductory, B is the first development, and B' is the second and completing development. In literary-structural terms, it is a perfect example of how Mark writes, and of how any rhetor might complete a sub-Series and a Series at the same time. We single out a few details for consideration. We read about a "considerable" crowd; it is the only time in the Gospel we read καὶ ὄχλου ἱκανοῦ. A blind beggar is named in contrast to the vast majority of characters who meet with Jesus in this Gospel and we read how he attracts Jesus' attention. The balance of Mark's presentation is impressive. And the Christological disclosures are no less impressive.

In Part A, we meet with a title for Jesus not used since Day One, 1.24: the blind man hears that "it is Jesus the Nazarene"[342] (v.47); and it is followed by another title not used at all before in the Gospel. In the first public and unrebuked recognition (by Jesus, that is) of its kind, this 'blind' man knows ('sees') who Jesus is: he is the "Son of David". Yes, the blind man is "rebuked"[343] by "many" which causes him "the much more to cry out, Son of David...". Firstly, we note that we have come across something like this before, in 7.36, in the same second sub-Series of the first of these two middle Sections, though there it is Jesus who is ordering silence. Secondly, we note that Mark's audience hear the title twice! Mark is promoting the application of this messianic title to Jesus[344]. Thirdly, the repetitions of "Son of David" occur as one would expect now with Mark, in the b and b' parts.

Part B begins with Jesus standing there and saying, "Call him". The Part is completed in its balancing b and b' parts: the blind man is called and he comes to Jesus.

Part B' begins with Jesus asking the man what he wanted. The blind man's answer, in b, is matched, in b', with his receiving his sight and his following Jesus on the way. Key to this healing is Jesus statement, "Go, your faith has made you whole". We can compare this, Ὕπαγε, ἡ πίστις σου σέσωκέν σε, with 5.34, the same words of Jesus to the woman who is healed, though ὕπαγε follows ἡ πίστις σου σέσωκέν σε: it is significant because Day Seven is the last Day of the first Series. Here is a parallel. Given the blind man begins to *follow* Jesus, we can compare the same with other references to "following" in this Series, in 8.35, 9.38 *bis*, 10.21, 28 and 32).[345]

As Hooker says, "The story is an appropriate climax to a section which has spelt out the meaning of discipleship... It is a final challenge to his (Mark's) readers to join Bartimaeus in following Jesus on the road (or 'way') of discipleship, even though that road leads to Jerusalem and all that happens there"[346]. It is a fitting climax too to the sub-Series of Days Nineteen, Twenty and Twenty-one which, after the middle Day's "testing" of Jesus by Pharisees, and its teaching on "receiving" the kingdom of God as a gift (in Day Eighteen, 10.1-16), returns to Christological matters and teachings on discipleship. This Day's setting well succeeds that of 10.32: Jesus is now only fifteen miles from Jerusalem and just a short distance, therefore, from his journey's goal.

This sub-Series of Days Nineteen, Twenty and Twenty-One exhibits another ABB' arrangement. Day Nineteen picks up the themes of the first sub-Series, after the Series' middle

---

[342]The term, "Jesus of Nazareth", is used sparingly and, therefore, significantly by Mark, in 1.24, 10.47, 14.67 and 16.6. It is to be found in an introductory sense in 1.9, "Jesus came from Nazareth...". In Chapter 8 we will judge its importance in Mark's presentation.

[343]I agree with Rienecker that the imperfect here represents continuous action, though it is border-line with inceptive. We read: Bartimaeus "begins to cry out and to say...", and judge "the crying out" continues; hence also the rebuking begins and continues too (Fritz Rienecker, *A Linguistic Key...*).

[344]The title, "Son of David" became a familiar title for the messianic king in later Jewish literature (its first known use is in Pss. Sol. 17.21) and would have been understood in that sense by Mark, who nevertheless demonstrates later that it is not a fully adequate title for Jesus (12.35-37).

[345]For a discussion on the importance of ἐν τῇ ὁδῷ see 1) under Day Fifteen.

[346]Hooker, *The Gospel...*, p.252.

Day's different emphases. It emphatically makes a new beginning "on the way", which becomes in the second Day (Day Twenty's telling) "the way up to Jerusalem", and in the third becomes "the way out of Jericho" (the last lap of the journey is *already begun*). Days B and B' in turn, in their introductory geographical statements, develop and announce with exactitude what was only an opening generality. I realise that this argument sits uneasily as we have learned previously not to define the structure of a threesome of Days, either by geographical location, or by which Days are consecutive, and not. Nevertheless, it would seem to be the case that Mark has indeed concluded this Series in this manner, simply because the Series itself does report Jesus' journey to Jerusalem as to the cross and glory. Clearly, to be consistent, however, we should look for an accompanying development in his presentation of Jesus' teaching of the disciples. It is this that established the ABB' structure of the first sub-Series.

The first day of this threesome establishes that the disciples have already left everything behind to follow Jesus. The rich man was not prepared to do that. The second day begins with Jesus spelling out what is going to happen to him in Jerusalem, but two of his disciples still want "glory" for themselves. Though they say that they are able to drink the same cup and be baptised with the same baptism as Jesus, they show they do not understand what Jesus is asking them. The third Day tells how a "blind man" who knows something of Jesus' status has "faith" to be healed. People with "faith" will have sight. People who understand will follow Jesus' way of suffering to glory. This story of the healing of blind Bartimaeus has the same function as the previous Series' concluding story, only now it is more simply interpreted; "understanding" comes through "faith". The second and third Days of this Series deal with this issue, and are to be seen as a pair in the sub-Series. The structure is ABB'.

A Summary of the Third Series of Seven Days:

This third Series of Seven Days is structured ABA', where, as before, A represents the first sub-Series/threesome of Days and A' the last sub-Series/threesome of Days around a central, pivotal Day, B. As is discussed under the middle Day, Day Eighteen, this fulcrum to the Series is established neither essentially by absences of Christological statement and oft-repeated phrases in the Series (such as $\dot{\epsilon}v\ \tau\tilde{\eta}\ \dot{o}\delta\tilde{\varphi}$), nor by elements of story-content which are included there and nowhere else in the Series, such as the "testing" of Jesus by Pharisees and the issues of marriage and divorce concerning which Jesus re-interprets the Mosaic Law. The Day is more than a buffer between the two sub-Series of three Days for which Jesus' own Christological statements about his suffering, death and resurrection and his servanthood undergird his teachings on discipleship. The middle Day both interprets and is interpreted by the Sub-Series. The kingdom of God is a gift to be received like a child, who trusts, and it is a gift of Jesus, as a result of his suffering, dying and resurrection, which promises repeated blessings. All discipleship hinges on receiving this gift.

We observe, therefore, in this Series, as in the first two, that the 'arrangement' of Days demonstrates application of ancient rhetorical conventions whereby there is a smoothing of the sharp edges of the transitional central turning point and the material around it. The accumulated evidence from the examination of the first three Series of the Gospel suggests the possibility of a modified annotation. Clearly, Mark's 'arrangement' could be summed up as three three-Day sub-Series which overlap, where the first sub-Series is described by ABB', the second by ABA', and the third by ABB':

$$\text{A} \quad \text{B} \quad \underline{\text{B}'} \qquad \underline{\text{A}} \quad \text{B} \quad \text{B}'$$
$$\underline{\text{A}} \quad \text{B} \quad \underline{\text{A}'}$$

All this is, of course, is an elaboration only of the summary ABA' Series form, but it does perhaps more clearly express Mark's method, that is, what he had in his mind as he composed his Series.

Other rhetorical features in this particular Series include the *inclusio* of "the Christ" in the first Day and "Son of David" in the last Day. The same is true also of 'rebukings', in both. We have seen already an *inclusio* in the first Series in the 'raisings from beds' in both the first and last Days. In the summary of the second Series, we have seen how a *link-motif* smooths the transition between this Series and the former one, 'the two-stage healing/the two-stage revelation'. Now an anastrophe functions in the same way between the ending of this Series and the beginning of the next: 'Son of David'/'our father David').

Clearly the defining of this Series, in literary-structural terms, establishes three points which are important to the assessment of the views of Wrede and many others on what constituted Mark's "leading idea", or purpose in constructing his Gospel. For them, it was on the basis that Jesus' messiahship was to be kept secret until after his resurrection (the key verse for which is 9.9). The three points are: 1) the first Day's telling of this Series, in 8.30, introduces the "*Messianic* secret" (specifically) into the Gospel for the first time; 2) the last Day's telling, in 10.47,48, implies that Jesus' Messianic *status* is a secret no longer (because Jesus himself did not rebuke Bartimaeus for what he was crying out); and 3) between these we read about disclosures which were for the disciples alone, about other aspects of Jesus' divine status, also his suffering, death and resurrection. What Mark has given his audience in his third Series is what (he thinks) Jesus wanted his disciples to know at this stage of his mission, and what at this stage he did not want the crowds to know. The logic Mark demonstrates clearly is that the people could not have been told what was going to happen to him in Jerusalem. And the logic continues surely: it could only be after his death and resurrection that all could know fully who he was and what his purpose had been from the beginning. The people could not have been expected *knowingly* to crucify their Messiah and the Son of God (to which 9.9 specifically refers), in order to establish a new Covenant between God and the world[347].

We will return to these matters in Chapter Eight. For the present, my view, shaped by the above and by other information which will be discussed, is that a restricting of public information about Jesus' messiahship, and certain aspects about it, simply *had* to be maintained until after Jesus' resurrection. Only then *could there truly be* "good news" for "the world"[348].

The title I give this Series, following the style of my titling of the earlier Series, is "The Days of Jesus' Journeying to Jerusalem, to the Cross and Glory."

Again, last of all, in summarising a Series we give consideration to the number of days Mark indicates that have passed, even though he has chosen to report only seven in full in a seven Day Series format. The information, where he supplies it, is exclusive to his Days' introductory pieces. Between the Second and the Third Series there is clearly no information about the number of days Jesus stayed in Bethsaida; he may have left there the day following Day Fourteen of Mark's plan, or he may have stayed some days. Further, the journey between Bethsaida and Caesarea Philippi of about 36 miles may have taken two days. Between the tellings of the first and second days, Mark informs his audience that "six" days passed (9.2). (Though he has been specific here we cannot be sure, however, that the number has not been adopted from Exodus 24.16, and that he used it typologically.) Not knowing where the mount

---

[347] 14.24 is supremely important in this regard. In the telling of the Passion, in the first Day's telling of the final sub-Series of the Gospel, we find this single, specific, Gospel reference to "the covenant". Jesus fulfils Zech. 9.11. In the first Day's telling of the Series and of the first sub-Series, therefore, Jesus' entry into Jerusalem fulfils Zech.9.9. We will discuss this and other features of Mark's balance in the following Chapter.

[348] We note aspects of Jesus' messiahship that *were* told to the crowd: see 8.38-9.1, in the context of 8.34. This verse establishes Jesus' want of the crowd to hear him on the issues too of 8.34-37. For 'the world' and 'the gospel', see 16.15. See Paul also, in Ro.1.4, where he says, Jesus is declared Son of God 'by his resurrection'.

of transfiguration was and not knowing how Mark defined Galilee (refer: 9.30) makes it impossible to assess the days of Jesus' journeying to Capernaum prior to the third Day's telling. The fourth Day's report is prefaced with the journey Jesus made from Capernaum to Judea and beyond the Jordan. He rises (10.1) 'from sleep' and began an 80 mile journey which could have taken him four to five days, or more if he had stayed in each place *en route*. At the beginning of the fifth Day's report, Jesus is "on the way", but we are not told where so there is no way of knowing here how many days had passed. The 'way' becomes the 'way to Jerusalem' (in 10.32) at the beginning of the sixth day; again not knowing the place of departure or the place of arrival before the day's report is given we are here stymied too. That Jesus and his disciples arrived in Jericho and likely stayed several days before leaving, at which point the event of the seventh day is told, we may estimate that the miles travelled between the end of day four and the beginning of day seven were 10 to 15 only, and therefore, that the passing of other, unreported days would have been due more to Jesus staying in places *en route* than on actual travelling.

The impression we gain overall is that Mark viewed this stage in Jesus' mission as covering a number of weeks. It is not so much the total number of days that counts, but the impression Mark gives, by his method of story-telling.

A Tabular Summary of the literary-structure of the Third Seven Days:

DAYS: number identified in series	1	2	3	4	5	6	7
number identified in Gospel	15	16	17	18	19	20	21
chapters and verses	8.27-9.1	9.2-32	9.33-50	10.1-16	10.17-31	10. 32-46a	10. 46b-52
SERIES' STRUCTURE	A			B		A'	
DAYS: in literary-terms, in series	A	B	B'	A	B	B'	
DAYS' sections	A B B'	A B B'	A B B'	A B B'	A B B'	A B B'	A
DAYS' sectional sub-divisions	A B B' A B B' A B B'	A B B' A B B' A B B'	A B B' A B B' A B B'	A B B' A B B' A B B'	A B B' A B B' A B B'	A B B' A B B' A B B'	A B B'
DAYS' number of verses	13	28	19	16	15	14.5	6.5
SUB-SERIES' number of verses	60				36		
SERIES' number of verses	112						

Addendum to the analysis of 'The Third Seven Days':

No new signifiers of literary-structural division between Days are identified in this Series' analysis that were not identified in the analyses of the first two Series. We do, however, spy a new entry to the telling of Day Twenty-One: it is a reversal of the usual departing and arriving. More usefully, in 9.40,41 and 10.40, I notice examples of word-usage and order, of the kind that I now find a lot in Paul's writings. But firstly, we note that Paul's insights on Christ are followed by Mark in this Series: Jesus in the flesh is a descendent of David and declared Son of God by his resurrection (see Ro. 1.3,4). Paul's writings, of course, precede those of Mark by about ten years. To read the Greek of Paul's Letters is to discover one is reading ancient rhetoric too, as with the Gospels, Acts and Revelation.[349] The feature I refer to here is that of repeating balancing words: *οὐκ* and *ἄν*, and *οὐκ* and *ἀλλα*, which are themselves further evidence that the ones who were writing these works were aware of the practices of (Hellenist) ancient rhetoric in their era.

In 9.40,41, we read two parts, b and b':

$$\text{ὃς γὰρ } \underline{οὐκ} \text{ ἔστιν καθ' ἡμῶν,} \qquad \text{b}$$
$$\text{ὑπὲρ ἡμῶν ἐστιν.}$$
$$\text{ὃς γὰρ } \underline{ἂν} \text{ ποτίσῃ ὑμᾶς ποτήριον ὕδατος ἐν ὀνόματι} \qquad \text{b'}$$
$$\text{ὅτι Χριστοῦ ἐστε,}$$
$$\text{ἀμὴν λέγω ὑμῖν}$$
$$\text{ὅτι οὐ μὴ}$$
$$\text{ἀπολέσῃ τὸν μισθὸν αὐτοῦ.}$$

And in 9.38, again we see two parts at work in a threesome:

$$\text{καὶ ὃς ἂν ἐμὲ δέχηται,} \qquad \text{a}$$
$$\underline{\text{οὐκ}} \text{ ἐμὲ δέχεται} \qquad \text{b}$$
$$\underline{\text{ἀλλὰ}} \text{ τὸν ἀποστείλαντά με.} \qquad \text{b'}$$

And again in 10.40, a closing piece of three parts, b and b' signified:

$$\text{τὸ δὲ καθίσαι} \qquad \text{a}$$
$$\text{ἐκ δεξιῶν μου}$$
$$\text{ἢ ἐξ εὐωνύμων}$$
$$\underline{\text{οὐκ}} \text{ ἔστιν ἐμὸν δοῦναι,} \qquad \text{b}$$
$$\underline{\text{ἀλλ'}} \text{ οἷς ἡτοίμασται.} \qquad \text{b'}$$

To our list, which carries over from Series A and B, we add for Series B', here, from Days Seventeen and Twenty: point 20) occupying b and b' positions: two opening words often used in succession (to the ear, it is a closing pair to any level of order presentation).

On the sizes of Mark's rhetorical units of Days we observe that the range is from 7 to 28 verses, a factor of four only, which may be compared with a factor of ten for the first Series and a factor of just less than six for the second Series. We may surmise that this demon-

---

[349] See my *New Testament: New Testimony to the Skills of the Writers and First Readers (Fifth: Illustrated Exhibition Edition)*, Ceridwen Press, Church Gresley, 2016, for my thesis in regard to all the books of the New Testament, that they all are works of ancient rhetoric that fulfil the rules and practices of their era,and can be charted in a Rhetorical Table of the New Testament.

strates that Mark exercised a greater control over the contents of his Day-presentations here than he did in the first two Series. It begs, of course, the question, "Why?" The answer may be that he *created* more of the contents of these Day's tellings than he did in the earlier Series. His repetitions, and developments of Jesus' predictions about his suffering, death and resurrection may well be said to be one signal that implies that he was short of 'tradition' here.

A Comparison of the Second and Third Series of Seven Days:

Now we have completed separate examinations of the literary-structures of the two middle Series of the Gospel, we can determine what if any relationship Mark deemed them to have in his overall Gospel scheme. At various points in the presentations of the two Series already, we have touched on some clear points of contact between them. Their titles again are: Series Two: "Days of Increase in the Mission of Jesus"; and Series Three: "The Days of Jesus' Journeying (to Jerusalem) to the Cross and Glory". As all the Series are structured in the same way as each other (A:B:A', where A and A' represent sub-Series of three Days, around a central pivotal Day, B) there is no structural argument for seeing Series Two and Three in parallel, save that their number of verses overall are 119 and 112 respectively and that they so compare more or less equally for size, when seen against Series One which has 172 verses, and Series Four which has 239 verses.

Under the examinations of Days Eight and Fifteen, we saw how these first Days of both Series begin remarkably similarly, and contain common subject matter on the questions raised in regard to the identity of Jesus (cf. 6.14b,15 and 8.28), and on the death of John the Baptist (in Day Eight) which prefigures what Jesus discloses, for the first time, about his own death (in Day Fifteen). Both opening Days introduce issues of 'discipleship' which are developed in the Series. Under the examinations of Days Fourteen and Twenty-one, the last Days of each Series, we noted the fact that nowhere else in the Gospel are there to be found stories of healings of blind people. These also, are illustrative of discipleship matters, as many scholars and commentators have judged previously. We note here, further, that these two Days, in their telling, are the shortest in the Gospel. Given that the central, pivotal Days in both Series begin in very similar ways (see under Days Eleven and Eighteen), the two middle Series not only begin and end in like manner but, therefore, also begin 'turning' at their centre in like manner. We observe also that the two middle Days raise issues of Jewish/Gentile tensions.

Further, literary-structural contact between the two middle Series is established by the contents of the second and sixth Days of each, in terms of their intra-Series and inter-Series relationships. The two 'feedings' of the Second Series (in Days Nine and Thirteen) and the two 'glory-episodes' of the Third Series (in Days Sixteen and Twenty) provide messianic disclosures of similar kinds. The middle Series also are beginning to look like they cover Old Covenant expectations in their first sub-Series of three Days and New Covenant expectations in the paralleling sub-Series of three Days, around a central Day which holds the two in tension. We will return to this later.

For now, it is reasonable to conclude, I think, that Mark composed these two middle Series, Series B and Series B', each with the other in mind, as parallel, central Series in his Gospel narrative scheme.

Chapter Six
The Fourth Series of Seven Days (11.1-16.8):

Day Twenty-two: 11.1-11:

The literary structure of Day Twenty-two is viewed as:

Καὶ ὅτε ἐγγίζουσιν εἰς Ἱεροσόλυμα	a	A	**A**
εἰς Βηθφαγὴ καὶ Βηθανίαν			
πρὸς τὸ Ὄρος τῶν Ἐλαιῶν,			
ἀποστέλλει δύο τῶν μαθητῶν αὐτοῦ [2]	b		
καὶ λέγει αὐτοῖς,	b'		
Ὑπάγετε	a	B	
εἰς τὴν κώμην			
τὴν κατέναντι ὑμῶν,			
καὶ εὐθὺς εἰσπορευόμενοι εἰς αὐτὴν	b		
εὑρήσετε πῶλον δεδεμένον			
ἐφ᾽ ὃν οὐδεὶς οὔπω ἀνθρώπων ἐκάθισεν·			
λύσατε αὐτὸν			
καὶ φέρετε. [3]			
καὶ ἐάν τις ὑμῖν εἴπῃ,	b'		
Τί ποιεῖτε τοῦτο;			
εἴπατε,			
Ὁ κύριος αὐτοῦ χρείαν ἔχει,			
καὶ εὐθὺς			
αὐτὸν ἀποστέλλει			
πάλιν ὧδε.			
καὶ ἀπῆλθον	a	B'	
καὶ εὗρον πῶλον			
δεδεμένον			
πρὸς θύραν			
ἔξω			
ἐπὶ τοῦ ἀμφόδου,			
καὶ λύουσιν αὐτόν. [5]			
καί τινες τῶν ἐκεῖ ἑστηκότων	b		
ἔλεγον αὐτοῖς,			
Τί ποιεῖτε			
λύοντες τὸν πῶλον; [6]			
οἱ δὲ εἶπαν αὐτοῖς	b'		
καθὼς εἶπεν ὁ Ἰησοῦς·			
καὶ ἀφῆκαν αὐτούς. [7]			

Καὶ φέρουσιν τὸν πῶλον πρὸς τὸν Ἰησοῦν,	A	**B**
καὶ ἐπιβάλλουσιν αὐτῷ		
τὰ ἱμάτια αὐτῶν,		
καὶ ἐκάθισεν ἐπ' αὐτόν. [8]	B	
καὶ πολλοὶ		
τὰ ἱμάτια αὐτῶν		
ἔστρωσαν εἰς τὴν ὁδόν,		
ἄλλοι δὲ		
στιβάδας		
κόψαντες ἐκ τῶν ἀγρῶν. [9]		
καὶ οἱ προάγοντες	B'	
καὶ οἱ ἀκολουθοῦντες		
ἔκραζον,		
Ὡσαννά·	a	
Εὐλογημένος ὁ ἐρχόμενος	b	
ἐν ὀνόματι κυρίου·		
Εὐλογημένη ἡ ἐρχομένη	b'	
βασιλεί τοῦ πατρὸς ἡμῶν Δαυίδ·		
Ὡσαννὰ ἐν τοῖς ὑψίστοις.	a'	
Καὶ εἰσῆλθεν	A	**B'**
εἰς Ἱεροσόλυμα		
εἰς τὸ ἱερόν·		
καὶ περιβλεψάμενος πάντα,	B	
ὀψίας ἤδη οὔσης τῆς ὥρας,		
ἐξῆλθεν	B'	
εἰς Βηθανίαν		
μετὰ τῶν δώδεκα.		

The first part, **A**, of the Day's telling, 11.1-6, describes the preparation for Jesus' entry into Jerusalem; the second part, **B**, 11.7-10, describes Jesus entering into Jerusalem surrounded and being greeted by crowds; and the third part, **B'**, 11.11, tells of his entry into Jerusalem and its temple. It is the venue for at least the following two days (see 11.12 and v.20).

The Day's initial setting is about two miles from Jerusalem and it is where the peparatory activity began. Jesus will enter on a colt. The two parts B and B', each in the customary three parts (of A, introductory, and B and B' as balancing completions), conclude the episode. Zech. 9.9 is clearly the primary Old Testament text in the backgound to this Day's telling. Jesus is Jerusalem's coming King[350]. With this O.T. allusion, the first Day of the final Series begins. Again it is the first Day of a three-day sub-Series. Significantly, in 14.24, in the first Day's telling of the balancing three-day sub-Series, we find an allusion to the same coming King, Zech. 9.11. In the setting of the last supper we read literally, "this is the *blood* of *me* of the (new) *covenant*"[351]. In

Below, I present the Day in literal English:

---

[350]For the direct references to "King" in the Gospel, as the title pertains to Jesus, see: 15.2,9,12,18,26,32. All these appear in Day Twenty-seven, the sixth Day of this Series, the Day of Jesus' crucifixion.
[351]The word "covenant" occurs only here in the Gospel, though covenant issues are addressed throughout. We will discuss this later. The word "new" is supported by some mss.

And when they draw near to Jerusalem,   a   A   **A**
        to Bethphage and Bethany,
        to the Mount of Olives,
    He sends two of his disciples   (see Day 26) b
    and he says to them,   b'
  'Go   B
        into the village
        opposite you,
    And immediately entering into it
          you will find a colt tethered
          on which no man yet has sat.
      Untie it,
      and bring it.
    And if anyone says to you,
        "Why are you doing this?"
      Say,
        "The Lord has need of it.
      And immediately
        he will send it
        again here."'
  And they went away,   B'
      and they found the colt
        tethered
        at a door
      outside,
      on the street,
      and they untie it.
    And some of the ones standing there
      said to them,
      'What are you doing,
      untying the colt?'
    And they said to them
      as Jesus said,
      and they let them go.
And they bring the colt to Jesus   A   **B**
      and they throw on
      it their garments.
  And he sat on it.   B
    And many
      their garments
      spread in the way.
    And others
      branches,
      cut from the fields.
  And the ones going ahead,   B'
      and the ones following,
      cried out,
    'Hosanna!   a
      Blessed is the one coming in the name of the Lord! b
      Blessed is the coming kingdom of our father David! b'
    Hosanna in the Highest!'   a'

	A	B'
And he entered		
into Jerusalem,		
into the temple.		
And looking around at everything,	B	
late now being the hour,		
he went out	B'	
to Bethany		
with the twelve.		

The Entry begins in the Day's Part **B** with the disciples, in the opening part, first bringing the colt to Jesus and preparing the colt; the second part tells of Jesus' sitting on it and 'the way' being prepared; the final part tells of the greeting Jesus receives.[352] It is important to note what Mark is doing here. At no point up till now in my reading of the Greek text of this Gospel have I discovered a chiasm, or concentric ring structure, but here there is one: Mark breaks briefly from his usual rhythm of abb' and supplies a four part chiasm, a,b,b',a'. The moment is one of major significance in Mark's scheme: the whole of the last Series covers Jesus' journeying to Jerusalem; and the Day's telling so far has been of the preparation for the entry. What the people cried continually, to Mark therefore, warranted a chiasm[353] for the sake of emphasis. To Ps.118.25, or more particularly to the parallel LXX, Ps.117.26, is added a central paralleling phrase, "Blessed is the coming kingdom of our *father* David". It is a description of David which is unknown in Judaism, but one which, overall, adds a messianic ingredient to the passover greeting. As we have seen also, in the summaries of Series Two and Three, it appears contrived by Mark to function as an anastrophe with "*Son* of David" in the final Day's presentation of the preceding Series.

Part **B'** completes the Day's telling: in A, the momentous words are recorded, "And he entered into Jerusalem, into the temple"; in parts B and B', a big hint of bathos appears to be struck: "looking around at all things, late now being the hour, he went out into Bethany with the twelve", having done no more than this. ('Bethany', in the first and last lines, is an *inclusio* for the Day's telling.) For Matthew this is unacceptable: to his parallel passage, he adds immediately Jesus' clearing of the temple. Luke follows Matthew in this[354]. But for Mark it is not bathos. O.T. prophecy is fulfilled again: see Mal. 3.1 ("Suddenly the Lord... will come to his temple.")[355]. It is a particularly important allusion, considering Mark's use of it in the opening of his Prologue. With the completion of the same he opens his final Series of the Gospel narrative. We will see below that the "temple" is truly the most important venue for the next two Days' presentations[356].

---

[352]Neirynck notes the chiasm also: *Duality...*, p.173.

[353]Contrary to many scholars who discern chiasms at sectional levels, I have identified only one chiasm before now: 5.3-5, which is at detail level. Mark clearly knows the technique as he applies it at the higher levels of literary order, but chooses to use it very sparingly indeed at this lower level.

[354]The view I take: Mark's Gospel was the first of the Synoptic Gospels to be written; in turn, Matthew created his, editing Mark and adding his own material; then Luke created his, based on Mark and Matthew, adding his own material. In *Sliced Bread...* (p.54), I support Farrer who said of Q source that, "To be rid of it we have no need of a contrary hypothesis, we merely have to make St Luke's use of St Matthew intelligible" (A.M. Farrer, "On Dispensing with Q", *Studies in the Gospels*, Ed. Nineham, Blackwell, London, 1955, p.66).

[355]O.T. allusions abound in Mark's Gospel. We noted a number of them in the Series prior to this; and already we have discovered Zech. 9.9 on this first Day of this new Series and Zech. 9.11 to be one of the fifth day's allusions.

[356]Nineham (*Saint Mark*, p.294) considers it likely that the tradition attached 'the cleansing', and that Mark, "in the interests of his time-scheme", and his wish to attach "the fig tree story", created v.11. Clearly, the matter of tradition and source (see note 7) is an open question.

Telford[357] studies particularly the relationship between the temple and the withered fig tree which will both feature in the two Days following. He cites a number of scholars' views concerning the integrity, at the redactional level, of 11.1-13.37, and he says of it that it exhibits "editorial organisation"[358]. He recognises the three-day structure as the chronological framework, and views it as a construct of Mark[359], which begins and ends on the *Mount of Olives*[360]. In my view, Mark does indeed set here for the reader/his audience his limits of this first sub-Series of his final Series, in this way. He has demonstrated to us already in his first three Gospel Series that this is his preferred method. What Telford does not recognise, however, is that Mark's chronological framework is also his literary framework.

Day Twenty-three: 11.12-19:

Days two and three of this Series (this Day Twenty-three and Day Twenty-four of the Gospel) begin with clear references to new Days which follow in sequence. For the first time in the Gospel, at 11.12, Mark uses the phrase, *Καὶ τῇ ἐπαύριον.* 11.20 sees a further use of the word *πρωΐ* compare 1.35 and the discussion and synopsis, under Day One, which notes its other uses at the beginning of Days at 15.1 and 16.2 (Days six and seven of this Series, Days Twenty-seven and Twenty-eight of the Gospel). 11.12 and 11.20 begin reports of Jesus' withering of the fig tree (told by Mark in two stages, but by Matthew in one whole as he likely conflates Mark's material again: compare Matthew's singular presentation above of Jesus' entry and the 'clearing' of the temple).

The literary structure of Day Twenty-three is viewed as:

<u>Καὶ τῇ ἐπαύριον</u>
   ἐξελθόντων αὐτῶν ἀπὸ Βηθανίας
   ἐπείνασεν. [13]   A   A
  καὶ ἰδὼν συκῆν   B
    ἀπὸ μακρόθεν
     ἔχουσαν φύλλα
  ἦλθεν
    εἰ ἄρα
    τι εὑρήσει ἐν αὐτῇ,
  καὶ ἐλθὼν ἐπ᾽ αὐτὴν
    οὐδὲν εὗρεν εἰ μὴ φύλλα·
    ὁ γὰρ καιρὸς οὐκ ἦν σύκων. [14]
  καὶ ἀποκριθεὶς   B'
    εἶπεν αὐτῇ,
    Μηκέτι εἰς τὸν αἰῶνα
     ἐκ σοῦ
     μηδεὶς καρπὸν φάγοι.
   καὶ ἤκουον οἱ μαθηταὶ αὐτοῦ.

---

[357]William R. Telford, *The Barren Temple and the Withered Tree*, JSNT Suppl. Series 1, JSOT Press, Sheffield, 1980.
[358]Telford, *The Barren Temple...*, p.39.
[359]Telford, *The Barren Temple...*, p.41.
[360]Telford, *The Barren Temple...*, p.39.

<u>Καὶ ἔρχονται εἰς Ἱεροσόλυμα.</u>   A   **B**
     καὶ εἰσελθὼν εἰς τὸ ἱερὸν   B
        ἤρξατο
           ἐκβάλλειν
             τοὺς πωλοῦντας
               καὶ τοὺς ἀγοράζοντας
           ἐν τῷ ἱερῷ,
        καὶ τὰς τραπέζας τῶν κολλυβιστῶν
          καὶ τὰς καθέδρας τῶν πωλούντων τὰς περιστερὰς
           κατέστρεψεν,¹⁶
    καὶ οὐκ ἤφιεν
      ἵνα τις διενέγκῃ σκεῦος
      διὰ τοῦ ἱεροῦ.¹⁷

καὶ ἐδίδασκεν   A   **B'**
     καὶ ἔλεγεν αὐτοῖς,
      Οὐ γέγραπται
    ὅτι Ὁ οἶκός μου οἶκος προσευχῆς κληθήσεται
      πᾶσιν τοῖς ἔθνεσιν;
     ὑμεῖς δὲ πεποιήκατε αὐτὸν σπήλαιον λῃστῶν.
   καὶ ἤκουσαν οἱ ἀρχιερεῖς καὶ οἱ γραμματεῖς,   B
     καὶ ἐζήτουν
      πῶς αὐτὸν ἀπολέσωσιν·
       ἐφοβοῦντο γὰρ αὐτόν,
    πᾶς γὰρ ὁ ὄχλος
      ἐξεπλήσσετο
      ἐπὶ τῇ διδαχῇ αὐτοῦ.
   Καὶ ὅταν ὀψὲ ἐγένετο,   B'
     ἐξεπορεύοντο
     ἔξω τῆς πόλεως.

And in literal English:

And on the next day,   A   **A**
     as they went out from Bethany,
     he hungered.
    And seeing a fig tree   B
      from afar,
       having leaves,
     he came
      if perhaps
      he will find something on it,
    and coming upon it,
      nothing he found except leaves,
      for it was not the season for figs.
    And answering,   B'
      he said to it,
    'No more in this age
      may anyone eat fruit
      from you!'
    And his disciples heard.

```
And they come to Jerusalem.                                         A    B
        And entering into the temple,                               B
                he began
                        to throw out/ the ones selling/ and the ones buying
                        in the temple,
                and the tables of the money-changers
                        and the seats of the ones selling doves
                        he overturned.
        And he did not permit                                       B
                that anyone should carry a vessel
                through the temple.

And he taught                                                       A    B'
                and he said to them,
                'Is is not written,
                "My house will be called a house of prayer for all the nations"?
                But you have made it a den of robbers!'
        And heard the chief priests and the scribes.                B
                And they sought
                        how they might destroy him
                        for they feared him.
                For all the crowd
                        was astounded
                        at his teaching.
        And when it became late,                                    B'
                they went out,
                outside the city.
```

Regularly, scholars speak of 11.12-25 as a Markan whole, with the fig-tree incident sandwiching the clearing of the temple. They cite 3.22-30 and 5.21-43 as other examples of Mark's predilection for sandwiches[361], but I have demonstrated already, in consideration of Days Five and Seven, that to Mark the latter, supposed examples are not 'sandwiches' as such in his rhetorical scheme, because they have their introduction in his introductory parts, A. That is, these units form, in the second of these, one of his B parts, and in the third, one of his B' parts of his ABB' three-part scheme. Whereas he locates these pericopae in his tellings of individual "Days", here the two stages of the fig tree incident are, significantly, the first episodes of new, successive "Days", in the greater B and B' scheme of his first sub-Series of three Days, ABB'. Days Twenty-two, Twenty-three and Twenty-four form his first full construction of his final Series of the Gospel. As we have already noted, these three Days link by reason of reference to the temple-setting, and the consecutive nature of the three Days. A further significant link between these last two Days of this final Series' first threesome of Days is that in the first of the two, Jesus "clears" the temple, and in the second of the two, Jesus speaks to his disciples of its impending, total destruction.

The detailed structure of this Day can be summarised as follows: Part **A** tells of their leaving Bethany (it becomes clear at the beginning of B that the destination is Jerusalem and the temple again, as the first day of the Series) and the first stage of the acted-out parable of the fig tree; Part **B** tells of Jesus' clearing of the temple of every trading or business activity;

[361]Bultmann, *The History...*, pp.232ff.; Taylor, *The Gospel...*, p.465; Nineham, *Saint Mark*, pp.297-303; Schweizer, *The Good News...*, pp.229-232; Hooker, *The Gospel...*, pp.260-266.

and Part **B'** records his explanation which causes the chief priests and scribes to begin seeking how "they might destroy" him. The Day concludes similarly to the Day before it, as it becomes late, ὀψέ.

We observe the first conflict story of this Series in this Day's telling. In seeing such episodes grouped in the First Series, in Days Three, Four and Five, I referred then (under Day Four) to those that we would find in Days two to six of this, the final Series. I discern an ordering on Mark's part of these major climaxes in each Day's telling of conflict, in Days two and three (completing the first sub-Series) and in Day four (the middle, pivotal Day of the Series):

Day two	(Twenty-three):	ἐζήτουν πῶς αὐτόν ἀπολέσωσιν	11.18[362]
Day three	(Twenty-four):	ἐζήτουν αὐτόν κρατῆσαι	12.12
Day four	(Twenty-five):	ἐζήτουν... πῶς αὐτόν ἐν δόλῳ κρατήσαντες ἀποκτείνωσιν	14.1
		ἐζήτει πῶς αὐτόν εὐκαίρως Παραδοῖ.	14.11
Day five	(Twenty-six):	παραδίδοται... ὁ παραδιδούς...	14.41,42
		καὶ ἐκράτησαν αὐτόν	14.46
		ἐζήτουν κατα΄ τοῦ Ἰησοῦ μαρτυρίαν εἰς τὸ΄ θανατῶσαι αὐτόν,	14.55
Day six	(Twenty-seven):	καὶ ἐσταύρωσαν αὐτόν.	15.25
		Καὶ τὸ΄ καταπέτασμα τοῦ ναοῦ ἐσχίσθη εἰς δύο ἀπ' ἄνωθεν ἕως κάτω	15.38

It would appear that Mark deliberately created a series of conflict climaxes in Days two, three and four to connect with Days five and six. An obvious link is made between Days two and six: in the first, they seek to destroy Jesus, and in the second they achieve their aim. In the table I have included another phrase also, 15.38, which would remind the reader and listeners, in Day six, of the temple-clearance of Jesus in Day two, and of the temple-destruction pending, in Day three. 14.58 and 15.29 further make the verbal link between the "temple" and "Jesus". Days three and five have their link too: in the first of these, they seek to seize Jesus, and in the second they achieve their purpose. The turning point in the Series, given these matters, is found in the middle day, Day four. The Day begins and ends with plottings: the chief priests and scribes seek how they may seize and kill Jesus, but the feast and the people are a difficulty to them. Judas' promise of betrayal is that which makes the difference. Particularly stimulating in this Series is the Markan structural and, therefore, rhetorical balance between Jesus' clearing of the temple of all things which pertain to the old sacrificial way of Old Israel, and the establishing of the new sacrificial way for New Israel, through his own sacrifice on the cross.

Under our discussion of the middle Day of the First Series, Day Four, we noted the comments of some scholars that the death plot of the Pharisees and the Herodians, in 3.6, appears "too early in the Gospel". I suggested a correspondence then between the conflict stories of the first Series and those of the last Series. The wording of 3.6 and the key phrase ὅπως αὐτόν ἀπολέσωσιν compares well with the first phrase of these conflict-climaxes. My case for seeing the First and Last Series of the Gospel in parallel in Mark's scheme is based on just such details, but also on thematic parallels and matters of scale. We will return

---

[362]Stephen H. Smith, "The Literary Structure of Mark 11.1-12.40", *NT* 31 (1989), pp.104-124: he sees the connection between 11.18 and 12.12, but because of the limits of his study, 11.1-12.40, he fails to see the others of our listing, and hence their structural significance. He further identifies the three days, but in the case of the third day (like Dewey, *Markan Public Debate...*, p.152) he wrongly sees it as ending at 12.44. Unless section limits are well set at first, rhetorical analysis can lead, and does lead, to all manner of views.

to such matters once we have completed the literary-structural reading of the remaining chapters.

A note may be added here, however, that the above correspondences in this seven-day Series, between days two and six, and days three and five, around a central turning point, day four, suggest a concentric/chiastic arrangement of the days:

$$1, 2, 3, 4, 5, 6, 7 \textit{ cf. } 1, 2, 3, C, 3', 2', 1'.$$

It is the very same issue which arose in my summarising of the first Series.

The issue can be resolved fully only when we have looked at the very clear relationships between days one and five of this Series. These suggest emphatically that Mark did in fact create only a three-part chiasm, by beginning two three-day sub-Series in similar ways and placing them around a central turning point, day four. Other common themes and details, of one to three, and five to seven, confirm that these days do form threesomes. I will demonstrate the evidence at the appropriate moments. For now, it may be said that the Series' structure is best described in the following terms:

$$\mathbf{A}(ABB') - \mathbf{B} - \mathbf{A}'(ABB').$$

Or in terms of the summary of Series Three, it can be expressed also by:

$$\begin{array}{ccc} A & B & \underline{B}' & \underline{A} & B & B' \\ & & \underline{A} & B & \underline{A}' \end{array}$$

where days three and five again (as underlined) smooth the sharp edges of the transitional central turning point, according to the conventions of ancient rhetoric. I would stress that both these methods of annotation are only elaborations of my summary ABA' annotation for this, and indeed all the Series.

Day Twenty-four: 11.20-13.37:

The Day's telling covers ninety-four verses, more verses than any other Day.[363] Nevertheless, the structure of the Day's telling is the same as every other day (so far), an ABB' form but here in its composit form ABB'/ABB'/ABB'. I present the outline structure below and we discuss the development of this analysis.

On the abb' principle of how the text divides, I was first led to one possible solution and then another and then another! It became a challenge to me to sort the teachings of this Day, because it could not be that there was no structure to them. That single thought kept driving me on as I attempted one sophisticated solution after another. Then suddenly it all fell into place. The introductory part is on what happens as Jesus returns to Jerusalem the next day; the first development of the Day is what happens inside the temple; and the second and concluding development is what happens outside the temple. The beginnings of the major divisions are as follows:

A	11.20	*Καὶ παραπορευόμενοι πρωῒ*
B	11.27	*Καὶ ἔρχονται πάλιν εἰς Ἰεροσόλυμα. καὶ <u>ἐν τῷ ἱερῷ</u> ...*
B'	13.1	*Καὶ ἐκπορευομένου αὐτοῦ <u>ἐκ τοῦ ἱεροῦ</u>...*

---

[363]The Day's telling is twenty-four more verses than the next Day which is Day Five. The third longest is Day Twenty-Six, with sixty-one verses.

In the first instance, I was identifying that neither Dewey nor Smith[364], in their studies on the literary structure of chapters 11 and 12, discerned any 'primary division' between 12.34 and v.35, or any correspondence between 11.27 and 13.1. Their schemes also overlook the primary Markan rhetorical structure of "Days" which delimits this third Day of this Series as 11.20-13.37. Smith and Dewey define "day three" as ending at 12.44. For them, there are no 'days' to consider here beyond those at 11.1-11, vv.12-19 and 11.20-12.44. They do not, therefore, have to postulate that 13.1 begins a new day. At that time I was toying with the following solutions:

My first proposal:		My second proposal:					
A	11.20-25	A	11.20-12.44	A	11.20-25		
B	11.27-33	B	11.27-12.17			A	27-33
B'	12.1-12					B	12.1-12
----------						B'	13-17
A	12.13-17						
B	12.18-27			B'	12.18-44	A	18-27
B'	12.28-34					B	28-34
						B'	35-44
A	12.35-44						
B	13.1-6	A'	13.1-37	A	13.1-6		
B'	13.7-17			B	13.7-17	A	7-10
						B	11-13
						B'	14-17
A	13.18-23			B'	13.18-37	A	18-23
B	13.24-31					B	24-31
B'	13.32-37					B'	32-37

We review now another attempt at that time at defining Mark's structuring of these chapters, that of Robbins[365]. I have agreed with him earlier on some of his three-step progressions, but here I cannot agree. He thinks he discerns two such progressions in this section of the Gospel: 10.46-48; vv.49-52; 11.1-11 and 13.1-2; vv.3-4; vv.5-37. For Robbins all such three-step progressions are clues to the formal structure of the Gospel. His analysis, therefore, leads him to the conclusion that the last two sections of the Gospel are 10.46-12.44 and 13.1-15.47. (To him, 16.1-8 is the Conclusion.) His position gains little support from my selected commentators and it gains no support from this literary-structural analysis which sees Day-presentations as all important in Mark's scheme. In our examination of Series Three, I show that 10.46b-52 ends that Series, and in terms of three-step progressions, I demonstrate that 11.1-11 is the first of three Days, in a specific sub-Series. Robbins' three-step progression of 10.46-11.11 is not what Mark had in mind. Neither is his 13.1-2, vv.3-4, vv.5-37 progression. In Markan rhetorical terms, 13.1,2 and vv.3,4 are the first two parts of a three-part progression, 13.1-6. The closing part is vv.5,6, not Robbins' vv.5-37.

Lastly, we review the contribution of Painter[366] to the structure and the functioning of 11.1-13.37 in Mark's scheme. His, most recent, commentary begins with his outline of Mark's Gospel. In his introduction, he says that he has given attention "to the arrangement of rhetori-

---

[364]Dewey, *Markan Public Debate...*, pp.152-167; Smith, "The Literary Structure...", pp.104-124.
[365]Robbins, *Jesus the Teacher...*, pp.41-47.
[366]John Painter, *Mark's Gospel: Worlds in Conflict*, Routledge, London and New York, 1997, pp.xiii, 154-179.

cally shaped stories into collections which shape the plot of the story"[367]. His sectionalising is as follows:

The coming of the King	11.1-11
A tale within a tale: fig tree and temple	11.12-25
Jesus' authority challenged in Jerusalem	11.27-12.12
Opponents and questions in Jerusalem	12.13-44
The temple and the Son of Man	13.1-37

Firstly, we note that Painter does not divide the material in terms of the 'three-days'. Indeed, on this matter he comments on 11.27ff.: "Jesus' return to the temple in Jerusalem is described but without any time reference." He appears not to consider that 11.20-26 is introductory, and continues, "Whether this was a day or days later is not significant for Mark..." It is not a promising start, given the three days that others have identified in 11.1-13.37[368], and all that I have been uncovering so far of the importance of Days in Mark's scheme. 11.20-25 in my reading is introductory to the whole Day's telling, Part **A**, 11.20-12.44. The second episode of the fig tree establishes the Day's beginning, just as the first episode does the previous Day's telling (for fig tree and temple, see below). Secondly, 11.27-33 in my reading is introductory to the telling of Part **B**, 11.27-12.44. Thirdly, rather unusually, we observe that two of his titles append "in Jerusalem". We now consider Painter's outline for 13.1-37:

The Lord abandons the temple and predicts its desolation	13.1,2
"When will these things be?"	13.3,4
Jesus' answer: "Watch out, be alert"	13.5-37
A^1 Warning: Don't be led astray, the end is not yet	13.5-8
B^1 Warning: You will be delivered up, betrayed	13.9-13
B^2 Warning: Flee to the mountains	13.14-20
A^2 Warning: False Christs, false prophets, signs and wonders	13.21-23
The end is the end	13.24-27
Learn a parable from the fig tree and other sayings	13.28-31
A parable and sayings about watchfulness	13.32-37

In the first three lines, Painter replicates Robbins (for my response to Robbins, see above). He then presents vv.5-23 as a chiasm, to which three-parts awkwardly attach, vv.24-37. Mark, it appears from literary-structural analysis, has been much more careful in his planning than this.

Because this Day is so long in verses, we will take it a section at a time: firstly then, my presentation of the literary structure of Day Twenty-four, Part A, 11.20-25:

---

[367]Painter, *Mark's Gospel...*, p.ix.
[368]See page 212 for Telford, page 218 for Smith and Dewey; also: R. Thiel, *Drei Markus-Evangelien*, (AKG, 26), Walter de Gruyter & Co. Ltd., Berlin, 1938, pp.53-59, 114, 170-175; E. Hirsch, *Frühgeschichte des Evangeliums. Das Werden des Markusevangeliums*, J.C.B. Mohr, Tübingen, (1940) 2nd ed. 1951, pp.121-126; K.L. Schmidt, *Rahmen...*, pp.274-303; M. Dibelius, *Die Formgeschichte des Evangeliums*, 5th ed. ed. G. Bornkamm, J.C.B. Mohr, Tübingen, 1966, p.225; Bultmann, *The History...*, pp.340-341; J. Schreiber, "Die Christologie des Markusevangeliums", *ZThK*, 58 (1961), pp.161-162; E. Wendling, *Die Entstehung des Marcus-Evangeliums*, J.C.B. Mohr, Tübingen, 1908, pp.144ff.

Καὶ παραπορευόμενοι πρωῒ   A   A
        εἶδον τὴν συκῆν
        ἐξηραμμένην ἐκ ῥιζῶν. [21]
    καὶ ἀναμνησθεὶς
        ὁ Πέτρος λέγει αὐτῷ,
        Ῥαββί,
  ἴδε
        ἡ συκῆ
            ἣν κατηράσω
        ἐξήρανται.
καὶ ἀποκριθεὶς   B
        ὁ Ἰησοῦς λέγει αὐτοῖς,
        Ἔχετε πίστιν θεοῦ, [23]
    ἀμὴν λέγω ὑμῖν
        ὅτι ὃς ἂν εἴπῃ τῷ ὄρει τούτῳ,
        Ἄρθητι
            καὶ βλήθητι
            εἰς τὴν θάλασσαν,
  καὶ μὴ διακριθῇ ἐν τῇ καρδίᾳ αὐτοῦ
        ἀλλὰ πιστεύῃ
            ὅτι ὃ λαλεῖ
            γίνεται,
        ἔσται αὐτῷ. [24]
διὰ τοῦτο λέγω ὑμῖν,   B'
      πάντα
        ὅσα προσεύχεσθε
        καὶ αἰτεῖσθε,
      πιστεύετε
        ὅτι ἐλάβετε,
        καὶ ἔσται ὑμῖν. [25]
  καὶ ὅταν στήκετε προσευχόμενοι,
      ἀφίετε
      εἴ τι ἔχετε κατά τινος,
  ἵνα καὶ ὁ πατὴρ ὑμῶν
        ὁ ἐν τοῖς οὐρανοῖς
      ἀφῇ ὑμῖν
        τὰ παραπτώματα ὑμῶν.

And in literal English:

And passing along early,   A   A
      they saw the fig tree,
      withered from the roots.
   And remembering,
      Peter says to him,
      'Rabbi,
  Behold!
      The fig tree
        which you cursed
      is withered!'
  And answering,   B
      Jesus says to them,
      'Have faith in God,
  Truly I tell you,
      whoever says to this mountain,
      "Be taken
        and be thrown
        into the sea",
  And does not doubt in his heart,
      but believes
        that what he says
        happens,
      it will be to him.
  Therefore, I tell you,   B'
      all things
        which you pray
        and ask,
      believe
        that you have received,
        and it will be to you.
  And when you stand praying,
      forgive,
      if anything you have against anyone,
  That also your father,
      the one in heaven,
      may forgive you
        your trespasses.'

     See Day Twenty-three for a discussion on the two parts and their placings of Jesus' withering of the fig tree. Essentially, this opening section of the Day's telling focuses on a teaching of Jesus on faith and prayer, but the fig tree, now "withered from its roots", is illustrative of Old Israel, its leadership, and even its temple, which are all under judgement for rejecting him[369] In the two B parts of this Day's telling, Parts **B** and **B'**, these matters are addressed.[370] It may be said that the illustration of "this mountain being hurled into the sea" is

---

[369]Our commentators agree though it is more because they see the so-called 'sandwich' of the fig tree and the temple: Taylor, *The Gospel...*, pp.458-460; Nineham, *Saint Mark*, pp.297-302; Schweizer, *The Good News...*, pp.229-233; Hooker, *The Gospel...*, pp.260-266.
[370]Telford sees the same connection: *The Barren Temple...*, p.59.

even comparable, for scale, with the temple which one of Jesus' disciples much admires, for its stones and buildings. It was itself, of course, standing on a mountain.

We now turn to Part **B**, 11.27-12.44. It begins, "And they come again into Jerusalem. And in the temple…". The sub-divisions are as follows:

A		And they come again into Jerusalem	11.27-33
B	a	And he began to speak	12.1-12
	b	And they send to him	12.13-17
	b'	And come Sadducees	12.18-27
B	a	And aapproaching, one of the scribes	12.28-34
	b	And answering	12.35-37
	b'	And in his teaching	12.38-44

Καὶ ἔρχονται πάλιν εἰς Ἱεροσόλυμα.   A
    καὶ ἐν τῷ ἱερῷ
        περιπατοῦντος αὐτοῦ
        ἔρχονται πρὸς αὐτὸν
           οἱ ἀρχιερεῖς
              καὶ οἱ γραμματεῖς
              καὶ οἱ πρεσβύτεροι [28]
      καὶ ἔλεγον αὐτῷ,
        Ἐν ποίᾳ ἐξουσίᾳ ταῦτα ποιεῖς;
        ἢ τίς σοι ἔδωκεν τὴν ἐξουσίαν ταύτην
          ἵνα ταῦτα ποιῇς;
    ὁ δὲ Ἰησοῦς εἶπεν αὐτοῖς,
        Ἐπερωτήσω ὑμᾶς ἕνα λόγον,
          καὶ ἀποκρίθητέ μοι,
          καὶ ἐρῶ ὑμῖν ἐν ποίᾳ ἐξουσίᾳ ταῦτα ποιῶ· [30]
      τὸ βάπτισμα τὸ Ἰωάννου
        ἐξ οὐρανοῦ ἦν
        ἢ ἐξ ἀνθρώπων;
      ἀποκρίθητέ μοι.
   καὶ διελογίζοντο πρὸς ἑαυτοὺς
        λέγοντες,
        Ἐὰν εἴπωμεν, Ἐξ οὐρανοῦ,
          ἐρεῖ,
          Διὰ τί οὖν οὐκ ἐπιστεύσατε αὐτῷ; [32]
      ἀλλὰ εἴπωμεν, Ἐξ ἀνθρώπων;
        ἐφοβοῦντο τὸν ὄχλον,
        ἅπαντες γὰρ εἶχον τὸν Ἰωάννην ὄντως
          ὅτι προφήτης ἦν.
    καὶ ἀποκριθέντες τῷ Ἰησοῦ
        λέγουσιν,
        Οὐκ οἴδαμεν.
    καὶ ὁ Ἰησοῦς λέγει αὐτοῖς,
        Οὐδὲ ἐγὼ λέγω ὑμῖν
        ἐν ποίᾳ ἐξουσίᾳ ταῦτα ποιῶ.

Καὶ ἤρξατο αὐτοῖς ἐν παραβολαῖς λαλεῖν,   a   B
     Ἀμπελῶνα ἄνθρωπος ἐφύτευσεν,
  καὶ περιέθηκεν φραγμὸν
    καὶ ὤρυξεν ὑπολήνιον
    καὶ ᾠκοδόμησεν πύργον,
  καὶ ἐξέδετο αὐτὸν γεωργοῖς,
    καὶ ἀπεδήμησεν. [2]
καὶ ἀπέστειλεν πρὸς τοὺς γεωργοὺς
    τῷ καιρῷ
     δοῦλον,
   ἵνα παρὰ τῶν γεωργῶν
    λάβῃ
      ἀπὸ τῶν καρπῶν τοῦ ἀμπελῶνος· [3]
  καὶ λαβόντες αὐτὸν
    ἔδειραν
    καὶ ἀπέστειλαν κενόν. [4]
καὶ πάλιν ἀπέστειλεν πρὸς αὐτοὺς ἄλλον δοῦλον·
    κἀκεῖνον ἐκεφαλίωσαν
    καὶ ἠτίμασαν. [5]
  καὶ ἄλλον ἀπέστειλεν,
    κἀκεῖνον ἀπέκτειναν,
  καὶ πολλοὺς ἄλλους,
    οὓς μὲν δέροντες
    οὓς δὲ ἀποκτέννοντες.
ἔτι ἕνα εἶχεν,
     υἱὸν ἀγαπητόν·
  ἀπέστειλεν αὐτὸν ἔσχατον πρὸς αὐτοὺς
    λέγων
    ὅτι Ἐντραπήσονται τὸν υἱόν μου.
  ἐκεῖνοι δὲ οἱ γεωργοὶ
    πρὸς ἑαυτοὺς
    εἶπαν
    ὅτι Οὗτός ἐστιν ὁ κληρονόμος·
   δεῦτε
     ἀποκτείνωμεν αὐτόν,
     καὶ ἡμῶν ἔσται ἡ κληρονομία. [8]
  καὶ λαβόντες
    ἀπέκτειναν αὐτόν,
    καὶ ἐξέβαλον αὐτὸν
     ἔξω τοῦ ἀμπελῶνος.
τί οὖν ποιήσει ὁ κύριος τοῦ ἀμπελῶνος;
    ἐλεύσεται καὶ ἀπολέσει τοὺς γεωργούς,
    καὶ δώσει τὸν ἀμπελῶνα ἄλλοις. [10]
 οὐδὲ τὴν γραφὴν ταύτην ἀνέγνωτε,
    Λίθον ὃν ἀπεδοκίμασαν οἱ οἰκοδομοῦντες,
     οὗτος ἐγενήθη εἰς κεφαλὴν γωνίας·
    παρὰ κυρίου ἐγένετο αὕτη,

καὶ ἔστιν θαυμαστὴ ἐν ὀφθαλμοῖς ἡμῶν;
καὶ ἐζήτουν αὐτὸν κρατῆσαι,
καὶ ἐφοβήθησαν τὸν ὄχλον,
ἔγνωσαν γὰρ ὅτι πρὸς αὐτοὺς
τὴν παραβολὴν εἶπεν.
καὶ ἀφέντες αὐτὸν
ἀπῆλθον.

Καὶ ἀποστέλλουσιν πρὸς αὐτόν   b
τινας τῶν Φαρισαίων καὶ τῶν Ἡρῳδιανῶν
ἵνα αὐτὸν ἀγρεύσωσιν λόγῳ. [14]
καὶ ἐλθόντες
λέγουσιν αὐτῷ,
Διδάσκαλε,
οἴδαμεν ὅτι ἀληθὴς εἶ
καὶ οὐ μέλει σοι
περὶ οὐδενός,
οὐ γὰρ βλέπεις εἰς πρόσωπον ἀνθρώπων,
ἀλλ᾽ ἐπ᾽ ἀληθείας
τὴν ὁδὸν τοῦ θεοῦ διδάσκεις·
ἔξεστιν
δοῦναι κῆνσον Καίσαρι
ἢ οὔ;
δῶμεν
ἢ μὴ δῶμεν; [15]
ὁ δὲ / εἰδὼς αὐτῶν τὴν ὑπόκρισιν
εἶπεν αὐτοῖς,
Τί με πειράζετε;
φέρετέ μοι δηνάριον
ἵνα ἴδω. [16]
οἱ δὲ ἤνεγκαν.
καὶ λέγει αὐτοῖς,
Τίνος ἡ εἰκὼν αὕτη
καὶ ἡ ἐπιγραφή;
οἱ δὲ εἶπαν αὐτῷ,
Καίσαρος.
ὁ δὲ Ἰησοῦς εἶπεν αὐτοῖς,
Τὰ Καίσαρος
ἀπόδοτε Καίσαρι
καὶ τὰ τοῦ θεοῦ
τῷ θεῷ.
καὶ ἐξεθαύμαζον ἐπ᾽ αὐτῷ.

Καὶ ἔρχονται Σαδδουκαῖοι πρὸς αὐτόν,　　　　　　　b'
　　　οἵτινες λέγουσιν ἀνάστασιν μὴ εἶναι,
　　　καὶ ἐπηρώτων αὐτὸν
　　　　　λέγοντες, [19]
　　　　　Διδάσκαλε,
　　　　Μωϋσῆς ἔγραψεν ἡμῖν ὅτι ἐάν τινος ἀδελφὸς ἀποθάνῃ
　　　　καὶ καταλίπῃ γυναῖκα
　　　　καὶ μὴ ἀφῇ τέκνον,
　　　ἵνα λάβῃ ὁ ἀδελφὸς αὐτοῦ τὴν γυναῖκα
　　　　καὶ ἐξαναστήσῃ σπέρμα
　　　　τῷ ἀδελφῷ αὐτοῦ. [20]
　ἑπτὰ ἀδελφοὶ ἦσαν·
　　　καὶ ὁ πρῶτος ἔλαβεν γυναῖκα,
　　　　καὶ ἀποθνῄσκων
　　　　οὐκ ἀφῆκεν σπέρμα· [21]
　　　καὶ ὁ δεύτερος ἔλαβεν αὐτήν,
　　　　καὶ ἀπέθανεν
　　　　μὴ καταλιπὼν σπέρμα·
　　καὶ ὁ τρίτος ὡσαύτως· [22]
　　　καὶ οἱ ἑπτὰ οὐκ ἀφῆκαν σπέρμα.
　　　ἔσχατον πάντων καὶ ἡ γυνὴ ἀπέθανεν. [23]
　ἐν τῇ ἀναστάσει
　　　τίνος αὐτῶν ἔσται γυνή;
　　　οἱ γὰρ ἑπτὰ ἔσχον αὐτὴν γυναῖκα.
ἔφη αὐτοῖς ὁ Ἰησοῦς,
　　　Οὐ διὰ τοῦτο πλανᾶσθε
　　　　μὴ εἰδότες τὰς γραφὰς
　　　　μηδὲ τὴν δύναμιν τοῦ θεοῦ; [25]
　　ὅταν γὰρ ἐκ νεκρῶν ἀναστῶσιν,
　　　οὔτε γαμοῦσιν
　　　　οὔτε γαμίζονται,
　　　ἀλλ᾽ εἰσὶν ὡς ἄγγελοι
　　　　ἐν τοῖς οὐρανοῖς. [26]
　　περὶ δὲ τῶν νεκρῶν
　　　ὅτι ἐγείρονται
　　　οὐκ ἀνέγνωτε ἐν τῇ βίβλῳ Μωϋσέως
　　　　　ἐπὶ τοῦ βάτου
　　　　πῶς εἶπεν αὐτῷ ὁ θεὸς
　　　　　λέγων,
　　　　Ἐγὼ ὁ θεὸς Ἀβραὰμ
　　　　　καὶ ὁ θεὸς Ἰσαὰκ
　　　　　καὶ ὁ θεὸς Ἰακώβ; [27]
　　　　οὐκ ἔστιν ὁ θεὸς
　　　　　νεκρῶν
　　　　　ἀλλὰ ζώντων·
　　πολὺ πλανᾶσθε.

Καὶ προσελθὼν εἷς <u>τῶν γραμματέων</u>   a   Β'
                    ἀκούσας αὐτῶν συζητούντων,
                    ἰδὼν ὅτι καλῶς ἀπεκρίθη αὐτοῖς,
          ἐπηρώτησεν αὐτόν, 0
          Ποία ἐστὶν ἐντολὴ πρώτη πάντων;
    Ἀπεκρίθη ὁ Ἰησοῦς
                              ὅτι Πρώτη ἐστίν,
                              Ἄκουε, Ἰσραήλ,
                    κύριος ὁ θεὸς ἡμῶν κύριος εἷς ἐστιν, [30]
                         καὶ ἀγαπήσεις κύριον τὸν θεόν σου
                                   ἐξ ὅλης τῆς καρδίας σου
                         καὶ ἐξ ὅλης τῆς ψυχῆς σου
                              καὶ ἐξ ὅλης τῆς διανοίας σου
                              καὶ ἐξ ὅλης τῆς ἰσχύος σου. [31]
               δευτέρα αὕτη,
                    Ἀγαπήσεις τὸν πλησίον σου
                    ὡς σεαυτόν.
               μείζων τούτων ἄλλη ἐντολὴ
                    οὐκ ἔστιν.
          καὶ εἶπεν αὐτῷ <u>ὁ γραμματεύς</u>,
                    Καλῶς,
                         διδάσκαλε,
                    ἐπ' ἀληθείας εἶπες
                         ὅτι εἷς ἐστιν
                         καὶ οὐκ ἔστιν ἄλλος πλὴν αὐτοῦ· [33]
               καὶ τὸ ἀγαπᾶν αὐτὸν ἐξ ὅλης τῆς καρδίας
                    καὶ ἐξ ὅλης τῆς συνέσεως
                    καὶ ἐξ ὅλης τῆς ἰσχύος
               καὶ τὸ ἀγαπᾶν τὸν πλησίον ὡς ἑαυτὸν
                    περισσότερόν ἐστιν
                    πάντων τῶν ὁλοκαυτωμάτων καὶ θυσιῶν.
          καὶ ὁ Ἰησοῦς
                    ἰδὼν
                    ὅτι νουνεχῶς ἀπεκρίθη
               εἶπεν αὐτῷ,
               Οὐ μακρὰν εἶ ἀπὸ τῆς βασιλείας τοῦ θεοῦ.
     Καὶ οὐδεὶς
          οὐκέτι ἐτόλμα
          αὐτὸν ἐπερωτῆσαι.

Καὶ ἀποκριθεὶς   b
    ὁ Ἰησοῦς ἔλεγεν
      διδάσκων ἐν τῷ ἱερῷ,
Πῶς λέγουσιν οἱ γραμματεῖς
      ὅτι ὁ Χριστὸς
          υἱὸς Δαυίδ ἐστιν;[36]
αὐτὸς Δαυὶδ εἶπεν ἐν τῷ πνεύματι τῷ ἁγίῳ,
    Εἶπεν κύριος τῷ κυρίῳ μου,
      Κάθου ἐκ δεξιῶν μου
    ἕως ἂν θῶ τοὺς ἐχθρούς σου
      ὑποκάτω τῶν ποδῶν σου.
αὐτὸς Δαυὶδ λέγει αὐτὸν κύριον,
    καὶ πόθεν αὐτοῦ ἐστιν υἱός;
Καὶ ὁ πολὺς ὄχλος ἤκουεν αὐτοῦ ἡδέως.

Καὶ ἐν τῇ διδαχῇ αὐτοῦ   b'
    ἔλεγεν,
    Βλέπετε ἀπὸ τῶν γραμματέων
τῶν θελόντων ἐν στολαῖς περιπατεῖν
    καὶ ἀσπασμοὺς ἐν ταῖς ἀγοραῖς[39]
    καὶ πρωτοκαθεδρίας ἐν ταῖς συναγωγαῖς
      καὶ πρωτοκλισίας ἐν τοῖς δείπνοις·[40]
οἱ κατεσθίοντες τὰς οἰκίας τῶν χηρῶν
    καὶ προφάσει
      μακρὰ προσευχόμενοι,
οὗτοι λήμψονται περισσότερον κρίμα.
Καὶ καθίσας
    κατέναντι τοῦ γαζοφυλακίου
    ἐθεώρει
      πῶς ὁ ὄχλος βάλλει χαλκὸν
      εἰς τὸ γαζοφυλάκιον·
καὶ πολλοὶ πλούσιοι ἔβαλλον πολλά·[42]
καὶ ἐλθοῦσα
    μία χήρα πτωχὴ ἔβαλεν λεπτὰ δύο,
    ὅ ἐστιν κοδράντης.
Καὶ προσκαλεσάμενος τοὺς μαθητὰς αὐτοῦ
    εἶπεν αὐτοῖς,
    Ἀμὴν λέγω ὑμῖν
ὅτι ἡ χήρα αὕτη ἡ πτωχὴ
    πλεῖον πάντων ἔβαλεν
    τῶν βαλλόντων εἰς τὸ γαζοφυλάκιον·[44]
πάντες γὰρ
      ἐκ τοῦ περισσεύοντος αὐτοῖς
      ἔβαλον,
    αὕτη δὲ
      ἐκ τῆς ὑστερήσεως αὐτῆς
      πάντα ὅσα εἶχεν ἔβαλεν,
    ὅλον τὸν βίον αὐτῆς.

And in literal English:

And they come again into Jerusalem.   A
> And <u>in the temple</u>,
>> as he walked about,
>> come to him
>>> the chief priests/ and the scribes/ and the elders.
> And they say to him,
>> 'By what authority do you do these things?
>> Or who gave you this authority that you may do these things?'

And Jesus said to them,
> 'I will question you one word,
>> and answer me,
>> and I will tell you by what authority I do these things.
> The baptism of John,
>> was it of heaven,
>> or of men?
> Answer me!'

And they debated among themselves,
>> saying,
> 'If we say, "Of heaven",
>> he will say, "Why then did you not believe him?"
> But may we say, "Of men"?
>> (They feared the crowd,
>>> for all held that John really was a prophet.)

And answering Jesus,
> they say,
> 'We do not know.'

And Jesus says to them,
> 'Neither I tell you
> by what authority I do these things.'

And he began to speak to them in parables,   a   B
       'A man planted a vineyard,
And he put a hedge around it,
    and dug a winepress,
    and built a tower.
And he let it out to tenants,
    and went away.
And he sent to the tenants,
        at the due time,
        a slave,
    That from the tenants
        he might receive
        of the fruits of the vineyard.
    And taking him
        they beat him
        and sent him away without anything.
And again he sent to them another slave,
        and that one they wounded on the head
        and insulted.
    And another he sent,
        and that one they killed.
    And many others,
        some beating,
        others killing.
  Still he had one,
          a beloved son:
        he sent him last to them,
           saying,
        "They will respect my son."
    But those tenants said to each other,
        "This is the heir.
         Come, let us kill him
            and ours will be the inheritance."
    And taking him,
        they killed him,
        and cast him outside the vineyard.
What will the lord of the vineyard do?
    He will come and destroy the tenants.
    And he will give the vineyard to others.
  Have you not read this scripture?
    "A stone which the builders rejected,/ this became the chief cornerstone.
    From the Lord was this,/ and it is marvellous in our eyes."
And they sought to seize him,
    But they feared the crowd,
        for they knew that to them
        he told the parable.
    And leaving him,
        they went away.

And they send to him   b
        some of the Pharisees and of the Herodians,
        that they might trap him in a word.
    And coming,
          they say to him,
          'Teacher,
      We know that you are true
          and it matters not to you
          who a person is,
      For you look not at the face of men,
          but in truth
          you teach the way of God.
    Is it lawful,
      to pay taxes to Caesar,
        or not?
      May we give,
        or may we not give?'
But he,
      knowing their hypocrisy,
        said to them,
      'Why do you test me?
    Bring me a denarius
      that I may see it.'
    And they brought it.
And he says to them,
        'Whose image is this,
         and the superscription?'
      And they tell him,
      'Caesar's.'
    So Jesus said to them,
      'The things of Caesar,
        render to Caesar,
      and the things of God,
        to God.'
    And they marvelled at him.

And come Sadducees to him,   b'
    who say that there is no resurrection,
    and they questioned him,
       saying,
       'Teacher,
Moses wrote for us that if a brother of anyone should die
    and leave behind a wife
    and not leave a child,
That his brother should take his wife,
    and raise up offspring
    for his brother.
Seven brothers there were.
    And the first took a wife,
       and dying
       he left no offspring.
    And the second took her,
       and he died,
       not leaving offspring.
    And the third similarly.
    And the seven left no offspring.
    Last of all also the wife died.
In the resurrection,
    which of them will she be wife,
    for the seven had her as wife?'
Said to them Jesus,
    'Are you not in error,
       because you do not know the scriptures,
       or the power of God?
For when they rise from the dead,
    they neither marry,
       nor are given in marriage,
    but are as angels
    in heaven.
But concerning the dead,
    that they are raised,
    Have you not read in the book of Moses
        at the bush
      how said to him God,
      saying,
     "I am the God of Abraham
      and God of Isaac
      and God of Jacob"?
    He is not God
      of the dead,
      but of the living!
    Much you are in error.'

And approaching,   a   B'
          one of the scribes,
          hearing them debating,
    Seeing
          that he answered them well,
          questioned him,
    'What is the first commandment of all?'
Answered Jesus,
            'The first is,
            "Hear, O Israel,
        The Lord our God is one Lord,
             and you shall love the Lord your God
             with all your heart,
        And with all your soul,
             and with all your mind,
             and with all your strength."
     The second is this,
         "You shall love your neighbour
         as yourself."
     There is no other commandment
         greater than these.'
And said to him the scribe,
            'Well said,
                Teacher,
            in truth you say
               that there is one,
               and there is no other besides him,
        And to love him with all the heart,
             and with all the understanding,
             and with all the strength,
        And to love the neighbour as himself,
             is greater than
             all the burnt offerings and sacrifices.'
And Jesus,
            seeing him,
            that he answered sensibly,
        said to him,
        'You are not far from the kingdom of God.'
And no-one
          anymore
          dared to question him.

And answering,   b
       Jesus began to say,
       <u>teaching in the temple,</u>
  'How do the scribes say
         that the Christ
         is the Son of David?
    David himself said in the Holy Spirit,
        "Said the Lord to my Lord, (*mou*)
          "Sit at my right (*mou*),
       Until I put your enemies (*sou*)
          under your feet (*sou*)."'"
    David himself calls him Lord,
      and how is he his son?'
  And the great crowd heard him gladly.

And in his teaching,   b'
       he began to say,
       'Beware of the scribes,
    of the ones wishing
        to walk about in robes,
        and greetings in the marketplaces,
     and chief seats in the synagogues,
        and chief places in the dinners,
    the ones devouring the houses of the widows,
        and under pretence praying at length:
    these will receive greater condemnation.
  And sitting opposite the treasury,
     he watched
     how the crowd threw money into the treasury,
  And many rich men threw in much.
  And coming,
     one poor widow threw in two lepta,
     which is a quadrans.
  And calling his disciples to him,
     he said to them,
     'Truly, I tell you,
   that this poor widow
     put in more than everyone
     of the ones throwing into the treasury,
   for everyone,
        out of their abundance,
        threw in,
   but this woman,
        out of her want,
   threw in all that she had,
        all her living.

In Part **B**, in the temple, in the opening piece, part A, the questioning and challenging of Jesus begins with a question put by the chief priests, scribes and elders concerning Jesus' authority for doing the things he does. They had not believed John the Baptist, and they were rejecting Jesus.

In part B, Jesus presents an allegorical parable ("told to/against *them*", 12.12) of the vineyard. Old Israel had rejected all whom God had sent to them: it would make the 'big mistake' of rejecting his Son also. The part ends on a climactic note of high drama, "And they sought how to seize him..." (see our table under Day Twenty-Three for the significance of this in the scheme of Days); it also sets up part B'. The leaders of Old Israel seek to "trap" Jesus "in a word", 12.13. They fail. He was too good a match for them: they would have to find another way. This indeed is the leading subject of the following Day, the middle and pivotal Day of the Series, Day Twenty-Five. The first questioners were 'sent' to Jesus by the chief priests, scribes and elders. We observe, therefore, the b,b' relationship of the two completing parts to part B, and we observe also the historical present of Mark with which he most frequently begins a new part and so introduces new characters. The questioners were the unusual alliance of 'heavies' of 3.6, who had wanted to destroy Jesus then; they were Pharisees and Herodians. Their question, on Caesar and the tax, is the kind of question that the Herodians would more likely have wanted to ask than the Pharisees, but the manner of the questioning suggests that it is the Pharisees who put it to Jesus. Jesus replies, asking for a denarius, a Roman coin... This part b ends with "their marvelling at him". Then Sadducees (mentioned here only in the Gospel), in the b' part, come with a wonderfully complicated question on the resurrection. Jesus replies, with reference to Moses, and does not resist concluding intimidatingly, "Much you are mistaken".

In part B', one of the scribes, in approaching Jesus, is more sympathetic than cautious. Having questioned Jesus on the principal commandment, he concurs with his reply and receives something of a commendation, "You are not far from the kingdom of God". The next part tells how Jesus, in his teaching in the temple, questions the scribes' understanding (consider 12.35, for the opening, *Καὶ ἀποκριθεὶς ὁ’Ιησοῦς ἔλεγεν διδάσκων ἐν τῷ ἱερῷ*) of the Christ as David's Son: he raises the issue between the Christ and David, as to whether the Christ is "Son" or "Lord" of David: he is Lord of David, and all his enemies "will be put under his feet" (the quotation is from Ps.110.1). "The large crowd heard him gladly." In the completing part (compare the opening with the previous part, *Καὶ ἐν τῇ διδαχῇ αὐτοῦ ἔλεγεν* for the common words, particularly, the imperfects, meaning 'he began to say'), Jesus addresses the issue of true devotion: the scribes are devoted to themselves, not to God and his purposes (theirs is the "greater condemnation"; they are the Lord's enemies); and when Jesus is located opposite the treasury he sees a poor "widow" (*χήρα* is a verbal link between the two passages) who, in contrast, is utterly devoted to God.

We now turn to Part B', 13.1-37. It begins, "And as he went forth, out of the temple...". The sub-divisions are as follows:

A		And he went forth	13.1-6
B	a	But <u>when</u> <u>you</u> hear	13.7-10
	b	And <u>when</u> they lead <u>you</u>	13.11-13
	b'	And <u>when</u> <u>you</u> see	13.14-16
B	a	But woe to the women	13.17-23
	b	But in those days	13.24-31
	b'	But about that day	13.32-37

Καὶ ἐκπορευομένου αὐτοῦ   A
        <u>ἐκ τοῦ ἱεροῦ</u>
        λέγει αὐτῷ
            εἷς τῶν μαθητῶν αὐτοῦ,
            Διδάσκαλε,
   ἴδε
        ποταποὶ λίθοι
        καὶ ποταπαὶ οἰκοδομαί.
     καὶ ὁ Ἰησοῦς εἶπεν αὐτῷ,
            Βλέπεις ταύτας τὰς μεγάλας οἰκοδομάς;
        οὐ μὴ ἀφεθῇ ὧδε λίθος ἐπὶ λίθον
        ὃς οὐ μὴ καταλυθῇ.
Καὶ καθημένου αὐτοῦ
        εἰς τὸ Ὄρος τῶν Ἐλαιῶν
        κατέναντι τοῦ ἱεροῦ
     ἐπηρώτα αὐτὸν
            κατ᾽ ἰδίαν
        Πέτρος
        καὶ Ἰάκωβος καὶ Ἰωάννης καὶ Ἀνδρέας, [4]
     Εἰπὸν ἡμῖν πότε ταῦτα ἔσται,
        καὶ τί τὸ σημεῖον
            ὅταν μέλλῃ ταῦτα συντελεῖσθαι πάντα.
ὁ δὲ Ἰησοῦς ἤρξατο λέγειν αὐτοῖς,
     Βλέπετε
        μή τις ὑμᾶς πλανήσῃ· [6]
     πολλοὶ ἐλεύσονται ἐπὶ τῷ ὀνόματί μου
        λέγοντες ὅτι Ἐγώ εἰμι,
        καὶ πολλοὺς πλανήσουσιν. [7]

<u>ὅταν δὲ ἀκούσητε</u>   a   B

       πολέμους
        καὶ ἀκοὰς πολέμων,
     μὴ θροεῖσθε·
δεῖ γενέσθαι,
ἀλλ᾽ οὔπω τὸ τέλος. [8]
ἐγερθήσεται γὰρ
      ἔθνος ἐπ᾽ ἔθνος
      καὶ βασιλεία ἐπὶ βασιλείαν,
    ἔσονται σεισμοὶ
     κατὰ τόπους
    ἔσονται λιμοί·
ἀρχὴ ὠδίνων ταῦτα.
βλέπετε δὲ
      ὑμεῖς
      ἑαυτούς·
    παραδώσουσιν ὑμᾶς εἰς συνέδρια
    καὶ εἰς συναγωγὰς δαρήσεσθε
καὶ ἐπὶ ἡγεμόνων καὶ βασιλέων σταθήσεσθε
     ἕνεκεν ἐμοῦ
     εἰς μαρτύριον αὐτοῖς. [10]
καὶ εἰς πάντα τὰ ἔθνη
    πρῶτον
    δεῖ κηρυχθῆναι τὸ εὐαγγέλιον. [11]

<u>Καὶ ὅταν ἄγωσιν ὑμᾶς</u>   b

    παραδιδόντες,
     μὴ προμεριμνᾶτε τί λαλήσητε,
ἀλλ᾽ ὃ ἐὰν δοθῇ ὑμῖν
    ἐν ἐκείνῃ τῇ ὥρᾳ
    τοῦτο λαλεῖτε,
οὐ γάρ ἐστε ὑμεῖς οἱ λαλοῦντες
    ἀλλὰ τὸ πνεῦμα τὸ ἅγιον.
καὶ παραδώσει ἀδελφὸς ἀδελφὸν εἰς θάνατον
    καὶ πατὴρ τέκνον,
    καὶ <u>ἐπ</u>αναστήσονται τέκνα <u>ἐπ</u>ὶ γονεῖς
      καὶ θανατώσουσιν αὐτούς· [13]
καὶ ἔσεσθε μισούμενοι
    ὑπὸ πάντων
     διὰ τὸ ὄνομά μου.
ὁ δὲ ὑπομείνας εἰς τέλος
οὗτος σωθήσεται.

<u>Ὅταν δὲ</u> ἴδητε τὸ βδέλυγμα τῆς ἐρημώσεως   b'
      ἑστηκότα ὅπου οὐ δεῖ,
    ὁ ἀναγινώσκων νοείτω,
    τότε οἱ ἐν τῇ Ἰουδαίᾳ
      φευγέτωσαν
      εἰς τὰ ὄρη, [15]
   ὁ ἐπὶ τοῦ δώματος
     μὴ καταβάτω
     μηδὲ εἰσελθάτω
      ἆραί τι
      ἐκ τῆς οἰκίας αὐτοῦ, [16]
  καὶ ὁ εἰς τὸν ἀγρὸν
     μὴ ἐπιστρεψάτω εἰς τὰ ὀπίσω
     ἆραι τὸ ἱμάτιον αὐτοῦ. [17]

Οὐαὶ δὲ ταῖς ἐν γαστρὶ ἐχούσαις   a   B'
    καὶ ταῖς θηλαζούσαις
    <u>ἐν ἐκείναις ταῖς ἡμέραις.</u> [18]
   προσεύχεσθε δὲ
     ἵνα μὴ γένηται
     χειμῶνος· [19]
   ἔσονται γὰρ <u>αἱ ἡμέραι ἐκεῖναι θλῖψις</u>
     οἵα οὐ γέγονεν τοιαύτη
    ἀπ' ἀρχῆς κτίσεως
     ἣν ἔκτισεν
     ὁ θεὸς
     ἕως τοῦ νῦν
     καὶ οὐ μὴ
     γένηται. [20]
  καὶ εἰ μὴ ἐκολόβωσεν κύριος τὰς ἡμέρας,
     οὐκ ἂν ἐσώθη πᾶσα σάρξ.
    ἀλλὰ διὰ τοὺς ἐκλεκτοὺς
    οὓς ἐξελέξατο
   ἐκολόβωσεν τὰς ἡμέρας. [21]
  καὶ τότε
    ἐάν τις ὑμῖν εἴπῃ,
     Ἴδε ὧδε ὁ Χριστός,
     Ἴδε ἐκεῖ,
    μὴ πιστεύετε· [22]
   ἐγερθήσονται γὰρ
     ψευδόχριστοι
     καὶ ψευδοπροφῆται
   καὶ δώσουσιν σημεῖα καὶ τέρατα
    πρὸς τὸ ἀποπλανᾶν, εἰ δυνατόν, τοὺς ἐκλεκτούς. [23]
   ὑμεῖς δὲ βλέπετε·
    προείρηκα ὑμῖν πάντα.

Ἀλλὰ *ἐν ἐκείναις ταῖς ἡμέραις*   b
        μετὰ τὴν θλῖψιν ἐκείνην
   ὁ ἥλιος σκοτισθήσεται,
      καὶ ἡ σελήνη οὐ δώσει τὸ φέγγος αὐτῆς,
     καὶ οἱ ἀστέρες ἔσονται ἐκ τοῦ οὐρανοῦ πίπτοντες,
     καὶ αἱ δυνάμεις
          αἱ ἐν τοῖς οὐρανοῖς
          σαλευθήσονται.
  καὶ τότε ὄψονται τὸν υἱὸν τοῦ ἀνθρώπου
     ἐρχόμενον ἐν νεφέλαις
      μετὰ δυνάμεως πολλῆς καὶ δόξης. [27]
  καὶ τότε ἀποστελεῖ τοὺς ἀγγέλους
     καὶ ἐπισυνάξει τοὺς ἐκλεκτοὺς αὐτοῦ
    ἐκ τῶν τεσσάρων ἀνέμων
       ἀπ' ἄκρου γῆς
       ἕως ἄκρου οὐρανοῦ.
 Ἀπὸ δὲ τῆς συκῆς μάθετε τὴν παραβολήν·
    ὅταν ἤδη ὁ κλάδος αὐτῆς ἁπαλὸς γένηται
     καὶ ἐκφύῃ τὰ φύλλα,
     γινώσκετε ὅτι ἐγγὺς τὸ θέρος ἐστίν. [29]
   οὕτως καὶ ὑμεῖς,
     ὅταν ἴδητε ταῦτα γινόμενα,
     γινώσκετε ὅτι ἐγγύς ἐστιν ἐπὶ θύραις. [30]
 ἀμὴν λέγω ὑμῖν
     ὅτι οὐ μὴ παρέλθῃ ἡ γενεὰ αὕτη
     μέχρις οὗ ταῦτα πάντα γένηται. [31]
   ὁ οὐρανὸς καὶ ἡ γῆ παρελεύσονται,
   οἱ δὲ λόγοι μου οὐ μὴ παρελεύσονται.

Περὶ δὲ <u>τῆς ἡμέρας ἐκείνης</u>   b᾽
  ἢ τῆς ὥρας
  οὐδεὶς οἶδεν,
  οὐδὲ οἱ ἄγγελοι ἐν οὐρανῷ
  οὐδὲ ὁ υἱός,
  εἰ μὴ ὁ πατήρ. 33
 βλέπετε
  ἀγρυπνεῖτε·
  οὐκ οἴδατε γὰρ πότε ὁ καιρός ἐστιν. 34
ὡς ἄνθρωπος ἀπόδημος
 ἀφεὶς τὴν οἰκίαν αὐτοῦ
  καὶ δοὺς τοῖς δούλοις αὐτοῦ τὴν ἐξουσίαν,
  ἑκάστῳ τὸ ἔργον αὐτοῦ,
 καὶ τῷ θυρωρῷ
  ἐνετείλατο
  ἵνα γρηγορῇ.
γρηγορεῖτε οὖν,
  οὐκ οἴδατε γὰρ
  πότε ὁ κύριος τῆς οἰκίας ἔρχεται,
   ἢ ὀψὲ
    ἢ μεσονύκτιον
   ἢ ἀλεκτοροφωνίας
    ἢ πρωΐ, 36
 μὴ ἐλθὼν ἐξαίφνης
  εὕρῃ ὑμᾶς καθεύδοντας. 37
 ὃ δὲ ὑμῖν λέγω,
  πᾶσιν λέγω,
  γρηγορεῖτε.

And in literal English:

And as he went forth,   A
        <u>out of the temple</u>,
        says to him,
     one of his disciples,
     'Teacher,
  Behold!
     What great stones!
     And what great buildings!'
  And Jesus said to him,
       'You see these huge buildings?
     There will not be left one stone on another,
     which will not be thrown down.'
And as he sat
     on the Mount of Olives
     opposite the temple,
  Began to question him,
       privately,
     Peter
     and James and John and Andrew
  'Tell us,
     when will these things be,
     and what will be the sign
       when all these things are about to be completed?'
And Jesus began to say to them,
   'Beware,
     lest anyone lead you astray.
  Many will come in my name,
     saying, "I am",
     and they will lead many astray.'

But when you hear   a   B
                of wars,
                and rumours of wars,
            do not be disturbed;
        it will necessarily happen,
        but it is not yet the end.
     For will be raised
           nation against nation,
           and kingdom against kingdom.
        There will be earthquakes
           in places
           there will be famines.
        The beginning/ of the birth-pangs/ these things.
    And beware,
                you,
                yourselves.
        They will deliver you to councils,
        and in synagogues you will be beaten,
      And before rulers and kings you will stand,
           for my sake,
           as a testimony to them.
      And to all the nations
           firstly
           it is necessary for the gospel to be proclaimed.

And when they lead you,   b
           delivering you,
           do not be anxious beforehand what you will speak.
      But whatever is given you
           in that hour,
           this speak.
      For you are not yourselves the ones speaking,
           but the Holy Spirit.
    And brother will deliver brother to death.
        And a father a child.
        And will rise up children against parents,
           and they will put them to death.
    And you will be hated
        by everyone
        on account of my name.
      But the one enduring to the end:
      this one will be saved.

And when you see the abomination of destruction   b'
                        stand where it ought not
       (the one reading,
              let him understand),
       then the ones in Judea
          let them flee
          to the mountains.
    The one on the roof
          let him not come down,
          nor let him enter
              to take anything
              out of his house,
   And the one in the field
          let him not return to things behind
          to take his garment.

But woe to the women who are pregnant   a   B'
              and to the ones who are breast-feeding
              in those days
        and pray
             that it may not happen
             in winter,
        for those days will be days of affliction,
                  of such a kind that has not happened
             since the beginning of creation
                which created
                God,
         until now
             and by no means
             may be.
   And except the Lord shortened the days,
          no flesh would be saved;
       but on account of the chosen
          whom he chose,
       he shortened the days.
   And then if anyone tells you,
                  'Behold here is the Christ!
                  Behold there!'
          Believe not!
       For will be raised
            false Christs
            and false prophets
          and they will do signs and wonders
          to lead astray, if possible, the chosen.
   But you beware!
          I have foretold to you everything.

But in <u>those days</u>   b
                  after that affliction,
            'The sun will be darkened,
                and the moon will not give its light,
            And the stars will fall out of heaven,
                and the powers
                      in the heavens
                      will be shaken.'
      <u>And then</u> they will see the Son of Man
            coming in clouds
            with much power and glory.
      <u>And then</u> he will send the angels
            and they will assemble the elect
            out of the four winds,
                from the extremity of earth
                to the extremity of heaven.
Now, from the fig tree learn the parable.
      When now its branch becomes tender
            and it puts forth its leaves,
            you know that the summer is near.
      So also you
            when you see these things happening,
            you know it is near, at the doors.
Truly I tell you,
            by no means passes this generation
            until all these things happen.
The heaven and the earth will pass away,
But my words will not pass away.

But about <u>that day</u>,   b'

> or hour,
> no-one knows,
> Not the angels in heaven,
> neither the Son,
> except the Father.
> Beware!
> Be awake!
> For you do not know when the time is.
> As a man away from home,
> Leaving his house,
> and giving authority to his slaves,
> to each his work,
> And the doorkeeper
> he commands
> to keep watch,
> Watch therefore
> for you do not know
> when the lord of the house comes,
> either late,
> or at midnight,
> or at cock-crowing,
> or early,
> lest coming suddenly
> he may find you sleeping.
> And what to you I say,
> I say to all,
> "Watch!'"

Part **B'** begins in 13.1,2 with Jesus going outside the temple. We note similarities in the ways the Day's three Parts work at their openings: the location is first given, then we are told Jesus is asked a question which attracts his response. We also notice the kind of details and constructions by Mark's hand that we have grown used to seeing at the beginning of new Days and new parts of Days:

11.20-22	*Καὶ παραπορευόμενοι... εἶδον τὴν συκῆν... λέγει αὐτῷ, Ῥαββί, ἴδε ἡ συκῆ... ὁ Ἰησοῦς λέγει αὐτοῖς...*
11.27-29	*Καὶ ἔρχονται πάλιν εἰς Ἰεροσόλυμα. Καὶ ἐν τῷ ἱερῷ... περιπατοῦντος αὐτοῦ... καὶ ἔλεγον αὐτῷ, Ἐν ποίᾳ ἐξουσίᾳ... ὁ δὲ Ἰησοῦς εἶπεν αὐτοῖς,*
13.1,2	*Καὶ ἐκπορευομένου αὐτοῦ ἐκ τοῦ ἱεροῦ λέγει αὐτῷ... Διδάσκαλε, ἴδε ποταποὶ λίθοι... ὁ Ἰησοῦς εἶπεν αὐτῷ ...*

The big news of Part **B'** is that it is the temple now which is going to be destroyed. Jesus cleared it the Day previously: the judgement of God is surely upon it. Peter, James, John and Andrew are present with Jesus. As Jesus now sits opposite the temple, they question him, "When will these things be?" and "What will be the sign...?". What we see in the layout and contents of Part **B'** is that the first question is answered firstly (see ὅταν in 13.7, v11 and v.14), and the second question is answered secondly (see τῆς ἡμέρας ἐκείνης and variations in 13.17-19, v.24 amd v.32). I think you will agree, when the texts are studied as I have parsed and presented them above, that Mark has come up with a very well ordered presentation here in Day Twenty-four which enables both understanding and memorising. We never should forget that 'memorability' was a key requirement of a first century work of Hellenist writing.

Parts A, B and B' of Part **B'** all play their role to Mark's usual high standard. The exposition of this part of the Day's contents has been a challenge and a fascination over the centuries. There is the warning that others will come to mislead, if possible, the elect. There will be "days of "distress" which will be "shortened" for the sake of "the elect". Affliction awaits, but the glorious finale will follow with the parousia and the angelic gathering up of the elect from every corner of the earth. People will be able to judge how near the event is, just as they know from the "parable" of the growth of a fig tree when summer is coming. All these things will happen *in this generation*: Jesus' word is to be trusted. The address finishes with teaching on 'that day'. Jesus may be talking only to Peter, James, John and Andrew, but his words are for "all" (so Mark presents): ὃ δὲ ὑμῖν λέγω, πᾶσιν λέγω, γρηγορεῖτε. We especially note that the teaching concludes with words like γρηγορεῖτε and καθεύδοντας, these feature again in Day Twenty-six, the chiastically corresponding Day of the Series, as Jesus gives instruction to Peter, James and John in Gethsemane.

We noted above the indicators of basic structure. Here we note how the content of Part **B'** has its correspondence in Part **B** with Jesus' allegorical parable of the vineyard: Old Israel will continue to "beat" and "put to death" God's representatives, but the one enduring ("for Jesus' sake", v.9; "proclaiming the Gospel", v.10; through whom "the Holy Spirit speaks", v.11) "will be saved", v.13.

If we are looking for correspondence elsewhere too in the Gospel, we only need to turn to the diagonally opposite Day Five (the second longest Day in the Gospel for its number of verses) and its teaching on the kingdom of God. In this Day's telling, we come across a very similar kind of construction to that of this Day Twenty-four, outside the temple. In Day Five, a scene begins, in the A part, with, "And he came into a house..." and his relatives are coming for him and scribes are coming from Jerusalem to him. In the following B part, Jesus answers the scribes and in the B' part, Jesus gives his answer to his family (but only to the crowd around him). This is in 3.20-35: just as Jesus is beginning to establish New Israel, his family think he is 'out of his mind'. Further, Days Five and Twenty-four do indeed set up the first diagonal connection between the First and last Series. Days Three and Twenty-six will set up the other, which together with this will form a *chi*, an X, at the centre of the Gospel's plan. (To this, we will return.)

Clearly, the length of this Day's telling, in terms of its verses, has been a challenge for establishing and presenting the Day's structure. Nevertheless, we are nearly ready to move on to the next Day. But before we go, we end our examination of Day Twenty-four with consideration of more minor matters of detail, but useful testings, however, of my analytical approach. Two chiasms have been said to exist: one at 12.10,11 and one at 12.35-37, both proposed by Marcus[371]. To recap, so far I have only encountered one chiasm, Mark's first in his Gospel, at 11.9,10, chosen by him to present the crowds' generous greetings of Jesus at his entry into Jerusalem. I am open to others being found, therefore.

---

[371]Marcus, *The Way of the Lord...*, pp.111f. and pp.130f.

Marcus's first chiasm is at 12.10,11: "The Rejected and Vindicated Stone", the quotation of Ps. 118.22-23 from the LXX (Ps.117):

> "Have you not read this scripture:
> 'A stone which the builders rejected   A
> this one was made the head of the corner B
> from the Lord this came to be   B'
> and it is astonishing in our eyes'?   A'

Marcus argues weakly, I think, that "parts B and B' speak of divine action of vindicating the stone", and that they are "framed by two human responses in parts A and A'."

The second is at 12.35-37: "David's Son and David's Lord": an arrangement around a quote from Ps. 110.1:

> And answering, Jesus said, teaching in the Temple,   A
> How do the scribes say that the Christ is the Son of David?   B
> David himself said in the Holy Spirit,   C
> The Lord said to my Lord/Sit at my right hand,   )   D
> Until I put your enemies/under your feet.   )
> David himself calls him "lord"   C'
> How then is he his son?   B'
> And the large crowd heard him gladly.   A'

My 'parsings' above, for this Day's texts in Greek and in literal English, can be compared. I cannot here agree with Marcus. Regarding Ps.118, the psalmist's lines are well accommodated in Mark's usual format and respected for their two parts per line. In the case of Ps.110, I am happy to stay with my presentation, as the two b parts both begin, very significantly, with 'David' and the whole presentation, again, sits comfortably in Mark's usual abb' format.

Day Twenty-five: 14.1-11:

Given that the first three Days comprise a sub-Series, this fourth Day's telling in Mark's final Series of seven Days occupies 'central' place. It behaves, as we might now expect, as a hinge, pivot or fulcrum to the material of the sub-Series of three Days each side of it. The Day relates two particular turning points, the plotting of Jesus' arrest and death, in which a disciple shares a part, in betraying him (see under Day Twenty-three, the table of conflict-climaxes), and the anointing of Jesus "for his burial" by a woman who will be remembered, "wherever the Gospel is proclaimed in all the world" (a unique clause in the Gospel narrative). In contrast to Judas Iscariot, literally "the one of the twelve", who will be remembered for his treachery, the woman who 'in one action anointed him Messiah, proclaimed his death and resurrection and made an act of total commitment to him as Lord'[372] is sadly unnamed.

The literary structure of Day Twenty-five may be viewed as:

---

[372]Hooker, *The Gospel...*, p.330.

Ἦν δὲ τὸ πάσχα　　　　　　　　　　　　　　　　　a　　　　　**A**
　　　　καὶ τὰ ἄζυμα
　　　　μετὰ δύο ἡμέρας.
καὶ ἐζήτουν οἱ ἀρχιερεῖς καὶ οἱ γραμματεῖς　　　　b
　　　　πῶς αὐτὸν ἐν δόλῳ κρατήσαντες
　　　　ἀποκτείνωσιν·[2]
ἔλεγον γάρ,　　　　　　　　　　　　　　　　　　b'
　　　　Μὴ ἐν τῇ ἑορτῇ,
　　　　μήποτε ἔσται θόρυβος τοῦ λαοῦ.

Καὶ ὄντος αὐτοῦ ἐν Βηθανίᾳ　　　　　　　　　a　　　A　　**B**
　　　　　ἐν τῇ οἰκίᾳ Σίμωνος τοῦ λεπροῦ
　　　　　κατακειμένου αὐτοῦ
　　　ἦλθεν γυνὴ
　　　　　ἔχουσα ἀλάβαστρον μύρου νάρδου　　　b
　　　　　πιστικῆς πολυτελοῦς·
　　　συντρίψασα τὴν ἀλάβαστρον　　　　　　b'
　　　　　κατέχεεν αὐτοῦ τῆς κεφαλῆς.
　　ἦσαν δέ τινες　　　　　　　　　　　　　　a　　　B
　　　　　ἀγανακτοῦντες
　　　　　πρὸς ἑαυτούς,
　　　Εἰς τί ἡ ἀπώλεια αὕτη τοῦ μύρου γέγονεν;[5]　b
　　　ἠδύνατο γὰρ τοῦτο τὸ μύρον　　　　　　　b'
　　　　　πραθῆναι ἐπάνω δηναρίων τριακοσίων
　　　　　καὶ δοθῆναι τοῖς πτωχοῖς·
　　καὶ ἐνεβριμῶντο αὐτῇ.　　　　　　　　　　a　　　B'
　　　　　　ὁ δὲ Ἰησοῦς εἶπεν,
　　　　　Ἄφετε αὐτήν·
　　　　　τί αὐτῇ κόπους παρέχετε;
　　　καλὸν ἔργον ἠργάσατο ἐν ἐμοί.[7]　　　　b
　　　　　πάντοτε γὰρ τοὺς πτωχοὺς ἔχετε μεθ' ἑαυτῶν,
　　　　　καὶ ὅταν θέλητε
　　　　　δύνασθε αὐτοῖς εὖ ποιῆσαι,
　　　　ἐμὲ δὲ οὐ πάντοτε ἔχετε.[8]
　　　ὃ ἔσχεν ἐποίησεν·　　　　　　　　　　　b'
　　　　　προέλαβεν
　　　　　　μυρίσαι τὸ σῶμά μου
　　　　　　εἰς τὸν ἐνταφιασμόν.[9]
　　　　ἀμὴν δὲ λέγω ὑμῖν,
　　　　　ὅπου ἐὰν κηρυχθῇ
　　　　　　τὸ εὐαγγέλιον
　　　　　　εἰς ὅλον τὸν κόσμον,
　　　　　καὶ ὃ ἐποίησεν αὕτη
　　　　　　λαληθήσεται
　　　　　　εἰς μνημόσυνον αὐτῆς.

Καὶ Ἰούδας Ἰσκαριὼθ   a   **B'**
    ὁ εἷς τῶν δώδεκα
    ἀπῆλθεν πρὸς τοὺς ἀρχιερεῖς
    ἵνα αὐτὸν παραδοῖ αὐτοῖς. [11]
οἱ δὲ ἀκούσαντες   b
    ἐχάρησαν
    καὶ ἐπηγγείλαντο αὐτῷ ἀργύριον δοῦναι.
καὶ ἐζήτει   b'
    πῶς αὐτὸν εὐκαίρως
    παραδοῖ.

The Day looks both backwards and forwards. Under Day Twenty-four I drew attention to the fact that the leaders of Old Israel set out to "trap" Jesus (12.13) but failed (12.13-34). They had to find another way. The Day's telling begins with their seeking how they might by stealth seize him and kill him: the Day's telling ends with the burden shifted onto Judas who now has to look for an opportunity to betray him. His chance comes the very next day.

The Day begins with what seems to be a simple and straightforward temporal reference[373], Ἦν δὲ τὸ πάσχα καὶ τὰ ἄζυμα μετὰ δύο ἡμέρας, but there is a problem, and it is not with the combining of the two feasts, for they had already become one[374]: it is with μετὰ δύο ἡμέρας. The key to understanding how Mark is counting, either inclusively meaning "the day before", or counting two whole days on, is found in Mark's references to Jesus' predictions that "after three days" he would rise (8.31, 9.31, 10.34). The three days are clearly Friday, Saturday and Sunday (see Days Twenty-seven, 15.1-47, and Twenty-eight, 16.1-8). He is counting inclusively. This Day's telling is located, therefore, on the day before the first Day of the Feast (14.12) which is Mark's Day Twenty-six which follows this one. At first sight, the Day may appear structured as a chiasm, but discerning Mark's usual ABB' method we see how A (vv.1,2) is introductory to the Day, and B (vv.3-9) and B' (vv.10,11) complete the Day's telling and hold together for reference to 'place', to 'money' and to 'true discipleship'.

On 'place': B begins: *Καὶ ὄντος αὐτοῦ ἐν Βηθανίᾳ ἐν τῇ οἰκίᾳ Σίμωνος τοῦ λεπροῦ*... (parechesis is observable in vv.2,3 but appears to function here more as an anastrophe to link vv1,2 and 3ff.); B' begins, *Καὶ Ἰούδας Ἰσκαριὼθ ὁ εἷς τῶν δώδεκα ἀπῆλθεν πρὸς*... On 'money': the annoyance with the woman "of some" of the disciples was that the ointment could have been sold for over "three hundred denarii" and given to the poor (vv.4,5); and the chief priests promised Judas "silver" (v.11). The closing two parts b and b', which balance as first and second developments, do lend support to the view that Judas betrayed Jesus for the money. Though Matthew does not mention the "three hundred denarii" in relation to the ointment, he does, alone of the Synoptists, put the figure of "thirty" on the pieces of "silver" (Matt. 26.9,15, see also Zech. 11.12, for 'thirty'). It would appear that both Mark and Matthew saw the monetary connection between the woman and Judas. On 'true discipleship': the greatest acts of generosity to Jesus express 'true discipleship'. Discipleship is not simply being listed among his followers, even his closest followers are capable of abusing his trust.

And now, the Day in literal English:

---

[373]See under Day Two for a listing of all Mark's Days which begin with temporal references.
[374]II Chron. 35.17; Josephus, *Antiquities*, XIV.2.1; XVII.9.3.

Now it was the Passover   **A**
     and Unleavened Bread
     in two days.
  And the chief priests and the scribes were seeking
     how in some sly way they might seize him
     that they might kill him.
  For they said,
     'Not at the feast
     lest there be a riot of the people.'

And as he was in Bethany,   **B**
       in the house of Simon the leper,
       as he sat at table,
    a woman came,
       having an alabaster phial of perfume,
       pure costly nard
    and breaking the alabaster phial,
       she poured it over his head.
  Now there were some present
       saying angrily
       to themselves,
    'Why has this waste of perfume happened?
    For could not this perfume
       have been sold for over three-hundred denarii,
       and have been given to the poor?'
  And they were indignant with her,
         but Jesus said,
       'Leave her alone!
       Why to her/ troubles/ cause?
    A good work/ she has performed/ on me.
       For always/ you will have the poor/ with you,
         and whenever you wish
         you can to them do well,
       but me/ not always/ you will have.
  She has done what she could.
       She has by anticipation/ anointed my body/ for burial.
       And truly, I tell you,
         wherever is proclaimed/ the gospel/ in all the world,
         also what this woman did/ will be told/ in memory of her.'

And Judas Iscariot, one of the twelve, went away   **B'**
     to the chief priests
     that he might betray him to them.
  And the ones hearing/ rejoiced,/ and promised to give him silver.
  And he sought/ how him suitably/ he might betray.

Day Twenty-six: 14.12-72:

The Day, the Gospel's third longest in the telling, begins Mark's final threesome/sub-Series of "Days". They are the most momentous of all his "Days". The hinge day of this Series, Day Twenty-five, in looking both backwards and forwards, may be considered to introduce the Passion narrative, but the Passion narrative as such actually *starts* here with the introductory section, 14.12-16, which begins with Mark's second reference to the Feast (see 14.1).

Of immediate interest, structurally-speaking, is the description of "preparation" which has its clear parallel at the beginning of the first Day of the first sub-Series, 11.1-6[375]. The two sub-Series mirror each other, in their openings. The common details are substantial. The Markan ABA' structure to the "Jerusalem Days", where A is the first and A' is the second sub-Series around the middle Day B, is well supported. We compare the Greek:

From 11.1-6:

α	ἀποστέλλει δύο τῶν μαθητῶν αὐτοῦ καὶ λέγει αὐτοῖς
β	Ὑπάγετε εἰς τὴν κώμην τὴν κατέναντι ὑμῶν
γ	Καὶ εὐθὺς εἰσπορευόμενοι εἰς αὐτὴν εὑρήσετε πῶλον δεδεμένον ἐφ᾽ ὃν οὐδεὶς οὔπω ἀνθρώπων ἐκάθισεν
δ	λύσατε αὐτὸν καὶ φέρετε
ε	εἴπατε, Ὁ κύριος
ζ	Καὶ ἀπῆλθον καὶ εὗρον πῶλον δεδεμένον
η	καὶ λύουσιν αὐτόν... ἐκεῖ
θ	οἱ δὲ εἶπαν αὐτοῖς καθὼς εἶπεν ὁ Ἰησοῦς

From 14.12-16:

α	καὶ ἀποστέλλει δύο τῶν μαθητῶν αὐτοῦ καὶ λέγει αὐτοῖς
β	Ὑπάγετε εἰς τὴν πόλιν
γ	καὶ ἀπαντήσει ὑμῖν ἄνθρωπος κεράμιον ὕδατος βαστάζων·
δ	ἀκολουθήσατε αὐτῷ
ε	εἴπατε τῷ οἰκοδεσπότῃ ὅτι Ὁ διδάσκαλος λέγει
ζ	καὶ ἐξῆλθον οἱ μαθηταὶ καὶ ἦλθον εἰς τὴν πόλιν καὶ εὗρον
η	καθὼς εἶπεν αὐτοῖς
θ	καὶ ἡτοίμασαν τὸ πάσχα

The repeating phrases, words and endings are many. The details and the constructions of these opening stories follow each other more or less in order, up to the last lines. There is no doubting that one story owes its current form to the other, and there is every good reason to argue here that Mark created one to match the other in order to signal the beginnings to this final Series' two threesomes of Days (11.1-13.37 and 14.12-16.8). To Schweizer, it is more likely 14.12-16 which Mark created because John's Gospel omits it[376]. To me, it is more likely 11.1-6. The account of 14.12-16 is much less repetitive in its detail than 11.1-6. Further, the details of 14.12-16 are important to the following reports in this Day's telling, whereas the details of 11.1-6 (which take up a large part of Day Twenty-two's telling) appear to have as their primary purpose the aim of affirming that the prophecy of Zechariah is fulfilled.[377]

---

[375]Neirynck identifies 11.1-7 and 14.12-16 as a 'Larger pericope Doublet', *Duality...*, p.135.

[376]Schweizer, *The Good News...*, p.294.

[377]See page 220 and my note 351, for an additional and very important link between these opening Days of these sub-Series: the allusions in both to the prophecy of Zechariah; in the first, Zech. 9.9 and in the second, 9.11.

The parameters of the Day are 14.12 and v.72[378], by way of the initial temporal reference and dating (see Day Twenty-five for a brief discussion), and because the following Day, which is consecutive, clearly begins at 15.1 with the words, *Καὶ εὐθὺς πρωΐ...* The literary-structure of Day Twenty-six is in the form of an ABB' scheme overall.

This Day is no different from all the others, structurally-speaking: it has three parts, Part **A** 14.12-31, Part **B** vv.32-46 and Part **B'** vv.47-72. It is a composite ABB' structure, which again shows the capacity of this style of writing to expand to contain the material appropriate to the Day's telling. Overall, it is an ABB'/ABB'/ABB' construction.

We examine Part **A**. Its first part, part A (vv.12-16) introduces the Day's date and the matter of the disciples' preparation for Jesus to eat the Passover in an upper room made ready for them. Its second par, part B (vv.17-25) tells how "when evening came" Jesus and the twelve shared the meal together (note *ἔρχεται*). At table the presence of the betrayer is the immediate issue: the two matters which complete the table-scene are Jesus' identification of his body and his blood of the 'covenant' with bread and wine; and that he will not drink wine again until "the day that" he drinks it "new" in the kingdom of God. The third part, part B' (vv.26-31) tells again of future events: on the Mount of Olives he tells them that they will be scattered, but that (1) after he is raised (2) he will go before them into Galilee (compare Day seven of this Series, the last Day of the Gospel narrative, at 16.7 for the telling of (1) and the reminder of (2)). The balancing concluding pieces link with the opening piece, through the word, *σκανδαλισθήσεσθε*. In the first, Peter claims he would not be like the others, but Jesus knows what will happen (as at the beginnings of this Day and Day Twenty-two, 11.1-11): he will deny him. In the second, Peter 'begins' to protest: what he says they all 'continue to say'.

I present the literary structure of Part **A**, 14.12-31:

---

[378]Heil views 14.1-52 as a nine-scene Markan whole, but because he fails to establish at the outset the beginning and end of a Markan presentation based on the beginning and ending of "Days", his "narrative structure" is immediately flawed. See John Paul Heil, "Mark 14.1-52: Narrative Structure and Reader-Response", *Bib.*, 71 no.3 (1990), pp.305-332.

Καὶ τῇ πρώτῃ ἡμέρᾳ   A   A
         τῶν ἀζύμων,
         ὅτε τὸ πάσχα ἔθυον,
    λέγουσιν
       αὐτῷ
       οἱ μαθηταὶ αὐτοῦ,
   Ποῦ θέλεις
       ἀπελθόντες ἑτοιμάσωμεν
       ἵνα φάγῃς τὸ πάσχα;
  καὶ ἀποστέλλει
       δύο τῶν μαθητῶν αὐτοῦ
       καὶ λέγει αὐτοῖς,
 Ὑπάγετε εἰς τὴν πόλιν,
         καὶ ἀπαντήσει ὑμῖν ἄνθρωπος
         κεράμιον ὕδατος βαστάζων·
   ἀκολουθήσατε αὐτῷ, [14]
         καὶ ὅπου ἐὰν εἰσέλθῃ
         εἴπατε τῷ οἰκοδεσπότῃ
   ὅτι Ὁ διδάσκαλος λέγει,
         Ποῦ ἐστιν τὸ κατάλυμά μου
         ὅπου τὸ πάσχα μετὰ τῶν μαθητῶν μου φάγω; [15]
   καὶ αὐτὸς
       ὑμῖν
       δείξει
    ἀνάγαιον μέγα
       ἐστρωμένον
       ἕτοιμον·
    καὶ ἐκεῖ
       ἑτοιμάσατε
       ἡμῖν.
  καὶ ἐξῆλθον οἱ μαθηταὶ
   καὶ ἦλθον εἰς τὴν πόλιν
    καὶ εὗρον
    καθὼς εἶπεν αὐτοῖς,
  καὶ ἡτοίμασαν τὸ πάσχα.

Καὶ ὀψίας γενομένης   B
      ἔρχεται
      μετὰ τῶν δώδεκα. [18]
  Καὶ ἀνακειμένων αὐτῶν
      καὶ ἐσθιόντων
        ὁ Ἰησοῦς εἶπεν,
      Ἀμὴν λέγω ὑμῖν
        ὅτι εἷς ἐξ ὑμῶν παραδώσει με,
        ὁ ἐσθίων μετ᾿ ἐμοῦ.
    ἤρξαντο λυπεῖσθαι καὶ λέγειν αὐτῷ
      εἷς κατὰ εἷς,
    Μήτι ἐγώ;
  ὁ δὲ εἶπεν αὐτοῖς,
      Εἷς τῶν δώδεκα,
      ὁ ἐμβαπτόμενος μετ᾿ ἐμοῦ εἰς τὸ τρύβλιον. [21]
    ὅτι ὁ μὲν
      υἱὸς τοῦ ἀνθρώπου ὑπάγει
      καθὼς γέγραπται περὶ αὐτοῦ,
    οὐαὶ δὲ τῷ ἀνθρώπῳ ἐκείνῳ
      δι᾿ οὗ ὁ υἱὸς τοῦ ἀνθρώπου παραδίδοται·
      καλὸν αὐτῷ εἰ οὐκ ἐγεννήθη ὁ ἄνθρωπος ἐκεῖνος.
  Καὶ ἐσθιόντων αὐτῶν
      λαβὼν ὁ Ἰησοῦς ἄρτον
    εὐλογήσας
      ἔκλασεν
      καὶ ἔδωκεν αὐτοῖς
    καὶ εἶπεν,
      Λάβετε,
      τοῦτό ἐστιν τὸ σῶμά μου.
    καὶ λαβὼν ποτήριον
      εὐχαριστήσας
      ἔδωκεν αὐτοῖς,
    καὶ ἔπιον ἐξ αὐτοῦ πάντες.
    καὶ εἶπεν αὐτοῖς,
      Τοῦτό ἐστιν τὸ αἷμά μου τῆς διαθήκης
      τὸ ἐκχυννόμενον ὑπὲρ πολλῶν· [25]
    ἀμὴν λέγω ὑμῖν
      ὅτι οὐκέτι
        οὐ μὴ
        πίω ἐκ τοῦ γενήματος τῆς ἀμπέλου
      ἕως τῆς ἡμέρας ἐκείνης
        ὅταν αὐτὸ πίνω καινὸν
        ἐν τῇ βασιλείᾳ τοῦ θεοῦ.

Καὶ ὑμνήσαντες   Β'

           ἐξῆλθον

               εἰς τὸ Ὄρος τῶν Ἐλαιῶν.

        καὶ λέγει αὐτοῖς ὁ Ἰησοῦς

      ὅτι Πάντες σκανδαλισθήσεσθε,

              ὅτι γέγραπται,

          Πατάξω τὸν ποιμένα,

         καὶ τὰ πρόβατα διασκορπισθήσονται·

     ἀλλὰ μετὰ τὸ ἐγερθῆναί με

          προάξω ὑμᾶς

          εἰς τὴν Γαλιλαίαν.

   ὁ δὲ Πέτρος ἔφη αὐτῷ,

     Εἰ καὶ πάντες σκανδαλισθήσονται,

     ἀλλ' οὐκ ἐγώ.

  <u>*Καὶ λέγει αὐτῷ ὁ Ἰησοῦς,*</u>

         Ἀμὴν λέγω σοι

         ὅτι σὺ σήμερον ταύτῃ τῇ νυκτὶ

            πρὶν ἢ δὶς ἀλέκτορα φωνῆσαι

            τρίς με ἀπαρνήσῃ.

    ὁ δὲ ἐκπερισσῶς ἐλάλει,

      Ἐὰν δέῃ με συναποθανεῖν σοι,

      οὐ μή σε ἀπαρνήσομαι.

    ὡσαύτως δὲ

        καὶ

        πάντες ἔλεγον.

And in literal English:

And on the first day   A   **A**
          of Unleavened Bread,
          when they sacrificed the Passover,
     they say
          to him
          his disciples,
    'Where do you wish
          we go and prepare
          for you to eat the Passover?'
  <u>And he sends</u>
          <u>two of his disciples</u>   (see Day 22)
          and he says to them,
    'Go into the city,
             and will meet you a man,
             carrying a pitcher of water.
          Follow him
             and wherever he enters,
             tell the house owner,
          "The teacher says,
             "Where is my guestroom,
              where I may eat the Passover with my disciples?"''
    And he
             you
             will show
          a large upper room
             furnished
             ready.
          And there
             prepare
             for us.'
And the disciples went forth,
     and they came into the city,
         and they found
         as he told them,
     and they prepared the Passover.

And when it was evening,
>> he comes
>> with the twelve.
> <u>And as they sat at table,</u>
>>>> and were eating,
>>> Jesus said,
>>> 'Truly I tell you,
>>>>> one of you will betray me,
>>>>> one eating with me.'
>> They began to grieve, and to say to him,
>>> one by one,
>>> 'Not I?'
>> And he said to them,
>>>>> 'One of the twelve.
>>>>> One dipping with me in the dish.
>>>> Because indeed,
>>>>> the Son of Man is going
>>>>> as it is written about him,
>>>> but woe to that man
>>>>> through whom the Son of Man is betrayed;
>>>>> better for him if that man had not been born.'
> <u>And as they were eating,</u>
>>>> taking Jesus bread,
>>> blessing it,
>>>> he broke it
>>>> and he gave it to them,
>>> and he said,
>>>> 'Take,
>>>> this is my body.'
>> And taking a cup,
>>>> giving thanks,
>>>> he gave it to them,
>>> and all drank from it,
>>> and he said to them,
>>>> 'This is my blood of the covenant,
>>>> being shed for many.
> Truly I tell you,
>> no more
>>>> by any means
>>>> will I drink of the fruit of the vine,
>>> until that day
>>>> when I drink it new
>>>> in the kingdom of God.'

B

And having sung a hymn   B'
            they went forth
                into the Mount of Olives
            and says to them Jesus,
        'You will all be <u>offended,</u>
                because it is written,
            "I will strike the shepherd,
             and the sheep will be scattered.
        But after I am raised,
            I will go before you
              into Galilee.'
     But Peter said to him,
        'Even if all will be <u>offended,</u>
           yet not I!'
    And says to him Jesus,
           'Truly I tell you,
           You today this night,
              before the cock crows twice,
              three times you will deny me.'
        But he more exceedingly said,
           'If it is necessary for me to die with you,
           by no means/ you/ will I deny.'
     And similarly
       also
          all were saying.

We continue with the Day's Part **B** (14.32-46). It is located wholly in Gethsemane. The opening part to tis Day's telling, in Part **A** (vv.12-31) has introduced two matters which have their fulfilment that night: the betrayal by Judas (from part B (vv.17-25)) is enacted in this Day's Part **B** (vv.32-46), and the scattering of the disciples and the denial of Peter (from part **B'** (vv.26-31), in Part A) are enacted in Part **B'** (vv.47-72). The Day is most certainly constructed to an ABB' part scheme.

Part **B** follows, firstly in the Greek and then in literal English:

Καὶ ἔρχονται   A   **B**
    εἰς χωρίον
    οὗ τὸ ὄνομα Γεθσημανί,
  καὶ λέγει τοῖς μαθηταῖς αὐτοῦ,
    Καθίσατε ὧδε ἕως προσεύξωμαι. [33]
καὶ παραλαμβάνει
    τὸν Πέτρον καὶ Ἰάκωβον καὶ Ἰωάννην
    μετ᾽ αὐτοῦ,
  καὶ ἤρξατο
    ἐκθαμβεῖσθαι
    καὶ ἀδημονεῖν, [34]
  καὶ λέγει αὐτοῖς,
    Περίλυπός ἐστιν ἡ ψυχή μου ἕως θανάτου·
    μείνατε ὧδε καὶ γρηγορεῖτε.
καὶ προελθὼν μικρὸν
    ἔπιπτεν
    ἐπὶ τῆς γῆς,
  καὶ προσηύχετο
    ἵνα εἰ δυνατόν ἐστιν
    παρέλθῃ ἀπ᾽ αὐτοῦ ἡ ὥρα, [36]
  καὶ ἔλεγεν,
    Ἀββὰ ὁ πατήρ,
      πάντα δυνατά σοι·
    παρένεγκε τὸ ποτήριον τοῦτο ἀπ᾽ ἐμοῦ·
      ἀλλ᾽ οὐ τί ἐγὼ θέλω
      ἀλλὰ τί σύ.

καὶ ἔρχεται   B
          καὶ εὑρίσκει αὐτοὺς
          καθεύδοντας,
      καὶ λέγει τῷ Πέτρῳ,
          Σίμων, καθεύδεις;
          οὐκ ἴσχυσας μίαν ὥραν γρηγορῆσαι; [38]
      γρηγορεῖτε
           καὶ προσεύχεσθε,
           ἵνα μὴ ἔλθητε εἰς πειρασμόν·
          τὸ μὲν πνεῦμα πρόθυμον
          ἡ δὲ σὰρξ ἀσθενής.
καὶ πάλιν ἀπελθὼν
          προσηύξατο
          τὸν αὐτὸν λόγον εἰπών. [40]
      καὶ πάλιν ἐλθὼν
          εὗρεν αὐτοὺς καθεύδοντας,
          ἦσαν γὰρ αὐτῶν οἱ ὀφθαλμοὶ καταβαρυνόμενοι,
      καὶ οὐκ ᾔδεισαν
          τί ἀποκριθῶσιν αὐτῷ.
καὶ ἔρχεται τὸ τρίτον
          καὶ λέγει αὐτοῖς,
          Καθεύδετε τὸ λοιπὸν καὶ ἀναπαύεσθε;
      ἀπέχει·
          ἦλθεν ἡ ὥρα,
          ἰδοὺ
            παραδίδοται ὁ υἱὸς τοῦ ἀνθρώπου
            εἰς τὰς χεῖρας τῶν ἁμαρτωλῶν. [42]
      ἐγείρεσθε
          ἄγωμεν·
          ἰδοὺ
            ὁ παραδιδούς με
            ἤγγικεν.

Καὶ εὐθὺς   Β᾽
             ἔτι αὐτοῦ λαλοῦντος
             παραγίνεται Ἰούδας
                  εἷς τῶν δώδεκα
        καὶ μετ᾽ αὐτοῦ ὄχλος
             μετὰ μαχαιρῶν
             καὶ ξύλων
        παρὰ τῶν ἀρχιερέων
             καὶ τῶν γραμματέων
             καὶ τῶν πρεσβυτέρων.
    δεδώκει δε
             ΄ ὁ παραδιδοὺς αὐτὸν
             σύσσημον αὐτοῖς λέγων,
        Ὃν ἂν φιλήσω
             αὐτός ἐστιν·
        κρατήσατε αὐτὸν
             καὶ ἀπάγετε
             ἀσφαλῶς. [45]
    καὶ ἐλθὼν
             εὐθὺς προσελθὼν αὐτῷ
             λέγει,
        Ῥαββί,
             καὶ κατεφίλησεν αὐτόν. [46]
        οἱ δὲ ἐπέβαλον τὰς χεῖρας αὐτῷ
             καὶ ἐκράτησαν αὐτόν. [47]

And they come   A   **B**
          to a place
          named Gethsemane.
    And he says to his disciples,
      'Sit here while I pray.'
  And he takes
          Peter and James and John
          with him,
    And he began
          to be greatly astonished
          and to be distressed.
    And he says to them,
          'Deeply grieved is my soul unto death.
          Stay here and watch.'
  And going forward a little,
          he fell
          on the ground,
    And he prayed
          that if it were possible,
          the hour might pass away from him.
    And he was saying,
          'Abba, Father,
             all things are possible to you,
          remove this cup from me,
             but not what I wish,
             but what you.'

And he comes   B
                    and he finds them
                    sleeping.
          And he says to Peter,
                    'Simon,
                              do you sleep?
                              Could you not watch one hour?
          Watch
                              and pray,
                              lest you come into temptation,
                    indeed the spirit is willing,
                    but the flesh is weak.'
And again going away,
                    he prayed,
                    saying the same word.
          And again coming,
                    he found them sleeping,
                    for their eyes were becoming heavy,
          And they did not know
                    what they might answer him.
And he comes the third time,
                    and he says to them,
                    'Sleep now and rest
          It is enough!
                    The hour has come!
                    Behold,
                              the Son of Man is betrayed
                              into the hands of sinners!
          Get up!
                    Let us go!
                    Behold,
                              the one betraying me
                              has drawn near!'

And immediately   B'
                              while he was still speaking,
                              arrives Judas,
                                        one of the twelve,
                        and with him a crowd
                              with swords
                              and clubs,
                        from the chief priests
                              and the scribes
                              and the elders.
              Now had given
                              the one betraying him
                              a signal to them saying,
                        'The one I kiss
                              is he.
                    Seize him
                              and lead him away
                              securely.'
              And coming,
                              immediately approaching him,
                              he says,
                        'Rabbi'
                              and fervently he kissed him.
                    And they laid their hands on him
                              and seized him.

Part **B** (vv.32-46, above), in its three parts, displays typically Markan introductions to each: the first begins with two historical presents; the second begins with three; and the third begins with *Καὶ εὐθὺς*.

In the first part A (vv.32-36), after the new setting and those with him are defined, Jesus first speaks to his three disciples and then, in prayer, to his father about his agony. The address to God is totally new in the Gospel, *Ἀββὰ ὁ πατήρ*. *Ἀββὰ*, the Aramaic and intimate expression for "father" is nowhere else found in the Gospels, but its use here, given the likely nature of Jesus' psychological state, is judged most appropriate. For "father" elsewhere, in respect to God, but nowhere else in the vocative, see 8.38, 11.25,26, and 13.32. The scene Mark paints allows the reader/listeners to witness the intimacy of the relationship Jesus has with with his Father and the three: we share a highly-charged moment.

In the second part B (vv.37-42), we see Jesus coming and going: three times he returns to the three. Each literary-part records a return of Jesus. It is a story beautifully, movingly and yet concisely told; and just as Jesus is beginning to accept that the three should be allowed their sleep, it ends dramatically with the betrayer coming near. We note the verbal correspondences with the conclusion of Jesus' apocalyptic teaching of chapter 13, γρηγορεῖτε and καθεύδοντας, for which see under Day Twenty-four: we can so compare the last Day of the first threesome of Days of this Series with this Day, the first Day of the second threesome.

The third part B' (vv.43-46) opens with the telling of the arrival of Judas and a threatening crowd from "the chief priests, scribes and elders" (of Day Twenty-four's telling again, 11.27). The betrayal is told in the two balancing and completing parts of this Day's telling. Part **B** ends: Jesus is to be seized.

We turn now to Part **B'** (14.47-72) which is linked to Part **B** by another anastrophe: we compare καὶ ἐκράτησαν αὐτόν, in 14.46, and καὶ οὐκ ἐκρατήσατέ με, in v.49. In part A (vv.47-54), in sub-part a Jesus is identified as a "robber" (see also 11.17 and 15.27 for λῃστήν in fulfilment of the scriptures (Isaiah 53.12[379]); in sub-part b Mark records the fleeing of Jesus' companions (in fulfilment of 14.27) and of the mysterious young man[380] who was nearly seized (v.51); and in sub-part b' the subjects for the remaining two parts, B and B' are introduced (in true Markan fashion, in A, his introductory piece), which in b'(a) is Jesus before the sanhedrin (part B), and which in b'(b) and (b') is Peter in the courtyard of the high priest (part B').

Part B (vv.55-65) tells of Jesus before the Sanhedrin. The opening piece a describes how the council sought any kind of witness against Jesus who remained silent in the face of false witness. The second piece b records the high priest's direct question, literally, "You are the Christ, the Son of the Blessed?"[381] Jesus gives a very direct answer. The high priest needed no other witness. Jesus is guilty of blasphemy. The third piece b' tells of the sentence: all condemned him to death; and then they began to mistreat him.

Part B' (vv.66-72) tells of Peter in the high priest's courtyard, in sub-part a, and later, outside in the forecourt, in sub-parts b and b', as he attempts to remove himself from the 'heat'. For each of the three sub-parts, read one 'denial', and note the common location for the last two parallel sub-parts, which also have in common the challenge: χομπαρε Οὗτος ἐξ αὐτῶν ἐστιν and Ἀληθῶς ἐξ αὐτῶν εἶ.

Part **B'** follows, firstly in the Greek and then in literal English:

---

[379]Marcus, *The Way of the Lord...*, p189: Marcus lists allusions to the Deutero-Isaian Servant Songs: 14.10,18,21,41-42, 15.1,10,15 (53.6,12); 14.24 (53.12); 14.61, 15.5 (53.7; 14.65 (50.6); 15.5,39 (52.15); 15.6-15 (53.6,12); I would add 14.48 (53.12).

[380]Compare 16.5: it appears to be indicated by Mark that the 'angel' who was later at the grave was first present at Jesus' arrest. We will return to this under Day Twenty-eight.

[381]Marcus puts the case for restrictive apposition in 14.61, that is that there ought to be no comma between "Christ" and "Son of the Blessed", that the latter phrase qualifies the first and that they should not be read as two separate titles. Mark's rhetorical method, however, does not allow the expressing of anything so delicate as this: it demands a breaking down of sentences to phrases and phrases to words. It is a process which cannot be stopped! I read a bb' pair: (b) Are you the Christ? (b') the Son of the Blessed? See, Joel Marcus, "Mark 14.61: "Are You the Messiah-Son-of-God?", *NovT*, 31, no.2 (1989), pp.125-142.

Εἷς δέ τις τῶν παρεστηκότων   A   **B'**
        σπασάμενος τὴν μάχαιραν
          ἔπαισεν τὸν δοῦλον τοῦ ἀρχιερέως
     καὶ ἀφεῖλεν αὐτοῦ τὸ ὠτάριον.
   καὶ ἀποκριθεὶς
       ὁ Ἰησοῦς εἶπεν
       αὐτοῖς,
      Ὡς ἐπὶ λῃστὴν
        ἐξήλθατε μετὰ μαχαιρῶν καὶ ξύλων
        συλλαβεῖν με; [49]
      καθ' ἡμέραν
       ἤμην πρὸς ὑμᾶς
         ἐν τῷ ἱερῷ
         διδάσκων
       καὶ οὐκ ἐκρατήσατέ με·
   ἀλλ' ἵνα πληρωθῶσιν αἱ γραφαί. [50]
καὶ ἀφέντες αὐτὸν
      ἔφυγον πάντες.
      Καὶ νεανίσκος τις συνηκολούθει αὐτῷ
       περιβεβλημένος σινδόνα
       ἐπὶ γυμνοῦ,
    καὶ κρατοῦσιν αὐτόν· [52]
       ὁ δὲ καταλιπὼν τὴν σινδόνα
       γυμνὸς ἔφυγεν.
Καὶ ἀπήγαγον τὸν Ἰησοῦν
       πρὸς τὸν ἀρχιερέα,
    καὶ συνέρχονται
    πάντες οἱ ἀρχιερεῖς
      καὶ οἱ πρεσβύτεροι
      καὶ οἱ γραμματεῖς. [54]
   καὶ ὁ Πέτρος
       ἀπὸ μακρόθεν
       ἠκολούθησεν αὐτῷ
    ἕως ἔσω
     εἰς τὴν αὐλὴν τοῦ ἀρχιερέως,
   καὶ ἦν συγκαθήμενος
     μετὰ τῶν ὑπηρετῶν
     καὶ θερμαινόμενος πρὸς τὸ φῶς.

οἱ δὲ ἀρχιερεῖς   B
        καὶ ὅλον τὸ συνέδριον
        ἐζήτουν κατὰ τοῦ Ἰησοῦ μαρτυρίαν
     εἰς τὸ θανατῶσαι αὐτόν,
     καὶ οὐχ ηὕρισκον·[56]
   πολλοὶ γὰρ ἐψευδομαρτύρουν κατ᾽ αὐτοῦ,
   καὶ ἴσαι αἱ μαρτυρίαι οὐκ ἦσαν.
καί τινες _ἀναστάντες_
     ἐψευδομαρτύρουν κατ᾽ αὐτοῦ
     λέγοντες[58]
   ὅτι Ἡμεῖς ἠκούσαμεν αὐτοῦ λέγοντος
     ὅτι Ἐγὼ καταλύσω τὸν ναὸν τοῦτον
       τὸν χειροποίητον
     καὶ διὰ τριῶν ἡμερῶν
       ἄλλον ἀχειροποίητον
       οἰκοδομήσω·
   καὶ οὐδὲ οὕτως ἴση ἦν ἡ μαρτυρία αὐτῶν.
καὶ _ἀναστὰς_
     ὁ ἀρχιερεὺς | εἰς μέσον
     ἐπηρώτησεν τὸν Ἰησοῦν | λέγων,
   Οὐκ ἀποκρίνῃ οὐδέν;
     τί οὗτοί σου καταμαρτυροῦσιν;[61]
   ὁ δὲ ἐσιώπα
     καὶ οὐκ ἀπεκρίνατο οὐδέν.
πάλιν ὁ ἀρχιερεὺς ἐπηρώτα αὐτὸν
       καὶ λέγει αὐτῷ,
     Σὺ εἶ ὁ Χριστὸς
     ὁ υἱὸς τοῦ εὐλογητοῦ;
   ὁ δὲ Ἰησοῦς εἶπεν,
     Ἐγώ εἰμι,
     καὶ ὄψεσθε τὸν υἱὸν τοῦ ἀνθρώπου
       ἐκ δεξιῶν καθήμενον τῆς δυνάμεως
       καὶ ἐρχόμενον μετὰ τῶν νεφελῶν τοῦ οὐρανοῦ.
   ὁ δὲ ἀρχιερεὺς
     διαρρήξας τοὺς χιτῶνας αὐτοῦ
     λέγει,
     Τί ἔτι χρείαν ἔχομεν μαρτύρων;[64]
   ἠκούσατε τῆς βλασφημίας·
   τί ὑμῖν φαίνεται;
οἱ δὲ πάντες κατέκριναν αὐτὸν
     ἔνοχον εἶναι
     θανάτου.[65]
   Καὶ ἤρξαντό τινες ἐμπτύειν αὐτῷ
     καὶ περικαλύπτειν αὐτοῦ τὸ πρόσωπον
       καὶ κολαφίζειν αὐτὸν
     καὶ λέγειν αὐτῷ,
     Προφήτευσον,
καὶ οἱ ὑπηρέται | ῥαπίσμασιν | αὐτὸν ἔλαβον.

Καὶ ὄντος τοῦ Πέτρου κάτω ἐν τῇ αὐλῇ   Β᾽
      ἔρχεται μία τῶν παιδισκῶν τοῦ ἀρχιερέως, [67]
    καὶ ἰδοῦσα τὸν Πέτρον θερμαινόμενον
      ἐμβλέψασα αὐτῷ
        λέγει,
      Καὶ σὺ μετὰ τοῦ Ναζαρηνοῦ ἦσθα
        τοῦ Ἰησοῦ.
    ὁ δὲ ἠρνήσατο
      λέγων,
      Οὔτε οἶδα
        οὔτε ἐπίσταμαι σὺ
        τί λέγεις.
  καὶ ἐξῆλθεν
      ἔξω
      εἰς τὸ προαύλιον. *
    καὶ ἡ παιδίσκη
      ἰδοῦσα αὐτὸν
      ἤρξατο πάλιν λέγειν τοῖς παρεστῶσιν
      ὅτι Οὗτος ἐξ αὐτῶν ἐστιν. [70]
    ὁ δὲ πάλιν ἠρνεῖτο.
  καὶ μετὰ μικρὸν
      πάλιν οἱ παρεστῶτες
      ἔλεγον τῷ Πέτρῳ,
      Ἀληθῶς ἐξ αὐτῶν εἶ,
      καὶ γὰρ Γαλιλαῖος εἶ.
    ὁ δὲ ἤρξατο
      ἀναθεματίζειν
      καὶ ὀμνύναι
      ὅτι Οὐκ οἶδα τὸν ἄνθρωπον τοῦτον
      ὃν λέγετε.
    καὶ εὐθὺς
      ἐκ δευτέρου
      ἀλέκτωρ ἐφώνησεν.
    καὶ ἀνεμνήσθη ὁ Πέτρος τὸ ῥῆμα
      ὡς εἶπεν αὐτῷ ὁ Ἰησοῦς
      ὅτι Πρὶν ἀλέκτορα φωνῆσαι δὶς
      τρίς με ἀπαρνήσῃ·
    καὶ ἐπιβαλὼν
      ἔκλαιεν.

Now a certain one of the ones standing by,   A   **B'**
        drawing his sword,
            he struck the slave of the high priest
        and he cut off his ear
    and answering,
            Jesus said
            to them,
        'As against a robber
            came you forth with swords and clubs
            to arrest me?
      Daily
            I was with you
                in the temple
                teaching,
            and you did not seize me,
     but that the scriptures may be fulfilled....'
And leaving him,
        they all fled.
    And a certain young man accompanied him,
        clothed in a linen cloth
        over his naked body,
    And they seize him,
        and he leaving the linen cloth,
        fled naked.
And they led Jesus away
            to the high priest,
        and they come together,
        all the chief priests
            and the elders
            and the scribes.
    And Peter,
            at a distance,
            followed him,
        as far as inside
        into the courtyard of the high priest.
    And he was sitting
        with the attendants,
        and warming himself by the fire.

Now the chief priests and all the Sanhedrin   B
       sought witness
         against Jesus,
           so that they might put him to death,
       but they found none,
     for many gave false testimony against him,
     and no testimonies were identical.
   And some standing up
       gave false testimony against him,
       saying,
     'We heard him saying,
       "I will destroy this temple
         made with hands
      and in three days
        build another,
        not made with hands."'
   And not so identical was their testimony.
   And standing up,
       the high priest,
         in the midst,
       questioned Jesus,
         saying,
     'Do you not answer anything
       that these men have testified against you?'
     But he was silent
       and did not answer anything.
 Again the high priest questioned him,
       and says to him,
     'You are the Christ,
     the Son of the Blessed?'
   And Jesus said,
     'I am,
     and you will see the Son of Man
       sitting at the right hand of power
       and coming with the clouds of heaven.'
   And the high priest,
       tearing his tunics,
         says,
     'What more need have we of witnesses?
   You heard the blasphemy!
   How does it appear to you?'
And they all condemned him/ to be worthy/ of death.
   And some began to spit on him
     and to cover his face
       and to maltreat him
     and to say to him,
       'Prophesy!'
   And the attendants
     struck him
     slapping him.

And as Peter was below in the courtyard,   B'
    there comes one of the maids of the high priest.
And seeing Peter warming himself,
    looking at him,
      she says,
    'And you were with the Nazarene,
      Jesus!'
But he denied,
    saying,
    'Neither do I know,
      nor do I understand
      what you are saying.'
And he went forth,
    outside,
    into the courtyard.*
And the maid,
    seeing him
    began again to say to the ones standing by,
    'This man is of them!'
But he again denied.
And after a little while,
    again the ones standing by
    began to say to Peter,
    'Truly, you are of them,
    for indeed you are a Galilean!'
And he began to curse and to swear,
    'I do not know this man,
    whom you are talking about.'
And immediately,
    a second time,
    a cock crew.
And Peter remembered the word
    as Jesus said to him, ..
    'Before a cock crows twice,
    three times you will deny me.'
And recalling it,
    he wept.

    * I comment on v.68: at this point some manuscripts include καὶ ἀλέκτωρ ἐφώνησεν, 'and a cock crowed': it has been added later, and not by Mark. Whilst it is supported by Codex Alexandrinus, it is not supported by Codices Sinaiticus and Vaticanus and many other witnesses. We may appreciate why it was added, but firstly, we observe its bad positioning in the story-line. The story flows better without it. Secondly, given the good story-telling position of the second cock crow immediately after the third denial (in (b')) of sub-part b'), its use in v.68 really does appear out of place, just after Peter changes location. My judgement is that Mark could have placed it after ὁ δὲ πάλιν ἠρνεῖτο to complete line (b') of verse 70. The reasoning is based on an understanding of his rhetorical scheme of (.a) (.b) (.b'). (Whoever added it in v.68 did not know Mark's style.) A third reason for judging that καὶ ἀλέκτωρ ἐφώνησεν is added in v.68 by another, is that it is arguable that Matthew and Luke identified the problem of the missing 'first-crowing' too, because they circumnavigated the problem by removing the word "twice" from Jesus' prediction: hence, "Before a

cock crows you will...". If there ever was a first reference to 'cock crow', which a copier subsequently failed to copy, I judge it would fit appropriately only after ὁ δὲ πάλιν ἠρνεῖτο, in the first line of v.70.

Whatever the case, the Day concludes with the contritional tears of Peter. Thinking on what Jesus had said he would do, "he begins to weep".[382] The implication of the Day's telling is that the last activities take place well into the night watches (a fire was lit, 14.54, around which people could warm themselves, in the cold night hours): Mark does not state which watch, but what he does say is that the events of the next Day begin early (see under Day One, for our discussion on the way Mark uses πρωΐ in a non-technical sense, of the fourth watch of the night, but co-incident, more or less, with sunrise).

Day Twenty-seven: 15.1-47:

The Day's telling begins Καὶ εὐθὺς πρωΐ... We identify a dramatic quickening of the pace of events. The form the Day's telling takes can be expressed as ABB' once more, or in its longer form, as ABB'/ABB'/ABB'.

The first part, Part **A**, 15.1-21 focuses on Jesus' audience with Pilate. It is systematically told in the three parts, A, B and B'. Part A (vv.1-5) tells how Jesus is delivered to Pilate, then for the beginnings of the b and b' parts we encounter:

for b   'And questioned him Pilate...'   and
for b'   'And Pilate again questioned him...'

Part B (vv.6-14) begins with the telling of a tradition 'at a Feast', then for the beginnings of the b and b' parts we encounter:

for b   'And Pilate answered them...'
for b'   'And Pilate again answering...'

We take note of the sequences and see the method of presentation repeated between them.
Part B' (vv.15-21) Pilate pleases the crowd: the Feast's tradition is served, Jesus is flogged, mocked and taken away for crucifixion, and a certain Simon from Cyrene carries Jesus' cross.

The second part, Part **B**, 15.22-41, begins with a historical present and a new location, Golgotha. It tells of the bleak scenes at the cross and is told again in three disciplined parts. In part A (vv.22-24) Jesus is brought, offered wine vinegar which he refuses and is fixed to his cross as his garments are shared. In part B (vv.25-32), at the third hour, he is crucified, 'King of the Jews', between two robbers, and is mocked by all. In part B' (vv.33-41), in the a part, at the sixth hour, darkness came over the land till the ninth hour when Jesus cries out, forsaken by all and even God; in the b part, people stand watching as he dies (at which point the temple curtain is torn in two and a centurion states, 'Truly, this man – a son of God was'; and in the part b', we are told that women were 'observing from afar', some are named, many had come up to Jerusalem with Jesus.

The third part, Part **B'**, 15.42-47, tells what happens as evening comes (just prior to the Sabbath beginning): in its three parts, firstly, a certain Joseph from Arimathea (one who was waiting for the kingdom of God to appear) goes to Pilate to ask for the body of Jesus; the next part, Pilate is surprised that Jesus is already dead and questions a centurion before he grants the corpse to Joseph; and so the burial takes place. Jesus is taken down from the cross, his body is wrapped in linen cloth and laid in a tomb hewn out of rock, and a stone is rolled against the doorway of the tomb. Two ladies called Mary, one of Magdala, observe.

---

[382]Under the discussion about the longer ending, we will look again at this Day's ending that leaves Peter weeping.

The literary structure of Day Twenty-seven is presented:

Καὶ εὐθὺς πρωῒ   A   **A**
      συμβούλιον ποιήσαντες
      οἱ ἀρχιερεῖς
   μετὰ τῶν πρεσβυτέρων
      καὶ γραμματέων
      καὶ ὅλον τὸ συνέδριον
   δήσαντες τὸν Ἰησοῦν
      ἀπήνεγκαν
      καὶ παρέδωκαν Πιλάτῳ.
  καὶ ἐπηρώτησεν αὐτὸν ὁ Πιλᾶτος,
      Σὺ εἶ ὁ βασιλεὺς τῶν Ἰουδαίων;
   ὁ δὲ ἀποκριθεὶς αὐτῷ λέγει,
      Σὺ λέγεις.
   καὶ κατηγόρουν αὐτοῦ
      οἱ ἀρχιερεῖς
      πολλά. [4]
  ὁ δὲ Πιλᾶτος πάλιν ἐπηρώτα αὐτὸν
      λέγων,
      Οὐκ ἀποκρίνῃ οὐδέν;
   ἴδε
      πόσα
      σου κατηγοροῦσιν.
   ὁ δὲ Ἰησοῦς οὐκέτι οὐδὲν ἀπεκρίθη,
      ὥστε θαυμάζειν τὸν Πιλᾶτον.

Κατὰ δὲ ἑορτὴν   B
     ἀπέλυεν αὐτοῖς ἕνα δέσμιον
     ὃν παρῃτοῦντο. [7]
  ἦν δὲ ὁ λεγόμενος Βαραββᾶς
     μετὰ τῶν στασιαστῶν δεδεμένος
     οἵτινες ἐν τῇ στάσει φόνον πεποιήκεισαν. [8]
καὶ ἀναβὰς
     ὁ ὄχλος ἤρξατο αἰτεῖσθαι
     καθὼς ἐποίει αὐτοῖς.
ὁ δὲ Πιλᾶτος ἀπεκρίθη αὐτοῖς
     λέγων,
     Θέλετε
        ἀπολύσω ὑμῖν
        τὸν βασιλέα τῶν Ἰουδαίων; [10]
ἐγίνωσκεν γὰρ
     ὅτι διὰ φθόνον
     παραδεδώκεισαν αὐτὸν οἱ ἀρχιερεῖς. [11]
οἱ δὲ ἀρχιερεῖς ἀνέσεισαν τὸν ὄχλον
     ἵνα μᾶλλον
     τὸν Βαραββᾶν ἀπολύσῃ αὐτοῖς.
ὁ δὲ Πιλᾶτος πάλιν ἀποκριθεὶς
     ἔλεγεν αὐτοῖς,
     Τί οὖν ποιήσω
        ὃν λέγετε
        τὸν βασιλέα τῶν Ἰουδαίων;
οἱ δὲ πάλιν ἔκραξαν,   (Mk. meaning: 'without any hesitation';
     Σταύρωσον αὐτόν.   see also: 2.13; 3.1 and 4.1)
ὁ δὲ Πιλᾶτος ἔλεγεν αὐτοῖς,
     Τί γὰρ ἐποίησεν κακόν;
οἱ δὲ περισσῶς ἔκραξαν,
     Σταύρωσον αὐτόν.

ὁ δὲ Πιλᾶτος   Β'
           βουλόμενος
             τῷ ὄχλῳ τὸ ἱκανὸν ποιῆσαι
    ἀπέλυσεν αὐτοῖς τὸν Βαραββᾶν,
    καὶ παρέδωκεν τὸν Ἰησοῦν
         φραγελλώσας
         ἵνα σταυρωθῇ.
Οἱ δὲ στρατιῶται ἀπήγαγον αὐτὸν
           ἔσω τῆς αὐλῆς,
            ὅ ἐστιν πραιτώριον,
    καὶ συγκαλοῦσιν ὅλην τὴν σπεῖραν. [17]
    καὶ ἐνδιδύσκουσιν αὐτὸν πορφύραν
      καὶ περιτιθέασιν αὐτῷ πλέξαντες ἀκάνθινον στέφανον· [18]
      καὶ ἤρξαντο ἀσπάζεσθαι αὐτόν,
          Χαῖρε,
           βασιλεῦ τῶν Ἰουδαίων· [19]
    καὶ ἔτυπτον αὐτοῦ τὴν κεφαλὴν καλάμῳ
        καὶ ἐνέπτυον αὐτῷ,
        καὶ τιθέντες τὰ γόνατα
           προσεκύνουν αὐτῷ. [20]
  Καὶ ὅτε ἐνέπαιξαν αὐτῷ,
      ἐξέδυσαν αὐτὸν τὴν πορφύραν
      καὶ ἐνέδυσαν αὐτὸν τὰ ἱμάτια αὐτοῦ.
    καὶ ἐξάγουσιν αὐτὸν
      ἵνα σταυρώσουσιν αὐτόν.
    καὶ ἀγγαρεύουσιν παράγοντά τινα
      Σίμωνα Κυρηναῖον
         ἐρχόμενον ἀπ' ἀγροῦ,
          τὸν πατέρα Ἀλεξάνδρου καὶ Ῥούφου,
      ἵνα ἄρῃ τὸν σταυρὸν αὐτοῦ. [22]

Καὶ φέρουσιν αὐτὸν   A   **B**
        ἐπὶ τὸν Γολγοθᾶν τόπον,
        ὅ ἐστιν μεθερμηνευόμενον
            Κρανίου Τόπος. [23]
      καὶ ἐδίδουν αὐτῷ ἐσμυρνισμένον οἶνον,
        ὃς δὲ οὐκ ἔλαβεν. [24]
      καὶ σταυροῦσιν αὐτὸν
        καὶ διαμερίζονται τὰ ἱμάτια αὐτοῦ,
        βάλλοντες κλῆρον ἐπ᾿ αὐτὰ τίς τί ἄρῃ.

ἦν δὲ ὥρα τρίτη   B
      καὶ ἐσταύρωσαν αὐτόν. [26]
      καὶ ἦν ἡ ἐπιγραφὴ
        τῆς αἰτίας
        αὐτοῦ ἐπιγεγραμμένη,
      Ὁ βασιλεὺς τῶν Ἰουδαίων. [27]
      καὶ σὺν αὐτῷ σταυροῦσιν δύο λῃστάς,
        ἕνα ἐκ δεξιῶν
        καὶ ἕνα ἐξ εὐωνύμων αὐτοῦ. [29]
      Καὶ οἱ παραπορευόμενοι ἐβλασφήμουν αὐτὸν
        κινοῦντες τὰς κεφαλὰς αὐτῶν
        καὶ λέγοντες,
      Οὐὰ
        ὁ καταλύων τὸν ναὸν
        καὶ οἰκοδομῶν ἐν τρισὶν ἡμέραις, [30]
      σῶσον σεαυτὸν
        καταβὰς ἀπὸ τοῦ σταυροῦ.
      Ὁμοίως καὶ οἱ ἀρχιερεῖς
        ἐμπαίζοντες πρὸς ἀλλήλους
        μετὰ τῶν γραμματέων ἔλεγον,
      Ἄλλους ἔσωσεν,
        ἑαυτὸν
        οὐ δύναται σῶσαι· [32]
      ὁ Χριστὸς ὁ βασιλεὺς Ἰσραὴλ
        καταβάτω νῦν ἀπὸ τοῦ σταυροῦ,
        ἵνα ἴδωμεν καὶ πιστεύσωμεν.
    καὶ οἱ συνεσταυρωμένοι
      σὺν αὐτῷ
      ὠνείδιζον αὐτόν.

Καὶ γενομένης <u>ὥρας ἕκτης</u>   Β᾽
    σκότος ἐγένετο ἐφ᾽ ὅλην τὴν γῆν
    ἕως ὥρας ἐνάτης. [34]
  καὶ τῇ ἐνάτῃ ὥρᾳ
      ἐβόησεν ὁ Ἰησοῦς
      φωνῇ μεγάλῃ,
    Ελωι ελωι
    λεμα σαβαχθανι;
  ὅ ἐστιν μεθερμηνευόμενον
    Ο θεός μου ὁ θεός μου,
    εἰς τί ἐγκατέλιπές με;
 καί τινες τῶν παρεστηκότων | ἀκούσαντες | ἔλεγον,
    Ἴδε᾽
    Ηλίαν φωνεῖ.
  δραμὼν δέ τις
      καὶ γεμίσας σπόγγον
      ὄξους
    περιθεὶς καλάμῳ
      ἐπότιζεν αὐτόν,
      λέγων,
    Ἄφετε
      ἴδωμεν εἰ ἔρχεται Ἡλίας
      καθελεῖν αὐτόν.
  ὁ δὲ Ἰησοῦς
      ἀφεὶς φωνὴν μεγάλην
      ἐξέπνευσεν.
    Καὶ τὸ καταπέτασμα τοῦ ναοῦ
      ἐσχίσθη εἰς δύο
      ἀπ᾽ ἄνωθεν ἕως κάτω. [39]
    Ἰδὼν δὲ
        ὁ κεντυρίων
        ὁ παρεστηκὼς
      ἐξ ἐναντίας αὐτοῦ
        ὅτι οὕτως ἐξέπνευσεν
        εἶπεν,
      Ἀληθῶς
        οὗτος ὁ ἄνθρωπος
        υἱὸς θεοῦ ἦν.
Ἦσαν δὲ καὶ γυναῖκες
    ἀπὸ μακρόθεν
    θεωροῦσαι,
  ἐν αἷς καὶ
    Μαρία ἡ Μαγδαληνὴ
      καὶ Μαρία
        ἡ Ἰακώβου τοῦ μικροῦ
        καὶ Ἰωσῆτος μήτηρ
      καὶ Σαλώμη, [41]
    αἳ ὅτε ἦν ἐν τῇ Γαλιλαίᾳ

ἠκολούθουν αὐτῷ
    καὶ διηκόνουν αὐτῷ,
καὶ ἄλλαι πολλαὶ
    αἱ συναναβᾶσαι αὐτῷ
    εἰς Ἱεροσόλυμα.

Καὶ ἤδη ὀψίας γενομένης,   A   **B'**
    ἐπεὶ ἦν παρασκευή,
    ὅ ἐστιν προσάββατον, [43]
    ἐλθὼν Ἰωσὴφ
        ὁ ἀπὸ Ἀριμαθαίας
    εὐσχήμων βουλευτής,
    ὃς καὶ αὐτὸς ἦν προσδεχόμενος
        τὴν βασιλείαν τοῦ θεοῦ,
τολμήσας
    εἰσῆλθεν πρὸς τὸν Πιλᾶτον
    καὶ ᾐτήσατο τὸ σῶμα τοῦ Ἰησοῦ. [44]

ὁ δὲ Πιλᾶτος ἐθαύμασεν   B
    εἰ ἤδη τέθνηκεν,
    καὶ προσκαλεσάμενος τὸν κεντυρίωνα
    ἐπηρώτησεν αὐτὸν
    εἰ πάλαι ἀπέθανεν· [45]
    καὶ γνοὺς ἀπὸ τοῦ κεντυρίωνος
    ἐδωρήσατο τὸ πτῶμα τῷ Ἰωσήφ. [46]

καὶ ἀγοράσας σινδόνα   B'
    καθελὼν αὐτὸν
    ἐνείλησεν τῇ σινδόνι
    καὶ ἔθηκεν αὐτὸν ἐν μνημείῳ
        ὃ ἦν λελατομημένον ἐκ πέτρας,
    καὶ προσεκύλισεν λίθον
        ἐπὶ τὴν θύραν
        τοῦ μνημείου. [47]
    ἡ δὲ Μαρία ἡ Μαγδαληνὴ
        καὶ Μαρία ἡ Ἰωσῆτος
    ἐθεώρουν
    ποῦ τέθειται.

And in literal English:

And immediately early,
      preparing a council,
      the chief priests
   with the elders
      and scribes
      and all the Sanhedrin,
   having bound Jesus
      led him away
      and delivered him to Pilate.
And questioned him Pilate,
      'You are the King of the Jews?'
  And he, answering him, says,
      'You say.'
  And accused him
      the chief priests
      many things.
But Pilate again questioned him,
      saying,
      'Do you not answer anything?
  Behold!
      How many things
      they accuse you.'
But Jesus no more answered anything,
      so that Pilate marvelled.

A   **A**

Now at a Feast B
    he released to them one prisoner
    whom they requested.
  And there was one named Barabbas,
    bound with the rebels,
    who in the rebellion had committed murder.
  And going up,
    the crowd began to ask *him to do*
    as he used to do for them.
And Pilate answered them,
    saying,
    'Do you wish
      that I release to you
      the King of the Jews?'
  For he knew
    that it was on account of envy
    that the chief priests had delivered him.
  But the chief priests stirred up the crowd,
    that rather
    he should release Barabbas to them.
And Pilate again answering
    said to them,
    'What then may I do
      to the one you call
      the King of the Jews?'
  And they,
    without hesitation, (See 2.13, 3.1 and 4.1: *palin*)
    cried out,
      'Crucify him!'
  But Pilate said to them,
      'Indeed what evil has he done?'
    And they the more cried out,
      'Crucify him!'

And Pilate,   B'
        resolving
        to satisfy the crowd,
    released to them Barabbas,
    and handed Jesus over,
        having him scourged,
        that he might be crucified.
  And the soldiers led him away
          inside the court,
          which is the Praetorium,
      and they call together all the cohort.
    And they put on him a purple robe
      and place on him a plaited crown of thorns,
      and they began to salute him,
         'Hail!
         King of the Jews!'
    And they struck his head with a reed,
      and spat at him,
      and getting on their knees,
        they worshipped him.
  And when they had mocked him,
      they took the purple robe off him
      and put his garments on him.
    And they lead him out
      to crucify him.
    And they compel one passing by,
      Simon from Cyrene,
        coming from the country,
        father of Alexander and Rufus,
      that he might carry his cross.

And they bring him   A   **B**
      to the place Golgotha,
      which is being interpreted,
            the place of a skull.
And they gave him wine spiced with myrrh,
      which he did not take.
And they crucify him,
      and they divide his garments,
      casting lots for them to determine who got what.

Now it was <u>the third hour</u>.   B
      And they crucified him.
      And was the superscription
            of the accusation
            written above him,
        'The King of the Jews'.
And with him they crucify two robbers,
        one on his right
        and one on his left.
And the ones going by blasphemed him
           shaking their heads
           and saying,
      'Ah!
           The one who was going to destroy the temple
           and rebuild it in three days!
      Save yourself!
           Come down from the cross!'
Likewise also the chief priests
           mocking to each other,
           with the scribes said,
      'Others he saved,
        himself -
        he cannot save!
      The Christ, the King of Israel,
           come down now from the cross
           that we may see and believe!'
And the ones crucified
    with him
    were reproaching him.

And when it was <u>the sixth hour,</u>   B'
        darkness came over all the land,
        until the ninth hour.
And at the ninth hour,/ cried out Jesus / in a loud voice,
        'Eloi, Eloi,
        Lama sabachthani?'
Which is being interpreted,
        'My God. My God.
        Why have you forsaken me?'
And some of the ones standing by,
           hearing,
           began to say,
      'Behold!
      He is calling Elijah.'
And one running,
          having filled a sponge
          with wine vinegar,
       placing it on a reed,
          gave it to him to drink,
          saying,
      'Leave,
         let us see if Elijah comes
         to take him down.'
But Jesus
        letting go a great cry,
        expired.
And the curtain of the temple
       was torn in two
       from top to bottom.
And seeing, / the centurion, / standing by,
       from opposite him,
          that he thus expired,
          he said,
      'Truly,
        this man
        a son of God was.'
And there were also women
      from afar,
      observing,
Among whom also
      Mary Magdalene
        and Mary
           the mother of James the less
           and of Joses,
        and Salome,
      who when he was in Galilee,
        followed him
        and served him,
And many other women
      having come up with him
      to Jerusalem.

And now when evening was coming,   A   **B'**
        since it was Preparation,
        which is the day before the Sabbath,
    Coming Joseph from Arimathea,
        an honourable councillor,
        who also himself was awaiting the kingdom of God,
    taking courage,
        went to Pilate
        and requested the body of Jesus.

And Pilate was surprised   B
        that he was already dead.
    And calling to him the centurion,
        he questioned him
        if he had been dead long.
    And knowing from the centurion,
        he granted the corpse to Joseph.

And having bought a linen cloth,   **B'**
        taking him down,
        he wrapped him in the linen cloth.
    And he laid him in a tomb
        which was hewn out of rock,
        and rolled a stone against the doorway of the tomb.
    And Mary Magdalene
           and Mary the mother of Joses
        observed
        where he was laid.

This presentation of the Day's literary structure demonstrates once more the Markan rhetorical abb' style, which he has employed throughout his Gospel and applied at all the principal and lower levels of literary order. What is different, however, is that some significant verbal details are confined to this Day's telling alone in the Gospel: some, of course, will be due more to the nature of the content (the crucifixion) of the Day's telling than to deliberate planning on Mark's part, but one title and phrase which Mark clearly did deliberately use is his term "King of the Jews", for Jesus. In all the Gospel it is only presented in 15.2, 9, 12, 18 and 26 (in v.32 it is "King of Israel"). As he has shown careful control over his presentations in the first three Series of the Gospel regarding the 'secret of the person of Jesus', and demonstrated the same careful control in dispensing with 'the secret' in his third Series after 10.47,48 (the public and unrebuked affirmation of Jesus' messiahship)[383], it is more logical to conclude that Mark deliberately used this title of Jesus here than that this term was already lodged (solely) in the tradition of the crucifixion, prior to his receiving it.

---

[383]See the discussion so far on the 'secret' and the third Series, page 215.

Up until this Series, the only specific application of the word "King" attaches (improperly) to Herod, in 6.14. I said in my note 35, page 146, that it may have been a deliberate wrong use of the term by Mark in order to set Jesus' kingship as greater. In 11.1-11, Mark begs his audience to interpret his first Day's telling of this Series in the light of Zech. 9.9. He begins this Series (and first sub-Series) with telling us that Jesus is the 'coming King'. In 14.24, in the Day's telling which begins this sub-Series, Days Twenty-six to Twenty-eight, Mark begs his audience to interpret it in the light of Zech. 9.11. Jesus' blood seals the 'kingly covenant'. What has been veiled until now, is spelt out here, in this Day's telling. It is the "King of the Jews" who is crucified.

Another word which is found here only in the Gospel, and only once unlike the phrase above, is located in 15.10, concerning Pilate:

$$\dot{\epsilon}\gamma\dot{\iota}\nu\omega\sigma\kappa\epsilon\nu \ \gamma\grave{\alpha}\rho \ \ddot{o}\tau\iota \ \delta\iota\grave{\alpha} \ \phi\theta\acute{o}\nu o\nu \ \pi\alpha\rho\alpha\delta\epsilon\delta\acute{\omega}\kappa\epsilon\iota\sigma\alpha\nu \ \alpha\mathring{\upsilon}\tau\grave{o}\nu \ o\acute{\iota} \ \dot{\alpha}\rho\chi\iota\epsilon\rho\epsilon\hat{\iota}\varsigma.$$

The word is $\phi\theta\acute{o}\nu o\nu$ meaning "envy", and it is immensely important because it explains why Jesus was crucified.[384]

It is worth first noting that we have already met with the singular use of two words in Mark's Gospel, in the previous Day's telling: in 14.36, $\mathrm{'}A\beta\beta\grave{\alpha} \ \acute{o} \ \pi\alpha\tau\acute{\eta}\rho$, and in 14.24, $\tau\hat{\eta}\varsigma \ \delta\iota\alpha\theta\acute{\eta}\kappa\eta\varsigma$. These terms too are of great importance for understanding Mark's Gospel, which carries in its narrative so much allusion to the Old Covenant which is being replaced by the New. It is surely the case that Mark chooses to make very clear what he has been leading up to all the time. Jesus is truly the Son of God (see also 15.39 of this Day's telling which speaks of 'a son of God'), and his death seals the new covenant.

The same important function applies also, in 15.10, to Mark's use of "envy". Hagedorn and Neyrey[385] demonstrate emphatically in their paper that they have been right to develop a full 'anatomy of envy' "to indicate how pervasive and culturally plausible envy is in a document of conflict such as Mark's Gospel". They, and we should, consider Jesus' 'growing fame and reputation' for its attraction of envy and 'the growing attacks on Jesus'.[386] Here, in a single use of the word, Mark makes clear both the *source* of the conflict he has been telling about throughout his narrative, *and its outcome*. As a result of envy, Jesus is crucified.

In regard to the 'arrangement' of Mark's presentation, it has been suggested that Ps. 22 has influenced in particular the course of the telling of 15.22-16.8 (according to literary-structural analysis, 15.22-47 covers the final two Parts of this Day's telling and 16.1-8 the telling of the final Day of Mark's narrative). It may well be the case. Marcus[387] sees the parallels between the psalm and 15.20b-16.7:

	Psalm 22:	Mark:
Suffering	vv.1-21	15.20b-37
Worship of Gentiles	v.27	15.39
Kingdom of God	v.28	15.43
----------------	--------------	------------
Resurrection	v.29	16.6
Proclamation to God's people	vv.30,31	16.7

---

[384] Anselm C. Hagedorn and Jerome H. Neyrey, " 'It was out of envy that they handed Jesus over' (Mark 15.10): The Anatomy of Envy and the Gospel of Mark", *JSNT* 69, (1998), pp.15-56.

[385] Hagedorn and Neyrey, "It was out of envy...", p.56.

[386] Additionally, Hagedorn and Neyrey would have us focus on 'envy which begins at home (Jesus' rejection at Nazareth)', 'the disciples' envy of a rival exorcist', 'envy among the disciples', 'Jesus' teaching on shunning honour and avoiding envy', 'secrecy and avoiding envy', 'refusing compliments', and 'the evil eye (of 7.21)'. "It was out of envy...", pp.47-54.

[387] Marcus, *The Way of the Lord...*, p.182.

The comparison of 15.43 and v.28 is an interesting one, given the nature of this Day's unique, but six times repeated, disclosure of the person of Jesus. The verse of the Psalm can be read: "The Lord is King, and he rules the nations" (from the Good News Bible, which is bolder than most translations). It may have influenced Mark in his choice of this Day's title for Jesus, and the teaching that pertains to it, therefore, on the person of Jesus. Given that v.29 of the psalm resonates with resurrection notices, it may well be that Mark intended the interpretation to be this, that whilst they put to death in the most awful way possible *their* Lord and King, he was raised as the Lord and King of *all nations*. It is an interpretation that squares well with indicators of this in the Series (see 11.17, 13.27, 14.9), and it looks like another final sub-Series' clarification of the kind that we have been seeing above.

Here, we may restart a discussion on the significant correspondences between this Day and its parallel Day in this Series, Day Twenty-three. We are comparing days 'two' of the three-day sub-Series which begin and end this final Series. For the main correspondence, we have what was hoped for in Day Twenty-three (specifically 11.18) and what is now the fulfilling of the desires of Old Israel's leaders. From my earlier table, we have:

Day two	(Twenty-three):	ἐζήτουν πῶς αὐτόν ἀπολέσωσιν	11.18[388]
Day six	(Twenty-seven):	καὶ ἐσταύρωσαν αὐτόν.	15.25
		Καὶ τὸ καταπέτασμα τοῦ ναοῦ ἐσχίσθη εἰς δύο ἀπ' ἄνωθεν ἕως κάτω	15.38

Under Day Twenty-three, we discussed the possibility that Mark may have deliberately paralleled Old and New sacrificial ways, of temple clearing and Jesus' death. Here in this Day's telling, we do find the clearest possible connection, in 15.38, regarding the tearing of the temple curtain right at the moment of Jesus' death. In Day Twenty-three, 12.1-8, we read the parabolic equivalent to the actual event of Jesus' death. Days two and six of this Series do connect significantly, just as under Day Twenty-six's examination we saw how Days one and five of this Series do. These common themes and details, and those like them, demonstrate not only the balance Mark creates between his first and last sub-Series of this Series, but also how, by his balance of presentations, they explain each other.

We may also see how Days Twenty-six and Twenty-seven connect, that is days five and six of this Series. In 14.22-25, we read about Jesus' institution of the Lord's Supper, and in 14.24a, we read about the particularly significant identification of his blood with the (Kingly) "covenant" of Zechariah's prophecy, Zech. 9.11. His death of Day Twenty-seven is the shedding of his blood of the covenant "for many", 14.24b. We noted too how Mark makes the further verbal link between Jesus and the temple, on destroying the temple and rebuilding it in three days, 14.58 and 15.29. The prophecy of 14.27 is fulfilled on the same day, Day Twenty-six, in 15.40, but the absence of male disciples is confirmed in Day Twenty-seven, in 15.40,41. These common themes and details, and those like them, establish these Days as the first and second of the final threesome.

Under the examination of Day Twenty-five, 14.1-11, we saw how this middle day of the Series looked both backwards and forwards. In 14.8, Jesus is anointed for burial. In the telling of Day Twenty-seven, in 15.42ff., Jesus' body is placed in a tomb. In 14.10,11 Judas plots to betray Jesus; in Day Twenty-six, Jesus addresses the issue of betrayal, 14.18, and later in the telling Judas betrays Jesus, 14.43-46.

---

[388]Stephen H. Smith, "The Literary Structure of Mark 11.1-12.40", *NT* 31 (1989), pp.104-124: he sees the connection between 11.18 and 12.12, but because of the limits of his study, 11.1-12.40, he fails to see the others of our listing, and hence their structural significance. He further identifies the three days, but in the case of the third day (like Dewey, *Markan Public Debate...*, p.152) he wrongly sees it as ending at 12.44. Unless section limits are well set at first, rhetorical analysis can lead, and does lead, to all manner of views.

The final Day of Mark's telling in his Gospel narrative, Day Twenty-eight, has its correspondences with Day Twenty-six. We observed above, the duality of 14.28 and 16.7; after he is raised, Jesus will go before the disciples into Galilee. Below, we will see a likely further correspondence, regarding "the young man" of 14.51,52. That Day Twenty-eight is the third day of the final threesome is established by the correspondence between the last pericope of the second day and the third day's three parts. In the opening parts of both, we read, in 15.42, about the onset of the "Sabbath" with the evening, and in 16.1 about the passing of the "Sabbath". In the third part of the one, in 15.46,47 we read about the laying of Jesus' body in the tomb, the stone that was rolled against its door, and the women who saw where he was laid. In the second part of the other, we read, in 16.2, about the women at the tomb, in 16.3,4 about the stone that was already rolled away from the door, and in 16.5,6, about the place where Jesus had been laid. In the third part of the last Day's telling, in 16.8, the women flee from the tomb.

Between days one and two of the sub-Series, we notice the connection between the lateness of the hour as the telling of the first Day ends, and the early beginning of the second Day. The final sub-Series is a threesome of Days best expressed again as in all the Gospel's sub-Series by ABB': where A is the first Day which is introductory; Jesus is going to die; but he will be raised; where B is the second Day, the first development; Jesus dies and is buried; and where B' is the third Day, the second and concluding development; the tomb is empty because Jesus is risen.

Day Twenty-eight: 16.1-8:

This Day's telling is seen as the last of the Gospel narrative of "Days". Many commentators include this resurrection announcement within the Passion narrative section; some separate it[389]. But whether they think it is included or excluded from the Passion account, most see it as concluding Mark's Gospel.

Given my literary-structural analysis, and the evidence for Mark's rhetorical scheme for his Gospel based on Days and Series of Days, 16.1-8 may be judged: 1) as the third Day of his final threesome of days, Jesus' Passion and Resurrection[390] (14.12-16.8, Days Twenty-six, Twenty-seven and Twenty-eight); and 2) as his seventh Day of a seven-day presentation of "Jesus' Jerusalem Days", his fourth and last Series. What particularly confirms this is that Mark's *first* Series ends on its last Day with a 'raising of the dead' (see Day Seven, 5.21-43). Nowhere else in the Gospel is such to be found. The outer two Series of the Gospel conclude on the same story-lines, just as the inner two Series conclude on the same story lines (on healings of blind people).

V.1 is introductory, and v.2 begins the Day's account with which Mark ends his Gospel Narrative on a note of climax. It is not without literary and theological significance that Mark presents this episode "very early on *the first day of the week... as the sun rose*"[391]. This last Day's telling, in the clearest possible way (compare all the other Days of his presentation) begins with the dawn of a new day and a new week[392] (a new age). It will have to be compared to the opening Day in Capernaum, which sees the sun setting on the old Sabbath, but more of that later.

Here, the literary structure of Day Twenty-eight is presented, first in Greek and then in literal English:

---

[389]See my table of my four selected commentators, in my Summary of this Series which follows this presentation of Day Twenty-eight.
[390]Compare Matthew who includes a Saturday account (Mt.27.62-66).
[391]For a discussion of this, see under Day One, page 43.
[392]Compare the Priestly story of creation, Gen. 1.1-2.4a: *creation* begins on the first day of the week.

Καὶ διαγενομένου τοῦ σαββάτου   A
    Μαρία ἡ Μαγδαληνὴ
        καὶ Μαρία ἡ τοῦ Ἰακώβου
        καὶ Σαλώμη
    ἠγόρασαν ἀρώματα
      ἵνα ἐλθοῦσαι
      ἀλείψωσιν αὐτόν. [2]

καὶ λίαν πρωῒ τῇ μιᾷ τῶν σαββάτων   B
        ἔρχονται ἐπὶ τὸ μνημεῖον
        <u>ἀνατείλαντος τοῦ ἡλίου</u>. [3]   (cf. 1.32, for significance)
      καὶ ἔλεγον πρὸς ἑαυτάς,
        Τίς ἀποκυλίσει ἡμῖν
        τὸν λίθον ἐκ τῆς θύρας τοῦ μνημείου;
      καὶ ἀναβλέψασαι
        θεωροῦσιν ὅτι ἀποκεκύλισται ὁ λίθος,
        ἦν γὰρ μέγας σφόδρα. [5]
    καὶ εἰσελθοῦσαι εἰς τὸ μνημεῖον
      εἶδον νεανίσκον
        καθήμενον ἐν τοῖς δεξιοῖς
        περιβεβλημένον στολὴν λευκήν,
      καὶ <u>ἐξεθαμβήθησαν</u>.
  ὁ δὲ λέγει αὐταῖς,
      <u>Μὴ ἐκθαμβεῖσθε·</u>
    Ἰησοῦν ζητεῖτε
      τὸν Ναζαρηνὸν
      τὸν ἐσταυρωμένον·
    ἠγέρθη,
      οὐκ ἔστιν ὧδε·
    ἴδε
      ὁ τόπος
      ὅπου ἔθηκαν αὐτόν. [7]
    ἀλλὰ ὑπάγετε
      εἴπατε τοῖς μαθηταῖς αὐτοῦ καὶ τῷ Πέτρῳ
      ὅτι Προάγει ὑμᾶς εἰς τὴν Γαλιλαίαν·
        ἐκεῖ αὐτὸν ὄψεσθε,
        καθὼς εἶπεν ὑμῖν.

καὶ ἐξελθοῦσαι   B'
    ἔφυγον
    ἀπὸ τοῦ μνημείου,
  εἶχεν γὰρ αὐτὰς
    τρόμος
    καὶ ἔκστασις·
  καὶ οὐδενὶ
    οὐδὲν εἶπαν,
    ἐφοβοῦντο γάρ.

And when the Sabbath was past,   A
    Mary Magdalene
        and Mary, the mother of James,
        and Salome
    bought spices,
        that coming,
        they might anoint him.

And very early on the first day of the week,   B
        they come <u>to the tomb</u>,
        as the sun was rising.
      And they were saying to themselves,
        'Who will roll away the stone for us
          from the doorway of the tomb?'
      And looking up,
        they saw that the stone had been rolled back,
        for it was exceedingly great.
    And entering into the tomb,
      they saw a young man,
        sitting on the right,
        clothed in a white robe,
      and they were <u>greatly astonished</u>.
    And he says to them,
        'Do not be <u>greatly astonished</u>.
      You seek Jesus
          the Nazarene,
          the crucified.
        He has been raised.
        He is not here:
          behold the place
          where they laid him.
      But go!
        Tell his disciples and Peter,
        "He goes before you into Galilee:
          there you will see him,
          as he told you."'

And going forth,   B'
      they fled
      <u>from the tomb</u>,
    for they were overcome
      with trembling
      and bewilderment
    and no one
      anything they told,
      for they were afraid.

Under the discussion of Day Twenty-seven, I drew attention to one connection that was to be made between the first and last Days of this last sub-Series, the "reminder" for the disciples (and the reader/listeners) of what Jesus had said (14.28), given at the tomb by the mysterious νεανίσκος to the women to relay (16.7). The νεανίσκος of 14.51,52 may be judged to be one and the same. That he was wearing a σινδόνα which he had to leave behind, and that Jesus' body was placed in one (15.46, in the Day's telling, prior to this) which he left behind does suggest some kind of a correspondence here. The 'young man' who was present at the tomb, significantly (to Mark, at least[393]) had been there at Jesus' arrest, though he was helpless to change the course of events over which Jesus had prayed, 14.35,36. For this reason, I judge Mark to have included this as a loving sign of God's reluctance to leave his Son to this fate.

Part A is introductory, in its telling what the women did when the Sabbath was over. It is a classically Markan rhetorical lead into a part B which tells what they find at 'the tomb'. Part B' well links with Part B in a classically Markan way again, in the manner of their leaving 'the tomb'. (The last imperfect of the gospel narrative is clearly of continuous action.)[394]

A Summary of the Fourth Series of Seven Days:

The Seven Days are presented by Mark as two sub-Series of threesomes of Days (to the 'arrangement' of ABB') around a central, fourth Day of the Series, to form another overall Series' ABA' scheme, where A and A' represent the outer sub-Series around the middle Day B which behaves as a fulcrum, pivot or turning point. All four Series, therefore, in terms of their arrangement of Days are constructed in the same way.

The Title to the Series, in the manner of the first three, with a view to brevity, can be stated simply as, "Jesus' Jerusalem Days: His Passion and Resurrection".

The first sub-Series of three Days are consecutive whereby: in the first, which is introductory, Jesus enters Jerusalem and the temple; in the second, he 'clears' the temple; and in the third, inside the temple, he faces various challenges, and outside the temple, he speaks of its coming destruction and the events that will occur at the last. The 'hinge', middle Day of the Series relates two particular turning points, the plotting for Jesus' death, in which a disciple shares a part in the plotting, and the anointing of Jesus for his burial by a woman who will be remembered, "wherever the Gospel is proclaimed in all the world". The balancing sub-Series of three days relates on the first Day, the Day the Passover is sacrificed, the passover meal which Jesus shares with his disciples, and his betrayal, arrest and trial before the Sanhedrin (Jesus will die, but he will be raised); the second tells of his trial before Pilate, his presentation to the people, his death by crucifixion, and his burial: and the third reports that he is risen from the tomb.

In terms of rhetorical conventions, we observed on page 223 the *inclusio* of 'the Mount of Olives' in the first sub-Series. Correspondences and details were established throughout the three day analyses: for a summary, see pages 225,226. The second sub-Series was established by correspondences of theme and detail: see in particular pages 295,296. The middle Day's rhetorical function was discussed on pages 256-259. A discussion on a possible Series' seven-day chiasm is found on page 227: such an alternative summary of Mark's scheme was rejected principally because Days one and five of the Series (Days Twenty-two and Twenth-six) were emphatically constructed each with the other in mind, as introductory Days to new sub-Series. On pages 255 and 274, we noted the major correspondences between Days three and five of the Series. Each side of the central Day their common details help

---

[393]Matthew and Luke omit Mk. 14.51,52.
[394]For a discussion of this Day and its relationship to the Passion and the longer ending, see Chapter Seven.

smooth the transition, after the manner of ancient rhetoric, from the first to the second sub-Series.

The structural scheme of this Series of seven Days is indeed best described by ABA', but here, we pick up the force of the impressive clarifications of the second sub-Series of three days, particularly of Days Twenty-six and Twenty-seven. The final Day, Day Twenty-eight, is, nevertheless, the crowning of the three. It was out of envy that the Old Covenant leaders handed Jesus over to the Gentiles to put him to death. Jesus died both as "Son of God" and "King of the Jews". With his death and resurrection (which affirmed him Lord and King of all nations) God sealed a New Covenant with the world.

We set these summaries against those of the first sub-Series. Jerusalem welcomes *its* Messiah. The fig tree episodes (which spelt judgement for Old Israel and its leadership) coupled with the temple clearing (of the Old Covenant sacrificial means of being made right with God), and the answers Jesus gave to the challenges put to him, which Mark follows with Jesus' telling of the temple's destruction, all spelt the end of Judaism.

The middle day's 'future' anticipation is the preaching of the Gospel throughout the world, while Jews plot against Jesus.

The dynamic of this, the last Series is represented by ABA', where:

A	communicates what will be the demise of the Old Covenant;
B	communicates the future preaching of the Gospel in the 'world', against the then plotting of the Jews; and
A'	communicates the events which establish the New Covenant.

In terms of Aristotelian Greek Tragedy: A is the 'complication'; B is the 'turning point'; and A' is the 'dénouement'. It reflects the rhetorical scheme of the First Series (pages 112-113). For further discussion on the comparison with Series One, see the end of this Chapter.

At this juncture, we usefully compare the limits of the Series' three parts (A,B,A') with those of the 'sections' of the commentators I have chosen to follow:

	A	B		A'	
From the above	11.1-13.37	14.1-11		14.12-16.8	
Taylor[395]	11.1-13.37			14.1-16.8	
Nineham[396]	11.1-12.44	13		14.1-15.47	16.1-8
Schweizer[397]	11.1-13.37			14.1-16.8	
Hooker[398]	11.1-13.37			14.1-15.47	16.1-8

Clearly, the delimiting of the first sub-Series of three consecutive Days coincides with all of them for its beginning, and with all but Nineham's at its close. My separation of the middle Day from 14.12-16.8 is because it behaves as a fulcrum or pivot to the whole Series' presentation. It appears that my reading is very different from the others, yet in 14.1-11, for all of us, the Passion narrative is introduced. For me, however, 14.1-11 also looks back to two Days' tellings of conflict and particularly the failure of the leaders of Old Israel to "trap" Jesus "in his words", which leads to the necessity of their plotting.[399] What I discern to be Mark's structure, therefore, is not so very different at this level of literary order from theirs.

---

[395]Taylor, *The Gospel...*, pp.110,111,450-610.
[396]Nineham, *Saint Mark*, pp.287-435,437-448.
[397]Schweizer, *The Good News...*, pp.226-363.
[398]Hooker, *The Gospel...*, pp.28-29, 255-387.
[399]See under Day Twenty-five for a fuller discussion.

It remains only to gather up the information of the introductory pieces of the seven Days' tellings of this Series to summarise the number of days which Mark's presentation covers in all, of the Jerusalem stage of Jesus' mission. Clearly, the three Days of the first sub-Series are consecutive *in his telling*. At the beginning of Day four (14.1), the central Day in the Series, his introductory information is different in form and style. It requires interpreting by recourse to 14.49, because Jesus says at his arrest, "Daily I was with you in the temple teaching and you did not seize me". We observe that the first sub-Series covers three days of Jesus' appearances in the temple, but only the second and the third qualify as days of his "teaching" there. The question is now: do these two Days constitute "daily"? As we understand the term today, they clearly do not. The story-line of this Series and the presentation of the three consecutive days require that we interpret that Jesus spent other days teaching in the temple which Mark has not reported. It follows that Day Twenty-four (11.20-13.37) is not necessarily representative of the last day that Jesus was teaching in the temple. Days likely pass, therefore, between the telling of days three and four of this Series.

Days Twenty-five (14.1-11), Twenty-six (14.12-72) and Twenty-seven (15.1-47) are clearly consecutive (see my discussions of the introductory pieces of these Days). On the activities of the Saturday following the Friday of Jesus' crucifixion, Mark simply summarises what the women do after the passing of the sabbath (at sunset). He does this in his introduction to Day Twenty-eight (16.1-8, see 16.1). We can be certain, therefore, that the Days' tellings of Twenty-seven and Twenty-eight cover three, inclusive of the Friday, the Saturday and the Sunday (refer also: 8.31, 9.31, 10.34).

To the seven Days of Mark's telling, therefore, we have only to add two or three days between the third and the fourth Days, and a day between the sixth and the seventh Days of his telling. The Jerusalem stage of Jesus' mission, which Mark told in just seven Days, may be judged to be about ten or eleven days in all. We observe that this Series which is by far the longest (in verses) in Mark's telling is, nevertheless, representative of the shortest stage in Mark's presentation of Jesus' mission.

A Tabular Summary of the literary-structure of the Fourth Seven Days:

DAYS: number identified	1	2	3	4	5	6	7
number identified in Gospel	22	23	24	25	26	27	28
chapters and verses	11.1-11	11.12-19	11.20-13.37	14.1-11	14.12-72	15.1-47	16.1-8
SERIES' STRUCTURE	A	A	A	B	A'	A'	A'
DAYS: in literary-terms, in series	A	B	B'	A	B	B'	
DAYS' sections	A	A	A B B'	A	A B B'	A B B'	A
DAYS' sectional sub-divisions	A B B'	A B B'	A B B' A B B' A B B'	A B B'	A B B' A B B' A B B'	A B B' A B B' A B B'	A B B'
DAYS' number of verses	11	8	94	11	61	46	8
SUB-SERIES' number of verses		113				115	
SERIES' number of verses				239			

Addendum to the analysis of 'The Fourth Seven Days':

We may consider from the table the range of verses of Mark's Day reports. The shortest Days in the telling are Days Twenty-three (11.2-19) and Twenty-eight (16.1-8) with 8 verses each. The longest Day, in the telling, of the Series (and of the Gospel) is Day Twenty-four (11.20-13.37) with 94 verses. I identify here a factor of difference of just less than 12. We further note that this is the largest of all the Series. Issues are raised. I think it can be said that Mark was much more interested in creating structural balance to his Series and Days than he was in achieving a balance by size (literally, size does not matter). But given that this Series is by far the largest in the Gospel, we have to ask, why? Is it because Mark had much more tradition to-hand on theses subjects than elsewhere (as from Paul's letters, or from the Old Testament scriptures, or from oral testimony, or from all of them)? The question is posed, at least.

Regarding other matters, it can be said that many of the propositions for the examination of the text of 11.1 to 16.8 were rehearsed in the presentations of the analyses of the first three Series. It is only in the telling of this Series, however, that Mark employs a number of rhetorical devices to signal the beginnings of his new Days' tellings. These are found at 11.12, 11.20, 14.1,12, 15.1 and 16.1,2:

At 11.12		*Καὶ τῇ ἐπαύριον*
11.20		*Καὶ παραπορευόμενοι πρωι*
14.1		*Ἦν δὲ τὸ πάσχα καὶ τὰ ἄζυμα μετὰ δύο ἡμέρας.*
14.12		*Καὶ τῇ πρώτῃ ἡμέρᾳ τῶν ἀζύμων, ὅτε τὸ πάσχα ἔθυον,*
15.1		*Καὶ εὐθὺς πρωῒ*
16.1-8	A	*Καὶ διαγενομένου τοῦ σαββάτου....*
	B	*καὶ λίαν πρωῒ τῇ μιᾷ τῶν σαββάτων ἔρχονται ἐπὶ τὸ μνημεῖον*
	B'	*καὶ ἐξελθοῦσαι ἔφυγον ἀπὸ τοῦ μνημείου*

All are discussed under the Days they begin, or referenced there if they were discussed under other Days because they added to the discussion of other Day beginnings. In every other way, historical presents and many imperfects, introductory presentations to sections (parts, sub-parts, and so on), correspondences between words (phrases and constructions) and thematic correspondences which are intra- and inter-sub-Series (in terms of their Days, Day-Parts, parts and so on), all serve again in combination to disclose Mark's compositional method and style.

A Comparison of the First and Fourth Series of Seven Days:

Now we have completed our separate examination of the literary-structure of the last Series of the Gospel, we can determine what if any relationship Mark deemed it to share with the first Series. Their titles again are: Series One: "Jesus' first Days of Mission, confined to Galilee and the Region of its Sea"; and Series Four: "Jesus' Jerusalem Days: His Passion and Resurrection".

Under the examination of Days Seven and Twenty-eight we paid attention to the fact that these alone in the Gospel tell stories about the raising of the dead. They are the concluding Days of the first and last Series. Days One and Twenty-two, which begin the Series exhibit correspondence too, in 1.21 and 11.11: for entry into a town, and into the synagogue/temple. We have noted above that the middle Days of the two series (Days Four and Twenty-five) correspond for the plottings against Jesus (3.6; 14.1,2; vv.10,11). In the fifth Days of each (Days Five and Twenty-six), Judas Iscariot is introduced (emphatically) as the 'betrayer' (in 3.19) and he 'betrays' Jesus (in 14.43ff.). The third days of both Series (Days Three and Twenty-four) raise the issue of Jesus' authority, by scribes (in 2.6f.) and answered by Jesus (in 2.8-10); and by chief priests, scribes and elders (in 11.27,28), though this time Jesus does not have to answer (11.29-33).

An impressive number of correspondences can be identified between the two Series, but then again we might expect such because they cover between them 410 verses of the 641 of the Gospel narrative (nearly two-thirds of the material). What is particularly impressive, however, is the way in which many of the common themes and details correspond *in order*, just like those we have mentioned already above. In 1951, Farrer saw this.[400]

He discerned a steady cyclic development in Mark's Gospel, and judged the structure of the Gospel to be:

---

[400]Austin M. Farrer, *A Study...*

1.1-6.56		Two double cycles, which he called, "Little Gospel"	
		1.1-2.12; 2.13-3.12 / 3.13-6.6; 6.7-6.56	
7.1-9.1		One double cycle: "Continuation of Little Gospel"	
		7.1-37; 8.1-26 (8.27-9.1)	
9.2-16.8		Two double cycles: "Fulfilment of Little Gospel"	
		9.2-10.31; 10.32-13.2 / 13.3-14.31; 14.32-16.8.	

The passage 8.27-9.1 is set in parenthesis because, rather oddly (for all his painstaking efforts) he was not able to place it with any sense of certainty. What he was assured of, however, was that the book is a unity; that it is composed in series and 'cycles'; that the whole scheme comprises a chiasm; and that, whatever his sources, Mark dominated them. The literary-structural analysis I have been doing supports these statements. Farrer likewise attempted a literary-analysis, but his approach differs from mine in that the object of his study was to follow "the symbolical and interpretative element in the Gospel to the farthest point"[401]. My aim has been only to identify Mark's signifiers of his Gospel plan and of his structures at every level of his literary presentation. The real point of difference between Farrer's results and mine stems from the fact that he identified healing miracles as the prime indicator of Markan ordering whereas I identify the importance of Days.

What is supportive of my analysis (and my view, therefore, that Mark created his first and last Series of the Gospel in parallel) is the number of correspondences which Farrer sees follow the same order, between 1.21 to 5.43[402] and 11.1-16.8 which are the limits of the outer two Series set by literary-structural analysis. Below, I list his observations[403]:

2.23-3.6	synagogue, David... destroy him crisis in the synagogue	11.1-19	temple, David destroy him crisis in the temple
3.1	withered	11.20	withered
3.6	Pharisees and Herodians	12.12,13	Pharisees and Herodians
3.7-12	left synagogue ascended mountain initiated disciples	13.1-3	left temple ascended Mount of Olives with the twelve
3.22-26	false prophets/kingdom	13.5-8	false prophets/Christs/kingdom
3.28-30	the Holy Spirit	13.9-11	the Holy Spirit
3.31-35	mother and brothers... dissociation	13.12,13	brother, father, child, parents... dislocation
4.1-20	the sower/endurance	13.13-20	endurance
4.26-29	harvest	13.24-27	harvest
4.35-41	sleeping/wake	13.32-37	sleep/watch/wake
5.25-34	woman who touched Christ	14.3-9	woman who anointed Christ
5.21-43	Jairus' daughter's resurrection	16.1-8	Jesus' resurrection

---

[401]Farrer, *A Study...*, p.10.

[402]What is particularly contradictory about Farrer's approach is that he sees the correspondences up to and between 5.21-43 and 16.1-8 but continues with an attempt to complete the first series at 6.56 (knowing there are no more parallels) on the basis of completing two double cycles.

[403]I summarise them from Farrer, *A Study...*, pp.159-168.

We can identify twelve correspondences of references (approximately twenty verbal/thematic correspondences) which are in order, verse to verse, from his study. We may observe that parallels found in 3.7-4.41, Day Five, lie diagonally opposite in Mark's scheme those which are found in 13.1-37, Day Twenty-four which is Day three of its Series. One parallel only lies in *Day to Day* order: it is 5.21-43 and 16.1-8. We can add to this those that have been mentioned in the analyses of Chapter 3 and this chapter. In day to day order (Series One and Series Four):

1.21	synagogue	11.11	temple
2.5-10	forgive	11.25,26	forgive
2.6-10	authority/reasoning	11.27-33	authority/reasoning
3.6	a plot against Jesus	14.1,10,11	a plot against Jesus
3.19	Judas Iscariot: betrayer	14.43ff.	Judas Iscariot: betrayal
3.29	liable	14.64	liable
4.35-41	sleeping/wake	14.32-42	sleep/watch/(wake)
5.1-20	Jesus' victory over great evil	15.1-16.8	(Jesus' victory over great evil)
5.20	all marvelled at Jesus	15.5,44	Pilate marvelled.

These are found in Days one, three, four, five, six and seven of both Series. Other correspondences which are not in day to day order include:

1.40	leper	14.3	Simon, the leper
2.7[1]	blasphemy	14.64[2]	blasphemy
2.19,20[1]	the bridegroom taken	14.46-15.47[2]	Jesus' arrest...
2.22[1]	wine	14.25[2]	vine
3.28,4.12[3]	forgive	11.25,26[4]	forgive
3.23,4.2-34[3]	teaching crowd in parables	12.1,12[4]	teaching crowd in parables
	explaining to disciples	13.3,28[4]	explaining to disciples
3.28-30[3]	the Holy Spirit	12.36[4]	the Holy Spirit
5.20	all marvelled at Jesus	12.17	they marvelled at Jesus.

Those that are denoted [1], however, occur in the last Day of the Series' first sub-Series while those that are denoted [2] (their parallels) occur in the first Day of the second sub-Series.

Those that are denoted [3] occur in the first Day of the second sub-Series, and those that are denoted [4] (their parallels) occur in the last Day of the first sub-Series.

That is they *are* ordered: they correspond cross-diagonally opposite each other around the central Days of the Series. This can hardly be a coincidence. With certainty, we may say that Mark deliberately wrote these connections into his narrative scheme in this way. With certainty too, we may say that he built his skeletal plan and matrix with seven Days across the page and four Series down the page. In Chapter 8, we will view this feature.

The number of references of common material has increased to about thirty, and the verbal and thematic details to approximately forty. Ten of these references demonstrate sequence, Day to Day (Series to Series). Sixteen of these hold relationship in diagonal pairings around the central Days. Clearly, Mark has balanced some of his material vertically Day to Day, and some diagonally Day to Day, between these Series. He has balanced sub-Series' material vertically too (that is the contents of the first sub-Series of both Series have their correspondence, likewise the second sub-Series of both Series). For a first sub-Series' example of one of these consider references to Jesus' "authority": 1.22,27, 2.10, against which compare 11.28,28,29,33. In regard to the middle Days and the last sub-Series, we can compare usefully the ways in which the two Series crescendo and climax.

After the middle Day's disclosure of a threat to Jesus' life, in the first Series, in the concluding sub-Series, we read firstly how all "Old Israel" gathers to Jesus who at that time lays down the foundations for a "New Israel". In the course of these Days he demonstrates great power and authority, stilling a raging storm, 'doing battle' with and (amazingly) succeeding over a whole 'legion' of evil spirits, healing an 'incurable' and showing himself to be a victor where death is concerned. The same crescendo and climax are seen in the turning point and latter half of the Fourth Series. After Jesus is anointed for burial, and one of his own has plotted with the leaders of "Old Israel" to betray him, he lays down the foundations of the "New Israel" (in the last supper, Gethsemane, through his capture and trial before the sanhedrin); on the Day of his death he 'does battle' with evil; and, at the last, he is victorious over death. Both Series conclude in ways that first-time listeners to the Gospel, with experience of first century rhetorical method, would have "marvelled". Using Farrer's terms, we may say that 11.1-16.8 'fulfils' 1.21-5.43.

Again, as for Series Two and Three, for suggesting a *formal* relationship, there is the literary-structural argument in the sense that these two outer series comprise significantly more verses than the middle two. They are 171 verses and 239 verses respectively. (Compare 119 and 112 verses for the two middle Series in turn.) There is also the rhetorical argument that the two Series exhibit similar interpretations of a 'complication', a 'turning point' and a 'dénouement'. In both Series the 'complication' is the clash between the 'old' and the 'new'; the 'turning point' includes plottings; and in the 'dénouement' is the resolution, the 'old' is going, the 'new' is come. We might consider, therefore, another kind of thematic summary, still more stimulating:

First sub-Series:	Turning point:	Second sub-Series:
Jews and the Old Covenant	Jews/Gentiles	the New Covenant and Gentiles

It is the case that this clearly reflects the last Series of the Gospel, but does it reflect the first?

The first sub-Series of the First Series establishes the beginnings of Jesus' mission in Jewish territory, to Jews, and raises immediately, on the first Day, Old Covenant leadership inadequacies (1.21,22). It ends in demonstrating that Jesus is replacing the Old Covenant means of being made right with God (2.5-7,10); Jesus will die (2.20); and the Old Covenant will be no more (2.21,22). The turning point concludes and climaxes with leaders under the Old Covenant (Pharisees) and leaders under the domination of Rome (Herodians) plotting together to kill Jesus (3.6). Mark is telling us that both Jews and Gentiles would be responsible for Jesus' death. The second sub-Series begins with Jesus' choosing a New Covenant leadership from the massive and totally Jewish assembly (3.7-19). Jesus' mission proceeds to Gentile country, where he shows himself powerful enough to defeat the world's evil. It ends in Jewish territory again, where Jesus shows himself to be victorious over death.

My summary thematic presentation *is* reflective of Mark's own presentational approach, for both of the outer two Series of his Gospel narrative. This immediately raises the question, "Do the central Series reduce thematically in the same way?" We re-read the literary-structural analyses of my Chapters 4 and 5.

In Series Two, the first sub-Series tells of events in Jewish territory, and its second Day records an open-air 'banquet' for Jews. The turning point is set in Gentile/Jewish territory and displays a Jewish/Gentile issue. The second sub-Series is set in Gentile territory for its first two days, but ends in Jewish territory on the third. The second Day reports an open-air 'banquet' for Gentiles. It is clearly the case that Mark has employed this same scheme in Series Two. (One Series remains to be judged.)

In Series Three, the first sub-Series may be said to be set in Jewish/Gentile territory, but it clearly associates Jesus with the Jews: in the first Day's telling, he is "the Christ"; and in the second Day's telling he is the one who fulfils Jewish end-time expectations. Mark sets the middle Day and turning point of his Series in ambiguous territory, apparently deliberately (10.1). It suggests both Jewish ("Judea") and Gentile ("beyond the Jordan": the Decapolis?/ Gerasene?) territories. And the Day's telling raises an issue of tension between Jews and Gentiles which Jesus addresses with reference to the "beginning of creation". The second sub-Series begins in the same territory as that of the middle Day's telling. Only at the second sub-Series' close is it clearly based in Jewish territory (compare the last Day of the first Series). In the second Day's telling of this second sub-Series the word "Gentiles" features significantly (this Day's detailed disclosures of Jesus' suffering at the hands of the Gentiles, we may note, are fulfilled on the parallel day in the final Series). This Series also follows the same plan.

In Chapter Eight, we will be able to gather up the results of all these analyses, and see the full 'matrix' of the Gospel which Mark devised before he wrote a single word of his Gospel. Here, for the first time, we can at least summarise the primary structure of the Gospel's narrative. The two outer Series are set in parallel, around two middle Series which parallel. Mark's overall scheme for 1.21-16.8, therefore, can be described as a chiasm: ABB'A', where:

A	represents	Series One;
B		Series Two;
B'		Series Three;
and A'		Series Four.

The analysis of the text of 1.1-16.8 is now complete, but for summary presentations. Mark's Prologue and Gospel Narrative are defined. A rigorous literary-structural analysis has been undertaken, and that analysis has been informed and interpreted both by the rules of ancient rhetoric in general, and by what has been discovered of Mark's use of such rhetorical conventions in particular.

Now we must give consideration to the fact that Greco-Roman Literature, the Aristotelian Greek Tragedy Play, and much Old Testament writing, all end with 'Epilogues'[404]. Rhetorical considerations require that we must go this one step further. 16.1-8 is no 'Epilogue' in ancient rhetorical terms. It has not the characteristics of an 'Epilogue'. 16.1-8 is fully integral with Mark's narrative; it is the seventh Day's telling of the last of four Series of seven Days. After all that has been discovered in 1.1-16.8, which accords with the rules of ancient rhetoric, it is inconceivable that Mark cheated rhetorical convention and his audience's expectations at the last by not producing an 'Epilogue'!

We can entertain two possible approaches: 1) we could assume that it is lost and try to create one ourselves, which would reflect his Prologue and complete his Gospel's presentation in the manner he suggests in his Narrative; or 2) we could risk an analysis of the longer ending, which most scholars today say is not Mark's, to see if there is anything which looks remotely like an Epilogue that he might have created (the other endings do not look too promising). I opt for 2). I will give consideration also to some of Mark's key words and phrases from his Prologue and his Narrative: such as "creation", "gospel", "world", "Gentiles", "covenant", and "Jesus of Nazareth", as well as his predilection for "twos".

---

[404]See the section of my Introduction, "The Cultural and Historical Context of the Gospel".

Chapter Seven
The Days Following (16.9-16, 19-20a):

The longer ending: 16.9-20:

Anyone who labels this longer ending 'Markan' and views it, therefore, as an original 'Epilogue', stands against a great weight of scholarly opinion[405]. Principally, the arguments go: it is absent from the most reliable, early manuscripts; it does not square with the preceding passage, 16.1-8; and its language is different from the rest of the text. We will consider these three basic points and then the issue of dependency, before proceeding to a literary-structural analysis after which we will give consideration to what has been raised since 1999.

1) The absence from reliable, early manuscripts:

The longer ending, 16.9-20, is clearly missing from the fourth century Codices Vaticanus and Siniaticus, which are in every other way deemed to be the 'reliable, early manuscripts'. Presented in three columns and by two hands, and in four columns and by three hands, respectively, they are the only two copies remaining of fifty that were made by Eusebius of Caesarea with the help of his friend Pamphilus (from a collection of earlier manuscripts to which they had access). An historical note of some consequence tells how they supplied Constantine at his request in the year 331 with fifty copies of the Greek Bible;[406] "fifty copies of the sacred scriptures" were "to be written on fine parchment in a legible manner and in a convenient portable form by professional scribes thoroughly accomplished in their art." It was Eusebius who says, "They were produced in threefold and fourfold forms." It follows, then, that our two most cherished manuscripts for Mark's Gospel, with characteristics of very fine vellum and size which conform to Constantine's request, were copies made at the same time, and in the same place, and from the same earlier manuscript collection.

Eusebius himself commented on the longer ending[407], and many scholars interpret what he had to say as indication that the longer ending was not Markan. When asked about the differences between Matthew 28.1 and Mark 16.9 on the timing of the resurrection, he replied: "They can be solved in two ways." (The first way here only.) "The person not wishing to accept this chapter (the passage under consideration) will say that it is not contained in all copies of the Gospel according to Mark. Indeed the accurate copies conclude the story ac-

---

[405]But see: B. Mariani, "Introduction", *Introduction à la Bible*, Eds. A Robert & A. Feuillet, Desclee & Co., Tournai, Belgium, 1959, p.73, and K.W Clark, "The Theological Relevance of Textual Variation in Current Criticism of the Greek New Testament", *JBL* 85 (1966), pp.9-12, who consider the question insoluble; E. Linnemann, "Der (wiedergefundene) Markusschluss", *ZThK* 66 (1969), pp. 255-259, whose hypothesis is that Mt 28.16f. + Mk. 16.15-20 was the original ending (the argument against his view is that his hypothesis is based on too many arbitrary assumptions); and W.R. Farmer, *The Last Twelve verses of Mark*, Cambridge University Press, Cambridge, 1974, who considers the question "still open" after attempting an explanation of the differences of style and vocabulary - when compared with the rest of the Gospel, on the basis that Mark in his epilogue handles the traditional material *differently* (the critical judgement of his work is that he did not present a strong enough case).

[406]Eusebius, *Life of Constantine*; Bruce M. Metzger, *The Text of the New Testament: Its Transmission, Corruption and Restoration*, Clarendon Press, Oxford, 1968, p.7; also *IntDB*, p.751.

[407]Jerome's letter to Hedibia (Jerome, *Letter*, 120.3).which deals with the same issues, a generation or so later, appears to be reiterating Eusebius' understanding. It is not judged to be a separate witness.

cording to Mark in the words of the young man seen by the women and saying to them Do not be afraid... for they were afraid. For the end is here in nearly all the copies of Mark. What follows is found but seldom, in some copies but by no means in all..."[408]

It is emphatic, even excessively so[409]. The longer ending was *not to be found* among his *best* Greek manuscripts. Nevertheless, manuscripts, which did include the longer ending, did exist, and he knew them. Clearly other manuscripts and other families of manuscripts did exist also at that time. He cannot have had access to them all[410]. Further, if Trocmé[411] *et al.* are right about the Gospel's place of composition, the *exemplar* would have started its life in Rome and likely have been there at that time (if it still existed then), and not immediately available to Eusebius in Caesarea. What manuscripts he did possess which included other endings did not survive[412] so we cannot assess his method of evaluation, nor his choice therefore, of the ones on which he based Codices Vaticanus and Sinaiticus. It is troubling to note, furthermore, that his judgement on other issues is questionable. Eusebius was not exactly free from error in his critical judgement of early material on the Eastern Church on which he wrote most, and what little he wrote on the Western Church does suggest that he knew much less about it, and its documents.[413]

At the opening of the biblical critical era, Codex D, Cantabrigiensis, and Codex A, Alexandrinus, were Europe's two most ancient Greek manuscripts of the New Testament and in both of them the longer ending of Mark was to be found. That it was missing in many manuscripts, however, was first drawn to everyone's attention through the critical and wholly dispassionate observations of Richard Simon, a French Priest, whose first critical studies of the New Testament were destroyed by the Catholic Church. He raised the matter in his *Critical History of the Text*[414] and presented 16.9-20 as 'the spurious ending of Mark'. In his *Critical History of the Translations*[415], he drew attention for the first time to the existence of an Old Latin translation that was earlier and differed from Jerome's Vulgate and added also that certain Greek manuscripts contained the chapter on which the oldest Latin and Syriac translations relied. At the last, having considered all things, Simon thought it right to base his judgement on the testimony of Irenaeus who showed that he knew 16.19. Simon's basic conviction was that exegesis should be concerned only with the truth. At approximately the same time also, John Mill, an Anglican scholar, was identifying variants of the texts (focusing mainly on the Greek) and discovering and numbering more than anyone had done before him. He challenged the *Textus receptus* (of Erasmus, which had been 'carelessly prepared from poor manuscripts'[416]), but only dared to place (his) variants in critical apparatus below the text, in his Greek New Testament of 1707 and 1710. Though he challenged the 'received text', he chose not to replace any of its words or phrases with those that came from his textual research. Johann Albrecht Bengel, a Swiss Lutheran pietist (who had been trained in Tübin-

---

[408]This record comes from a previously lost work known to us as *Gospel Questions and Solutions Addressed to Marinus*, which was found last century. See Johannes Quasten, *Patrology, Volume 3. The Golden Age of Greek Patristic Literature: from the Council of Nicaea to the Council of Chalcedon*, (Utrecht, 1960) repr. Newman Press, Westminster, Md., 1986, p.337.

[409]We probably have all heard about the preacher's sermon margin notes which say, "Shout louder here, argument weak."

[410]The family of Italy and Gaul, from which came Codex Bezae; and the family of Carthage, from which came Codex Washingtonianus.

[411]Trocmé, *The Formation...*, p.242.

[412]No manuscript exists today from before the fifth century which includes the longer ending: see for fifth century examples: Codices Alexandrinus (A), Ephraimi Syri (C), Washingtonianus (W), and the 5th/6th century Bezae (D).

[413]"Eusebius", *The Oxford Dictionary of the Christian Church*, ed. F.L. Cross, 3rd Ed. Oxford University Press, 1997.

[414] Richard Simon, *Critical History of the Text of the New Testament*, Rotterdam, 1689

[415] Richard Simon, *Critical History of the Translations of the New Testament*, Rotterdam, 1690

[416] W.G. Kümmel, *The New Testament: The History of the Investigation of its Problems*, tr. Gilmour & Kee, SCM Press Ltd., 1972: the quote is Kümmel's, p.40.

gen) followed Simon and showed greater courage in preparing his Greek New Testament of 1734 and his own more organised critical apparatus. Furthermore, when Bengel produced his *Gnomon*[417] in 1742, he pointed exegesis in the direction of context and grammar and specifically in the identification of chiasmus as a common characteristic of the texts. He was persuaded on grammatical grounds that the longer ending of Mark was genuine.

In a wonderfully titled book, *The Last Twelve verses of the Gospel According to S. Mark Vindicated against Critical Objectors and Established* (1871)[418], Burgon properly appealed to patristic evidence as Simon had done, which is earlier than the manuscript evidence of Eusebius. We can appeal to it too. V.20 of the longer ending was known to Justin (*Apology*, 1.45) in about AD 155. Vv.14,16,19 were known to Tatian (*Diatessaron; the Persian Gospel Harmony*) in about 165. As above, Irenaeus knew v.19 (*Against Heresies*, 3.11.6) in about 180: he knew that it came from Mark's Gospel for he writes, "At the end of the Gospel Mark says And so the Lord Jesus after he had spoken to them, was taken into heaven, and sat down at the right hand of God". Hippolytus, whose life and work spanned the turn of the second century, knew v.16 (*Apostolic Constitutions*, 6.15) and vv.17,18 (*Ap. Con.*, 8.1). We can conclude, therefore, that manuscripts of the Gospel with the longer ending *were* circulating in the second century. What we cannot conclude is that any Gospel manuscript which finished at 16.8 was circulating as early as this.

We cannot know what happened to Mark's own *exemplar* and its earliest copies. Certainly, plenty of evidence does exist which shows that the leaves of early manuscripts did become worn or torn, and that outer leaves became totally separated[419]. In such a manner, 16.9-20 could have been lost, and the re-discovering of it later because the Gospel had been memorised is quite feasible (see my Introduction, for the mnemonic qualities of ancient rhetoric). Less feasible to some, however, is that this last leaf contained these verses only. But it may be the case that Mark wrote his Prologue on one leaf, and gave his Epilogue similarly a separate page. Clearly it is not for us to know, and the reasonable counter argument to all of this, of course, is that the *exemplar* would have been copied before it disintegrated.

Other possibilities also can be entertained. Farmer raises one. He asks, "Were there conditions obtaining in Alexandria under which the last twelve verses could have been omitted from copies of Mark deliberately?"[420] He argues cogently from patristic documents that the discrepancies between the endings of the Gospels were causing innumerable problems. The timing of the resurrection was one of them, and in this matter, Matthew's Gospel was viewed as the tradition. Vv.17,18 were causing a particular problem too. It was not anything to do with the resurrection as such, but to do with spiritual gifts and their exercise. The church attempted to deal with their troublesome influence by containment[421], but there is no evidence that they succeeded with this approach. Expurgation of vv.9-20 *may* have been the church's only considered recourse.

In summary of this section, we must simply conclude that there is, therefore, no sure evidence against Markan authorship of the longer ending based on its absence from 'reliable, early manuscripts'. Scholars who maintain that the last twelve verses of Mark's Gospel are written by someone other than Mark cannot appeal to manuscript evidence.

[417] Johann Albrecht Bengel, *The Greek New Testament*, 1734, *The Gnomon*, 1742 (popularised in Europe by John Wesley under the title, *Explanatory Notes Upon the New Testament*, 1754, but robbed of its technical content)
[418] J.W. Burgon, *The Last Twelve Verses of the Gospel According to S. Mark Vindicated against Critical Objectors and Established*, G. Bell & Son, Oxford and London, 1871.
[419] For example: Luke's Gospel, Bodmer Papyrus XIV, P75 (175-225AD) V. Martin & R. Kasser (eds.) Cologny-Geneve 1961.
[420] Farmer, *The Last...*, p.59.
[421] Farmer, *The Last...*, pp.66-72. Farmer quotes from *The Ante-Nicene Fathers*, vii, pp.479-481. Farmer observes also the Alexandrian attempt to introduce a 'cut' in Homer's work.

2) It does not square with the preceding passage, 16.1-8:

The break itself, between 16.8 and v.9, has been an issue which many have attempted to resolve by recourse to the argument that vv.9-20 were added later, and not too cleverly at that. But the break is justifiable simply, given my analysis of 1.21-16.8, on literary-structural grounds because at 16.8 the narrative (organised from 1.21-16.8 on the basis of a presentation of "Days" in four "Series of seven Days") ends. Further, in the last Day's report, 16.1-8, Mark's application of his ABB' rhetorical structure is identified again as fully completed. If Mark had written anything beyond 16.8 it *would have shown* a disjunction of some kind with 16.1-8.

The argument that Mary Magdalene is introduced afresh in v.9 as though she were not already on stage[422] evaporates. The Day of resurrection is begun to be retold in a new way (and with several repetitions: see not only the mention of Mary Magdalene, but also that of the day and also the timing of Jesus' resurrection). We note the obvious: Jesus was not 'on stage' himself in Day Twenty-eight's telling; but now he is, in v.9. The 'Epilogue', if that is what vv.9-20 represent, is, therefore, introduced with a recapitulation of details, but for a new purpose. If this is of Mark, then we must judge that he established both an appropriate break in his text, and a new beginning. Regarding what may have been his purpose, we can deduce from the longer ending that it may have been to inform his audience about Jesus' appearances and his final commands. For a suitable 'Epilogue', these do not seem out-of-place aims.

Mark's last presentation in his twenty-eight Day narrative did, of course, communicate to his audience the Gospel's most amazing happening of all. Its ending, with the report that the women fled from the tomb and told no-one anything because they were afraid (16.8), would have been totally understandable. (That there is no resumption of the theme of fear and silence in v.9 *is* a further sign of disjunction, but it is no signal that Mark himself is not writing.) To Hooker, "It is Mark's final irony. In the rest of the story, Jesus has commanded men and women to say nothing about the truth they have glimpsed, and they have frequently disobeyed. Now that the time has at last come to report what has happened, the women are silent!"[423] Whether or not this is truly ironical, we may judge later. What is raised here is a question of approach, for Hooker goes on to represent the views of many when she says that the longer ending "does not attempt to deal with the problems caused by Mark's abrupt ending (the women's silence and the unfulfilled promise to the disciples that they would see Jesus in Galilee) and it shows no reliance on vv.1-8."[424]

To me, the focus is wrong. The last sub-Series of the Gospel narrative, 14.12-16.8, provides us our text in the first place for interpreting the longer ending, not 16.1-8. Further, before we can say whether or not this is truly Mark's 'Epilogue' we will have to interpret it in the light of all that he has written previously, in his Prologue, his Series and sub-Series. The first task is my business here; the second will follow at the end of this chapter.

From the longer ending, we note that the first post-resurrection appearance, to Mary Magdalene, takes place in Jerusalem on the day of the resurrection (16.9). In the Passion Narrative, Mark is concerned to tell us that she and other women who had "followed and served" Jesus in Galilee[425] were present, when no male disciple was anywhere at all to be seen, because they had all "scattered" and "fled" (see 14.27,50). The women (Mark tells us these things because his choice of scripture fulfilment necessitated this: as a result no male disciple could be present) were witnesses to Jesus' crucifixion, 15.40f., and to his burial, 15v.47; they prepared themselves to go to the tomb and anoint the corpse, 16.1; and they only were witnesses to the empty tomb, 16.2-7. The men who had followed with Jesus (beginning in Gali-

---

[422]D.C. Parker, *The Living Text of the Gospels*, Cambridge University Press, Cambridge, 1997, p.138.
[423]Hooker, *The Gospel...*, p.387.
[424]Hooker, *The Gospel...*, p.389.
[425]Compare 1.31 for another woman serving Jesus.

lee, like the women) were nowhere to be found at these times. Mary Magdalene and the other women, at least, were still in Jerusalem on the day of Jesus' resurrection.

The logic of the story-line of the longer ending is that Mary Magdalene first had to find the others who had been with Jesus before she could report to them Jesus' appearance to her. It is the case also that she, and the other women who had been at the tomb with her, would have had to have found the disciples before they could report the message they had been given by the "young man" at the tomb. Mark says in v.8 that the women said nothing to "anyone because they were afraid". We can interpret from the Gospel's final sub-Series, the Passion Narrative, that they could not report immediately either to "the disciples" as they were no longer in the city, or to "Peter", who, after his humiliation (in 14.70) is nowhere stated to be present on the day of Jesus' crucifixion. The last time we heard of Peter, he was a broken man. He was left "weeping", in the Gospel account of 14.72. Not surprisingly, perhaps, when Mary reaches them with the message of Jesus' appearance (16.10), she finds all "those who had been with him (Jesus) mourning and *weeping*". Further, the message the women had received earlier was for "the disciples and Peter" (16.7) and not just "anyone" (16.8). The ending of the last Day (16.1-8) of Mark's telling may be interpreted, therefore, as one of apparent irony only, not one of "Mark's final irony"[426].

The 'longer ending' indeed does not tell, as does the shorter (and much later) ending[427], that the women broke their silence and so gave their message. What it does tell, in 16.10, is that Mary Magdalene had to "go" to report. We ask, "Go where?" According to 14.28 and 16.7, the answer is somewhere on the way to Galilee. In 14.28, it would seem that Jesus expected his disciples to go to Galilee, after their "scattering" (see 14.27). 14.28 does not look like a disguised command of Jesus to his disciples to go there, nor could it have been a command of any such kind when, as it is expressed by Mark, their "scattering" would be a fulfilling of the scripture. The logic of the story-line, therefore, is that before the women were able to report the young man's message, from the tomb, to Peter and the disciples, Jesus' appeared to Mary Magdalene, with the result that she had the message of his appearance to tell as well as the message of the young man (*cf.* Mt.28.5-9). In the longer ending, the message of Jesus' appearance eclipses the message of the young man. (The message of the young man (16.7), in its repetition of Jesus' earlier statement to the disciples now looks more like a literary device on Mark's part, than a matter of true record[428].) The drift of the longer ending is freed from 'journey' and 'day' concerns; it can concentrate on the real point for Mark's audience: the believing of those who had seen the risen Jesus.

The longer ending, therefore, tells how the risen Jesus was three-times his own witness, and how the disciples twice reacted *reasonably,* but *unbelievingly*, to reports of his being seen. (We observe that the empty tomb does not feature in this account.) Vv.9-11, vv.12-13, and v.14 tell of appearances of the risen Jesus. The first two tell of the reports which are then given and the responses they attract. In the third, in which Jesus appears to the eleven, we are told of Jesus' extreme annoyance that the reports were not believed. In fact, three times the audience of the writer of the longer ending hears that the reports of witnesses to the risen Lord were not believed (vv.11,13,14).

The empty tomb was not in itself evidence of resurrection (Matthew picks that one up: see 28.11-16 for a possible alternative reason for its being empty). The message of a young

---

[426]See page 312 for Hooker's reference to the phrase.
[427]Found in L Y 099 0112 274^{mg} 579 k sy$^{hl\,mg}$ and in some MSS. of sa bo aeth.
[428]Compare Mark's handling of the story of the withered fig tree. It appears likely that he created 11.11 for his purpose of creating a break (a Day's break, in this instance) so that he could introduce his next Day's telling with the first episode of the fig tree incident. The tradition of Jesus' entry into Jerusalem may well have connected with his clearing of the temple. Likewise, the fig tree incident may have been one whole story in the tradition. The teaching that attaches to the second episode (11.20-25) looks to be a Markan additon.

man in a white robe was evidence of a kind[429] (but with Mark's account we are left wondering who he was anyway; when we read Mt. 28.2 and Lk. 24.4ff. we helpfully find *angelic* developments). But the fact that Jesus appeared to certain people who could be identified, that could be called evidence, though it was still evidence which could be rejected. Hence, therefore, we observe the force of the risen Jesus' remonstrating with his disciples, in 16.14, which has its precursor in 8.17f.; and his most severe remonstration is not for his disciples alone but for *all* who would deny[430] the veracity of the report of witnesses to a face-to-face meeting with him, after his resurrection.[431]

The longer ending records that Mary Magdalene did report Jesus' appearance to her to his disciples. If we interpret that Mary Magdalene delivered her report immediately, we interpret wrongly. We now ask, "How could she have done?" We can only deduce that the first section of the longer ending (vv.9-11) covered several days, as she sought out Jesus' disciples, either in Galilee, or on their way to Galilee (Jerusalem to the Sea of Galilee is about 87 miles). Likewise, the second section of the longer ending (vv.12,13), we may deduce, is intended to convey what happened after a further interval of time, and in a place quite different from Jerusalem. The second appearance takes place as "*two* of them were walking... going into (the) country". And we note, "they went away from there" (the place of the meeting) to report. Of the greatest support for Markan authorship of this piece is Mark's repeated motif of "twos" in his Prologue and in each of his Gospel narrative Series. (So many scholars readily argue dependency on Lk. 24.13-35, and ignore this connection. See pages 64,65.)

It would appear that the "country" of Galilee is the setting for the second section's story. The third section of the longer ending (16.14), in that case, would be similarly set. The timing of the appearance of Jesus to the eleven would be possible, therefore, anytime after the two had been able to return to the group and report. The longer ending, given the sifting of its inherent logic (taking into account information from the Passion Narrative), reports events which cover (like the Prologue) a number of days, and which take place in settings on the way to Galilee and in Galilee.

The longer ending is clearly condensed and abbreviated, but it is in the style of the Gospel as a whole in that respect[432]. (Brevity particularly in "an Epilogue" is a quality which Aristotle commends[433].) When the longer ending is interpreted in the light of the contents of the last sub-Series of the Gospel (Days Twenty-six, Twenty-seven and Twenty-eight) it is observed that it not only attaches well to what has been told before it, but also what has been told before it prefaces it and, therefore, interprets it. The longer ending, or its first section at least, is looking like it is Mark's composition. What we have seen above demonstrates, whoever the writer is, that the story lines and details that we have focused upon are complete without temporal and geographical details of journeyings (such would have cluttered the presentation; and such, we might judge, were unnecessary anyway given the twice repeated location in the final sub-Series). Essentially therefore, the writer has been able to focus upon the two important issues that follow on from Jesus' death and resurrection: the need of the church to believe the witnesses of the risen Christ; and the need of the church to preach the

---

[429]Likely the same mysterious young man of 14.51f.: compare the first and last days of the final threesome of days of the gospel and note the verbal similarities: in 14.51f., νεανίσκος... περιβεβλημένος σινδόνα, and in 16.5, νεανίσκον... περιβεβλημένον στολὴν λευκήν, for further references to σινδόνα see 15.46, in the passage of the entombing of Jesus. See also under the examination of Day Twenty-eight.

[430]It is a feature of Mark's Gospel that the disciples' place in the company of Jesus is exemplary to the listener.

[431]We note how the Prologue is not just written to inform but to draw the listener into taking a stand: it would appear that the longer ending fulfils a similar role.

[432]David Hall (*The Gospel Framework...*, p.54) draws attention to this characteristic of abbreviation in the gospels as a whole. One of his attacks on Schmidt's thesis is based on this.

[433]Aristotle, *Ars Rhetorica*, III.19 1420[b]: consider his example, "I have done. You have heard me. The facts are before you. I ask for your judgement."

good news everywhere (vv.15,20a). For the moment we have given attention only to the first of these.

3) Its language is different from the rest of the text:

Over the years, much has been written about the differences of the vocabulary, style and grammar of the longer ending over and against that of the rest of the gospel[434]. Farmer[435] judges that the most exhaustive studies have been made by scholars who have wished to disprove authenticity. He argues that they have been selective of the evidence. In singling out Morgenthaler's 'word-statistical' research on the longer ending[436] for special attention, Farmer demonstrates that it does not lead to 'clear results', as claimed. On the use of καί and δέ in the longer ending, for example, Morgenthaler notes that καί is used 'on average' half what it is elsewhere in Mark, and δέ is used over twice as often. Morgenthaler notes that these frequencies do vary in different parts of the Gospel, but still concludes that this feature 'certainly speaks for the unauthenticity' of vv.9-20. Farmer points out that Morgenthaler's own statistical results show that the use of καί is greater in the first half of Mark than the second, while the use of δέ is greater in the second half. Farmer[437] judges that the use of καί and δέ in the longer ending is in keeping with these tendencies in the Gospel.

Many scholars[438] have concluded with Morgenthaler that "A style is written here (in vv.9-20) completely different than appears elsewhere in Mark's Gospel." It is clearly the case that only one of the nine sentences begins with καί. For comparison's sake, Morgenthaler looked at the section 15.46-16.8, and noted that eight out of the sixteen uses of καί begin sentences. Farmer, however, looked at 15.35-45, and noted that out of the fourteen uses of καί only two begin sentences. He further observes that καί is used twelve times after 15.39 before it is used a second time to begin a sentence. Farmer counters, therefore, "It is the case that καί is used with greater frequency to begin sentences in Mark, especially in the early chapters. But it is not true that the use of καί and δέ in 16.9-20 is 'completely different than appears elsewhere in Mark's Gospel'."[439]

Fascinatingly, it would appear that this is not all there is to the matter. What scholars have continued to overlook is the rule of ancient rhetoric on the Epilogue which states that its style *should be different* from what precedes it. Aristotle's final and emphatic point on the Epilogue[440] may be translated: 1) "The end of the whole ought to be free from conjunctions, to make the hearers aware that our discourse is at its close"; 2) "Asyndeton is appropriate for the end of the discourse since this is an *epilogos* not a *logos*"[441]; and 3) "For the conclusion, the disconnected style of language is appropriate, and will mark the difference between the oration and the peroration"[442]. It would appear that the writer of the longer ending was aware

---

[434]E.g. and so henceforth: Wellhausen, *Das Evangelium...*, 1909; Taylor, *The Gospel...*, 1952; and W.G. Farmer, *The Last...*, 1974.
[435]Farmer, p.79.
[436]Robert Morgenthaler, *Statistik des Neutestamentlichen Wortschatzes*, Gotthelf Verlag, Zurich, 1958
[437]Farmer, *The Last...*, p.81.
[438]My selected commentators, Taylor, Nineham, Schweizer and Hooker, all agree on this matter. And Paul Ellingworth, "The Dog in the Night...", p.127, says, "The frequency of the non-καί sentences increases sharply in the alternative endings of Mark, confirming that they are not part of the original Gospel."
[439]Farmer, *The Last...*, p.83.
[440]*Ars Rhetorica*, III.19 1420[b] (*Aristotelis Ars Rhetorica*, ed. Rudolfus Kassel, Walter de Gruyter, Berlin, 1976).
[441]*Aristotle on Rhetoric: A Theory of Civic Discourse*, tr. George A. Kennedy, Oxford University Press, New York/Oxford, 1991, p.282.
[442]W. Rhys Roberts,"Rhetorica", *The Works of Aristotle, Translated into English*, tr. ed. W.D. Ross, Vol. XI, Clarendon Press, Oxford, 1924, III.19 1420[b].

of this rule. The lack of καί introductions to sentences is no reason to judge that it was not Mark who was writing.

Farmer examined all the verses. We note his conclusions: "Evidence for non-Marcan authorship seems to be preponderant in verse 10. Verses 12, 14, 16, 17, 18 and 19 seem to be either basically, or in balance neutral. Evidence for Markan authorship seems to be preponderant in verses 9, 11, 13, 15, and 20."[443] For Parker[444], who addresses these matters in less than a single page, the significant feature is that "as many as seventeen words in this short passage of twelve verses are either not found in Mark 1.1-16.8, or are used here in a non-Markan sense." For him, "the argument about style and word usage is cumulative."

On word usage, in particular, we have seen in the analysis of the final sub-Series of the Gospel narrative how Mark is still introducing there new words and phrases. The ones that were identified on pages 294,295 are: "covenant", "Abba", "envy", "King of the Jews", and King of Israel". We judged that he had chosen deliberately to set these new words in his final sub-Series because he was sharpening his audience's focus on the strands of his earlier narrative which have their fullest interpretation in the Passion account. It follows that if Mark did write the longer ending, or much of it, he could have continued with the same in writing an Epilogue. Additionally, the subjects that we find in vv.9-20 are new to the Gospel's telling, and include post-resurrection appearances, and final commands. New themes require new vocabulary. Still on evidence of word usage, we also noted how Mark's Days' tellings in his final Series began in ways that were different from those of his earlier Series (see page 303). An Epilogue's sectional beginnings, we might judge, would require introductory descriptions that were different from the Narrative's text, but similar maybe to the Prologue's text. Already we have seen the introductory function of v.9. We shall consider below the supposed non-Markan words of Μετὰ δὲ ταῦτα (v.12) and Ὕστερον δέ (v.14) in their *story* context, for that is the only way to assess them properly.

Firstly, we may observe John's use of the first of these phrases, Μετὰ δὲ ταῦτα. In his Gospel it is much in evidence. Only once does it have the sense of "immediately following" (in Jn. 19.28). Only once does it have the sense of "very soon after" (19.38). Elsewhere in John's Gospel, it has the sense of "next", "next in what is related", and what is more, it infers a passage of days between the pericope which precedes it and the one which it introduces. New sections and sub-sections begin[445] in John's Gospel at Jn. 2.12, 3.22, 5.1, 6.1, 7.1 and 21.1. Interestingly, we note, in regard to the last of these references (21.1), the setting leaps to "the sea of Tiberias" without any explanation at all. In Mark's Gospel, by way of contrast, we have explanation of what will be the setting of "Galilee" (in 14.28, 16.7), but no mention of the place when the stories are being told. The phrase, Μετὰ δὲ ταῦτα, in the longer ending behaves as in the majority of cases in John's Gospel, but it does not look as if it is dependent on John. We may observe, in 1.14 of Mark's Gospel, by way of introduction to the third section of the *Prologue*, something very similar to it, Μετὰ δὲ τό, which is followed by an aorist passive infinitive. A passage of days takes place there, before the introductory phrase to 1.14-20. We have also by way of comparison, in 16.19, Ὁ μὲν οὖν... μετά τό, followed by an aorist active infinitive. The use of Μετὰ δὲ ταῦτα at v.12 in the longer ending cannot be considered non-Markan. It functions in the way that the passage requires, given its setting in a threesome of events which covers several days in the telling.

The second of the two introductions may read as "Finally..." or "At the last...", as in Matthew's use of ὕστερον at 4.2, 21.30,32,37, 22.27 (*cf.* Luke, in his parallel, 20.32), 25.11 and 26.60. The writer of the longer ending, therefore, uses the word which is the one most appropriate. In the threesome of stories, it introduces the last of the three scenes (v.14). In terms of the Gospel as a whole, of course, it introduces the last of all its scenes. If it is Mark

---

[443]Farmer, *The Last...*, p.103.
[444]D.C. Parker, *The Living Text...*, pp.141,142.
[445]See Palmer, *Sliced Bread...*, pp.87ff.

who has written this longer ending, or the greater proportion of it, then it may be said that he has chosen for the opening of his last presentation-piece of the Gospel a word he has not used before in all its verses. It would have to be acknowledged also that he has chosen the most suitable word available to him.

In terms of the continuing story-line of the Gospel narrative and the longer ending, we might read, therefore, "*At the last*, he appeared to the eleven as they sat at table..." (v.14) When interpreted in the light of the Passion Narrative, 14.11-16.8, the scene clearly reflects that of the last supper, beginning at 14.17,18. Also, the prediction of Jesus, in 14.25, is now about to be fulfilled: "Truly I tell you, No more will I drink the fruit of the vine, until *that* day when I drink it new in the Kingdom of God." This is the scene of his ascension, according to the longer ending, and we may interpret that it is then that he enters the Kingdom of God[446]. Again it has to be argued that the longer ending is interpreted correctly against the back-drop of the Passion Narrative. Similarly, the lack of a place-name for this scene in the longer ending is not problematic because Mark has stated twice already that they would see the risen Jesus in Galilee[447]. Further, with Mark's use of $\dot{\epsilon}\kappa\epsilon\acute{\iota}\nu\eta\varsigma$ in 14.25, we have a verbal connection of sorts with $\dot{\epsilon}\kappa\epsilon\acute{\iota}\nu\eta$, in v.10, and $\dot{\epsilon}\kappa\epsilon\acute{\iota}\nu\sigma\varsigma$, in vv.13,20, which others say are not 'used absolutely' at all in 1.1-16.8. To Farmer[448], this fact is one of the features that sets v.10 aside as non-Markan. I note, however, that it is 'used absolutely' in 7.20: there $\dot{\epsilon}\kappa\epsilon\acute{\iota}\nu\sigma$ is clearly the singular subject of the verb.

Given the analysis of the literary-structural method of Mark for his narrative based on "Days", we do find changes of place at the beginnings of the second and third parts of many of his three-part presentations, but because they are confined to introducing new events on the same, particular "Days" we do not find conjunctions of the kind that we meet here in the longer ending which reports a series of events which take place over a series of days. Indeed, both, in the Prologue and in the longer ending, we discover conjunction- constructions which are not used anywhere else in the Gospel at major *sub-structural* points. Consider 1.9, "And it came to pass in those days, came Jesus..."; and 1.14, "And after John was delivered, came Jesus...". The literary-constructional requirements of both Prologue and the longer ending are different from the rest of the Gospel, because they each cover a number of days within their three-fold structures.

It would seem, therefore, that it is not enough for scholars to describe these sub-structural introductions in the longer ending as non-Markan simply because they had not been used before in the gospel. Their function in the longer ending is to introduce the second and third closing sections to the gospel and so report events which took place over several days. There is no reason why Mark himself could not have employed the terms. The matter of authorship of the longer ending, to Farmer, is still an open question[449]. Given the above, authorship cannot be settled by reference to differences with 1.1-16.8, in regard to its vocabulary, style and grammar.

4) Dependency:

On the issue of dependency, Parker begins by stating that the longer ending is "best read as a cento or pastiche of material gathered from the other Gospels and from other sources"[450]. He

---

[446]See 14.62, also 8.38, 9.1: for Mark's understanding of the Kingdom of God, as coming from heaven, while Jesus sits at the right hand of power.
[447]The first is at 14.28 and the "reminder" is at 16.7 (on the first and third days in the telling of Mark's last sub-Series of days).
[448]Farmer, *The Last...*, pp.85,86.
[449]Farmer, *The Last...*, p.109.
[450]Parker, *The Living Text...*, p.138.

says he will go through the longer ending "verse by verse", but in practice he groups some together. On vv.9-11, he speaks of the 'universal tradition', as found in Mark 16.2, as the initial source for the writer of the longer ending. He says that Jesus' appearance to Mary Magdalene is Johannine tradition. He says that vv.10,11 are based on Luke 24.10b-11 (with John 20.18 as another parallel). He says that the reference to "mourning and weeping" is "an expansion of the tradition" and adds a note, "the oldest version, the Freer Gospels, lacks the second verb, so that this expansion can be shown to have grown by stages". He starts his argument, and launches into it as if the issue of non-authenticity is beyond question. Many commentators do the same and assume that the longer ending is dependent on Luke 8.2 for the statement that Jesus saved Mary Magdalene from "seven demons", on John 20.11-18 for Jesus' appearance to Mary Magdalene, on Luke 24.11 for the failure of the disciples to believe her report (note: of the empty tomb), on Luke 24.13-35 for a much shorter story about "the two" (the stories, I note, conclude in different ways), on Matthew 28.19, Luke 24.46-49 or Acts 1.8 for a commissioning of the disciples (and in the case of the Lukan parallel, a heavenly co-operation, for which compare 16.20b), on Acts 2.4, etc. for speaking in new tongues, and on Acts 28.3-6 for picking up snakes.

No case is put by any of the four commentators, to whose work I have been principally referring, for believing dependency is this way about. The principle has been established already above. If the longer ending is to be assessed for authenticity, it has in the first place to be interpreted by the Passion Narrative, and in the second by Mark's Gospel as a whole. Only when that has been done might we be able to say that we have established a sure result. Up till now I have been following, in the main, only the first path, and it has been a worthwhile journey. Connections abound which suggest the authenticity of the majority of the verses of the longer ending. But putting aside this methodolgy for the moment, there is still a case to be put for thinking that the longer ending is authentically Markan, and that dependency is that of Matthew and Luke upon it, for their endings of their gospels as for the rest of their gospels.

Matthew tells how before the women (Mary Magdalene was one of them) could report their message (the same as in Mark) from the tomb, Jesus met with them on their way (Mt. 28.8,9 cf. Mk.16.8,9). In his v.8, Matthew, it appears, simplified Mark's v.8 and made it less difficult to handle, in terms of continuing story. It might be said that in his v.9, Matthew dispensed with the longer ending's opening phrase, Ἀναστὰς δὲ πρωῒ πρώτῃ σαββάτου, and replaced 'Mary Magdalene' with the 'two women' for a clearer correspondence with the previous passage on the 'two' (not the Markan 'three') women at the tomb, 28.1-7. We could say that he thus demonstrated again as elsewhere *his* predilection for pairs, see 8.28, 21.2,5, and so on). Matthew then created his v.10 from Mark's v.7 and his own earlier development of it in his own v.7, and created in near juxtaposition, therefore, a pair of messages about seeing the risen Jesus in Galilee (the first from the angel, the second from the risen Jesus) for the women to deliver to the disciples. It appears very much like a clarifying of the geographical setting of the longer ending, as does also Matthew's rather mundane, repetitive mention (by comparison) of Galilee again, in his v.16. In vv.11-15, it may be argued that Matthew addressed a flaw in Mark's witness of the empty tomb (Jesus' body could have been stolen by his disciples), and that he then rejected the longer ending's ascension scene in order to present an already exalted Christ who, in this state, re-visited the eleven (and presumably could visit them and the church again and again) from heaven[451]. The longer ending's Jesus, in contrast, lacks this (later added) facility because he takes a one way route to heaven to return only on the Day appointed. In the scene of Jesus' post-resurrection meeting with his disciples, Matthew records "some doubted"[452], and it does look as though it might have had its origin in the longer ending's v.12, ἐφανερώθη ἐν ἑτέρᾳ μορφῇ. Further, Matthew's v.17 expunges to-

---

[451]For example of which, see Saul's conversion in Acts 9 (and its two further tellings, in chapters 22 and 26).
[452]See the end of Mt. 28.17, "but some doubted".

tally any reproach Jesus may have had for his disciples (the longer ending's vv.11-14) which does look like a typically Matthaean gospel development of Mark, in presenting Jesus' disciples in a better light. Also Matthew's 'great commission' (vv.18-20a) looks more refined than the longer ending's vv.15,16, so the longer ending could have supplied him with the idea. Lastly, Matthew's final statement (v.20b) looks like a development of the longer ending's final statement because it reads as an unmistakable promise to the continuing church of Jesus' continuing presence. The longer ending could be interpreted as limited to the time of the apostles.

Luke tells events in detail which the longer ending tells only briefly. Luke reads the longer ending as if it only covered one day, and represents it that way (Lk.24). Further, it would not be untypical of Luke to develop a story based on 16.12,13, and to develop a "commissioning scene" based on 16.14-20 in order to set the two in parallel, for his own literary purposes[453]. At some stage, of course, Luke was persuaded to write a second book: the longer ending could have suggested it to him, but in regard to Mk.16.17,18 it looks more like the dependency is the other way about. Lastly, the reference to Mary Magdalene's 'seven' demons (Mk. 16.9, *cf.* Lk. 8.2) discloses a numerological/numerical interest which may be judged to be not untypically Markan[454].

A case could be put, therefore, for a dating of the longer ending, 16.9-20, earlier than Matthew's and Luke's Gospels, and for these Gospels to be dependent upon it, that is, the majority of its verses[455].

A Summary Statement of Today's Predominating Views on 16.9-20:

Issues of dependency in regard to the synoptic gospels, Mark's Gospel and longer ending content and style considerations, and most importantly manuscript evidence have all been judged in this century to establish that the Gospel was intended to end at 16.8, as it does in Codex Vaticanus and Codex Siniaiticus and a number of later manuscripts. The inclusion of the shorter ending[456] between the gospel and the longer ending in some manuscripts has also served to support the view that the longer ending was added later, and not by Mark. Further to this, while many scholars have recognised that a number of the themes and details of the longer ending have their contact with the gospel as a whole, this fact has been used to justify "the abrupt ending".

Some of the longer ending material on the role of the disciples has its clear mention in chapter 3. "Preaching" and "believing" in the longer ending *are* much covered elsewhere[457]. That Jesus would be raised from the dead *is* severally stated in the narrative, and that he would be seen by his disciples in Galilee after his resurrection is twice stated.[458] The otherwise closing statement that the women did not report what they were told to report "because they were afraid" has had its objectors. The answer that they have received, and properly so, is that the response of fear to a report of his resurrection, is entirely in keeping with responses

[453]See Palmer, *Sliced Bread...*, pp.83f., for parallels between Lk. 24.13-32 and 33-53, and for much evidence of Luke's ability to create stories as well as re-tell stories with new purposes.
[454]Compare: the woman with the issue of blood..., and Jairus' daughter, both 'twelve' years (5.25,42) and the feedings of the five- and four-thousands (6.30-52 and 8.1-21), for a variety of numbers.
[455]Kümmel (*Introduction...*, p.100) argues that Matthew and Luke demonstrate uneasiness that Mark could not end at 16.8: but their divergence beyond shows that Mark already ended there. My reading above, however, takes account of Matthew's and Luke's different approaches to the work of writing their gospels; Kummel's does not.
[456]See note 427.
[457]We observe that "baptism", outside of the Prologue, is only mentioned metaphorically (10.38,39).
[458]We note, however, that Jesus' violent death is predicted three times in direct manner, and a number of other times indirectly (see, for example 2.20), but no-one suggests that Mark did not intend Jesus' death to be included. Indeed, Jesus' death and resurrection are three-times predicted together (see 8.31; 9.31; 10.34).

found elsewhere in the gospel, to the healings and miracles of Jesus. Likewise, the objection that a gospel would not end with γαρ has been met with examples of paragraphs ending this way[459]. It is the case that since 1903, when Wellhausen first suggested that Mark intended to end his gospel at 16.8, objections to his proposal have been addressed to the satisfaction of most scholars and commentators.

This compounding of the justification that the gospel was always intended to end at 16.8, because the longer ending material is much to be found already in the Gospel, tends to the following kind of views:

i) The story ends with the invitation to all to "go to Galilee", the place of discipleship, and that "if you want to see Jesus then follow where he leads. This is the end of Mark's story because it is the beginning of discipleship"[460];

ii) "Readers or hearers of Mark know the disciples did see Jesus; they also know that they themselves experience his powerful presence...; we have always to return to the beginning in Galilee... It is a continual pilgrimage".[461]

iii) "The *modern reader* will not be misled by the call (16.7) to follow Jesus who has gone before. Discipleship is following in the way of Jesus..."[462] (I interpret this writer to mean that Mark's *first audiences* of 1.1-16.8 also were not misled.)

Clearly, these similar views are representative of the inevitable end of currently accepted scholarship on the issues addressed in 1) to 4) above. Rather, my studies of these issues lead me to judge that the longer ending *is* the place to look for what may be Mark's original 'Epilogue'. Contrary to Painter, I do not think that the longer ending is "clearly secondary"[463]; I cannot say that it does not do "anything to illuminate Mark"[464]; and I cannot accept that "Whoever compiled this ending does not display Mark's dramatic skills."[465] We turn now, therefore, to the text of the longer ending and subject it to the same literary-structural analysis that the text of 1.1-16.8 has undergone.

Literary-structural Evidence:

Below, I present the literary-structure of the longer ending, 16.9-20, as it exists now and as it was parsed in 1999. It demonstrates two halves consisting of three-part presentations of the kind we have encountered elsewhere in Mark's Gospel. But it is in the form A:A', when every other piece of the Gospel is arranged as ABB'. Before, it looked like an expanded form of ABB':ABB'. All three sections of the first half are linked by resurrection appearances, reportings and their being met with "disbelief".

In the first half, part A (vv.9-11) introduces, by first report, the theme for the other two parts, and focuses on Jesus' "first" appearance, to Mary Magdalene: she reports to "those who had been with him..."; they *disbelieve*. Part B (vv.12,13) records "next" the appearance of Jesus "to two of them" who then report "to the rest" who *disbelieve*. Part B' (v.14) records "at the last", Jesus' appearance "to the eleven", and his upbraiding them for *disbelieving* those who had seen him. There is no direct speech in any of these reports up to this point; they are compact third-person reports of the writer.

In the so-described second half, part A (vv.15,16), as it stands now, includes direct speech: Jesus sends the eleven out into the world to preach the gospel. A pair of sayings, on

---

[459]For examples: see Lightfoot, *Locality and Doctrine...*, pp.1-48, and *The Gospel Message...*, pp.80-97; and Hooker (*The Gospel...*, p.391) who cites Menander's *Dyscolos*, lines 437-8. Others are still adding to the list.
[460]Hooker, representing the views of others (*The Gospel...*, p.394).
[461]Best, presenting his own view (*Mark: The Gospel...*, pp.132f).
[462]Painter, *Mark's Gospel...*, p.216.
[463]Painter, *Mark's Gospel...*, p.215.
[464]Painter, *Mark's Gospel...*, p.216.
[465]Painter, *Mark's Gospel...*, p.215.

those "*believing*" and those "*not believing*" occupy the two balancing, closing parts b and b'. Of the two remaining parts, part B (vv.17,18) tells of "signs" which will follow those who "believe", and these are listed (covering three parts), and part B' (vv.19,20), as it stands now, records Jesus' ascension (in the first part), his heavenly seat (in the second) and the eleven's mission and his working with them with "signs" accompanying (in the third). We consider:

'Αναστὰς δὲ πρωΐ πρώτῃ σαββάτου   A
  ἐφάνη πρῶτον Μαρίᾳ τῇ Μαγδαληνῇ,
  παρ' ἧς ἐκβεβλήκει ἑπτὰ δαιμόνια.¹⁰
 ἐκείνη πορευθεῖσα
  ἀπήγγειλεν τοῖς μετ' αὐτοῦ γενομένοις
  πενθοῦσι καὶ κλαίουσιν·¹¹
 κἀκεῖνοι ἀκούσαντες
  ὅτι ζῇ καὶ ἐθεάθη ὑπ' αὐτῆς
  ἠπίστησαν.¹²
Μετὰ δὲ ταῦτα δυσὶν ἐξ αὐτῶν περιπατοῦσιν
  ἐφανερώθη ἐν ἑτέρᾳ μορφῇ
  πορευομένοις εἰς ἀγρόν·¹³
 κἀκεῖνοι
  ἀπελθόντες
  ἀπήγγειλαν τοῖς λοιποῖς·
 οὐδὲ ἐκείνοις ἐπίστευσαν.¹⁴
Ὕστερον δὲ ἀνακειμένοις αὐτοῖς τοῖς ἕνδεκα ἐφανερώθη,
 καὶ ὠνείδισεν τὴν ἀπιστίαν αὐτῶν καὶ σκληροκαρδίαν
 ὅτι τοῖς θεασαμένοις αὐτὸν ἐγηγερμένον οὐκ ἐπίστευσαν.

Καὶ εἶπεν αὐτοῖς,   A'
  Πορευθέντες εἰς τὸν κόσμον ἅπαντα
  κηρύξατε τὸ εὐαγγέλιον πάσῃ τῇ κτίσει.¹⁶
 ὁ πιστεύσας καὶ βαπτισθεὶς σωθήσεται.
 ὁ δὲ ἀπιστήσας κατακριθήσεται.
Σημεῖα δὲ τοῖς πιστεύσασιν ταῦτα παρακολουθήσει·
 ἐν τῷ ὀνόματί μου δαιμόνια ἐκβαλοῦσιν, γλώσσαις λαλήσουσιν καιναῖς,
 καὶ ἐν ταῖς χερσίν ὄφεις ἀροῦσιν.
  κἂν θανάσιμόν τι πίωσιν οὐ μὴ αὐτοὺς βλάψῃ,
  ἐπὶ ἀρρώστους χεῖρας ἐπιθήσουσιν καὶ καλῶς ἕξουσιν.
Ὁ μὲν οὖν κύριος Ἰησοῦς
  μετὰ τὸ λαλῆσαι αὐτοῖς
  ἀνελήμφθη εἰς τὸν οὐρανὸν
 καὶ ἐκάθισεν ἐκ δεξιῶν τοῦ θεοῦ.
 ἐκεῖνοι δὲ ἐξελθόντες ἐκήρυξαν πανταχοῦ,
  τοῦ κυρίου συνεργοῦντος καὶ τόν λόγον βεβαιοῦντος
  διά τῶν ἐπακολουθούντων σημείων.

This longer ending, as it stands now, has the appearance of a Markan composition, but for its AA' form. That is the first thing we can say about it. The second is that it is most economical in its presentation. In each of its parts, it is not at all wasteful of words. As a candidate for an 'Epilogue' (after the manner of ancient rhetoric) it is suitably succinct and to the point. But now we must ask if it is possible that another writer has re-worked it, and included material which is strange to Mark. In section 1) of this chapter, we noted the possibility that the whole of the longer ending was expunged from the text because vv.17,18, of all the verses, were problematic to the church in patristic times. In section 2) the longer ending was interpreted by a re-reading of the Passion Narrative, 14.11-16.8. No connection between vv.17,18 and the Passion commend themselves. In section 3) attention was paid to key features of the vocabulary, style and grammar of the longer ending. We may here consider the fact that of the seventeen words/phrases which are not found elsewhere in Mark, or are handled differently, eight[466] appear in these two verses. In section 4) I noted, in regard to dependency, that it was more likely that vv.17,18 were constructed by reference to Luke's writings than the other way about. Additional to these considerations, there is the principle in writing today, that 'one does not introduce new material into one's conclusion'. It appears that it was one of the rules of ancient rhetoric[467]. Vv.17,18 (and 20bc, therefore), on "signs", *do* represent 'new material'. Any possible link with 6.7-13 is tenuous. Further to this, these verses contradict what Mark expresses in 8.12 ("*no sign* will be given" this generation). Equally, the reference in 13.22, is not exactly positive about "signs and miracles", in the church's mission programme. No, the force of the first half of this longer ending is emphatically on "believing" the reports of Jesus' appearances after his death. "Believing" and "being baptised", in the second half's telling of the longer ending, alone reflect this and the Prologue's similar revelations, if, that is, we read correctly that "baptism" will continue to be a sign of "repentance". "Preaching", here, is the fundamental task of the 'eleven', and it is reflective of the same, simple introduction of Jesus' mission, in the Prologue (1.14).

It is true that as they stand the 'signs passages' balance each other in their current positions and as such have *the appearance* of Markan arrangement, though I have to say that the last lines, of v.20 itself, are too cumbersome for a Markan construction; the καί is superfluous. Nothing like it exists elsewhere in the Gospel text. A simultaneous, double removal of vv.17,18 and vv.20bc immediately creates a better balance between the introductory phrases Καὶ εἶπεν αὐτοῖς and Ὁ μὲν οὖν κύριος Ἰησοῦς μετὰ τὸ λαλῆσαι αὐτοῖς, which have the appearance of intended balance, in the normal Markan positions of B and B'. By removing from the existing second half those passages which speak of "signs" that will follow "the ones believing", and "signs" that "accompanied", we observe a number of interesting results.

Since the publication of this thesis in 1999, I have again revisited the literary-structural analysis of all the major components that make up this Gospel presentation. Not one of them is an A:A' (parallel) structure. All are ABB' structures. Over the years, of exploring the constructions of the Books (the four gospels, Acts and the Revelation) and the Letters of the New Testament, my reading of ABB' formations has improved, to the point that I may now be reading a text as well as any reader in the first centuries of the Christian era. What this means, clearly, is this: what I present now is my firm proposal for careful consideration of what may have been the original Epilogue. That there was one is not in doubt in my mind. No one would ever have left an auditorium if a recital of *this* Gospel had ended *without an Epilogue*. It is just as today, as after a performance, any audience expects something more!

Following my presentation of the Greek text for Mark's Epilogue, I present a literal English translation which shows what is visible in the text to any Greek reader. And, added to this, I want to pint out right now how the first word of this Epilogue, 'Rising', is a key word in this Gospel. The two Middle Days of the two Inner Series of the Gospel include it in their openings (though both are unrecorded in The New International Version and the Good News Bible). The major first and last days of the Gospel's narrative employ it also. It is a key word, a key matter, a matter of real importance to the good news (the 'bravo news'?) of Mark's Gospel.

---

[466] παρακολουθήσει, γλώσσαις λαλήσουσιν καιναῖς, ὄφεις, θανάσιμόν, τι (separated from the conditional particle), πίωσιν, βλάψῃ, καὶ καλῶς ἕξουσιν.

[467] One of the purposes of the Epilogue was to "review *what you have already said*", another was "to magnify or minimize your leading facts", *Ars Rhetorica* III.19. See also note 25, on the issue of brevity.

Ἀναστὰς δὲ   a A
   πρωῒ
   πρώτῃ σαββάτου
  ἐφάνη πρῶτον Μαρίᾳ τῇ Μαγδαληνῇ,
  παρ᾽ ἧς ἐκβεβλήκει ἑπτὰ δαιμόνια. [10]
ἐκείνη   b
   πορευθεῖσα
   ἀπήγγειλεν
     τοῖς μετ᾽ αὐτοῦ γενομένοις
     πενθοῦσι καὶ κλαίουσιν· [11]
κἀκεῖνοι   b'
   ἀκούσαντες
    ὅτι ζῇ
    καὶ ἐθεάθη ὑπ᾽ αὐτῆς
ἠπίστησαν. [12]

Μετὰ δὲ ταῦτα   a B
   δυσὶν ἐξ αὐτῶν
   περιπατοῦσιν
  ἐφανερώθη ἐν ἑτέρᾳ μορφῇ
   πορευομένοις εἰς ἀγρόν· [13]
κἀκεῖνοι   b
   ἀπελθόντες
   ἀπήγγειλαν τοῖς λοιποῖς·
οὐδὲ ἐκείνοις ἐπίστευσαν. [14]   b'

Ὕστερον δὲ   a B'
   ἀνακειμένοις αὐτοῖς
   τοῖς ἕνδεκα
  ἐφανερώθη,
   καὶ ὠνείδισεν τὴν ἀπιστίαν αὐτῶν
   καὶ σκληροκαρδίαν
  ὅτι τοῖς θεασαμένοις αὐτὸν
   ἐγηγερμένον
   οὐκ ἐπίστευσαν.
καὶ εἶπεν αὐτοῖς,   b
   Πορευθέντες εἰς τὸν κόσμον ἅπαντα
   κηρύξατε τὸ εὐαγγέλιον πάσῃ τῇ κτίσει. [16]
  ὁ πιστεύσας καὶ βαπτισθεὶς σωθήσεται.
  ὁ δὲ ἀπιστήσας κατακριθήσεται. [17-18 omitted] [19]
Ὁ μὲν οὖν κύριος Ἰησοῦς   (a) b'
   μετὰ τὸ λαλῆσαι αὐτοῖς
   ἀνελήμφθη εἰς τὸν οὐρανὸν
  καὶ ἐκάθισεν   (b)
   ἐκ δεξιῶν
   τοῦ θεοῦ. [20a (b omitted)]
ἐκεῖνοι δὲ   (b')
   ἐξελθόντες
   ἐκήρυξαν πανταχοῦ. (*parechesis:* cf. 1.1; 1.2; 6.1 and 8.27)

```
Rising/ early/ on the first day of the week,        (a)    a    A
        he appeared/ firstly/ to Mary Magdalene,    (b)
        from whom/he had expelled/seven demons.     (b')
    That one (ekeine)                                       b
        going,
        reported to those who had been with him
                who were mourning
                and weeping.
    And those (kakeinoi)                                         b'
        hearing/ that he lives/ and was seen by her
        disbelieved.


After these things/ to two of them/ walking,        (a)    a    B
        he appeared in a different form              (b)
        as they were going into the country.         (b')
    And those (kakeinoi)                                    b
        going away
        reported to the rest.
    Neither those (ekeinois) they believed.                     b'


Last of all,/ to them sitting at table,/ to the eleven,  (a)  a   B'
        he appeared                                  (b)
        and reproached their disbelief
        and their hardness of heart,
        because the ones seeing him                  (b')
                having been raised
                they did not believe.
    And he said to them:                                    b
        'Going into all the world,
                preach the Gospel to all creation:
        the one believing/ and being baptized/ will be saved;
        the one disbelieving/ will be condemned.'
    The Lord Jesus therefore,                                   b'
                after speaking to them,
                was taken up into heaven,
        and he sat down
                at the right hand
                of God (theou),                      // 'ou' – sound
        but those (ekeinoi)
                going out
                preached everywhere (pantachou).     //
```

The literary-structure, with the removal of vv.17,18 and v.20b,c becomes that of a three-part, ABB', presentation, where all three sections behave consistently with previous form and now contain resurrection appearances, reportings, and a focus on matters of belief. It results in the word ἐκεῖνοι appearing in a repeated and emphatic position at, or very near the beginning of the last line of each section. The amendment further, and most interestingly, restores what were very likely the syllable-sounds to the endings of the last two parts of the

Gospel, so echoing the way the Gospel begins[468], τοῦ θεοῦ and πανταχοῦ [469]. The questionable παρ᾽ ἧς ἐκβεβλήκει ἑπτὰ δαιμόνια occupies a (b') setting, and appears to sit in true Markan fashion quite comfortably in the text. It can be maintained that it is Markan for its reference to "demons", and its numbering of them. "Seven", as elsewhere used in the Gospel, in first century understanding, represented 'fulfilment' and 'completion'. It would not have been beyond Mark's intention to affirm and emphasise Jesus' power to defeat evil, in this way and here too. It is a sure indicator that Jesus has fully and completely defeated evil now, by his dying and his rising[470].

It would appear, therefore, that we have a case for considering this reduced longer ending to be Mark's original Epilogue. It reflects Mark's method of structuring better than the longer ending as a whole does. Even though there is not much balance between the two B sections for size, there is nothing new in that. (Compare, for example, Day Twenty-eight's presentation.) This case will be strengthened, of course, if it can be shown that the Prologue and this Epilogue behave similarly as framing pieces to the Gospel's narrative.

Prologue (1.2-20) and reduced longer-ending (16.9-16,19-20a) compared:

In my presentations of both Prologue and longer ending I have given some attention to the fact that they both do more than present a story-line: they both engage the listener in identifying with the disciples. Now we can see how both Prologue and reduced longer ending each break down structurally into three parts. We have noted above how they each employ introductory pieces to their parts which are not found elsewhere in the Gospel. We have just seen that there is a common employment of *parechesis*, at the beginning of the Prologue and in the concluding of the reduced longer ending. In my summary on the Prologue, I estimated that it covered fifty days or thereabouts, as a minimum. We may judge that the period the reduced longer ending covers is at the very least seven days (see page 314). We note that Church tradition, after Luke, suggests forty days, and forty days, of course, has its parallel in the Prologue's forty days of Jesus' time in the desert. Clearly, the reportings of these two framing elements contrast with those which make up the gospel narrative (1.21-16.8). These both cover a number of days each, whereas the other primary elements cover one Day at a time. Thematically and in some verbal details we do find significant correspondences between the Prologue and this reduced longer ending. They are listed:

1)   The mission of the one coming before Jesus is spoken about in the Prologue: the mission of those coming after Jesus is spoken about in the reduced longer ending.
2)   In the Prologue, disciples are called to follow and a promise is made by Jesus regarding their future function; in the reduced longer ending, they are commissioned and sent out.
3)   In the Prologue, the heavens open and the Spirit descends on Jesus; in the reduced longer ending, Jesus himself ascends into heaven.
4)   The little-used term in the Gospel, of "Lord", is applied to Jesus in both the Prologue and the reduced longer ending, see 1.3 and 16.19 for a variant, "Lord Jesus".
5)   The phrase "preaching the gospel" is common also to both: in 1.14, it is what Jesus is doing "in Galilee"; in 16.15, he is commanding his disciples to do the same; and in 16.20a the reduced longer ending indeed concludes with their preaching "everywhere".

---

[468]For this feature, turn to the examination of the Prologue, and also to the examinations of the opening Days to the two middle Series, and of Day Twenty-four, the longest in the telling of all Days (13.1/3 where the same οῦ sound would appear to confirm the beginning of the second half in the presentation).
[469]The word πανταχοῦ is used by Mark previously in 1.28.
[470]For the connection between the dying of Jesus and the defeat of evil, see my summaries at the end of Chapter Six.

6)   The word "baptism" is common to both: in both Prologue and reduced longer ending, it is understood to have salvific importance for all people.

7)   "Belief" is also important in both: in the Prologue, at 1.15, Jesus says, "Repent and believe the gospel of God"; in the reduced longer ending, at 16.16, he makes a two-fold statement, "The one believing and being baptised will be saved: but the one who disbelieves will be condemned"[471].

8)   Three geographical names and settings of the Prologue are interpreted in the reduced longer ending from the passion: Jerusalem, Judaea and Galilee.

9)   In the Prologue, Jesus calls two sets of two brothers to be his disciples; in the reduced longer ending, he appears to two disciples.

10)   As with Homer's *Iliad*, the Prologue and the Epilogue each cover a multiplicity of Days.

It can be said, therefore, that the Prologue of twenty verses and the reduced longer ending of nine-and-a-half verses connect in these ways. What remains to be done is to give consideration to some of Mark's key words and phrases, and to consider his use of them throughout his Gospel as they reflect his development and completion of his themes, and his 'arrangement' of them in his Prologue, Narrative and Epilogue. If the reduced longer ending is Mark's Epilogue, it will demonstrate a sympathetic use of them.

We observe firstly an important and most significant difference between the Prologue and the possible Epilogue. It is that the Prologue emphasises in several ways that Jesus' mission is to the Jews. It is they who are repenting and preparing themselves for his mission. It is Old Covenant scripture and Jewish expectations which are being fulfilled. And it is Jewish territory, principally, in which Jesus is set. In the proposed Epilogue, it is Galilee in which the stories are set, but the mission of the disciples is now to the "world" and to "all creation", with the result that they "preached everywhere". Clearly, this difference between the Prologue and the proposed Epilogue can be judged to be a feature which well expresses the thrust of Mark's narrative. It is a story which has begun with the Jews, but which ends with the "world".

This description of this framing well establishes the paradigm for the narrative itself, for which for each of its Series, Mark presents Jesus' mission: in its first sub-Series, to the Jews in respect to the Old Covenant; at the turning point, in respect to Jewish/Gentile tension which focuses upon him; and in the second sub-Series, in respect to the New Covenant and to Gentiles.

We have seen, under the examination of the Passion Narrative in Chapter Six, how the word, "covenant" is used only once in the Gospel, in 14.24, but that Mark's use of the term, where it does appear, spells out the truth for the very first time, that Jesus' death establishes the (New) Covenant. Up till then, the Gospel's first three Series' second sub-Series had been pointing to this truth, only by allusion and in veiled terms. The reference in the Epilogue, in 16.15, to the "world" and to "creation" puts it beyond any doubt that the New Covenant is not just for the Jews but for the world, for Gentiles. The word "world" is first found in 8.36 (in the first Day's teaching of Jesus on discipleship, in Series Three). Significantly, it is next found in 14.9 (the middle Day and turning point of the Fourth Series). Here the "world" and the "gospel" are linked by "preaching", which is what we find in the Epilogue at 16.15. The Epilogue is in harmony with the Fourth Series, which at its centre and 'turning point' reveals (in true ancient rhetorical style) the significance of what is taking place.

Earlier use of the word "creation" is found in 10.6 (the turning point of Series Three), and in 13.19 (in the apocalyptic teaching of Jesus, of Day three in the final Series). There is more than a hint in the Prologue and the Narrative that Mark understands Jesus' mission as that of establishing a New Creation. In the Introduction, we noticed the possibility that his 'ar-

---

[471]We note that Luke, in his parallel opening and closing sections to his Gospel makes much of "believing and disbelieving", see Palmer, *Sliced Bread...*, pp.82ff.

rangement' and 'style' had been influenced by the Genesis accounts of creation and new creation, in Gen. 1-11 (pages 10,11). His Gospel opens in Genesis' style. The Prologue begins the telling of 'twos' in the Gospel (compare animals entering the ark) and the proposed Epilogue (16.12) completes the telling of "twos":

in the Prologue	we observe two calls of two named individuals, four in all;
in the first Series	they are named again in the first day, Day 1, 1.29;
in the second Series	the first day, Day 8, the disciples are sent out "two by two", 6.7;
in the third Series	'two', who are named, meet with Jesus at his transfiguration on the second day, Day 16, 9.4, and in the balancing day of the series, Day 20, 'two' who are named ask to sit either side of Jesus in his glory, 10.37;
in the fourth Series	on the days beginning both sub-series of three days, Days 22 and 26, 11.1 and 14.13, Jesus sends 'two' (not named) each time to make preparations for him; and
in the longer ending	Jesus appears to 'two' (not named), 16.12.

That is a lot of 'twos', and it is also a reasonably well balanced distribution of the same. For a possible significance, we need to return to the Introduction, and to matters raised on page 10 in regard to the motif of the flood which we observed might have had an influence on Mark's compositional arrangement. Clearly, in the flood story, it is animals which go into the ark and are saved from God's judgement in order that they might "multiply on the earth and be fruitful and increase in number upon it" (Gen. 8.17). The story-line does appeal, nevertheless, as a parallel to judgement and salvation, and to mission, as they pertain to followers of Jesus. The narrative of the Flood for its 'twenty-seventh day' (Gen. 8.14ff.) which marks the moments of the completion of God's judgement of the world and its evil (v.21), and of his work of new creation (see particularly v.17) parallels exactly Mark's Twenty-seventh Day's telling of Jesus' death. (In 13.30,31, in the context of "this generation", Jesus' "words" - *cf.* Gen. 1.3,6,9 and so on - contrast with the passing away of "the heaven and the earth".) The proposed Epilogue's reference to "creation", in 16.15, is indicative of the opportunity the world now has for 'recreation', and it is synonymous with what the Gospel as a whole indicates.

The word "gospel" is, of course introduced in the opening line of the Prologue. In pages 13-15 of the Introduction, we considered political and historical issues which might have caused Mark to begin writing. We interpreted there that the late 60's, and the year 70 in particular, were "bad news" for the Jews, but that he had "good news" to share with the world, with both Jews and Gentiles. God had made a New Covenant with the world, which was more than a replacement for the Old Covenant which was suffering its demise. The Prologue makes clear in the first instance, in 1.14,15, that the "gospel" was for the Jews. The next mentions of the word "gospel" are not until 8.35 (in the first Day's telling of the first sub-Series of the Third Series, which goes on to tell, in the second day, about Old Covenant fulfilments pertaining to the Jews) and 10.29 (in the first Day's telling of the second sub-Series of Series Three, which goes on to tell, in its second day, about New Covenant foundations laid down at the hands of the Gentiles). Both read "for the sake of me and the gospel". The next use of the word "gospel" appears in 13.10 (in Jesus' apocalyptic teaching): it is to be preached to all the "Gentiles/nations". In 14.9 (the turning point of Series Four), it appears again, as we noted above: it will be "preached" in all the "world". The word "gospel", then, is found extra to the Prologue, at significant structural points in the Series' tellings, and in the apocalyptic teaching of Jesus. Its use in the proposed Epilogue is entirely in keeping with Mark's employment of the word elsewhere. His emphasis, at the last, in 16.15, that the "gospel" is for all the "world" and for all "creation" is entirely in keeping with his development and his completing of his Gospel.

We have begun to see already above the significance also of the word "Gentiles" in Mark's Gospel. We noted in the summaries at the end of Chapter Six that the first allusion to Gentiles is at the turning point of Series One, in regard to the Herodians (who are under Roman authority) and their plotting with Pharisees (under the Old Covenant) against Jesus, 3.6. Gentiles and Gentile country are also only alluded to in the First Series' second sub-Series. In the Second Series, after the turning point mention of the Greek woman, Gentile country and Gentiles are alluded to again, but more strongly than before (notably again in the second sub-Series). It is not until 10.33 and 10.42, in Series Three's second sub-Series, that we encounter uses of the word itself. Most significantly, the first mention of the word "Gentiles" links them with the suffering and death of Jesus (cf. 3.6, for the first hint of this): Jesus will be handed over to "the Gentiles" who will mock, spit, whip and kill him. Gentiles indeed do all these things to Jesus, according to report in Series Four's second sub-Series, on the same sixth Day of that Series. Further, at the scene and at the moment of Jesus' death, it is a Gentile, "a centurion", 15.39, to whom understanding is given. (I have pointed out before that on the sixth Day of the First Series, Jesus demonstrates that he is victorious over great evil. That Day's telling anticipates this. On that Day, evil is expressed as "Legion", a Gentile word with the same characteristic as that of "centurion".) Further employments of the word "Gentiles" appear in the Fourth Series' first sub-Series, in 11.17 (the Temple was always intended for "all Gentiles/nations": Jesus replaces the temple with himself, 14.58, 15.29, and rights a wrongful practice), and in the apocalyptic discourse again, in 13.8, 13.10 (in the first, in relation to wars soon to be engaged, and in the second, as above, in relation to the "preaching of the gospel"). The word "Gentiles" from that point becomes eclipsed by the more inclusive word, "world" (for which, see above; it is indisputably inclusive of both Jews and Gentiles). The use of the word "Gentiles", only towards the end of the Gospel narrative, sharpens the focus on what we can call Mark's scheme, by which the "gospel" is presented firstly to the Jews, but which by the involvement of Gentiles becomes the "gospel" for the "world". The proposed Epilogue well concludes this scheme.

Finally, we consider Mark's use of the phrase, "Jesus of Nazareth" (lit. "Jesus the Nazarene"). In the Prologue, Jesus is presented as the one who "came from Nazareth", 1.9. The term "Jesus of Nazareth" is first found in 1.24 (in the First Day's telling of the narrative). It is last found in 16.6 (in the Last Day's telling). It serves in one sense as an *inclusio* in the narrative. It is found also in 10.47 (in the last Day's telling of Series Three): here Mark makes it plain that "Jesus of Nazareth" is accorded messianic status. It is also found in 14.67 (in the first Day's telling of the last Series' second sub-Series), where it corresponds with the final use of the term, in 16.6, as an anastrophe (in the last Day's telling of the same sub-Series). In 16.6, "Jesus of Nazareth" who was crucified is risen; he is not there in the tomb. In the proposed Epilogue, Jesus is not actually named at all until the final scene, where just as he is "taken up" into heaven, in 16.19, he *is* named, and titled, "the Lord Jesus", for the first and only time in the whole Gospel. (The longer ending's use of this term is not as strange, or as foreign to Mark, as scholars have supposed, given the setting, and given also the earlier uses of the former title for Jesus.) In other words, in the narrative, Mark presents Jesus as "Jesus of Nazareth". In the Prologue, Mark tells us where he has come from, and titles him simply "Jesus". In the proposed Epilogue, Mark tells us where he is going, and addresses him "the Lord Jesus", just at the point of his going up to heaven. There is evidence of Markan intention here, and of a Markan systematic use of titling for Jesus. The Epilogue's reverencing of Jesus with the title "Lord", at the last, and at such a moment, is entirely in keeping with the story-line of the Gospel which in its Prologue, in the scripture quotation in 1.3, identifies Jesus with the "Lord" of prophecy. (For other references to "Lord" as it pertains to Jesus in the narrative, consider for possibilities: 2.28, 5.19, 7.28, 11.3, 12.37.)

With these word-studies, I near the conclusion of my presentation of the evidence for viewing my reduction of the longer ending as the original Epilogue of Mark's Gospel. It is that of 16.9-16,19-20a and it is as important to Mark's Gospel as his Prologue. It completes the framing of the Narrative, and it completes, therefore, Mark's presentation. It is not just the rhetorical structure of the Gospel that require it, but, further to this, it is also confirmed within the Greek text as having a belonging and, for this, it is detailed in the text, put deliberately there by the rhetor for the reader to check that he is reading the work as the writer intended. The 'helps' for the reader are found in the last part of three in the Prologue (the B' part) and the first part of three in the Epilogue (the A part), that is in the immediately framing pieces to the Narrative. This is not peculiar to Mark's Gospel alone. All the Gospels evidence the same kind of 'helps', deliberately well-placed by the writers/rhetors.[472] So, with Mark, the essential Prologue ends with an introduction of 'two pairs of brothers' and the essential Epilogue begins with a mention of 'seven' demons because the Gospel comprises two pairs of sections (two middle and two outer) of seven Days each.

Presented below, in conformity with Chapters Three and Six, are summaries of the common, basic literary-structural features of these components of the Gospel:

A Tabular Summary of the literary-structures of the Prologue and the revised longer ending, the original Epilogue:

DAYS: before and after	$\mathrm{P.}$ Prologue	$\mathrm{E.}$ Epilogue
chapters and verses	1.1-20	16.9--16, 19-20a
Sections: for comparison with the narrative text	A B B'	A B B'
	A B B'	A B B'
Number of verses	20	9 1/2

Conclusion:

In 1903, since Wellhausen[473] raised his objections to the longer ending and proposed that Mark ended his Gospel at 16.8, many have added to the arguments and I have now introduced mine. New information comes out of a literary-structural analysis of the text itself. Reference to the rules and practices of ancient rhetoric repays generously; they have been long neglected. And if Mark had written more, it would have been an account about an appearance (or appearances) of the risen Jesus, of one or more to the disciples, and set in Galilee. Our *reduced longer ending*, as laid out above, satisfies these three criteria. Further, it has to be seen

---

[472] With Matthew, for a single example, it is in the opening piece that the numbers 3 and 14 are introduced and in the closing piece that the number 11 is first given. Both are excellent checks for the reader, reader/reciter: Matthew's Gospel comprises 'eleven' sections (chiastically-arranged) where a standard section comprises 'fourteen' pieces and two major teaching sections comprise 'three times fourteen' pieces. See my *New Testament: New Testimony...*

[473] J. Wellhausen, *Das Evangelium Marci*, Reimer, Berlin, 1903. But notice: Eusebius got there before him by a 'few' centuries and Simon too in the C17th: see pages 310 and 311.

in the light, not of its relationship to the report of the last Day alone (16.1-8), but of its relationship to the reports of the last threesome of "Days" (of the gospel narrative). Furthermore, in regard to Mark's overall Gospel plan and purpose, the *reduced longer ending* much completes what the Prologue begins and what the Gospel narrative develops.

As a result of literary-structural analysis and the attendant investigations of the Gospel of Mark, 1.1-16.20, I accept, therefore, that the *reduced longer ending*, 16.9-16,19-20a, is the original 'Epilogue", or one that is very near to it which Mark himself did indeed write to complete his Gospel.

If we now ask the question, "Did Matthew and Luke know Mark's original Epilogue?" we can at least answer that this reducing of the content of the longer ending *takes nothing away* from the possibility that they did. Only, in regard to Luke's second book, and as to what inspired him to write it, have we been considering the possibility that he knew the "longer ending" in its entirety, with vv.17,18 and v.20b. But, as we have argued in Section 4) above, it is more likely that it was the other way about, that Luke's second book inspired the *editor* of the longer ending to add to it.

What is fascinating to consider, is that new arguments *can be added* now to the discussion under section 4). We were there reviewing the possibility of Matthew's and Luke's re-handling of the longer ending. Given the reduced longer ending, it is not the removal of vv.17,18 that particularly raises new issues, but the removal of v.20b that does. The ending of Mark's 'Epilogue' reports the ascension of Jesus, and the eleven's leaving to preach everywhere. (We have considered already Matthew's possible reasons for rejecting the ascension scene.) It may well be that Matthew reacted to Mark's ending (or Matthew's church did) which clearly could be interpreted, without v.20b, that Jesus 'is not here anymore'. Without v.20b, there is no 'accompanying Jesus'. The argument might go this way that Matthew replaced the ending of vv.19,20a with one which assured the church of Jesus' continuing presence (see Mt. 28.20b).

Finally, given my arguments and my conclusions for believing that Mark's Epilogue is now 'found', I present what I consider is a likely re-construction of the events which led to its becoming 'lost' in the Longer Ending. It is mostly *suggested* by the historic documents and the manuscripts to which we have access today:

Mark's Gospel, 1.1-16.16,19,20a, was circulating in the churches from the early seventies. It was the first compilation of its kind. It was received gladly, but it attracted a number of criticisms, chief among which was that its Epilogue *could be* interpreted that "Jesus was no longer present in his church"[474]. This and other deficiencies prompted the contributions of both Matthew and Luke. In addition, these two writers had much more teaching tradition to share than Mark had included.

Sometime after Luke's second book, the Acts of the Apostles, was written, Mark's Epilogue was revised, by addition only of vv.17,18 and v.20bc. It was carried out by someone who was sympathetic to his style, but who was not aware of his *parachesis*, or who thought it comparatively unimportant. The amendment attempted to resolve the chief deficiency, as described above. It attempted also to give the church a warrant for experiencing signs and miracles in its mission work. Material for the amendment came from the editor's reading of the Acts, and a legend on drinking poison without harmful effect (as in 16.18: a second reference to which is not found anywhere in the New Testament[475]).

---

[474]Compare Mt.28.16-20 (for which see my earlier arguments), and Luke's second book for the "Acts of the Holy Sprit". Consider also that Mark expected Jesus' early return. Matthew does likewise, and his emphasis on obedience (28.20) is as important as the other changes he makes to Mark's ending.

[475]But mentioned by Papias (Eus. *HE*, 3.39) of Barsabbas and in a well-known legend concerning St. John (Acts of John, xx, cf. M.R. James, *The Apocryphal New Testament*, Clarendon Press, Oxford, 1924), and in many stories attested by Theophylact (v. H.B. Swete, *The Gospel according to St. Mark*, 3rd Ed. Macmillan, London, 1913, p.406).

Mark's Gospel with this longer ending (vv.9-20) began to circulate in the early part of the second century. During this phase of the Gospel's life, patristic scholars began noticing and addressing the difficulties caused by differences between the longer ending and Matthew's Gospel in matters of the timing of Jesus' resurrection (by then Matthew's Gospel was being viewed as the tradition)[476]. Vv.17,18, also began to attract criticism for the trouble that they were causing in the church (regarding spiritual gifts and their exercise). Attempts to contain this trouble failed. It was decided eventually by the Church leaders in Alexandria that the longer ending should be expunged altogether[477].

Copies of the reduced Gospel, 1.1-16.8, then began to be made and to be circulated. A few copies of the Gospel with its amended Epilogue existed. They were not destroyed. They simply lay in storage. No copies of the original Gospel were being made by then. Copies had been so well read that they had disintegrated with use, and they were beyond further useful reference. In various centres throughout the mission field, collections of manuscripts began to be made.

In the fourth century, Eusebius had access to one such collection of manuscripts. Most of his copies, and his best copies at that, were of 1.1-16.8, but he did have some copies of the version with the longer ending. In the year 331, Constantine requested "fifty copies of the sacred scriptures". Eusebius, naturally, made copies of the best manuscripts available to him. *Gospel Questions and Solutions Addressed to Marinus*[478] and Codices Vaticanus and Siniaticus are testimony to this.

A century later, in Alexandria, the "longer ending", the *edited original* Epilogue, resurfaced and vv.9-20 included. Codex Alexandrinus is testimony to that. Elsewhere, by then other endings were being written and attached, with the result that copies began to be made and to circulate with more than one ending. Other manuscripts are evidence of this.

A Final Comment:

In summary of the analyses and conclusions of this Chapter (contrary to the great weight of scholarly opinion), it can be stated that Mark did write an epilogue and that the Epilogue which is original to Mark has lain undiscovered *in* the longer ending. It is 16.9-16,19-20a. It is as important to Mark's Gospel as his Prologue. The Prologue and the Epilogue provide framing to the Gospel, and the Epilogue completes, therefore, Mark's presentation. It needs to be read because it contributes much to our understanding of the writer's purposes and his reasons for writing.

---

[476]See notes 407 and 408.
[477]Refer to note 418.
[478]See note 408.

Chapter Eight
So, what is Mark's Gospel?

Firstly, we gather up the results of the literary-structural analyses of Chapters Two to Seven. We chart everything as we go and assess the ways that the text works. For further evidence, we summarise Mark's method and the rhetorical devices he used, as discovered in the analyses of the Days and of the Series of Days. We then check it all against the Rules of Hellenist (ancient) rhetoric. At this point, we will be able to answer the question posed, 'What is Mark's Gospel?' When we have done this, we will re-visit the fundamental questions in the Study of Mark's Gospel and at the same time assess new studies that have taken place since 1999 that relate to this work and contribute to our thinking on this Gospel. We will explore what the book requires now in regard to exegesis, its exposition and interpretation. And lastly, we will think about the importance and significance of this work for New Testament studies today.

The Results of Literary-structural Analysis:

The Table below summarises my findings in regard to the schematic arrangement of Days and Series of Days in the Gospel Narrative, 1.21-16.8.

Table 1: The Primary Schematic Structure of the Gospel Narrative:

a	1	2	3	4	5	6	7	8	9	10	11	12	13	14	15	16	17	18	19	20	21	22	23	24	25	26	27	28
b	1	2	3	4	5	6	7	1	2	3	4	5	6	7	1	2	3	4	5	6	7	1	2	3	4	5	6	7
c	A	B	B'		A	B	B'	A	B	B'		A	B	B'	A	B	B'		A	B	B'	A	B	B'		A	B	B'
d		A			B			A'				A			B			A'				A			B		A'	
e				A							B							B'							A'			
f	1						172	2						119	3						112	4						239

Key:	a	Days of the Gospel narrative;
	b	Days of the Series of seven days;
	c	Days in sub-Series of threes;
	d	Series of Days: the three sections of each;
	e	Series of Days of the Gospel narrative;
	f	number of verses of the four Series.

The information for this table is found in the written and tabular summaries of Chapters Three to Six. Clearly, what is demonstrated is a regular and systematic presentation on Mark's part in his construction of the Series, in the number of Days they comprise, and in the arrangement of the Days within the Series. In terms of the Series' numbers of verses, the middle two Series balance for size (compare verses 119 and 112) and the outer two reasonably balance as the larger presentations (172 and 239 respectively).

Again, from the written and tabular summaries, but this time taken from Chapters Two to Seven, we can establish Mark's Series' theme plan and basic structure for the whole of his Gospel:

Table 2: The Gospel's Series' Theme Plan and Basic Structure:

Title 1.1
Prologue: 1.2-20

SERIES A: Jesus' First Days of Mission, confined to Galilee and the Region of its Sea:

Day 1	Day 2	Day 3	Day 4	Day 5	Day 6	Day 7
1.21-38	1.39-45	2.1-22	2.23-3.6	3.7-4.41	5.1-20	5.21-43

Sub-Series: A: 1.21-2.22   B: 2.23-3.6   A': 3.7-5.43

SERIES B: Days of Increase in the Mission of Jesus:

Day 1	Day 2	Day 3	Day 4	Day 5	Day 6	Day 7
6.1-29	6.30-52	6.53-7.23	7.24-30	7.31-37	8.1-21	8.22-26

Sub-Series: A: 6.1-7.23   B: 7.24-30   A': 7.31-8.26

SERIES B': The Days of Jesus Journeying to Jerusalem:

Day 1	Day 2	Day 3	Day 4	Day 5	Day 6	Day 7
8.27-9.1	9.2-32	9.33-50	10.1-16	10.17-31	10.32-46a	10.46b-52

Sub-Series: A: 8.27-9.50   B: 10.1-16   A': 10.17-52

SERIES A': Jesus' Jerusalem Days: his Passion and Resurrection:

Day 1	Day 2	Day 3	Day 4	Day 5	Day 6	Day 7
11.1-11	11.12-19	11.20-13.37	14.1-11	14.12-72	15.1-47	16.1-8

Sub-Series: A: 11.1-13.37   B: 14.1-11   A': 14.12-16.8

Epilogue 16.9-16, 19-20a

Table 3: The Gospel's Fixed and Repeating Arrangements:

The Prologue: The Gospel appears to be for the Jews

The scheme for each of the four Series:

The first sub-Series: Jews and the Old Covenant
The turning point: Jews/Gentiles, Old Covenant/New Covenant
The second sub-Series: The New Covenant and Gentiles

The Epilogue: The Gospel is for the World.

I risk stating this too simply. Some will say that there is mention of "Jews" here, and allusions to "Gentiles" there. Yes, but the above does, nevertheless, reflect Mark's purpose for the three parts of each of his four Series' presentations, and it does reflect the effect that his narrative has upon the difference between the foci of his Prologue and Epilogue. We discovered much of the evidence for this consideration in my summaries of Chapters Six and Seven. It was there that we found the 'rhetorical plan' of Mark could be represented as simply as this. The charts below will show this discovery more clearly.

Additionally, in the outer Series, as I have identified in my summaries of the four Series, Series A and A' display Markan 'arrangement' after the manner of an Aristotelian understanding of the structure of a Greek Tragedy: the first sub-Series is the 'complication', the middle day is the 'turning point', and the second sub-Series is the 'dénouement'. The middle two Series, B and B', however, simply display the same balance of contents structurally. It is tempting to describe them in Aristotelian fashion, but I judge that would be to force the argument. Clearly, issues of "rigidity" and "flexibility" on Mark's part arise with such summaries as these.

According to Best[479], both Farrer and Carrington envisaged "rigid planning" on Mark's part, though they came to very different conclusions. Farrer[480] suggested a scheme based on numerology in relation to miracles and five-paragraph sectionalising. Carrington[481] pursued the possibility that the order of the material was dictated by the liturgical needs of the church. The arrangement (or matrix) which is presented here (Prologue, four Series of seven Days, Epilogue) might properly be described as "rigid", and Mark's presentational method, for its ABB' form, one that might be termed "rigid" also, but the evidence shows flexibility, nevertheless, on Mark's part, as he composed his Day-reports. His "rhetorical" and "rigid" plan did not strait-jacket him. We consider this feature in the next few summary tables:

Table 4: Number and Order of Verses of "Days":

	Day 1	2	3	4	5	6	7
Series A	13th 18 verses	24th 7	10th 22	19th 12	2nd 70	12th 20	8th 23
B	6th 29	8th 23	7th 27	24th 7	24th 7	11th 21	28th 5
B'	18th 13	5th 31	14th 16	14th 16	16th 15	17th 14.5	27th 6.5
A'	20th 11	22nd 8	1st 94	20th 11	3rd 61	4th 46	22nd 8

---

[479]Best, *Mark: the Gospel as Story*, p.107.
[480]Farrer, *A Study in St Mark...*
[481]P. Carrington, *The Primitive Christian Calendar: A Study in the Making of the Markan Gospel*, Cambridge University Press, Cambridge, 1952.

The range of verses is from 5, for the seventh Day of Series B, to 94, for the third Day of Series A'. The factor of difference is nearly 19. On this basis alone, it would be improper to call Mark's compositional approach "rigid". Even when we consider the numbers of verses of Days within the Series themselves (as we perhaps should, judging their weight within the local setting of each Series and not the Gospel as a whole) the ranges are still more variable and the factors of difference are still greater than we might have expected them to be in a planned presentation:

	Range:	Factor of difference:
Series A:	7 to 70 verses	10
Series B:	5 to 29	just less than 6
Series B':	6.5 to 31	just less than 5
Series A':	8 to 94	just less than 12.

From these results, because the factors of difference are less for the two middle Series, we may judge that Mark exercised greater control over these Series than the outer two.

Table 5: Number and Order of Verses over all:

Series:	A A : B : B'	B	A' A : B : B'	Totals:
A	6th 47	12	2nd 113	2nd 172
B	4th 79	7	8th 33	3rd 119
B'	5th 60	16	7th 36	4th 112
A'	2nd 113	11	1st 115	1st 239

Again we discern a Series' range overall of 112 verses for Series B' and 239 verses for Series A', and a sub-Series range of 33 verses for the second (A') of Series B and 115 verses for the second (A') of Series A'. Mark's "rhetorical plan" has not strait-jacketed him: where he has had more material to present, his rhetorical method has been flexible enough to cope with it. As was discussed in the summaries of the analyses of each Series, it is necessary to conclude that Mark was not as interested in quantitative balance of composition as he was with completing his constructions, whether at the level of ABA' (for sub-Series A, pivotal Day B, sub-Series B'), or at the level of ABB' (for the sub-Series: Day A, Day B, Day B'), or at the level of his Day compositions (which we will summarise below). Though we have noted above already that the inner two Series compare well for overall size and the outer two also, it is not so much in terms of their number of verses, but rather in terms of their contents, both thematic and detailed, that balance is perceived in turn between the inner two Series, the outer two Series, and also the Prologue and Epilogue.

Table 6a: Artwork showing Fundamental Correspondences:

MARK'S GOSPEL

Vertically, for example:
In the two middle series, B and B': compare
the first days of each: for Jesus' identity: in both, he is John the Baptist, Elijah, a prophet;
the last days of each: for stories of healings of blind people (the only two in the Gospel);
the middle days: for common openings: 'And from there', rising up', 'into the region'.
In the two outer series, A and A': compare
the first days of each: Jesus enters a city and the principal place of Jewish worship there;
the last days of each: these are stories of resurrection (the only two in the Gospel);
the middle days: they tell of plots against Jesus (the first and the last in the Gospel).
Horizontally, for example: in
the first Days of each three day sub-series (Days 1 and 5):
the First Series we read about healings and casting out of demons (the demons are to be quiet);
the Last Series we read about 'two' disciples being sent by Jesus who foresees things.
the second Days of each sub-series (Days 2 and 6):
the First Series we read about individual men to whom Jesus ministered;
the Second we read about desert banquets, of 5,000 in the first and 4,000 in the second;
the Third we read about 'two' with Jesus in glory and 'two' wishing to be with him in glory;
the Fourth we read about the clearing of the temple of the old sacrificial means of being
made right with God and, in turn, about the new means of being made right with God.
Diagonally, for example, consider:
First Series, Fifth Day and Last Series, Third Day, for 'teaching', and also
First Series, Third Day and Last Series, Fifth Day, for 'sitting at table' content.

I have chosen to show the new Table 6a before my previous Table 6b

Table 6b: Fundamental Correspondences:

P J		1		2	3		4	5		6	7
A	k t	1		2 m	3 I x (y)		4 H	5 G t x (z)		6 n	7 F
B	A s	1		2 B	3 w		4 C	5 s w		6 D	7 E
B'	A r	1		2 B	3 v		4 C	5 r v		6 D p	7 E
A'	k q	1		2 m	3 I u (z)		4 H	5 G q u (y)		6 n p	7 F
E J											

With this table, I first attempted to represent: by same capital letter annotation, the primary correspondences between Days in the balancing Series; by same lower case letter, significant further correspondences Day to Day; and by bracketed, lower case letters, the principle diagonal relationships of Days. The table attempts to summarise those correspondences that we observed in the Series' summaries (see the concluding presentations of Chapters Five, Six and Seven). Mark has employed rhetorical techniques whereby correspondences establish: in the first place, the beginnings and ends of his Series; in the second, the beginnings of his Series' sub-Series; in the third, 'transitional smoothings' in Days three and five of his Series, around a central Day four; and in the fourth, relationships between his outer Series which are of a diagonal kind. Further, consider my extended list of Farrer's identifications, of progressive and corresponding details in the comparison of the First and the Fourth Series of Seven Days (in Chapter Six): many do not correspond Day to Day. Mark has exercised freedom too, and has not been bound to balancing every detail and sub-theme in his scheme. But what it clearly suggests is that as he composed one Series, he had the other to hand as he did so. He was guided by it, but he did not feel required to follow it slavishly. It is, of course, impossible to summarise here all the many correspondences, and the functions of them all. My analyses of the Days themselves will have to be gone through again and again.

In the same vein, we can consider the structures of Mark's Days, Prologue and Epilogue, as taken from the summary tables in Chapters Two to Seven:

Table 7a: The Structures of the Gospel's Component Parts (1999):

P	A						
A	1 A/A'	2 A	3 A/A'	4 A/A'	5 AA'/AA'	6 A/A'	7 ABB'
B	1 A/A'	2 ABB'	3 ABB'	4 A	5 A	6 A/A'	7 A
B'	1 A/A'	2 AA'/AA'	3 ABB'	4 A	5 A	6 A	7 A
A'	1 A/A'	2 A	3 A/A'	4 A	5 ABB'	6 A/A'	7 A
E	A						

Table 7b: The Structures of the Gospel's Component Parts (2020):

P	ABB'						
A	1 ABB'	2 A	3 ABB'	4 ABB'	5 ABB'	6 ABB'	7 ABB'
B	1 ABB'	2 ABB'	3 ABB'	4 A	5 A	6 ABB'	7 A
B'	1 ABB'	2 ABB'	3 ABB'	4 A	5 A	6 A	7 A
A'	1 ABB'	2 A	3 ABB'	4 A	5 ABB'	6 ABB'	7 A
E	ABB'						

I have deliberately chosen to show the two tables, thus recording the changes to my analyses that have been required over the past twenty-one years. It is the case that it has taken me time to become a first-century reader of texts presented in columns of rows of letters (but practically speaking, taking the best texts available today and ignoring all punctuation, sentence and paragraph divisions, etc.). Over the last years, I have been doing the same with all the texts of the New Testament. I have been improving, therefore, my skills and learning how to read like a first-century reader.[482]

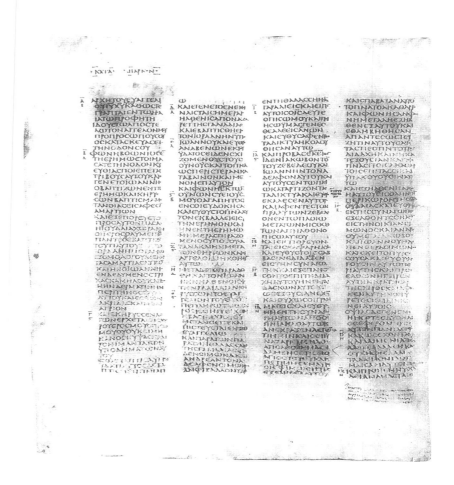

Above, I present the first folio of Mark's Gospel from Codex Sinaiticus, possibly produced in AD 331. What greeted the reader, therefore, were columns of lines of letters with no gaps between words, no punctuation and only the occasional edentation (protruding single, or half letters) in the left hand margin with an attendant space in the preceding line, which was used to denote a paragraph, or new section beginning. We would be a little upset today to be presented with such a paper to read, I guess!

Below, I present my own *Sinaiticus-type Version* of a well-known children's story, in English. Even though I have not included edentations (I found them too difficult to put in using the software I have), my expectation is that you will be near to reading it perfectly after expending a little effort only.

---

[482] See David G. Palmer, *New Testament: New Testimony to the Skills of the Writers and First Readers*, the Fifth - Illustrated Exhibition – Edition, Ceridwen Press: Church Gresley, 2016, for the results of my analyses of all the books of the New Testament.

THELITTLEREDHENANDTHEGRAIN	HEATASKEDTHELITTLEREDHENNO	WHOWILLHELPMETOTAKETHISFL
SOFWHEATONCEUPONATIMETHE	TISAIDTHECATNOTISAIDTHERATN	OURTOTHEBAKERTOBEMADEINT
REWASALITTLEREDHENWHOLIVE	OTISAIDTHEPIGTHENISHALLCUTT	OBREADASKEDTHELITTLEREDHEN
DINAFARMYARDONEDAYTHELITTL	HEWHEATMYSELFSAIDTHELITTLE	NOTISAIDTHECATNOTISAIDTHERA
EREDHENFOUNDSOMEGRAINSOF	REDHENSOSHEDIDTHEWHEATISN	TNOTISAIDTHEPIGTHENISHALLTA
WHEATSHETOOKTHEMTOTHEOT	OWREADYTOBEMADEINTOFLOUR	KETHEFLOURTOTHEBAKERMYSELF
HERANIMALSINTHEFARMYARDW	SAIDTHELITTLEREDHENTOHERSEL	SAIDTHELITTLEREDHENSOSHEDID
HOWILLHELPMETOPLANTTHESEG	FASSHESETOFFFORTHEFARMYAR	THELITTLEREDHENTOOKTHEFLOU
RAINSOFWHEATASKEDTHELITTLE	DWHOWILLHELPMETOTAKETHEW	RTOTHEBAKERANDTHEBAKERMA
REDHENNOTISAIDTHECATNOTISAI	HEATTOTHEMILLTOBEGROUNDIN	DEITINTOBREADWHENTHEBREAD
DTHERATNOTISAIDTHEPIGTHENIS	TOFLOURASKEDTHELITTLEREDHE	WASBAKEDTHELITTLEREDHENTO
HALLPLANTTHEGRAINSMYSELFSAI	NNOTISAIDTHECATNOTISAIDTHER	OKITTOTHEOTHERANIMALSINTHE
DTHELITTLEREDHENSOSHEDIDEVE	ATNOTISAIDTHEPIGTHENISHALLT	FARMYARDTHEBREADISNOWREA
RYDAYTHELITTLEREDHENWENTTO	AKETHEWHEATTOTHEMILLMYSEL	DYTOBEATENSAIDTHELITTLEREDH
THEFIELDTOWATCHTHEGRAINSOF	FSAIDTHELITTLEREDHENSOSHEDI	ENWHOWILLHELPMETOEATTHEB
WHEATGROWINGTHEYGREWTALL	DTHELITTLEREDHENTOOKTHEWH	READIWILLSAIDTHECATIWILLSAID
ANDSTRONGONEDAYTHELITTLERE	EATTOTHEMILLANDTHEMILLERGR	THERATIWILLSAIDTHEPIGNOYOU
DHENSAWTHATTHEWHEATWASR	OUNDITINTOFLOURWHENTHEWH	WILLNOTSAIDTHELITTLEREDHENI
EADYTOBECUTSOSHEWENTTOTH	EATHADBEENGROUNDINTOFLOU	SHALLEATITMYSELFSOSHEDID
EOTHERANIMALSINTHEFARMYAR	RTHELITTLEREDHENTOOKITTOTHE	
DWHOWILLHELPMETOCUTTHEW	OTHERANIMALSINTHEFARMYARD	

A well known children's story - presented in the way that a first century reader would expect to be given it

What helps? Clearly, it is the familiar letters of familiar words, familiar syntax, or arrangement of words. The title can be separated from the narrative, because the narrative opens with the well-worn entry, 'Once upon a time…'. Line by line, you begin to define the structure of the whole narrative and its beautifully repeating pieces: 'Who will help me…?, Not I said the cat, Not I said the rat, Not I said the pig', etc., with the repeating ending to each section, 'Then I shall… myself. So she did.' It is really rather delightful for its repetitions. As it is in English, anyone who speaks English will be able to discern the narrative structure of five sections. And not one will miss the twist at the end! All reading-method is learned.

Overleaf is the table that summarises the literary-orders of Mark's Gospel. I record now in 2020 that Mark has "rigidly" stayed with the same presentational pattern for each component part of his scheme. It is to be observed that A and ABB' represent the same structure, where A denotes a simple ABB' scheme and ABB' a composite scheme of ABB'/ABB'/ABB'. Why did Mark do this? There is only one single clear answer. He did it to help his readers interpret his text, like the one shown opposite (and above), which had been laid out in columns of rows of letters without spaces between words. It raises, of course, why texts were ever produced like this in the first place. It was so, it seems to me, that they could be copied very simply, by scribes who knew their Greek letters and were able to add letter upon letter to their vellum as the reader directed. It was a low-skilled tedious job, yes? But, I think it will have worked very well in this way.

Mark writes methodically, therefore, and presents a disciplined arrangement. (We could think of him as a first-century Methodist, yes?) Even his title is a three-part, abb' presentation! As soon as the reader begins reading, therefore, he is led, by the Title and, subsequently, by the Prologue to read the work as the writer required, all the way through from its beginning to its end. How good is that! And how useful for today! Why has no one seen this, until now? And why has no one since 1999 picked this up?

Table 8: The Gospel's Literary Orders:

1	**P:A:B:B'A':E**	The Gospel: comprising Prologue, Gospel Narrative and Epilogue
2	**A : B : B' : A'**	The Series of the Gospel Narrative
3	**A : B : A'**	Series, in sub-division
4	**(ABB') (X) (ABB')**	Days in Series of sevens
5	A, ABB'	Days' , P. and E. Parts
6	**ABB'**	Days' Part sub-divisions
7	abb', a:a'	sub-sectional divisions
8	(a) (b) (b'), (a) (a');	parts
9	.a .b .b', .a .a'	sub-parts
10	..a etc.	sub-sub-parts
11	...a etc.	sub-sub-sub-parts

We briefly open up a discussion on Mark's presentational method. Undoubtedly, his preferred method of presentation is that of ABB' (or abb') where A is the introductory part, B is the first development, and B' is the second, paralleling and completing development. In the lowest levels of literary order, we find parts a:a' (etc.) which either lie in simple parallelism or where the second part a' simply completes the first, a.

What this chart does not do is tell us where *chiasmus* is found. One single detailed chiasm is found in the whole of the text: we discovered it at the point of Jesus' entry into Jerusalem. Here Mark demonstrates a preference to accentuate the telling of the shouts of the crowd with this characteristically distinct form of construction, presumably, for maximum effect. So we can say that in his Gospel he used 'chiasms' very sparingly indeed! Contrary to Dewey, Marcus *et al*, who read many chiasms, or concentric structures in Mark's Gospel, in the details and in the 'medium-structures' (we shall call them), my literary-structural examination of the text has revealed only one, at 11.9b,10. In the planning of his Series, however, Mark did employ chiasm in that he established a middle, pivotal Day as his 'turning point', around which he created sub-Series of three Days, in balance. And in the planning of the Gospel's framework, he also employed chiasm, centring two balancing middle Series, around which he placed two balancing outer Series, all of which he framed with the Prologue and the Epilogue. Chiasm is one of Mark's literary tools, but his employment of it is almost only restricted to the higher levels of literary order, and not the middle or lower orders.

As with chiasms so also Mark used 'listings' very sparingly: I find them only:

in Series A,	at 3.16-19:	the appointing of the 'twelve';
	at 4.3b-8:	the parable of the 'sower';
	at 4.14-20:	the interpretation of the parable;
in Series B,	at 7.21b,22:	six plural and
		six singular terms (on 'what defile').

Five listings, in four references, are all that Mark created. (In the Letters, there are many.)

In the analysis of the Gospel text (in my Chapters Two to Seven) I identified a number of rhetorical devices which Mark employed as signifiers of his structuring, in opening new Days' tellings and in organising his Days' reports into parts. They were discussed as they arose out of the text and were summarised at the conclusions of the presentations of the Series in which they were identified. (See particularly the Addendums of the first, second and fourth Series.) We review only one of these devices here, that of parechesis, Mark's repetitions of the ou sound. Examples are found at:

Title	1.1	
Prologue:	1.2-3	the opening of the Gospel;
Series B:	6.1	the opening;
Series B':	8.27	the opening;
(Series A'	12.36	quote from Ps110.1 in Day 24;
	13.1/3	the opening of Day 24's Part **B'**;
	14.2/3	the opening of Day 25);
Epilogue:	16.19b,20a	the closing of the Gospel.

It may be recognised, of course, that the genitive absolute wherever it is used repeats the *ou* sound, but the identification of parechesis depends on other than this in the above cases. The genitive absolute is found at 16.1, the beginning of a new Day's telling (the last in Mark's presentation), but the *ou* sound there is not developed by Mark: he does not intend his audience to differentiate it there from other sounds. Parechesis is a feature of Mark's presentation with which he, literally, begins and ends his Gospel, and with which he identifies for his audience the two openings to his middle Series. In the longer, concluding Series A', he retains one usage which he finds in a quotation from the Psalms (12.36), he introduces one (which we may note is not complete, for reasons of v.2's separating of the sounds) to begin the second half of his longest presentation of a Day (Day Twenty-four, 11.220-13.37, 94 verses), and includes another (which is not complete, for reasons of v.1's omission of the sounds) at the beginning of the middle Day's telling (Day Twenty-five, 14.1-11). It may be judged that Mark's creation of parechesis, where it is complete, is wholly consistent. It so proves to be an important rhetorical device, which we can find amongst historical presents, imperfects, three-step progressions, opening formulae, etc., in his well-equipped (rhetorical) tool box. Without it, we would be without major supporting evidence of structural division.

Rhetorical devices that have been identified as we have gone through our analysis of the text can be at least listed here, even if we do not discuss them. It is an impressive list and shows us, in summary, that Mark was consciously in control of his writing work.

Table 9: Mark's Rhetorical Devices:

We begin with a listing from the Days' analyses:

Under Day One:	1)	Mark's understanding of the Hebrew/Palestinian day (see also Introduction: An Interest in "Days");
	2)	Mark's definition of "Day" which he uses for the purpose of his presentation: the civil day beginning with sunrise (see also Introduction: An Interest in "Days" and note 60);
	3)	*πρωΐ* and other times of day;
Under Day Two:	4)	Temporal links;
	5)	Geographical links which behave temporally;

	6)	Historical Presents;
Under Day Three:	7)	*Καὶ πάλιν,*
Under Day Four:	8)	*Καὶ* and parataxis;
	9)	non-*καὶ* sentences;
	10)	*Καὶ εὐθὺς,*
	11)	Chiasm: an alternative to it, part I (see also Introduction: The Cultural and Historical Context... and Chapter Two: The Days beginning the Gospel);
Under Day Five:	12)	Three-step progressions and formal structure;
	13)	Sandwich construction: an alternative to it, part I (see also Introduction: an Interest in "Days");
	14)	Chiasm: an alternative to it, part II;
	15)	Numbers of verses and the versatility of ABB' to accommodate varying numbers of lines (3 to 243?);
Under Day Six:	16)	"Night-crossings of the sea of Galilee": new Days begin with new locations and new activities after sunrise;
Under Day Seven:	17)	Sandwich construction: an alternative to it, part I;
	18)	Mark's numerological interest.
Under Day Eleven:	19)	The leaving of the place of the earlier Day's telling and the arriving in another: an introductory formula.
Under Days Seventeen and Twenty:	20)	occupying b and b' positions: two opening words often used in succession (to the ear, it is a closing pair to any level of order presentation).

Under all the Days of the Fourth Series, A', we observed new rhetorical devices to signal the beginnings of the new Days. These are found at 11.12, 11.20, 14.1,12, 15.1 and 16.1,2:

At 11.12		*Καὶ τῇ ἐπαύριον*
11.20		*Καὶ παραπορευόμενοι πρωι*
14.1		*Ἦν δὲ τὸ πάσχα καὶ τὰ ἄζυμα μετὰ δύο ἡμέρας.*
14.12		*Καὶ τῇ πρώτῃ ἡμέρᾳ τῶν ἀζύμων, ὅτε τὸ πάσχα ἔθυον,*
15.1		*Καὶ εὐθὺς πρωῒ*
16.1-8	A	*Καὶ διαγενομένου τοῦ σαββάτου....*
	B	*καὶ λίαν πρωῒ τῇ μιᾷ τῶν σαββάτων ἔρχονται ἐπὶ τὸ μνημεῖον*
	B'	*καὶ ἐξελθοῦσαι ἔφυγον ἀπὸ τοῦ μνημείου*

The same is true also for the Epilogue's introductory pieces:

A	*Ἀναστὰς δὲ πρωῒ πρώτῃ σαββάτου*
B	*Μετὰ δὲ ταῦτα*
B'	*Ὕστερον δὲ*

And as we said, in Chapter Seven: there was no more suitable opening for the final piece of the final Part of the Gospel than that that Mark chose.

Finally, it was noticed that the last part of the Prologue revealed the numbers 'two plus two' and the first part of the Epilogue disclosed the number 'seven'. Between them, they described the structure of the Narrative they cradled which is of two inner series within two outer series of seven days each. It is a rhetorical feature that it is not just known to Mark.

Table 10: Mark's Number of Days (estimated from the text):

Fundamental to completing the exercise of gathering up the results of literary-structural analysis is a consideration of what Mark understood to be the total number of days Jesus' mission covered. In his telling of only four Series of Seven Days, there is indication that he presented his work so as to suggest that he was telling only the most significant. At the conclusion of the analysis of each of the Series, I explored the introductory pieces to each of the Days which are the only points in the Gospel narrative where Mark included information of this kind. Because the Prologue and the Epilogue each cover a number of days, their full texts had to be considered also.

Prologue:	fifty days;
Series A:	many weeks;
Series B:	several weeks;
Series B':	several weeks;
Series A':	ten/eleven days minimum;
Epilogue:	seven days minimum.

Due to the fact that Mark has not attempted to define the passing of days with the same exactitude in all cases (as in 1.13, 8.1/2, 9.2, 11.12, 20, 14.1, 12, 15.1, 16.1/2), and due to the fact that some of these may be more symbolic, or typological than historical (e.g. 1.13: "forty days"; and also 9.2: "And after six days"), we should not attempt to add up the days and the weeks of Jesus' mission with a calculator, and pretend that we have an exact view on how long it actually took. Rather, this is as far as this exercise can properly go. We may estimate only that Mark might have understood the story he tells (in Prologue, twenty-eight Days, and Epilogue) to have covered possibly nine to ten months, or so[483].

Mark's Travelogue of Jesus:

Details of Jesus' journeying are given in the Prologue and the Days, and not directly in the Epilogue. For the Epilogue, the information, '(H)e will go before you into Galilee…', is twice told in Jerusalem (in 14.28 and 16.7). A map follows, on the next page, which plots the Gospel's geographical place names: the regions, cities, towns and villages. Commentators in the past have referred to the writer's lack of knowledge regarding the geography of Jesus' journeying. The matter relates to where they think the Gospel was written. Some think it was in Galilee; they, therefore, see no major problems with the writer's travelogue. Others speak of Rome, Italy, Antioch and Egypt as being possible, because of ancient historical references to each. For reasons as we will see towards the end of this chapter, the likeliest place is Rome. Whatever the case, we can be certain that Mark wants us to see his Prologue, four Series and Epilogue as geographically defined. The titles for the Series which suggest themselves from the text demonstrate this. Mark's presentation of Jesus' life and mission clearly benefits from the spatial and temporal information he provides.

---

[483]Schmidt suggests a minimum of one year: *Der Rahmen…*, p.190. He and Hall (*The Gospel Framework…*, p.55) make much of 2.23-28, for its suggesting a harvest time in the year previous to the Passover. Without it, they both say that Mark's telling could have covered only a few months. *IntDB* Vol. 2, on "Harvest", p.527, suggests a date up to the end of June: that would suggest an occurrence for this scene, nine to ten months before the Passover.

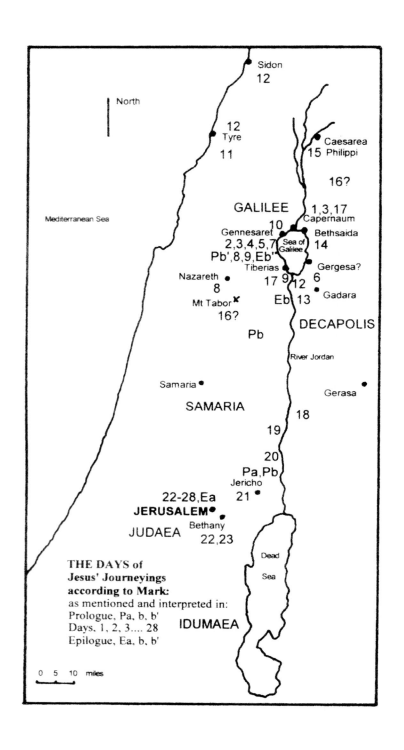

North

Sidon
12

12
Tyre
11

Mediterranean Sea

Caesarea
15 Philippi

16?

GALILEE
10
Gennesaret
2,3,4,5,7
Pb',8,9,Eb'
Tiberias

1,3,17
Capernaum
Sea of
Galilee

Bethsaida
14

Nazareth
8

17 9 12
Eb 13

Gergesa?
6

Mt Tabor
16?

Gadara

Pb

DECAPOLIS

River Jordan

Samaria

SAMARIA

Gerasa

18

19

20

Pa,Pb
Jericho

22-28,Ea
JERUSALEM
JUDAEA   Bethany
22,23

21

Dead
Sea

**THE DAYS of
Jesus' Journeyings
according to Mark:**
as mentioned and interpreted in:
Prologue, Pa, b, b'
Days, 1, 2, 3.... 28
Epilogue, Ea, b, b'

IDUMAEA

0 5 10 miles

The Rules of Ancient Rhetoric:

Lastly, in completing our summary of the data collected from this analysis of Mark's Gospel, we reflect on the writer's adherence to the Classical Rules of Ancient Rhetoric, introduced in Chapter One. For the purpose of this critique, we consider the five aspects of the practice of ancient rhetoric, as presented in my Introduction: 'invention', 'arrangement', 'style', 'memory' and 'delivery'. I have two reasons for taking this approach. Though my analysis of Mark's text has been openly literary-structural from the beginning, it has been informed increasingly by the rules of ancient rhetoric as Mark more and more demonstrated himself to be an exponent of the ancient writing art and discipline. A judgement appears now possible and I think it is furthered by this kind of concluding examination. Additionally, it must be the case that any proper assessment of Mark's skills and abilities is only appropriately made with due regard to the practice and purpose of writing in the first century. My analysis does demonstrate that Mark was well schooled in ancient rhetoric[484]. His skills and abilities in literary and theological matters cannot be properly compared with twentieth century scholarship, in the first instance.

'Invention':

'Invention' in ancient rhetoric is the first stage of composition when thoughts and arguments are marshalled, and when basic themes are chosen. The 'leading idea', or the purpose of the book is established at this stage. 'Invention' was the conceptual stage in the process of composition. Decisions had to be taken on the subject to be elaborated, and how it was going to be promoted.

Table 3 above may be said to disclose what Mark chose primarily for his literary and theological task. And it will have been one task. The theme of his book was "Good News" (or "bravo" news, see $\varepsilon\dot{v}$). His book would demonstrate how, in the beginning, it was presented by Jesus to the Jews, but in the end, it was for presenting to the whole World. The Prologue would cover the former, the Epilogue the latter, and in his narrative between, he would develop a series of presentations which would begin with the Jews and Old Covenant issues; they would develop through a turning point concerned with both Jews and Gentiles (Old Covenant and New Covenant); and he would end them with the Gentiles and New Covenant issues. The "bad news" that he would counter would be the Fall of Jerusalem, the destruction of the temple, the deaths of over a million and what appeared to be the end of Judaism. He would re-interpret it as Good News for both Jews and Gentiles.

His exchange of the word "world" for "Gentiles" in the concluding of his last Series, and his use of the word "world" in his Epilogue would show that the New Covenant was for all, not just the Gentiles. He would show how both Jews and Gentiles were complicit in the death of the story's central character. Through this death, his audience would be shown that God established a New Covenant with them. In presenting Jesus, at the point of his dying, as 'a Son of God', he would demonstrate that for the "world" it was an act of new creation like that at the time of Noah. The creation account would have its reference and allusion. He would show that God had dealt with evil in the world in this new way.

---

[484]Best, *Mark: the Gospel...*, p.107; see also Kennedy, *New Testament Interpretation...*, p.102: in discussing whether or not Mark may have used the methods of the rhetoricians, they say, 'We must allow that even if Mark had not attended a school where rhetoric was taught *and it is most unlikely that he had*, some of the broader principles of composition would have percolated down from these schools to the general public.' My analysis shows that we can be more certain than this.
We recall Tolbert's arguments (*Sowing the Gospel...*) for the two major formative influences of Greco-Roman rhetoric and popular culture, on Mark. See my Introduction, pages 20,21.

For his supporting arguments, he would explore possibilities in the Old Covenant scriptures, particularly the Genesis account of creation, and 1 and 2 Kings for the earlier prophets, but also the Psalms and the Prophets as well, which he would use by allusion and direct quotation, and maybe by reference too.

For his presentation of his argument, he would choose to tell his story in Series of "Days", as in the creation account[485]. The 'twenty-seventh day' in his account would replicate that in the account of Noah[486], as a day of new creation. The book would be expressive of the "Day of the Lord"[487], a day of both judgement and salvation. A telling in Days would be understood not only by the Jews, but also by the Greeks who had their epic[488] about their origins, which was told in Days.

'Arrangement':

'Arrangement' was as important and creative a process as 'invention'. In actual practice, each influenced the other in the work of composition. The task was to establish order so that the themes, their content, and their development could be expressed clearly. There were standard skeletal outlines to choose from, but developments of these were possible. Once established, the outline would normally have been hidden so that the story unfolded smoothly.

Tables 1 and 2 represent Mark's 'arrangement'. Tables 4 to 8 qualify his 'arrangement' with descriptions of the end results of his compositional process. He chose for his narrative, 1.21-16.8, a scheme of four Series of seven Days; and for each of his Series, he chose two sub-Series of three Days which would lie each side of his middle Day and 'turning point' of the Series. It is likely that Mark lifted this Series' scheme simply 'off the peg'. It is representative of Homer's scheme for his *Iliad* (Books 2-8; 9; 10-23: three Days; one Day; three Days)[489], and we can deduce, therefore, that it had been used many times over in the intervening eight centuries. In creating his four Series in the form of ABB'A', it is again likely that he chose it from a stock of standard outlines. Both these 'arrangements' are described today as chiastic[490].

Table 2 demonstrates Mark's use of this 'arrangement' for presenting *four stages* in Jesus' Mission. As we have seen in the summaries of Chapter Six, the outer two Series balance, by way of a prefiguring in the former, and a fulfilling in the latter. The summaries of Chapter Five, demonstrate the balance between the two middle Series. Mark demonstrates employment of 'chiasm' (like Homer[491]) in his larger constructions. His use of them elsewhere, in

---

[485]See my Introduction, pages 10-12, and Chapter Seven, page 328, but also page 144: Mark does not present a 'week' of days as such for each Series; rather he presents a 'stage'/'phase' in the mission of Jesus, which is 'completed' by his telling of specifically 'seven' Days.

[486]See Gen. 8.14-9.17.

[487]See note 306 in the examination of the Third Series and Day Fifteen, and discussion in the text on the suggestion of Best, and in particular of Marcus who considers the Gospel to be "The Way of the Lord". For "the Day of the Lord" and "the Day of Judgement", see Isaiah, Jer., Lam. Ezk., Hos., Joel, Amos, Zeph. and Zech.; for "the coming of the great and dreadful day", see Mal. 4.5.

[488]Homer's *Iliad*. It has been viewed as the 'Old Testament' of the Greek's (A. Sinclair, p.xiii) because it is judged to have presented to an ancient people their origins - in ancient myths, legends and, as a result of archeological discoveries, much history too. We may judge from the contents of his Gospel that Mark's theological work similarly and creatively combines these three elements too, for the purpose of presenting the origins of what was expected to be (and what has proved to be) a new, universal nationhood. See also my Introduction, pages 12,13.

[489]See my Introduction, page 12.

[490]For earlier designations for 'chiasm', see Ian H. Thomson, *Chiasmus...*, pp.12-16.

[491]For examples of balance we have: from Homer's first book, 'the treatment of Chryses', and from his last book (the twenty-fourth) 'the treatment of Priam'; and from the same books in turn also, 'the burning of the Achaian ships' and 'the burning of Hector's body'. From book three, 'the meeting of Menelaos and Paris', compare from book twenty-two, 'the meeting of Hector and Achilles'. And from book six, 'the arming of Paris', compare from

what I describe as the lower levels of literary order, is restricted to one (Jesus' entry into Jerusalem).

Because Mark creates a compound of the two chiastic forms, and creates a 'four times seven' scheme, we have to consider if he intended that his scheme carried meaning[492]. As we have seen already, under Day Thirteen, in Series Two, Mark does well demonstrate an interest in numerology (see 8.16-21). He sets the numerical details of the 'feedings' in such a fashion as to create a numerological conundrum which requires solution by those who are listening (for my solution, see under Day Thirteen). As 'seven' is a sacred number in many of the world's religions, and as it stands for 'fulfilment' and 'completion' in Hebrew-usage[493] we, who have not been encouraged in the modern Western world to think in these terms, do have to consider seriously Mark's reason for using it in his rhetorical plan. Given also the meaning of 'four' which is another sacred number expressing 'universality' in many of the world's first century religions (in Hebrew-terms expressive of the 'four winds' and, therefore, the four points of the compass), we do have to consider the possibility that Mark intended a 'deep meaning' for his 'four' by 'seven' narrative scheme. Such symbolical arithmetic translates, 'the fulfilment for the world of the divine plan'. It does at least accord with the leading idea expressed above.

Finally, we observed in the summaries of Chapters Three and Six, and in the summary above that the three-part arrangement of Mark's outer Series can be read as the 'complication', the 'turning point', and the 'dénouement' of a Greek Tragedy. It is another well-tested approach to writing which he could have lifted simply 'off the peg'.

'Style':

'Style' was also a matter of choice to the rhetor. There were many methods he had to choose from to present his material in the course of his composition. Mark's first choice is unmistakably an ABB' presentation. See Table 1, for his application of this in his sub-Series of Days. See Table 7, for his use of it for structuring his Gospel's main components: Prologue, Days and Epilogue. Compounds of the same are used in a variety of ways. See Table 8, for its use at levels of literary order, 4 down to 11.

Again we have to ask if he meant any significance in using it. I have, however, found it now in use throughout the New Testament's books and letters[494] so I am less interested in this possibility than before. The number three might naturally suggest "the idea of completeness - of beginning, middle and end".[495] But it is more likely that Mark adopted it because of its use elsewhere, as in the Genesis 'creation account', and 1 and 2 Kings[496]. Whatever is the case, having introduced it in his Title and his Prologue, Mark commits himself to using it for the whole of his work and this is for the sake of his reader's interpretation of a script of words in rows in columns, etc.

'Style' too refers to the matter of a rhetor's choice of grammar, syntax, and the selection of balancing/connecting words. At the end of Chapters Three to Six, I have summarised those features of 'style' that Mark chose to employ to signify new Days. Elsewhere, we have

---

book sixteen, 'the arming of Patroclos'. Homer's chronological scheme makes the balancing "absolutely explicit". See page 12 again.

[492]Consider Rev. 18.11ff.: "the merchants of the *earth* will weep and mourn"; no-one will buy any of their 'twenty-eight' items of trade. Or consider the 'twenty-eight' days of the lunar month: here the possibility that Jesus, or his mission, is likened to "the *lesser* light to govern the night" (Gen. 1.16) is not too likely; compare the "sun of righteousness" (Mal. 4.2).

[493]*Int.DB*, 1961, Twelfth reprinting 1981, p.564.

[494]See: *New Testament: New Testimony...*

[495]*Int.DB*, Vol. 3, p.564.

[496]See my Introduction, pages 10,11 and 13.

seen how Mark has a whole armoury of rhetorical conventions to hand. He uses parechesis, anaphoras, anastrophes, historical presents, imperfects, inclusios, dualities, non-καὶ sentence-beginnings, three-step progressions and so on to define the components of his composition and signal their inter- and intra-relationships.

'Style' like 'arrangement' was important as a matter of aesthetic, also for its mnemonic value and for its persuasive effect. Mark's use of much parataxis and koine Greek will have been a choice he made in order to ensure 'popular' attention to his presentation.

The abb' choice of Mark is seen in Table 8 to operate from the higher literary level of Four to the lowest, of Ten or Eleven. We take a little longer on the matter.

I present the Prologue in the Greek and in literal English. It is in the Prologue that I first saw how the writer was facilitating a reading of his work, in terms of abb' and ABB', but I only grasped this when I laid the three parts side by side and saw the whole, as it were, in a chart. (Why do New Testament scholars rue charts, I wonder?) In the past, the Prologue was assessed on contents alone, but now we see how the writer declares his commitment to his writer to present a disciplined work, from beginning to end, so that a presentation like that of Codex Sinaiticus can be read as the writer intended.

Being able to see the connections between the parts in each construction has been the key to my analysis. The writing style of ABB' and abb' at every level of literary, down from level Four help me to discern the parts and the pieces that make up the wholes of this text. It may be that we ought to name Mark's choice of style 'dactylic' after the Greek, δακτυλνσ, for 'finger'. In the literary sense, of course, a dactyl is a 'foot' which is viewed as a long syllable followed by two short ones. In the case of our fingers, A is the longer part and the B and B' parts are the remaining shorter, more equal sized ones. Homer's Iliad was written in dactylic hexameter. It may be, therefore, that it is Mark's conscious choice of matching it as near as he could.

THE PROLOGUE TO THE GOSPEL OF MARK, 1.2-20

(1.1 is the 'Title' by my reading. For many, 1.1-13 describes the Prologue.)

PART A	PART B	PART B'
Καθὼς γέγραπται	Καὶ ἐγένετο ἐν ἐκείναις ταῖς ἡμέραις	Μετὰ δὲ τὸ παραδοθῆναι τὸν Ἰωάννην
ἐν τῷ Ἡσαΐᾳ	ἦλθεν Ἰησοῦς	ἦλθεν ὁ Ἰησοῦς εἰς τὴν Γαλιλαίαν
τῷ προφήτῃ,	ἀπὸ Ναζαρέτ	κηρύσσων τὸ εὐαγγέλιον τοῦ θεοῦ [15]
Ἰδοὺ ἀποστέλλω τὸν ἄγγελόν μου	τῆς Γαλιλαίας	καὶ λέγων
πρὸ προσώπου σου,	καὶ ἐβαπτίσθη	ὅτι Πεπλήρωται ὁ καιρὸς
ὃς κατασκευάσει τὴν ὁδόν σου·	εἰς τὸν Ἰορδάνην	καὶ ἤγγικεν ἡ βασιλεία τοῦ θεοῦ·
φωνὴ βοῶντος ἐν τῇ ἐρήμῳ,	ὑπὸ Ἰωάννου. [9]	μετανοεῖτε καὶ πιστεύετε ἐν τῷ εὐαγγελίῳ.
Ἑτοιμάσατε τὴν ὁδὸν κυρίου,	Καὶ εὐθὺς	Καὶ παράγων
εὐθείας ποιεῖτε τὰς τρίβους αὐτοῦ.	ἀναβαίνων	παρὰ τὴν θάλασσαν
Ἐγένετο Ἰωάννης	ἐκ τοῦ ὕδατος	τῆς Γαλιλαίας
ὁ βαπτίζων	εἶδεν σχιζομένους τοὺς οὐρανοὺς	εἶδεν Σίμωνα
ἐν τῇ ἐρήμῳ	καὶ τὸ πνεῦμα	καὶ Ἀνδρέαν
καὶ κηρύσσων βάπτισμα μετανοίας	ὡς περιστερὰν καταβαῖνον εἰς αὐτόν· [11]	τὸν ἀδελφὸν Σίμωνος
εἰς ἄφεσιν ἁμαρτιῶν. [5]	καὶ φωνὴ ἐγένετο ἐκ τῶν οὐρανῶν,	ἀμφιβάλλοντας ἐν τῇ θαλάσσῃ·
καὶ ἐξεπορεύετο πρὸς αὐτὸν	Σὺ εἶ ὁ υἱός μου ὁ ἀγαπητός,	ἦσαν γὰρ ἁλιεῖς. [17]
πᾶσα ἡ Ἰουδαία χώρα	ἐν σοὶ εὐδόκησα.	καὶ εἶπεν αὐτοῖς ὁ Ἰησοῦς,
καὶ οἱ Ἱεροσολυμῖται πάντες,	Καὶ εὐθὺς	Δεῦτε ὀπίσω μου,
καὶ ἐβαπτίζοντο ὑπ' αὐτοῦ	τὸ πνεῦμα αὐτὸν ἐκβάλλει	καὶ ποιήσω ὑμᾶς γενέσθαι ἁλιεῖς ἀνθρώπων. [18]
ἐν τῷ Ἰορδάνῃ ποταμῷ	εἰς τὴν ἔρημον.	καὶ εὐθὺς
ἐξομολογούμενοι τὰς ἁμαρτίας αὐτῶν. [6]	καὶ ἦν ἐν τῇ ἐρήμῳ	ἀφέντες τὰ δίκτυα
Καὶ ἦν ὁ Ἰωάννης	τεσσεράκοντα ἡμέρας	ἠκολούθησαν αὐτῷ.
ἐνδεδυμένος τρίχας καμήλου	πειραζόμενος ὑπὸ τοῦ Σατανᾶ.	Καὶ προβὰς ὀλίγον
καὶ ζώνην δερματίνην	καὶ ἦν μετὰ τῶν θηρίων,	εἶδεν
περὶ τὴν ὀσφὺν αὐτοῦ,	καὶ οἱ ἄγγελοι διηκόνουν αὐτῷ.	Ἰάκωβον
καὶ ἐσθίων		τὸν τοῦ Ζεβεδαίου
ἀκρίδας		καὶ Ἰωάννην
καὶ μέλι ἄγριον. [7]		τὸν ἀδελφὸν αὐτοῦ,
καὶ ἐκήρυσσεν		καὶ αὐτοὺς
λέγων,		ἐν τῷ πλοίῳ
Ἔρχεται ὁ ἰσχυρότερός μου		καταρτίζοντας τὰ δίκτυα. [20]
ὀπίσω μου,		καὶ εὐθὺς
οὗ οὐκ εἰμὶ ἱκανὸς		ἐκάλεσεν αὐτούς.
κύψας		καὶ ἀφέντες
λῦσαι τὸν ἱμάντα τῶν ὑποδημάτων αὐτοῦ· [8]		τὸν πατέρα αὐτῶν
ἐγὼ ἐβάπτισα ὑμᾶς ὕδατι,		Ζεβεδαῖον
αὐτὸς δὲ βαπτίσει ὑμᾶς ἐν πνεύματι ἁγίῳ.		ἐν τῷ πλοίῳ
		μετὰ τῶν μισθωτῶν
		ἀπῆλθον
		ὀπίσω αὐτοῦ.

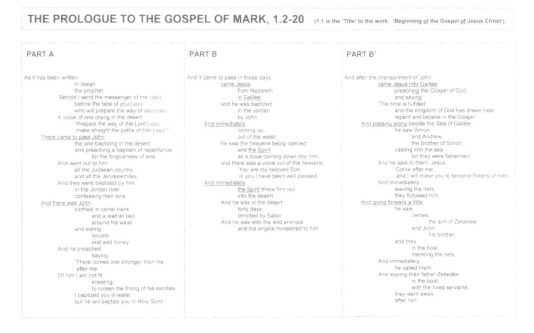

THE PROLOGUE TO THE GOSPEL OF MARK, 1.2-20 (1.1 is the 'Title' to the work: 'Beginning of the Gospel of Jesus Christ')

PART A

As it has been written
    in Isaiah
    the prophet.
    Behold I send the messenger of me (-ou)
        before the face of you (-ou),
        who will prepare the way of you (-ou).
    A voice of one crying in the desert.
        'Prepare the way of the Lord (-ou),
        make straight the paths of him (-ou).'
There came to pass John,
    the one baptizing in the desert
    and preaching a baptism of repentance
        for the forgiveness of sins.
And went out to him
    all the Judaean country
    and all the Jerusalemites
And they were baptized by him
    in the Jordan river,
    confessing their sins.
And there was John,
    clothed in camel hairs,
        and a leather belt
        around his waist,
    and eating
        locusts
        and wild honey.
And he preached,
        saying,
    'There comes one stronger than me,
    after me.
Of him I am not fit,
        kneeling,
    to loosen the thong of his sandals.
    I baptized you in water;
    but he will baptize you in Holy Spirit.'

PART B

And it came to pass in those days,
        came Jesus
        from Nazareth
        in Galilee,
    and he was baptized
        in the Jordan
        by John.
And immediately,
    coming up
    out of the water,
    he saw the heavens being opened,
        and the Spirit
    as a dove coming down into him,
    and there was a voice out of the heavens,
    'You are my beloved Son,
    in you I have been well pleased.'
And immediately,
        the Spirit threw him out
        into the desert.
And he was in the desert
    forty days,
    tempted by Satan.
And he was with the wild animals,
    and the angels ministered to him.

PART B'

And after the imprisonment of John
        came Jesus into Galilee,
        preaching the Gospel of God
        and saying,
    'The time is fulfilled
    and the kingdom of God has drawn near,
    repent and believe in the Gospel.'
And passing along beside the Sea of Galilee,
        he saw Simon
        and Andrew,
        the brother of Simon,
        casting into the sea,
        for they were fishermen.
And he said to them, Jesus,
    Come after me,
    and I will make you to become fishers of men.'
And immediately,
        leaving the nets,
        they followed him.
And going forward a little,
        he saw
        James,
            the son of Zebedee,
        and John,
            his brother,
        and they
        in the boat,
            mending the nets.
And immediately,
    he called them.
And leaving their father Zebedee
        in the boat,
        with the hired servants,
    they went away
    after him.

'Memory' and 'Delivery':

We take 'memory' and 'delivery' together. Mark's Arrangement' and his choice of an ABB' 'style' will have greatly assisted any reader's memorising of the story, for 'believable' and purposeful delivery[497], taking account of breathing rhythms, the need for movements of quiet, reflective presentation, and others for dramatic crescendo and climax. We have identified some such moments in the text. The last three Days of the First Series build and quicken; they were clearly written in this way to evoke in the hearers the response of wonder. Another kind of dramatic moment is found between 10.46a and 10.46b: here a pause is certainly intended, as suggested in the abb' presentations, and it has to do with the entering and leaving of Jericho. Mark clearly has produced his "Gospel" for public performance in an oral/aural culture. By following the rules of ancient rhetoric, his work had a usefulness for its day. It was prepared for a first-century reader and *his* audience, but, clearly, it can be re-packaged for today, for a world that likes charts, illustrations and artworks! Meaning and the disclosure of its leading ideas flow from the text in structured and disciplined ways.

So, what is Mark's Gospel?

It is most certainly a work of ancient rhetoric, prepared to function as a popular drama, similar to that of an Aristotelian Greek Tragedy, with a twist at its climax.

---

[497]In her article on "The Gospel of Mark as an Oral-Aural Event: Implications for Interpretation", *The New Literary Criticism and the New Testament*, eds. Edgar V. McKnight and Elizabeth Struthers Malbon, Trinity Press International, Valley Forge, Pennsylvania, 1994, Joanna Dewey usefully reminds us that Mark's composition would only take an hour and a half to two hours to read. She describes it as a "quite customary duration for oral performances... Furthermore, good storytellers could easily learn the story of Mark from hearing it read or hearing it told." (p.146) But she goes on to conclude that "in oral-aural cultures before there is any written text, or when a written text is recycled back into oral circulation, *there is no fixed text* that is used in oral performance." (p.157) This must be a matter for conjecture, surely?

For the past century at least, the view of most New Testament scholars had been that the gospels had nothing, or very little, to do with Hellenist (ancient) rhetoric. A piece of work, that summarised that view and groomed younger scholars to accept it, has had a huge influence. I quote from a Paper in a much recommended and much re-printed single volume commentary on the Bible, entitled, 'The Literature and Canon of the New Testament'.[498] It states: 'The New Testament can hardly be considered as literature at all, except in the most general sense of the term.... The aesthetic motive and the desire to produce fine writing as something worthwhile in itself are foreign to its authors whose aims were urgent and practical.... Lk 1.1-4 echoes the cadences and repeats *the conventional claims of the Hellenistic historians*, but there the resemblance ends.... Their comparative indifference to pagan literature was on the whole an advantage to the writers of the New Testament. They gained thereby in freshness and *freedom from stale conventions* and *artificial rhetoric*. They were *not conscious literary artists*, *obeying a convention* and *imitating the correct models*, *like Hellenistic authors*, but rather practical men falling into familiar forms when these happened to provide them with effective means of expression... The *Literature of the New Testament* is *in the main something new*.' On *speeches and sermons*, the writer admits that Thucydides put speeches into the mouths of his principal personages at appropriate moments and so '*set an unfortunate precedent*', but that 'Luke didn't follow the precedent'. I want to ask: how did views like these ever work their way into mainstream New Testament scholarship? The statements are not based on an actual reading of the Greek texts, but on supposition, surmise and wishful thinking.

---

[498] J.N. Sanders, 'The Literature and Canon of the New Testament', in *Peake's (single volume) Commentary on the Bible*, eds. Matthew Black and H.H. Rowley, Thomas Nelson & Sons Ltd, 1962, pp.676-677.

Since I completed my pen and ink drawing in 1989 (see Table 6a), I prepared the presentation above in 2013 (in Double AO, in acrylics on wood). It was for a two-year touring exhibition around Great Britain titled, 'The New Testament, but not as you know it'. It was at its near completion that I stood back and looked at the way in which the Narrative of 1.21-16.8 was cradled between the closing part of the Prologue and the opening part of the Epilogue and that the narrative's composition could be said to be described in those two parts by the numbers they contained. In my artwork, I immediately added, therefore the numbers '2 +2' to the artwork of the former and '7' to the latter. I did so with confidence, because I had been discovering similar 'checks for readers' in my analyses of other gospels.

Contrary to the opinions of very many scholars in the past, this gospel is a work of ancient rhetoric which is disciplined in the literary sense and described by the rules of Hellenist writing which shaped it, the rules of idea, structure, writing style, memory and performance. This whole text, when parsed and rhetorical analysed, exhibits symmetrical arrangements of the features that characterise it, the many dualities, repeating introductory formulae, repeating and balancing themes and sub-themes, word repetitions, etc., etc. We can celebrate, therefore, that for the very first time we have an objective way of looking at this document. It really is 'Good-bye' to opinions and 'Hello' to facts about this text.

Consider Psalms 67 and 119: they can be described in particular ways. Ps.67 is in the form of the menorah (the seven-branched lampstand). Ps.119 is in the form of an alphabetical acrostic (with eight lines per Hebrew letter). Both psalms can be defined in the same ways by everyone, because these descriptions are objective and not subjective. We can have opinions about them, but their structures are clear for everyone to see and describe in exactly the same ways. In the same way now, Mark's Gospel can be described and defined objectively too!

So, with newly established data on this Gospel, we have opportunity to look differently into what this Gospel is and what it was meant to do for the church. We pick up firstly on questions posed in the Introduction to this book.

Fundamental Questions in the Study of Mark's Gospel:

In my Introduction, I presented the case that fundamental questions remained unanswered in regard to Mark's Gospel, even though the methodological tool-box of biblical critics was full to overflowing. A brief survey of the findings of scholarship on Mark's leading idea, and on his theological, literary and compositional abilities shows that there is the widest possible range of views, and much contradiction. Though many had been examining Mark's Gospel by many different approaches, an analysis of the text of Mark's Gospel, that is *the text alone*, was still needed, if progress was to be made on these issues.

Mark's Literary and Compositional Abilities:

For Mark's audience, there is order in the presentation, but it is not tedious. In the Introduction, we asked, "How was a Gospel to function" in a first century world of few readers and of few book-owners? We may deduce that Mark's plan and method were much influenced by the requirements then. If any literature was to stand a chance of popular success, it had to have a good story-line. It also had to be written in such a way that it could be well presented orally. It needed, therefore, a rhythmic, repetitive structure and an engaging style. We may judge that Mark's Gospel had 'the story' and the technical qualities for popular listening then.

Mark has been credited in the past, with creating a new, literary genre, Gospel, but we note Bultmann's judgement which has been supported by many over the years, that "Mark is not sufficiently master of his material to be able to venture on a systematic construction himself."[499] Meagher, much more recently, has judged Mark's Gospel to be "a clumsy construction", that it has "an air of great ordinariness" and that it "is not egregiously bad... nor memorably good" as a literary work[500]. It would seem that not a few judgements of Mark's literary and compositional abilities will need to be revised. Mark should be credited not only with creating a new literary genre, but also with taking from Greco-Roman rhetorical technique all that he needed to 'create' a connected narrative[501] which would popularise, in the first century cultural milieu, his church's message.

Contrary to what many scholars have said, Mark's Gospel does have the appearance of being a kind of 'day-to-day' account of the story of Jesus, as from his baptism and focused on his mission, passion and resurrection[502]. The Gospel does appear to consist of Days as if taken from a diary, and as such this would seem to be expressive of Mark's intention, to present his story of Jesus, from its beginning to its end, as a heavenly story which is, nevertheless, well-earthed in the human space- (Palestine) and time-frame (Days). That Mark gave his serialised story an artificial structure, as Schmidt suggested long ago, cannot be in doubt: the many correspondences of his themes and details demonstrate that his presentation is schematic.

It would seem that his primary literary purpose was to create a 'connected narrative' which would tell the Good News of Jesus Christ ('the Son of God' – later added). In his Prologue, Mark tells how Jesus came to begin his mission and begin calling followers to himself. In his first Series, he describes the first days of Jesus' mission and demonstrates the authority and power of Jesus and his ability to draw crowds to himself: he also shows how his presence and activities stirred up the leaders of Old Israel against him, and how Jesus laid the foundations for New Israel which would grow from small beginnings to be big in the world. In the second Series, Mark demonstrates how Jesus' mission extended, and how, by recourse to numerological presentation, Gentiles were not excluded from the New Israel in formation; further, the crowds stayed longer with him and were larger in number. In the third Series, he demonstrates that the Messiah necessarily took the way of suffering, death and resurrection, in order to establish New Israel. Jesus had much to teach his would-be followers about the way they should live too. In the fourth Series, Mark tells of the events in Jerusalem that led up to and included Jesus' passion and resurrection by which, in his own person he replaced the institution of the old temple (which in AD 70 was destroyed[503]) and its sacrificial means of being made right with God. He secured new foundations for a New Israel. The Epilogue tells how the disciples came to be commissioned and how, after Jesus' ascension, they began continuing Jesus' mission in the world. Mark's Good News *is* for both Jew and Gentile.

Mark's Gospel contains an evangelistic appeal, which would provoke commitment on the part of the hearers, but, principally, it appears more to be a re-writing of Christian Faith. It had to adapt to what God had been doing in Jerusalem in AD 70. The Day of the Lord had begun with the start of Jesus' mission. We move from literature considerations to theological ones. In the past, it has been judged likely that Mark's reasons for writing when he did were to do with the fact that eye-witnesses of the life of Jesus were dying out (see the Introduction, pages 14,15). But, I think it will be acknowledged that it was more to do with the fact that they had died in the pogrom that accompanied the fall of Jerusalem and the destruction of the temple. It is likely that Mark was writing soon after and seized his opportunity to promote the

---

[499]Bultmann, *The History...*, p.350.
[500]See note 26 in the Introduction.
[501]See Luke 1.1,2: "connected narrative" would seem to be a Lukan description of Mark's work.
[502]See note 81 in the Introduction, and the discussion in the text.
[503]I hold to the view, with Hooker (*The Gospel...*, p.303), that Mark was writing soon after the fall of Jerusalem and the destruction of the temple in AD70. 13.21-23 suggests it is so, for the 'false signs' that will further be. See also 14.58, 15.29 and v.38 for an identification of Jesus with the temple.§

new universal faith out of the 'ruins' of its forebear, and provide his 'good news' for the universal[504] church's dissemination.

To us today, who have never before been so fully introduced to the writing of a gospel to the rules of ancient rhetoric, it seems at first incredible that anyone would write as Mark did, creating such a plan as has been uncovered here. Amazing too is the way in which Mark employed a style of presentation at so many levels of literary order simultaneously. Not least surprising, however, is that these features of his work would appear to have lain hidden over so many centuries. We may now marvel at Mark's literary and compositional abilities, but if we are tempted to describe him as some special 'literary artist', we should be aware that his composition is simply equal to that of many first-century writers, whose schooling initially had been in Homeric rhetoric[505] and Aristotelian Greek Tragedy, but was guided by the every-day rules of Hellenist (ancient) rhetoric and its writing practices.

Mark's Theological Abilities:

In my Introduction, I noted the wide range of opinion that there is on Mark's theological abilities. To Bultmann, Mark was simply a collector or hander on of traditions, "not a theologian"; whereas, to Marxsen and Schweizer, in turn, he was a profound interpretor, whose theology may also be used on the contemporary scene. (See pages 2-5 of the Introduction, for these and other views too.) Literary-structural analysis has made the difference on a number of previously open issues in regard to Mark's Gospel; we ask now, "In what ways, if any, might it influence our attitudes to Mark as a theologian?"

Literary-structural analysis clearly establishes that Mark exercised full control over his presentation. Tradition did not control him. The evidence demonstrates that Mark was the writer of his Gospel and not simply the editor of tradition. It follows, therefore, that he himself exercised full control over the Gospel's theological developments and that he was solely responsible for his 'leading idea' which is both literary and theological. He has to be credited, therefore, with selecting and developing Old Testament texts and with applying titles to Jesus where he thought they were appropriate to his Gospel scheme.

In the past, a number of scholars have confidently separated so-called "tradition" from Mark's so-called "editorial hand" or "construction" (though they have displayed little agreement). The process was hazardous enough, but given that the stamp of Mark's rhetorical method and purpose can now be seen on all the Gospel material, the separating of what is tradition from what is editing will be a task which few will dare to tackle. The bottom line is that Mark is to be credited with full compositional control over the tradition and the theology of his Gospel. It follows, therefore, that if we discover any lack of "a coherent and consistent theology"[506], it is down to Mark himself, or it is down to us, either for misreading Mark, or for expecting too much refinement in what is, when all is said and done, the first writing ever of a Gospel. And his Gospel, of course, was written not for the purpose of twentieth century study, but for first century proclamation of the Good News of *Jesus Christ* (1.1). It was Good

---

[504]It is presently the case that many commentators and scholars are content to think of Mark as writing for a 'particular' community (see Hooker, *The Gospel...*, p.4) as a pastor and theologian. Literary-structural analysis which exhibits the influence of ancient rhetoric shows him to be more likely a writer/theologian (whether a 'disciple of Peter or not') who was commissioned like Luke was (Lk.1.3). Mark's universalistic leading idea contains no distinctively local appeal, and his naming of only Jairus, Bartimaeus and Simon the leper, out of all those to whom Jesus ministered, hardly can be said to display knowledge of any local church's membership. He was likely writing in Rome and could even have witnessed the return of Îtitus with the spoils from the temple. (See note 72 in the Introduction for Trocmé's support of Rome as the place of Mark's writing, but also for the emphasis again that the Gospel was for 'his church's own use').

[505]See Introduction, note 42, A. Stock.

[506]Best, *Disciples...*, pp.46f.

News which *in the beginning* was presented by Jesus to the Jews, but *in the end* was to be presented by his disciples to the world. The Good News was that God had made a new Covenant with the world. Jesus' death and resurrection sealed the New Covenant, and it signalled a time of new creation for the world. The Good News countered the 'Bad News' of Jerusalem's fall, the temple's destruction, and the apparent demise of the Old Covenant, so much so, given Mark's theme plan, that one wonders if there would have been any 'Good News', any gospel at all, without the Jewish War.

Under 'Invention' above, I am satisfied that I have captured the salient theological features of Mark's leading idea for his Gospel. In this regard, we consider Wrede's work of 1901, principally because it has continued to be influential throughout the biblical-critical era. His judgement was that Mark's leading idea was the constructing of his Gospel on the basis of a dogmatic theory of a messiahship which was to be kept secret until after his resurrection. On page 215, I join forces with Wrede, and address the problem with which Mark had to grapple in his presentation. Jews and Gentiles could not knowingly crucify the *Messiah* and *Son of God* in order to establish a New Covenant between God and the world. Equally, it could not be that they had no opportunity of knowing who Jesus was during his Mission. Mark's problem *and* his solution are immediately apparent. In the third Series, these matters are given an airing by Mark. After the confession, "You are the *Messiah*", silence is demanded (8.30). After the mountain disclosure of Jesus *'my beloved Son'*, silence is demanded until after the resurrection (9.9). Telford, in his work on *The Barren Temple and the Withered Tree*[507] says of 10.46-12.37 (which bridges the third and fourth Series), that "it is in many respects damaging" to Wrede's thesis, "The Secrecy motif rather than presenting Jesus as the concealed Jewish *Messiah*, serves to present him as the concealed *Son of God*." Given these observations, we may make another, of the greatest importance. It would appear that Mark presents Jesus to the *Jews* as their *Messiah*, and that he presents Jesus to the *Gentiles* as the *Son of God*.

We do a short word-study. It completes an examination of Mark's key words, begun on pages 326-328:

For "The Christ"/"Son of David"[508], as designations for Jesus, see 1.1, 8.29, 9.41, 10.47,48, 11.10, 12.35-37, 14.61,62, and 15.31,32.

In 1.1, its use has no specific attachment, either to Jews, or Gentiles as such; in 8.29* and 9.41, it is for the disciples to know; in 10.47,48, Bartimaeus knows; in 11.10, Jerusalem's crowds know; in 12.35-37, the temple crowds know; in 14.61,62, the high priest wants to know, and Jesus tells all the Sanhedrin; and in 15.31,32, chief priests and scribes mock (they really did not know, they could not believe Jesus for his answer).

For "Son of God" (and variations) as a designation for Jesus, see 1.11, 3.11, 5.7, 9.7, 12.6 *bis.*, and 15.39.

In 1.1 and vv.2-11, its use has no specific attachment, either to Jews, or Gentiles as such; in 3.11, Jews *and* Gentiles are present and hear, "You are the Son of God" (3.7,8 define the crowd mix; *cf.* 3.8 and 10.1 for "beyond the Jordan"; and 3.8 and 7.24 for "Tyre and Sidon"; in both the connecting stories, Gentiles are present, and the issues are Jewish/Gentile ones); in 5.7, Gentiles hear, "Jesus, Son of God of the Most High" (it is Gerasene and "pig" country); in 9.7*, it is like 1.11, but it is for Peter, James and John only to know, until after the resurrection (9.9); in 12.6, the use of "son" is parabolic and allegorical, for the temple crowd; in 15.39, Jesus' dying provokes the Gentile "centurion" to affirm Jesus "a son of God", which takes the audience in the direction the writer is directing it.

---

[507] Telford, p.262

[508]The titles for Jesus, in Day Twenty-seven, of "King of the Jews" (15.2,9,12,18 and 26) and "King of Israel" (15.32) attach further messianic status to Jesus. See my page 241. The Royal Psalms (for example, especially Ps. 2, to which Mark refers in Day Twenty-seven's telling) were interpreted "in later times as thoroughly messianic": *IntDB*, Vol. 3, p.361.

It is significant that the references in 8.29, to Peter's identification of Jesus as "the Christ", and in 9.7, to the reference to Jesus as "my beloved Son" (hence, my asterisks above), occupy the first and second Days respectively of Series Three. The central point of Mark's gospel scheme has just been passed.

Both Jews and Gentiles were complicit in Jesus' death, but to Mark they do 'associate' with Jesus in these particular ways. It is astute of Mark. The connection between the Jews and the Messiah is supported by Old Covenant scriptures (he could appeal to these). He had, however, to create the connection between the Gentiles and Jesus. But it was easy to do. Caesar Worship[509], and Emperor Worship[510] were such that the *sacramentum* of the Roman Soldier was "Caesar is Lord"; Caesar was a "Son of God". Mark chose to affirm to Gentiles that Jesus was the one to "follow". Additionally, we observe, in 12.13-17, that Pharisees (leaders under the Old Covenant) and Herodians (leaders of Israel under Roman authority) together try to trick Jesus over paying tribute to Caesar.

We have noted already, in Chapter Two, that literary-structural analysis does not defend the phrase "Son of God" textually, in 1.1. In this Title to his Gospel, Mark is saying something in terms that Jews will understand, giving reference to their Christ. A scribe has been too quick to add the term that transmits something more meaningful to Gentiles. Mark has written his Gospel so that both Jew and Gentile, in their different ways, may know the Good News about Jesus. The secrecy motif[511], of Jesus' Messianic status and his status as Son of God, which Wrede identified, is not Mark's leading idea as such. Yes, it was clearly the case, as has been said above, that the Jews could not have knowingly killed their Messiah and the Gentiles the one who was to be Caesar's replacement, the actual and true Son of God. Mark had this to accommodate. But in the last Day's telling of Series Three, we noted that the unrebuked shouting, 'Son of David, Jesus...', 'Son of David, have pity on me', demonstrated at least by that stage in the Gospel's revelations, that the secrecy motif was no longer a feature or characteristic of the text.

What we have discovered so far about Mark's Gospel, due to this literary-structural analysis, demonstrates well Mark's profound and creative theological ability. He may not have written his Gospel to everyone's abiding satisfaction[512], but it was the first to be written, and as such its importance to the Church's *understanding* about its beginnings is without parallel. Yet, when we have discussed the work undertaken by others since 1999, we will want to pay a little more attention to what it is that Mark has actually given us. It matters very much: did he have lots of oral and written tradition to work with, or did he have very little, maybe just the historical references to Jesus' life, ministry, death and resurrection as he found them in Paul's Letters?

---

[509]*IntDB*, Vol. 1, p.479.

[510]*IntDB*, Vol. 2, pp.98,99.

[511]The *restricting of information* (on the Kingdom, on who Jesus is, and on what he has been doing, or will be doing) is found in the Gospel only in the Days of the first three Series:

Series One:	**1**	**2**	3	**5**	6	7	
Series Two:	8	9	10	11	**12**	13	**14**
Series Three:	**15**	**16**	*17*	18	19	*20*	21

All the underlined Days contain a secrecy command of Jesus. Only the underlined Days in bold contain a command to keep quiet about his identity specifically (at 1.25,34, 3.12, 8.30, 9.9). Additionally, Days 5, 17 and 20 which are italicised contain expressions which inform Mark's audience that it was for the disciples alone, and not the crowds, to know certain things, such as the meanings of the parables, and the matters about Jesus' suffering, death and resurrection, before events took place. Others, who had been *healed*, had been told not to say anything, at 1.44, 3.12, 5.43 (witnesses to the raising), 7.36 (witnesses to the healing), and 8.26. These are to be found in the telling of Days 2, 5, 7, 12 and 14, some of which are represented by a single underline, that is where they do not contain other 'secrecy' statements.

[512]Consider: 1) the first re-writing of his Gospel with additions, by Matthew; 2) in turn, Luke's second re-writing of his Gospel and of Matthew's simultaneously; 3) the amendments to, and then the expurgation of the original epilogue; 4) its neglect over the centuries, as it was viewed as subordinate to Matthew's and Luke's; and 5) the judgements of scholars over the last one hundred years concerning Markan inconsistencies.

Work undertaken by others on Mark's Gospel since 1999:

David Friedrich Strauss said in the nineteenth century that these gospels were 'mere myths'[513]. I argue otherwise. So too does Bauckham[514] but for different reasons. Following ancient tradition, he says Mark is Peter's eye-witness report, and that because of this, a good proportion of the other gospels are eye-witness report too. I will show that this is very unlikely. Burridge[515] says they are ancient 'bioi', 'lives'. I can partially agree, but they are more than 'lives'; they are written that others live their lives to a new Creed. MacDonald[516] says that, for contents, Mark is influenced by Homer's Odyssey and the Iliad. I myself recognise Homer's influence on the structure of Mark, which MacDonald does not, and I am open to being persuaded of a little of the other, but only a little. And a student of literature[517], on the internet, says they are 'fictions'. I will argue that this is not what any of the four evangelists would have said they were writing.

Augustine said a long time ago[518], and if you accept it, it was his advice for any would-be biblical critic in any future age: before you can know the meaning and purpose of a text, you have to know its form, that is, its structure and style. For me, Strauss has been hugely influential for good. He did more than anyone else to set a new agenda for critical (analytical) studies. But he led others, nevertheless, into making the same mistake as he. It is not possible to get out of a text what the writer put there, if you have no idea of what the writer was doing and what he thought he was doing. The text has to be allowed to be what it is. Indeed, what scholars say about the ideas and abilities of the gospel writers is worthless if *their* views (those of *these* scholars) are not based on an analysis solely of the texts. The goal of every New Testament scholar, I think, should be to be able to say that he or she can read any text of the New Testament in the way that its author, writer or rhetor intended.

Literary scholars are rightly upset with their New Testament counterparts for their lack of literary interest[519] and for their blinkered want to preserve the uniqueness of the gospels at all costs[520]. In his chapter on 'The Bible as Literature: A Brief History', in the Complete Literary Guide to the Bible[521], Leland Ryken first speaks of a paradigm shift for both biblical and literary scholars. He states, 'Among biblical scholars, literary approaches have increasingly replaced traditional ways of dealing with the Bible.' But towards the end of his presentation[522], he seems to contradict himself. He says, 'Increasingly absent is the practice of explicating biblical texts – close readings of biblical texts as literary wholes, allowing the texts to set the agenda of topics to be covered and including a sequential reading of the text at some point.' For me, the purpose of any literary approach is the explication of the text as a

---

[513] David Friedrich Strauss, *Das Leben Jesu: kritisch bearbeitet* (2 vols., First Ed. Tübingen, 1835-36, Fourth Ed., Tübingen, 1840) tr. George Eliot, *The Life of Jesus Critically Examined* (SCM Press, London 1973) p.782.

[514] Richard Bauckham, *Jesus and the Eyewitnesses: The Gospels as Eyewitness Testimony* (Eerdmans, Grand Rapids, Michigan/Cambridge, 2006): on pages 217-221, he argues for a haphazard arrangement, for no arrangement on Mark's part of the material he is supposed to have received from Peter. This is contradicted by my PhD Thesis in every way.

[515] Richard A. Burridge, *What are the Gospels? A Comparison with Graeco-Roman Biography,* Second Edition (Eerdmans, Grand Rapids, Michigan/Cambridge, 2004).

[516] Dennis R. MacDonald, *The Homeric Epics and the Gospel of Mark* (Yale University Press, New Haven and London, 2000).

[517] Incognito?

[518] Augustine, *De Doctr. Christ.*, ii, II

[519] Robert Alter & Frank Kermode, Eds., *The Literary Guide to the Bible* (Wm Collins, London, 1987); Leland Ryken & Tremper Longman III, Eds., *A Complete Literary Guide to the Bible* (Zondervan, Grand Rapids, Michigan, 1993) p.49

[520] Peake, see note 498

[521] Leland Ryken & Tremper Longman III, Eds., *A Complete Literary Guide to the Bible* (Zondervan, Grand Rapids, Michigan, 1993) p.49

[522] Ryken, p.64

whole, and is not in any way at all to be limited to the descriptions only of the pieces and parts that make up the whole text.

For support for the view that the gospels are the work of the Holy Spirit also, visit any of the catechisms of the church's denominations. The gospels can never be treated solely as an academic subject, though they do need to be subjected to the full force of academic inquiry. Judge, then, how the gospels include, either by direct reference or allusion, consideration of the earlier texts of Old Covenant faith. Look at how these texts are believed to have been fulfilled in the life and mission of Jesus Christ and specifically in regard to his death and resurrection. Look also at the writers' choice of proof texts. Consider the purpose of their focus and inclusion. Include in your examination also, the things 'foretold' in the gospels which took place before they were written: 1) the catastrophic loss of life, including that of 'the elect', which would accompany the Fall of Jerusalem; 2) the provision God had already made for the replacement of its Temple; and 3) for the surviving church, the comforting vision of a Lord who had returned, with his angels, to gather up the elect (or in Luke, who says, 'to bring about their redemption'), rescuing them out of this first century pogrom. When anyone makes these explorations, they do not fail to acknowledge that, to the Early Church, these gospels were sacred texts.

Over the years, there have been many attempts to affirm that the Gospels are sacred for their eye-witness report. One of the most recent is from Richard Bauckham[523]. He judges Mark's Gospel to be the unadulterated and untreated historical jottings of one who has received his information from the apostle Peter. Throughout his book (pp. 203, 207, 217-221, 227-228, 410, 423-424, *et al*), he pleads for this view on the grounds that Mark did not create a Greek-type of 'history' that was unreliable, as he might have done if he himself were an eye-witness, a writer *and* a historian, because *he gives no order* to the material he received. Mark's Gospel is Mark's jottings, therefore, of what he learned from Peter.

That Mark's Gospel is not in any *note form* is very clear to me and, I think, now, maybe, to anyone who is reading this book. My artwork summarises a lot of the evidence. My PhD work in the 1990s shows considerable support for a clearly *ordered* matrix, where the author appears in every way to have been in total control of his material *and* to have learned his trade from Homer and, for good reason, mimicked his compositional approach to the *Iliad*. The Gospel is about the beginnings of Christianity and about how it became a world religion. It cannot be associated simply with 'bioi'. It is important for its stress on the eternal worth of believing and committing to Jesus. The 'original' Epilogue is important here for these two conclusions, see 16.15,16. And Jesus' death coupled with his resurrection is fundamental to his story of the salvation of humankind. But it is what Paul had said before him. By telling his story of Jesus in 'four series' of 'seven days', he is the first ever (it seems) to have put days and dates to Paul's thought (consider: 1 Cor. 11.23-26; 15.3-5). For its meaning, our writer says Jesus' death is to be understood as associated (in thought) with the Passover (see 1 Cor. 5.7). Hence, the new era begins at dawn on the first day of the new week that follows after the Passover. This is myth-making at its best, surely? Through Jesus' blood-shedding and death, God passes over the sins of those who believe Jesus to be the Christ and Son of God. Read too between the sixth days' accounts of the two outer series, 5.1-20 and 15.1-47: as Jesus dies upon the cross he is doing battle with 'Legions' of evil spirits. In the 'matrix' of the story-telling, powerful truths are exposed. The book essentially presents eternal truth, what is eternally true, for would-be believers.

The tradition associated with Papias, which says Mark was not a disciple of Jesus, but of Peter who wrote down what he learned from Peter is important[524]. This appears to have

---

[523] Bauckham, *Eyewitness...* : in many pages, we find the words: 'perhaps', 'maybe', 'possibly' and the like; his investigation is the epitome of much evangelical scholarship based on supposition and wishful thinking.

[524] ...according to the tradition of John the Elder and passed on, in about 130 CE, by Papias, Bishop of Hierapolis, and recorded by Eusebius in his *Historia Ecclesiastica* iii.39.15.

been the view of those who wanted in their day to read this Gospel as history. They appear to have known nothing of this book's literary form and the writer's literary task and endeavour. People could have told the story of a historical Jesus, that is, if they had lived till after AD 70 and moved away from Jerusalem, or out of Judea, before the slaughter, but even then, it seems, the early focus was on the Christ of faith. For this, Paul appears responsible; Paul shows great reluctance to surrender his Gospel in any way to Peter (see: Gal. 1.11-2.21). In his letters, we have bits and bobs in regard to Jesus' person, a last supper, a betrayal (though not at the hands of a disciple – the 'twelve' see him raised, I Cor. 15.5), his death, burial, resurrection and a likely ascension (Eph. 4.7-13), the 'twelve' disciples, mentions of scripture fulfilment, teachings (Ro. 8.31, 13.1-7, 8-10; I Cor. 15.12-14, 25, 35-51; Gal. 5.14) and a firm belief in Jesus as the Christ-Redeemer. It is these that have been gathered up in a single production here, it seems. Paul's writings, rather than Peter's reminiscences, gave the principal thoughts and details to this Good News.

In every way, this Gospel, exhibits indebtedness to the writing rules of ancient Greco-Roman literature. My joy, then, had been to discover another who in parallel with me (but quite separately) had imagined himself to be the first to see a link between the Gospel of Mark and Homer. He introduced his thesis in the same way as I do, with the belief that readers of the Gospel of Mark had seen nothing of what they should have been seeing. Here, I refer to the work of Dennis R. MacDonald[525]. I have been checking what he has had to say alongside what I have had to say. His overall thesis is that Mark's Gospel is much influenced *for its content* by both Homer's *Odyssey* and the *Iliad*: in fact, he says Mark imitated the whole of the *Odyssey* for the Gospel, and two books of the *Iliad*, Books 22 and 24, for the death of Jesus. Yet like Bauckham, he too demonstrates no knowledge of the Gospel's structure. Neither does he appear to show any interest in the structures of the *Odyssey* and the *Iliad*. Indeed, he shows no inkling that Mark's Gospel, for structure, imitates Homer's for the *Iliad* - four times over. We have found different things?

I applaud every challenge to accepted currents and consensuses in biblical scholarship. In his valedictory address to the Conference of the British New Testament Society in 2013 at the University of St Andrews, in a paper, *Fashions, Fallacies and Futures in NT Studies*, Larry Hurtado sought to bury 'Structuralist Exegesis'. But structuralism and ancient rhetoric share something of the same DNA. What none of us can escape is the influence of Homer's requirement of structure on first century writing, either BC or AD. My own PhD work on Mark's Gospel focused on it in the 1990s. The review[526] of the 1999 version of the *The Markan Matrix...* elicited in 2001, 'Much as one respects the scholarship and conviction which has gone into this book, *sadly it runs counter to too many currents and consensuses* in Markan scholarship...' (my italics).

Both Bauckham and MacDonald have been much rewarded for their work, likewise also Richard A Burridge[527]. As a classics graduate, he transferred to theological studies and built a solid argument: the gospels in general are no longer to be viewed as *sui generis*; rather, they are Greco-Roman Bioi (Lives, Biographies). First published in 1992, his doctoral work attracted much interest from those who did not have his advantage of studying classics. In 2004, he reproduced his earlier text (with some revisions) and added a chapter. The latter gave him his opportunity to deal with the earliest objections to his work and the chance to gather up the supportive comments of others. He was able also to record the new developments of others that were based on his work. It is disappointing, therefore, to find that he makes no reference to MacDonald's work (published in 2000), nor indeed also to Mack's (published in 1990) on Rhetoric and the New Testament, nor to my own on the Markan Matrix (published in 1999). And lastly, I ask, 'Does his thesis help with our reading of the text?'

---

[525] MacDonald, *Homeric...*
[526] *JTS*, vol.52, April 2001
[527] Burridge, *What is a Gospel...*

There is no comfort for Bauckham in what I have been presenting, but there is much supporting evidence for what both Burridge and MacDonald write about. I think D.F. Strauss[528] would have been helped too, one-hundred-and-eighty-five years ago, if he had known then, what we can know now. But, please give me one more word on Burridge's thesis. In a word, this gospel is more than an example of a Greek *bios*. Its thesis is 'salvation for the world, for all creation' (if we accept as I think we should, the Epilogue which I have produced out of the longer ending). It is saying how this new world religion came into being. The New Covenant is God's replacement for the Old Covenant. The writer tells eternal truth. He presents creed in story form.

When it came to the biblical critical era, the interpretation of the New Testament was everything: on the one hand there were the supernaturalists and on the other, the rationalists. They reached an impasse. Into this milieu, David Friedrich Strauss tossed his revolutionary third way – of interpreting the Gospels[529] (*Das Leben Jesu...*). The Gospels were not eye-witness accounts, but myths, 'mere myths', he said.

There was a furious response from biblical scholars. (Strauss suffered. And his career suffered.) By turning eventually to a form critical approach, Tübingen scholars sought to defend the Gospels' historicity by establishing the *sitz-im-leben* of every one of the units that made up the gospels, thinking that everything in the gospels came from oral tradition and had, therefore, a first setting in life before being incorporated in a Gospel presentation. For a time, form criticism kept scholars happily occupied, but in time new approaches had to be tried, such as different forms of literary criticism and redaction criticism.

By the mid twentieth century, however, the old views still prevailed (that is, of the pre-biblical-critical era). Modern interpreters, like those before them, saw no reason to look to the Hellenists for help in understanding the literature they were handling. Scholarship had been persuaded that New Testament Literature was new literature.

So, can our liberation from false premises be celebrated without fear of anyone losing faith? My answer is 'yes'! I actually believe we will all benefit now, including those who in the past have said, 'But this I can't believe,' and walked away. One-hundred-and-eighty-five years ago, there was a stand-off between supernaturalists and rationalists. Today, a mythic interpretation of the gospels is needed to give us an informed centre for faith sharing.

Furthermore, I believe that if the New Testament writers had not written as they did, to the classical rules of ancient rhetoric, there would have been no Christian faith in the world to be celebrating today. No one would have respected the texts enough in the first two centuries to even make an attempt at reading them! We can say that the writer of Mark's Gospel chose his approach well. Homer's epics were clearly known to him, as to every writer and reader and every non-reading audience in his era. Homer's myths had their appeal. They had power; they communicated and inspired. Furthermore, they had been well tried and tested by others who used them as models for their own new works over the centuries. Myth may appear awkwardly to us to historicize events that were not historical, but in its usage in the Gospels it communicates what the writers believed to be eternal truth. Myth is not to be derogated in this context: let no one *today* say, the Gospels are 'mere myth'. Myths offer much. They may not be histories, and that may be disappointing and somewhat disarming for some to learn, but they are more than history: they are a valuable means for communicating important and inspiring truth, of the kind that will help people decide on the course they want their lives to take.

---

[528] Strauss, *Life of Jesus...*
[529] Strauss, *Life of Jesus...*, p.782

Ridding the Gospel of Chapter and Verse:

Given my new title to this work, I need firstly to say a word about Langton's chapters. Yes, I am offering my book as a definitive literary analysis of the Gospel of Mark. And yes, I am keen to make my point that it has never before been graced with the study it has been given here and for which it has been begging, seventeen-hundred years. So yes, I think my sub-title for this book is apt: 'Chapter and Verse'. But the chapters of Stephen Langton can go, for what we have unearthed here is evidence that Mark's text provides its own reference system. It never did need anyone (least of all the church) to impose another!

Currently, many read the gospels as if they were intended from the beginning to be read from the printed page. Anyone today, who is able to read, can read them for themselves and in their own time. Plenty of copy, plenty of printed versions are available. It was not so in the beginning and we will come back to this point. Rather for now, between the time of the writing of the gospels and today, we can track times when the church really did try to assist people with their reading and their understanding of them. Within two centuries of their writing, church leaders were translating the texts of the New Testament from the Greek into Latin (though often with limited skill, Augustine informs us[530]). Their aim was to make the texts more available to the majority of the people of the Mediterranean area of the Roman Empire, who spoke Latin much more than they did Greek. (This indeed was also the case with Augustine, who, though a Professor of Rhetoric in Latin in Alexandria, had squandered his earlier-life opportunity to master Greek Rhetoric.) Without anyone knowing, this translation into Latin led to the loss of many of the signifiers of structure that were cradled in the Greek texts. Gone, lost to the church, so early in its life, were the reading helps that the writers embedded in their works.

In the Middle Ages, these indicators of literary form were buried a little deeper when the church imposed Stephen Langton's chapter and verse on the texts. Though his method of versification[531] was to be replaced quite quickly, his chapters have remained. The intention of the church was a good one. The inclusion of chapters meant that a useful referencing was added to the texts and people were enabled to go to the same piece of text quite quickly and simply. But over the years, these chapter additions have attracted complaint. One wrote that they had been made 'very incorrectly, often separating things that are closely joined, and joining those things that are entirely distinct from each other.' John Wesley wrote this, on the 4th January, 1754, in his Preface to his 'Explanatory Notes...'[532].

In modern times, what stands out more than anything else is the proliferation of translations and editions. One has followed another, promising something different. Those that have been prepared for reading in church have undergone word-changes! Check, for example, the evolving wording of Luke 11.27. Different editions also separate one bit of text from another in different ways. Most editions introduce 'editorial headings' to the text which editors think suitable, whether or not they have an understanding of the text and whether or not they are trained for such work. Additionally, people are encouraged to read the gospels, not to the writers' designated plans and methods, but to those of others, because they, in fact, do not know what the writers' intentions were. Reading schemes are produced by all kinds of well-meaning experts. The church's own 'lectionaries' are of this ilk. Joint commissions even, of the churches, have endeavoured to provide congregations and preachers alike with a meaningful route through the biblical texts over weeks and months, and up to a year for a gospel and three years for the whole set. But what has it done? What is the result? A significant number of appointed readings begin and end in places that the writers themselves would never have chosen, or agreed to! Indeed, some lectionary-designated passages in the letters

---

[530] Augustine, *De Doctr. Christ.*, ii II.
[531] At seven verses per chapter: a,b,c...g.
[532] John Wesley, *Explanatory Notes Upon the New Testament,* 1976 Edition (Epworth Press, London)

begin halfway through a piece and end halfway through the following piece, giving license to the preacher that Sunday to say just about anything about anything!

Clearly, this literary-structural exercise demonstrates that there is now much further work to be done. A re-appraisal of all critical methodologies and of much Markan scholarship appears to be required. Of the tools of critical investigation, it is plain that structural and rhetorical criticism have proved much more valuable in this exercise than source, form and redaction criticism. The Commentaries of Taylor, Nineham and Schweizer, which were chosen for their different approaches, and with that of Hooker, for their scholarship and insight, proved most valuable in the process of examining the text, but their usefulness lay more in their detailed consideration of Mark's writing than in their understanding of how the Gospel was put together. Because of this discovery of the Gospel's form, it does mean that much Markan scholarship will need to be re-visited and re-assessed. And much that is presented immediately above, based on the results of literary-structural analysis, will require a great deal of further consideration too.

Effort, in the past, has been expended on an ever-increasing range of tasks: it may be that it can be more focused now. Also, what has been done here for Mark, requires to be done for other writers. Clearly, all books that were produced in the latter half of the first century, whether or not they found their way into the canon of Holy Scripture, require similar structural and rhetorical analysis. The work has been begun, of course, and I have made my own contribution too, before now, on the Gospels, Acts and the Revelation to John[533], but the development of the study of book-structures is a matter of the greatest importance if we are to understand the theology of these writers[534], and, therefore, what it is that their books represent. It is plain, as a result of this exercise, that we should suspend all judgement on any writer's purpose or leading idea, theology, compositional and literary skills, until we have established his book-framework and his rhetorical style. We need not be hesitant: all the writers of these books did have a plan, and a presentational method.

For the replacing of chapter and verse, I propose use of Mark's Series, Days and parts of the telling of the Days: hence, from ABB'A', 1-7, ABB', for example, B4A.

On Reading and Understanding Mark now:

Principally, for the purpose of reading Mark now, the work of textual criticism can be developed. What is not of Mark, and what is of Mark, from the many mss., because of the uncovering of his rhetorical method, can be more easily assessed than before. In the analysis, for example, of Day Twenty-six, in 14.68, the phrase, "and the cock crowed" in the Nestle-Aland text (which is not supported by Codices Vaticanus and Sinaiticus) simply does not fit Mark's abb' scheme. (See under Day Twenty-six for my interpretation that the phrase once had its place at v.70.) It is simply one of those phrases which some mss. witness to and others do not.

Translation is the next job of work on my list, if Mark's Gospel is to be read and heard as it was meant, by more than ancient-Greek scholars. For now, I have provided my literal English version of the Greek to communicate what can be communicated of the Greek to non-Greek readers. It would be a hugely challenging task to repeat Mark's abb' rhetorical style (if not to the eleventh level of literary order, at least to the ninth or tenth) in a good English translation, but it would be the first to be respectful of the writer's endeavours.

Presentation comes next. The Gospel is deserving of a completely revised presentation, of paragraphs, annotations, headings and sub-headings. Readers today should have access to its structure, and, therefore, have opportunity to read according to it. Literary-

---

[533]Palmer, *Sliced Bread...*, 1988; also *New Testament: New Testimony...*, 2004-2016.
[534]Others who are saying the same, from their standpoints, are: N. Perrin, "The Evangelist as Author: Reflections on Method in the Study and Interpretation of the Synoptic Gospels and Acts", *BR* 17 (1972), pp.5-18; Stephen H. Smith, "The Literary Structure...", 1989; Greg Fay, "Introduction to Incomprehension...", 1989.

structural analysis further demonstrates that the Gospel has its own lectionary scheme built in: no other reading schemes are needed now, save that for church purposes of Sunday public-readings and for group study there remains a need to allot the Gospel's elements for serialised reading.

And the Gospel is waiting to be taught. The Book, according to my detailed analysis of the Greek text, comprises twenty-eight Days that have the appearance of being taken from a diary. The 'four times seven' scheme has to be interpreted in the light of what numbers meant when the gospel was being written. The sacred number 'seven' stood for perfection, completion and fulfilment. The number 'four' had its association with the four winds. (For us today it is the four points of the compass.) Overall, the book's 'four' times 'seven' structure exhibits a 'perfect universalism': this Gospel is for *All the World* and *All Creation* (says also the likely original Epilogue, at 16.15). The rhetor intended this meaning in his presentation of Days. But to clarify an important point, the writer is not saying Jesus was a '28-day wonder'. The book infers that there were many more days to these stages, or phases, in Jesus' mission than just the 'seven' each time. Nine to ten months is postulated for the whole presentation. There is no exactitude in judging this. 'Seven' is used for each series, it seems, because it symbolised 'completeness'. Each series' presentation, therefore, is complete in itself. But there is yet more to this arrangement.

The seven days, as has been stated above, have their arrangement in Homeric fashion, as in the *Iliad* which reads as three days, a turning point and three days, hence ABB'XABB', where A is introductory, B is the first development and B' is the concluding second development, and where X is, in the case of the Gospel of Mark, a middle turning point day. This middle day looks both backwards and forwards, between what is passing and what is coming. I have come to see that 'Mark' means this: that what is passing is the Old Covenant which Jesus' presence and mission fulfils; and that what is coming is the New Covenant which Jesus by his presence and his mission, death, resurrection and ascension is establishing. The first 'three days' of each series tell of the completing of the Old Covenant. The second 'three days', after the middle days, tell of the establishing of the New Covenant. The middle days of each series show the Old and New Covenants in tension.

For the sake of the reader, the rhetor describes in his first day's telling (1.21-38) a full 24-hour period (then, of twelve daylight hours and four watches of the night). Mark's choice of 'day' is the Civil Day that begins with sunrise and continues to just before sunrise on the next day. What is of note, again on this first day, is that the rhetor acknowledges the Jewish Day too, one that begins with sunset. He tells that when the sun set and the Sabbath restrictions were lifted, the people gathered for their healings in large numbers.

It needs to be observed that with Mark's Gospel scheme the sun sets (see 1.32) on the first day and the sun rises (see 16.2) on the last day of the narrative. Nowhere else in Mark's gospel does the story-line speak of sunrise or sunset. Such references are for the first and last days of the narrative only. We may note also that 'the first day' is the old 'Sabbath' on which the sun sets and 'the last day', on which the sun rises, on the first day of the week, is the Christian, new 'Sabbath'. (I have tried to capture this detail in my acrylic artwork and show the sun's rays over the Days included.) It really is 'cool' story-telling!

It needs to be observed that with Mark's Gospel scheme the sun sets (see 1.32) on the Old Covenant and its Sabbath day and the sun rises (see 16.2) on the New Covenant and the new Sabbath day. This, I think, is the interpretation that the writer means us to give to the arrangement. It is the over-riding purpose for his narrative, to take us from the one to the other. It is what drives him in his writing. It is his key idea, his leading idea. We focus on its meaning and purpose.

This first-century rhetor gave much thought to the purposes for which he was writing, as well as to his construction of his composition. Ancient rhetoric required a systematic and meaningful approach. If anyone were to chart my progress with my publications, with *Sliced*

Bread in the 1980s, *The Markan Matrix* in the 1990s and my earlier editions of *New Testament: New Testimony* in the 2000s, as also on my websites, they would see that my understanding of this gospel has been growing with each decade. It is in my near literal English translations, of my own 'parsing' and rhetorical analysis of the Greek text, that I have been attempting to demonstrate the development of my thinking on the Prologue, and why I view it to be 1.2-20, and the Epilogue, and why I view it to be 16.9-16,19-20a as a match for the Prologue. I look back upon this journey over the years and I still find it incredible that there is nothing comparable to read, that shares anything like these things. There is no secondary literature to match this. The joy I have had with Mark's Gospel is beyond words. Every moment of discovery has been a thrill in its own way.

In my more colourful artwork on the cover of this book, with the colour palette of 'desert', which supersedes the earlier pen and ink drawing for accuracy, I include the numbers, '2+2' in the last part (the B' part) of the Prologue and '7' in the first part (the A part) of the likely Epilogue. The references which I am making are to those parts which actually boarder the narrative. The inclusion of these numbers in the artwork is because they will likely have had real significance for the first-century reader. It is going to seem really far-fetched to those who are reading this for the first time, but rhetors are known to have inserted confirmatory numbers in their texts. They, these numbers, gave readers chance to check that they had interpreted the structure correctly. The rhetors of the Gospels of Matthew, Luke and John all do the same. In Mark's Prologue, 'two' brothers are called and after them another 'two' brothers are called. The framework of the gospel is of 'two' outer series and 'two' inner series. In the Epilogue, 'seven' demons are exorcised from Mary Magdalene. All four series comprise 'seven' days.

You will see from my pen and ink drawing and the notes that attend it that this gospel's framework is a 'matrix' which works vertically, horizontally and even diagonally, the latter forming a *chi*, X.

Consider with me the two middle series. On the first days, Jesus' identity is questioned in the exact, same ways and the same three alternatives are mentioned in each and in the same order. Here is a duality that goes unobserved in many Commentaries on Mark. This duality is hugely important for its structural significance. Twice over people think Jesus is John the Baptist (raised from the dead), or Elijah, or another prophet (see 6.14,15 and 8.28). Further, both middle series end in the same way, with in-sight/physical-sight interplay (for this, see 8.22-26 and 10.46-52). These are the only two healings of blind people in the gospel. Central to the Gospel's message is Christ's atoning sacrifice. It is just past the middle of the book that we have the acknowledgement by Peter that Jesus is 'the Christ' and it is then that we start learning of what will be Jesus' complete victory over sin, Satan, sickness, evil and death which will clear the way for believers (his followers) to enter the coming Kingdom of God (and avoid hell). Up till this point in the presentation, these things have been indicated in what Jesus has been doing from the first day and even, indeed, during his 40-day sojourn in the desert where he first took on Satan.

The centres of the two middle series are in balance. At the beginnings of each middle day we encounter common Greek words in the same sequence. There is no repetition of this elsewhere in the gospel: 'And thence, rising up *he went away/he comes* into the district of...' I will point out first of all that the Greek word *anastasis* appears in both *middle days* of the *middle series* of the gospel. The writer is saying something! The gospel he presents hinges ultimately on Jesus' *anastasis*, his resurrection. And the word does not even get translated in the NIV, or the GNB. Readers, without ancient Greek, have no chance of seeing this.

In the first (7.24-30), the focus is on the gulf between Jew and Gentile, the people of the Law and the people not of the Law. It is set directly between the feedings of the five- and four-thousands. In the past, Gentiles were willing to receive the scraps from the children's table, but now Jesus is here, things are changing. God feeds the Jews through Jesus' hands as he once fed his own through the hands of Moses, Elijah and Elisha. Furthermore, because of Jesus' presence, Gentiles are to receive the same as the Jews. See how the Feedings of the Five- and Four-thousands lie opposite each other. Dualities are key in this gospel to establishing this rhetorical structure. The rhetor declares that God is even-handed and generous to all. Through Jesus' hands there is more than enough for everyone's needs. The age old interpretation of the numbers, the '5,000' representing the Jews and the '4,000' the Gentiles, is supported by this reading which recognises the balances in the presentation. We interpret too that Jesus' ministry is firstly to the Jews.

The middle day (10.1-16) of the second middle series focuses on Jesus being tested on the Law. He replies that the Law was given for a purpose, for when their 'hearts were hardened'. Clearly, Jesus expects better in the future, when there will be no need of such a law to protect mothers and their children. To conclude the scene, Jesus goes out of his way to welcome representative mothers and children. The first century Gentile-Jewish tension in the church over Law is being addressed in these two middle days. It is a theme that Matthew will develop, for example, in Mt. 5.21-48.

The outer two series begin in named towns and the places of worship. They turn on plottings against Jesus' life, the first in the gospel (see 2.23-3.6) and the last in the gospel (see 14.1-11). The climactic note is struck in the ending of both days' tellings. And we note that these outer two series conclude with a focus on the only two 'resurrections' of the gospel. These outer series, like the middle series, similarly begin, turn and end.

It is to the fourth series we now turn, for post AD 70 teachings on the atonement that the rhetor of Mark's Gospel himself supplies to the church. The focus is on the destruction of the Old Temple and the building of the New Temple. It is a new concept, not found anywhere else before this. The balance that is struck between the first three days and the last three days of this series is what is most instructive. Firstly, we see how both Days A, Days 1 and 5, begin with 'two disciples' being sent off to make preparation. (This is a duality that gives structural clarity to the reading of the text that is rarely noted by commentators.) Further, Jesus can 'see' things as they will be, firstly in regard to the ass he needs and secondly in regard to the room he needs. Zechariah has its influence in both too, see Zech. 9.9 and 9.11. As regards the 'twos' MacDonald sees a link with their usage in the *Odyssey*. I see the rhetor's focus on 'twos' throughout his work: in the Prologue, the Narrative and also in the likely original Epilogue. I have an idea that there's a reference here to the Noahic covenant and to salvation then as it was expressed when the animals went in and out of the ark, 'two by two'.

With Day 1, day A, 11.1-11, Jesus fulfils ancient prophecy by entering Jerusalem on an ass and he is greeted with, 'Save we pray!' (It is what he is there for!) As it is late he just enters the temple to look around before leaving with the twelve for Bethany for the night. Thus is the sub-Series begun without the clearing of the temple on the same day as Jesus' arrival, as in Matthew's and Luke's Gospels. It is enough for this rhetor. He has Day 2, day B, to tell of Jesus' clearing of the temple for a first development (it is the place of sacrifice where a person could be made right with God, but it has come to the end of its usefulness to God), and Day 3, day B', to tell of the destruction of the temple for a second and completing development (the temple would be destroyed in the last days). The rhetor well links Days 5, 6 and 7 with what has gone before in Days 1, 2 and 3. In 14.58, towards the end of Day 5, at the trial before the Sanhedrin, the connection between Jesus and the temple is made, and also in 15.29 towards the end of Day 6, as Jesus is mocked on the cross. Day 7 in the telling of this Final Series completes the presentation: through dying, through visiting death, rather than saving himself by coming down from the cross, Jesus creates the new temple. His risen body is his broken body (of 14.22-25). His is the 'blood of the (new) covenant which is poured out *for many.*' See, therefore, 10.45 which clearly tells that he 'came not to be served, but *to serve* and to give his life as *a ransom for many.*' For the parallel to this, in the opposite day to

Day 6 in the second middle series, see Day 2, 9.2-32: it speaks of what will be able to be announced after Jesus' resurrection.

For the arrest, trials, death, burial and resurrection of Jesus, our rhetor gives the time frame as beginning with the *Evening of Passover* and ending with *the dawn* of the *first day* of the *new week*. Until Mark's Gospel is written there is no evidence of an Easter as we know it. Is he to be credited with inventing it? The symmetries of the book as a whole and of this series seems to be suggesting that he is. And I ask, if anyone of us had been required to present the meaning and the significance of such a series of events, would we not have written similarly, with symbolic and powerful effect, not because our details, or our datings are particularly (historically) true, but because the eternal truth that 'one died *for all*' mattered so much more? It ushered in a new age on the earth! *Inventio* and *dispositio* play a huge part in ancient rhetoric. This rhetor knows it and he is responsible, more than any other, for the story that we continue to tell. This is the position that I take, given the evidence of the writer's method and prowess.

His picture of Calvary resonates with much that is found in Psalm 22, Isaiah's Servant Passages (42.1-9; 49.1-7; 50.1-11; 52.13-53.12) and other ancient prophetic writings. Of the three pictures painted in our four gospels, his is by far the bleakest. Jesus is deserted by his friends and also by God. The two who are crucified with Jesus add their mocking to those of others. The day is presented as 'night', in four quarters, as if watches of the night: there is mention of the third, sixth and ninth hours. Darkness extends over the earth from the sixth to the ninth, at which moment, Jesus, the 'King of the Jews', dies. His body is taken down and laid in a tomb as the day ends. God's disappearance is expressed at Jesus' arrest. He demonstrates reluctance to go. He is personified in the fleeing 'young man' (of 14.51-52). Who then re-appears in the tomb (when it is all over)? The same representative of God, wrapped in a white robe and with an announcement to make (in 16.5-7). It is the focus of the last day of the narrative.

For a structural parallel to Day 6 of the last series, look at Day 6 of the first series which tells of a man 'out of the tombs'. Days 7 of both these series are created as deliberate parallels - for their resurrection happenings. In Days 6, therefore, we read that it is in this rhetor's mind that on the cross, Jesus does battle with Satan and the 'legions' of evil spirits. Alone in the darkness (of sin-bearing?) and in suffering the pain and the mocking, Jesus sacrificially does battle with all that oppresses humankind and prevents people's access to God and their communion with him.

The next thing we notice is that at the point of Jesus' death, the rhetor chooses to have a 'centurion' comment, 'Truly this man was a son of God.' (We note Luke's change to the words here, 'Truly this man was righteous.') Says MacDonald of Mark's account, these words interpret as further mocking. MacDonald is looking for another one of Mark's Homeric parallels as he knows them, that immediately after the death of Hector in the *Iliad* dear Hector is mocked. Yet can this be the interpretation here? Matthew's Gospel repeats the scene and the saying, and it is a moment of the same dramatic disclosure in both these gospels, isn't it? The fact that it is a Gentile speaking, I think, is significant. The gospel is written for both Jews and Gentiles, but at the moment of Jesus' death all Gentiles are given a spokesperson in the centurion. It is for all Gentiles, along with the centurion, to acknowledge Jesus in this way. Further, I think MacDonald overlooks the part the darkness plays in the painting of this picture.

Another feature to consider is that 'centurion' and 'legion' have their correspondence, as Roman army terms. They are the only two such references in the gospel. (To me, the GNB's use of 'mob' for 'legion' as a name is totally unacceptable.) This verbal link connects the sixth day of the first series with the sixth day of the fourth series. In the first of the two, one comes from 'among the tombs' and confronts Jesus, who casts out 2,000 (*cf.* the number of pigs?) demons from him. In the second of the two, the rhetor is inviting us to see Jesus on the cross doing battle with all Satan's armies of organised evil before he dies and is himself placed 'in a tomb'.

That at the moment of Jesus' dying the temple curtain is said to have been torn from top to bottom tells the reader that the link made between Jesus and the temple is assured. His dying and rising body is at once both the temple and the sacrifice. In the Epilogue, in 16.16, we read that Jesus' atoning work is to be believed in: 'Whoever believes and is baptised will be saved, but whoever does not believe will be condemned'. It reads as a typically Markan, b/b' arrangement. It is the requirement of any ancient rhetor to handover, at the last, the responsibility for decision to his audience. With startling clarity and simplicity, our rhetor does this! It is one of the principle purposes of his Epilogue, his epilogue, that is, according to my analysis.

But for now, we turn to yet another matter. In the larger picture that the rhetor paints, at the turning point of this last series, the rhetor introduces a woman who would be remembered 'wherever the gospel is preached' (14.10) who broke open a flask of very expensive perfume and poured its contents liberally over Jesus (Jesus says, for his burial). Are we meant to think on the significance of this still further, that Jesus was aware of the aroma and was comforted by it, therefore, as he suffered and died some 48 hours later? Or is it to do with Paul's choice of words, 'a *fragrant* offering, an acceptable *sacrifice*, pleasing to God', in Phil 4.18? (See also Eph. 5.2.) It is highly expressive language and it is exactly the kind of correspondence which would lead scholars to think this Gospel owes more to Paul's theology and writings, than it does to Peter's experiences and recollections. Until Mark's Gospel appeared, the church possessed no document on the Life of Jesus. It only had Paul's writings and in it some scattered details about Jesus. Again we list them: his descent from David, his being declared 'Son of God' at his resurrection, the last supper, a betrayal, a cross, his death ('for our sins, according to the scriptures'), his resurrection three days later ('according to the scriptures'), witnesses to the resurrection and a reference to a possible ascension (according to the scripture, Ps. 68.18, for which the writer reverses the giving and the receiving). It is illuminating also to see the teachings that are common to both Paul and Jesus, the teachings which Paul's letters and this gospel share. Is there evidence that Paul's writings are the gospel's source? I think so.

Mark 13 interests me most of all as something that the church will need to look into again. It describes a whole succession of events: wars and earthquakes are mentioned, Jesus' disciples and followers will suffer; many will die; the sun 'will be darkened and the moon will not give its light....'; the son of man will come on the clouds...'; he and his angels will gather up the elect. Uncomfortably for every commentator, it then states that 'all these things will happen *in this generation*'. Something very similar is found also in the Gospels of Matthew and Luke. Three of our four gospel writers are saying in the same words that Jesus was returning in that 'generation'. The church's interpretation is contradictory to this, but the clear indication in these three gospels is that Jesus returned as Lord to his own people. With 'his angels', he gathered up 'the elect' at the time many Jews and Christians alike were losing their lives (and their wish to live?) in the civil war of divided families and the famine that preceded the attack of the Roman army, and in the ensuing fall of Jerusalem and Judea in AD 70. The hills (the mountains), not Jerusalem's walls, would save them (Mk. 13.14).

We need to note that this rhetor, in his Prologue, has '*all* the Judean countryside' and '*all* the Jerusalemites' coming out to John the Baptist for his 'baptism of repentance for the forgiveness of (their) sins'. Isn't it these who perished in AD 70? Mark's Gospel shows an alertness, from its opening, it seems, to the historical happenings that reshaped the lands of the Jews and saw their capital and holy city destroyed. In Mark 13, the rhetor quotes from Isaiah 13 and so uses extravagant language that suits what was historically the early church's most horrendous experience. I note that the rhetor of the Revelation uses the same prophetic piece from Isaiah 13 as he speaks of 'the great tribulation' out of which the faithful are brought. Traditionally, the church has seen Rome as Babylon, of course, but the support for 'old' Jerusalem is stronger with this reading of Mark's Gospel and of the Revelation. That Christ returned to and for his own people is a comfort for the church, surely, that this writer wanted future generations to have? (Over the years, Jewish children have been taught in synagogue Hebrew classes that 'no fewer than one million people lost their lives during the siege.'[535]) We are identifying here another leading idea of this gospel's writer.

In Mk 12.1-12, the Parable of the Tenants says that the owner of the vineyard 'will come and kill those tenants and give the vineyard to others.' MacDonald makes much of this, Jesus' vineyard parable, to demonstrate that it was in Mark's mind that those who were putting Jesus to death were bringing destruction on themselves and on Jerusalem. As I see it now, he is entirely right to do so. I read all the prophecies of 13.2-37 as being fulfilled before the writing of the gospel. The gospel begins with Judeans and Jerusalemites going out to John the Baptist for 'a baptism of repentance' for the remission of their sins; it is they, in the end, in historical terms, who are wiped out. As Jerusalem falls, a million die. The gospel writer tells that the believers among them who suffered so terribly and died so awfully (historically, through famine, civil war and slaughter) were gathered up to be with Jesus who personally returned for them, with his angels. The dramatic language of earlier prophecies from Isaiah is applied. The interpretation is that the kingdom of God is begun on earth in AD 70. The inference is that Jesus will come again similarly to all who are his own at their deaths. (I appreciate that what I state here is a decent discussion starter. This reading suggests that in the past we have got it wrong when we have said that Jesus was mistaken, or that the gospel writers were mistaken, or that Paul was mistaken, or even that the writer of the Revelation was mistaken, and also Peter, James and, yes, all the rest!) With Luke, we see the greater interest in God's judgement of Jerusalem. In Mark, we have only the parable of the tenants. And further, Luke irons out some of the difficulties of timing and sequence when he introduces a new thought, that 'Jerusalem will be trodden down by the Gentiles, until the times of the Gentiles are fulfilled' (Lk. 21.24).

To Mk. 12.1-12, we add consideration of Mk. 9.1,2: And he said to them, 'Truly, I tell you, there are some standing here who will by no means taste death until they see the kingdom of God coming in power.' The writer, again, is using the future tense to tell what has already happened. He is interpreting the events of the mayhem and slaughter associated with the destruction of Jerusalem. It is the work of God, of his power, of his judgement. The writer is reminded of Jerusalem's history, of its fall to the Babylonians in 587 BC and its fall to the Romans in 63 BC and of the interpretations that the Jews themselves gave to these events. He links also the fire of Rome in AD 64 and Nero's blaming it on the Christians, the deaths of Peter (in Rome in 64) and Paul (in Rome in 67?). The histories of Jews and Christians are now entwined in happenings in Jerusalem and Judea. He cannot gloss over the fact that the church was caught up in it all. The principle, founding 'mother church' of the Christian community that had spread itself already around much of the Roman Empire was now itself destroyed. The rhetor is able to give his own positive interpretation, nevertheless: before it all happened, God made every provision for the disciples of his Son, for the well-being of their souls in eternity.

Is this a reconstruction we can live with? If it is, the church will need to reconsider Christ's future coming and 'the coming kingdom of God'. John's Gospel, chapter 14, clearly emphasises Jesus' returning at the time of any disciple's death. The ending of John's Gospel could be said to be supportive of the reconstruction: there were issues in the church regarding whether or not Jesus would return before the death of his beloved disciple (John?). The door is left open to the above interpretation. Should the liturgy read, therefore: Christ has died, Christ is risen, Christ will come again and again?

---

[535] Jack M. Myers, p.113

Now, of the kingdom of God, it is often stated that it has already come with Christ, but will come fully only when he comes again. Luke (21.31) links the nearness of the Kingdom of God with these end-of-the-age events, which interprets as the age of the Spirit, given the Promise with which this gospel ends and the force of the Acts as it continues the story of the Christian faith. The Apostle Paul's description of the kingdom of God as a kingdom 'of justice (righteousness), peace and joy in Holy Spirit' (Ro. 14.17) is not in any way impugned by this interpretation. Do you want to interpret this way: the Christian enters the kingdom of God on earth, but fully enters it in heaven where there is no evil? Or, of God's kingdom on earth, do Christians not presence it by giving God rule in their hearts and, therefore, in their communities and the world? Mark's Gospel is telling us God's kingdom is here now and has been here since AD 70. My heart responds: to wait for more help than we have been given already is to nullify what we have already experienced: we are the New Covenant community built (and building) on Christ and the Holy Spirit.

What stands out for me is that the rhetor of Mark's Gospel is writing *after* the Fall of Jerusalem in AD 70 and that he has built on what the Apostle Paul has written before him. He is not following Peter's reminiscences as a part of the tradition suggests. The following may well be what this rhetor built upon: Ro. 1.3-5; I Cor. 5.7; 11.23-25; 15.1-5; Phil.4.18b and Eph. 4.8 (?) and 5.2 (?). Our rhetor of Mark's Gospel adds his own presentation of Jesus as the 'new temple', but like Paul he shows Jesus as the 'Passover... sacrifice', a '*fragrant* offering and sacrifice to God' (see Mk. 14.3-9 for a link that no commentator discusses). The balance in the final series of Mark's Gospel is around the central 'fragrancing' of Jesus. The two ABB' arrangements of days begin with two disciples being sent out by Jesus to make preparation. Zech. 9.9 and 9.11 are fulfilled in these days, in succession. The B and B' days are linked: the first pair through the fig-tree, the clearing of the temple and the destruction of the temple; the second pair by Jesus' death and resurrection (which are indivisible in the psyche of the church). The second days of each focus on 'sacrifice'. Jesus, in the first of the two, clears the Temple of the old sacrificial means for people being made right with God under the Old Covenant; in the second of the two, he becomes the sacrifice by which all are made right with God under the New Covenant. His death is a fragrant offering and sacrifice to God, so says the rhetor as he presents Jesus as the new Passover sacrifice. 'Raised from death', Jesus 'ascends into heaven' and 'sits down at the right hand of God', while the eleven 'go out and preach everywhere'. In completing his gospel's Epilogue in this way, in its original final two lines, with a rhyming couplet of '*ou*' sounds (in the Greek), this rhetor well demonstrates that he has been undervalued and underestimated as a writer and theologian for far too long!

Certainly, old issues can now be re-addressed and many of them put to bed! Is Mark a theologian, writer, or both? Plenty of scholars have said he is neither writer nor theologian, but now we see the writer's hand in the creation of this literary work and in its exposure of New Covenant doctrine, it is looking like Mark is to be credited with being both an effective writer and superb theologian. We can credit him with the dating of Jesus' death and resurrection, with the presenting of Jesus as the new temple, the replacement for the old that would be destroyed in AD 70. What is the answer to the question: is Mark's Gospel eye-witness report? It is No, it is not. Is this Gospel the remembrances of Peter? No, it is not, it is eternal truth told in stories, but based on the bits and pieces of historical information that Mark found in Paul's letters, the literature of the church that preceded Mark's own. What is to be done in regard to exegesis, exposition and interpretation? Preachers will need to look again at their sermons, to see what it is that they base them upon. Teachers and lecturers will need to review their notes and ask if they take proper account of Greek influences on the text.

The Significance of this Analysis for New Testament Studies:

Clearly, Mark's Gospel is central to our understanding of the Literature of the New Testament. If his work cannot be viewed as eye-witness, what then of the other gospels that build on his work? And what also of the later works, the Letters that criticise or interpret these gospels differently from each other?

Here, I want to raise discussion on the importance of Mark's work in the church's development of its understanding of itself and of its message and of how the message could be shared through literature. What I presented 'new' in 1999 provoked a long review in 2001 which concluded with appreciation of my scholarship, but ended with 'Sadly...'[536] Over all my forty years of research, I have not found it easy to persuade New Testament scholars of anything they thought unusual, extraordinarily new, or unexpected! It may be that my thoughts about that *JTS* review propelled me five weeks ago to re-write *The Markan Matrix*, revise it and add to it. It has bothered me also for some time now that scholars and publishers of New Testament studies display an aversion to tables, artworks and illustrations of any kind. As an Architect in my former life, they were the stuff of every-day communication. And all of this is a reminder to me that Mark faced similar difficulties of his own. Fascinatingly, we can see today how in the New Testament there *are* negative reactions to his work *as well as* differing responses of a more positive kind.

Mark's Gospel does not just hold the key to our understanding of the writings of the New Testament, it *is* the key. This has become very clear to me over the twenty years since *The Markan Matrix* was published. Prior to Mark's work, the church possessed only the writings of Paul, of the 50s and early 60s. It was Paul who had set out the terms of Christian Faith in his Letters. In his letter to the Galatians, he declares his source: he received his gospel 'by revelation from Jesus Christ' (Gal. 1.12). He also says he is the corrector of Peter (Gal.2.11)! In the 70s, after a civil war, famine, the Fall of Jerusalem, the Destruction of its Temple and the deaths of over a million, Mark shared his 'good news' ('bravo' news) in a 'world' that was reeling over the carnage and destruction in Jerusalem and Judea.[537] That 'world' was the Roman Empire and one section of it had just been totally destroyed, a huge number killed, many taken to the slave auction that was awash with them, others taken off to Rome and the weak and maimed abandoned, displaced and lost. To that which Mark took from Paul's letters, he simply gave his own days and dates as he shaped his presentation. He was tasked with telling eternal truth in story-form, with presenting Christian Creed in memorable and dramatic imagery and showing that what was prophesied in the Old Covenant was fulfilled. Those who could have given him eye-witness accounts were dead, they had died in the pogrom. Others had died previously through execution and even crucifixion. So, to produce his Epic and tell his tale, he chose to follow best practice, as laid down by Homer in the *Iliad*.

For a time, the church encouraged similar gospels to be written, adding teachings to Mark, shaping one gospel particularly for Jews and another for Gentiles. Another, with a totally different time-frame and dating, was written to aid the church's spiritual understanding of Jesus. Those who had had only Paul's Letters were initially troubled by these new texts, their stories, their conflicting genealogies and their contrary claims. They had their writers, so they put them to work (see, 1 and 2 Timothy and Titus). Later, partly in response to *these* writings, one wrote saying that these gospels were saying what really happened (see, 2 Peter). What all the New Testament writers, including Luke, were stating, however, was that the end (the Apocalypse) was imminent! The gospel writers, after Mark, all clearly taught that it was going to happen in their generation. And according to Mark it did, because he wrote after the event, explaining what had happened in the future tense: provision had been made for those

---

[536] *JTS*, April 2001
[537] "This upheaval, as I said, was the greatest of *all* time...", so wrote Josephus in his Preface, 1,7, *The Jewish War*, tr. G.A. Williamson, Rev. Ed., Penguin Books, Harmondsworth, 1980.

who had not sought to save their own lives, but had died in the pogrom: they had been gathered up into heaven by the returning King himself and his angels. This was comfort for the early church, reeling from its sufferings and losses. We could identify this as the pastoral function of Mark's Gospel.

To this day, the church struggles with the New Testament, not knowing what this literature is, and what it is for. It struggles with the gospels in particular, between interpretations of 'myth' and 'history', juggling with different views on just about everything to do with the way we read and the way we live. And all this time, it has been failing to present its texts for reading as the writers intended. Mark's purposes have been frustrated for far too long. All he ever wanted was to make his appeal; the old world had gone for ever and the new world had already come. (Today, many dream of 'the world' that might follow the pandemic.) Mark had witnessed (possibly?) in Rome, the return of the triumphant General Titus with spoils from the temple (its value so great that Rome could build its Colliseum) and a train of suffering, hurting, dejected and fearful humans. He could not have expected that one day in the city where he was to write his gospel, a future Emperor would acknowledge his Empire's right to the Christian Faith. God was establishing his rule in AD 70 through his judgement on Jerusalem and his provision in Christ Jesus to see 'new things' happen. We could call this the prophetic function of Mark's Gospel. The replacement of the Old Covenant with the New which the Old foresaw as coming is evidence. The events of AD 70 are evidence. Rome's future acceptance of Christianity is evidence in a way, evidence of God's commitment to the world and all creation in Christ Jesus, his Son.

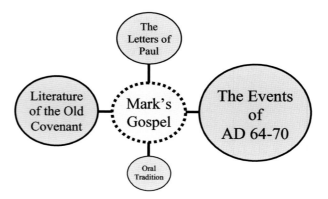

Mark's Gospel displays the influences of Homeric and Aristotelian rhetoric upon its form and the influences of the above, proportionally, upon its contents and themes:

Christianity launched itself into the world in the 30s, after the death 'of one'. In the 70s, after the deaths 'of a million', it re-launched itself with the help of Mark's Gospel. Its writer could not have known just how useful his work was going to be to the fulfilling of God's purposes. Or could he?

If the church and academe are taking note, the current 'chapter and verse' will be gone in a jiffy, for shame and for joy!

Bibliography:

Achtemeier, Paul J., "Toward the Isolation of Pre-Markan Miracle Catenae", *JBL* 89 (1970), pp.265-291

Achtemeier, Paul J., "The Origin and Function of the Pre-Markan Miracle Catenae", *JBL* 91 (1972), pp.198-221

Aharoni, Yohanan & Avi-Yonah, Michael, *The Macmillan Bible Atlas*, Rev. Ed., Macmillan Publishing, New York & Collier Macmillan Publishers, London, 1977

Allen, R.E. (ed.), *Concise Oxford Dictionary of Current English*, Clarendon Press, Oxford, 8th ed. 1990.

Alter, Robert & Kermode, Frank, Eds., *The Literary Guide to the Bible* (Wm Collins, London, 1987); Leland Ryken & Tremper Longman III, Eds., *A Complete Literary Guide to the Bible* (Zondervan, Grand Rapids, Michigan, 1993) p.49

Bailey, K.E., *Poet and Peasant: A Literary Cultural Approach to the Parables*, Eerdmans, Grand Rapids, 1976

Bandstra, Barry L., *Reading the Old Testament: An Introduction to the Hebrew Bible*, Wadsworth Publishing Co., International Thomson Publishing Inc., 1995

Barclay, Wm., *Mark*, Daily Study Bible, St Andrew Press, Edinburgh, 1954

Barthes, Roland, "Introduction to the Structural Analysis of Narrative", *Image - Music - Text*, ed. & tr. Stephen Heath, Hill and Wang, New York, 1977

Bauckham, Richard, *Jesus and the Eyewitnesses: The Gospels as Eyewitness Testimony*, Eerdmans, Grand Rapids, Michigan/Cambridge, 2006

Beach, C., *The Gospel of Mark: Its Making and Meaning*, Harper & Bros., New York, 1959

Belo, Fernando, *A Materialist Reading of the Gospel of Mark*, Maryknoll, New York, 1981

Bengel, Johann Albrecht, *The Greek New Testament*, 1734,

Bengel, Johann Albrecht, *Gnomon Novi Testamenti*, Tübingen, 1742

Best, Ernest, *Mark: the Gospel as Story*, T. & T. Clark, Edinburgh, 1983

Best, Ernest, *Disciples and Discipleship: Studies in the Gospel according to Mark*, T. & T. Clark, Edinburgh, 1986

Bettensen, H. (ed.), *Documents of the Christian Church*, Oxford University Press, London, 2nd ed. 1963

Bilezikian, Gilbert G., *The Liberated Gospel: A Comparison of the Gospel of Mark and Greek Tragedy*, Baker, Grand Rapids, 1977

Blass, F. & Debrunner, A., *A Greek Grammar of the New Testament and other Early Christian Literature*, tr. & rev. R.W. Funk, University of Chicago Press, Chicago, 1957

Blomberg, Craig, "Midrash, Chiasmus, and the Outline of Luke's Central Section", pp.217-259, *Gospel Perspectives (Studies in Midrash and Historiography)* Vol. III, eds. France & Wenham, JSOT Press, Sheffield, 1983

Bowman, J., "The Gospel of Mark: The New Christian Passover Haggada", *StPB* 8 (1965)

Brown, Colin (ed.), *The New International Dictionary of New Testament Theology*, The Paternoster Press Ltd., Exeter, 1975

Bultmann, Rudolf, *Die Geschichte der Synoptischen Tradition*, Gottingen, 1931, *TheHistory of the Synoptic Tradition*, tr. John Marsh, Basil Blackwell, Oxford, 1972

Burgon, J.W., *The Last Twelve Verses of the Gospel According to S. Mark Vindicated against Critical Objectors and Established*, G. Bell & Son, Oxford and London, 1871

Burridge, Richard A., *What are the Gospels? A Comparison with Graeco-Roman Biography,* Second Edition, Eerdmans, Grand Rapids, Michigan/Cambridge, 2004

Buth, Randall, "Mark's use of the Historical Present", *Notes on Translation* 65 (1977), pp.7-13

Carrington, P., *The Primitive Christian Calendar: A Study in the Making of the Markan Gospel*, Cambridge University Press, Cambridge, 1952

Carrol, Robert, Book Review: Leach & Aycock, "Structuralist Interpretations of Biblical Myth", *RS*, 21/1 (1985), pp.116-118

Clark, David J., "Criteria for Identifying Chiasm", *LB* 35 (1975), pp.63-72

Clark, K.W., "The Theological Relevance of Textual Variation in Current Criticism of the Greek New Testament", *JBL* 85 (1966), pp.9-12.

Cranfield, C.E.B., "The Gospel of Mark", *IntDB*, Abingdon, Nashville, 1962

Cranfield, C.E.B., *The Gospel According to St. Mark*, gen. ed. C.F.D. Moule, The Cambridge Greek Testament Commentary, Cambridge University Press, Cambridge, 1959, rev. 1977

Cross, F.L.& Livingstone, E.A. (eds.), *The Oxford Dictionary of the Christian Church*, 3rd Ed., Oxford University Press, Oxford, 1997

Culpepper, R.A., "An Outline of the Gospel According to Mark", *R&E* 75 (1978), pp.619-622

Deeks, David, "The Structure of the Fourth Gospel", *NTS* 15 (1968-69), pp.107-129

Dewey, Joanna, *Markan Public Debate: Literary Technique, Concentric Structure, and Theology in Mark 2.1-3.6*, SBLDS 48, Scholars Press, Chico CA, 1980

Dewey, Joanna, "The Gospel of Mark as an Oral-Aural Event: Implications for Interpretation", *The New Literary Criticism and the New Testament*, eds. Edgar V. McKnight and Elizabeth Struthers Malbon, Trinity Press International, Valley Forge, Pennsylvania, 1994

DeWitt Burton, Earnest, *Syntax of the Moods and Tenses in New Testament Greek*, 3rd ed., T. & T. Clark, Edinburgh, 1955

Dibelius, M., *Die Formgeschichte des Evangeliums*, 5th ed. ed. G. Bornkamm, J.C.B. Mohr, Tubingen, 1966

Di Marco, Angelico, "Der Chiasmus in der Bibel: 1. Teil", *LB* 36 (1975), pp.21-97

Di Marco, Angelico, "Der Chiasmus in der Bibel: 3. Teil", *LB* 39 (1976), pp.37-85

Dodd, C.H., "The Framework of the Gospel Narrative", *ExpT* 43 (1932), pp.396-400.

Drury, John, "Mark", *The Literary Guide to the Bible*, Eds. Robert Alter & Frank Kermode, Collins, London, 1987, pp.402-417

Drury, John, "Mark 1.1-15: An Interpretation", in *Alternative Approaches to New Testament Study*, ed. A.E. Harvey, SPCK, London, 1985

Ellingworth, Paul, "How Soon is 'Immediately' in Mark?", *BT* 29 (1978), pp.414-419

Ellingworth, Paul, "The Dog in the Night: A Note on Mark's non-use of KAI", *BT* 46 (1995), pp.125-128.

English, Donald, *The Message of Mark: The mystery of faith*, BST, The Bible Speaks Today, Inter-Varsity Press, Leicester, 1992

Fanning, Buist M., *Verbal Aspect in New Testament Greek*, Clarendon Press, Oxford, 1990

Farmer, W.R., *The Last Twelve Verses of Mark*, Cambridge University Press, Cambridge, 1974

Farrer, Austin M., *A Study in St. Mark*, Dacre Press, Westminster, 1951

Farrer, Austin M., "On Dispensing with Q", *Studies in the Gospels*, Ed. Nineham, Blackwell, London, 1955

Faw, C.E., "The Outline of Mark", *JBR* 25 (1957), pp.19-23

Fay, Greg, "Introduction to Incomprehension: The Literary Structure of Mark 4.1-34", *CBQ* 51 (1989), pp. 65-81

Fenton, John C., "Inclusio and Chiasmus in Matthew", *Studia Evangelica*, International Congress on New Testament Studies, ed. Kurt Aland, et al., Akademie-Verlag, Berlin, 1959 Vol. 73, pp.174-179

Fischel, Henry A., "Story and History: Observations on Greco-Roman Rhetoric and Pharisaism", *AOS, Middle West Branch, Semi-Centennial Volume*, ed. Dennis Sinor, pp.59-88, 1969

Fowler, R.M., *Loaves and Fishes. The Function of the Feeding Stories in the Gospel of Mark*, SBLDS 54, Scholars Press, Chico CA, 1981

Funk, R., *Language, Hermeneutic, and the Word of God*, Harper & Row, New York, 1966

Gamba, Giuseppe G., "Considerazioni in margine alla poetica di Mc.2.1-12" *Salesianum* 28 (1966), pp.324-349

Gamble, Harry Y., *Books and Readers in the Early Church: A History of Early Christian Texts*, Yale University Press, New Haven and London, 1995

Gerhardsson, Birger, *Memory and Manuscript: Oral Tradition and written Transmission in Rabbinic Judaism and Early Christianity*, tr. Eric J. Sharpe, C.W.K. Gleerup, Uppsala, 1961

Gnilka, J., "Das Evangelium nach Markus", 1-2, *EKK* 2/1-2, Neukirchen (1978-79)

Goulder, M.D., *The Evangelists' Calendar (A Lectionary Explanation of the Development of Scripture)*, SPCK, London, 1978

Goulder, M.D., "The Chiastic Structure of the Lucan Journey", *TU* 87 (1963), pp.195-202

Güttgemanns, E., *Offene Fragen zur Formgeschichte des Evangeliums*, Christian Kaiser Verlag, Munchen, 1970

Hagedorn, Anselm C. & Neyrey, Jerome H., " 'It was out of envy that they handed Jesus over' (Mark 15.10): The Anatomy of Envy and the Gospel of Mark", *JSNT* 69 (1998), pp.15-56

Hall, David R., *The Gospel Framework: Fiction or Fact? (A critical evaluation of Der Rahmen der Geschichte Jesu)*, Paternoster Press, Carlisle, 1998

Harris, William, *Ancient Literacy*, Harvard University Press, Cambridge, Mass., 1989

Hawkins, J.C., *Horae Synopticae, Contributions to the Study of the Synoptic Problem*, Clarendon Press, Oxford, 2nd ed. 1909

Heil, John Paul, "Mark 14.1-52: Narrative Structure and Reader-Response", *Bib* 71, 3 (1990), pp.305-332

Hengel, Martin, *Studies in the Gospel of Mark*, SCM Press, London, 1985

Hengel, Martin, *Judaism and Hellenism*, tr. J. Bowden, Fortress Press, Philadelphia, 1974

Hirsch, E., *Frühgeschichte des Evangeliums. Das Werden des Markusevangeliums*, J.C.B. Mohr, Tübingen (1940) 2nd ed. 1951

Hooker, Morna D., *Beginnings: Keys that open the Gospels*, SCM Press, London, 1997

Hooker, Morna D., *The Gospel according to St. Mark*, Black's New Testament Commentaries, A. & C. Black, London, 1991

Isaaksson, A., *Marriage and Ministry in the New Temple*, C.W.K. Gleerup, Lund, 1965

Jenkins, Luke H., "A Markan Doublet", *Studies in History and Religion: Presented to Dr. H. Wheeler Robinson*, ed. Ernest A. Payne, Lutterworth, London, 1942

Jeremias, J., *Infant Baptism in the First Four Centuries*, tr. by D. Cairns, SCM Press, London, 2nd ed. 1971

Jeremias, J., *The Prayers of Jesus*, tr. J. Bowden *et al*, SCM Press, London, 1967

Jeremias, J., *New Testament Theology*, tr. J. Bowden, SCM Press, London, 1971

Juel, Donald, *Messiah and Temple: The Trial of Jesus in the Gospel of Mark*, SBLDS 31, Scholars Press, Missoula, Montana, 1977

Keck, L.E., "The Introduction to Mark's Gospel", *NTS* 172 (1966), pp.352-70

Kennedy, G.A., *New Testament Interpretation through Rhetorical Criticism*, University of North Carolina Press, Chapel Hill, NC, 1984

Kingsbury, J.D., *The Christology of Mark's Gospel*, Fortress Press, Philadelphia, 1983

Koch, Dietrich-Alex, *Die Bedeutung der Wundererzahlungen fur die Christologie des Markusevengeliums*, BZNW 42, Walter de Gruyter, Berlin, 1975

Kolenkow, Anitra Bingham, "Beyond Miracles, Suffering and Eschatology", *1973 Seminar Papers*, ed. George MacRae, SBLSP 109 (1973) pp.155-202

Kuhn, Heinz-Wofgang, *Ältere Sammlungen im Markusevangelium*, Studien zur Umwelt des Neuen Testaments 8, Vandenhoeck & Ruprecht, Göttingen, 1971

Kümmel, W.G., *Introduction to the New Testament*, SCM Press, London, 1979

Lambrecht, J., "Jesus and the Law: an Investigation of Mark 7.1-23", *EphThL* 53 (1977), pp.24-79

Lambrecht, J., *Marcus Interpretator: Stijl en Boodschap in Mc.320-4.34*, Desclee de Brouwer, Brugge-Utrecht, 1969

Lang, Friedrich G., "Kompositionsanalyse des Markusevangeliums", *ZThK* 74 (1977), pp.1-24

Leach, Edmund, *Genesis as Myth and Other Essays*, Cape, London, 1969

Leach, Edmund & Aycock, D. Alan, *Structuralist Interpretations of Biblical Myth*, Cambridge University Press, Cambridge, 1983

Lightfoot, R.H., *The Gospel Message of St. Mark*, Clarendon Press, Oxford, 1950

Lightfoot, R.H., *Locality and Doctrine in the Gospels*, Hodder & Stoughton, London, 1938

Linnemann, E., "Der (wiedergefundene) Markusschluss", *ZThK* 66 (1969), pp.255-259

Lohmeyer, E., *Das Evangelium des Markus*, Vandenhoeck & Ruprecht, Gottingen, 11th ed. 1951, Orig. 1937

MacDonald, Dennis R., *The Homeric Epics and the Gospel of Mark*, Yale University Press, New Haven and London, 2000

Mack, Burton L., *Rhetoric and the New Testament*, Fortress Press, Minneapolis, 1990

Malbon, E.S., "Galilee and Jerusalem: History and Literature in Marcan Presentation", *CBQ* 44 (1982), pp.242-248

Marcus, Joel, *The Way of the Lord: Christological Exegesis of the Old Testament in the Gospel of Mark*, T. & T. Clark, Edinburgh, 1993

Marcus, Joel, "Mark 14.61: Are You the Messiah-Son-of-God?", *NovT,* 31, 2 (1989), pp.125-142

Mariani, B., "Introduction", *Introduction à la Bible*, eds. A. Robert & A. Feuillet, Desclee & Co., Tournai, Belgium, 1959

Marxsen, W., *Introduction to the New Testament*, tr. G. Buswell, Blackwell, Oxford, 1968

Marxsen, W., *Mark the Evangelist*, (1956), tr. J. Boyce, Abingdon Press, Nashville, 1969

Matera, Frank J., *What are they saying about Mark?*, Paulist Press, New York/Mahwah, 1987

Matera, Frank J., "The Prologue as the interpretative Key to Mark's Gospel", *JSNT* 34 (1988), pp.3-20

Meagher, J.C., *Clumsy Construction in Mark's Gospel: A Critique of Form- and Redaktionsgeschichte,* Toronto Studies in Theology 3, Edwin Mellen, New York, 1979

Metzger, Bruce M., *The Text of the New Testament: Its Transmission, Corruption and Restoration*, Clarendon Press, Oxford, 1968

Minette de Tillesse, G., *Le secret messianique dans l'Evangile de Marc*, LD 47, Editions du Cerf, Paris, 1968

Morgenthaler, Robert, *Statistik des Neutestamentlichen Wortschatzes*, Gotthelf Verlag, Zurich, 1958

Moulton, J.H. & Milligan G., *The Vocabulary of the Greek Testament* (London, 1914-29), Eerdmans, Grand Rapids, 1972

Mourlon Beernaert, Pierre, "Jésus controversé: Structure et theologie de Marc 2.1-3.6", *NRT* 95 (1973), pp.129-149

Myers, Jack M., *The Story of the Jewish People*, London, Kegan Paul, Trench, Trubner & Co Ltd., London, 1922

Neirynck, Frans, *Duality in Mark: Contributions to the study of the Markan Redaction*, Rev. Ed., Leuven University Press, Leuven, 1988

Nineham, D.E., *Saint Mark*, The Pelican Gospel Commentaries, Penguin, Harmondsworth, 1963

Noble, D.F., *An Examination of the Structure of Mark's Gospel*, PhD Thesis, University of Edinburgh, 1972

Osburn, Carroll D., "The Historical Present as a Text-Critical Criterion", *Bib* 64 (1983), pp.486-500

Painter, John, *Mark's Gospel: Worlds in Conflict*, Routledge, London and New York, 1997

Palmer, David G., *Sliced Bread: The Four Gospels, Acts & Revelation: Their Literary Structures*, Ceridwen Press, Cardiff, 1988

Palmer, David G., *New Testament: New Testimony to the Skills of the Writers and First Readers*, the Fifth - Illustrated Exhibition – Edition, Ceridwen Press: Church Gresley, 2016

Parker, D.C., *The Living Text of the Gospels*, Cambridge University Press, Cambridge, 1997

Parunak, H., "Oral Typesetting: Some uses of Biblical Structure", *Bib* 62 (1981), pp.153-168

Perelman, Chaim & Olbrechts-Tyteca, L., *The New Rhetoric: A Treatise on Argumentation*, University of Notre Dame Press, Notre Dame, Ind., 1969

Perrin, N., "The Evangelist as Author: Reflections on Method in the Study and Interpretation of the Synoptic Gospels and Acts", *BR* 17 (1972), pp.5-18.

Pesch, Rudolf, *Das Markusevangelium 1. Teil: Einleitung und Kommentar zu Kap. 1.1-8.26*, Herders Theologischer Kommentar zum Neuen Testament II, Herder, Freiburg, 1976

Petersen, N.R., *Literary Criticism for New Testament Critics*, Fortress Press, Philadelphia, 1978

Petersen, N.R., "The Composition of Mark 4.1-8.26", *HThR* 73 (1980), pp.185-217

Quasten, Johannes, *Patrology, Volume 3. The Golden Age of Greek Patristic Literature: from the Council of Nicaea to the Council of Chalcedon* (Utrecht 1960) repr. Newman Press, Westminster, Md., 1986

Räisänen, Heikki, *The "Messianic Secret" in Mark*, tr. Christopher Tucket, "Studies of the New Testament and Its World", ed. John Riches, T. & T. Clark, Edinburgh, 1990

Rhoads, D. & Michie, D., *Mark as Story. An Introduction to the Narrative of a Gospel*, Fortress Press, Philadelphia, 1982

Richardson, A., *The Miracle Stories of the Gospels*, SCM Press, London, 1941

Riches, John.K., *A Century of New Testament Criticism*, The Lutterworth Press, Cambridge, 1993

Rienecker, Fritz, *A Linguistic key to the Greek New Testament: Matthew-Acts*, tr. & rev. Cleon L. Rogers, Jr., Bagster & Sons, London, 1977

Robbins, Vernon K., *Jesus the Teacher (A Socio-Rhetorical Interpretation of Mark)*, Fortress Press, Philadelphia, 1984

Ryken, Leland & Longman III, Tremper (eds.), *A Complete Literary Guide to the Bible*, Zondervan Publishing House, Grand Rapids, Michigan, 1993

Sanders, J.N., 'The Literature and Canon of the New Testament', in *Peake's (single volume) Commentary on the Bible* (eds. Matthew Black and H.H. Rowley, Thomas Nelson & Sons Ltd, 1962) pp.676-677

Schmidt, K.L., *Der Rahmen der Geschichte Jesu, Literarkritische Untersuchungen zur altesten Jesusuberlieferung*, Trowitzsch & Sohn, Berlin, 1919

Schmithals, W., "Das Evangelium nach Markus", 1-2, *ÖTK* 2/1-2, Gütersloh (1979)

Schreiber, J., "Die Christologie des Markusevangeliums. Beobachtungen zur Theologie und Komposition des zweiten Evangeliums", *ZThK* 58 (1961), pp.154-183

Schweizer, Eduard, *The Good News according to Mark*, tr. Donald H. Madvig, John Knox Press, Atlanta, 1970

Schweizer, Eduard, "Die Frage nach dem historischen Jesus", *EvTh* (1964), pp.403-419

Schwyzer, Eduard, *Griechische Grammatik*, vol. ii, *Syntax und syntaktische Stilistik*, ed. Albert Debrunner, C.H. Beck, Munich, 1950

Scott, M.P., "Chiastic Structure: A Key to the Interpretation of Mark's Gospel", *BThB* 15 (1985), pp.17-26

Simon, Richard, *Critical History of the Text of the New Testament*, Rotterdam, 1689

Simon, Richard, *Critical History of the Translations of the New Testament*, Rotterdam, 1690

Smith, Stephen H., "The Literary Structure of Mark 11.1-12.40", *NovT* 31, 2 (1989), pp.104-124

Souter, Alexander, *A Pocket Lexicon to the Greek New Testament*, Clarendon Press, Oxford, 1976

Standaert, Benoit, *L'Évangile selon Marc: Commentaire*, Lire la Bible 61, Les Éditions du Cerf, Paris, 1983

Stock, A., "Chiastic Awareness and Education in Antiquity", *BThB* 14 (1984) pp.23-27

Stock, A., "Hinge Transitions in Mark's Gospel", *BThB* 15 (1985), pp.27-31

Strauss, David Friedrich, *Das Leben Jesu, kritisch bearbeitet*, 2 vols., 1st ed. Tübingen, 1835-36, 4th ed. Tübingen, 1840; tr. George Eliot, *The Life of Jesus Critically Examined*, SCM Press, London, 1973

Swete, Henry Barclay, *The Gospel According to St. Mark*, 3rd Ed., Macmillan, London, 1913

Talbert, Charles H., *Literary Patterns, Theological Themes, and the Genre of Luke-Acts*, SBLMS 20, Scholars Press, Missoula, Montana, 1974

Tannehill, Robert C., "The Disciples in Mark: The Function of a Narrative Role", *JR* 57 (1977), reprinted in *The Interpretation of Mark*, ed. W.R. Telford, SPCK, London, 1985

Taylor, Vincent, *The Gospel according to St. Mark*, Macmillan, London, 1952

Telford, William R., *The Barren Temple and the Withered Tree*, JSNT Suppl. Series 1, JSOT Press, Sheffield, 1980

Thackeray, H. St. John, *The Septuagint and Jewish Worship: A Study in Origins*, 2nd edn., The Schweich Lectures, Oxford University Press, London, 1923

Thiel, R., *Drei Markus-Evangelien*, (AKG, 26), Walter de Gruyter, Berlin, 1938

Thomson, Ian H., *Chiasmus in the Pauline Corpus*, JSNT, Sheffield Academic Press, Sheffield, 1995

Tolbert, Mary Ann, *Sowing the Gospel: Mark's World in Literary-Historical Perspective*, Fortress Press, Minneapolis, 1989

Trocmé, Étienne, *The Formation of the Gospel According to Mark*, tr. P. Gaughan, SPCK, London, 1975 (first pub. in Fr. 1963)

Vanhoye, A., *La Structure Litteraire de l'Epitre aux Hebreux*, Desclee de Brouwer, Paris-Bruges, 1976

Vermes, G., *Jesus and the World of Judaism*, SCM Press, London, 1983

Via, Dan O., *The Parables: Their Literary and Existential Dimension*, Fortress Press, Philadelphia, 1974

Via, Dan O., *Kerygma & Commedy in the New Testament: A Structuralist Approach to Hermeneutic*, Fortress Press, Philadelphia, 1975

Watt, I., "The First Paragraph of the *Ambassadors*: An Explication", in *Contemporary Essays on Style: Rhetoric, Linguistics, and Criticism*, eds. G. Love & M. Payne, Scott Foresman & Co., Glenview, Ill., 1969, pp.266-283

Wellhausen, J., *Das Evangelium Marci*, Reimer, Berlin, 2nd ed. 1909, orig. 1903

Wendling, E., *Die Entstehung des Marcus-Evangeliums*, J.C.B. Mohr, Tubingen, 1908

Wesley, John, *Explanatory Notes Upon the New Testament,* 1976 Edition, Epworth Press, London

Wilson, T. McL., "Mark", *Peake's Commentary on the Bible*, Matthew Black & H.H. Rowley (eds.), Nelson, Sunbury-on-Thames, 1977, pp.799-819

Williams, J.G., *Gospel against Parable. Mark's Language of Mystery*, Sheffield Academic Press, Sheffield, 1985

Wrede, W., *The Messianic Secret*, tr. J.C.G. Greig, James Clarke & Co., Cambridge and London, 1971

Zerwick, Max & Grosvenor, Mary, *A Grammatical Analysis of the Greek New Testament*, Biblical Institute Press, Rome, 1981

Texts:

Nestle-Aland, ***Novum Testamentum Graece***, UBS4(5) Deutsche Bibelstiftung, Stuttgart, 27th ed. 1993

Brenton, Sir Lancelot C.L., ***The Septuagint with Apocrypha: Greek and English***, Regency Ref. Lib., Zondervan Publishing House, Grand Rapids, Michigan (orig. pub. S. Bagster & Sons, London, 1851)

Codex Vaticanus, Roma, Bibl. Vatic., Gr. 1209

Codex Sinaiticus, London, Brit. Mus., Add. 43725

Codex Alexandrinus, London, Brit. Mus., Royal 1 D. VIII

Ancient Authors and Writings:

The Acts of John (tr. ed. M.R. James, *The Apocryphal New Testament*, Clarendon Press, Oxford, 1924)

Aristotle, *Poetics*

Aristotle, *Ars Rhetorica* (*The Art of Rhetoric*, tr. J.H. Freese, Loeb Classical Library, Harvard University Press, Cambridge, Mass., 1926; also: *Aristotelis Ars Rhetorica*, ed. Rudolfus Kassel, Walter de Gruyter, Berlin, 1976; *Aristotle on Rhetoric: A Theory of Civic Discourse*, tr. George A. Kennedy, Oxford University Press, New York/Oxford, 1991; and "Rhetorica" by W. Rhys Roberts, *The Works of Aristotle, Translated into English*, tr. ed. W.D. Ross, Vol. XI, Clarendon Press, Oxford, 1924)

Augustine, *de Doctr. Christ.*, ii II

Cicero, *De inventione*

Demetrius, *On Style*

Eusebius, *Historia Ecclesiastica* iii.39.15

Eusebius, *Life of Constantine*

Eusebius, *Gospel Questions and Solutions Addressed to Marinus* (See J. Quaston, *Patrology, Volume 3. The Golden Age of Greek Patristic Literature: from the Council of Nicaea to the Council of Chalcedon*, (Utrecht, 1960) repr. Westminster, Md., 1983)

Hermogenes, *On Invention* (ed. H.Rabe, *Rhetores Graece* Vol. 6, Bibliotheca Scriptorum Graecorum et Romanorum, Teubneriana, Leipzig, 1913)

Herodotus, *The Histories*

Homer, *Iliad* (tr. by W.H.D. Rouse, with Intro. and Appreciation by Andrew Sinclair, Heron Books/Thomas Nelson, London; also tr. by Robert Fagles, with Intro. and Notes by Bernard Knox, Viking Penguin, 1990 & The Softback Preview, 1997)

Homer, *Odyssey*

Jerome, *Letter to Hedibia*

Josephus, *Contra Apionem*, 2.204, *Antiquities*, IV.211; XIV.2.1; XVII.9.3, *The Jewish War* (tr. G.A. Williamson, Rev. Ed., Penguin, Harmondsworth, 1980)

Justin Martyr, *Apology*, 1.67

Lucian, *De conscribenda historia* (tr. D.A. Russell, in *Ancient Literary Criticism: the Principal Texts in New Translations*, eds. D.A. Russell & M. Winterbottom, Clarendon Press, Oxford, 1972)

Philo, *Ad Gaium*

Rhetorica ad Herennium (tr. Harry Caplan, Loeb Classical Library, Harvard University Press, Cambridge, Mass., 1954)

Theon, *The Progymnasmata* (see Christian Walz, ed., *Rhetores Graeci*, 5 vols., Cottae, Stuttgart, 1832-36)

Virgil, *Eclogues, Georgics* and *Aeneid*

Xenophon of Athens, *Memorabilia*